THE MAKING OF MODERN IMMIGRATION

THE MAKING OF MODERN IMMIGRATION

AN ENCYCLOPEDIA OF PEOPLE AND IDEAS

Volume 2

Patrick J. Hayes, Editor

ABC-CLIO

Santa Barbara, California • Denver, Colorado • Oxford, England

Library of Congress Cataloging-in-Publication Data

The making of modern immigration : an encyclopedia of people and ideas / Patrick J. Hayes, editor.

p. cm.

Includes bibliographical references and index.

ISBN 978-0-313-39202-3 (hardcopy : alk. paper) — ISBN 978-0-313-39203-0 (ebook)   1. United States—Emigration and immigration—History—Encyclopedias.   2. Immigrants—United States—History—Encyclopedias.   3. National characteristics, American—History—Encyclopedias.   I. Hayes, Patrick J., 1966–

JV6450.M364   2012

304.8'73003—dc23   2011026347

ISBN: 978-0-313-39202-3
EISBN: 978-0-313-39203-0

16 15 14 13 12   1 2 3 4 5

This book is also available on the World Wide Web as an eBook. Visit www.abc-clio.com for details.

ABC-CLIO, LLC
130 Cremona Drive, P.O. Box 1911
Santa Barbara, California 93116-1911

This book is printed on acid-free paper ∞

Manufactured in the United States of America

Contents

Immigration Reform and Control Act of 1986

Jean-Paul R. deGuzman

During the first season of the American smash-hit comedy-drama television show, *Ugly Betty,* the eponymous protagonist and her family were shocked to find out their father was, in fact, an undocumented immigrant.[1] Immediately after the Suarez family patriarch revealed this, Betty asked why he did not simply avail himself of the "amnesty" in 1986. While the rest of the plot focused on the particulars of Ignacio Suarez's life, unfolding a convoluted tale of love, murder, and migration, Betty's quick invocation of the Immigration Reform and Control Act of 1986 and its pathway toward legalization underscored the significance of that legislation for a generation of immigrants to the United States.[2]

The Immigration Reform and Control Act (Pub. L. No. 99–603, 100 Stat. 2259), also known as the Simpson-Mazzoli Act and popularly referred to as IRCA, is an act of the U.S. Congress, signed into law by President Ronald Reagan in 1986.[3] While IRCA contained restrictive measures such as sanctions for employers who knowingly hired undocumented labor and the militarization of the U.S.-Mexico border—designed to stem the flow of undocumented migration—it also featured a new status for seasonal agricultural labor and, most notably, a mass legalization program that allowed some 3.1 million undocumented immigrants to seek citizenship. Although the passage of IRCA was firmly situated within a nexus of increasing Mexican immigration and domestic economic problems, it also inherited a long legacy of diverse immigration laws that, at different epochs, excluded and welcomed immigrants to the United States.

IRCA in Context: Closing and Opening the "Golden Door"

IRCA fits into a long trajectory of U.S. immigration laws that have shifted from the systematic exclusion of groups based on race (and, to a lesser extent, sex, health, ability, and political ideology) to liberalized policies based on hemispheric ceilings. Before World War II, those fortunate enough to be able to enter the "Golden Door" of freedom, the United States, nevertheless witnessed a litany of nativist

President Reagan signs the Immigration Reform and Control Act of 1986. (Ronald Reagan Library)

immigration acts designed to sharply curtail immigration from Asia as well as Eastern and Southern Europe.[4] The "Golden Door" was a narrow passage and its threshold seemed to be continuously withdrawn. Most notably, the Johnson-Reed Immigration Act of 1924 instituted national origins quotas to achieve restrictionist goals. A major group of immigrants, however, were not included in the 1924 Act. Foreshadowing the complex relationship between Mexican labor and American business interests that structured immigration debates leading up to and beyond IRCA, "The powerful lobby of southwestern agribusinessmen tempered the nativists' quest for a 'whites-only' immigration policy by supporting an exemption from the national quota system for all immigration from countries in the Western Hemisphere," according to historian Kelly Lytle-Hernandez. "Mexico's immigrant workers, therefore, were allowed to continue entering the United States without any preset numerical limit."[5] Following the geopolitical realignments wrought by World War II and the Cold War, U.S. law—most notably the Hart-Celler Act of 1965—liberalized the immigration system, facilitating the mass migration of new waves of Asians and Latino/as to the United States.[6] These reforms, however, did not anticipate increasing undocumented immigration from Mexico and Latin America beginning in the 1970s.

The Rise of Mexican Immigration and the Coming of IRCA

Although the United States and Mexico have long shared an entangled history of immigration, labor exchanges, and borderlands contacts and conflicts, the period from the 1960s to the 1980s witnessed a meteoric rise in Mexican migration.[7] For example, during the 1940s, approximately 60,589 Mexicans immigrated to the United States comprising a mere 6 percent of all immigrants. Twenty years later, Mexican immigrants formed approximately 14 percent of all immigrants coming into the United States in the 1960s. Twenty years after that, by the dawn of the 1990s, 23 percent of immigrants were of Mexican descent.[8] A variety of global and domestic factors facilitated this exponential growth in Mexican migration.

Following World War II, the Mexican economy suffered a series of boom and bust cycles. Rapid industrialization successfully drove both steady population growth and a widening gap between the rich and poor. The global recession of the 1970s also exacted a harsh toll on the people of Mexico. Although there may have been hope for financial salvation in the oil boom of the late 1970s, the fall in oil prices by the early 1980s quickly dashed any such dreams. Additionally, rather than boosting the Mexican economy, the oil boom wrought periods of staggering inflation. In addition to these harsh economic crises, the Mexican people faced a looming foreign debt and a combined underemployment and unemployment rate of 50 percent. Within this context, migration to the United States became not so much a choice as a financial necessity.[9] Although many Mexicans crossed the border legally, settling down in the United States to establish new lives and communities, the specter of undocumented migration catalyzed passionate, and often rancorous, debates that led to new national discussions of once again reforming the immigration system.

By the 1970s, immigrants pushed out of Mexico by dire economic forces sought refuge in the United States. Living lives in the shadows of American life and politics, undocumented immigrants found employment niches in the sprawling complexes of light industry and the service sector in America's urban landscapes in addition to joining the ranks of agricultural labor in, what trailblazing lawyer and activist Carey McWilliams had long ago called, the "factories in the field."[10]

Toiling in America's informal economies, undocumented immigrants became a lightning rod for debates ranging from border security to criminality, to acrimonious claims about the "Hispanicization" of America to anger over the perception that such immigrants were draining the nation's public services (namely, education and welfare). To some scholars, policy makers, commentators, and members of the general public these "illegal aliens" were nothing more than an unequivocal bane to native-born workers who drove down wages, lowered the American standard of living, and created an unfair pool of labor competition. These arguments, of course, were nothing new and had previously been launched at a variety of ethnic and racial "others" ranging from Chinese miners in the gold fields of California, to African American freedmen and freedwomen during Reconstruction, to Italians and other Southern and Eastern Europeans in America's Gilded Age urban areas.[11] Former American Federation of Labor president Samuel Gompers popularly said, for example, "immigration is, in its fundamental aspects, a labor problem," a sentiment that reverberated through debates well into the 20th century.[12] Socially, undocumented immigrants became increasingly stigmatized as threats to U.S. domestic prosperity. A 1977 letter to the editor of *Texas Monthly* encapsulated many of those views. In response to a sympathetic portrayal of undocumented immigration, an Austin resident opined:

> I read your article on opening the flood-gates to Mexican illegal aliens—and that's what it would be: a flood of poor, illiterate people would not be content to fill the menial jobs. They would demand to be fed, clothed, and educated. If we don't try to take care of the home folks first instead of trying to support the whole damn world, not only will there not be a bigger pie to divide up, there just won't be any pie at all.[13]

Rhetoric that suggested undocumented immigrants were "taking our jobs" filled editorial pages and airwaves throughout the 1970s and 1980s. Moreover, foreshadowing the provisions of IRCA, some commentators, including a *New York Times* editorialist, noted, "Since the incentive is economic, the most effective penalty has to be economic. Congress is out to impose stiff civil penalties on any employer who hires an illegal alien."[14]

To others, undocumented immigrants simply filled positions that native-born workers would not take and in doing so became a critical labor supply and helped revitalize an otherwise crumbling labor movement.[15] Although labor unions had antagonized undocumented workers, the winds slowly began to change in the 1970s. Indeed, as early as 1975, the International Ladies Garment Workers Union, which had a tradition of organizing immigrant women, moved to unionize undocumented workers.[16] The *Los Angeles Times* noted, "The new ILGWU policy marks one of the first breaks in the heretofore united stand U.S. labor unions have taken against the employment of illegal aliens by American industry."[17] Defenders of undocumented immigrants emphasized their contributions to the economy, taking jobs that were either eviscerated by deindustrialization and de-unionization in the 1970s or were characterized by unsafe workplace conditions considered unsavory by American-born workers. In 1978 *The New York Times* painted a more humane vision of the lives of undocumented workers: "the life that often awaits" such immigrants—"poisoned by poor employment prospects and crushing personal hardship—is something that few aliens expect to find when they set out for

America."[18] Even in conservative bastions such as Orange County, California, a few supporters in 1980 highlighted how "Cutting off a supply of workers could be disastrous for the community ... in which agriculture is a thriving business. Others may not be able to keep their jobs because there is nobody to clean the house or watch children for a nominal wage," gesturing toward the diverse and quotidian ways in which undocumented workers contributed to the economy.[19] This discourse on immigration that emerged from the 1970s and 1980s powerfully informed the evolution of legislation that culminated in IRCA.

Despite some support for the undocumented, historian Roger Daniels argues that the years leading up to IRCA were filled with an escalation of nativism akin to the 1850s and the rise of the Know-Nothing Party or the 1920s, when immigration from Asia and Southern and Eastern Europe was effectively put to an end.[20] An increasingly conservative zeitgeist concerning immigration swept across the United States as President Jimmy Carter appointed a Select Commission on Immigration and Refugee Policy in 1979 comprised of a variety of political and public leaders. The commission's chair, University of Notre Dame president Rev. Theodore M. Hesburgh, charged his colleagues to "walk the fine line between honoring America's tradition of being a land of opportunity and dealing with today's harsh realities."[21] Following a series of hearings conducted across the country, and reflective of Hesburgh's original sentiment summarized above, the commission presented a report that featured both restrictive and inclusive measures. *U.S. Immigration Policy and the National Interest* recommended, on the one hand, "that Border Patrol funding levels be raised to provide for a substantial increase in the numbers and training of personnel, replacement sensor systems, additional light planes and helicopters and other needed equipment."[22] However, the report emphasized that "the reunification of families continue to play a major and important role in U.S. immigration policy," reaffirming, that is, a major thrust of the McCarran-Walter Act (1952) and the Hart-Celler Act (1965).[23]

Critically, the report also recognized that the structure of the U.S. economy helped facilitate the movement of undocumented immigrants. "In a sense," the report noted, "our society has participated in the creation of the problem. Many undocumented/illegal migrants were induced to come to the United States by offers of work from U.S. employers who recruited and hired them under protection of present U.S. law."[24] Acknowledging the complicity of American employers in hiring undocumented labor with impunity, the commission presented another, far more controversial, set of recommendations. In addition to instituting sanctions against employers who knowingly hired undocumented workers, Hesburgh and his colleagues recommended a legalization program for those "who have settled in this country and who are otherwise qualified."[25] Anticipating criticism for this recommendation, the report elucidated the general benefits of a legalization program, noting, among other issues, "Hard-working, law-abiding persons with a stake in the U.S. society will come out into the open and contribute much more to it."[26] The commissioners accepted rhetoric that undocumented immigrants fundamentally drained the economy; thus legalization suggested, "they no longer [would] contribute to depressing U.S. labor standards and wages."[27] Likewise, framing legalization as a means to combat undocumented migration, the report noted that an amnesty could potentially provide "New and accurate information about migration routes and the smuggling of people into the United States [which would] contribute to the targeting of enforcement resources to stop illegal migration in the future."[28] These collective recommendations that at once sought to curb undocumented immigration patterns while retaining the liberal, inclusive dimensions of previous immigration reform set the stage for IRCA.

Debating and Codifying IRCA

Wyoming's Republican Senator Alan Simpson, one of the members of the Select Commission on Immigration and Refugee Policy, became a key figure as the recommendations set forth in *U.S. Immigration Policy and National Interest* reached the halls of Congress. While the Select Commission's report contained potentially liberating features—such as the amnesty program—that were translated into IRCA legislation, Simpson made it a personal crusade to introduce more stringent measures into the crafting of immigration reform. Animated by fears that Latino/a immigrants would harm the fabric of American cultural life, Simpson rehearsed, although in a more sophisticated manner, the arguments of 1920s-era nativists. "A substantial portion of these new persons and their descendants do not assimilate satisfactorily into our society," Simpson wrote in a *Washington Post* editorial following the publication of the Select Commission's report. He proceeded to stress how those "new persons" had the potential to "create in America some of the same social, political, and economic problems that exist in the countries from which they have chosen to depart. Furthermore, if language and cultural separation rise above a certain level, the unity and political stability of our nation will—in time—be seriously eroded."[29]

As the 1980s progressed, Senator Simpson, along with Democratic Kentucky Representative Romano Mazzoli, introduced several proposals—generally called the Simpson-Mazzoli bills—to Congress designed to initiate immigration reform along the lines of the Select Commission's recommendations. Notably, even going beyond the purview of immigration policy concerned with the undocumented, Simpson suggested the complete abolition of the mechanisms that facilitated the chain migration of Latino/as and Asians—that is, the preference categories that included family members of U.S. citizens. Justifying this recommendation, Simpson returned to his rhetoric, evident in his earlier *Washington Post* article, that cast immigrants as culturally distinct and possibly threatening to native-born European

Americans. Addressing a congressional hearing, he argued that "the family preference categories should be based on the U.S. concept of the nuclear family and not on the definition of such a family as expressed in other nations."[30] Although this provision did not appear in the final IRCA, its logic spoke to the anxieties about increasing immigration and reflected the more conservative nature of the Simpson-Mazzoli bills relative to the Select Commission's proposals and the final structure of IRCA.[31]

As the debates evolved, increasing numbers of individuals and agencies lent their support to what eventually became IRCA. The Immigration and Naturalization Service (INS) enthusiastically welcomed legislation to enhance border security. Various media outlets claimed that balancing border enforcement and punishing employers who hired undocumented labor with a possible amnesty might comprise the magic combination to solve the nation's immigration issues. Advocates of the bill, capitalizing on the sluggish economy of the early 1980s underscored how the potential IRCA could wrestle employment opportunities away from undocumented labor and redeem native-born Americans. Thus, in addition to marketing IRCA as a type of immigration reform, those advocates also cast the legislation as a "jobs bill."[32]

Keenly aware of the needs of agribusiness, President Ronald Reagan—the former governor of California, a state with a sprawling and powerful agricultural industry—early on endorsed the amnesty program as well as provisions to adjust the status of agricultural workers. In a 1981 policy statement, the president noted, "We must also recognize that both the United States and Mexico have historically benefitted from Mexicans obtaining employment in the United States."[33] His reflection upon the historic relationship between the two nations pivoted, however, on surveying the contemporary needs of the U.S. economy. He continued:

> A number of our States have special labor needs, and we should take these into account. Illegal immigrants in considerable numbers have become productive members of our society and are a basic part of our work force. Those who have established equities in the United States should be recognized and accorded legal status. At the same time, in doing so, we must now encourage legal immigration.[34]

In addition to the amnesty provisions for undocumented immigrants who had established informal residence in the United States, IRCA also provided for the option of legalization for seasonal agricultural workers, inducing greater numbers of migrants to the lucrative agricultural fields of California. Reflective of the demands of the sweeping agricultural industries of California and other Southwestern states and designed to attract the support of congressional representatives of those areas, California's Republican Senator Pete Wilson added to IRCA the terms under which an agricultural worker could "perform seasonal agricultural services in the United States for at least 90 man-days" between May 1985 and May 1986 to begin citizenship procedures.[35]

By 1986, lawmakers settled upon a series of provisions that one historian called "a schizoid measure reflecting the deep divisions in Congress over immigration policy."[36] IRCA, in its final iteration, contained a variety of measures that were both restrictive and punitive as well as liberal and inclusive. Most notably, IRCA set up a system of sanctions of employers who knowingly hired or recruited undocumented immigrants as well as increased border enforcement. These dimensions of the law stood in contrast to the well-known legalization of status program, popularly known as an amnesty, for undocumented immigrants who could prove "continuous unlawful residence since 1982."[37] In a move to allow agricultural growers to circumvent employer sanctions, agribusiness allies in Congress pushed through the creation of a new categorization and pathway to legalization for seasonal agricultural workers. Finally, IRCA enacted an "authorization of additional visas" to "nonpreference immigrants."[38] During 1987 and 1988, some 5,000 visas were distributed to immigrants from nations that did not witness great outmigration patterns as a result of the 1965 Immigration and Nationality Act. These provisions did not identify particular nations as recipients of the lion's share of visas; however, one historian calls this dimension of IRCA nothing less than "a kind of affirmative action for certain white persons"—that is, Irish immigrants.[39] Indeed, after Ireland's economy declined in the early 1980s, members of the Massachusetts congressional delegation, including Representative Brian Donnelly and Senator Edward Kennedy, lobbied their colleagues to diversify the distribution of visas. Their negotiations worked as immigration officials awarded Irish nationals over 40 percent of the new visas during 1987 and 1988.[40] To bring all these terms to fruition, Congress allocated an additional $422 million for 1987 and in 1988 another $419 million to the INS, augmenting its existing $600 million budget.[41]

Thus, by the end of 1986, lawmakers presented the nation with a package marketed as a great remedy for the nation's immigration ills. Needless to say, the evolution of IRCA continued to attract its fair share of critics. More hawkish commentators, including Bill McCollum, a Republican representative from Florida, like many others, viewed the amnesty as little more than a dual reward for criminals and punishment for law-abiding immigrants.[42] Meanwhile, Latino/a organizations criticized employer sanctions and felt that immigration reform should focus instead on ensuring that employers adhere to federal labor laws to prevent the illegal exploitation of workers, documented or otherwise.[43] Other critics highlighted how the cutoff dates for establishing residency could potentially tear families apart in the event one family member migrated before 1982 while another came to the United States afterward (this dilemma was later rectified by the Immigration Act of 1990).[44]

In the end, however, Simpson and Mazzoli's allies prevailed in both chambers. With an affirmative vote of 63–24 in the Senate and 238–173 in the House of Representatives, IRCA was well on its way to President Ronald Reagan's desk. Representative Mazzoli simply remarked, "I'm really happy that this thing is done."[45] President Reagan, upon signing IRCA into law in 1986, hailed what he saw as the bipartisan spirit of the law and reiterated the dual goals of IRCA—the pathway to legalization coupled with increased employer sanctions and border enforcement—calling it "the most comprehensive reform of our immigration laws since 1952" (curiously omitting the 1965 Hart-Celler Act). He continued, "In the past 35 years our nation has been increasingly affected by illegal immigration. This legislation takes a major step toward meeting this challenge to our sovereignty. At the same time, it preserves and enhances the Nation's heritage of legal immigration. I am pleased to sign the bill into law."[46] As outlined earlier, while a variety of constituencies—including the INS, policy makers, and media pundits—invested high hopes in IRCA as a bulwark against undocumented immigration and as a nascent jobs bill, its effects were ambiguous at best.

Effects of IRCA

Institution of IRCA's most prominent provisions—an amnesty, employer sanctions, and increased border enforcement—had a variety of anticipated and unanticipated effects on U.S. immigration and society. Notably, immediately after IRCA became federal law, the number of applicants for amnesty fell below the anticipated numbers. Some critics charged that the INS did not adequately outline eligibility standards for amnesty applications, thus delaying responses. Likewise, following years of living in the shadows of American society, many undocumented immigrants developed a deep suspicion of the INS along with other state institutions and therefore feared that IRCA was designed as an attempt to catalogue such residents in preparation for deportations. Legal scholar Gerald P. López, for example, highlights the case of a low-income Latina mother called María Elena, who, despite dreams of providing the best for her children—including U.S. citizenship—felt remarkably ambiguous about IRCA. "It wasn't so much that the decision demanded that she resolve complex feelings about national allegiance; instead, it seemed to require that she make their lives vulnerable to law, lawyers, and to government bureaucracy," López found. "For diffuse reasons, María Elena has come to regard law and lawyers as more dangerous than helpful. And time and time again she has experienced governmental bureaucracies as inscrutable, senseless, and unchangeable."[47] As a response to these anxieties, "provisions were made," as social work scholar Wilbur Finch noted, "for applicants to seek help from a network of more than 800 social service, community, and legal aid groups across the country who were designated 'qualified certified entities' for the purpose of helping [undocumented immigrants] meet application requirements."[48]

It should be noted that, while the vast majority of amnesty applicants between 1986 and 1988 were of Mexican descent (almost 70 percent), other undocumented immigrants from El Salvador, Guatemala, Colombia, the Dominican Republic, Nicaragua, Haiti, Poland, and Iran also stepped forward to adjust their immigration status.[49] Social scientists have found that IRCA also created a pathway to citizenship for a number of undocumented immigrant groups including Chinese, Filipino/as, and, to a lesser extent, South Asians.[50] Legal scholar Bill Ong Hing found that after the 1965 Hart-Celler Act, the majority of undocumented immigrants were Filipino/as (who, as former colonial subjects, had a long and complicated history of immigration to the United States).[51] One might infer that a good number of these Filipino/a immigrants were medical professionals who did not pass restrictive U.S. medical licensure examinations—which some claimed were implicitly biased again foreign nurses—and were thus subject to deportation.[52] Some 15,995 Filipino/as applied for legal status through IRCA.[53] The next largest Asian immigrant group to adjust their status was Chinese, as 11,737 undocumented immigrants from China, Taiwan, and Hong Kong utilized the liberal provisions of IRCA.[54]

Applying for amnesty was only one step, however, in a larger process of moving toward citizenship. After two and a half years, applicants were expected to file for permanent residency. To obtain that status, applicants should demonstrate a clean criminal record, financial responsibility, proficiency in English and U.S. history, and, reflective of public health anxieties in the 1980s, test negative for AIDS. Following this step, applicants as permanent residents had to wait five years before formally applying for citizenship.[55] Despite these obstacles, some 3.1 million undocumented immigrants took advantage of the legalization program to seek a pathway to citizenship.[56]

IRCA's impact upon undocumented immigration has proven to be ambiguous. While collecting data on undocumented migration is an inherently problematic endeavor, a comparison of the records of Border Patrol apprehensions before and after 1986 indeed revealed that, in the short run, IRCA did momentarily curb undocumented migration.[57] *Immigration Reform: Employer Sanctions and the Question of Discrimination,* a 1990 report published by the U.S. General Accounting Office, likewise found that IRCA "has apparently reduced illegal immigration and is not an unnecessary burden on employers."[58] Specifically, one can trace the dip in migration to the amplified difficulties associated with financial and personal risks crossing the border as well as trouble finding employment.[59] However, following the immediate impact of the passage of IRCA, undocumented immigration rose once more. Assessing IRCA's immediate effect, one scholar writes that it "served as a formidable if ephemeral barrier to undocumented Mexican migration."[60]

Although undocumented immigration continued to rise following the short-term influence of IRCA, the INS invested massive amounts of time, energy, and capital into the provisions directed toward the enforcement of immigration laws along the U.S.-Mexico border. Less than a decade after Congress passed IRCA, the border-lands between the United States and Mexico witnessed what one historian calls "a stunning militarization."[61] The multibillion-dollar construction of walls and fences in addition to the development of technologically innovative forms of surveillance in the 1990s did not fulfill the objectives of IRCA's authors in forestalling undocumented immigration. Rather, crossing the border to the United States simply became increasingly more difficult and dangerous. As a result, the underground economy of human smuggling has grown while injuries and deaths have increased among those who attempt the trek through barren deserts that separate the United States and Mexico.[62]

Just as IRCA's stipulations could not contain the flows of undocumented migrants, the terms of employer sanctions likewise fell short of the expectations laid out by the law's authors. Although the rhetoric of criminalizing employers who knowingly hired undocumented labor may have appealed to many, the massive apparatus of maintaining detailed files on employee citizenship was too much for some firms to endure, thus highlighting the complicity of the business sector in fomenting a subclass of illegal labor. Likewise, immigration law lacked the architecture to systematically enforce IRCA's call for employer sanctions, particularly in sectors such as agribusiness that had long exploited undocumented Latino/a workers as a major labor source.[63] One could argue as well that Congress never intended to completely indict growers and other agribusiness leaders who often had important political connections.[64] Examining the full text of IRCA reveals, for example, how the law's authors included restrictions upon "warrantless entry in the case of outdoor agricultural operations."[65] That is, while IRCA may have allowed for INS raids of urban sweatshops that relied upon undocumented workers, growers could employ such labor with virtual impunity. The text of the law emphasized that "an officer or employee of the [Immigration and Naturalization] Service may *not* enter without the consent of the owner (or agent thereof) or a properly executed warrant onto the premises of a farm or other outdoor agricultural operation for the purpose of interrogating a person believed to be an alien as to the person's right to remain in the United States" (emphasis added).[66]

Some employers, however, did seriously heed IRCA's warnings against knowingly hiring undocumented workers. Preliminary findings from the U.S. General Accounting Office in 1990 found, for example, that an unanticipated result of IRCA's provisions for employer sanctions included a noticeable rise in racial discrimination among employers. The report found that "An estimated 227,000 employers reported that they began a practice, as a result of IRCA, not to hire job applicants whose foreign appearance or accent led them to suspect that they might be unauthorized aliens."[67] Additionally, some 346,000 employers divulged that rather than systematically screening all employees to ascertain their immigration status, they rather "applied IRCA's verification system only to persons who had a 'foreign' appearance or accent."[68] Moreover, another government report found, "employers who are not thoroughly informed about all the documents that can establish an individual's work authorization may prefer familiar documents such as social security cards, U.S. passports, or green cards, to the less familiar work authorization documents that are frequently held by new migrants and refugees."[69] Legal scholar Angelo Ancheta, drawing on U.S. Commission on Civil Rights reports, additionally found that the employer sanctions provision fueled the "racialization" of immigrants—legal and undocumented—as perpetual foreigners.[70] Indeed, the 1992 report, *Civil Rights Issues Facing Asian Americans in the 1990s*, dedicated an entire section to "Discrimination Caused by the Immigration Reform and Control Act" and noted that, "If employers assume that more individuals in ethnic groups with high proportions of immigrants are likely to be unauthorized workers, then they may be more suspicious of the work authorization of *all* members of the group, and they might be reluctant to hire *any* members of that group at all" (emphasis in original).[71] Surveying the literature on the impact of the 1986 law on employment, historian David Reimers asserts, "The discrimination issue remains troubling … and indicated how shaky that IRCA was."[72]

In the same ways that IRCA was unable to enact a program of employer sanctions, it likewise faced difficulties in sealing the U.S.-Mexico border. The recent rise in xenophobia and anti-immigrant sentiment directed against Mexicans and other Latino/as speaks to the failures of IRCA's stated goals of curbing undocumented immigration. Less than decade after IRCA was formally adopted as public law, groups antagonistic toward undocumented immigrants secured an initiative on the California ballot that, if passed, would effectively bar undocumented immigrants from seeking public social services ranging from medical care to public education. Although Proposition 187, otherwise known as the evocative "Save Our State" Initiative passed as a 1994 ballot proposal with some 60 percent of the vote, federal courts found the measures unconstitutional in 1997. Two years later, the newly elected Democratic governor, Gray Davis, immobilized efforts to appeal the federal court's decision.[73]

Moreover, throughout the mid-2000s a variety of policy makers and public figures continued to stoke the flames of nativism. One of the more recent flashpoints, reflective of the same economic and cultural anxieties that led to IRCA in the 1980s, included the introduction of House Resolution 4437 by James Sensenbrenner, a Wisconsin Republican. Popularly known as the Sensenbrenner bill, H.R. 4437 featured strengthening of the U.S.-Mexico border, the federal apprehension of undocumented individuals who had originally been detained by local officials, and, quite controversially, criminalizing anyone or any agency that assisted undocumented immigrants.

Viewed as unduly draconian and tinged with nativism, the Sensenbrenner bill galvanized a mass protest movement across the United States on May 1, 2006. Billed as a "day without immigrants," Latino/a immigrants and their allies such as organized labor, the Catholic Church, student groups, and civil rights organizations took to the streets of major cities to illustrate the political and economic significance of those who ventured to the United States from a different land.[74] Unable to escape the national mobilization of immigrant labor, Congress did not pass H.R. 4437. Anti-immigrant sentiment did not evaporate after the defeat of the Sensenbrenner bill, however. In the spring of 2010, the state of Arizona passed a particularly far-reaching and virulent anti-undocumented immigrant law—S.B. 1070. The new law criminalizes individuals who do not carry documentation of their legal status. Supporters laud the law as an aggressive stance on undocumented immigration. Critics, however, charge that the new law is tantamount to a mandate for racial profiling, because local law enforcement agents, "with reasonable suspicion," may interrogate individuals about their immigration status and detain undocumented immigrants.[75] Only time will tell the fate of S.B. 1070; in any event, comprehensive immigration reform remains an enduring and contentious issue in contemporary U.S. politics.

While IRCA may not have been able to deliver its lofty promises of stemming the tides of undocumented immigration, its significance as humanitarian legislation endures. Roger Daniels argues that:

> In the final analysis, IRCA was not "reform legislation" in either the original or the contemporary meaning of the term. Nor was it, as had been claimed, a measure that would reduce immigration. It was clearly a failure administratively, but, in human terms, it gave some 3 million human beings a better chance for a successful life.[76]

Notes

1. I use the term *undocumented immigrant* to humanize these individuals and avoid the pejorative connotations associated with the term *illegal alien*. As historian Mae Ngai points out, "To be sure, [that] phrase suggests a diminution of personhood and is particularly associated with racism towards Mexicans and other Latinos and Latinas." Although she persuasively makes the case to "locate the historical *origins*" of the legal rhetoric of the "illegal alien," for this short and introductory entry, I continue to use "undocumented" (emphasis in original). See Mae Ngai, *Impossible Subjects: Illegal Aliens and the Making of Modern America* (Princeton, NJ: Princeton University Press, 2004), xix.
2. See the episodes "The Lyin,' the Watch and the Wardrobe" (October 26, 2006) and "Trust Lust Must" (November 2, 2006).

3. *Immigration Reform and Control Act of 1986,* Pub. L. No. 99–603, 100 Stat. 2259 (1986), https://www.oig.lsc.gov/legis/irca86.htm.

4. See, for example, the Chinese Exclusion Act (1882), Gentleman's Agreement (1906), Asiatic Barred Zone Act (1917), and the Tydings-McDuffie Act (1934).

5. Kelly Lytle-Hernandez, *Migra! A History of the U.S. Border Patrol* (Berkeley and Los Angeles: University of California Press, 2010), 28.

6. See Roger Daniels, *Guarding the Golden Door: American Immigration Policy and Immigrants Since 1924* (New York: Hill and Wang, 2004), 113–144.

7. See, for example, Juan Gómez-Quiñones, *Roots of Chicano Politics, 1600–1940* (Albuquerque: University of New Mexico Press, 1994) and *Chicano Politics: Reality and Promise, 1940–11990* (Albuquerque: University of New Mexico Press, 1990); George J. Sanchez, *Becoming Mexican American: Ethnicity, Culture, and Identity in Chicano Los Angeles, 1900–1943* (New York: Oxford University Press, 1993); and Gilbert González, *Mexican Consuls and Labor Organizing: Imperial Politics in the American Southwest* (Austin: University of Texas Press, 1999).

8. Statistics taken from Daniels, *Guarding the Golden Door,* 181.

9. David Reimers, *Still the Golden Door: The Third World Comes to America,* 2nd ed. (New York: Columbia University Press, 1992), 132–139.

10. Carey McWilliams, *Factories in the Field: The Story of Migratory Farm Labor in California* (1935; reprinted Berkeley and Los Angeles: University of California Press, 2000).

11. See, for example, Vernon Briggs, *Immigration and American Unionism* (Ithaca, NY: Cornell University Press, 2001). On historical animosities against a variety of migrants, see Alexander Saxton, *The Indispensible Enemy: The Anti-Chinese Movement in California* (Berkeley and Los Angeles: University of California Press, 1971); Amy Dru Stanley, *From Bondage to Contract: Wage Labor, Marriage, and the Market in the Age of Slave Emancipation* (Oxford, UK, and New York: Oxford University Press, 1998); John Higham, *Strangers in the Land: Patterns of American Nativism, 1860–1925* (New Brunswick, NJ: Rutgers University Press, 1955).

12. Samuel Gompers, *Seventy Years of Life and Labor: An Autobiography,* Vol. 2 (New York: Dutton, 1925), 157.

13. M.A. Holcomb, "The Roar of the Crowd" (letter to the editor), *Texas Monthly* (December 1977): 8.

14. William V. Shannon, "The Illegal Immigrants," *The New York Times* (January 14, 1975), 32.

15. See, for example, Ruth Milkman, *LA Story: Immigrant Labor and the Future of the US Labor Movement* (New York: Russell Sage Foundation, 2006); Janice Fine, *Workers Centers: Organizing Communities at the Edge of the Dream* (Ithaca, NY: Cornell University Press, 2006); Jennifer Gordon, *Suburban*

Sweatshops: The Fight for Immigrant Rights (Cambridge, MA: Harvard University Press, 2005).

16. See George J. Sanchez, "Forging a New Politics of Opposition," in Sanchez, *Becoming Mexican American,* 227–252; and Frank Del Olmo, "Illegal Aliens Union Targets," *Los Angeles Times* (January 30, 1975), 8A.

17. Del Olmo, "Illegal Aliens Union Targets."

18. David F. White, "Strangers in the Land," *The New York Times* (January 29, 1978), WC3.

19. Valerie Halleen, "The Illegal Alien Problem: Crossing the Border into a Catch 22 Situation of Exploitation and Secrecy That Has Defied a Government Solution," *Orange Coast* (February 1980): 101.

20. Roger Daniels, *Coming to America: A History of Immigration and Ethnicity in American Life*, 2nd ed. (New York: Perennial, 2002), 422.

21. Theodore M. Hesburgh quoted in Daniels, *Coming to America*, 389.

22. *U.S. Immigration Policy and the National Interest: The Final Report and Recommendations of the Select Commission on Immigration and Refugee Policy with Supplemental Views By Commissioners* (Washington, DC: Congress of the United States, Select Commission on Immigration and Refugee Policy, 1981), xvi.

23. Ibid., xix.

24. Ibid., 12.

25. Ibid., 13.

26. Ibid., 13.

27. Ibid., 13.

28. Ibid., 13.

29. Alan Simpson quoted in Daniels, *Coming to America*, 391.

30. Alan Simpson quoted in Daniels, *Guarding the Golden Door*, 224.

31. Daniels, *Coming to America*, 392.

32. Reimers, *Still the Golden Door*, 242.

33. Ronald Reagan quoted in Daniels, *Guarding the Golden Door*, 223.

34. Ronald Reagan quoted in Daniels, *Guarding the Golden Door*, 223.

35. *Immigration Reform and Control Act of 1986,* Pub. L. No. 99–603, 100 Stat. 2259 (1986), https://www.oig.lsc.gov/legis/irca86.htm.

36. Daniels, *Guarding the Golden Door*, 224.

37. *Immigration Reform and Control Act of 1986,* Pub. L. No. 99–603, 100 Stat. 2259 (1986), https://www.oig.lsc.gov/legis/irca86.htm.

38. Ibid.

39. Daniels, *Guarding the Golden Door*, 230.

40. Ibid., 230–231.

41. Lisa May, "President Signs Alien Bill Amid Funding Worry," *Los Angeles Times* (November 7, 1986), A5.

42. Reimers, *Still the Golden Door*, 245.

43. Ibid.

44. Ibid., 249.

45. Romano Mazzoli quoted in May, "President Signs Alien Bill," A5.

46. "Statement on Signing the Immigration Reform and Control Act of 1986." *The Public Papers of President Ronald W. Reagan.* Ronald Reagan Presidential Library, http://www.reagan.utexas.edu/archives/speeches/1986/110686b.htm.

47. Gerald P. López, "The Work We Know So Little About," in *The Latina/o Condition: A Critical Reader*, eds. Richard Delgado and Jean Stefancic (New York: New York University Press, 1998), 341.

48. Wilbur A. Finch Jr., "The Immigration Reform and Control Act of 1986: A Preliminary Assessment." *Social Service Review* 64, no. 2 (June 1990), 249.

49. Daniels, *Coming to America*, 394.

50. Pyong Gap Min, "Asian Immigration: History and Contemporary Trends," in *Asian Americans Contemporary Trends and Issues*, ed. Pyong Gap Min (Newbury Park, CA: Pine Forge Press, 2006), 16; Nazli Kibria, "South Asian Americans," in *Asian Americans Contemporary Trends and Issues*, ed. Pyong Gap Min (Newbury Park, CA: Pine Forge Press, 2006), 208.

51. Bill Ong Hing, *Making and Remaking Asian America through Immigration Policy, 1850–1990* (Stanford, CA: Stanford University Press, 1994), 112. On Filipino/a migration, see Linda Espana-Maram, *Creating Masculinity in Los Angeles' Little Manila: Working-Class Filipinos and Popular Culture, 1920s–1950s* (New York: Columbia University Press, 2006); Yen Le Espiritu, *Home Bound: Filipino American Lives Across Cultures, Communities, and Countries* (Berkeley and Los Angeles: University of California Press, 2003); and Catherine Ceniza Choy, *Empire of Care: Nursing and Migration in Filipino American History* (Durham, NC: Duke University Press, 2003).

52. See Catherine Ceniza Choy, "Conflict and Caring: Filipino Nurses Organize in the United States," in Choy, *Empire of Care*, 166–185.

53. Hing, *Making and Remaking Asian America*, 112.

54. Ibid.

55. Daniels, *Coming to America*, 393.

56. Ibid., 393.

57. Richard C. Jones, "Immigration Reform and Migrant Flows: Compositional and Spatial Changes in Mexican Migration after the Immigration Reform Act of 1986," *Annals of the Association of American Geographers* 85, no. 4 (December 1985): 715–730.

58. *Immigration Reform: Employer Sanctions and the Question of Discrimination. Report to the Congress* (Gaithersburg, MD: U.S. General Accounting Office, 1990), 3.

59. Jones, "Immigration Reform and Migrant Flows," 718.
60. Ibid., 717.
61. Ngai, *Impossible Subjects*, 266.
62. Ibid., 266.
63. Daniels, *Coming to America*, 395, and *Guarding the Golden Door*, 225.
64. Daniels, *Guarding the Golden Door*, 225.
65. *Immigration Reform and Control Act of 1986,* Pub. L. No. 99–603, 100 Stat. 2259 (1986), https://www.oig.lsc.gov/legis/irca86.htm.
66. Ibid.
67. *Immigration Reform: Employer Sanctions and the Question of Discrimination*, 6.
68. Ibid., 6.
69. United States Commission on Civil Rights, *Civil Rights Issues Facing Asian Americans in the 1990s: A Report of the United States Commission on Civil Rights* (Washington, DC: U.S. Government Printing Office, 1992), 149.
70. Angelo Ancheta, *Race, Rights, and the Asian American Experience*, 2nd ed. (New Brunswick, NJ: Rutgers University Press, 2006), 79.
71. United States Commission on Civil Rights, *Civil Rights Issues Facing Asian Americans*, 149.
72. Reimers, *Still the Golden Door*, 250.
73. See Linda Bosniak, "Undocumented Immigrants and the National Imagination," in *The Latina/o Condition*, eds. Richard Delgado and Jean Stefancic (New York: New York University Press, 1998), 99–105.
74. See Victor Narro, Kent Wong, and Janna Shadduck-Hernández, "The 2006 Immigrant Uprising: Origin and Future," *New Labor Forum* 16, no. 1 (Winter 2007): 49–56.
75. Nicholas Riccardi, "Arizona Passes Strict Illegal Immigration Act," *Los Angeles Times* (April 13, 2010), http://www.latimes.com/news/nationworld/nation/la-na-arizona-immigration14–2010apr14,0,4677282.story.
76. Daniels, *Guarding the Golden Door*, 231.

Bibliography

Primary Sources

Del Olmo, Frank. "Illegal Aliens Union Targets." *Los Angeles Times*, January 30, 1975, 8A.

Gompers, Samuel. *Seventy Years of Life and Labor: An Autobiography*, vol. 2. New York: Dutton, 1925.

Halleen, Valerie. "The Illegal Alien Problem: Crossing the Border into a Catch 22 Situation of Exploitation and Secrecy That Has Defied a Government Solution." *Orange Coast*, February 1980, 94–101.

Holcomb, M.A. "The Roar of the Crowd." Letters to the editor. *Texas Monthly*, December 1977, 8.

Immigration Reform and Control Act of 1986, Pub. L. No. 99–603, 100 Stat. 2259 (1986). https://www.oig.lsc.gov/legis/irca86.htm.

Immigration Reform: Employer Sanctions and the Question of Discrimination: Report to the Congress. Gaithersburg, MD: U.S. General Accounting Office, 1990.

May, Lisa. "President Signs Alien Bill Amid Funding Worry." *Los Angeles Times*, November 7, 1986, A5.

Riccardi, Nicholas. "Arizona Passes Strict Illegal Immigration Act," *Los Angeles Times*, April 13, 2010. http://www.latimes.com/news/nationworld/nation/la-na-arizona-immigration14–2010apr14,0,4677282.story.

Shannon, William V. "The Illegal Immigrants." *The New York Times*, January 14, 1975, 32.

"Statement on Signing the Immigration Reform and Control Act of 1986." *The Public Papers of President Ronald W. Reagan.* Ronald Reagan Presidential Library. http://www.reagan.utexas.edu/archives/speeches/1986/110686b.htm.

United States Commission on Civil Rights. *Civil Rights Issues Facing Asian Americans in the 1990s: A Report of the United States Commission on Civil Rights.* Washington, DC: U.S. Government Printing Office, 1992.

U.S. Immigration Policy and the National Interest: The Final Report and Recommendations of the Select Commission on Immigration and Refugee Policy with Supplemental Views by Commissioners. Washington, DC: Congress of the United States, Select Commission on Immigration and Refugee Policy, 1981.

White, David F. "Strangers in the Land." *The New York Times*, January 29, 1978, WC3.

Secondary Sources

Ancheta, Angelo. *Race, Rights, and the Asian American Experience*, 2nd ed. New Brunswick, NJ: Rutgers University Press, 2006.

Bosniak, Linda. "Undocumented Immigrants and the National Imagination." In *The Latina/o Condition*, edited by Richard Delgado and Jean Stefancic, 99–105. New York: New York University Press, 1998.

Briggs, Vernon. *Immigration and American Unionism*. Ithaca, NY: Cornell University Press, 2001.

Choy, Catherine Ceniza. *Empire of Care: Nursing and Migration in Filipino American History*. Durham, NC: Duke University Press, 2003.

Daniels, Roger. *Coming to America: A History Immigration and Ethnicity in American Life*, 2nd ed. New York: Harper Perennial, 2002.

Daniels, Roger. *Guarding the Golden Door: American Immigration Policy and Immigrants since 1882*. New York: Hill and Wang, 2004.

Espana-Maram, Linda. *Creating Masculinity in Los Angeles' Little Manila: Working-Class Filipinos and Popular Culture, 1920s–1950s*. New York: Columbia University Press, 2006.

Espiritu, Yen Le. *Home Bound: Filipino American Lives across Cultures, Communities, and Countries*. Berkeley and Los Angeles: University of California Press, 2003.

Finch, Wilbur A. Jr. "The Immigration Reform and Control Act of 1986: A Preliminary Assessment." *Social Service Review* 64, no. 2 (June 1990): 244–260.

Fine, Janice. *Workers Centers: Organizing Communities at the Edge of the Dream*. Ithaca, NY: Cornell University Press, 2006.

Gómez-Quiñones, Juan. *Chicano Politics: Reality and Promise, 1940–1990*. Albuquerque: University of New Mexico Press, 1990.

Gómez-Quiñones, Juan. *Roots of Chicano Politics, 1600–1940*. Albuquerque: University of New Mexico Press, 1994.

González, Gilbert. *Mexican Consuls and Labor Organizing: Imperial Politics in the American Southwest*. Austin: University of Texas Press, 1999.

Gordon, Jennifer. *Suburban Sweatshops: The Fight for Immigrant Rights*. Cambridge, MA: Harvard University Press, 2005.

Higham, John. *Strangers in the Land: Patterns of American Nativism, 1860–1925*. New Brunswick, NJ: Rutgers University Press, 1955.

Hing, Bill Ong. *Making and Remaking Asian America through Immigration Policy, 1850–1990*. Stanford, CA: Stanford University Press, 1994.

Jones, Richard C. "Immigration Reform and Migrant Flows: Compositional and Spatial Changes in Mexican Migration after the Immigration Reform Act of 1986." *Annals of the Association of American Geographers* 85, no. 4 (December 1985): 715–730.

Kibria, Nazli. "South Asian Americans." In *Asian Americans Contemporary Trends and Issues*, edited by Pyong Gap Min, 206–227. Newbury Park, CA: Pine Forge Press, 2006.

López, Gerald P. "The Work We Know So Little About." In *The Latina/o Condition: A Critical Reader*, edited by Richard Delgado and Jean Stefancic, 339–346. New York: New York University Press, 1998.

Lytle-Hernandez, Kelly. *Migra! A History of the U.S. Border Patrol*. Berkeley and Los Angeles: University of California Press, 2010.

McWilliams, Carey. *Factories in the Field: The Story of Migratory Farm Labor in California*. Berkeley and Los Angeles: University of California Press, [1935] 2000.

Milkman, Ruth. *LA Story: Immigrant Labor and the Future of the US Labor Movement*. New York: Russell Sage Foundation, 2006.

Min, Pyong Gap. "Asian Immigration: History and Contemporary Trends." In *Asian Americans Contemporary Trends and Issues*, edited by Pyong Gap Min, 7–11. Newbury Park, CA: Pine Forge Press, 2006.

Narro, Victor, Kent Wong, and Janna Shadduck-Hernández. "The 2006 Immigrant Uprising: Origin and Future" *New Labor Forum* 16, no. 1 (Winter 2007): 49–56.

Ngai, Mae M. *Impossible Subjects: Illegal Aliens and the Making of Modern America*. Princeton, NJ: Princeton University Press, 2004.

Reimers, David. *Still the Golden Door: The Third World Comes to America*, 2nd ed. New York: Columbia University Press, 1992.

Sanchez, George J. *Becoming Mexican American: Ethnicity, Culture, and Identity in Chicano Los Angeles, 1900–1943*. New York: Oxford University Press, 1993.

Saxton, Alexander. *The Indispensible Enemy: The Anti-Chinese Movement in California*. Berkeley and Los Angeles: University of California Press, 1971.

Stanley, Amy Dru. *From Bondage to Contract: Wage Labor, Marriage, and the Market in the Age of Slave Emancipation*. Oxford, UK, and New York: Oxford University Press, 1998.

Immigration and Religion

Patrick J. Hayes

If, according to Oscar Handlin's classic definition, immigration history is the history of America, then the religious history of immigrants is the foundational pillar. Religion and immigration are inextricably linked—particularly in the monotheistic faiths that comprise the mainstream of American society.[1] Conceptualizing the relationship between immigration and religion has been explored by various authors in a number of fields such as religious studies and theology but also anthropology, sociology, and history.[2] Anyone who has traversed New York Harbor and gone through Ellis Island—no longer the relic it once was but now a national park—will know that in their satchels and bundles immigrants carried amulets and crucifixes, rosaries, and tefillin. Awaiting them were scores of reception officers from benevolent and ethnic societies, many of whom were organized or cooperated with the umbrella organizations run by churches and synagogues. Many lodged at Catholic or Protestant way stations and the seamen who ferried them to the United States enjoyed the hospitality of church-affiliated hostels. Transition into American life was colored by the neighborhoods built up by certain ethnic groups, whether on the West or East Coasts, and these invariably grew around the neighborhood church, planted like oaks to stabilize the newcomer.

Some would argue that religion was at the margin of the experience of most immigrants to the United States. The intensity of the experience was too often driven by economic concerns and basic sustenance. More immediate questions such as "where will my next meal come from and how will I pay for it?" dominated the immigrant's thinking. But in the dark moments where one wondered about shelter and the basic necessities of life, immigrants could be found praying to God for guidance and strength. Since the founding of the Republic, this private prayer has infused so much courage and charity that it is quite apt to suggest the marked religiosity of the American people these last two centuries and more. There is no unanimity on the approach of religious traditions in their dealings with immigrants to the United States. Not only do the various policy statements of religious bodies often diverge, they are also sometimes entirely mute on the subject. This partly reflects the disposition of their members' politics, but it also signals how their theology informs the attitudes and actions of their respective congregations. In terms of the members' own abilities to absorb immigrant communities into their ranks, the results are often mixed. Some, however, have recognized the potential power of immigrants in the public square, and sociologists are beginning to understand the ways in which local churches are using recent immigrants to promote civic engagement.[3] In their three-year study on immigrant worship communities in and around Washington, DC, Dean Hoge and Michael Foley noted how the presence of such communities has forced church groups to respond with social services and greater political engagement. In their findings, the authors suggest that the deeper the ethnic presence of immigrants, the greater the likelihood of civic action. This cuts across both Christian and non-Christian denominations.

It is not the point of this essay to canvass all of the religious bodies, but it does survey some of the major religious denominations in the United States for their institutional practice and policy toward immigrants. A more extensive segment treats the Roman Catholic Church in the United States, whose formal handling of immigration issues was necessitated largely through the gargantuan numbers of co-religionists from Europe between the 1830s to the aftermath of World War II. They have also had an overwhelming impact on the kinds of services provided to immigrants to the United States through the Church's various charitable mechanisms both at the local and national levels.

Episcopalians (Anglicans)

Among the older Christian churches in the United States is the Episcopal Church in the United States of America (ECUSA), which today constitutes a significant part of the worldwide Anglican Communion. The membership of the church in the United States numbers only a fraction of the total population, with just over 2 million members, making it the 15th largest denomination in the country.

The present immigration policies of the ECUSA fall under the purview of the Episcopal Public Policy Network (EPPN), a body charged with various social ministries. This is an outgrowth of the Episcopal Migration Network, an advocacy arm. The EPPN's primary goal is to give information through its website (www.episcopalchurch.org). During Lent 2010, for instance, it promoted a comprehensive overview of the immigration problem and showed how for church members the immigrant was a special object of hospitality. It is also quite ecumenical in its approach to immigration reform. The church partners with the Interfaith Immigration Network and the United States Conference of Catholic Bishops in promoting just and fair responses to immigration legislation.

Within its own polity, the Episcopal Church has routinely given attention to immigration issues that come before its General Conventions. In 1982, at the

67th General Convention, it encouraged relief for refugees by commending efforts to resettle them and to have the Church accept them into their communities. Of particular interest were the fair treatment of Salvadoran and Haitian refugees and the need for recognition by civil authorities for those political and economic refugees seeking permanent status. Also at this convention, the Church supported changes in immigration laws that would permit greater numbers of Amerasian children to enter the country. At the following convention in 1985, the Church reaffirmed a call for safe haven for Central Americans seeking temporary refuge from the civil strife in their countries. The undocumented members of American society were also a special object of concern, and the hope of the Church was that Congress would enact legislation that broadens the definition of those seeking asylum, especially from political repression. As the 1980s closed, the 69th convention made provisions for refugee Anglican bishops and clergy from parts of the world in which conflict was prevalent and from which they were forced to flee their ministries.

By 1997, at the 72nd convention, Episcopalians began to realize that the immigration issue was becoming increasingly rancorous. A more systematic approach to immigration problems was required, with the force of a new series of Church initiatives. Not satisfied with simply creating new resolutions, Episcopalians formed the Episcopal Migration Ministries to develop a widespread action agenda. This agenda not only included comprehensive educational and informational programs for Church members, but also plotted with legislators for continued improvements in immigration reform bills before Congress. The Episcopal Migration Ministries also developed the Episcopalians' policy statement, "The Alien Among You," which was adopted in 2006 at the 75th General Convention.[4]

This document is a short but powerful statement on the Church's commitment to the immigrant, particularly in the wake of 9/11. Issued by the Standing Commission on Anglican and International Peace with Justice Concerns, the theological underpinnings are clear and echo Leviticus 19:33–34: "When an alien resides with you in your land, you shall not oppress the alien. The alien who resides with you shall be to you as the citizen among you; you shall love the alien as yourself, for you were aliens in the land of Egypt." Unlike other statements from within the Christian community, however, the Episcopal Church has indicted the national past for having gradually developed immigration policies that have been at times "glaringly racist and exclusionary." The antidote to this is to possess a vocation toward welcoming the stranger and offering hospitality. The statement notes how, since 9/11, the immigration rate has been halved and refugees who arrive are generally victims of the perpetrators of terror, not the perpetrators themselves. Open and responsible resettlement is called for through comprehensive immigration reform, a goal that the Church supports, particularly for separated families and "millions of undocumented aliens—especially agricultural workers and others who perform unskilled or low skilled jobs that are critical to the American economy." The Standing Committee therefore recommended some concrete policy initiatives for the Church. First, it supports immigration reform that is rooted in the biblical notion of hospitality to the stranger. While acknowledging the right of sovereign nations to protect their borders, support is also given for a "responsible and humane process for inclusion of people who come to the United States seeking economic opportunity, refuge from persecution and family reunification." Several principles of just and fair immigration policies were enumerated:

1. Undocumented aliens should have reasonable opportunity to pursue permanent residency.
2. Legal workers should be allowed to enter the United States to respond to recognized labor force needs.
3. Close family members should be allowed to reunite without undue delay with individuals lawfully present in the United States.
4. Fundamental U.S. principles of legal due process should be granted all persons.
5. Enforcement of national borders and immigration policies should be proportional and humane.

With respect to this latter point, the convention adopted a resolution that "deplores any action by the Government of the United States which unduly emphasizes enforcement, including militarization of the border between the United States and Mexico, as the primary response to immigrants entering the United States to work."

Southern Baptists

The Southern Baptist Convention (SBC) is the largest group of Baptists in the United States and second only to Catholics in terms of their numbers. Traditionally they have been politically conservative, though more and more survey data suggest that there is a progressive streak running through the Convention on issues of climate change and environmental awareness. The SBC has a number of issues it judges to be worthy of the membership, not least is to take positions on the immigration question. As such, the membership is in stark contrast to other religious groups insofar as it advocates for strict prohibitions.

In March 2006, Eric Land, the president of the SBC's Ethics and Religious Liberty Commission, along with others (including representatives of the Salvation Army and the Catholic Church), told then President George Bush that Southern Baptists would not support any type of guest-worker program if the immigration laws were not enforced. The meeting came at a time just before Senate hearings on the topic. With nearly 12 million illegal immigrants in the country, "Land said he told the president Southern Baptists 'are deeply offended at a very basic level when the government doesn't enforce the law. And it's clear that the government is not rigorously enforcing the law at the border or in the country when it comes to illegal immigration. As Southern Baptists, we believe that Romans 13 teaches the government is to punish those who break the law and reward those who obey the law.'"[5] While Land reported that the overwhelming majority of Southern Baptists sought more secure borders, they did not advocate a closed-border policy but better control of who comes in and who goes out. This was a clear agenda item during the administration of President George W. Bush, and then Senate Majority Leader Bill Frist, over the objections of Senate Democrats, pushed it through (without a guest-worker component to the bill). The repercussions of a staunch border enforcement strategy are still with us.

The United Church of Christ (Congregationalists)

The United Church of Christ (UCC) is a mainline Protestant body with concentrations in the Northeast. Its immigration policies have been proposed through the synod, a formal body constituted to address issues affecting the polity of the Church. A number of "witness resolutions" have been drawn up in these synod statements. In General Synod XIII (1981), for instance, the UCC adopted a

pronouncement on immigration calling upon all settings of the church to:

1. advocate for the rights of immigrants;
2. aid undocumented immigrants in attaining legal status;
3. aid immigrants in reunification with their families and in placement in areas of the country most favorable for their productive participation in society;
4. assist in meeting the social welfare needs of immigrants; and
5. be inclusive of immigrants in existing and new churches.

Additionally, in General Synod XXIV, the UCC adopted a resolution supporting Humane Borders, a faith-based group that offers assistance to those in need by maintaining water stations on and near the border. In effect, Congregationalists seek to ground biblical theology with everyday praxis with the latest set coming at General Synod XXVI.

In their "Call for a More Humane U.S. Immigration Policy; End Migrant Deaths; Support Immigrant Communities," a series of resolutions points up this admixture of the biblical commands and lived reality. Noting that the words of Jesus and other scriptural texts are clear when they identify the "stranger" as deserving of love and compassion, they wish to see all borders destroyed insofar as they render us unable to envision each person as a child of God living in "one world." The UCC recognizes that in its actions the federal government detains immigrants, prosecutes the undocumented worker, and fractures families, even prosecuting those who would give them assistance. They further find it a consequence of the "blockade strategy of border enforcement" that, subsequent to its implementation, 3,000 men, women, and children have died attempting to cross the United States–Mexico border. Border control is a right of sovereign nations, but it is not absolute, particularly when it helps drive an underground market for smuggling individuals across. They hoped to show continued solidarity with new immigrants in local communities, which included getting to know the stories of their new neighbors, however temporary they happened to be. Pastors were called upon to link with established ministries serving immigrant populations, such as Border Links, Presbyterian Border Ministry, Samaritan Patrols, Illinois Maya Ministry, the New Sanctuary Movement, and the Center for Education and Social Transformation. A consciousness-raising campaign in the church would be facilitated by reflection sessions on such films as *El Norte* and *Babel* and books such as *The Devil's Highway* by Luis Alberto Urrea. They believe it is shameful that 12 million undocumented immigrants have had to live "covertly, without rights, and in vulnerable situations all over the United States." Pointing to the economics of immigration, the UCC statement calls for the righting of inequities on both sides of the border and extending to all of Latin America. They resolved that the United States had an "ineffective and inhumane" policy of "militarized border enforcement." They called upon UCC congregations to advocate with their congressional representatives for a "policy that allows immigrant workers and their families to live and work in a safe, legal, orderly and humane manner through an Employment-Focused immigration program (as opposed to employer focused) that guarantees basic international workers' rights to organization, collective bargaining, job portability, religious freedom, easy and safe travel between the United States and their homeland, achievable and verifiable paths to residency, and a basic human right of mobility."

United Methodist Church

After Catholics and Baptists, the United Methodist Church is the third largest religious denomination in the country. English in origin, today its membership is concentrated in the South, though it is a global church with more than 14 million members. Within the United States there are five ethnic advocacy groups within the Methodist Church. Among them is MARCHA—Methodists Associated Representing the Cause of Hispanic Americans. This caucus has often critiqued the U.S. government for its lack of comprehensive immigration policy. In 2007, for instance, it derided the Immigration Reform Act (1996), noting in a resolution that it "severely restricted the opportunity for immigrants in this country to be reunited with their families and obtain permission to work legally and avoid being exploited by unscrupulous employers and employment practices."

These sentiments build upon a strongly worded statement adopted by the church's general assembly in 2000, "Opposition to the Illegal Immigration Reform and Immigration Resolution Act." Like Episcopalians, Methodists are concerned with scriptural foundations for their position and have issued policy statements (such as "Love the Sojourner"), but they go a step further and see the ethic of their work as rooted in the Universal Declaration on Human Rights, the United Nations Charter, and documents concerning immigration of the Geneva Convention. The statement called for amnesty for the undocumented members of the Hispanic community living in the United States and to reverse the governmental attitude that being undocumented is somehow a crime. The conclusion reached in this statement does not brook compromise: "*Therefore, be it resolved*, that we, The United Methodist Church, declare that the *Illegal Immigration Reform and Immigrant Resolution Act* is evil and unjust, and that the enforcement thereof results in immediate and insufferable human rights violations, discrimination, and oppression."[6]

Methodists have also taken to lobbying Congress for immigration reform as a way of combating the rise of hate groups around the country. Bishop Elias Galván, the executive director of MARCHA has called for vigilance against vigilantism. In 2007, his group opposed the Comprehensive Immigration Reform Act, calling the Senate version of the bill a "grand bargain." An opposition letter was signed by the chief executives or other officers of the United Methodist Board of Church and Society, Board of Global Ministries, Women's Division of Global Ministries, General Commission on Religion and Race, National Plan for Hispanic/Latino Ministry, Methodists Associated to Represent the Cause of Hispanic Americans, and National Federation of Asian American United Methodists.

Islam

No one community or organization speaks for Islam in the United States, and, given the relative newness of the Muslim presence within the United States, one can hardly expect a concerted effort to form in alleviating the trials of immigration. However, with the post-9/11 backlash faced by many American Muslims, particularly those with a recent immigrant past, many Islamic centers around the country are taking account of the numerous instances of discrimination that have befallen their members. Few, however, have filed formal complaints with authorities, and fewer still have been prosecuted, though the Federal Bureau of Investigation has noted a 17-fold increase in the numbers of hate crimes cases filed between 2000 and 2001.[7] Systemic change is not imminent. This is in part due to the lack of a viable network of immigration advocates to lobby on Muslims' behalf. Perhaps this explains why Arsalan Iftikhar can point to four prominent cases (among over 1,200 in the aftermath of 9/11) of apparent injustice visited upon Muslims: Captain James Yee, who spent seventy-six days in solidarity confinement, being labeled a "spy" in most media circles—despite the fact that he was never convicted of any offense. The second case involves Brandon Mayfield, who was falsely linked by the FBI to the Madrid train bombings of March 11, 2004. The third and fourth cases involve Professor Tariq Ramadan and Yusuf Islam (formerly Cat Stevens) who were placed on the Transportation Security Administration's terrorist suspect "no fly" list. Each of these cases provides a different insight into the ethno-religious profiling and egregious violations of civil liberties and legal rights that have been experienced by thousands of American Muslims since the attacks of September 11, 2001.[8]

It is perhaps understandable to puzzle over Muslim immigration to the United States due to a variety of reasons. The records are scant. The personalities that typified Muslim interests were often not recognized by others within the Islamic community itself. Within the Muslim sector of the American population, there is no outward agenda for influencing policy or, indeed, of making one's voice heard in the public square. Until the aftermath of World War II, Islamic immigration was but a trickle, though today one can point to a large number of Palestinian refugees who arrived after the creation of Israel in 1948. Muslim migrants have fled oppressive regimes in Egypt, Iraq, and Syria; and South Asian Muslims, as from Pakistan, have sought economic opportunity. By the 1990s, Muslims had established more than 600 mosques and centers across the United States.[9]

Judaism

American Jewry has a long and illustrious history stemming from the earliest settlers in 1654 in New York City through the emergence of new forms of Jewish life and culture, some of which is uniquely American.[10] By 1776, some 2,000 Jews could be found throughout the former colonies. By 1820, the first wave of Jewish immigrants had come to a completion, with fewer than 15,000 Jews seeking religious tolerance on these shores, with most coming from Western Europe. Their communities were coastal in the main, with synagogues established in New York; Newport, Rhode Island; Charleston, South Carolina; Savannah, Georgia; and Philadelphia. But the next 60 years saw a considerable jump in numbers, as some quarter million German Jews made their way to the United States.[11] By 1881, it was apparent that formalized structures were needed to absorb all of the immigrants coming from Eastern and Central Europe. In that year the Hebrew Immigrant Aid Society was formally constituted and has remained the primary aid agency for Jewish immigration around the world, helping millions with resettlement. During this period, there was a "perception of emigration as banishment," a notion that contains biblical tropes, though most immigrants were actually of the secular sort—unafraid of breaking out of a more parochial life in the shtetl.[12] But many saw American as a new frontier that opened on all manner of possibility. A primer issued in 1907 for those undergoing the bar mitzvah instructed a Jewish boy that he should pray the following: "For my God and for my faith, I shall struggle . . . to the last drop of my blood. I am in the land of liberty, in America where Jews enjoy equal rights with all other nations; but I shall always keep in mind my brethren from other parts of the world where Justice is being trampled upon. Being a good citizen of America I shall also be a good Zionist, and strive to revive our holy land."[13]

In 1914, nearly 140,000 Jews fled Eastern Europe for the United States, trying to escape the oncoming catastrophe of World War I. But so many had come that the new arrivals were often branded as being politically suspect. Epithets of communism or anarchism followed these individuals, so that in November 1919, the so-called Palmer Raids rounded up thousands of Jewish "agitators." And still they came. Whereas in 1870 the Jewish population in the United States hovered around 200,000, by the mid-1920s, more than 4 million had arrived, with the heaviest volume coming between 1904 and 1908 (650,000 entrants, mostly from Eastern Europe).[14]

Considerable funding of immigration of Jewish co-religionists began in earnest in the early 20th century with the formation of groups like the American Jewish Committee and the United Jewish Appeal. The American Jewish Committee was founded in 1906 by a group of prominent American Jews in response to anti-Jewish riots in Russia. It was to be a defense and advocacy group, but practically all of its efforts have been to undertake programs that quash anti-Semitism, including the rescue of Jews in harm's way. Additionally, the American Jewish Joint Distribution Committee (also known as the JDC) was founded in 1914 to facilitate and centralize the collection and distribution of funds by American Jews for Jews abroad. Although the JDC was at first reluctant to aid individuals directly, this became necessary after the outbreak of World War II.

Between 1922 and 1960, more than 350,000 Jews fled Hitler's Europe or came to the United States as refugees seeking permanent residency. Most of these were in displaced persons camps scattered throughout Europe. Survivors of the war felt a special bond with one another and have passed on the responsibility of remembering to their children and to all persons of goodwill through such monuments as the United States Holocaust Memorial Museum. While the work of such institutions remains circumscribed, it nonetheless gives attention to the plight of refugees everywhere, especially those fleeing the dehumanizing effects of war and racism.

It is not possible to give adequate attention to Jewish immigration history in this short space, but of all the individuals who might be singled out for contributions to this cause, the name of Cecelia Razovsky has yet to claim its due.[15] Born May 4, 1886, in St. Louis, Missouri, she was an educator for the Jewish Educational

Alliance there until 1917, during which time she also taught evening classes to foreigners in public school for the St. Louis Board of Education. Eventually, in 1921, she was hired by the National Council of Jewish Women's Department of Immigrant Aid as its executive secretary, a post she held until 1932. She also edited its publication, *The Immigrant*, and published her own pamphlet, *What Every Emigrant Should Know*. This work enabled her to travel throughout Europe, surveying conditions for Jewish refugees in European ports. She undertook similar duties in Cuba, establishing a community center and refugee program in Havana. In 1927, she wed Dr. Morris Davidson but retained her maiden name. In 1929, she served as an official delegate to the International Association for the Protection of Migrants, an advisory committee of the League of Nations.

Razovsky became chairperson of the committee of the National Council on Naturalization and Citizenship in 1931 and was charged with investigating the fee structure for applicants to the United States. In that same year, she visited Soviet Russia to study its social services. In 1933, she chaired a committee of specialists appointed by Secretary of Labor Frances Perkins to advise policy makers on conditions at Ellis Island. Between 1933 and 1936, she chaired the General Committee of Immigrant Aid at Ellis Island and New York Harbor. In early 1934, with the crisis in Germany reaching epic proportions, she authored a document giving the general framework for the National Coordinating Committee, an umbrella group that assisted in securing passage from German occupied lands of hundreds of thousands of Jews to safe haven in various parts of the world. Eventually, she became the Executive Director of the National Coordinating Committee. In June 1939, she witnessed the attempted debarking of the SS *St. Louis*, a ship carrying 930 Jewish refugees, but which was eventually turned back from Cuba. While on board, she tried to prevent suicide attempts. In September 1940, she helped to negotiate safe landing for the SS *Quanza*, which had been denied admission in Mexico.

In 1939, Razovsky began the directorship of the Migration Department of the National Refugee Service, an affiliation she held until 1943. For the remainder of the war, she was attached to the United Nations Relief and Rehabilitation Administration (UNRRA) and worked on loan from the UNRRA in the Paris office of the American Jewish Joint Distribution Committee (AJDC), where she saw to the relocation of several thousand Jews from Western Europe and eventually their welfare while in displaced persons camps. In 1946, she devoted herself solely to this work under the auspices of the AJDC and helped to arrange massive resettlement programs in South America. Although she retired in 1948, this was short-lived. Her work on intergroup relations helped launch a new career as a field representative for the United Service for New Americans, where she toured the southern tier of the country inviting Jewish communities to accept new arrivals. Through the 1950s, Razovsky made visits to Israel, Brazil, Chile, Columbia, Ecuador, Panama, Paraguay, and Peru and spent the early part of the 1960s assisting Cuban refugees from Castro's revolution. She continued her Central and South American travels even while in semiretirement before she died in 1968.

Roman Catholics

Unlike any other religious body, the vast numbers of Catholics coming to U.S. shores has been a story fraught with heartache and joy, trial and triumph. Upon assuming the office of the presidency, George Washington wrote to Catholics (in the person of the Archbishop of Baltimore, John Carroll), "As mankind become more liberal they will be more apt to allow that all those who conduct themselves as worthy members of the community are equally entitled to the protection of civil government. I hope ever to see America among the foremost nations in examples of justice and liberality. And I presume that your fellow-citizens will not forget the patriotic part which you took in the accomplishment of their Revolution, and the establishment of their government; or the important assistance which they received from a nation in which the Roman Catholic faith is professed."[16] But in the 19th century, against the backdrop of nativism, which had infected local communities for a lengthy portion of the nation's history, Catholic immigrants had to fend for themselves.[17] Tied to their priests, these immigrants sought out sacramental relief wherever it could be found—a balm for their plight as penniless newcomers. "Who was this priest?" Michael Gannon has wondered.

> Originally, he was, in the main, Anglo-American and a former member of the English Province of the suppressed Society of Jesus. About twenty-five in number, this select body of the clergy was the total force of clergy available to Father John Carroll upon the latter's appointment as Superior of the American missions in 1784. The faithful to whom these priests ministered tended to be well-established Anglo-American families centered principally in Maryland. Very quickly, however, this clergy, to whom not only the English language but also the English traditions in literature and politics were native, yielded prominence to French and Irish immigrant clergy. Father François Nagot led the first group of French émigré priests to this country in the summer of 1791. Refugees from a France where the Civil Constitution of the Clergy, promulgated the year before, to all practical purposes severed the French Church from the See of Rome, this first group of four priests and five seminarians, all members of the Society of Saint Sulpice, founded the mother seminary of the American Church, St. Mary's, in Baltimore. Not only their seminary but also the Sulpician faculty, a considerable number of whom went out to the frontier as missionaries during the next quarter century, had an important and salutary influence on the state of the Church during the early national period.[18]

The Church's people self-identified by both their ethnic heritage and their ecclesial allegiances, creating a transnational and thick description of themselves, their neighborhoods, and their worldviews. Transnationalism could be seen at work among the Irish communities in the United States as early as 1880, when Michael Davitt told a group of Irish Americans gathered at New York's Cooper Union that if they wanted respect in their new homeland, they ought to aid those Irish across the Atlantic who were themselves struggling. "Aid us in Ireland to remove the stain of degradation from your birth and the Irish race here in America will get the respect you deserve."[19]

Catholics in the United States often found their bishops or other members of the hierarchy decrying particular legislative actions, particularly if they were perceived to exclude Catholic populations from immigrating to these shores. For instance, in 1914 and 1915, periodic attempts by Congress to insert literacy tests into the requirements for entry were met with denunciations from Cardinal James Gibbons of Baltimore or the Vatican itself.[20] However, Catholics were slow to take up the challenge of putting formal and comprehensive measures in place to assist new arrivals or to lobby on their behalf, but a vast network has since sprung up, particularly from the beginnings of the U.S. bishops' national headquarters in Washington, DC, launched as the National Catholic War Council (NCWC) in 1919. The following year, it established the Bureau of Immigration Affairs with a layperson, Bruce Mohler, as director. A decorated veteran of World War I and a diligent assistant for the American Red Cross in postwar Poland, the Ohio native brought a wealth of organizational and technical expertise to the job.

With nearly 50 years of service to the world's émigrés, Bruce Mohler's work for the National Catholic Welfare Conference helped to assist over a million people immigrate and resettle in the United States between 1920 and 1967. (Center for Migration Studies Coll. #023 Box 58)

Early in his tenure—which would last nearly five decades—Mohler brought on an Irish native, Thomas Mulholland, to run the NCWC's port office in New York. The two were constant correspondents, sending notes and memoranda nearly everyday for the entirety of their careers. There was no aspect of immigration on which the two men were not thoroughly briefed. Three important moments in U.S. history were shaped by their service. The first involves the massive exodus of Mexicans fleeing the turmoil there in the 1920s. Part of the difficulty in caring for these thousands was a lack of information on the ground, so

Mohler, at the behest of the apostolic delegate to the United States, Monsignor Pietro Fumasoni-Biondi, sent him to Mexico City. There Mohler delivered a letter from the Pope to the archbishop of Mexico City, José Maria Mora del Rio, in which the Pope observed the schismatic nature of the government of Mexico. The release of a pastoral letter on Mexico would be imminent, and when it came it blasted the government for its religious intolerance. The letter itself was smuggled in by Mohler, unbeknownst to the government, and was read out in all the churches in Mexico. The consequence was increased repression, the expulsion of the Archbishop, and untold numbers of Mexican Catholics (easily more than 200,000 per year), including scores of clergy, who came to the United States in what was the first massive migration crisis in the aftermath of World War I.[21] Consequently, Mohler established a border office at El Paso, Texas, to care for these refugees, and the Mexican border regions have been a priority area for the U.S. Catholic bishops ever since.

The second major involvement of Mohler in American immigration history involves the role he played in directing Catholic efforts to secure the release of Catholic non-Aryans from Germany. Like his counterpart Cecelia Razovsky, Mohler involved himself deeply in the rescue of thousands of persons escaping Nazism. The response came in two phases and was coordinated through several committees and offices of the NCWC. The first phase was prewar migration, which came steadily from the moment Hitler was elected chancellor in 1933. With the passage of the Nuremberg Laws, non-Aryan Catholics started coming en masse in 1935. The Evian Conference in the summer of 1938, which held out so much hope for European refugees, fell to pieces. Mohler worked diligently to secure the safe passage of thousands of German non-Aryans and shared information with Razovsky for the betterment of Jewish refugees. Although it was delayed in coming, the War Refugee Board was established to assist, and Mohler worked tirelessly with Archbishop Joseph Rummel of New Orleans to provide as much assistance as possible to this agency.

The third moment in which Mohler played a significant role came in the debates over the McCarran-Walter Act in 1951. In spring of that year, the National Catholic Welfare Conference was asked to give testimony before the Joint Subcommittee on Immigration and Naturalization on this bill. Mohler supplied lengthy commentary to the subcommittee and ultimately endorsed McCarren-Walter. Speaking for the whole episcopate, Mohler noted that the following provisions of the bill found favor: "the removal of racial barriers to admissibility and naturalization; the abolishing of sex discrimination in the various immigration procedures; recognition of the desirability and need for uniting and keeping family units intact; the simplification of processes to accord permanent residence, if desired, to qualified non-immigrants while they are residing within the country; and the policy of providing selectivity to certain persons whose services are urgently needed here."[22] Mohler's testimony reveals that he was especially concerned with family stability and the ability of foreign priests to enter the United States for ministry. The act passed in 1952, and, although the exclusivity of the act was widely felt, Mohler was pleased to report to the bishops that provisions that encouraged family reunification already had brought together tens of thousands of immigrants with their kin. And yet he remained unsatisfied and hoped these numbers would increase. When in 1953 the Refugee Relief Act was reexamined and new provisions established for the unification of spouses and children with heads of households living in the United States, Mohler was again alerted to the potential to advance a Catholic position, though on this legislation he had much less influence. Thanks largely to legislation of Senator John Kennedy of Massachusetts (signed by the president as PL 85–316 on September 11, 1957), the Refugee Relief Acts limitations would come under review, and Kennedy himself invited Mohler's Department of Immigration Affairs to prepare a noncontroversial measure that would "terminate many of the inadequacies of the present law."[23] Mohler took the opportunity not only to stress the importance of family reunification, for which there would be an immediate benefit for some 33,000 people, but he also sought to undo the disastrous effects of a national origins quota system, which the U.S. bishops had continuously opposed since the 1920s. His ideas stimulated the progressive move toward elimination of national origins quotas that eventuated in the Hart-Celler Act of 1965. It was about this time that Mohler stepped down from his service at the bishops' conference headquarters, but his record remains a lasting legacy. Without exaggeration, well over 2 million immigrants and their families were assisted in some way by his office during his tenure.

The activities of the Department of Immigration Affairs were consolidated in 1966 to include many programs—resettlement, care for orphans, Cuban refugees, and the more traditional concerns affecting immigrants to the United States. Today the Church has its primary focus on the border to the south, in part because border communities themselves are primarily Catholic. Indeed, in its last major pastoral letter on immigration, the U.S. bishops joined their Mexican counterparts in a joint statement, "The Stranger Among Us."[24] This deep connection between the Church and the immigrant has not been lost on the popular mindset, and the denomination's membership has been vociferously pro-immigrant, even risking legal action for its advocacy. For instance, as a sign of his displeasure with a border security bill, "in early 2006 a priest from a large Catholic church [in El Paso] posted a big sign on a roof facing the Interstate 10 freeway which read, 'Immigrants Welcome, No to House Bill 4437.'"[25]

As the Catholic Church in the United States is also part of a worldwide ecclesial body, it also takes direction from and works with other particular churches within its communion and international organizing bodies such as the International Catholic Migration Commission (ICMC). The latter organization has charge of the World Day of Migrants and Refugees. In January 2010, the governing committee of the ICMC celebrated its 60-year anniversary. It has operations in 40 countries and represents the Holy See in several international organizations, including pertinent bodies of the United Nations in New York and Geneva. It tackles such issues as human trafficking, refugee protection and integration, migrant rights and responsibilities, children's issues, and, lately, it has turned its attention to advocacy issues, such as the lessening of xenophobia and racism toward migrants.

Additionally, the Holy See guides episcopal conferences such as the one in the United States with periodic policy statements. One branch of the Roman Curia is the Pontifical Council for the Pastoral Care of Migrants and Itinerant Peoples. In 2004, it issued *Erga Migrantes Caritas Christi*, a document that has promoted awareness of the difficulties of migration and that is constructive in its efforts to organize local churches to act in defense of immigrants, the displaced, and refugees, as well as all those itinerant peoples that traverse the earth.[26] It has been implemented by many groups working especially with immigrant populations around the globe, including the Society of Jesus, a religious order.[27] In the United States, the Jesuits have attempted to engage Congress and the White House over immigration reform and have personally lobbied on Capitol Hill.[28] Even in the face of perceptibly unjust laws that adversely affects immigrants' rights, some Catholic leaders—notably Cardinal Roger Mahoney, the emeritus archbishop of Los Angeles—has threatened civil authorities with massive disobedience. On Good Friday 2006, Catholic bishops in New York State called upon Congress to pass legislation that "provides for a pathway to permanent legal status for undocumented workers" and makes a provision for "rational and fair temporary worker" programs. The attitudes of most Catholics, according to a 2006 Zogby poll, showed strong opposition (49 percent) to the granting of a blanket amnesty for the undocumented; only 34 percent supported it; 15 percent were unsure.[29]

These attitudes and activity are supplemental to what the United States Conference of Catholic Bishops (USCCB) attempts to do in influencing policy. While it acknowledges the willingness of President Barack Obama to move on comprehensive immigration reform, the USCCB has continually called for action on the part of Congress. In June 2010, for instance, the Episcopal conferences of the entire Western Hemisphere gathered in Washington, DC, and requested that government officials do all in their power to provide the requisite legal protections and recognition for migrants of all types.[30]

Conclusion

"In the United States, immigration and religion are inextricably linked," concludes a recent group of scholars.[31] One could add that the glue that holds them together is politics. In 2005, religious leaders were so adamant about securing comprehensive immigration reform that they decided to come together and sign a joint statement that has all but fallen on deaf ears. Nevertheless, it is significant that so many have come into the public square on this issue. In their "Interfaith Statement,"[32] these leaders pointed to both the Biblical and Qur'anic texts that undergird the mission to the immigrant. Among their demands, the leaders wished their officials to put in place in any future legislation "an opportunity for hard-working immigrants who are already contributing to this country to come out of the shadows, regularize their status upon satisfaction of reasonable criteria and, over time, pursue an option to become lawful permanent residents and eventually United States citizens" and "significantly reduce waiting times for separated families who currently wait many years to be reunited." Among the signatories were the Anti-Defamation League, the American Friends Service Committee, the American Jewish Committee, the American Society for Muslim Advancement, Islamic Circle of America, the United Methodist Committee on Relief, and the USCCB. Symptomatic of a closer vision among the people of the land, perhaps one day the idea of a just immigration policy will be made reality.

Notes

1. See Yvonne Yazbeck Haddad, Janie I. Smith, and John L. Esposito, eds., *Religion and Immigration: Christian Jewish, and Muslim Experiences in the United States* (Walnut Creek, CA: AltaMira Press, 2003).
2. See especially, Richard Alba, Albert J. Raboteau, and John DeWind, eds., *Immigration and Religion in America* (New York: New York University Press, 2009), from which the present article draws liberally.
3. See, for example, Dean R. Hoge and Michael W. Foley, *Religion and the New Immigrants: How Faith Communities Form Our Newest Citizens* (New York: Oxford University Press, 2007).
4. See http://www.madreanna.org/immref/alien.pdf.
5. See Tom Strode, "S. Baptists Want Immigration Enforcement, Land Tells Bush," *Baptist Press* (March 24, 2006).
6. See the entire statement at http://www.umc.org/site/apps/nlnet/content3.aspx?c= lwL4KnN1LtH&b=2072519&ct=3978987.
7. See Anju Mary Paul, S.V., "Scapegoating of Arab and Muslim Americans," in *Battleground Immigration*, vol. 2, ed. Judith Ann Warner (Westport, CT: Greenwood Press, 2009), 753.
8. Arsalan Iftikhar, "Presumption of Guilt: September 11 and the American Muslim Community," in *Keeping Out the Other: A Critical Introduction to Immigration Enforcement Today*, eds. David C. Brotherton and Philip Kretsedemas (New York: Columbia University Press, 2008), 108.
9. See: http://nationalhumanitiescenter.org/tserve/twenty/tkeyinfo/islam.htm.

10. Naomi Werner Cohen, *Encounter with Emancipation: The German Jews in the United States, 1830–1914* (Philadelphia: Jewish Publication Society of America, 1984).

11. From http://www.jfrej.org/Jewish.Immigration.Timeline.html.

12. See Matthew Frye Jacobson, *Special Sorrows: The Diasporic Imagination of Irish, Polish, and Jewish Immigrants in the United States* (Berkeley: University of California Press, 2002), 25.

13. Jacobson, *Special Sorrows*, 72, citing G. Selikowitz, *Der yiddisher-amerikaner redner* (New York: Hebrew Publishing, 1907), 34–35.

14. See Calvin Goldsheider, "Immigration and the Transformation of American Jews: Assimilation, Distinctiveness, and Community," in *Immigration and Religion in America*, eds. Richard Alba, Albert J. Raboteau, and John DeWind (New York: New York University Press, 2009), 201.

15. The papers of Cecelia Rasovsky are housed at the American Jewish Historical Society at the Center for Jewish History in New York. An online finding aid, with an excellent biographical summary, is available at http://findingaids.cjh.org/index2.php?fnm=CeciliaRazovsky&pnm=AJHS.

16. Washington to Carroll, March 15, 1790, in *The Papers of George Washington*, vol. 5, eds. Dorothy Twohig, Mark A. Mastromarino, and Jack D. Warren (Charlottesville: University of Virginia Press, 1996), 301.

17. See, for example, Tyler Anbinder, *Nativism and Slavery: The Northern Know-Nothings and the Politics of the 1850s* (New York: Oxford University Press, 1992).

18. See Michael V. Gannon, "Before and After Modernism: The Intellectual Isolation of the American Priest," in *The Catholic Priest in the United States: Historical Investigations*, ed. John Tracy Ellis (Collegeville, MN: Saint John's University Press, 1971), 299. Gannon continued: "It was the Irish, however, who eventually would predominate, in numbers, in manner, and in influence. Irish priests—Augustinians, Capuchins, Dominicans, and seculars—filtered into the seaboard towns during the late 1780s and already by 1792 had changed the composition of American clergy in their favor. . . . With them and ahead of them came thousands of their fellow countrymen: a total of 1,783,791 from the time of Carroll's death in 1815 until the close of the Civil War in 1865. Before the next century they could be found everywhere in the young nation" (300).

19. See Thomas N. Brown, "The Origins and Character of Irish-American Nationalism," in *Irish Nationalism and the American Contribution*, ed. Lawrence McCaffrey (New York: Arno Press, 1976), 334. Jacobson, *Special Sorrows*, also notes at 67: "One historian [Emmet Larkin] has recently suggested that, given the centrality of the Catholic Church in 'sustaining the ongoing Irish

identity' against the encroachments of Anglicization, 'it was inevitable that Irish and Catholic over time would become virtually interchangeable terms.'"

20. For a review of the chronology, see Catholic University of America, *U.S. Catholic Bishops and Immigration: Chronology* (Washington, DC: Catholic University of America), http://libraries.cua.edu/achrcua/immigration/immigration_chron.html.

21. See Mohler to Fumasoni-Biondi, April 2, 1926, in Center for Migration Studies, Staten Island, New York, Bureau of Immigration Affairs, Restricted Files from Box 56: Mexico/Mr. Mohler's Trip 1926.

22. See Mohler's testimony in Center for Migration Studies, Staten Island, New York, Bureau of Migration Affairs, Box 48: McCarran-Walter Act.

23. Mohler to the apostolic delegate to the United States, Archbishop Amleto Cicognani, September 17, 1957, in Center for Migration Studies, Staten Island, New York, Bureau of Migration Affairs, Box 48: McCarran-Walter Act.

24. See the entire statement at United States Conference of Catholic Bishops, *Strangers No Longer: Together on the Journey of Hope* (Washington, DC: USCCB, 2003), http://www.usccb.org/mrs/stranger.shtml.

25. Kathleen Staudt, "Bordering the Other in the U.S. Southwest El Pasoans Confront the Local Sheriff," in *Keeping Out the Other: A Critical Introduction to Immigration Enforcement Today*, eds. David C. Brotherton and Philip Kretsedemas (New York: Columbia University Press, 2008), 300. Staudt calls attention to the sentiments of several scholars that "it is not the church that saves the immigrant. Because of their faith, their dependence on God and their faithful witness amidst adversity, the immigrant saves the church."

26. Pontifical Council for the Pastoral Care of Migrants and Itinerant Peoples, *Erga Migrantes Caritas Christi* (Vatican City, 2004), http://www.vatican.va/roman_curia/pontifical_councils/migrants/documents/rc_pc_migrants_doc_20040514_erga-migrantes-caritas-christi_en.html.

27. William O'Neill, "What We Owe to Refugees and IDPs: An Inquiry into the Rights of the Forcibly Displaced," in *Refugee Rights: Ethics, Advocacy, and Africa*, ed. David Hollenbach (Washington, DC: Georgetown University Press, 2008), 27–49.

28. See the letter of the Jesuit Conference of the United States at http://www.jesuit.org/index.php/home/jesuits-men-for-others/immigration/immigration-letter. Jesuits have been pondering the immigration question, arguably, since the 1600s. A more recent reflection may be found in Jesuit Refugee Service, *Everybody's Challenge: Essential Documents from the Jesuit Refugee Service, 1980–2000* (Rome: JRS, 2000).

29. For analysis of the April 2006 Zogby poll, see "Catholic Bishops to Left of Flock on Immigration," *The Washington Times,* April 17, 2006, http://www.washingtontimes.com/news/2006/apr/17/20060417-104414-6805r/.

30. See "Bishops to US: Reform Your Immigration Laws: Calls for Just and Humane Treatment of Migrants," June 11, 2010, http://www.zenit.org/article-29582?l=english. See also http://www.usccb.org/comm/archives/2010/10-118.shtml.
31. Haddad, Smith, and Esposito, *Religion and Immigration*, 1.
32. See "Interfaith Statement in Support of Comprehensive Immigration Reform" (October 14, 2005), http://worldrelief.org/Page.aspx?pid=1524.

Bibliography

Abrams, E., ed. *The Influence of Faith: Religious Groups and U.S. Foreign Policy.* Lanham, MD: Rowman & Littlefield, 2001.

Bau, I. *The Ground Is Holy: Church Sanctuary and Central American Refugees.* Mahwah, NJ: Paulist Press, 1985.

Becker, P., and N. Eiesland, eds. *Contemporary American Religion: An Ethnographic Reader.* Walnut Creek, CA: AltaMira Press, 1997.

Burns, J., E. Skerrett, and J. White, eds. *Keeping Faith: European and Asian Catholic Immigrants.* Maryknoll, NY: Orbis Books, 2000.

Cadge, Wendy, and Elaine Howard Ecklund. "Immigration and Religion." *Annual Review of Sociology* 33 (2007): 359–379.

Dolan, J. *The Immigrant Church: New York's Irish and German Catholics.* Baltimore: Johns Hopkins University Press, 1975.

Dolan, J., and A. Deck, eds. *Hispanic Catholic Culture in the U.S.: Issues and Concerns.* Notre Dame, IN, and London: University of Notre Dame Press, 1997.

Ebaugh, H., and J. Chafetz. *Religion and the New Immigrants: Continuities and Adaptations in Immigrant Congregations.* Walnut Creek, CA: AltaMira Press, 2000.

Eck, D. *A New Religious America: How a "Christian Country" Has Become the World's Most Religiously Diverse Nation.* San Francisco: Harper Collins, 2001.

Gleason, P. "Immigration, Religion, and Intergroup Relations: Historical Perspectives on the American Experience." In *Immigrants in Two Democracies: French and American Experience*, edited by D.L. Horowitz and C. Noiriel, 167–187. New York: New York University Press, 1992.

Joselit, J. *Immigration and American Religion.* New York: Oxford University Press, 2001.

Levitt, Peggy. *God Needs No Passport: Immigrants and the Changing American Religious Landscape.* New York: New Press, 2009.

Matovina, T., and G. Poyo, eds. *Presente! U.S. Latino Catholics from Colonial Origins to the Present.* Maryknoll, NY: Orbis Books, 2000.

Menjfvar, C. "Religious Institutions and Transnationalism: A Case Study of Catholic and Evangelical Salvadoran Immigrants." *International Journal of Politics, Culture, and Society* 12 (1999): 589–612.

Min, P., and J. Kim, eds. *Religions in Asian America: Building Faith Communities.* Walnut Creek, CA: AltaMira Press, 2002.

Ng, D., ed. *People on the Way: Asian North Americans Discovering Christ, Culture, and Community.* Valley Forge, PA: Judson Press, 1996.

Smith, T. L. "Religion and Ethnicity in America." *American Historical Review* 83 (1978): 1155–1185.

Spinner-Halev, J. *Surviving Diversity: Religion and Democratic Citizenship.* Baltimore: Johns Hopkins University Press, 2000.

Tomasi, S. M. "The Ethnic Church and the Integration of Italian Americans in the United States." In *The Italian Experience in the United States*, edited by S. M. Tomasi and M. H. Engel, 163–193. New York: Center for Migration Studies, 1970.

Tweed, T., ed. *Retelling U.S. Religious History.* Berkeley: University of California Press, 1997.

Tweed, T., and S. Prothero. *Asian Religions in America: A Documentary History.* New York: Oxford University Press, 1999.

Villa, P. *Crossing Borders, Reinforcing Borders: Social Categories, Metaphors, and Narrative Identities on the U.S.-Mexico Frontier.* Austin: University of Texas Press, 2000.

Warner, R. S., and J. G. Wittner, eds. *Gatherings in Diaspora: Religious Communities and the New Immigration.* Philadelphia: Temple University Press, 1998.

Yang, Y. *Chinese Christians in America: Conversion, Assimilation, and Adhesive Identities.* University Park: Pennsylvania State University Press, 1999.

Yoo, D., ed. *New Spiritual Homes: Religion and Asian Americans.* Honolulu: University of Hawaii Press, 1999.

Thomas Jefferson (1743–1826): "A Right Which Nature Has Given to All Men"

Mary Elizabeth Brown

Born in the British colony of Virginia on April 13, 1743, Thomas Jefferson played a role in Virginia's, and the American nation's, fight for independence and then remained politically active until his death on July 4, 1826. During his life, he held many honors: governor of Virginia, minister plenipotentiary to France, first secretary of state of the United States, and second vice president of the United States. As a candidate for office, he helped to found both the two-party system and an ancestor of the modern Democratic Party. As president, he approved the Louisiana Purchase and the subsequent Lewis and Clark expedition. In private life, he was known for his interest in just about everything, and the home he designed, Monticello, is a tourist attraction. He remains a popular and controversial biographical subject.

Jefferson wanted to be remembered for other achievements. He designed his own gravestone, an obelisk mounted on a rectangular base. He asked that the base be engraved with his three favorite accomplishments: author of the Declaration of Independence, author of the Virginia Statute of Religious Liberty, and founder of the University of Virginia. These pointed not so much to deeds as to ideas and values: self-government, freedom of conscience, and liberal education.

How are those values reflected in Jefferson's stance on immigration? Jefferson's writings on immigration show his intellectual side, his interest in trying to think a problem through. They also show his emotional side, his ability to shrink from his own conclusions. Finally, they show where his loyalties lay in the conflict between how he felt and what he thought, between what he termed, in another context, his heart and his head.

Jefferson began writing on immigration late in 1774. In 1773, Bostonians had staged a protest against a tax Parliament said the colonists were supposed to pay for tea, dumping several chests of tea leaves into Boston Harbor. Parliament reacted to this destruction of property, and to the attitude of disobedience underlying it, with a series of laws that it called the Coercive Acts and that Massachusetts labeled the Intolerable Acts. Massachusetts appealed to the other colonies for support, and

Thomas Jefferson, third president of the United States. (Library of Congress)

a Continental Congress was called to determine a course of action. Virginia held a convention at Williamsburg to elect and instruct delegates to the Continental Congress.

Jefferson was supposed to participate, but when he left his home at Monticello, he found the winter roads impassable, and he also took sick. All of this may have confirmed his sense of how best to participate in the Williamsburg meeting. Jefferson was never good at public speaking. He could not speak loudly, and any time he spoke for a long period, he developed a hoarse, raspy voice. He also got flustered easily; he was not very good at thinking on his feet and answering objections on the spot. He preferred to write. In this case, he wrote what he intended to say at the meeting and entrusted copies to two other delegates, Patrick Henry and Peyton Randolph. Randolph had a house in Williamsburg and read Jefferson's writing to delegates assembled informally there. Shortly thereafter, Jefferson's thoughts were published in a pamphlet titled *A Summary View of the Rights of British America*.

The first right Jefferson covered was the right to leave one country for another: The Saxons had abandoned Northern Europe, taken over the sparsely inhabited island of Britain, and established a government there. Whatever government they had left behind in Northern Europe never claimed them for a colony. In the American case:

> [Our] ancestors, before their emigration to America, were the free inhabitants of the British dominions in Europe, and possessed a right which nature has given to all men, of departing from the country in which chance, not choice, has placed them, of going in quest of new habitations, and of there establishing new societies, under such laws and regulations as to them shall seem most likely to promote public happiness.[1]

It is most likely that Jefferson got this idea from an earlier pamphlet: Richard Bland's 1766 *Inquiry into the Rights of the British Colonies*.[2] Readers may notice that Jefferson, characteristically, was skipping some problems. The Saxons in Britain and the British in America encountered natives to whom they denied the rights of life, liberty, and the pursuit of happiness. Another notable point is that Jefferson used some ideas here that he used again later. The first was the idea of natural rights. It is not clear here whether a right is a liberty (the freedom to do something) or a power (the ability to do it), but whichever it is, it is, a priori, as if there were already a person present before any of the accidents of birth were added. Persons were free. Once those persons were born as girls, there were limitations put upon them. Once society cast some into slavery, there were some limitations put on those people. Once persons organized governments, they put limits on themselves for the sake of the community. But all men were *created* equal.

Sex, and probably race, put limits on individuals that, as far as Jefferson was concerned, no human effort could remove. Governments, which came after people and were created by them, were supposed to be less powerful. Historical accidents had given some governments, notably despotic crowned heads, powers they were not really supposed to have. History, though, had been kind to the Saxons on the island of Britain. They were able to hew closely to natural law in erecting their government. When those born in Great Britain left for North America, they erected their own governments, based on their understanding of the natural law that was preserved and exemplified in British history. And, Jefferson claimed, unlike the Saxons leaving Europe, these emigrants "thought proper" to continue their union with the crown, who became "the central link connecting the several points of the empire thus newly multiplied." Here, again, Jefferson overlooked some historical facts. Contrary to claims Jefferson made in his pamphlet, the colonies would not have been founded without a certain minimum of royal assistance, such as a charter. Although colonies, notably Massachusetts, tried to distance themselves from the royal government, the royal government was involved in colonial administration. These historical inaccuracies may have been deliberate distortions, written to win over delegates in Williamsburg. They do not undermine the fact that Jefferson saw expatriation as a natural right.

Within the newly established governments, participation was to be as broad as possible, as demonstrated by one of the wilder passages in *A Summary View of the Rights of British America*. Having established to his satisfaction the colonists' right to form their own governments and to obey only their own laws, Jefferson launched into a lengthy indictment of how Parliament and the crown tried to force their laws on colonies. Specifically, he claimed:

> The abolition of domestic slavery is the great object of desire in these colonies, where it was unhappily introduced in their infant state. But previous to the enfranchisement of the slaves we have, it is necessary to exclude all further importations from Africa; yet our repeated attempts to effect this by

prohibitions, and by imposing duties which might amount to a prohibition have been hitherto defeated by his majesty's negative.[3]

Again, Jefferson is ignoring historical fact. It was not just that the British wanted to sell slaves; it was that traders based in the colonies wanted to trade them and that colonists wanted to use their cheap labor. What is important here is that Jefferson used *abolition* and *enfranchisement of the slaves* as synonyms. No halfway status was identified between slavery and full citizenship, no free blacks languishing without the vote or civil rights.

As it happened, *A Summary View of the Rights of British America* enhanced Jefferson's reputation as a political writer. By the time the delegates chosen at the Williamsburg convention arrived in Philadelphia, matters in Massachusetts had run far ahead of their instructions. On April 18, 1775, a battle broke out between British troops stationed in Boston and militia in Boston and surrounding towns. The Continental Congress had already dissolved, so a Second Continental Congress was called to determine how to meet the crisis. Jefferson was chosen a delegate from Virginia to the Second Continental Congress. Arriving at the Philadelphia meeting place of the new Congress in the spring of 1776, he was put on a committee to draft what became known as the Declaration of Independence.

Although the declaration is shorter, its structure is similar to *A Summary View of the Rights of British America*. It has a short preamble, then the statement of principles that begins with "We hold these truths to be self-evident." It then lists specific examples of how crown and Parliament had violated these principles. In his draft, Jefferson again introduced his charge that King George III had prevented colonists from abolishing slavery. His fellow delegates did not find the accusation sufficiently convincing, and besides, they were writing a justification of their reasons for opposing the crown; it was no time to be accusing themselves of similar bad behavior. Out went the clause regarding slavery. However, Congress did permit another of Jefferson's charges to remain, one that took the same issue of the colonists' efforts to extend the privileges of citizenship but used immigrants as the example: "He has endeavoured to prevent the population of these States; for that purpose obstructing the Laws of Naturalization of Foreigners; refusing to pass others to encourage their migration hither, and raising the conditions of new Appropriations of Lands."[4]

After the Second Continental Congress adopted the Declaration of Independence on July 4, 1776, Jefferson resigned his position as a delegate and returned to Virginia. Once the Declaration was signed, Virginia was no longer a colony. It was a state, a self-governing entity. Specifically, it was a commonwealth, whose people chose their rulers rather than acquiescing to a hereditary aristocracy or a royal line. Its laws needed an overhauling befitting its new status. Jefferson was already involved in this project. In June 1776, besides the draft of the

Declaration of Independence, he had produced a draft of a constitution for Virginia. Between 1776 and 1779, he gathered copies of all the laws passed under the colonial government—no easy task given that, before easy means of making copies, there was only one copy of some of these laws in the entire colony. He studied the laws and made recommendations for new ones. Among these recommendations were several regarding immigration to Virginia, acquiring citizenship there, and expatriating from the commonwealth.

Consistent with his belief that migration was a human right, Jefferson made immigration, citizenship, and expatriation easy. Insofar as citizenship for the native-born was concerned, he adopted the tradition of English common law, known as jus soli, or the law of the soil, which ruled that anyone born in Virginia was a citizen of the commonwealth. Because Virginia had slavery, there was an exception to jus soli: Those born of slave mothers inherited their mothers' slavery and were neither free nor citizens of the commonwealth. There were no restrictions on who could enter Virginia. All immigrants could take oaths or make affirmations (some religions forbade the taking of oaths, and Jefferson, respecting freedom of conscience, made provisions for variations in religious practice) that they intended to reside in Virginia for two years (later increased to seven by the legislature) and that they intended to subscribe to Virginia's fundamental laws. With that oath or affirmation, they had the same rights as free native Virginians. All sane men aged 21 or older and possessing a certain amount of land (the legislature later set the amounts at one-quarter of an acre in a town or 25 acres of rural territory) could vote. Citizens could divest themselves of citizenship by declaring—using means admissible in court—that they intended to expatriate.[5] Citizens of the other 12 states in the new United States were extended the same rights, privileges, and immunities of Virginia citizens.[6] This was during a time when few other countries had provisions for accepting immigrants, for making them citizens, or for letting native-born citizens leave.[7]

Some evidence suggests that Jefferson understood that his proposals were generous and that he considered them an inducement to migration. He was heard to suggest that Virginia might offer money and land to those willing to migrate to it.[8] Encouraging migration, though, was never one of Jefferson's main themes. During the early years of the United States, he was decidedly ambiguous about it.

After completing the revision of the laws for the newly independent Virginia, Jefferson was elected to a one-year term as governor of the commonwealth. His term was made difficult by the fact that the Revolutionary War had moved south. Traitor Benedict Arnold, now commanding British troops, was in advance of a British force heading north from Savannah, Georgia. During Jefferson's administration, Arnold invaded Virginia, ultimately unsuccessfully. Arnold's failure was not due to Jefferson's astute wartime leadership. Jefferson did ride and shoot, but, unlike his Virginia colleague George Washington, he had no intellectual interest in military affairs. Instead, while the invasion was going on, his term of office ended, and he did not even stay in Richmond (the capital he had chosen when revamping the laws for its central location in the state) to hand over the reins of government to his successor. He headed back to Monticello and to a new project, a book that he eventually titled *Notes on the State of Virginia*.

The *Notes* are organized as if Jefferson was responding to an interested student's or visitor's questions about his state. It has 23 chapters, each titled "Query," because each asked about a different aspect of the commonwealth. Query VIII concerns Virginia's population. Jefferson explained that he considered Virginia underpopulated. The two usual ways of augmenting population are by natural increase—by people having babies—and by immigration. With the attention to detail typical of him when he was engaged in such problems, Jefferson gave the population of *all* Virginians, slave and free, men and women. In 1782, the latest date available to him, the total was 567,614. He then calculated how many people Virginia could hold; he put the figure at 4.5 million. He determined it would take Virginia until three-quarters of the way through 1862 to reach its maximum population if it relied solely on natural increase, and until midway through 1835 if a number of people equal to the number of births immigrated each year. Then Jefferson subtracted 1782 from October 1862 and also from June 1835 to get the relative difference between using natural increase and using natural increase plus immigration to attain his population goals. His conclusion: It would take 81.75 years for Virginia to reach 4.5 million people if it relied on natural increase alone and 54.5 years if it relied on both natural increase and immigration. Finally, Jefferson subtracted 54.5 from 81.75, to reach 27.25.[9]

Was immigration worth the savings of 27 years to achieve Virginia's population goals? Jefferson thought not.

It is for the happiness of those united in society to harmonize as much as possible in matters which they must of necessity transact together. Civil government being the sale object of forming societies, its administration must be conducted by common consent. Every species of government has its specific principles. Ours perhaps are more peculiar than those of any other in the universe. It is a composition of the freest principles of the English constitution, with others derived from natural right and natural reason. To these nothing can be more opposed than the maxims of absolute monarchies. Yet, from such, we are to expect the greatest number of emigrants. They will bring with them, the principles of the governments they leave, imbibed in their early youth; or, if able to throw them off, it will be in exchange for an unbounded licentiousness, passing, as is usual, from one extreme to another. It would be a miracle were they to stop precisely at the point of temperate liberty. These principles, with their language, they will transmit to their children.

In proportion to their members, they will share with us the legislation. They will infuse into it their spirit, warp and bias its direction, and render it a heterogeneous, incoherent, distracted mass.[10]

This is hardly a flattering portrait of immigrants. Buried in it, however, is an interesting statement: "In proportion to their members, they will share with us the legislation." As with the example from his writings on slavery, cited above, Jefferson had no halfway status. He would not admit that a government could protect itself by preventing people with dubious backgrounds and opinions from voting. (He argued, though, that it should protect itself from immigrants, and from its own people's worst tendencies, with a system of free public education from the elementary to the university level.) Even if their previous experience under European monarchies had left immigrants improperly prepared to exercise their natural rights, they still retained these rights.

Shortly after completing the work that led to the *Notes on the State of Virginia*, Jefferson was called to service by the new national government operating under the Articles of Confederation. He was sent to Paris as minister plenipotentiary. While there, he was asked to review an article on the new Étas-Unis for a French publication, the *Encyclopedie Methodique*. The article criticized the United States for permitting indentured labor, in which individuals contracted to provide several years of labor, free of charge except for their living expenses, in exchange for passage to the United States. Jefferson observed that this was hardly the Americans' fault:

So desirous are the poor of Europe to get to America, where they may better their condition, that being unable to pay their passage, they will agree to serve two or three years on their arrival here, rather than not go. During the time of that service, they are better fed, better clothed, and have lighter labor, than while in Europe. Continuing to work here a few years longer, they buy a farm, marry, and enjoy all the sweets of a domestic society of their own. The American governments are censured for permitting this species of servitude, which lays the foundation of the happiness of these people. But what should the governments do? Pay the passage of all who choose to go into their country? They are not able; nor, were they able, do they think the purchase worth the price? Should they exclude those people from their shore? Those who know their situations in Europe and America, would not say that this is the alternative which humanity dictates.[11]

Jefferson's capacity to fudge the facts shines through here. There is some debate as to the relative difficulty of indentured servitude in the United States and labor in Europe. There was no doubt he was correct in asserting that socioeconomic mobility was more likely in the United States than in Europe. What is interesting is

Jefferson's comments about a possible alternative to indentured servitude, that the U.S., or a state, government pay the passage of potential immigrants. He wondered if the federal or state governments would really consider these people a bargain. Yet although he was not willing to pay for these people to migrate, he ruled out excluding them. Their natural right to migrate outweighed the governments' interest in selecting immigrants.

One final bit of evidence regarding Jefferson's thoughts on immigration comes from a suggestion he made to John Adams in 1785. He proposed to make citizenship between contracting nations reciprocal. U.S. citizens living abroad would have all the rights, immunities, and privileges of their host countries, and immigrants would automatically have all those of the United States. For all practical purposes, there would be no immigration; the crossing of national borders would pose no problem. Even Jefferson admitted this was far outside the accepted way of doing things, but it is an example of his commitment to the idea that movement, even international movement, was a basic human right.[12]

The Alien and Sedition Acts of 1798 moved Jefferson from a philosopher debating the proper laws for immigration to participant in the debate. The Alien and Sedition Acts were four in number. The Sedition Act had to do with the right to criticize, in print or in speech, elected officials and their policies. The Alien Enemies Act permitted the federal government to detain noncitizen immigrants in cases in which the United States went to war against their home countries. The Alien Act permitted the president to order out of the country any noncitizen immigrant, to detain those who refused to leave, and to deport those whose detention proved difficult, for whatever reason the president chose. The Naturalization Act superseded a previous act of 1795, which required five years' residence in the United States before an immigrant applied for citizenship. The new law required 14 years' residence.

There were two motives behind the Alien and Sedition Acts that are significant here. The first was a military motive. The Alien and Sedition Acts were passed because there was a chance the United States would be caught in a war between France and England—specifically, that the United States might declare war on France to protect the rights of neutral ships on the high seas. This was the first time the United States was faced with this situation, and the new country needed legislation to regulate immigrants during the war. In fact, the Alien Enemies Act is still on the books and could be activated in time of war.

The second motive was partisan politics. The Alien and Sedition Acts were passed shortly after the first two political parties, the Federalists and Jefferson's Democratic Republicans, were formed. The Federalists controlled the presidency. The Jeffersonians interpreted the Alien and Sedition Acts as directed against themselves. For example, the Alien Act was set to expire on June 25, 1800, and the Sedition Act on March 3, 1801. These expiration dates gave the Federalists the power to suppress opposition to their rule during the presidential campaign of 1800. The best evidence of a Federalist plot to suppress Jeffersonians was the Naturalization Act, with its lengthy waiting period for citizenship. It was thought that recent immigrants voted for the Jeffersonians, and the Naturalization Act made it look as though the Federalists were determined to deny immigrants citizenship, and voting rights, until they got over their Jeffersonian leanings.[13]

It was Jefferson's private opinion that the Alien and Sedition Acts were unconstitutional extensions of executive power. A personal protest, though, would not be very effective. Someone with authority had to rule the laws were unconstitutional. This was before John Marshall, in *Marbury v. Madison*, set the precedent on which the Supreme Court ruled as to the constitutionality of laws. At that point, the only precedent had been set by George Washington. When he was president, Washington would receive bills passed by Congress. If he was uncertain about their constitutionality, as he was when Congress authorized a national bank, he would ask for advice from his cabinet and then make a ruling. According to this precedent, John Adams was now charged with responsibility for ruling on the constitutionality of the law. However, it was unlikely that Adams would rule as Jefferson desired; Adams was more sympathetic toward the Federalists. Anyway, Jefferson had his own candidate for the proper authority for ruling on the constitutionality of laws. The states, which until the Fourteenth Amendment stood outside the Constitution, could judge it.

Jefferson drafted a document laying out this theory and applying it specifically to the Alien and Sedition Acts. Introduced into the Kentucky legislature by his associate, John Breckenridge, and approved on November 16, 1798, they became known as the Kentucky Resolves. In his document, Jefferson made only two references directly to immigration. He pointed out that the Constitution did not say anything about aliens whose home countries were not at war with the United States. Under the principle of strict construction, that meant that Congress could pass no legislation regarding "alien friends." The states in which they lived passed any legislation necessary. The only power over migration that the Constitution gave Congress was in Article I, Section 9: "The Migration or Importation of such Persons as any of the States now existing shall think proper to admit, shall not be prohibited by the Congress prior to the Year one thousand eight hundred and eight." Jefferson knew this had been inserted as a compromise over the slave trade, but taken literally, the clause referred only to immigration. Fortunately for Jefferson, he was writing this in 1799, not after 1808, when this section expired and Congress had greater power. For the present, Congress had to follow state law. If a state admitted a person, Congress could not pass a law permitting the president to expel or detain that person.

It is worth emphasizing that immigration was of secondary concern in the Kentucky and Virginia Resolves. Jefferson used the Alien and Sedition Acts to show that Congress had exceeded its constitutional mandate. However, to say that immigration was of secondary importance is not to say it was of no importance. When he became president, Jefferson, like the Federalists he criticized, used the powers of the office to urge action on immigration issues.

On December 8, 1801, Jefferson delivered his first annual message to Congress, assessing his presidency and laying out plans for the future. He suggested action on the remaining sore point from the Alien and Sedition Acts, the Naturalization Act:

> Considering the ordinary chances of human life, a denial of citizenship under a residence of fourteen years is a denial to a great proportion of those who ask it, and controls a policy pursued from the first settlement by many of these States, and still believed of consequence to their posterity. And shall we refuse the unhappy fugitives from distress that hospitality which the savages of the wilderness extended to our fathers arriving in this land? Shall oppressed humanity find no asylum on this globe? The Constitution, indeed, has wisely provided that, for admission to certain offices of important trust, a residence shall be required sufficient to develop character and design. But might not the general character and capabilities of a citizen be safely communicated to everyone manifesting a *bona fide* purpose of embarking his life and fortunes permanently with us?[14]

Congress obliged, restoring the previous requirement of five years' residence in order to become a U.S. citizen. During his second administration, Jefferson had one last chance to act specifically on behalf of immigrants, and his actions showed his consistent adherence to his earliest principles. France and Great Britain were at naval war. The British had the stronger navy. British naval ships stopped other nations' ships, naval and commercial ships, even ships from countries with which England was not at war. The commanders ascertained where the ships were going. If they were going to England's enemies, the commanders had the ships searched and carried off any contraband or materials that would directly aid the enemy war effort. The commanders also searched the ships for people who could be subjected to British impressment laws. Life in the British navy was so notoriously harsh that the navy faced a constant labor shortage. This is where the issue of immigrants again came in. The British did not permit native-born men to abandon their citizenship and take on that of some other country. They considered any English-born man, even one who had become a naturalized U.S. citizen, to be English and thus subject to impressment laws. The United States, though, followed the Jeffersonian principle that an individual could leave one country and become a citizen in a second, that naturalized English-born sailors were Americans, and thus the sailors should not be impressed into the British navy. These conflicting issues of citizenship were as much an issue as neutral rights on the high seas.

The issue was still unsettled when Jefferson finished his second term as president; eventually, it contributed to the War of 1812. By then, James Madison was almost ready to run for his second term. Jefferson had watched his successor take the oath of office in 1809, and then he returned to Monticello. Much of the rest of his life was taken up with the founding of the University of Virginia, which he thought of as a "wonderful hobby for a septuagenarian," and his personal affairs. Jefferson was constantly in debt. He sold his library to the federal legislature (where it became the basis for the Library of Congress) and was supposed to use the money to pay off debts and start afresh, but soon he was back to his old habits of buying books, redesigning Monticello, experimenting with new plants in his garden, and ignoring the effect of his discretionary spending on his budget. He slipped back into debt and never emerged from it.

Jefferson never again dealt with immigration as a public issue. Having worked out his thoughts in the 1770s, he stuck to these principles throughout his life. On June 12, 1817, in a private letter, he gave them one last expression: "If [God] has made it a law in the nature of man to pursue his own happiness, he has left him free in the choice of place as well as mode; and we may safely call on the whole body of English jurists to produce the map on which Nature has traced, for each individual, the geographical line which she forbids him to cross in pursuit of happiness."[15]

This was indeed a radical position in that it was based on an analysis of the root issues of which rights took precedence—the rights of nations or the rights of individuals. It was also radical in that it was one of Jefferson's basic principles to which he adhered through 50 years of political activity as a writer, partisan leader, and president. In fact, it may have been Jefferson's consistency that gave rise to the charge that he was inconsistent, impractical, and unable to see the real issues involved. Many other people, contemplating the immigration of people who might not make good citizens, would unhesitatingly protect those people from their own inevitable mistakes in self-government, and protect the nation, by prohibiting immigration. Jefferson, too, flinched at the prospect of immigrants bringing in strange languages and stranger political principles. However, he reminded himself that all men are, indeed, created equal and that this was the moral basis on which he should act.

Notes

1. [Thomas Jefferson], *A Summary View of the Rights of British America* (Williamsburg, VA: Clementin A. Rind, 1774), in Paul Leicester Ford, comp. and ed., *The Works of Thomas Jefferson*, 12 vols. (New York: G. P. Putnam's Sons, 1904), 2:64.
2. David N. Mayer, *The Constitutional Thought of Thomas Jefferson* (Charlottesville: University Press of Virginia, 1994), 338–339.

3. Jefferson, *A Summary View*, 79.

4. "The Declaration of Independence," in Henry Steele Commager, ed., *Documents of American History*, 8th ed., 2 vols. (New York: Appleton-Century-Croft, 1968), 1:101.

5. Samuel K. Padover, comp., *The Complete Jefferson* (New York: Duell, Sloan and Pearce, 1943), 659.

6. Thomas Jefferson, 1776 draft of constitution for Virginia, in Ford, *The Works of Thomas Jefferson,* 2:176, 180; Merrill D. Peterson, *Thomas Jefferson and the New Nation: A Biography* (New York: Oxford University Press, 1970), 153–154.

7. John Sharp Williams, *Thomas Jefferson: His Permanent Influence on American Institutions* (New York: Columbia University Press, 1913), 91.

8. William Eleroy Curtis, *The True Thomas Jefferson*, The "True" Biographies and Histories Series (Philadelphia: J. B. Lippincott, 1901), 302; Peterson, *Thomas Jefferson and the New Nation*, 153–154.

9. Thomas Jefferson, *Notes on the State of Virginia*, ed. William Pedan (Charlotte: University of North Carolina Press, 1954; reprint, New York: W. W. Norton, 1972), 83–84 (page citations are to the reprint edition).

10. Ibid., 84–85.

11. Padover, *The Complete Jefferson*, 55. Jefferson's notes on the article were written on June 22, 1786.

12. Peterson, *Thomas Jefferson and the New Nation*, 310.

13. An example is the community of Anglo-Irish lawyers that migrated to New York. See Walter L. Walsh, "Religion, Ethnicity, and History: Clues to the Cultural Construction of Law," in *The New York Irish*, ed. Ronald H. Bayer and Timothy J. Meagher (Baltimore and London: Johns Hopkins University Press, 1996), 48–69.

14. Padover, *The Complete Jefferson*, 393.

15. Thomas Jefferson to John Manners, n.p., June 12, 1817, cited in Mayer, *The Constitutional Thought of Thomas Jefferson*, 80.

Bibliography

Jefferson's writings are available in several formats, including Paul Leicester Ford, comp. and ed., *The Works of Thomas Jefferson*, 12 vols. (New York: G. P. Putnam's Sons, 1904); Andrew Lipscomb and Alber Ellery Bergh, eds., *The Writings of Thomas Jefferson*, 20 vols. (Washington, DC: Thomas Jefferson Memorial Association, 1904); and Samuel K. Padover, comp., *The Complete Jefferson* (New York: Duell, Sloan and Pearce, 1943). Jefferson himself wrote one book; the edition used here was *Notes on the State of Virginia*, ed. William Pedan (Charlotte: University of North Carolina, 1954; reprint, New York: W. W. Norton, 1972). Jefferson also has many biographers. Among the best is Joseph J. Ellis, *American Sphinx: The Character of Thomas Jefferson* (New York: Alfred A. Knopf, 1997); Dumas Malone, *Jefferson and the Ordeal of Liberty* (Boston: Little,

Brown, 1962); and Merrill D. Peterson, *Thomas Jefferson and the New Nation: A Biography* (New York: Oxford University Press, 1970). Jefferson worked out his thoughts on immigration in the context of his general work on law, and there are useful monographs on this subject, such as those of David N. Mayer, *The Constitutional Thought of Thomas Jefferson* (Charlottesville: University Press of Virginia, 1994) or Peter Onuf, *Jefferson's Empire: The Language of American Nationhood* (Charlottesville: University Press of Virginia, 2000). A helpful monograph on the historical context in which Jefferson worked out his ideas is Stanley Elkins and Eric McKitrick, *The Age of Federalism: The Early American Republic, 1788–1800* (New York: Oxford University Press, 1993).

Denis Kearney (1847–1907): "The Chinese Must Go!"

Mary Elizabeth Brown

Open a survey of Chinese American or California history to the index, and one will probably find "Kearney, Denis" (or "Dennis") followed by one reference. Go to that reference, and one will probably find out that Kearney spearheaded a campaign that ultimately led to the 1882 Chinese Exclusion Act. The ubiquity of this information is matched by the paucity of any other. There is no modern biography of Kearney, and the one biography that ever was in book form consisted of 3 pages in a 100-page political pamphlet, with one of those pages being devoted to a picture of him.

Yet Kearney shaped the U.S. debate on immigration in numerous ways. He shifted the debate geographically, moving it from the East Coast and Old Northwest to the West Coast, from a discussion of Irish and German migration to a discussion of Chinese migration. Being Irish himself, he changed the sides in the debate from natives versus immigrants to one group of immigrants versus another. He was the first since the debate over the importation of slaves to raise the issue of immigrants of different races. To get across his viewpoint, Kearney had to involve himself in other issues. He had to break up the regular two-party system and convince voters to support a third party, the Workingmen's Party of California (WPC). He had to organize the party so that it followed his guidance and not that of rival would-be leaders. And then he had to be on the winning side in a series of other conflicts: the power of the state legislature versus that of a constitutional convention, state power versus federal power, and the power of one country against another.

Denis Kearney was born in Oakmont, County Cork, Ireland, on February 1, 1847. He was the second of seven boys in a family so poor that they did not send him to school. Then the family situation worsened. When Denis was 11 years old, his father died. His mother sent him to sea to earn his living. At some point early in his career, he began to work under the American flag. He worked his way up from cabin boy to first officer. He sailed into San Francisco in 1868 as first officer aboard a coastal steamer, the *Shooting Star*, decided to make the city

Denis Kearney spearheaded a campaign that ultimately led to the 1882 Chinese Exclusion Act. (Courtesy of the Bancroft Library)

his home base, and took a job with Messrs. Holladay and Brennan, a steamship firm. In 1870 he married Mary Ann Leary, with whom he eventually had four children. In 1872, he gave up seafaring and purchased a dray business. A dray was a low wagon, without sides, used for heavy loads such as full beer barrels. He eventually acquired three drays and hired others to help do all the hauling that came his way.[1]

Because some might consider him an entrepreneur, it is worth emphasizing that Kearney called himself a workingman. Nor was he unusual in this. Those who worked with him in the Workingmen's Party of California had similar backgrounds. Frank Roney was born in Ireland and had been active in Irish trade unions and in the movement to liberate Ireland from England; he migrated to the United States when he was threatened with arrest and execution in Ireland. William Wellock, second vice president of the Workingmen's Party of California, was born in England and apprenticed to a boot and shoemaker; he immigrated to the United States in 1872 and to California in 1876. Henry M. Moore, the party secretary, was born in New York State, apprenticed to a tailor, and later became a lawyer. Thomas Donnelly was born in County Tyrone in 1848 and emigrated in 1857; at the time he was involved in Workingmen politics he was in the coal business. Lawyer Clitus Barbour was the son of Irish, German, and Welsh immigrants, although he himself was born in Illinois. Also a lawyer was Charles J. Beerstecher, who was born in Urach, Württemberg, Germany, and came to the United States when his father's involvement in '48er politics meant the family had to leave the country. Grocer John Dunn was born in County Cavan, Ireland, but raised in the United States.[2] Critics charged that the adoption of the workingman identity was politically motivated; Kearney attracted voters by claiming, falsely, to be one of them.

Political opportunity does not seem to have been Kearney's reason for calling himself a workingman. Kearney was involved in the Draymen and Teamster's Union. The business he owned was the Irish immigrant equivalent of the stereotypical Chinese laundry, a business that did not require a great deal of capital to start or a great deal of skill to operate. Kearney truly relied on his own labor.

He inherited nothing from his family and apparently did not marry into wealth. And he would work for a long, long time to support himself, because he had no retirement earnings. In fact, critics charged that Kearney's interest in politics stemmed from a failed effort to enhance his own earnings; some people claimed he invested his savings in the stock market and lost all.[3] In short, even though he owned his own business, Kearney's life was as insecure as it would have been had he worked for wages, and in that sense he was a workingman.

Work, though, whether in one's own business or for wages, was not the core of self-definition for Kearney and his colleagues. Their pamphlets explained why they were "real" workingmen and the Chinese, who seemed equally industrious, were not:

> The intelligent American laborer in seeking employment in California, for the purpose of providing for his wife and children the necessary raiment for covering their nakedness, food for their mouths, and education enough to enable them to successfully fight the battle of life after him, contends with a race who know nothing of these necessities in their lives, who live upon the very refuse of the land, and who make this very absence of responsibilities and the low depravity of their own lives the means of successfully underbidding the labor of our own people.[4]

For the "intelligent" workingmen, work was not an end to itself but a means to an end. It was the way to earn money to achieve middle-class status, measured by the acquisition of comforts for oneself and by one's ability to secure more education and more options in terms of careers and professions for one's offspring. Ironically, the workingmen resembled the Chinese more closely than they knew; it was just that the Chinese had their families back home in China, where the overall cost of living, and their own families' standard of living, was indeed lower. Rather than reach across the races, though, and form one large union, Kearney and his associates turned to familiar and traditional tools, to their trade unions and to politics, to preserve their status in society.

The conditions that led Kearney into politics started in 1873. That year, the New York Stock Exchange collapsed, partly because financier Jay Gould tried to corner the gold market and drove up prices with his purchases. When the stock market crashed, investors held on to their money until more secure investments presented themselves. That meant that businesses could not obtain the capital to start up or to expand, and thus they could not hire new workers. Businesses that depended on other businesses' expansion, such as forges that turned out steel for railroads, had to lay off their workers. There was no safety net for these workers, no unemployment insurance. What saved the situation for a while was that the same year the stock market crashed, the Comstock Lode silver vein was discovered in Nevada.

For a few years, renewed mining opportunities drew more people west. By 1877, the West was sharing in the depression that ground on year after year. In January of that year, the Comstock Lode missed paying a dividend to its stockholders. Its stock slipped. The stock market sank, and the economy started to unwind: no business expansion, no new jobs; soon, the existing jobs disappeared, too.

Unemployment was not an either/or situation. During the good weather, men fanned out across California. Periods of employment planting a crop or filling in on a railroad gang alternated with periods of tramping to the next possible work site. As the weather turned bad, workers began to drift, like autumn leaves falling off a tree, down the hills and into San Francisco. They competed against each other for jobs that were only as numerous as the city's normal population. Consistent losers sank into hunger and homelessness. Winners lived from job to job, working a few days here and there, eating from day to day and paying the rent nightly or weekly. The semi-employed filled up any spare space in the city, presenting an opportunity for more settled families to make fast money by taking in a boarder or lodger. They spent their time together, sharing information on job possibilities, spending money when they had it, discussing what it was that had brought them to this condition.

The Workingmen's Party of the United States put forth one attractive theory. This party had been formed a year earlier on the East Coast. Its members had previously been involved in the First Internationale, Marxism, and other socialist groups. However, it would be premature to see the Workingmen as equivalent to the Communist Party of the 20th century. The most communist-like thing that could be said about them was that they thought that the government was stacked against the workers. They parted with the communists in that they thought it was still possible to use the political system to restack the government in favor of the workers. The next summer, the Workingmen's Party became interested in a labor-state conflict taking place in Pittsburgh. On July 16, 1877, the Baltimore and Ohio railroad announced a 10 percent wage cut. Baltimore and Ohio workers at Martinsburg, West Virginia, responded by halting railroad traffic through their town. The Baltimore and Ohio managers asked the governor of West Virginia for assistance, and the governor called out the state militia. When state troops proved ineffective and the strike spread to other cities, President Rutherford B. Hayes authorized the use of the United States Army. Truly, the government seemed to favor the railroad over the workers.

On July 23, some people who were interested in starting a San Francisco unit of the Workingmen's Party of the United States called an open-air meeting to show support for the Baltimore and Ohio workers. About 6,000 people came to the meeting.[5] The meeting was held near city hall at a sandlot, a tract cleared for construction and covered with sand until a building could be erected on it. Speeches about the Baltimore and Ohio workers, even speeches about the dangers of capital and a capitalist-dominated government that could apply more directly to the San Franciscans, were insufficiently compelling. Groups hived off from the audience and went marauding in nearby Chinatown. On July 23, they attacked Chinese laundry rooms. The next night, they set fires and murdered Chinese before the police intervened. The third night, they set fire to a lumberyard near the docks of the Pacific Mail Steamship Company, which transported many Chinese to California. Apparently, the rioters were attempting to burn down the docks. When firefighters arrived, the arsonists tried to prevent them from doing their work, and the result was a riot in which several men were killed.

City officials regained control with the aid of a volunteer, an entrepreneur who had helped out in previous anti-Chinese violence, William T. Coleman. Coleman formed a Vigilance Committee to patrol the streets for several weeks to discourage rioting. He also prepared a report on the causes of the riot and made suggestions for preventing another one. His chief proposal was that the federal government should seek to amend the Burlingame Treaty with China so as to exclude Chinese immigration to the United States. Coleman's report came out the day before the state elections scheduled for early September. The effect was to give the voters a new task to impose on their elected officials. It was at this point that Kearney burst upon the scene. As Kearney later explained:

> In September, 1877, immediately after the general State, municipal and congressional elections, I called a meeting of working men and others to discuss publicly the propriety of permanently organizing for the purpose of holding the politicians up to *the* pledges made before the election. . . . I made up my mind that if our civilization—California civilization—was to continue, Chinese immigration must be stopped, and I saw in the people the power to enforce that "must." Hence the meeting. This meeting resolved itself into a permanent organization, and "resoluted" in favour of a "red-hot" agitation. I was, in spite of my earnest protests, elected president of this new organization, with instructions from the meeting to "push the organization" throughout the city and state without delay. Our aim was to press Congress to take action against the Chinese at its next sitting.[6]

On August 18, 1877, the nucleus of the San Francisco branch of the Workingmen's Party held a small meeting at Charter and Oak Hall. They announced a platform party members were dedicated to promoting. Its key features were abolishing assessments on candidates for office, holding state and local officials accountable for their action, establishing a bureau of labor statistics, regulating the hours of labor, and pressing the state legislature to create a convention on labor with its headquarters at San Francisco. On Sunday, September 16, the leaders called a meeting at the sandlot by city hall in order to appeal to the masses; the meeting attracted about 500 people. Considering the meeting reasonably successful, the leaders called a second meeting for Friday, September 21. At this meeting, Kearney changed the direction of the entire political movement by making racism a reasonable response to capitalist exploitation, claiming that "the capitalists who employ Chinese are robbing the working people with their system."[7]

On October 4, word reached San Francisco that a group of Chinese at Rocklin had murdered a group of whites. Kearney used the resulting spike in the anti-Chinese fever to call a meeting at Dashaway Hall on October 5. He led the audience in forming a Workingmen's Party of California. Its first party platform plank showed its affinity for the Workingmen's Party of the United States, proposing "to wrest the government from the hands of the rich and place it in the hands of the people where it naturally belongs." The second plank added a specifically California twist: "We propose to rid the country of cheap Chinese labor as soon as possible, and by all the means in our power, because it tends still more to degrade labor and aggrandize capital."[8]

The Workingmen's Party embarked on a series of open-air meetings. Critics complained that the choice of the open-air format indicated that Kearney was nothing more than a demagogue attracting unemployed loiterers. Kearney replied: "It was only when the city authorities, who while persecuting us, either hired all of the halls or frightened their owners or lessees into not allowing us to hire them, that we were driven to the Sand Lots."[9] When Kearney's claim is balanced against the actual meeting record, a pattern appears that indicates the secret of his success. Others vying for party leadership often met indoors, hiring a variety of halls. Kearney, though, excelled at sandlot addresses, dominated the open-air meetings, and sometimes used the crowds he mobilized there to back him in getting the other would-be leaders to agree to do things his way.

During the month of October, the Workingmen's Party of California became the talk of San Francisco and the specter that haunted the city's officials. On Sunday, October 7, a sandlot meeting attracted 4,000, eight times the number that came in mid-September. By the end of the month, the mob had moved off the sandlots and closer to the homes and offices of the well-to-do and the entrepreneurs. On Monday, October 29, Kearney addressed a crowd at the city's Nob Hill. Kearney later complained that the newspapers distorted his speeches, but in this case, parts of the speech were reprinted in a Workingmen's Party of California pamphlet, and one can see that it was replete with slurs upon the Chinese and with reminders of previous acts of violence visited upon capitalists who oppressed the workers. On November 1, All Saints' Day for himself and his many Irish Catholic followers, he addressed another crowd at the Irish-American Hall. Kearney's remarks were not recorded, but the officials either heard it or heard about it. On November 3, they issued a warrant for his arrest for "using language tending to incite his hearers to deeds of violence." Bringing the warrant with them, the police found Kearney speaking at a street-corner meeting and carried him off in midsentence.[10]

Instead of solving their problems, the city officials created a martyr. On November 14, officials had to release Kearney because the ordinance under which the arrest warrants were issued was ruled illegal. They immediately re-arrested him under a different charge, inciting a riot. A judge heard the case November 15–21 and acquitted Kearney on the grounds that there had, in fact, been no riot following Kearney's address. On January 9, 1878, Kearney was arrested a third time, for violating a new law, another attempt to ban language tending to incite public disorder. This time the case went to a jury, which, on January 22, found Kearney not guilty. Each time he was cleared, it was an occasion for celebration and for attracting new adherents to the Workingmen's Party of California.[11]

The appearance of one party encouraged yet another, the Grangers, who found support in rural California. The Grangers also criticized the regular politicians and parties for being in the pay of the corporations. Railroads, the Grangers complained, charged farmers more for hauling their produce than they charged the big corporations for hauling their larger shipments of industrial goods. Grain elevator owners similarly gave price breaks to big customers and gouged the small ones. Banks lent money at low interest to big industries but charged high rates to farmers. If the Workingmen and Grangers could get together and discuss their economic programs, perhaps they could unite and form a stronger party movement that would benefit them both.

During the 1875–1876 legislative session, the state legislature had decided to have voters elect delegates to a convention to write a new state constitution. California was operating under a constitution drafted in 1849. The Civil War and its attendant constitutional amendments, state population growth, the completion of the transcontinental railroad, and the development of the economy made a new one desirable. The legislature's action was a boon for the Workingmen and the Grangers, giving both a chance to guide public policy. At this point, the Workingmen's Party of California had to organize itself to create a united front at the California constitutional convention and to ally itself with the Grangers so that the two groups could dominate the convention. However, efforts to create unity nearly broke down over Kearney's insistence on retaining power.

By early 1878, Kearney had a serious rival for power in the Workingmen's Party of California: Frank Roney. Roney wanted an organization that reflected his experience in Ireland and in San Francisco. He proposed that the Workingmen's Party structure itself by creating a statewide central committee composed of five representatives from each senatorial district and one from each trade union in the state. This, he thought, would strike a balance between competing goods: allowing the diverse voices in the party to be heard and their various interests to be aired and securing leadership from experienced, competent people who could choose among themselves who would run for available political offices. Kearney objected that all of Roney's plans simply guaranteed more politics as usual. The district and trade union representatives would be more interested in their positions, and in the lucrative bribes and kickbacks industries routinely offered political leaders, than they would be in representing their constituents. Kearney proposed that no one already an officer in the party should accept a position as a candidate for office. Kearney won, mostly on the strength of his superior skills at rousing oratory and ad hoc leadership; he would speak at a local political meeting, give a speech, and the next thing Roney knew, his experienced and competent leaders were being dumped for putting their personal advancement above party concerns and were being replaced with leadership loyal to Kearney. Maybe Roney's system of carefully building a disciplined party whose leadership represented diverse views would have prevailed, but time was too short for him to fight back. Roney was so thoroughly routed that he abandoned his political efforts and left the city.

Why was it so important to Kearney to dominate the Workingmen's Party of California? Perhaps he was simply power hungry. But there is another possible explanation, and that is that Kearney did not trust anyone else to give the same priority to anti-Chinese legislation that he did. People like Roney would be too willing to work with the Grangers on general economic issues and would not press for anti-Chinese laws. Support for this view comes from a look at the constitution the delegates drafted in September 1878.

Rather than cooperation between the Grangers and the Workingmen's Party of California on legislation important to both, there was a division. The economic laws written into California's constitution were of particular concern to the Grangers. The Grangers thought government was corrupt, and they tried to prevent such corruption by putting elected officials on short leashes, by limiting the state legislature to enacting laws that carried out priorities set in the constitution, and by making it a felony to attempt to bribe a state official. The Grangers distrusted big business even more than big government and so introduced regulations for the stock market, the telegraph business, the gas business, the water business, and the railroad and established in the constitution the principle that the government could legislate to prevent corporations from conducting business in such a way as to infringe on public welfare. Finally, the Grangers thought the previous constitution distributed the tax burden unfairly and so legislated a different system, authorizing a state study of property holdings for tax purposes, taxing uncultivated land (which corporations had been holding as investments), and authorizing the state to levy an income, in addition to a real estate, tax.

The Workingmen got their anti-Chinese legislation. Their program was spelled out in the four sections of Article XIX. Section 1 was directed at immigrants generally. It listed the categories of immigrants for which the state could enact legislation and described the types of activities the state could engage in. The second section spoke directly to the Workingmen's most pressing concern, job competition:

No corporation now existing or hereafter formed under the laws of this State shall, after the adoption of this Constitution, employ, directly or indirectly, in any capacity, any Chinese or Mongolian. The Legislature shall pass such laws as may be necessary to enforce this provision.

Section 3 also discussed job competition, this time in the public sector: "No Chinese shall be employed on any State, County, municipal, or other public work, except in punishment for crime." Section 4 indicated that the Workingmen's anti-Chinese sentiment drew strength from racism as well as from economic concerns:

The presence of foreigners ineligible to become citizens of the United States is declared to be dangerous to the well being of the State, and the Legislature shall discourage their immigration by all means within its power. Asiatic coolieism is a form of human slavery, and is forever prohibited in this State; and all contracts for coolie labor shall be void. All companies or corporations, whether formed in this country or any foreign country, for the importation of such labor, shall be subject to such penalties as the Legislature may prescribe. The Legislature shall delegate all necessary power to the incorporated cities and towns of this State for the removal of Chinese without the limits of such cities and towns, or for their location within prescribed portions of those limits; and it shall also provide the necessary legislation to prohibit the introduction into this State of Chinese after the adoption of this Constitution. This section shall be enforced by appropriate legislation.[12]

Upon completion of its work, the convention called for a statewide referendum to ratify or reject the drafted constitution. The ratified constitution became California's fundamental law in 1879. Almost immediately, the state constitution came into conflict with the U.S. Constitution. Pursuant to Article XIX, Section 2, the 1879–1880 California state legislature made it a misdemeanor for a corporation to employ Chinese. The Sulphur Bank Quicksilver Mining Company challenged the law. The case went to the Supreme Court, which ruled that Article XIX was an unconstitutional violation of the recently (1868) ratified Fourteenth Amendment to the U.S. Constitution, which guaranteed equal protection under the law.[13]

Thus, all the anti-Chinese provisions that the Workingmen's Party of California had managed to have added to the California state constitution became null and void. In response, the party became even more thoroughly anti-Chinese. Frank Roney, for example, had earlier had his doubts about the party's anti-Chinese thrust. According to Roney, when the anti-Chinese issue first took over San Francisco politics, "[I] agreed to sail under the flag so emblazoned in order that I might in time have other and real subjects considered by the people, which I deemed to be of far greater importance to their permanent well-being."[14] However, later in his career, Roney borrowed a leaf from Kearney's book. After his quarrel with Kearney cooled, he returned to San Francisco and organized 40 labor unions into a League of Deliverance that called on employers to discharge Chinese workers and asked consumers to boycott goods made by Chinese immigrants. Kearney had demonstrated that being anti-Chinese was the way to get ahead in California politics.

Kearney now rode astride two horses—one being the Workingmen's Party of California and the other the effort to participate in the national anti-Chinese movement. After the ratification of the constitution, Kearney busied himself selecting California Workingmen's Party candidates for the 1879 elections. As candidate for mayor of San Francisco, Kearney chose a former New England abolitionist named Isaac Kalloch. Kearney's choice caused a split among his followers. Charles De Young, editor and publisher of the San Francisco *Chronicle*, had wanted to promote his own candidate. De Young tried to achieve his goals by shooting candidate Kalloch. Kalloch survived the assassination attempt, won the election, and continued the anti-Chinese agitation locally.

For his part, Kearney began to campaign nationally. After the summertime election of the constitutional convention delegates in 1878, Kearney headed east to campaign against the Chinese there. He returned to California in 1879 to stump the state on behalf of the constitution and to prepare for the September elections. In January 1880, after Kalloch was installed as mayor, Kearney went back east. He recalled these trips as "a brilliant success. In less than a year I had succeeded in lifting the Chinese from a local to a great national question."[15]

Kearney was correct that Chinese immigration had become a national issue, although making it so came at a cost. While Kearney was reaching new audiences in the East, he was losing them in California. He missed the winter in San Francisco, when the unemployed gathered in the city. When they went to the sandlots, the unemployed heard new speakers: L. J. Gannon and Anna Smith. The Workingmen's Party also suffered a scandal. When Kalloch recovered from his assassination attempt, judicial officials concluded there was no further reason to hold his would-be assassin and freed De Young. Kalloch's son then distributed the sort of rough justice frontier California had been famous for, shooting, and this time killing, De Young.

Kearney also should have shared with others the credit for making opposition to Chinese immigrants a national cause. A quarter century of anti-Chinese legislation and agitation in California had not been lost on the federal government. In 1877, a Joint Congressional Committee to Investigate Chinese Immigration interviewed numerous Californians and concluded that economics indicated continued Chinese immigration was indeed undesirable. In 1880, the Chinese imperial government and the United States signed an agreement to revise the Burlingame Treaty, with new provisions for the limitation or temporary suspension of Chinese immigration. The next year, the U.S. Congress tried to suspend Chinese immigration for

20 years; it was prevented from doing so by President Chester Alan Arthur's veto. On May 6, 1882, Congress got its way, passing the first of a series of laws that excluded Chinese immigration almost entirely.

Anti-Chinese sentiment did have its opponents. Two years after the Joint Congressional Committee to Investigate Chinese Immigration issued its report, an anonymous minority report appeared; rumor had it the report was authored by the Joint Committee's chair, the late Oliver Morton, who had been active in Reconstruction. The report charged that the real opposition to Chinese migration stemmed not from the supposed economic concerns but from racism. An editorial in *The New York Times* fairly dripped with sarcasm trying to communicate its theory that the reason the Chinese were so mistreated was because their government was too weak to enforce its treaty claims. The United States, the *Times* claimed, honored its agreements with France and England, countries strong enough to force such respect. When there was no one around to compel respect, when it was a matter of dealing with Indians or Chinese, the United States showed its true attitude toward the importance of its treaties.[16]

Some critics of the anti-Chinese movement found it ironic, or perhaps fitting, that Kearney should be so thoroughly identified with it. Racial discrimination was so contrary to the Declaration of Independence proclamations of equality, so un-American, that it had to come from somewhere else. William Lloyd Garrison heaped on Kearney the venom he previously reserved for slaveholders and their supporters: "that most ignorant, profane, strike-engendering and besotted declaimer Denis Kearney—himself a foreigner, or of foreign descent, and much more entitled to be in a lunatic asylum than running at large."[17] W. H. Barton of the *California Independent* saw "a Historic Parallel." At the same time as the anti-Chinese excitement, Germany experienced an outbreak of anti-Semitism, with prominent Germans calling for Jewish exclusion on the grounds that Jews filled the universities and colleges, worked their way to the top in business, and excelled in the arts. Similarly, Kearney and his companions "say the Chinese are intemperate, industrious, economical, ingenious and apt in intellectual acquirement, and are, therefore proving themselves more the equal in the race of life with the Irish; hence the cry: 'The Chinese must go!'"[18]

Kearney himself thought he had nothing to apologize for. When critics taunted that his star fell as rapidly as it had risen and that he had no career in politics, he answered them serenely:

> I stopped agitating after having shown the people their immense power, and how it could be used. The Chinese question was also in a fair way of being solved. The plains of this State were strewn with the festering carcasses of public robbers. I was poor, with a helpless family, and I went to work to provide for their comfort. Common sense would suggest that if I sought office,

or the emoluments of office, I could easily have formed combinations to be elected either governor of my State or United States Senator.[19]

Kearney was correct that he spent the rest of his life out of the public eye. He remained interested in his reputation; most of the quotes from him cited above come from a long letter he sent to Lord Bryce when he saw a chapter on "Kearneyism in the United States" in Bryce's case study of American political science, *The American Commonwealth*. Kearney died at Alameda, California, on April 24, 1907.

Kearney's influence on the debate over immigration continued long after his death. The laws against Chinese migration remained on the books until 1943. When the Republic of China was allied with the United States to defeat the Empire of Japan in World War II, it seemed contradictory to regard the Chinese as suitable allies but not suitable immigrants. Accordingly, the Chinese were given a national quota of 105 immigrant visas per year. The Chinese achieved parity with other nations in 1965, when all national restrictions on migration were lifted. Even then, questions remained about the desirability and possibilities for assimilation of immigrants of different colors and races.

Notes

1. J.C. Stedman and R.A. Leonard, *The Workingmen's Party of California: An Epitome of Its Rise and Progress* (San Francisco: Bacon, 1878), 95.
2. Ibid., 103ff.
3. James Bryce, *The American Commonwealth*, 2 vols. (New York: Macmillan, 1910), 2:432; "The Anti-Chinese Movement—Important Statements, Letter from a Trades Unionist," *Labor Standard* (June 23, 1878), reproduced in Philip S. Foner and Daniel Rosenberg, eds., *Racism, Dissent, and Asian Americans from 1850 to the Present* (Westport, CT: Greenwood Press, 1993), 173–174.
4. Stedman and Leonard, *Workingmen's Party*, 11.
5. Elmer Clarence Sandmeyer, *The Anti-Chinese Movement in California* (Urbana: University of Illinois Press, 1939; reprint, Urbana: University of Illinois Press, 1991), 64 (page citation is to the reprint edition).
6. Bryce, *American Commonwealth*, 2:937–938.
7. Stedman and Leonard, *Workingmen's Party*, 16–19.
8. Ibid., 20–21.
9. Bryce, *American Commonwealth*, 2:938–939.
10. Stedman and Leonard, *Workingmen's Party*, 22–27.
11. Ibid., 31–33, 49–53.
12. "The Constitution of the State of California, 1879," quoted in William L. Tung, *The Chinese in America, 1820–1973: A Chronology and Fact Book* (Dobbs Ferry, NY: Oceana Publications, 1974), 57.

13. Mary Roberts Coolidge, *Chinese Immigration* (New York: Henry Holt, 1909; reprint, New York: Arno, 1969), 124 (page citation is to the reprint edition).

14. Frank Roney, *Frank Roney: Irish Rebel and California Labor Leader*, ed. Ira B. Cross (Berkeley: University of California Press, 1931), 287, quoted in Alexander Saxon, *The Indispensable Enemy: Labor and the Anti-Chinese Movement in California* (Berkeley: University of California Press, 1971), 122.

15. Bryce, *American Commonwealth*, 2:938.

16. "The Chinese Must Go," *New York Times* (February 26, 1880), reprinted in Foner and Rosenberg, *Racism, Dissent, and Asian Americans*, 106–108.

17. Letter to the editor, William Lloyd Garrison, Boston, February 15, 1879, reprinted in Foner and Rosenberg, *Racism, Dissent, and Asian Americans*, 105.

18. W. H. Barton, "A Historic Parallel," *California Independent* (March 13, 1880), reprinted in Foner and Rosenberg, *Racism, Dissent, and Asian Americans*, 109–110.

19. Bryce, *American Commonwealth*, 2:938.

Bibliography

Kearney had no biography but is represented in the *Dictionary of American Biography*. Besides coverage in the newspapers of the day, useful primary material is in J. C. Stedman and R. A. Leonard, *The Workingmen's Party of California: An Epitome of Its Rise and Progress* (San Francisco: Bacon, 1878); and Philip S. Foner and Daniel Rosenberg, *Racism, Dissent, and Asian Americans from 1850 to the Present*, Contributions in American History No. 148 (Westport, CT: Greenwood Press, 1993). James Bryce, *The American Commonwealth*, 2 vols. (New York: Macmillan, 1910), includes excerpts from a letter from Kearney to the author and cites the author's own interviews in San Francisco in 1880. It discusses Kearney from the perspective of political science. Useful secondary material includes Mary Roberts Coolidge, *Chinese Immigration* (New York: Henry Holt, 1909; reprint, New York: Arno, 1969); Elmer Clarence Sandmeyer, *The Anti-Chinese Movement in California* (Urbana: University of Illinois Press, 1939; reprint, Urbana: University of Illinois Press [Illini Books], 1991); and Alexander Saxon, *The Indispensable Enemy: Labor and the Anti-Chinese Movement in California* (Berkeley: University of California Press, 1971). A useful chronology of anti-Chinese legislation in California is in William L. Tung, *The Chinese in America, 1820–1973: A Chronology and Fact Book* (Dobbs Ferry, NY: Oceana Publications, 1974). Ronald Takaki, *Strangers from a Different Shore: A History of Asian Americans* (New York: Penguin, 1989), offers good coverage on Chinese, and other Asian, immigration from a perspective other than Kearney's; unlike most such surveys, Kearney is not even in the index.

Edward M. Kennedy (1932–2009): Immigration as a Solution to Other Problems

Mary Elizabeth Brown

Edward M. (Ted) Kennedy emerged as a prominent shaper of the debate over immigration almost as soon as he won his brother President John F. Kennedy's former seat as Massachusetts Senator in 1962 and remained such until his death from brain cancer in 2009. Throughout his career, Kennedy accepted immigration as having positive benefits for the individuals involved and for the United States. He focused on the practical details of legislation for immigrants and was prominent in the effort to identify refugees as a distinct category of immigrants. He used immigration policy to address issues in U.S. and world affairs.

Immigration was part of Kennedy's own family story. His forbears came from Ireland to Boston in the 19th century. Both grandfathers entered politics. His paternal grandfather, Patrick, was an unelected leader who guided constituents from his position as owner of a neighborhood saloon. His maternal grandfather, John "Honey Fitz" Fitzgerald served as mayor of Boston and congressional representative. His father, Joseph Patrick, made a fortune in finance and then entered political service; Franklin D. Roosevelt appointed him founding chairman of the Securities and Exchange Commission in 1933 and U.S. ambassador to England in 1938, recalling him when it became clear that he differed from the president in his willingness to commit to war against Nazi Germany. His mother, Rose, reared nine children. At that time, the four boys in the family were expected to have public careers. The oldest, Joseph Jr., died in action in an air raid over Germany in World War II, and the family's career in elected politics thus began with second son John.

In his autobiography, Ted described himself as wanting to "catch up" with his brothers.[1] When John was elected president and named brother Robert "Bobby" as Attorney General, Ted began to think of elective office for himself. When he turned 30, the minimum age the constitution required for a senator, he declared his candidacy for Senator from Massachusetts. No sooner had he won than he went to Washington, DC, to get started in his new job, which included getting his committee assignments. One of those assignments was to the Senate Judiciary Committee's Subcommittee on Immigration and Nationality.

Ted was thus in a position to offer his presidential brother support on the latter's proposals for immigration legislation. In *A Nation of Immigrants*, John Kennedy had complained that the 1952 Immigration and Nationality Act, sponsored by Senator Pat McCarran (D-NV) and Representative Francis Walter (D-PA), hampered U.S. global leadership. The United States wanted allies around the world but did not accept immigrants from some of these sought-after allies. It claimed to practice a more ethical form of government than did its communist opponents, but it practiced an immoral form of discrimination. As president, John used his position to advocate for less racist policies. On June 11, 1963, the same day he delivered a major address on civil rights, he welcomed delegates to a conference of the American Committee for Italian Migration to the White House and expressed his support for a fairer distribution of immigration visas, with greater attention to be given to family reunification.[2] The president had already asked his attorney general to prepare a legislative proposal. Bobby turned the task over to Justice Department aide Adam Walinsky. On July 23, 1963, John sent Walinsky's draft to Congress. Philip Hart (D-MI) introduced it into the Senate on July 24. Emanuel Celler (D-NY), who had been calling for such legislation since the 1920s, introduced it to the House soon after. The bill stalled, partly because it was competing for attention with civil rights legislation and partly because racially conservative legislators found it as problematic as other civil rights legislation, fearing it would lead to an increased immigration of nonwhites. President Kennedy's assassination on November 22, 1963, the transition to President Lyndon B. Johnson, and Johnson's focus on civil rights and on his own Great Society programs further slowed progress.

In November 1964, Johnson won the presidency in his own right, and the Democrats won large majorities in both houses of Congress, raising the possibility that many pending bills would now move more quickly. Ted Kennedy had already made gestures of goodwill to the Johnson administration. He used his first speech in the Senate to speak in favor of the administration's civil rights bill and to assure Congress that it was indeed what his brother would have wanted. He also offered to be the floor manager for the Hart-Celler immigration bill. Johnson agreed, although it was unusual to give such responsibility to a senator of only two years' experience.

Ted Kennedy's handling of the Hart-Celler bill demonstrated his effectiveness as a Senator. His first accomplishment was getting along with the Chair of the Judiciary Committee, Senator James Eastland (D-MS), who suspected the immigration bill would end up benefiting nonwhites. Nevertheless, Eastland had appointed Kennedy chair of the Judiciary Committee's Subcommittee on Immigration and Nationality, empowering him to conduct hearings. The hearings ran from February 10 to August 3, with time off from mid-March to the end of May for consideration of the Voting Rights Act. Kennedy later recalled the objections raised by those testifying at the hearings. The most pressing was the "ethnic and racial pattern."[3] Two senators on the committee, Everett Dirksen (R-IL) and Sam Ervin (D-NC), later of Watergate fame, opposed upsetting the racial balance.[4] The Daughters of the American Revolution, the National Association of Evangelicals, the Liberty Lobby, and the American Committee on Immigration Politics went on record to oppose the bill, at least partly because it would change the demographic composition of the U.S. population.

Other groups supported the bill after weighing their options. The American Legion and the American Coalition of Patriotic Societies realized that important persons favored change and concentrated on modifying the bill rather than defeating it. For the American Federation of Labor–Congress of Industrial Organizations (AFL-CIO), the fact that many members descended from immigrants outweighed any threat that immigrants admitted under this bill might pose in the way of competition for jobs. The bill also made a change in the distribution of employment visas that benefited U.S. labor. Previously, visas went to potential laborers unless the Labor Department determined there was already an oversupply of persons qualified for the jobs the immigrants were qualified for; the new bill forbade the distribution of visas for particular kinds of workers unless the Labor Department had certified there was a shortage of qualified help. Finally, while the bill would increase the number of visas available to countries historically discriminated against, it would reduce the number available to Ireland. The authors of the 1920s laws, not wanting to name specific European countries, had drafted laws to maintain the U.S. ethnic status quo, and the Irish had started migrating so early in the 19th century that they ended up with more visas than historic prejudice against them might have suggested. Kennedy recalled having to calm the fears of his Irish American constituents; over time, he would have to do more than that.

Outright support came from three sources. Some organizations represented people from countries that historically had been given few visas or had been forbidden to send migrants. The American Committee for Italian Migration and the Japanese American Citizens League favored ending discriminatory quotas. The National Catholic Welfare Conference Department of Immigration and the National Council of Jewish Women favored the new law, because the laws that reduced immigration from certain countries had the side effect of reducing immigration of Catholics and Jews, but in addition, these groups argued against discrimination on moral grounds. Finally, people such as Bobby Kennedy, who in 1964 had resigned as Attorney General and had won one of New York's Senate seats, argued that being morally right had pragmatic purposes. The United States could not lead the free world against communism and then tell allies their nationals were not welcome as immigrants.

Ted Kennedy ensured that opponents and proponents of the bill aired their views at his subcommittee's hearings. He then got the resulting bill approved by the subcommittee, the Judiciary Committee, and the Senate. When the House approved a different version of the bill, a reconciliation committee brought the two versions into harmony, and then Kennedy got the reconciled version through the Senate. On October 3, 1965, President Johnson sat at a desk placed at the base of the Statue of Liberty in New York Harbor to sign the Hart-Celler bill into law. Johnson argued on that occasion that the bill would not change immigration itself. What it changed was U.S. law, bringing it into line with moral condemnations of racial and national discrimination.[5]

Johnson's signature did not end the debate over the bill, which contained some important innovations. One was the way it treated the Western Hemisphere. For the first time, there was an annual limit, of 120,000, on the number of migrants from countries in the Americas. The Johnson administration originally took the position that limiting hemispheric migration violated the historic relationship the United States had with surrounding countries. However, racially conservative members of Congress preferred to break with diplomatic tradition rather than risk altering the racial status quo. Johnson acquiesced to their demand to get other legislation, including the 1964 termination of the Bracero Program that brought Mexicans across the border for temporary, transient agricultural labor. What these laws could not change, however, were the conditions that fueled migration. People from the Western Hemisphere, especially Mexicans, continued to migrate, even outside of the legal framework. In 1974, Kennedy proposed legislation to sanction employers who took advantage of undocumented workers and to create a process by which the undocumented workers could become legal permanent residents, suggestions that found their way into the 1986 Immigration Reform and Control Act.[6]

A second problem stemmed from the emphasis on family reunification. Since the 1920s, U.S. law permitted the migration of all wives and children of male U.S. citizens regardless of other considerations. The McCarran-Walter Act made the law gender neutral, and the 1965 law expanded the categories of relatives to include parents. There was a potential for an increase in the total number of immigrants. For example, the 1920s laws admitted 150,000 immigrants with visas. If all of those immigrants were male and all became citizens and sponsored wives, there would be an additional 150,000 migrants. The new law admitted 290,000 immigrants under various categories. If each became a citizen and sponsored one spouse and two parents, that would be an additional 870,000 migrants, and that does not count the children.

Another problem was also related to the emphasis on family reunification. The new laws established a seven-level preference system. Five of those levels gave preference to people with relatives already in the United States. This same law also established a maximum of 170,000 immigrants from outside the Western Hemisphere and 20,000 from any one country. Dividing 170,000 by 20,000 yields 8.5, far below the real number of countries outside the Western Hemisphere. People with relatives in the United States quickly began to use up most of the visas not only for their own countries but for the entire hemisphere. The situation was the same in the Western Hemisphere: 120,000 divided by 20,000 is only 6. Placating countries that could not send immigrants posed a diplomatic problem for the United States, while at the same time anti-immigrant forces in the United States complained that the new law admitted too many immigrants.

In 1965, though, Ted Kennedy came under criticism because the new law admitted too few immigrants. Specifically, it overlooked refugees. When Kennedy first entered the Senate, there was no general legislation concerning refugees, because few people thought of refugees as an ongoing migrant stream. Refugees were created by unexpected events such as wars. Most were admitted under presidential parole: President Eisenhower paroled Hungarians fleeing the Soviet crushing of their 1956 rebellion, and both President Kennedy and President Johnson paroled Cubans fleeing Castro; Johnson used his remarks upon signing the immigration bill to welcome Cuban refugees. Congress also initially passed specific laws for specific refugees, such as the 1948 Displaced Persons Act to assist those who had fled the fighting or the advancing Soviet Union in World War II. The 1965 law included provisions for refugees. It defined a refugee in a way consistent with U.S. foreign policy, as a person fleeing communism or unrest in the Middle East, and created a block of 50,000 visas to be used for them.

A combination of circumstances led Ted Kennedy to expand his interest in migrants to include refugees. The 1964 election created tension between liberal and conservative Democrats, who tended to be older and to chair the committees. The senior members handled this tension by creating subcommittees for the junior members to chair. Senator Eastland assigned Kennedy to chair the Senate Judiciary Committee Subcommittee on Refugees and Escapees from Communism, later renamed the Subcommittee on Refugees. This gave Kennedy a power base from which to operate.

A second issue was Vietnam. Ted Kennedy missed the Senate's early involvement in the war. On June 19, 1964, he, Senator Birch Bayh (D-IN), and Mrs. Bayh hurried out of the final roll call vote on the Civil Rights Act to catch an airplane for Westfield, Massachusetts, to attend a party convention in West Springfield. The plane crashed, the pilot and a Kennedy aide died instantly, and Senator Bayh rescued himself, his wife, and Kennedy. Kennedy suffered a punctured lung, two broken ribs, and three cracked vertebrae, putting him in New England Baptist Hospital. He was there when, on August 7, 1964, Congress passed the Gulf of Tonkin resolution, permitting President Johnson independence in determining how to assist South Vietnam resist communist advances from North Vietnamese seeking to reunite the country under their government. Kennedy's biographer, James MacGregor Burns, has argued that had Kennedy voted, he would have agreed with the resolution, for the liberal Democrats were also Cold Warriors.[7]

Shortly after Johnson signed the 1965 immigration act, Subcommittee on Refugees staff member Dale de Haan called Kennedy's attention to a new issue. The

International Red Cross reported that fighting in South Vietnam was forcing people to flee their homes. Even though the people had not yet left South Vietnam—technically, they were "displaced" rather than "refugees"—it sounded like a proper topic for Kennedy's subcommittee to investigate. Kennedy asked the State Department to plan a trip to South Vietnam for himself, administrative assistant David Burke, Senator Joseph Tydings (D-MD), Representative John Tunney (D-CA) and Representative John Culver (D-IA). During the trip, which took place in October 1965, Kennedy made one observation that raised a problem in his mind. One could argue that the hardships of the war would be temporary, and once the communists were defeated, the South Vietnamese would not have to flee. Kennedy was not so sure; what he observed indicated those in power in South Vietnam were not interested in the people they governed. Also, even if the war was supposed to be temporary, it still affected people, and the U.S. government had no plans to help those people. Kennedy began to suspect that something was wrong in Vietnam. His suspicions were deepened by a conversation with French journalist and Vietnam expert Bernard Fall, who, sitting in his own study in Washington, DC, and using only the information the U.S. government published, raised doubts about the information military officers and diplomats had given Kennedy on his trip. How to reconcile the official story with Fall's? Kennedy chaired the Subcommittee on Refugees, with the power to hold hearings. During 1965, people working in Vietnam testified before the subcommittee. In the summer of 1966, Kennedy proposed additional hearings and began to articulate the notion that Vietnamese military victory would be incomplete without social reform.

Kennedy's questions about South Vietnamese refugees led to a power struggle between himself and President Johnson. Johnson created a Special Assistant to the Secretary of State for Refugee and Migration Affairs to address the issues Kennedy raised. Kennedy raised more issues. During 1967, he called for more hospitals for the civilian casualties in South Vietnam. In August of that year, a panel of six U.S. physicians issued a report critical of the way the South Vietnamese government handled refugees. Aid to International Development, a U.S. State Department agency, countered with a report claiming that South Vietnam was managing its refugee situation satisfactorily. Kennedy announced that these conflicting views were reason enough to hold more hearings on "Civilian Casualty, Social Welfare and Refugee Problems in South Vietnam," which he did from October 9 to October 16. In December 1967, he made a second fact-finding trip to South Vietnam. This time, he did not ask the State Department to arrange his itinerary. Upon arriving in Saigon, he declined the initial briefings from U.S. officials. When he returned from a week visiting military bases and refugee camps, the officials tried to brief him again, but Kennedy claimed their report did not describe the situation he saw in the countryside. Back in the United States in early 1968, Kennedy gave several speeches trying to puncture optimism about Vietnam. When the U.S. Army vanquished its enemies and left Vietnam, how long would the victory last if only the ruined society of South Vietnam was there to uphold it?

The burgeoning antiwar movement stole Kennedy's thunder, raising many more objections to the war than what it was doing to the Vietnamese people. On November 30, 1967, Senator Eugene McCarthy (D-MN) challenged President Johnson for the Democratic nomination to the presidency. The January 31, 1968, Tet Offensive, in which communist South Vietnamese forces called the Viet Cong launched simultaneous coordinated attacks on some 30 targets across South Vietnam, provided yet another reason to oppose the war; it seemed Johnson was not waging it very well. McCarthy did better than expected in the New Hampshire primary, coming in second to the president himself. However, neither Bobby nor Ted Kennedy thought McCarthy was presidential material; he opposed the war, but he had no positive plans for domestic reform. On March 16, Bobby Kennedy entered the race for the Democratic presidential nomination. Lyndon Johnson dropped out of the race on March 31, and for the next few weeks Robert Kennedy and McCarthy competed for primary victories. Bobby had just snatched a victory in the California primaries from McCarthy on June 5, when Sirhan Sirhan, an Arab American opposed to Bobby's support for Israel, assassinated him.

Ted Kennedy did not give another Senate speech until September 23, 1968, when he resumed advocating for refugees. In 1967, Biafra had declared its independence from Nigeria, which refused to recognize the right of succession and declared war to regain the territory. Biafrans suffered from violence, disease, and starvation. Kennedy took to the Senate floor to urge the United States to aid the Biafrans and then lobbied the State Department until aid was sent.

In 1969, Kennedy did something that forever limited his political career. On July 18, he stopped by a party for some of Bobby Kennedy's office staff, held at Chappaquiddick, a small island east of the larger one of Martha's Vineyard. When he left, another partygoer, Mary Jo Kopechne, said she would also like to leave, and Kennedy offered to drive her to the ferry that would take her back to her hotel. Instead, he drove the car off a bridge into Massachusetts Bay. He was able to swim free of the car and return to his hotel, but he failed to notify authorities of the accident. By the next morning, when fishermen discovered the car, Kopechne had died. Convicted of leaving the scene of an accident in which he caused an injury, Kennedy received a two-month suspended sentence. The lapse in judgment and the rumors of drunken driving and extramarital affairs followed Kennedy for the rest of his life, intensifying whenever it was suggested he might run for president.

Richard M. Nixon, the winner of the 1968 presidential election, negotiated a withdrawal that led to removal of U.S. troops from South Vietnam on January 28, 1973. On April 30, 1975, communist forces defeated the South Vietnamese army and extended the government of North Vietnam throughout the country. Indochina remained unstable throughout the 1970s, partly because the internally displaced people Kennedy saw in 1965 had become true refugees seeking asylum in nearby countries ill prepared to receive them and partly because the Vietnam conflict contributed to a brief border war between Vietnam and the People's Republic of China and to a longer civil war between communist and anticommunist factions in Cambodia.

Kennedy's Subcommittee on Refugees held hearings on the situation in Indochina every year from 1969 to 1975, inclusive, and Congress passed a steady stream of legislation addressing the Indochinese refugee issue. The Indochina Migration and Refugee Assistance Act of May 23, 1975, created a resettlement program for those who left Cambodia and Vietnam. Laotians became eligible for the program under a June 21, 1976, law. An October 28, 1977, law permitted refugees admitted under the 1975 act to adjust their status to that of permanent residents, a step toward citizenship, and extended the time period for which the refugees were entitled to assistance. A law passed on December 22, 1987, addressed the issue of children born to members of the U.S. armed forces consorting with Vietnamese by permitting the children, mothers, and siblings to come to the United States outside of national ceilings on visas and with the benefits given to refugees. On November 21, 1989, Congress passed its last law to protect refugees from the Vietnam conflict, permitting former Soviet and Indochinese nationals who had been admitted to the United States on presidential parole to become permanent residents.

Meanwhile, Kennedy began to call for amendment of the 1965 immigration law as it concerned refugees.[8] In 1968, the United States signed the United Nations Protocol Relating to the Status of Refugees, agreeing to abide by its standards. The United Nations (UN) had a different definition of refugee than the United States did. The UN definition was that refugees were people fleeing persecution at the hands of any government, not just a communist government or unrest in the Middle East. In 1969, Kennedy and Representative Michael Feighan (D-OH) introduced a bill substituting the UN definition for the U.S. definition in its law. At that point, Nixon was in office and the Vietnam War was an important issue; the bill died without action being taken. After Nixon withdrew U.S. troops from Vietnam, Representative Peter Rodino (D-NJ) introduced legislation to admit refugees without regarding to the 20,000-visas-per-country limit. However, at that point, the Watergate scandal took precedence. Then, after the fall of Saigon, there was a flood of refugees, and Congress concentrated on laws tailored to their specific needs rather than to general laws. In 1976, Jimmy Carter was elected president; in October 1978, he sent proposed refugee legislation, similar to that favored by Kennedy, to Congress. In February 1979, Kennedy and Representative Elizabeth Holtzman (D-NY), the successor to Emanuel Celler, formally introduced the bill to their respective houses of Congress. Action on general legislation for refugees was finally under way.[9] The Refugee Act became law on March 17, 1980. It changed the definition of a refugee to conform to the definition the United States agreed to when it signed the UN protocol. It placed the admission of refugees in a separate category, apart from the national and worldwide limits. Instead, the president and the Congress were to agree annually on a total number of refugees for that fiscal year (from October 1 of one calendar year to September 30 of the next). The law established a program for working with family sponsors and not-for-profit agencies in resettling refugees in the United States. There were also provisions for readjusting the status of refugees, those who fled a country with the announced intention of coming to the United States, and of asylees, those who came to the Untied States and then asked to be admitted permanently for fear of persecution at home. Finally, there were provisions for emergencies.

Shortly after the passage of the Refugee Act, the Cuban government announced that all people who wished to leave for the United States could try to go. The United States was swamped with newcomers. When the U.S. government tried to determine whether individuals were admissible under U.S. law, the people asked to be admitted as refugees. There were rumors that some applicants were, in fact, criminals who were ineligible for admission. However, until the facts were known, each individual had to have a court appearance, and until the appearances could be scheduled, the applicants had to be kept in the United States. Kennedy again used his position as subcommittee chair to hold hearings on the subject.[10] In November of that year, an earthquake demolished part of southern Italy and left many people without homes or jobs. Kennedy urged President Carter to admit some Italians as refugees from natural disaster.[11]

Kennedy also remained active in the field of immigration legislation. During the early 1980s, one of the provisions of the 1965 law began to cause problems. The relevant provision was the one that gave preference to family reunification, which made getting visas difficult for people who did not have relatives in the United States. When the Irish economy weakened, the Irish people resorted to a traditional coping pattern, migration. However, the lack of recent Irish migration meant many Irish had no living relatives to enable them to get family-preference visas.

The idea that the United States would not help Ireland in its economic difficulties by permitting its people to migrate had implications for diplomatic relations between the two countries and political implications for people who depended on Irish American voters. Kennedy supported the efforts of Representative Brian Donnelly (D-CT) to develop legislation that would permit more Irish to migrate. The most straightforward way would have been to set aside visas for people who had no relatives in the United States, but the absence of relatives would be difficult to prove, making for a time-consuming and expensive law. The next most straightforward way would have been to create an Irish relief bill, but that would raise the specter of discriminating in favor of the Irish and would have ignored people with the same problem but from other countries. Congress settled on a pilot program included in the November 6, 1986, Immigration Reform and Control Act (IRCA) that

House and Senate conferees meet at the start of their first session on the immigration reform bill on Capitol Hill, Washington, DC, September 13, 1984. From left are, Democratic Senator Edward Kennedy of Massachusetts, Republican Senator Alan Simpson of Wyoming, Democratic Representative Romano Mazzoli of Kentucky, Republican Representative Hamilton Fish of New York, and Democratic Representative Peter Rodino of New Jersey. (AP/Wide World Photos)

set aside 5,000 visas each for 1987 and 1988 for persons from countries adversely affected by the 1965 law. Individuals applied for visas, which were then distributed by a special system that gave preference to people who came from countries with low recent immigration, to people with skills and education that would enable them to get jobs in the United States, and to people who spoke English.

IRCA was the first sign of a situation in which the extremes defeated the middle, blocking new immigration legislation. Intended to reduce the numbers of undocumented workers, IRCA failed, because on the one hand there were people who thought of undocumented workers as poor people driven to desperate measures in search of jobs, and on the other hand there were people who opposed government intrusion into the labor market, especially intrusions that might make labor more expensive. The situation was not so bad in 1990 that Kennedy could not reach across the aisle to work with Alan K. Simpson (R-WY) on that year's Immigration and Nationality Act. However, it grew steadily worse. The 1990s and 2000s saw a steady increase in the number of people in government who were more interested in maintaining ideological purity or party loyalty than in compromising in the interests of action. The terrorist attacks of September 11, 2001, planned by 20 immigrants, some of whom had entered the country legally but then had over-stayed their visas, led some people to prize security above all else. The economic downturn that accompanied 9/11 tore voters in two directions: for some, immigrants represented job competition; for others, they represented inexpensive labor. In 2005, the administration of President George W. Bush put forward its proposals for immigration, including a revival of the IRCA provision granting a "fast track to citizenship" for those who met certain requirements. The provision attracted opposition from those who denounced undocumented immigrants as lawbreakers who did not deserve such consideration. Added to those who had security concerns, those who did not think undocumented immigration was such a crime, and those who overlooked the crime in order to obtain the labor, and the law was tied down like Gulliver among the Lilliputians. Among Kennedy's last contributions to immigration reform was a June 9, 2007, visit to Senate Majority Leader Harry Reid to try to buy the bill more time.[12]

On May 16, 2008, Kennedy suffered a spell of unconsciousness in his home in Hyannis Port, on Cape Cod in Massachusetts. Tests revealed a malignant brain tumor. Following the diagnosis, Kennedy took three steps. First, he underwent surgery to try to control the tumor. Second, he used his illness to point out the difference between a person like himself, with a job that carried health insurance and the ability to pay for what the insurance did not cover, and the millions of Americans who did not have health insurance and therefore did not have his options; he became identified with an ultimately successful effort to pass comprehensive legislation reforming health insurance. Finally, he cast his support to the candidate in the 2008 Democratic primary elections who seemed to him most likely to carry on his philosophy of using the power of government to benefit people, and was an early supporter of Barack Obama. Kennedy died August 25, 2009.

Kennedy's record on immigration may seem inconsistent. He oversaw the passage of the 1965 amendments to the Immigration and Nationality Act, which was based on the idea that all nations were being treated fairly if they were all treated equally, with the same number of visas available to citizens of each nation. He also changed that law drastically in 1990, eliminating national caps on visas completely, and relied on a pool of "diversity" visas to make up for any imbalances that occurred in the sources of immigration. Over time, he concerned himself with the Vietnamese and Southeast Asians generally, with Biafrans, and with the Irish. Kennedy himself saw an ideological consistency in his work. He was a liberal in the sense that he thought the government should use its powers to benefit the people it served. Sometimes people needed to migrate in search of jobs; sometimes refugees needed to escape. Immigration was never the problem; it was the solution to problems.

Notes

1. Edward M. Kennedy, *True Compass: A Memoir* (New York and Boston: Twelve/Hachette Book Group 2009), 22, 162.
2. John F. Kennedy, "Remarks to the Delegates of the American Committee on Italian Migration," Washington, DC, June 11, 1963, John Woolley and Gerhard Peters, *The American Presidency Project*, University of California, Santa Barbara, http://www.presidency.ucsb.edu/ws/index.php?pid=9269.
3. Edward M. Kennedy, "The Immigration Act of 1964," *Annals of the American Academy of Political and Social Science* 367 (September 1966): 137–149.
4. Burton Hersh, *The Education of Edward Kennedy: A Family Biography* (New York: William Morrow, 1972), 221–225.
5. Lyndon B. Johnson, "Remarks at the Signing of the Immigration Bill, Liberty Island, New York, October 3, 1965," John Woolley and Gerhard Peters, *The American Presidency Project*, University of California, Santa Barbara, http://www.presidency.ucsb.edu/ws/index.php?pid=27292&st=immigration&st1=.
6. Austin T. Fragomen Jr., "Legislative and Judicial Developments: Regulating the Illegal Aliens," *International Migration Review* 8, no. 4 (Winter 1974): 567–572.
7. James MacGregor Burns, *Edward Kennedy and the Camelot Legacy* (New York: W.W. Norton, 1976), 133.
8. Edward M. Kennedy, "Foreword," *San Diego Law Review* 14, no. 1 (December 1976): 1–5. This is an introduction to a special issue of the journal concerning immigration law.
9. Deborah E. Anker and Michael H. Posner, "The Forty Year Crisis: A Legislative History of the Refugee Act of 1980," *San Diego Law Review* 19, no. 1 (1981): 9–89.
10. Graham Hovey, "Kennedy Plans a Hearing Monday on Cuba and Haiti Refugee Crisis," *The New York Times* (May 9, 1980), Marymount Manhattan College via ProQuest.
11. "Earthquake Survivors in Naples Seize Apartments and Money," *The New York Times* (December 3, 1980), Marymount Manhattan College via ProQuest.
12. Carl Hulse, Robert Pear, and Jeff Zeleny, "Kennedy Plea Was Last Gasp for Immigration Bill," *The New York Times* (June 9, 2007), Marymount Manhattan College via Lexis-Nexis.

Bibliography

Along with the articles cited, Kennedy's writings discussing his own immigration legislation include "Immigration Law: Some Refinements and New Reforms," *International Migration Review* 4, no. 3 (Summer 1970): 4–10. In addition to the biographies cited in the notes, other useful biographies on Kennedy are Burton Hersch, *The Shadow President: Ted Kennedy in Opposition* (New York: Steerforth, 1997); William H. Honan, *Ted Kennedy: Profile of a Survivor* (New York: Quadrangle Books 1972); and Theo Lippman Jr., *Senator Ted Kennedy* (New York: W.W. Norton, 1976). For more on the Kennedy family, see Doris Kearns Goodwin, *The Fitzgeralds and the Kennedys* (New York: Simon & Schuster, 1987). For material on the 1965 Immigration and Nationality Act, see, in addition to the sources cited, David M. Reimers, "An Unintended Reform: The 1965 Immigration Act and Third World Immigration to the United States," *Journal of American Ethnic History* 3, no. 1 (Fall 1983): 4–28, and Reimers's *Still the Golden Door: The Third World Comes to America*, 2nd ed. (New York: Columbia University Press, 1992). For context on refugees, see Gil Loescher and John A. Scanlan, *Calculated Kindness: Refugees and America's Half-Open Door, 1945–Present* (New York: Free Press, 1986). Regarding the tangle of ideology and party in immigration, see Daniel J. Tichenor, "Strange Bedfellows: The Politics and Pathologies of Immigration Reform," *Labor: Studies in Working Class History of the Americas* 5, no. 2 (Summer 2008): 39–60.

Henry Cabot Lodge (1850–1924): Immigration Restriction as National Policy

Mary Elizabeth Brown

Henry Cabot Lodge presents a divided face to American history students. Most encounter him when they study World War I, when he defeated Woodrow Wilson and the Versailles Peace Treaty. In this role, Lodge appears to be governed partly by personal passions and short-term considerations: his own dislike of Wilson, the rivalry between his Republicans and Wilson's Democrats, and his guardianship of Senate prerogatives in foreign affairs over and against an increasingly powerful presidency. However, even if one grants these issues figured in Lodge's opposition to the treaty, one still has to concede that Lodge and Wilson had substantial differences in the field of foreign affairs, with Wilson arguing for international equality and cooperation and Lodge defending the United States from the limits to its independence that he feared in the League of Nations covenant.

On the other hand, if one reads monographs about immigration legislation, Lodge appears to base his work almost wholly on personal prejudices and passions. Lodge is presented as someone who was well born, well off, and well educated but whose social status was slipping as other people came to dominate U.S. politics and economics. He projected his fears of status loss onto the immigrants, as if the lowly, impoverished, illiterate foreign born might topple the elite from their places. To this end, he led an early, and underhanded, effort to legislate the exclusion of particular immigrants on the basis of ethnicity, race, or national origin.

It might be possible to develop a unified field theory of Henry Cabot Lodge, one in which immigration restriction and his other accomplishments—in U.S. tariff policy as well as in foreign policy—can be brought together. Lodge was a protectionist in the largest possible sense of the word.[1] He aimed to bring the United States to the status of a Great Power, which required attention to the economy, international affairs, and population characteristics. In this scenario, the fact that immigration restriction had a personal appeal for Lodge becomes less important. After all, certain aspects of the defeat of the Versailles Treaty—the opportunity to put Wilson in his place, for example—had a personal appeal, too.

Influential Republican Senator Henry Cabot Lodge from Massachusetts was a strong advocate of U.S. expansionism and urged U.S. intervention in Cuba. (Library of Congress)

There is a quatrain that used to be well known in Boston:

And this is good old Boston
The home of the bean and the cod
Where the Lowells talk only to Cabots
And the Cabots talk only to God.

That verse, silly as it is, might be helpful to understanding Lodge. He was born in Boston on May 12, 1850. His father, John Ellerton Lodge, was a prosperous merchant who owned a fleet of clipper ships and engaged in the China trade. His mother, Anna, was the one who connected him to the Cabots; she was the granddaughter of Federalist politician George Cabot. Lodge was so pleased with that connection that he preferred using his middle name. If a proper Bostonian can be pictured jumping through hoops, Lodge jumped through all the proper ones. He was educated at E.S. Dixwell's Latin School in Boston, where he met other young boys of good family and comfortable income. He then moved on to Harvard. Upon graduation, he married his cousin, Anna Cabot Miller Davis, the daughter of Rear Admiral Charles H. Davis. During 1871–1872, the couple spent a year in Rome. Upon their return to Boston, the young husband entered Harvard Law School. None of this was done with any firm plan in mind; these were all steps other men of his class took. In most cases, the young men's ancestors had already achieved status and money. Keeping up the family reputation was not quite as exciting as making it, and it was not as easy. One could always slip up and lose it all. Young men such as Lodge had no reason to hurry and good reasons not to. The result was that some young men failed because they did not even try; they kept waiting for opportunities appropriate to their station to come along, or they kept bemoaning the passing of the "good old days," when their family name, wealth, education, and cultured backgrounds automatically commanded respect.

In Lodge's case, an assist came from a man like himself. Henry Adams had also been born in Boston. (The opening pages of his *Autobiography*, while not so quotable as the rhyme above, are a far more elegant evocation of the same notion of being born to the head of society.) He also had famous relatives; his great-grandfather was President John Adams, his grandfather was President John Quincy Adams, his father was Civil War Minister to England Charles Francis Adams, and his brother was railroad regulation pioneer Charles Francis Adams Jr. The family home was in Quincy, Massachusetts, but Charles Francis Adams maintained a town house on Beacon Hill. The Adamses had money: John Adams had bequeathed John Quincy land, John Quincy bequeathed Charles Francis more real estate and some canal stock, and Charles Francis invested in the modern industries of his age, the railroads. Charles Francis's sons were also faced with the problem of how to hold on to their status as social and political leaders, and at one point Henry Adams chose to exercise his influence through journalism. He was the editor of the *North American Review*, a monthly magazine that printed thought-provoking articles on the issues of the day. In 1873, Adams asked Lodge to be his assistant. Lodge received his law degree in 1874 and was admitted to the bar in 1875 but never practiced his profession, preferring his career in editorial work and then in doing research and writing on his own. In 1876, Harvard granted him the first doctorate in political science it ever awarded. Characteristic of his interest in preserving his heritage, he produced a dissertation entitled "The Anglo-Saxon Land Law." From 1876 to 1879, he lectured at Harvard, and throughout the 1880s he produced a series of historical and biographical works on the Revolutionary and Federalist periods of U.S. history, including an 1877 biography of his great-grandfather.

In 1879, Lodge moved into politics. On the one hand, it was a tradition; the Boston "Brahmins," as the town's elite were called, had come to their position partly through their leadership during the Revolution, the Federalist period, the development of the abolitionist movement, and the Civil War. On the other hand, it was not a tradition that many of Lodge's peers took personal steps to preserve. Most of them went into business, law, college and university education, or publishing or lived off their family income while writing or pursuing cultural or philanthropic interests. They disdained politics. Gilded Age politics was the antithesis of ancestor worship. Candidates were judged on how they personally appealed to voters, not on the basis of what their ancestors had done in the past. In the Boston area, it was even necessary to appeal to the Irish Catholic working class; shortly after Lodge began his political career, Hugh O'Brien became the first Irish American Catholic mayor of the English Puritan's city on a hill, and Lodge served a term in Congress with John Fitzgerald, John F. Kennedy's maternal grandfather, as a colleague. Lodge, though, turned out to be a canny, shrewd, partisan young man who could play the political game as if he were one of the Irish ward heelers he so much disliked. He built a considerable personal power base in his voting district and used it to sustain a long career.

Lodge won election to the Massachusetts State House of Representatives in their election of 1879. He was reelected in 1880 and also elected one of the delegates to the Republican National Convention, where he participated in nominating James Abram Garfield for what turned out to be a successful presidential candidacy. The next year, he left his House seat for an unsuccessful bid for the Massachusetts Senate, and the year after that saw another setback, as he was defeated in a try for the U.S. House of Representatives. Then, in 1883, he became campaign manager for the Republican candidate for governor of Massachusetts, George D. Robinson. Lodge helped Robinson to defeat Benjamin F. Butler. Butler was a tough opponent because he had a Civil War record (it helped in Massachusetts that people in New Orleans, where Butler served, referred to him as "General Beast Butler"), and he was a Democrat who could command the vote of numerous Irish throughout the commonwealth.

The year after that, Lodge really proved his political savvy. Elected delegate-at-large to the 1884 Republican National Convention, he went to the meeting fighting the candidacy of James G. Blaine. Boston Brahmins thought of themselves as being on the morally correct side of political questions ranging from the Revolution to the labor-capital disputes of the Gilded Age, and Blaine had an unsavory reputation for showing favoritism to railroad magnates. Lodge opposed Blaine—until Blaine won the majority necessary to become the Republican presidential candidate. A group of Republicans bolted the party to bolster the support of the Mugwumps, a splinter political group that criticized both major parties as corrupt. Lodge closed ranks and remained a regular Republican. Because the Republicans divided into regulars and Mugwumps, Blaine lost his campaign to Democrat Grover Cleveland. Lodge also lost his race for a congressional seat in 1884. But because he had been loyal, the Republicans nominated him again in 1886, by which time the Mugwump revolt was over. He won by a narrow majority and was reelected in 1888 and 1890, serving from 1887 to 1893.

During Lodge's tenure in the House, the definition of a regular Republican changed. One of the early bills Lodge drafted and tried to get through Congress was the 1890–1891 "Force Bill." Had it passed, this legislation would have established federal control over polling places, thus breaking southern opposition to black voting. This would have been a way of standing up for traditional Republican interests and also increasing Republican votes. However, instead of having his legislation become law, Lodge found that even Bostonians had given up on helping southern blacks to secure the vote. Lodge was also well known for supporting the Sherman Antitrust Act and for promoting civil service reform, specifically for getting Theodore Roosevelt to serve on the federal Civil Service Commission. These activities showed that he did indeed understand the Republican agenda at the end of the Gilded Age and the beginning of the Progressive Era. The new Republican conscience combined a critique of politics and economics with snobbery and partisanship. A properly run civil service would sabotage machine politics, patronage, and favoritism, which would help the Republicans' chances. Antitrust legislation would undermine the basis on which the nouveau riche were building their fortunes, thus preventing them from challenging the most established Republicans for leadership. There were other challenges to the American way of life. Lodge began addressing them as early as 1888, when he gave a speech imploring, "[L]et us have done with British-Americans and Irish-Americans and German-Americans, and so on, and all be Americans."[2]

In 1891, an event prompted a major consideration of immigration. The story begins in New Orleans, with Police Chief David Hennessey. On the night of October 15, 1890, Hennessey was honored at a banquet for his assistance in controlling organized crime among the city's Italians. As he headed up his street at 11:30 that night, he was assassinated by a group of men that had been hiding behind a parked cart. He died on October 16. People watching at his deathbed heard him say that "the dagoes" had got him. Officials concentrated their efforts on the Italian community, particularly among the people who felt oppressed by Hennessey's anticrime activities. On November 9 of that year, the city indicted 19 Italians. On March 13, 1891, a jury acquitted 13 and reported that it could not render a decision regarding the other 6. Although cleared in the case, those on trial were returned to jail pending the completion of the necessary legal forms. The next night, March 14, a mob broke into the jail and summarily executed every Italian it could find. Eleven Italians died in the lynching, seven connected with the trial and four who were in jail that night on other charges.

Lodge wrote an article on "Lynch Law and Unrestricted Immigration," explaining why the massacre took place. He offered one minor reason, that corrupt government in New Orleans gave people good reason to distrust even jury decisions. Then, ignoring anything he had learned in law school, he skipped over the question of whether the accused had murdered Hennessey to point out that there was indeed a mafia operating in New Orleans, established by criminals migrating from Sicily. For good measure, he then went on to accuse the immigrants of bringing diseases and of increasing the pool of unskilled labor and thus lowering wages. He leapt over the last logical barrier to present his solution to problems immigrants presented: "Some such fair and restrictive test as that of the ability to read and write."[3] Specifically, the idea was that every adult male immigrant had to be able to read and write in the language of the country from which he came.

Lodge got the idea for a literacy test from Edward W. Bemis, who lectured on this subject in 1887. An economist, Bemis was concerned with the problem of competition between immigrants and native workers for jobs. The law of supply and demand suggested that the sheer numbers of job seekers would lead employers to conclude they could keep wages low. Immigrants were also widely suspected of having an additional advantage. Their lack of culture and refinement gave them a competitive edge in the job market, for they would accept wages that were too low to support a good lifestyle and never realize what they were missing. A literacy test would solve two problems. It would reduce the pool of eligible immigrants by about half. The remaining immigrants and natives would compete on a more level playing field, as the literate immigrants presumably had a standard of living closer to that of the natives. Bemis, though, was not just an economist. Like many people in his day, he was convinced of the importance of heredity. It was for him a happy coincidence that the places with the least desirable national groups—Italy, Poland, Greece, Russia, and so on—also had the least inclusive educational systems and that many immigrants from these places were unable to read.

Over the years, Lodge considered, and dismissed, other ways to limit migration. A high head tax would seem to be the most direct way to eliminate the impoverished immigrants, but, Lodge claimed, "it would have excluded the desirable as well as the objectionable immigration," and there was no necessary corollary between wealth and citizenship qualifications. Lodge also investigated the idea of having U.S. consular officials examine the potential immigrants while they were still in their homelands and issue certificates for those who passed the examination. However, it turned out that most countries objected to having U.S. officials exercise that much authority outside their own national boundaries. Also, the countries that were willing to cooperate were most interested in having the United States help them prevent the young men of military age from immigrating, whereas it was in the best interest of the United States to admit such healthy young men at the peak of their labor power. The literacy test, though, would bar exactly the kind of people Lodge wanted to limit, without his having to come right out and object to any immigrants on the grounds of national origins or poverty.[4]

In all this, Lodge sounds like he either was, or was trying to pose as, a friend of the worker. Immigration restriction was a variant of the protective tariff. The tariff supposedly preserved American jobs at decent wages by keeping cheaply made foreign goods off the U.S. market. Restriction kept the same foreigners from manufacturing the cheaply made goods in the United States. (This was before potential immigrants could stay in their home countries and compete with U.S. workers by manufacturing inexpensive goods in U.S.-owned plants there.) However, one should also note that Lodge had grounds for complaint. Mass immigration gave a boost to employers, allowing the captains of industry to reduce costs, rake in more profits, move up in society—and challenge Henry Cabot Lodge and his Boston Brahmins for social leadership much faster than a bunch of recently arrived illiterates ever could. Immigrants' votes fueled Lodge's political rivals' campaigns.

Lodge had identified a new issue, but he had no time to press it in the House. In 1892, Lodge declined to run for Congress again, partly because a window of opportunity had opened for a higher office. Henry Laurens Dawes was getting too deaf to fulfill his duties as a U.S. senator, and under the rules that applied until the Seventeenth Amendment to the Constitution replaced them, the commonwealth's legislature had to elect a successor; it chose Lodge early in 1893. It is worth comparing Dawes and Lodge. They were both born in Massachusetts of New England families. They both went to Ivy League schools, Dawes graduating from Yale.

Both had editorial experience, were admitted to the state bar, started their political careers in the state legislature, and moved to the U.S. House of Representatives and then to the Senate. They had slightly different legislative records. Dawes is best known for the Dawes Severalty Act of 1887. The law is controversial in U.S. history, because it was based on the idea of breaking up Native American tribes and weaning individual Indians away from their inherited identities. The point here is that Dawes did not see a need to protect his own heritage from pollution. While it may have been chauvinistic of him to think others *should* assimilate into it, it is, in the light of his successor's career, interesting to note that he thought others *could* assimilate. Lodge was less optimistic about the possibility that others could assimilate and more concerned about setting boundaries between himself and outsiders.

Lodge was not the only one who doubted the possibility of assimilation and desirability of immigration. In the spring of 1894, about a year after Lodge replaced Dawes, the Immigration Restriction League of Boston formed. The Restriction League was founded by a group of Bostonians much like Henry Cabot Lodge, albeit somewhat younger; they were just finishing their studies at Harvard's graduate or professional schools and were trying to preserve their places near the top of society. Charles Warren, the one who gathered the others into the organization, was the descendant of a colonial family and the son of a politician who had gotten as far as port collector of the Port of Boston before his personal advance and his reform proposals were blocked by local Irish Democratic politics. Robert DeCourcy Ward's mother was Anna Saltonstall, another descendant of a colonial family that remained politically active through the 20th century, and his father was Henry Veazie Ward, a merchant whose middle name indicated his ancestors had come to Massachusetts in the 17th century. Prescott Farnsworth Hall was the son of merchant Samuel Hall and Elizabeth Farnsworth. The Immigration Restriction League advocated a literacy test before the public and in the halls of Congress. It was so effective that it aroused opposition. Hull House, a Chicago settlement headed by Jane Addams and famous for its interest in its immigrant neighbors, organized the Immigrants' Protective League, which lobbied Congress and the public on behalf of generous immigration laws.

Lodge continued to write against immigration and in favor of a literacy test as the fastest, fairest way to reduce it. He combed the census for figures to support his contention that immigrants were a burden on taxpayers. The foreign born and native born of foreign parents (second-generation immigrants) accounted for 38 percent of the national population in 1890 but supplied 52 percent of all penitentiary inmates, 61 percent of all juvenile delinquents, and 59 percent of all almshouse residents.[5] Lodge was not above manipulating the data to get the desired effect. In 1890, police reporter Jacob A. Riis published *How the Other Half Lives*, a lengthy indictment of New York City's officials and landlords for overcharging impoverished and uncomprehending immigrants for tenements in which they lived in squalor. Lodge ignored the forces of law and economics and blamed the immigrants themselves:

> Anyone who is desirous of knowing in practical detail the degrading effect of this constant importation of the lowest forms of labor can find a vivid picture of its results in the very interesting book just published by Mr. Riis, entitled *How the Other Half Lives*. The story which he tells of the condition of a large mass of the laboring population of New York is enough to alarm every thinking man; and this dreadful condition of things is intensified everyday by the steady inflow of immigration, which is constantly pulling down the wages of the working people of New York and affecting in a similar way the entire labor market of the United States.[6]

As Lodge moved from the House to the Senate, the political climate changed and thwarted his restrictionist ambitions. Any anti-immigrant sentiment unleashed by the New Orleans episode had dissipated by the 1892 congressional elections, which went heavily Democrat. The depression of 1893 had a longer effect; voters still remembered it in 1894, when they replaced Democrats with Republicans in many districts in the fall elections. However, the rules in force at the time meant that the Congress elected in November 1894 did not sit until December 1895, by which time it faced an issue it considered of pressing importance: the 1896 elections. The election of William McKinley as the next president in November 1896 gave Lodge confidence, and he got the literacy bill through the House and the Senate and to lame-duck President Grover Cleveland. Cleveland vetoed it. He was a Democrat, but he was more than that. He was a conservative, and legislation that compromised the American tradition of relatively free migration offended his conservatism. He did not like the idea that someone might be pulling the wool over his eyes, and this bill seemed clearly designed to do that, legislating a literacy test when supporters speechifying about it usually skipped right over literacy and promised the law would limit the immigration of undesirable races. Finally, he did not like the invidious distinctions between different types of European-descended peoples.

During the late 1890s and early 1900s, Lodge tried to get the literacy test into law several times but was blocked by his colleagues on Capitol Hill. Once McKinley had actually taken the oath of office and would be available to sign the bill into law, Lodge tried to send the bill through Congress again, but opponents to the bill had been alerted by the first campaign and were now mobilized against it. McKinley's assassination brought the subject of immigration restriction up again. The assassin, Leon Czolgosz, was himself born in the United States, but his parents had been born elsewhere, and that was close enough. Also, Czolgosz professed to be an anarchist, and there seems to have been a sentiment that he could not have picked up such ideas just through reading; he must have learned the ideology by contact with foreign-born anarchists. In 1902, Congress went to work on a bill prohibiting immigrant anarchists. Lodge got his literacy test appended to the bill, but his amendment had to be removed to get the law passed. The anti-anarchism bill became law, without his literacy test, on March 3, 1903.

The issue of literacy tests came up again during the period when Theodore Roosevelt was in the White House. Whether Roosevelt would have signed such a bill is open to question. He considered Lodge a close friend, and they were in agreement in other matters, such as the direction they wanted U.S. foreign policy to take. Although the president did not deliver a formal State of the Union address then, Roosevelt did mention the literacy test favorably in his constitutionally required written State of the Union message. As president, though, Roosevelt was the lightning rod attracting the protests of those opposed to the literacy test. He understood that he was president only because McKinley had been assassinated. If he wanted to be elected president in his own right, he had to avoid gratuitously antagonizing big voting blocs. Whether Roosevelt would have signed the bill remains academic. Speaker of the House Joseph G. Cannon, a Republican from Illinois, prevented an immigration bill from being reported to the floor of the House with the literacy test as a component. Yet the bill did contain other clauses Lodge wanted to see enacted, such as a requirement that Japanese immigrants present passports to U.S. officials at their ports of entry. (There was a diplomatic understanding with the Empire of Japan that the government would issue passports only to the very few Japanese the United States wanted to admit.) Lodge removed the literacy test to get the rest of the bill through, and it became law on February 20, 1907.

Behind Cannon's actions was a complicated assessment of voting behavior. Cannon's home district was a mining area composed of wealthy mine owners and largely ethnic miners. Cannon already had ties to the mine owners, and he knew they were interested in a large labor pool that would allow them to set low wages. However, he knew the miners had votes, too, and he wanted to avoid antagonizing them. In this case, it so happened that the mine owners' interest in a large labor pool coincided with the ethnic voters' interest in relatively open immigration.

That ironic agreement hides another layer of issues. Perhaps the reader could draw a stick figure representing one of Cannon's mine worker constituents. Draw a circle around that miner such that the miner appears at the extreme right of the circle, then label the circle "worker." Draw a second circle, also around the stick figure, but this time making the circle so that the figure is on the extreme left (in other words, a Venn diagram with the figure in the overlap). Label the second circle "ethnic." Cannon's mine workers—and millions of other voters—belonged to both circles, claimed both identities. They were workers and might presumably be expected to vote their pocketbooks—that is, for candidates and legislation that raised their wages, provided them with public schools, and made their socioeconomic advancement easier. They also identified with their particular ethnic group, and that brought another set of interests. They wanted to see a member of their group receive political honors; they wanted to practice their home religion freely (which might mean sending their children to denominational schools); they wanted their compatriots to be free to migrate; and, if their home country went to war, they wanted it to emerge victorious. When Lodge wrote against immigration, he appealed to the worker identity and acted as if he opposed immigration chiefly because it pushed down wages. This was partly a ploy, but it also reflected Lodge's deepest values: He wanted to emphasize American economic interests. Politicians such as Cannon either used the opposite ploy or sincerely held opposite values. Either they were willing to appeal to the voters as the voters indicated they wanted to be appealed to—through their ethnic pride—or they thought the United States could easily accommodate people with pride in their ethnic heritages.

After 1912, Lodge had gained sufficient control over Congress that he was able to get literacy test bills through the House and Senate. By then, however, the presidency was against him. Lame-duck President William Howard Taft vetoed a literacy bill in 1913, on the grounds that the United States needed as many laborers as it could get. Woodrow Wilson vetoed a literacy bill in 1915 on the grounds that during his campaign he had indicated to foreign-born voters he would do so. Still operating on the theory that his campaign promises meant something, Wilson vetoed the law a second time in 1917. This time, though, the House and Senate overrode the veto and the bill became law on February 5. The difference that led to victory in 1917 was the new concern about the depth of foreign-born loyalty in the event of war, and Wilson did ask Congress for a declaration of war against imperial Germany on April 2.

Evaluations of the 1917 literacy test law agree that it was nearly useless as soon as it passed, but they differ as to why. One line of thought emphasizes the low standard of literacy and the exemptions. Europe had made some progress in literacy since the law was first proposed in the early 1890s. Yet the law required only that every immigrant over 16 years of age be able to read one 50-word passage in the language of the immigrant's choice. There was a provision that if a family was migrating together, one person could take the test for all family members, so one school-age child who could read secured admission for a family of illiterate adults. There was also an exemption for groups fleeing religious persecution, which Russian Jews, not one of Lodge's favored groups, used heavily. A second line of thought emphasizes the timing. The same war that secured passage of the literacy test law also did more to reduce migration than the law ever could.

On the other hand, one might ask not what the law accomplished but what it intended to accomplish. It intended to shape migration along the lines of national origins, disguising the real criteria with a literacy test that members from undesirable groups were not expected to pass. It reflects a shift from exclusion on a case-by-case basis (an anarchist here, a trachoma sufferer there) to exclusion on prejudicial grounds (reducing the immigration of undesirable groups without worrying about the merits of particular individuals). Viewed this way, Henry Cabot Lodge had finally helped to effect a major change in immigration policy.

Lodge, though, was not in a position to rest on his laurels. The United States was at war, and he was a member of the Senate, the branch of Congress the Constitution charges with the role of "advice and consent" in foreign affairs. By 1919, he was the senior member and chair of the Foreign Relations Committee. Soon after he entered the Senate, he had taken part in important episodes in international affairs and always with a view to making the United States a Great Power, with a sphere of influence extending from the Western Hemisphere to the Pacific Rim and the ability to stand up to European Great Powers. Wilson's proposals for the basic equality of nations threatened Lodge's long-term commitment to making the United States *unequal*, to making it a Great Power.

Immigration was an element in the debate over the League of Nations in two ways. First, Lodge argued, perhaps simply to scare people, that if the United States joined the League, it would no longer be able to govern itself but would have to abide by League rulings. What if the League followed Thomas Jefferson's logic and ruled in favor of the worldwide freedom to migrate? The Chinese Exclusion Act would then be unenforceable, the United States would be swamped with cheap labor, and wages and living standards would go down.[7]

Second, different ethnic groups had varied and sometimes conflicting agendas. Jews, aware of the anti-Semitic tendencies of Czar Nicholas II and his court and advisers, did not want Russia to win the war. Poles hoped that their birthplace could be reconstituted as an independent state. The Italians wanted to use the war to further their policy of reclaiming the irredenta, the Italian-speaking populations living just over the Italian border in the Austro-Hungarian Empire. The Irish tried to use the fact that the British were engaged elsewhere to their advantage and staged an uprising in the spring of 1916. When this Easter Rebellion failed, they pinned their hopes on postwar negotiations. His experience dealing with ethnic expectations "served to confirm Lodge in his opinion that the composition of the American population placed a severe limitation on the country's ability to pursue a consistent foreign policy."[8] Lodge wanted to identify and pursue American interests, but he could not continue to hold political office without at least acknowledging that some Americans had multiple interests and as yet saw no reason to choose between them.

It is a measure of Lodge's political ability that, although he disapproved of groups of citizens putting their particular interests in Fiume or Free Ireland ahead of the U.S. national interest, he still found a way to turn this regretable state of affairs to his advantage. He encouraged the ethnic groups when he could. Privately, he worried that Irish agitation for independence might antagonize the British, with whom he hoped to cooperate. Personally, he thought the Italians a bit chauvinistic in their insistence on Fiume. However, he could use their agitation to call attention to issues in the postwar negotiations that he thought important. And, after all, Wilson had set himself up as *the* negotiator of the Versailles Treaty, going to Paris without Lodge, without any senators, and with few Republicans. Let ethnic voters bring their complaints to Wilson. Let them nibble away at the treaty day after day, week after week. Let them plant in the minds of the general public the notion that the treaty was flawed. This was not the whole of Lodge's strategy, but it did not hurt. In 1920, he managed to defeat the Versailles Treaty in the Senate and to have his counterparts defeat it in the House.

It was at this point that immigrant quotas, the kind of national origins legislation that Lodge had disguised with literacy tests, dropped their disguise and came out in the open. Lodge, though, was not a champion of them. It is difficult to determine cause and effect at this point. Did Lodge's sense that other people were getting ahead of him in political leadership depress him and further the aging process, or was Lodge getting old and therefore irrelevant, even to the rather conservative 1920s?

It is a fact that Lodge's role in politics diminished after 1920, right at the peak of his most famous victory. Other factions of the Republican Party secured the nomination of Warren G. Harding of Ohio as a Republican candidate for president in 1920. The Republicans did nominate Calvin Coolidge, also of Massachusetts, as vice president, but Coolidge came from a different wing of the Republican Party. Harding died in office, Coolidge took his place as president, and in 1924 the Republicans nominated Coolidge for a presidential term in his own right.

While other Republicans were convening, Lodge was in the Charlesgate Hospital in Cambridge, Massachusetts, in failing health. He never left the hospital. On October 20, his physicians performed surgery. On November 9, he suffered a stroke that killed him that same night.

Notes

1. William C. Widenor, *Henry Cabot Lodge and the Search for an American Foreign Policy* (Berkeley: University of California Press, 1980), 57–58: "To Lodge immigration restriction was an integral part of any intelligent protective policy, and protection transcended the interests of individual manufactures and had a national purpose."
2. Karl Schriftgiesser, *The Gentleman from Massachusetts: Henry Cabot Lodge* (Boston: Little, Brown, 1944), 114.
3. Henry Cabot Lodge, "Lynch Law and Unrestricted Immigration," *North American Review* 152 (May 1891): 602–612.
4. Henry Cabot Lodge, "A Million Immigrants a Year, Part I," *Century* 67 (January 1904): 466–469.

5. Henry Cabot Lodge, "The Census and Immigration," *Century* 24 (September 1893): 737–739.

6. Henry Cabot Lodge, "The Restriction of Immigration," *North American Review* 152 (January 1892): 27–36.

7. Schriftgiesser, *Gentleman from Massachusetts*, 290.

8. Widenor, *Henry Cabot Lodge*, 342.

Bibliography

Lodge's papers are at the Massachusetts Historical Society. Lodge produced one pamphlet on his thoughts on immigration, *The Question of Immigration: A Lecture before the Massachusetts Society for Promoting Good Citizenship* (Boston: Massachusetts Society for Promoting Good Citizenship, 1892). He also produced articles for the periodical press, including "The Census and Immigration," *Century* 24 (September 1893): 737–739; "Lynch Law and Unrestricted Immigration," *North American Review* 152 (May 1891): 602–612; "A Million Immigrants a Year, Part I," *Century* 67 (January 1904): 466–469; and "The Restriction of Immigration," *North American Review* 152 (January 1892): 27–36. Lodge's biographies include John Garraty, *Henry Cabot Lodge: A Biography* (New York: Alfred A. Knopf, 1953); Charles Stuart Graves, *Henry Cabot Lodge: Statesman* (Boston: Small, Maynard, 1925); and Karl Schriftgiesser, *The Gentleman from Massachusetts: Henry Cabot Lodge* (Boston: Little, Brown, 1944). There is also a helpful monograph of a specific aspect of Lodge's career: William C. Widenor, *Henry Cabot Lodge and the Search for an American Foreign Policy* (Berkeley: University of California Press, 1980). A monograph helpful for the anti-immigration aspect of Lodge's work is Barbara Miller Solomon, *Ancestors and Immigrants: A Changing New England Tradition* (Chicago: University of Chicago Press, 1956) as well as a senior honors history thesis of a Harvard student, Daniel Isaias Freeman, "Stay Those Who to Thy Sacred Portals Come: Henry Cabot Lodge and the Intellectual and Legislative Origins of Immigration Restriction, 1850–1924." Lodge also figures in a helpful political case study: Richard M. Abrams, *Conservatism in a Progressive Era: Massachusetts Politics, 1900–1912* (Cambridge, MA: Harvard University Press, 1964). A helpful article is John Higham, "Another Look at Nativism," in *Send These to Me: Jews and Other Immigrants in Urban America* (New York: Atheneum, 1975), 102–115. For a monograph on the 1891 New Orleans lynching, see Richard Gambino, *Vendetta* (New York: Doubleday, 1977). Lodge often charged that "birds of passage," or transient workers, impoverished the United States by taking their wages out of the country to spend or invest elsewhere; for more on this, see Neil Larry Shumsky, " 'LET NO MAN STOP TO PLUNDER!' American Hostility to Return Migration, 1890–1924," *Journal of American Ethnic History* 11, no. 2 (Winter 1992): 56–76.

Patrick Anthony McCarran (1876–1954): Cold War Immigration

Mary Elizabeth Brown

The term *McCarthyism* sums up a part of the early 1950s. It takes its name from Joseph R. McCarthy, who was first elected to the U.S. Senate in 1946. There were already signs, such as the investigation of communism in Hollywood, that people feared that the Communist Party, directed by officials in the Soviet Union, had subversive influence in U.S. life. McCarthy took that fear to new levels, charging that high U.S. authorities had been lax in preventing communist infiltration of the executive branch of the federal government. He became a leader in speaking out against such communist subversion, and when he was given charge of a Senate committee, he investigated communism ruthlessly, without regard for the rights of the accused or for people's reputations. For a while, it seemed that the government spent much of its time trying to counter a communist menace.

Before there was McCarthy, there was Patrick Anthony McCarran. McCarthy and McCarran had a few biographical details in common. They both projected images of informal camaraderie: It was Pat McCarran and Joe McCarthy. They were both Roman Catholics. They were both of Irish extraction. They both hailed from outside the Northeast and Mid-Atlantic states that dominated politics; McCarthy was from Wisconsin and McCarran from Nevada. They both fell in with the majority party in their states—the Republicans for McCarthy and the Democrats for McCarran. They were both members of the U.S. Senate. They were both identified with the post–World War II anticommunist crusade.

However, there were some important differences. McCarran was older than McCarthy and had been in the Senate longer. His career helps to illuminate the connection between pre– and post–World War II policies in foreign affairs and in immigration. The Republicans were not completely united around McCarthy's anticommunism, but anticommunism did provide an issue that up-and-coming Republicans such as McCarthy (and Richard M. Nixon) could use to advance their careers. By contrast, McCarran's anticommunism revealed how fragile the supposedly invincible Democratic coalition really was. As a young senator, McCarthy had only so many ways to affect public policy. He made the most of the

Senator Pat McCarran, Democrat of Nevada, was a post–World War II anticommunist crusader. (Library of Congress)

opportunities handed him to conduct investigations. As a senior senator, McCarran was an example of the paradoxes of the American political system. He maintained his office because he served his native Nevada well, but as he maintained it, he advanced in seniority and thus had his pick of committee assignments in which he could shape not only Nevada's fate but the nation's and the immigrants' as well.

McCarran's father, also Patrick McCarran, was born in Ireland about 1832 and stowed away on a ship during the famine year of 1848. In the United States, he joined the army's cavalry, fought the Paiute Indians, and then settled in Nevada to become a homesteader and a sheep rancher. He married Margaret Shea, who had come from County Cork as a domestic servant. On August 8, 1876, this couple had their only child. He was educated in the local schools, graduating from Reno High School in 1897 as class valedictorian. He began putting himself through the University of Nevada with a job as a janitor but had to quit in his senior year when his father suffered a disabling illness.

It is a measure of his energy and ability that McCarran found other ways to achieve his goals. He made an advantageous marriage, in 1903, to Martha Harriet Weeks. Her Elko, Nevada, family was also in ranching. They were Episcopalians, and McCarran's bride had been a school teacher prior to her marriage. They eventually had five children: a son, Samuel, and daughters Mary, Margaret, Norine, and Patricia. McCarran also studied law on his own. He was admitted to the bar in 1905 and practiced law for the next 30 years.

The only area in which his ambitions were thwarted was in politics. He secured a seat in the Nevada state legislature in 1902. Between 1907 and 1909, he was the district attorney general for Nye City. Between 1913 and 1918, he was on the Nevada Supreme Court; during 1917 and 1918, he was the chief justice. What he really wanted to be, though, was a senator. He made his first effort in 1916, when he challenged Democrat Key Pittman for the party nomination. It is not clear whether he thought he had a chance because Pittman himself had been in the Senate only since 1912 or whether he was so ambitious as to be reckless. All he gained, though, was an enemy. Pittman defeated him for the nomination easily. Thereafter, they needled each other as long as they were both in politics. In 1924, they were both in Nevada's delegation to the Democratic National Convention. The convention deadlocked over the choice between William McAdoo and Alfred E. Smith. Pittman, the delegation leader, was irritated with McAdoo and Smith for insisting on staying in the race but more irritated with McCarran, who was undermining Pittman's attempts to broker a deal whereby both men forswore the nomination. McCarran countered Pittman's claims of neutrality by publishing results of Nevada's delegates' straw poll, which showed Pittman really favored McAdoo. When McCarran ran for the Senate again, in 1926, Pittman did not make a move to help his fellow Democrat, and McCarran was defeated.

McCarran's big opportunity came in 1932, when the Great Depression led to a wholesale rejection of Republicans and the election of Democrats of whatever kind. This is an important point. The more McCarran saw of Franklin D. Roosevelt's New Deal, the less he liked it. Soon, he had distanced himself from Roosevelt and thus could not rely on administrative support for future political campaigns. Key Pittman was still one of Nevada's two senators and still in control of the state Democratic Party. Pittman and McCarran had another quarrel when Pittman thought McCarran tried to undermine Pittman's ultimately successful 1934 reelection bid. With no regular party support, McCarran had to develop his own organization.

To ensure his continuity in office and in influence, McCarran tended to his constituents assiduously. Early on, he identified aviation as a new industry that it would be in isolated Nevada's interest to cultivate, and he worked hard for it. (He was rewarded by having the Las Vegas international airport named in his honor.) When it benefited his constituents, McCarran could favor immigration. On March 3, 1949, he introduced Senate Bill 1165, which assisted Nevada's sheep-ranching industry by permitting skilled shepherds to enter the United States outside of the quota restrictions.[1] The bill became law on June 30, 1950. McCarran's work for Nevada ensured his reelection for the rest of his life. Eventually, his longevity in the Senate brought him seniority, which meant he could take his pick of prestigious committees that wrote laws not just for Nevada but for the United States. In 1943, after 10 years in the Senate, he became chair of the Senate Judiciary Committee and also head of the Appropriations Subcommittee, which introduced to the Senate funding bills for the Commerce, State, and Justice Departments.

In the Senate, the lines between Democrats and Republicans were crosscut by other lines. There was a loose coalition of conservatives—people who were divided into Democrats and Republicans and also divided in terms of regional or economic interest but who were united by the sense that the New Deal was a dangerous innovation. The New Deal transferred power from the legislature to the executive branch of the federal government. It threatened the balance between federal and state power. It advocated the redistribution of wealth, which challenged capitalist notions that the individual, not the government, should take the lead in society and also challenged traditional moral views that people should earn their own way (and should be permitted to keep what they earned). For Nevada's senators, the New Deal shift in foreign policy was an important point. Seniority had given Key Pittman the post of chair of the Senate Foreign Relations Committee. This was a powerful position from which to urge the country to isolate itself from the growth of communism, the rise of fascism, the expansion of the Empire of Japan, and the possibility of another war. McCarran never supported Pittman publicly, but he shared Pittman's sentiments. By the time World War II came, Pittman was dead. (He passed away on November 10, 1940, five days after his reelection to the Senate.) McCarran supported the war patriotically and then resumed his isolationist policies.

Yet McCarran reverted to isolationism in new circumstances. During World War II, the United States and the Soviet Union allied to defeat the Axis alliance of Nazi Germany and fascist Italy, but the alliance was always tentative, dependent on Franklin Roosevelt's personal contacts. After World War II, the United States and the Soviet Union entered into a Cold War that lasted until the 1991 Soviet collapse. Roosevelt's former secretary of agriculture and Iowa politician Henry A. Wallace argued that the Cold War need not exist and that the United States should aim for normal relations with the Soviet Union. He was in the minority, but he was part of a spectrum. George F. Kennan, who was no communist sympathizer, argued for cultivating diplomatic relations with the Soviets, too. He argued that the Soviets had no system for transferring leadership from one generation to the next; when the present leadership died out (he gave it 15 years), the Soviet Union might collapse. Until then, the United States had to remain active in world affairs, using diplomacy, economic sanctions, and perhaps sometimes military means to "contain" Soviet expansionist tendencies within historic borders. (Hence, Kennan's theory is called "containment.") When longtime isolationist Senator Arthur Vandenburg of Michigan began advocating greater involvement in world affairs, it would seem that the United States had abandoned its historic isolationism. Actually, people such as Pat McCarran remained isolationist, albeit in another sense—trying to isolate the United States from succumbing to international communism.

The Cold War was a new kind of war. It had battlegrounds, such as Korea and Vietnam. The United States and the Soviet Union were also rivals in a battle that took place in laboratories and atomic weapons testing grounds. Most important for McCarran was the possibility that individual members of the Communist Party active in the United States could deliver the country to the Soviets.

McCarran first raised this possibility during debates over postwar Europe. Wars always create some refugees as civilians flee advancing troops. During World War II, the Nazis deliberately uprooted more than 20 million civilians. Some were sent directly to extermination camps such as Auschwitz, specifically built to kill people. Others were put to work as slave labor in agriculture and industry under lethal conditions; denied adequate food, clothing, shelter, and medical care; and worked under the supervision of guards who beat and tortured them. They died at their slave labor camps, or, as they wore out, they were transported to the death camps. Altogether, 12 million captives (including nearly 6 million Jews) died before the Allies defeated the Nazis and put an end to their system. The Allies then went to work breaking up the concentration camps and getting the newly freed inmates in sufficient health to return home. However, more than a million survivors of this vast uprooting could not return to their homes. In the case of Jews, Nazis had often leveled their towns after transferring or deporting them, and there was no home to return to. In other cases, the advancing Soviets had replaced the retreating Nazis. In the part of Germany and Austria occupied by American troops, the United States Army transferred the displaced persons (DPs) from their concentration camps and slave labor quarters to the best accommodations they could find, which were often the barracks the Nazis had lived in while they were guarding their prisoners. They provided as much as they could and appealed to the American public for more food and for clothing. The DPs were able to augment the food supply by growing vegetables in patches of ground between their barracks. The DPs scrounged their camps for furniture and fabric so that, as families reassembled, they could curtain off the corners of their barracks into family areas, although they still had to eat at the common mess and take their recreation in public areas, because they did not have the facilities for kitchens or for play space. The DPs also scrounged for work, supporting themselves by keeping their camps as clean as they could, providing each other with petty services, and helping the American authorities. World War II ended in Europe on May 8, 1945. However, for several years thereafter, some DPs remained in their camps, freed from Nazi tyranny and restored to health but without homes or jobs.

Harry Truman wanted to move at least some people from Germany and Austria, and also people displaced by the war in Italy, to the United States. Some DPs could be integrated into European society but not all. Italy had historically been an immigrant-sending country; its economy was even weaker than usual right after World War II. Germany was getting a new wave of refugees—*Volksdeutsch*, ethnic Germans who had lived in the Soviet Union, Poland, and Czechoslovakia but who were being expelled as a result of Nazi occupation of those countries. The DPs could not all find jobs in the German or Austrian economy, and there was still a certain amount of ethnic prejudice and anti-Semitism. Some DPs might prefer to go to other countries, such as Israel, which became an independent state in May 1948. Truman did not want to force anyone to return to Soviet-dominated areas who did not want to go, and after three years, it was clear these people did not want to. Encouraging migration to the United States would relieve the kind of unemployment and economic depression that made Europeans vote for the Communist Party. It would also, Truman thought, be handled in a way that was safe to the United States, taking, for example, people who had relatives who could help them find work and homes and assist them in adjusting to the United States, or confiding them to the care of agencies, such as the Hebrew Immigrant Aid Society, that would perform the same functions.

Truman managed to get some of what he wanted in the Displaced Persons Act of June 25, 1948. Truman had wanted to admit the DPs outside of existing quota laws. Congress worded the Displaced Persons Act to permit 205,000 people to enter the United States over a two-year period. Their visas were charged against future quotas. Italy had a quota of about 5,000 people annually. If 205,000 immigrants went from Italy to the United States between 1948 and 1950, Italy would use up the next 41 years of quotas and would not be able to send another immigrant until 1992 (205,000 divided by 5,000 is 41, the number of years of quotas). Thus, the law took care of an emergency without increasing immigration in the long run.

In Europe, DPs now had something new to fill their time. They had to gather documents that would allow them to get passports and visas. Documentation was no easy task, because many had lost their homes and had all their personal possessions taken from them when they entered concentration camps. DPs did not have to conform to the quota system but did have to fulfill all the requirements regarding immigration that the United States had imposed since the 1880s. They had to swear they were not anarchists or polygamists. They had to take literacy tests. They had to take medical tests that checked them for loathsome and contagious diseases. (This was a serious barrier, because the concentration and DP camps were conducive to tuberculosis.) If they had relatives in the United States, they had to contact them and convince them to be sponsors. They also had to do the paperwork for the agency that transported them from the DP camp to the port at Bremerhaven in northern Germany and chaperoned them on the steamship that carried them to an American port—usually New York City but sometimes Boston or New Orleans.

McCarran never supported the DP program. Even if all it did was permit countries to use future quotas in this short, two-year period, it was still going to alter the ethnic and racial composition of the United States. Ireland, which had no DPs, could not take advantage of the program. Also, he feared that in the rush of immigrants, communist spies and saboteurs might pose as refugees, be admitted to the United States, and carry out subversive activities. Truman argued that the danger of spies and saboteurs was minimal. This led to a confrontation between the executive and legislative branch, and between wings of the Democratic Party, on the issue of control of subversives.

People concerned about civil liberties were already suspicious of the executive branch's record. Even before World War II started, the Alien Registration Act of June 28, 1940, required immigrants older than 14 years of age who had not become citizens of the United States to register and be fingerprinted and permitted deportation of people who had been members of radical political organizations. In 1942, Roosevelt sanctioned the relocation of Japanese immigrants and their American-born children from their California homes to camps in the interior, where they were held, without trial, until 1944. German and Italian immigrants who were not citizens were required to register as enemy aliens and to obey a separate code of laws. Throughout the war, Congress had given the executive branch power to restrict immigration in the name of national defense.

Truman authorized each department of the executive branch to conduct investigations into the loyalty of department employees and to fire those deemed security risks. The loyalty reviews may have removed security risks but at a cost to innocent people. It attacked individuals who were not members of the Communist Party but who had personal information (such as homosexuality) they wished to keep private. Fearing the communists would blackmail such people and thus force them to become spies, the authorities deemed the people security risks and fired them.

A series of events in 1950 suggested the executive branch had not been thorough enough in its search for communist spies. In December 1948, while the first groups of U.S.-bound DPs were boarding U.S. Army transport ships, the House Un-American Activities Committee (HUAC) was watching *Time* magazine editor Whittaker Chambers produce evidence that he claimed proved that State Department official Alger Hiss was a Soviet spy. Chambers himself had been a member of the Communist Party. He left the party in fear of his life, when he began to see how ruthless Stalin was about ensuring loyalty. To protect himself from retribution from his former colleagues, he had saved microfilmed copies of documents his spy ring had passed to the Soviets. To protect the documents from thieves, he had hidden them in a hollowed-out pumpkin in a patch in his farm in Maryland. Called to testify before HUAC, Chambers mentioned that Hiss had been part of the spy ring. When Hiss denied it, Chambers waded out into his pumpkin patch, uncorked the pumpkin, and pulled out what he said was the incriminating microfilm. Hiss sued Chambers for libel. Hiss ended up being convicted of perjury—specifically of lying under oath about his communist affiliations—on January 21, 1950. Hiss served his time in the federal penitentiary and then went about his life, maintaining until his death that he was innocent. Only after the Soviet Union collapsed did historians obtain documents in Soviet archives indicating that Hiss was indeed a spy.

Shortly after a jury convicted Hiss of perjury, the Federal Bureau of Investigation (FBI) began to arrest individuals connected with a ring of atomic spies. Their story started on February 5, 1950, when British authorities announced that Klaus Fuchs, a German-born British citizen, had confessed to passing to the Soviets reports on the work being conducted at Los Alamos, New Mexico, where scientists were supposedly building an atomic bomb in total secrecy. Fuchs gave the name of his courier, an army sergeant named David Greenglass who had been stationed at Los Alamos. Greenglass in turn named the other people in the ring, including his brother-in-law Julius Rosenberg and his sister Ethel. In this case, it was the release of secret U.S. files a generation later that indicated Julius Rosenberg transferred secret documents between U.S. and Soviet agents and that the agents at the time thought Ethel supported her husband's work by typing notes. The Rosenbergs were not confronted with the evidence at their trial, because authorities thought that making their files public would reveal too much about their counterespionage techniques. Instead, the Rosenbergs were executed in 1953 without being able to see the evidence against them.

On February 9, 1950, right after the FBI began arresting Fuchs's associates, McCarthy delivered an address to the Wheeling, West Virginia, Women's Republican Club. McCarthy called into question the executive branch's and the Democrats' commitment to eradicating communism by charging that there were still communists working in the U.S. State Department. Anticommunism and Republicans were like a magnet and iron filings. Republicans came together on the issue that they were better at being anticommunist than the Democrats were. The same issue had the opposite effect on the Democrats. Truman argued that he had been sufficiently vigilant against communists and that McCarthy's charges were a red herring. McCarran agreed with McCarthy and weighed in with his opinion through his sponsorship of a new internal security bill that made it clear what the United States was up against:

> There exists a world Communist movement which, in its origins, its development, and its present practice, is a world-wide revolutionary movement whose purpose it is, by treachery, deceit, infiltration into other groups (governmental and otherwise), espionage, sabotage, terrorism, and any other means deemed necessary, to establish a Communist totalitarian dictatorship in the countries throughout the world through the medium of a world-wide Communist organization.[2]

Because "[t]he direction and control of the world Communist movement is vested in and exercised by the Communist dictatorship of a foreign country," it was necessary to pay special attention to the possibility that communists would sneak in among legitimate immigrants. To that end, McCarran's bill specifically prohibited immigrants who were members of communist parties. In case communists changed their name, another paragraph denied admission to aliens who adhered to any doctrines common among communists or who belonged to any organizations that adhered to these doctrines. The law empowered attorneys general to deport aliens without hearings about the justice of their cause. Denying immigrants hearings covered situations similar to that in the Rosenberg trial, in which authorities had access to confidential documents but could not declassify and publish them. Attorneys general could not deport immigrants to countries where they faced lethal persecution, but they could exercise a great deal of discretion in determining a deportation destination. New procedures were established to carry out the new supervision of the domestic and immigrant populations.

McCarran's bill went through the Senate and House and to President Truman. Truman vetoed it and published his reasons. He objected to the bill on practical grounds, claiming that new procedures would hamper the ones already in place for identifying subversives. He also objected to it as presenting complications in foreign relations. Although the United States was not a totalitarian country, it did have relations with countries that were (specifically fascist Spain and communist, but nonaligned, Yugoslavia), and it could not pass anti-totalitarian legislation so thorough as to require termination of diplomatic relations with countries that, while admittedly imperfect, were not Stalinist. Finally, Truman questioned the judgment of those sponsoring this legislation; the United States, he wrote, did not need "hysterical" legislation.[3] Nevertheless, McCarran's bill passed the Senate and the House over Truman's veto, and it became law on September 29, 1950. Conflict lines were drawn: between president and Congress, between one wing of the Democrats and the other, between those who thought of foreign affairs as a place where the United States should exercise leadership and those who thought the United States should isolate and protect itself.

The same year, McCarran, through a Senate Judiciary Subcommittee, proposed a new immigration law. The new law would bring the previous laws together in one code eliminating obsolete laws, reinforcing ones that were still useful, and addressing new issues. It took more than a year to draft the proposed Immigration and Nationality Act, which meant that the bill was introduced at a critical time. In 1952, while McCarran was overseeing the drafting of the immigration bill, the United States was in the midst of campaigns to elect a president, one-third of the Senate, and the entire House of Representatives. Truman was eligible to run for the presidency again, but after doing poorly in early primaries, he bowed out. Adlai Stevenson was the Democratic nominee but was thoroughly identified with the Truman, rather than the McCarran, wing of the party. This might be the year the Democrats fell apart, creating a vacuum into which the Republicans could step. McCarran's immigration law, then, could be a factor in attracting or repelling voters.

McCarran's law was comprehensive enough to contain something for everyone. For those concerned about the complexity of government, all immigration laws were now brought together in one place. For those who thought the laws antiquated in the face of modern tendencies to travel and to go on foreign vacations, there was a long list of nonimmigrant categories (such as tourist or student) and procedures for transferring between categories (so that a nonimmigrant could become a permanent resident). For those who worried about labor shortages, the bill introduced a new procedure for selecting immigrants on the basis of the skills they would bring to the United States. For those worried about labor competition, the bill generally skirted conflict with the Bracero Program (which admitted Mexican workers on a temporary basis) but in other cases had qualifications that prohibited labor migration. For those who worried about communists, the law increased the list of reasons for excluding or deporting aliens. For those who worried about civil rights, it outlined the procedures to safeguard those subject to deportation. For those concerned about discrimination, it eliminated sexual discrimination in immigration and racial discrimination in naturalization, and it ended the prohibitions on immigration from East Asia. For those who thought racial differences were important, it kept the quotas on European immigrants, assigned quotas to countries now permitted to send Asian immigrants, and limited colonial people's ability to enter the United States on the quotas of the countries that colonized them (e.g., people from the Belgian Congo could not enter as Belgians).

Yet instead of satisfying everyone, McCarran's bill raised an outcry. Circumstances called tremendous attention to the portions of the bill bearing on race and ethnicity. World War II had been fueled by Nazi racism. The mass movement for civil rights was still a few years away, but there were already signs (Jackie Robinson's baseball career, Truman's desegregation of the U.S. armed forces) that ending racism was an important issue in the United States. The argument Truman made about the relationship between the treatment of immigrants and the ability to conduct foreign policy was still valid. There were also some DPs still in Europe; escapees from the Iron Curtain were replacing survivors of Nazi concentration camps. Guardians of civil liberties were even more concerned about the threat McCarran's bill posed than they had been about the Truman administration's actions, and with good reason. Later, McCarran's legislation would be used to justify excluding people from the United States on the grounds that they had written unfavorably about the U.S. government and favorably about communism, even though to the people involved, such writing seemed to be simply an exercise of constitutionally protected freedom of the press.[4]

Liberal Democrats fell over each other to suggest alternatives. On March 25, 1952, Truman proposed the United States revive its displaced persons legislation and permit 300,000 refugees to enter the country over the next three years.[5] On April 2, Emanuel Celler, a House Democrat from Brooklyn, introduced a bill worded similarly to Truman's.[6] In the Senate, Minnesota Democrat Hubert H. Humphrey and New York Democrat Herbert Lehman also proposed legislation. If one believed *The New York Times*, no one supported McCarran's bill. The *Times* editorialized against it and reported that none of the foreign-language press in New York favored it.[7] The American Federation of Labor and railroad heir W. A. Harriman were on the same side, with one urging acceptance of Truman's proposal for 300,000 DPs and the other urging a veto of the McCarran law.[8] The Jewish Labor Council and the National Council of Churches agreed in opposing McCarran. The Catholics split, with the National Catholic Welfare Council supporting it and the Catholic Association for

International Peace opposing it.[9] The Polish-American Congress opposed it. A New York Italian politician named Fortunato Pope warned that the Italians were going to vote for Stevenson because of it.[10] A nasty fight broke out when the intensely partisan Truman accused the Republicans of supporting racist legislation. Actually, Republican candidate Dwight D. Eisenhower urged repeal of racist legislation.[11]

However, McCarran was an experienced politician who knew how to get legislation passed. On this occasion, he worked with another conservative Democrat, Francis Walter of Pennsylvania, who, as chair of the House Judiciary Committee Subcommittee on Immigration, introduced the bill in the House. The Senate tacked on 21 amendments but, on May 23, 1952, passed the bill. In the House, New York Republican Jacob Javits (an example that the Republicans had the same ideological split as the Democrats) tried to force a roll call vote and get the bill returned to committee, but the bill passed there, too, on June 11.

Truman vetoed the bill on June 25. It took him so long not because he had to make up his mind but because he drafted a lengthy veto message. Part of the message was addressed over the heads of Congress, to people watching from overseas. Truman assured Asians that he would like to sign legislation permitting them to immigrate. "But now this most desirable provision comes before me embedded in a mass of legislation which would perpetuate injustices of long standing against many other nations of the world," the president said, referring specifically to the quotas against European countries.[12] The rest of the message was addressed directly to its supporters. As with the Internal Security Act, Truman complained that the procedures being introduced would complicate, not facilitate, the achievement of intended goals. More importantly, he pointed out that the real problem was the quota system. "It repudiates our basic religious concepts, our belief in the brotherhood of man, and in the words of St. Paul that 'there is neither Jew nor Greek, there is neither bond nor free, . . . for ye are all one in Christ Jesus.'"[13] It flew in the face of the egalitarianism inscribed in the Declaration of Independence. It negated the compassion proclaimed by the Emma Lazarus poem on the base of the Statue of Liberty.

McCarran responded that Truman's veto was "one of the most un-American acts I have witnessed in my career."[14] Back in the Senate, he rallied his colleagues: "In God's name, in the name of the American people, in the name of America's future, let us override this veto." The Senate passed the bill by the two-thirds majority necessary to counter the presidential veto, as did the House. The bill became law on June 27, 1952, two days after Truman's veto. Obliged to enforce it, Truman began to make arrangements to admit Asians according to the new quotas. He also used his position to make one last attack on McCarran. On September 4, 1952, he appointed a committee to study immigration and naturalization and to report to him. On January 1, 1953 (they had to hurry; Eisenhower had been elected president in November 1952), the committee returned a report titled *Whom We Shall*

Welcome. This was not a question, "Whom shall we welcome?" It was a declaration of fact, drawn from a statement by George Washington, on December 2, 1783: "The bosom of America is open to receive not only the Opulent and Respectable Stranger, but the oppressed and persecuted of all Nations and Religions; whom we shall welcome to a participation of all our rights and previlege [*sic*], if by decency and propriety of conduct they appear to merit the enjoyment."[15] It was obvious that the battle over immigration would go on.

However, the extreme anticommunists had little time left to lead it. While McCarran was passing legislation, his colleagues Richard Nixon and Joe McCarthy were getting most of the public attention by investigating communism in various executive branch offices. Eisenhower accepted Nixon as his running mate. Nixon came from the populous state of California; he was identified with the new people in Congress and with the new concerns. But Eisenhower was always cool toward McCarthy. And McCarthy was becoming a liability. One of McCarthy's aides, David Schine, was drafted into the U.S. Army. McCarthy tried to get an exemption for him, but the army turned it down. McCarthy then decided someone in the army must want to hamper his ongoing anticommunist investigations. Who was it and what was the purpose? In 1954, McCarthy began to investigate the possibility of communist infiltration of the army, a sensational enough charge that the hearings were carried on television, a medium that did not put McCarthy in his best light. The army also had good lawyers and, of course, distinguished veterans of World War II to testify on its behalf; it turned back McCarthy's investigation. Then, McCarthy's colleagues in the Senate appointed a committee to consider censuring the senator for his behavior.

McCarthy's army hearings took place during a congressional election year. While he agreed with McCarthy's opinions, McCarran was hoping to use them to improve conservative Democratic changes in the upcoming elections. He made peace with the other Democrats in the state, including Vail Pittman, the brother of the late Key Pittman, McCarran's perpetual rival. On September 27, McCarran was in Washington, testifying before an ad hoc Senate committee about why McCarthy should not be censured. On September 28, he was at the Civic Center of Hawthorne, Nevada, speaking at a political event. He finished his speech, descended the platform, and was walking up a side aisle when he collapsed from a heart attack and died.

McCarthy was condemned for conduct unbecoming a senator. He died in 1957. By then, he had given his name to an era. But McCarran had given that era its immigration laws.

Notes

1. *Congressional Index, Eighty-first Congress, 1949–1950* (Chicago, Washington, DC, and New York: Commerce Clearing House, 1948), 855.

2. Henry Steele Commager, *Documents of American History*, 8th ed. (New York: Appleton-Century-Crofts, 1968), 2:555.

3. Ibid., 2:558–562.

4. C. J. Grossman, "The McCarran-Walter Act: War against Margaret Randall and the First Amendment," *Crime and Social Justice* 27–28 (1987): 220–233, and Trevor Parry-Giles, "Stemming the Red Tide: Free Speech and Immigration Policy in the Case of Margaret Randall," *Western Journal of Speech Communication* 52, no. 2 (1988): 167–183. Margaret Randall was a U.S. journalist who voluntarily surrendered her U.S. citizenship in 1966, then requested a tourist visa in 1986. Acting on the authority of the 1952 Immigration and Nationality Act, the Immigration and Naturalization Service denied her a visa.

5. *The New York Times* (March 25, 1952), 1.

6. *The New York Times* (April 2, 1952), 12.

7. *The New York Times* (May 29, 1952), 29; and *The New York Times* (June 18, 1952), 11.

8. *The New York Times* (May 23, 1952), 10; and *The New York Times* (June 26, 1952), 16.

9. *The New York Times* (March 22, 1952), 10; *The New York Times* (June 16, 1952), 5; *The New York Times* (June 25, 1952), 16; and *The New York Times* (August 3, 1952), 4.

10. *The New York Times* (June 2, 1952), 5; and *The New York Times* (October 29, 1952), 24.

11. *The New York Times* (October 17, 1952), 19.

12. Commager, *Documents of American History*, 2:581–582.

13. Ibid., 2:583. There is a small logical error in using this to support Truman's position. Paul was not arguing for tolerance. The full passage claims that it was common acceptance of Christ as Messiah that made Jews, Greeks, slaves, and free people equal. More interesting is that the original quote, Galatians 3:28, also includes a phrase about there being neither male nor female. The omission may have been deliberate. In 1944, the Republicans introduced the Equal Rights Amendment into their party platform, and it remained there until 1980. The Democrats did not support the amendment because they were afraid it would render unconstitutional the body of legislation they had passed to protect women workers from exploitation; for them, there had to be a difference between male and female.

14. *The New York Times* (June 26, 1952), 14.

15. *Whom We Shall Welcome: Report of the President's Commission on Immigration and Naturalization* (Washington, DC: U.S. Government Printing Office, 1953), frontispiece.

Bibliography

The most accessible of McCarran's papers are at the Nevada State Archives in Carson City. McCarran's biographer, Jerome E. Edwards, has published several works, including *Pat McCarran: Political Boss of Nevada*, Nevada Studies in History and Political Science No. 17 (Reno: University of Nevada Press, 1982). The *Nevada Historical Society Quarterly* has devoted much space to McCarran. McCarran's daughter, Sister Margaret Patricia McCarran, published a two-part memoir in 1968 and 1969; Jerome E. Edwards published "Nevada Power Broker: Pat McCarran and His Political Machine," in volume 27, no. 3 (1984): 182–198; and Christopher Gerard published "On the Road to Viet Nam: 'The Loss of China Syndrome,' Pat McCarran and J. Edgar Hoover," in volume 37, no. 4 (1994): 247–262. Monographs that include reference to McCarran but deal more generally with McCarthyism include William F. Buckley Jr. and L. Brent Bozell, *McCarthy and His Enemies: The Record and Its Meaning* (Chicago: H. Regnery, 1954); Robert Griffith, *The Politics of Fear: Joseph R. McCarthy and the Senate* (Lexington: University Press of Kentucky for the Organization of American Historians, 1970); and Yelong Han, "An Untold Story: American Policy toward Chinese Students in the United States, 1949–1955," *Journal of American-East Asian Relations* 11, no. 1 (1993): 77–99. For the conservative Democratic context, see James T. Patterson, *Congressional Conservatives and the New Deal: The Growth of the Conservative Coalition in Congress, 1933–1939* (Lexington: University Press of Kentucky for the Organization of American Historians, 1967). For the Nevada context, see Russell Elliott, with the assistance of William D. Rowley, *History of Nevada*, 2nd ed., rev. (Lincoln: University of Nebraska Press, 1987); and Fred L. Israel, *Nevada's Key Pittman* (Lincoln: University of Nebraska Press, 1963).

The Melting Pot versus Tapestry Debate

Alexander I. Stingl

In 1908, a play by Israel Zangwill titled *The Melting Pot* popularized what would be one of the most influential metaphors in the American immigration debate. The reasoning behind the metaphor was that immigrants assimilate into American culture as though they were melting with one another in a crucible. The metaphor, though popularized by Zangwill, had been around in the form of similar images and was the product of an international academic debate on culture and civilization that was conducted throughout the latter half of the 18th century and all of the 19th century. With the academic debates reaching a popular level and public discussion mediated through authors like Zangwill, John Dewey, and Horace Kallen, the debate turned up a number of social conflicts that had remained implicit powder kegs in U.S. society. Some conservative critics of immigration in general opened up to nationalism and racism, while over time the melting pot metaphor was criticized by liberal thinkers in line with what would be called multiculturalism, arguing that American culture resembled more a salad bowl, mosaic, or tapestry.

In many ways, this conflict has been reheated today, first with feminism and the question of sexuality and gender justice, second as a problem of civil society and religion after September 11, and third, in the question of the digital divide.

Intellectual History

To properly understand the rise, the use, and the discontents of the metaphor of the melting pot, one must view it in light of the history of ideas and the intellectual and scholarly exchange between Europe and the United States since the mid-18th century. In the late 18th century, the major philosophical disputes in Europe—and, in particular, in Germany—posed the question "what connections exist between reason, progress, government, history, language, and civilization?"

Immanuel Kant (1724–1804), famous for his three critiques of pure reason, of practical reasoning, and of judgment, also wrote at length about the idea of cosmopolitanism in relation to the natural evolution of humans in history and in relation

Israel Zangwill's play, *The Melting Pot*, popularized what would be one of the most influential metaphors in the American immigration debate. (Library of Congress)

to peace between peoples. In sum, and glossing over a few of the more intricate details of the contemporary philosophical debate, we may summarize that, in Kant's view, the evolution of men, part of the new field of anthropology, entailed the goal of a truly cosmopolitan state as its final end.

In the version of his former students and admirers Hamann and Herder (both later turning into harsh critics), much depended on the question of language and its origin. For them, language is the source of reason, and the question of the differences in languages and, respectively, cultures, turns up in the wake of these philosophical discussions. Herder's model of cultures as enclosed spheres remains one of the most influential ideas in the debates on the transactions of cultures even today. It is the basis, for example, of Samuel Huntington's famous thesis regarding the clash of civilizations (1992), which guided some of the ideological positions of the administration of George W. Bush.[1]

Huntington predicted that cultural and, above all, religious identities and values would incite and continually fuel conflicts on a global scale. He intended to answer utopian visions that arose after the fall of communism, arguing that the "victory of capitalism over communism" did not indicate a victory of capitalism and democracy in general but a return to the "normal situation" of cultural conflict. While a heated debate ensued, Huntington's influential position as an internationally renowned author, university professor at Harvard, and former foreign policy advisor to President Jimmy Carter, leant credit to his views, which were received with open arms as fodder for conservative politicians who argue that security goes before liberty. Hawkish members of the George W. Bush administration not only found justification for their positions in Huntington's discussion, but also Huntington's work escalated their ideologies.

Two centuries prior, when Kant, Herder, and others wrote furiously to resolve these questions philosophically, which for them were wrought with religious and social consequences, Michel Guillaume Jean de Crevecoeur (1735–1813), who had changed his name to John Hector St. John de Crevecoeur after moving from

France to New York at the age of 20, became credited with one of the first descriptions of the United States as a crucible in his *Letters of an American Farmer*. These essays were published in London after Crevecoeur's return to European soil. They received wide acclaim and are considered to be the first literary success of an American author in Europe. For Crevecoeur, the idea of a mixture in America was described as a "mixture of blood," but he was referring, more importantly, not so much to a mere fact of customs mixing or coexisting than he was alluding to the outwardly peaceful coexistence of different Christian denominations. This harmonious state of religious coexistence seemed unthinkable in Europe. Thus, for him, "being an American" meant to be part of "the finest system of populations" and embracing a "new mode of life."

Another French voice was that of Alexis de Tocqueville (1805–1859), whose *Democracy in America* (1835) is still standard reading for humanities and social science students today.

He had traveled to the United States at a time of many social, economic, and political transformations. De Tocqueville described the ambiguities of American society and democracy that he experienced with a sharp analytical eye but also from the point of view of a French citizen who came from a political culture of centralism and a philosophy highly distrustful of individualism, which he saw on the rise in America's economic individualism. However, he repeatedly expressed his puzzlement over the fact that Americans, despite the existence of genuine inequalities and the pursuit of individualism, seemed eagerly engaged in open criticism of these inequalities and the negative consequences that individualism could have.

American writers of political philosophy, theological reflection, and literature such as the Transcendentalists—among them Theodor Parker (1810–1860); Orestes Brownson (1803–1876), who coined the concept "Americanization"; Margaret Fuller (1810–1850); and, above all, their herald, Ralph Waldo Emerson (1803–1882)—would create their own "intellectual crucible" in bringing forth a convergence between the writings of men such as Crevecoeur, the European philosophers such as Kant, and, to some degree, the British and German Romanticists. Emerson and the Transcendentalists helped promote the education of American students in French, British, and, above all else, German scholarship.

In *The American Scholar*, Emerson declares that man can exist in one of two states. Either he can be divided and therefore be in a state of degeneration, or he can be in the "right state," one with all of mankind.[2] To be forged in the crucible of Americanization, therefore, can be viewed as an intellectual idealization of producing the right state. Emerson's position did rest on the ideas of "harmonious equilibrium," "indifference," and "compensation," which were used interchangeably in philosophy, medicine, economics, politics, and physics by diverse authors beginning with Kant but also including F. W. J. Schelling (1775–1854), Joseph Louis Lagrange (1736–1813), and A. A. Cournot (1801–1877). Few current or recent authors in the history of political ideas, sociology, or philosophy have paid attention to this significant and crucial detail of European-American exchange ideas; philosopher Odo Marquard is one of the few exceptions.[3]

While Emerson was producing his work, in Europe a new generation of scholars trained in philosophy, medicine, and psychology began to theorize about the differences of the customs, cultures, and spirit of peoples, eventually leading to the creation of cultural psychology, sociology, and anthropology as academic disciplines in their own right. The leading figure was Rudolf Hermann Lotze (1817–1881), who taught physiology and philosophy at the University of Goettingen and whose courses were frequented by scores of American students who had to take an obligatory year or two of studying abroad. While he is nearly forgotten today, Lotze's books, such as his famous *Microcosm* (three volumes, 1856–1864), were required reading for American psychologists and philosophers well into the first decades of the 20th century.[4] Another German experimentalist, Wilhelm Wundt (1832–1920), received equal prominence among American students of physiology, psychology, and philosophy. Cultural anthropology, ethnology, and cultural psychology are largely the intellectual creation of the scholarship of Lotze and Wundt. The discussion that these emerging disciplines began in Germany became also very influential in the United States, with its focus on the question of the role that culture plays for the unity and prosperity of a nation. Their significance in the American context reinforced certain aspects of their discussion in Germany. However, while their institutionalization was promoted in the United States, the increasing nationalist tendencies and academic shortsightedness of those in charge of higher education and research administration in Germany slowed down the progress of these fields significantly.

Largely, the overall intellectual discussion can be felt in the work of men such as William James on the one hand and in the important role that one German immigrant, Franz Boas (1858–1942), played in particular. "Although German born," writes George Stocking, "and deeply rooted in the intellectual traditions of his homeland, Franz Boas, more than any other man, defined the 'national character' of anthropology in the US."[5]

Boas was rooted in the tradition of Kant and Herder, whose works he had studied intensely while in Berlin under the tutelage of the physiologically oriented anthropologist and anatomist Rudolph Virchow (1821–1902), who was a follower of the evolutionary theory of Lamarck, as well as ethnologist Adolf Bastian (1826–1905), who believed in a fundamental unity of mankind based on his belief in a mutual intellectual potential shared by all humans. Boas developed his ideas toward an understanding of the "cultural other" in what was known as historical particularism, a school of thought accredited with being the intellectual forerunner of the culture-personality movement, the culture-as-text idea, and, above all, multiculturalism in American anthropology and social theory.[6] In 1887, Boas began working in the United States, starting his teaching career at Clark University a year later.

Meanwhile, Adolf Bastian's contemporaries, Moritz Lazarus (1824–1903) and Heymann Steinthal (1823–1899), helped in the foundation of influential German journals in cultural psychology (*Voelkerpsychologie*), which was largely associated with the works of psychologist Wilhelm Wundt, whose work was very influential on William James, and with the ideas developed by philosopher and sociologist Georg Simmel (1858–1918), who tutored essayist, philosopher, and William James's protégé George Santayana (1863–1952) and Brown University's psychology major domo Edmund Burke Delabarre (1863–1945).

These are but a few examples of the connections between European anthropology and Americanscience. The connections are noteworthy because of the important position people such as William James or Delabarre had, not just as authors or public figures but as university teachers. Intellectual leaders in science, society, and politics of the early 20th century studied with these men and their likes. Their ideas of what American society should or could look like was largely shaped by their teachers. The intellectual climate that determined their education and, in turn, their understanding of what a symbol like "the melting pot" meant was not to be separated from the ideas of American pragmatism and the idea that each and everyone could influence their own fate in the face of a nation's progress and that this form of freedom meant contributing to progress itself.

In his 1920 collection *Character and Opinion in the United States*, Santayana would describe his perception of an oppressive nature associated with the American melting pot:

> You must wave, you must cheer, you must push with the irresistible crowd; otherwise you will feel like a traitor, a soulless outcast, a deserted ship high and dry on the shore. . . . This national faith and morality are vague in idea, but inexorable in spirit; they are the gospel of work and the belief in progress. By them, in a country where all men are free, every man finds that what most matters has been settled beforehand.[7]

The German anthropological discussion revolved around two principle ideas of culture: particularism versus universalism (whether culture was meant to come together in a thickening or "melting"—what Lazarus called *Verdichtung*) or whether culture was part of what Max Weber believed was a larger *Gewebe*—a netting, fabric, or tapestry.

In the American context, the thought of scholars such as William James, Josiah Royce (1855–1916), who had studied under Lotze in Goettingen, and John Dewey (1859–1952) was largely shaped by their European teachers and counterparts. This does not mean, however, that their contributions were not original and brilliant in their own right. For American scholars in the late 19th century and in the wake of Emerson, the concept of utility became a way of resolving the

Max Weber was a sociologist who conceptualized the theory of the Protestant work ethic and wrote about its influence on capitalism. (Library of Congress)

differences emerging from the Puritan roots and modern demands on the one hand and between collectivism and individualism one the other. Utility, as found in American pragmatism, meant a general optimism that, indeed, community actions could solve any problem, because the conflict between individuals and the collective was only a conflict if one did not accept mutually shared values, with utility at the core of this set of values. For Josiah Royce, the individual self was left in the middle of the social world, which gave rise to a need for a concept of loyalty that became constitutional of the positive idea of community.

In his quasi-religious arguments, Royce considered loyalty to be the superhuman quality of the united lives, represented in the acts of individual selves. In U.S. society, with its high influx of foreigners, the teaching and maintenance of loyalty was, therefore, a social engineering project of installing personal devotion to the American cause in every citizen. While not sharing Royce's more idealistic notions, the constant "inner dialogue" that people led inside their mind, according to Royce, to resolve issues of devotion was mirrored in James's conception of intersubjectivity. By *devotion*, Royce referred to the idea that one's devotion to an object mattered more than the inherent values and effects of that object; respectively, loyalty is the supreme moral good in his conceptions. To provide an example, loyalty is something that one should look for in a friend, because such a person is our friend not for the fact that he *is* a friend but because he is loyal to us.[8]

Intersubjectivity refers to the problem that each of us has a subjective perspective of the world. In short, we cannot know someone else's mind. Yet, somehow people have to interact with one another, and the question arises about what we share of the world that allows this interaction to function properly on the one hand and that allows everybody to retain a unique personal identity on the other.

For James, a central aspect of the solution to this problem was not loyalty but the problem of truth. In his view, we all are seekers of truth, which is constituted by its usefulness. As such seekers, we rely on our "social others"—the other members of society—to help verify these truths, for they also seek truth. Therefore, others are "benevolent seekers of the same truth," which becomes the constitution of an idea of community that can remain person-centered.

This means that everyone's perspective is of value and considered a contribution to the search of useful truths, as long as we all stand ready to correct our views when a more useful truth is discovered. Therefore, a member of another culture might bring an individual contribution with him or her that is more useful than what we know and how we do business. On the other hand, our way of conducting our business may prove to be more useful, and that person should, ideally, adapt.

John Dewey extended the discussion of pragmatism and intersubjectivity to include democracy and the idea of "the public." Dewey defined the public as the sphere of shared experiences. By sharing experiences with one another, we have a basis for a communication-centered learning process. In his perspective, the existence of the abstract entity he named "the public" leads to democracy as the basis of community, because we must allow for debate to share our different experiences. The question that would eventually hit the American public was, what are these shared experiences and will they lead to possibilities for personal growth or limit freedom?

The Melting Pot Metaphor in the Early 20th Century

In general, the concept of the melting pot is used metaphorically to describe the form of integration of several groups of immigrants who assimilate a prevalent national culture of the society they have migrated into by process of fusing a common culture from their different cultural streams. The United States has been considered for a long time to be the embodiment of this ideal; implicitly during the 19th century and explicitly after the melting pot concept was made popular by Israel Zangwill's play in 1907. Zangwill (1864–1926), a British writer and friends with famous novelists such as H. G. Wells, was a political writer and supported many causes, some of which gained expression in his novels and plays, including the fate of people living in ghettos, the emancipation of Jewish people and Zionism, and women's suffrage, an issue he became involved with through his wife and mother of his three children, Edith Ayrton. Zangwill was also friends with Theodor Herzl (1860–1904), the international leader of the Zionist movement. He broke with the movement in 1905, founding his own Jewish Territorialist Organization, based on the belief that the geographic location of a Jewish state did not matter as long as such a state and safe haven could be founded. In 1926, he was reported to have considered all his political ideals as having evidently failed and, subsequently, died from "a broken heart."

His play, *The Melting Pot,* hit American stages in 1908 and became an instant success; it is still staged today. In late 1909, President Theodore Roosevelt saw the play in Washington, DC, and his reactions were reported to have been ecstatic.

The plot of the drama vividly describes the experience that many immigrants have had in the United States. Drawing on real historic events, Zangwill's lead character, David Quixano, was depicted as the survivor of the Kishinev pogrom that happened in the Russian empire in 1903. While this event, from our historic point of view, cannot compare to the atrocities of the fascists starting three decades after the events described in Zangwill's play, the Kishinev pogrom made international news in its time, and Roosevelt, in explaining his position on the Monroe Doctrine (the so-called Roosevelt Corollary), cited it as a sample case that, in the event it happened in Latin America, it would be a justification for U.S. intervention.

In *The Melting Pot*, David has lost his family in the pogrom and immigrates, grief stricken, to the United States. He is a composer and finds solace in working on his "American symphony." In the play, David's monologues feature declarations of the hopes he has for America as the fabled city upon a hill, where humanity will be reborn: "America is God's crucible, the great melting pot where all of Europe's races are melting and reforming."[9] In a Shakespeare-inspired plot twist, David meets and falls in love with a Christian woman from Russia, Vera. However, it turns out that Vera is the daughter of the officer who is responsible for the pogrom that killed David's family and sent him to flee. At first, David is horrified and unable to follow his ideal of overcoming the past, engaging in reconciliation, and of "melting in the pot." Consequently, he breaks up with Vera, but the lovers are reunited and at the end of the play. They watch the sun setting behind the Statue of Liberty together while uttering declarations of hope for America's future and prosperity. The play touched a nerve, and the melting pot became a crucial metaphor that entered into national political events, becoming the subject of heated debate in the 1910s and 1920s.

Tapestry versus Melting Pot

While the melting pot seemed an ideal worth striving toward for some and a presumed reality for others, one set of critics argued in favor of cultural pluralism, fearing that the melting would pose limits to freedom; yet another set of critics argued that too much melting would annihilate the true American spirit; an offshoot group of the latter were groups that were racially biased, for the idea of the melting pot certainly raised the question whether the melting included non-Europeans, in particular whether this meant "biological melting" with those of "other races."[10] Those ascribing to the nationalist perspective have become known as jingoists, a metaphor that came in use in the United States after the sinking of the USS *Maine* that precipitated the Spanish-American War of 1898. Even Theodore Roosevelt was occasionally accused of being a jingoist and saw himself forced to address this matter in an interview with *The New York Times* on October 8, 1895. Such aspects certainly lead one to reflect on the ambiguities of the melting pot ideal and the problem of integration as assimilation. Assimilation can mean both the mutual assimilation of a national and foreign culture, preserving both, but it can also mean that the national culture eradicates the foreign elements in the process—that is, it melts them away.

The problems of immigration and the cultural contribution of foreigners were discussed in many countries, and some of the most influential texts have been written by French and German scholars—most notably Max Weber and Georg Simmel. But one of the most groundbreaking and influential essays was written by Charles Chesnutt. Chesnutt (1858–1932), was considered in the southern U.S. states legally black by the so-called one-drop rule and, on occasion, declared himself to be "seven-eighths white African-American." Many of his short stories focus on black characters that spoke in local dialects, thereby introducing a novelty into the literature genre. At the start of the 20th century, Chesnutt was politically active, working with famous advocates such as Booker T. Washington and W.E.B. DuBois. In 1900, Chesnutt published the landmark essay, "The Future American," which is an exemplary specimen of the debates of the time.[11] The essay deals with the discussion among many public writers at the time regarding the emergence of the "future American race." Chesnutt thought these writers were consciously or unconsciously avoiding the issue. This Emersonian theme was forged into a "popular theory" that is the version, he says, where the American race will be a "harmonious fusion of the various European elements, which now make up our heterogeneous population." Although, this seems to indicate that some "undesirable traits" need to be bred out.

He goes on to state that, indeed, for identification of these traits, science can find no "denominator" in physiognomy, language, or race. And, as science shows, the "amalgamation" of races will produce the future American race or "ethnic type." Amalgamation was the contemporary term for interethnic or interracial marriage and procreation. This is, however, a slow process, and, given the South, he states that the colored people will achieve equal status by "becoming white" in the way of a biological melting pot, which some tried to circumvent by means of face bleaching and so forth.

Clearly, Chesnutt saw the reality of the melting in 1900 being deeply racially biased and, more often than not, biases were unspoken. Some foreign scholars working in the United States, such as Harvard psychologist Hugo Muensterberg in *American Traits from a German Point of View* (1901), tried to paint a balanced picture but were often scorned for some of their more critical comments. In Muensterberg's case, he had retained his German citizenship and was occasionally accused of spying. However, the public climate remained mostly optimistic, whatever version of the melting pot different authors and speakers ascribed to, until World War I broke out, and the allegiances of many ethnic or "hyphenated Americans" came into question when they began to take different sides.

In 1915, Horace M. Kallen posed the problem in a "study of American nationality" as "Democracy versus the Melting-Pot."[12] Kallen (1882–1974) was a student and then assistant of George Santayana and famous for having coined the term "cultural pluralism," which became even more popular through John Dewey's later works. In his perspective, the optimistic philosophy that was spread publicly would have to lead to severe conflicts because differences were kept under the rug until they multiply and break out more violently. Instead, according to Kallen, differences and arguments should be addressed openly as they occur in society.

In his essay, which is a reaction to sociologist Edward Ross's (1866–1951) writings, whom he singles out as an example, Kallen opens the discussion by comparing the situation of 1776 to 1914. In 1776, the enemy was the British, against whose patronizing acts the Declaration of Independence was directed. In contrast to the past, the 1914 "enemy" from Europe is not identified as a "superior force" by writers like Ross; instead it is declared to be an "inferior" enemy of "Americanism." Democracy, in Ross's version, seems to be in need of defense against the melting pot.

In Randall Bourne's *Transnational America* (1916), the diagnosis is that the American public has become aware of a failure of the melting pot.[13] Bourne mirrors Kallen in his attitude that any overemphasis of the Anglo-Saxon core of Americanism will not lead toward the resolution of conflict. However, he did not ascribe to Kallen's quick appreciation of difference. While he referred to the fact that, regardless of where people lived geographically, they often upheld "a spiritual cultural heritage" that differed from the society that surrounded them, he felt that a cosmopolitan attitude should be possible that allowed for the coexistence of the spiritual and the local without clashing. Following William James and arguing against Dewey and Kallen, Bourne wondered "what democracy is and what are the justifications for a democratic" state?[14] He delineated the argument of what democracy is supposed to mean in a pluralistic nation instead of using democracy as a constitutive fact that is an unquestioned end that justifies any kind of means—a trait that he saw practiced in the United States' participation in World War I.

Multiculturalism, Salad Bowls, and Tapestries

On a theoretical level, the positions regarding the incorporation of cultural groupings that were pitted against one another included supremacist theorists who were arguing the existence of a core Anglo-American culture that immigrants and ethnic minorities had to assimilate to by subversion; at the heart of this debate was the conflict of whether this was also a racial issue.

Another position was the idea that German Americans, Irish Americans, Italian Americans, and so on represented semiautonomous subcultures. Finally, multiculturalism emerged from the idea of cultural pluralism, arguing that different cultural groups do and should retain their native cultural identity and that U.S. society would be better considered as a tapestry, salad bowl, mosaic, symphony, or rainbow. A key consideration in this debate is not just the question of mere cultural identity but of language and language education, which is deemed to be the heart of any cultural heritage. The discussion was and still is fierce in the United States, whether English should either be made the national language as the only and exclusive national language, or whether there should be several national languages, or whether it should be made certain that every child and every person living in the United States does speak English, or even whether every child should learn English as her first language.

The correlated idea of the "hyphenated American" is dated to a newspaper article from 1889 written by Charles W. Penrose, a high-ranking member of the Church of Latter Day Saints.[15] It was used to distinguish differences in ethnicity, race, and nationality. For the first few decades, however, it was used as a slur or insult, which was then taken up by the respective ethnic groups and transformed into a positive identity. During World War I, politicians used the hyphenation to address groups of German Americans, Irish Americans, and so on to urge them to remain neutral.

The transition from assimilation and hyphenation to the idea of multiculturalism and the tapestry or mosaic rests, perhaps, on two essential pillars of American social structure: the idea of individual achievement and distrust of government. U.S. society and public policy are built around the individual as a free agent in a free market who builds his own fortune. In addition, following from the first settlers' reasons to leave Europe and the religious oppression from governments and the experiences that led to the Declaration of Independence and the conflicts that followed, the role that government should play in the lives of U.S. citizens has remained a disputed issue until today. The general attitude, however, is a heightened distrust of government. At the very least, assimilation in these two respects is subliminally expected from every immigrant or U.S. citizen.

In the 1950s and 1960s, the question of ethnic, racial, and cultural heritage entered a new domain of public discussion and scientific interest—the question of social justice. Certainly, the fate of African American citizens, which led to the civil rights debates and the installment of policies such as affirmative action, was an important engine of social change. However, the question of social justice did not stop at the plight of citizens of color. The stakes for an increasing number of people was abolition of social inequalities due to race, ethnicity, gender, and cultural and religious background of any kind. On the front stage of the social sciences, the publication of a legion of studies in publicly accessible ways shed new light on the fate of minority cultures. Social scientists and their work found a growing audience outside of academia and began to become an influential force in immigration and integration politics.

Notably, a series of essays written by Nathan Glazer and Daniel Patrick Moynihan in the late 1950s and early 1960s, collected in the landmark *Beyond the Melting Pot: The Negroes, Puerto Ricans, Jews, Italians, and Irish of New York City* (1963), not only investigated these minority cultures in detail; Glazer also proved that, even in their third and fourth generations, the original cultures of these immigrants were still vividly alive and no or little melting had taken place.[16] Moreover, these minorities were indeed subject to severe social inequalities. While the book, and many like it following in its wake, did much to bring the problems to public consciousness and change American social science, Glazer himself has argued that the book and its successors have, in the decades since, not effected a real change in the social realities these ethnic groups have to live in and that social justice and equality are still largely out of reach for many cultural and ethnic groups. When he published his controversial *We Are All Multiculturalists Now* in 1997, Glazer asserted that, while assimilation was now politically incorrect to practice or even speak of, the idea of multiculturalism had pervaded the education curriculum of the nation along with affirmative action and similar policies, but effectually these strategies have not only failed to alleviate inequality, they may have even made the situation worse.[17] Due to his ambivalence regarding multiculturalism, Glazer has become the target of both conservatives and liberals, such as Dinesh D'Souza and John Fonte.[18]

At the same time, the discussion of multiculturalism has long surpassed the discussion on immigration alone and has branched out like a hydra and crept into emerging fields of study. For instance, both feminist discourse and gay activism have produced strong and influential voices in the debate on multiculturalism. At the very heart of the matter of multiculturalism is not just the question of political allegiance or skin color. More importantly, the question of which forms of living are "acceptable" or are considered "normal" in a society and which forms of living produce reactions of intolerance or, worse, lead to exclusion from social benefits or from society at large are the stakes of the contemporary debate. With regard to health care, the new questions that also need to be considered are age and "patient cultures." With an increasing number of people reaching very old age, their needs and their forms of life represent strong interest groups, which often pertain to completely different cultural ideals than younger generations do, including different ideas of what multiculturalism means. As for patient groups, children and adolescents, their parents, and adults suffering physiologically and socially from different kinds of ailments—and, in consequence, from social stigmatization—group together and create new life forms centered around the pathologies in question. These new forms of culture, often involving organization via the Internet, form a new "tapestry," including different patient groups, parental internet activism, and they form a new melting pot, a "digital crucible" referring to the need to adapt to "digital culture" (new generations of young Americans are often referred to as "digital natives").[19] However, these developments produce a new form of inequality known as the "digital divide." We often find that it follows old patterns and that Glazer's judgment that specifically for blacks, Puerto Ricans, and Latin Americans, the situation has not really improved but worsened.

Multicultural Diversity and Its Discontents

Language still remains a key problem in all these debates and developments. Other issues are, of course, expression of religious belief and cultural symbols and their use in public, ranging from ritual festivities, holidays, and certain garments. The Muslim hijab, the head scarf that women are supposed to wear according to some interpretations of the Qur'an and the hadith, has been the subject of debate in many nations, before and after September 11. The United States, with its history of religious tolerance, has, of course, taken a very liberal position in questions of freedom of expression of one's faith. However, after the terrorist attacks, many have questioned this practice, and, once again, the question of freedom and democracy is in the throes of a debate on culture, its forms, and its discontents.

The question of symbolic expression has been at the center of sociological and political theory for quite a while. Herbert Gans and Mary Waters are two prominent scholars who have researched the matter thoroughly and have argued that often the symbolic expression does not fully reflect the actual cultural meaning because of mere demographic developments of cultural intermarriages. It is suggested that people uphold symbols and rituals, but the reasons and meanings behind them are forgotten, and, therefore, the cultural heritage is not re-actualized. Respectively, newer generations do not have a cultural or ethnic heritage. They get to chose between options as they please.

What is a demographic fact about the future of the United States is that by 2050 the majority of Americans will have a Hispanic ethnic background, and the white population that seems to dominate the images of American mass-media culture will be a genuine minority. Multiculturalism will need to be redefined as a consequence of these facts. One of the most ambitious projects discussing the role of culture in society, integration, and social justice in our time of mass media and globalization, is Jeffrey Alexander's *The Civil Sphere*.[20] He argues in favor of a broad humanistic ideal of solidarity based on his conviction that there is a grain of free will in every human action and that social criticism can reveal the factors that hold us back from establishing solidarity on a global range. The global range is, in his view, a necessity even for national civil society, because the dangers to any civil society are largely globalized to begin with. Alexander's new melting pot or new American race is, therefore, not so much found in an Anglo-Saxon American core but at the heart of a global construct of humanity.

Alexander's book is an example of the kind of learned work that draws from the past to create a solution for contemporary problems. Alexander manages to discuss the discontents and the successes of America's history of immigration and integration in light of modern theories of democracy, governance, and mass communication. His aim is to show that a mode of integration of different cultural and interest groups is possible that does not negate the heritage and ideals of these groups. Instead, it leaves them intact and turns them into a force for productive communication. Second, he manages to create a solution that integrates the national and the global levels of problems in governance. For him, in other words, it is not the problems of immigration and integration that are decisive but our ways of overcoming them that can be turned into a force for more global democracy and solidarity.

Notes

1. Samuel Huntington, *The Clash of Civilizations? The Debate* (New York: Foreign Affairs, 1996).
2. Ralph Waldo Emerson, *Essential Writings* (New York: Random House, 2000).
3. Odo Marquard, *Farewell to Matters of Principle* (Oxford, UK: Oxford University Press, 1989), 38.
4. Rudolf Hermann Lotze, *Microcosm* (Edinburgh, Scotland: T.&T. Clark, 1885).
5. George W. Stocking Jr., *The Shaping of American Anthropology: A Franz Boas Reader* (New York: Basic Books, 1974), 1.
6. The idea that cultures are like texts is a powerful idea found, for example, in the work of anthropologist Clifford Geertz. It means that cultures and certain events or processes associated with a culture can be interpreted through linguistic clues that indicate symbolism. Symbols indicate public meaning. In a multiculturalist perspective, the differences in attitudes and knowledge that arise from different symbolic systems are accepted, whereas the assimilation perspective would argue that these differences should be negated. In referring to culture as text, multiculturalists would argue that the interpretation of a cultural text may indeed differ, whereas proponents of assimilation would argue that people need to agree on a common interpretation. See Clifford Geertz, *The Interpretation of Culture* (New York: Basic Books, 1977).
7. George Santayana, *Character and Opinion in the United States* (New York: Charles Scribner's Sons, 1921), 211.
8. In a similar fashion, Kant argued that we have to adhere to moral principles, not because that kind of adherence will make us happy, but only by acting morally will we attain a disposition toward being able to achieve happiness. Georg Simmel argued in a similar fashion with regard to the use of money. Money is not valuable in itself; it is only valuable in use, because we are "devoted" to the

idea that it has value and can function as a medium for the exchange of goods and services.

9. Israel Zangwill, *The Melting Pot—A Drama in Four Acts* (New York: Macmillan, 1914).

10. Tim Prchal, "Reimagining the Melting Pot and the Golden Door," *Melus* 32 (2007): 29.

11. Charles W. Chesnutt, "The Future American," *Boston Evening Transcript* (August 18, 1900).

12. Horace M. Kallen, "Democracy versus the Melting Pot," *The Nation* (February 25, 1915).

13. Randall Bourne, "Transnational America," *Atlantic Monthly* 118 (July 1916): 86–97.

14. Ibid., 86.

15. Charles William Penrose, "Letter from 'Junius,'" *Deseret Weekly: Pioneer Publication of the Rocky Mountain Region* 39 (July 6, 1889): 53.

16. Nathan Glazer and Daniel Moynihan, *Beyond the Melting Pot: The Negroes, Puerto Ricans, Jews, Italians, and Irish of New York City*, 2nd ed. (Cambridge, MA: MIT Press, 1970).

17. Nathan Glazer, *We Are All Multiculturalists Now* (Cambridge, MA: Harvard University Press, 1997).

18. See Dinesh D'Souza, *The Enemy at Home* (New York: Doubleday, 2007) and John Fonte's testimony, "It Is Time for Americanization," before the House Judiciary Committee Immigration Subcommittee (May 16, 2007), http://www.hudson.org/files/publications/Fonte_CongressionalTestimonyMay_07.pdf

19. John Palfrey and Urs Gasser, *Born Digital* (New York: Basic Books, 2010).

20. Jeffrey Alexander, *The Civil Sphere* (Oxford, UK: Oxford University Press, 2006).

Kerby Miller and the Study of the Irish Immigrant in America

Bryan McGovern

Kerby Miller, a renowned historian, has written numerous books and articles on Irish and Irish American history and has served as historical consultant for numerous documentaries. He is best known for his seminal work, *Emigrants and Exiles: Ireland and the Irish Exodus to North America* (1985), which was later used as the basis for the documentary, *Out of Ireland: The Story of Irish Emigration to America*. In *Emigrants and Exiles*, Miller introduced the exile motif to explain how the Irish Americans implemented traditional cultural values from their home country in their adjustment to American society.[1] Despite some criticism, it remains the most important work in the field to this day.

Miller was born in Phoenix, Arizona, in 1944, and attended Pomona College in Claremont, California. Miller, currently Curator's Professor of History at the University of Missouri-Columbia, finished his doctoral work in 1976 at the University of California, Berkeley, where he studied with Kenneth Stampp, the eminent historian of African American slavery and the Civil War era. Miller, who is not of recent Irish descent, originally set out to compare and contrast race relations in the American South with Latin America in his dissertation, but, on the recommendation of Stampp, he decided to examine Irish American racism and the New York draft riot of 1863. After examining numerous immigrant letters, he noticed a theme of exile and alienation and decided to focus his dissertation on how the Irish viewed their emigration and how that was reflected in their adaptation to their new lives in the United States. The dissertation would become the framework for *Emigrants and Exiles*.[2]

Emigrants and Exiles remains Miller's most prominent work. The book won numerous prestigious awards, including the Merle Curti Award presented by the Organization of American Historians as the best book in U.S. social history, the Theodore Saloutos Award for the best book in immigration and ethnic history, and it was a finalist for the Pulitzer Prize in History. Miller's main contribution to the historiography was his reliance on immigrant letters. Amassing one of the largest collections of Irish immigrant letters in the world, Miller was one of the

Kerby Miller, a renowned historian, has written numerous books and articles on Irish and Irish American history, and is the Curator's Professor at the University of Missouri. (Kerby Miller)

first historians to focus on how emigrants perceived their flight from Ireland. Miller emphasized the transatlantic nature of immigration, examining how Irish culture influenced expatriates in the United States. He discovered that Irish immigrants perceived themselves as exiles forced out of Ireland by malfeasant British rule and a corrupt landlord system. Irish emigrants, he argued, left because they felt they had been forced out of their homeland. They took with them their cultural mores, such as collectivism, Catholicism, and fatalism, which often meant they faced great difficulty in acculturating into American society, which emphasized individualism and capitalism.

Much of the criticism on *Emigrants and Exiles* stemmed from its lack of historiographical convention. It was neither nationalist nor revisionist in scope, meaning that he did not interpret Irish history from the Catholic nationalist nor the Protestant Unionist perspective. Miller, like many non-Irish scholars working in the field, was seen as an outsider, incapable of understanding the intricacies of Irish cultural, societal, and historical debates. Perhaps the most profound critique offered focused on Miller's grounding the work in Antonio Gramsci's notion of cultural hegemony and Marx's views on class. The villains in Miller's story are the capitalists and imperialists, while the Catholic poor represented a traditional people struggling in a modern world, especially after arriving in the United States. Miller emphasized class conflict as paramount to the story of the Irish and utilized Gramsci's writings to maintain that middle-class values of individualism and capitalism permeated Anglo-Irish and American society, marginalizing the more communal Gaelic Catholic Irish, whose values seemed antiquated in a modern world. This led some centrist and conservative historians to criticize Miller for ignoring the material success of the Irish throughout the world. Donald Akenson, for example, argued that Irish Protestants and Catholics experienced similar and relatively prosperous assimilation to the new world. Akenson, who focuses on the Irish in Canada, asserted that Miller's hypothesis focuses only on those immigrants who ended up in urban centers and ignores the immigrants who became rural bourgeoisie, which, according to Akenson, made up the predominant group of Irish expatriates. Akenson focused on the economic successes of the Irish in other parts of the world and criticized Miller's emphasis on Irish Catholic culture.[3]

Miller has also been at the forefront of critiquing the "two traditions" in Irish history. According to the two-traditions thesis, espoused either implicitly or explicitly by many historians, Ireland's narrative has been the story of two groups—Protestants and Catholics—and rarely do these histories overlap or intertwine. From the loyalist or Protestant perspective, Anglican and Presbyterian socioeconomic status and political successes have stemmed from their Weberian value system (what Weber called the Protestant work ethic) that spurred their capitalistic and imperialistic triumphs. Protestant Irish have often assumed that the Act of Union (1800), which made Ireland part of the United Kingdom, has provided them with opportunities unavailable in an independent Ireland. The partition of Northern Ireland in 1922 from a semi-independent Irish Free State (later the Republic of Ireland) has protected them from the vagaries of the majority Catholic population. They viewed Catholics historically as lazy, spiritually weak, beholden to the Pope, and unable to cope in a modern Anglo society. Catholics, often identified as nationalists, however, have perceived Protestants as greedy, imperialistic, and morally corrupt. Catholics have assigned Protestant imperialist intruders as thieves of their land. While Protestants have interpreted the Great Famine (1845–1849), which they argued affected only Catholics, as providential or self-inflicted due to laziness, papal fidelity, and antiquated values, Catholics blamed the Great Hunger on Protestant landowners and British malfeasance. The two-traditions thesis played itself out in other related historical issues. Modern immigration has been represented as a Catholic phenomenon, and nationalist movements are often portrayed as sectarian, violent, and inherently irrational. Miller has attempted to deviate from the two traditions by demonstrating that neither Catholics nor Protestants were monolithic. In Irish history, there are numerous examples of Catholics who have remained loyal to the British crown, while many Protestants have been at the forefront of republican movements. There have also existed divisions within each group, and both groups have experienced their share of pains and successes, including those that accompanied immigration.[4]

As Miller and other scholars have demonstrated, immigration has become the enduring historical legacy of Ireland. In 1995, Irish president Mary Robinson, at her inauguration, claimed to symbolically represent "the 70 million people world-wide who can claim Irish descent."[5] The Irish ended up in the 19th-century penal colonies of Australia, the ports of South America, England, and North America, where, from the 17th century to the 1920s, more than 7 million expatriates migrated.[6] The Irish, mostly Presbyterians, or what later became known as the "Scotch Irish," began coming to America during the colonial period. The earliest Protestant arrivals were typically religious dissenters such as the Quakers, who began arriving in the 1680s, but the largest group was the Presbyterians. This group was typically descended from Scots settlers to the north of Ireland during the Plantation of Ulster in the early 17th century. After a few generations in Ireland, they emigrated to the

United States, where they sought out economic opportunity and a chance to escape the harsh penal laws that precluded them from reaching the highest rungs of the socioeconomic ladder. These penal laws mostly affected Catholics, but some of them were also sometimes applied to Presbyterians (but not Anglicans). By the time of the founding of the United States, many Presbyterians sought political, economic, and religious freedom, including a number of political dissidents who fled Ireland after a failed rebellion by the United Irishmen in 1798. The Ulster Presbyterians typically migrated to the Appalachians from Pennsylvania down to Georgia. The historian David Doyle maintains that, in 1790, roughly one-fifth of the white South was of Irish stock. In Georgia and South Carolina, the Irish made up over one-fourth of the white population, while in Kentucky and Tennessee, it was around one-third. Doyle estimates that two-thirds of these Irish expatriates were what later would be called the Scotch Irish or Scots Irish. The other third was either Anglican or Catholic, many of whom converted to Presbyterianism either before or soon after they emigrated to the United States. Some have asserted that the Scots Irish have maintained a particular culture that defines the southern parts of the United States or, at the very least, Appalachian America. While this is highly debatable, the fact remains that the Scots Irish impact on the United States has been large.[7]

It was from the Scots-Irish community and their descendants that the Irish made their earliest, and perhaps greatest, impact on American society and politics. Andrew Jackson, Woodrow Wilson, and Ronald Reagan are a few of the presidents who come from Scots Irish stock. Andrew Jackson was hardly typical of descendents of the Scots-Irish, but his story certainly reflects much of what we know about this group. His parents emigrated in 1865 from Carrickfergus in County Antrim in what is now Northern Ireland. Jackson was born in 1867 in Waxhaws, South Carolina, where he received limited schooling. His father died shortly after his birth, his brother died after contracting smallpox as a British prisoner during the American Revolution, and his mother also passed due to disease during the Revolution. Jackson, orphaned as a teen, gambled, drank, and caroused. After some maturation and some apprenticeship, he became a country lawyer in the western region of North Carolina (currently Tennessee) and eventually made his way toward Nashville. There, he became a judge, a slave owner, a military hero (against the British and various native groups), a politician, and then President of the United States. Jackson represented the stereotypical Scots Irishman on the American frontier: independent, fierce, violent, self-sufficient, racist, and socioeconomically mobile. Portions of this stereotype are perhaps unfair and certainly exaggerated, but the notion that there existed and exists a Scots-Irish identity in the United States continues to remain one of the more fascinating historiographical questions regarding this group.[8]

It has been Irish Catholic immigration, however, that historians have mostly emphasized. In fact, most historians of Ireland, Irish America, and immigration have often equated Irish immigration with Catholic immigration. While Irish Catholics have been emigrating to the United States since the 17th century, it was not until the end of the Napoleonic Wars that larger numbers of Irish Catholics came to the United States. The earliest Catholics were often involuntarily transported for forced labor in the Caribbean and Chesapeake by Oliver Cromwell's forces that had devastated the Irish countryside during the 17th century. A product of the violent sectarianism that has strained Irish society since the Protestant Reformation in the early 16th century, these Catholic servants typically acclimated to the American South after the expiration of their indentured servitude. The Catholic Church, which was typically outlawed throughout the colonies, remained a nonentity throughout early America, especially in the South, which led to many Catholics converting to a Protestant faith.[9] The end of the Napoleonic Wars in Europe in the early 19th century, however, would result in greater emigration from Catholic Ireland. The Irish had experienced relative economic prosperity while supplying the British army and parts of the continent with grain as Napoleon attempted to conquer Europe. After the war, a depression ensued, and many Irish began to migrate to North America. By the 1830s, most of the Irish immigrants coming to the United States were Catholic.

Catholic emigration to the United States increased dramatically during and immediately after the Great Famine (1845–1949). Between 1847 and 1851, about 1.8 million Irish arrived in the United States, the vast majority of them Catholics. Blight destroyed much of the potato crop, on which the peasant farmers relied heavily for nutrition. The average Irish man ate nearly 14 pounds of potatoes per day, and the loss of the crop resulted in mass starvation and disease. More than 1 million Irish men, women, and children perished. The Famine Irish who arrived were poorer, less skilled, and many spoke Irish as their primary if not sole language. Fifty thousand people emigrated with assistance from the local government, church, or landlords. Others benefited from remuneration sent by relatives who had already lived in Ireland but emigrated to America. Thousands died on the way over, sailing on rickety, unsafe "coffin ships," sometimes surrounded by other passengers with deadly, communicable diseases like typhoid. While previous groups of Irish immigrants came to the United States looking for economic opportunity, the Famine Irish simply wanted to survive. One Sligo woman pleaded with her father in Canada to "[P]ity our hard case. . . . For God's sake take us out of poverty, and don't let us die with the hunger." Those who did make it to the United States faced a nativist response that led to a vociferous protest against the entry of so many sickly, Catholic peasants. The media portrayed them as subhuman simians, and the American Party (Know-Nothings) was created to fight the onslaught of foreigners. Protestant Irish Americans began to refer to themselves as Scots Irish to distinguish themselves from the new arrivals. It was clear early on that the famine Irish were not welcome in their new homeland.[10]

Irish Catholics typically entered the United States on or near the near bottom rung of the socioeconomic ladder. Although typically arriving from rural areas of Ireland, they mostly migrated to urban areas such as New York, Boston, Chicago, and San Francisco. Twelve percent of the United States' Irish population lived in New York City, and 26 percent of that city's population had been born in Ireland.[11] David Doyle maintains that, in 1870, almost 75 percent of all Irish immigrants resided in urban areas or industrial and mining towns. In Boston, they were ostracized by the blue-blooded Brahmins. The Irish in Philadelphia, despite Dennis Clark's contention that they adapted relatively easily and took advantage of opportunities in the United States, faced great hostility, as evident by the anti-Irish riots of the mid-1840s. The Irish tended to fare better the farther west they traveled, where the Protestant establishment was less entrenched and there were more economic opportunities as well as a greater chance for social mobility. In St. Louis, for example, the Catholic infrastructure allowed expatriates to adjust to society with limited native hostility present. In Butte, Montana, the Irish-owned copper mines led to stability and relative prosperity for Irish workers during the late 19th century. San Francisco was in great transition due to the population influx from the Gold Rush in the late 1840s, so when the Irish arrived, the lack of a stable community meant that they faced less enmity than in eastern cities, which were well established. In San Francisco, which by 1870 was the 10th largest city in the United States, the foreign-born population almost equaled the native-born population, thus enabling foreigners such as the Irish to acculturate with relative ease.[12]

The Irish brought with them their disdain for Britain, and nationalist organizations were established throughout the United States. The refugees of the United Irish rebellion of 1798 had set up clubs and fraternal societies throughout the United States, including in the South, that advocated the liberation of Ireland from its imperial oppressor. After the failed Young Ireland rebellion of 1848, a number of political expatriates joined the mass of Famine immigrants, many of whom blamed the London government for the death and destruction caused by the Famine. In many ways, Irish American nationalism was more radical and more prone to advocate violent rebellion because its adherents had been displaced by the Famine, on which they blamed British imperialism and malfeasance for their predicament. Young Irelander John Mitchel espoused in the "genocide thesis" that the British utilized the potato blight to eradicate the Irish from their land to allow landlords the ability to transfer their holdings from unprofitable tenant farms to lucrative sheep and cattle grazing. Mitchel and Thomas Francis Meagher were at the forefront of early Irish American nationalist organizations such as the Irish Civil and Military Republican Union and the Irish Military and Civil Association. Both ventures never really gained immense popularity, but they did set the stage for a later organization—the Irish Republican Brotherhood (Fenians), which became the standard bearer for all future nationalist organizations in the United States and Ireland. In the United States, Fenianism attracted immigrants from the lower rungs of the socioeconomic ladder. Whereas the United Irishmen and Young Ireland had mostly attracted middle-class, educated Irish from different religious perspectives, the Fenians were mostly Catholic, although somewhat anticlerical. Organized in 1858, Fenianism later attracted a number of veterans from the American Civil War and achieved greater popularity after the war. Three failed invasions of Canada and another failed rebellion back home in Ireland in 1867, as well as fracturing within the organization, doomed the Brotherhood, but it also set a precedent that Irish independence through violent rebellion would become the hallmark of later nationalist movements.

Historians have debated the significance and foundation of Irish nationalist organizations in the United States. Thomas Brown argued in the late 1960s that nationalist movements helped Irish immigrants to adjust to American society. The fight for an independent Irish republic allowed the Irish to demonstrate they were interested in participating legitimately in a republican society, despite nativist assertions that, as Catholics, the Irish were beholden to the Pope and not their new nation. For Brown, Irish American nationalism was a product of the American experience, a reaction to the hostility and loneliness they faced in their new country, and not a result of their previous experiences in Ireland. In the 1980s, Eric Foner and David Montgomery asserted that Irish American nationalism was really working-class radicalism, because Irish workers associated and identified Irish land issues with American class issues, allowing the Irish to assimilate into working-class society. Kerby Miller disagreed with Brown that Irish American nationalism was strictly an American phenomenon and, similar to his expositions on immigration, argued that nationalism had its roots in issues that affected the Irish at home. More recently, historians have emphasized the transatlantic nature of nationalism, evinced by the close, if sometimes contentious, relationship between American Fenians and the Irish Republican Brotherhood, as well as the connection between Clan na' Gael (and later the Irish Northern Aid Committee [NORAID]) and the Irish Republican Army. The importance of transatlantic ties cannot be overestimated. While Irish American nationalism has been a product of its environment, the desire to see a free and united Ireland certainly remained the impetus of such groups. Clearly, the American experience, including the contentious nativist environment, had an impact on Irish Americans. However, the links to the home country and the desire to truly see Ireland independent from British shackles played a large role as well.[13]

As Miller has demonstrated, Irish immigrants, while they might have appreciated the opportunities the United States offered, often yearned for the home of their childhood and remained connected to Ireland in real and abstract ways. John Reilly, an immigrant from County Cavan in the midlands of Ireland, wrote to his father, Edward, back home in Ireland, "the stern reality comes before me of my absence, away, away from all I love dear and checks my reverie—waking me up to an aching heart and moistened eye . . . my heart still lingers in dear native Erin."[14]

Irish immigrants also tended to shun those who became too American. William Downes, an Irish immigrant, wrote from Brooklyn disavowing those expatriates who had attempted to "shake off everything Irish in their appearance." Writing to James Shaughnessey in 1887, Downes asserted, "Ireland does not suffer in the least by such people disowning it, as they are either grossly ignorant, or have done something of which, Ireland would have cause to hang her head for giving birth to such cowards and traitors."[15] Clearly for Downes, a true Irishman remained faithful and loyal to Ireland despite the physical distance.

Another Irish American debate between historians revolves around whether the Irish were active contributors or innocent victims of racial prejudices in the United States. The Irish clearly faced hostility in the United States from a society that tended to distrust newcomers, especially those of the Catholic faith. Cartoonists such as Thomas Nast portrayed the Irish as apelike creatures unprepared to assimilate into American society. However, there is a darker side, where the Irish became even more oppressive to minorities than nativists were to them. Historians such as Noel Ignatiev and David Roediger assert that the Irish chose "whiteness" to distinguish themselves from African Americans and elevate their position in society. In other words, they accepted and embraced the racial antipathy toward blacks in order to expedite their assimilation. The Draft Riots of 1863, in which Irishmen simultaneously protested against Civil War conscription and Lincoln's Emancipation Proclamation with violence against blacks and prominent Republicans in New York City, demonstrated that Irish Americans had embraced the racial proclivities of Americans, especially the Democratic Party. However, Ignatiev and Roediger fail to take into account that the actions of the Irish were influenced more by the structures of the United States as they were the racial views they transported with them across the Atlantic. As Kevin Kenney has maintained, Irish Catholics arrived to a United States in which the racial hierarchy already existed. Even if they had attempted, the Irish would have been unable to change that. Still, they did come from a country where racialism permeated the culture. The British, like many nativists in the United States, relegated the Irish as racial inferiors, closer to ape than man. The cultural and racial stigmas of laziness, dirtiness, and immorality were all heaped upon Irish Catholics as an explanation for their poverty. The British press and politicians even went so far to blame the Irish for the Great Famine of the 1840s, either claiming that their barbarian ways led to the destitution or arguing that God was punishing them for their depraved ways. Like African Americans, Irish Catholics were dehumanized in both their home and new nations. Even Irish nationalists such as Thomas Davis and John Mitchel (who supported Southern slavery and the Confederacy in America) emphasized the link between culture and race, asserting that the Irish race was defined by embracing Gaelic culture. So the Irish were familiar with the importance of race and culture and how those categories fit into socioeconomic status. However, to claim that they accepted whiteness and racist ideology to further their own ambitions is neither fair nor accurate. The Irish accepted and acculturated American notions of race into their own lives, and many accepted racism against blacks as a normal aspect of life in the United States. Still, it was the influence of 19th-century American values and the tie to a Democratic Party that opposed abolitionism and promoted the superiority of whites that had led most Irish men and women to accept racism against blacks as socially acceptable.[16]

The symbiotic relationship between the Irish and the Democratic Party remained a significant political and cultural factor in the expatriate community until the middle of the 20th century. During the early republic, Irish Protestants tended to side with the Jeffersonian Democratic-Republicans, the party they believed protected the interests of small farmers and good republicans. When Andrew Jackson became president, he was soon opposed by a group who referred to themselves as Whigs, and Jackson's party became known as the Democrats, which some saw as the ideological successors to the Jeffersonian values that opposed New England manufacturing, Protestant evangelical morals, and abolitionism. The Irish typically sided with the Democrats, not as much for ideological reasons as for cultural similarities. Whereas Whigs and Republicans absorbed the evangelical and abolitionist movements in the United States, which tended to be anti-Irish and anti-Catholic, Democrats were more amenable to Irish Catholic culture, including a general opposition to temperance and the emancipation of slaves. Also, the Irish faced hostility from the Whigs/Republicans over the control of public schools, particularly the use of the Protestant King James Bible, which Irish Catholics opposed. The bloody sectarian riots in Philadelphia resulted from nativist Protestants attempting to thwart Irish Catholic social and cultural influence in the city and schools. Later riots in Louisville in 1855 occurred when the Irish and German Catholics tried to assert their right to vote for the Democratic candidate. Nativists, who had begun the Know-Nothing (American) Party, attempted to wrest complete control of their cities and hoped to marginalize Irish Catholics to maintain their own cultural hegemony. The Irish looked to the Democratic Party as a way to combat this.

Within the Democratic Party, the Irish took advantage of their large numbers in the United States and utilized their experience with grassroots political movements back in Ireland to seize power, especially in urban centers. Daniel O'Connell, considered by some to be the father of modern democracy, built up a massive movement in Ireland during the early 19th century to advocate first for Catholic emancipation and then for repeal of the Act of Union. By charging only one penny to join his political organizations, common Irish peasants became politicized and familiar with the importance of mass political movements. In New York, Boss Tweed, of Scots Irish descent, built up the Tammany machine and allowed Irish Americans such as George Washington Plunkett to rise to political power through political corruption and manipulation of the electoral system. On one hand, the political machines utilized their power to amass large fortunes and maintain political hegemony. On the other hand, these machines served a social welfare purpose for newly arrived immigrants and indigent natives. When the Irish reached shore, it was the representatives of political machines that often supplied access to employment, housing, and even coal during the winter months. Of course, in response, the immigrants were expected to demonstrate loyalty to the party—typically the Democrats but in some cities the Republicans—that had assisted them. The Democratic Party especially was able to garner the loyalty and votes of Irish immigrants, and Irish politicians were able to offer civil service jobs to some of those very immigrants.

The Irish also were at the forefront of the labor movement. The Irish controlled the Knights of Labor, as Leon Fink has demonstrated. Terrence Vincent Powderly, the eventual head of the Knights of Labor, was a son of Irish immigrants and active in the nationalist movement the Clan na' Gael. More importantly, the connection between Irish nationalists, particularly those who supported land reform in Ireland, was strong. Patrick Ford, Michael Davitt, and Powderly, all of whom were associated with the Irish National Land League, had implemented tactics used by the Land League in Ireland in labor movements like the Knights of Labor. Mother Jones, born to a peasant family in Cork, became a well-known union agitator and organizer after she lost her iron-worker husband and four children to yellow fever and experienced the loss of her dressmaking business during the Great Fire in Chicago. She later joined the United Mine Workers, where she led strikes to protest against the working conditions in various mines. Patrick Ford's newspaper, the *Irish World and Industrial Liberator*, tied together the strands of Irish American nationalism and radical labor politics and became the most popular Irish weekly in the United States during the 1870s and 1880s. We also see the importance in Irish American communities of labor unions, nationalist organizations, and fraternal societies in David Emmons, *The Butte Irish: Class and Ethnicity in an American Mining Town, 1875–1925*. Marcus Daly, who founded and headed the Anaconda Copper Mine in Butte, was born in Ballyjamesduff in County Cavan, Ireland. Throughout the late 19th century, Daly was inclined to hire his fellow expatriates, many of whom had experience working in the copper mines of Cork and Waterford. By 1900, more than one-quarter of Butte had been born in Ireland, making it the most Irish town in the United States.[17]

Besides the association with the Democratic Party, another important component of Irish American life was the Catholic Church. The Church remained relatively weak throughout the 18th and early 19th centuries, and it was the Irish who directed and grew the Church into what would soon become the largest religious denomination in the country. The Catholic Church in Ireland had been the dominant institution in guiding the everyday life of ordinary Irish Catholics. Despite this, many Irish people were not churchgoing, and their rituals were often defined as much by traditional Gaelic culture as it was by the Papacy in Rome. The "devotional revolution," which took place in the middle of the 19th century in Ireland, had led to greater attachment of the people to the Church. This devotional revolution also affected the Irish in the United States, and the nativist hostility they faced led them to become more insular and isolated but also more devoted to the Church for protection and cultural identification. In response, the Irish Catholic Church built churches, schools, and hospitals to inculcate and protect their community. In New York City, Archbishop Hughes was at the forefront of establishing Irish Catholic institutions. He created hospitals, schools, and fraternal associations that protected and insulated Irish Catholics from the larger community.[18]

The American Civil War, as much as any event, transformed the Irish in American society. More than 200,000 Irish fought for the Union, and roughly 30,000 took up arms for the Confederacy. Thousands died fighting in all-Irish regiments like the 69th New York, led by Waterford native General Thomas Francis Meagher, which were massacred at Fredericksburg and Antietam. Fighting and dying for their new countries, the Irish demonstrated their loyalty as well as their desire to behave as good republican citizens. Before the Civil War, many Americans believed that the Irish were more loyal to their homeland or the Pope and that their Catholicism precluded them from becoming good republican Americans. The Irish became more assertive as well and attempted to demonstrate their republican bona fides through nationalist efforts to free Ireland from British imperial shackles. The Fenians, also known as the Irish Republican Brotherhood, founded in 1858, became particularly popular with Civil War veterans, especially in the North. While the Fenians seemed intent on freeing Ireland, and many Irish Americans took part in an 1867 rebellion back in Ireland as well as three separate invasions of British Canada, members of the organization seemed as interested as using their involvement as a way to climb the socioeconomic ladder in the United States. Fenianism gave the Irish a chance to demonstrate their republican attributes, and the organization allowed working-class Irish the chance for social mobility through social networking. The transformation from indigent, unwelcomed immigrants to respectable middle-class citizens did not happen immediately, but by 1900, the Irish in the United States had equaled the status of native-born Americans in every occupation but agriculture. The Irish, it appeared, had assimilated. Perhaps Richard O'Gorman, the nationalist Young Irelander who became a successful attorney and politician in New York, was perhaps prescient when he asserted that his involvement in upper-class American society was to "serve Ireland" by convincing Americans through gentle guidance that Ireland needed the assistance of the United States.[19]

Irish American immigration experienced a small spike again in the early 1880s as a land war broke out in Ireland in 1879. Immigration began to taper somewhat during the late 19th and early 20th centuries as more Irish took ownership of the land. Also, Irish immigrants were more likely to migrate to other destinations, particularly England, and "new" immigrants such as Eastern Europeans, and later Asians and Hispanics, started to arrive in the United States, replacing the Irish in the lower-paying jobs. The Irish continued to come to the United States, but in much smaller numbers. As the United States codified immigration laws to restrict immigration in the 20th century, more and more illegal Irish entered urban settings such as Boston and New York, where they could find a job tending bar in the local saloon or working construction, and they fit into their local environs without suspicion. The Irish today make up the third largest group of illegal immigrants in the United States, and many Irish immigrants, legal and illegal, went back to Ireland during the economic boom known as the Celtic Tiger in the 1990s. With much of the world in recession in 2010, Ireland is once again seeing some of its best and brightest leave for economic opportunity but continues to welcome many other Irish emigrants home from sojourns in other nations.[20]

During the 1970s and 1980s, Irish Americans, including second- and third-generation immigrants, began to trumpet their Irish identity. Irish Americans began to discover their roots, travel to the old sod, and embrace all things Irish (or perhaps even faux Irish), and St. Patrick's Day has become popular with all ethnicities and races. It is once again acceptable, if not laudable, to be Irish, even for the descendents of those who once eschewed such a label. As Kerby Miller has demonstrated, Irish identity was much more fluid during 18th- and early 19th-century America, including in the antebellum South, where Protestant and Catholic Irish often intermarried and most Catholics (and Anglo-Irish) became Presbyterian. With the mass exodus of the Famine Irish to the United States, some of those formerly Catholic families even embraced a Scotch-Irish identity to disassociate themselves from their Catholic countrymen and -women. *Gone with the Wind* and the O'Hara family reflect in literature the Southern family with a Gaelic surname that embraced the Protestant culture of the South. Actual Protestant families such as the Hills of Abbeville, South Carolina, also demonstrate a trend in Irish immigration of Ulster Protestants who once came to the United States with a strong sense of Irish identity. William Hill, who arrived in the United States in the early 19th century from County Antrim in Ulster, demonstrated a devotion to his homeland. He named his son after an Irish nationalist and continued in the United States to condemn British imperialism in Ireland. He was also, however, mortified by the arrival of indigent Famine Irish and made a clear point to distinguish himself from the "real Irish, of papist stock." His more immediate descendents would continue to distance themselves from their Irish roots, as demonstrated by his granddaughter's school essay that asserted her family was "Scotch Irish" rather than Irish. However, in the 1990 census, many of Hill's descendents identified themselves as strictly Irish. By the end of the 20th century, families such as the O'Haras and the Hills that once claimed a Scots-Irish identity began to drop the Scots part and embrace their Irish heritage.[21]

The 400-year history of Irish immigration to the United States has been a tumultuous, multifaceted, and interesting narrative, and more research is needed to explain fully the story of the immigrant Irish. No historian has done a better job of reflecting the complexities of this narrative than Kerby Miller. The story of Irish immigration is no longer strictly Catholic nor parochial. Thanks to historians like Miller, the study of Irish immigration to the United States has become transatlantic in scope while incorporating various religious groups. It tends no longer to be as hagiographic or sectarian. Unfortunately, the history of Ireland and the Irish in the United States has been trivialized at most institutions of higher learning. Despite the immense popularity of Irish culture, the vast number of Americans with Irish roots, and the significant contribution of the Irish to U.S. culture and society, jobs teaching Irish history are scarce. Universities rarely offer classes on Irish history and Irish immigration. We still have a great deal to learn about this history, and our interpretations are bound to continue to change over time. Many questions remain, and debates continue to rage over assimilation, acculturation, nationalism, religion, and identity, and historians will hopefully continue to delve into these subjects in scholarly fashion.

Notes

1. Kerby Miller, *Emigrants and Exiles: Ireland and the Irish Exodus to North America* (New York: Oxford University Press, 1985).
2. Marion Casey, "The Genealogy of Scholarship: An Oral History with Kerby Miller, David Doyle, and Bruce Bolling," *Radharc: The Chronicles of Glucksman Ireland House at New York University* 5–7 (2006): 312–316.
3. Donald Akenson, *The Irish in Ontario: A Study in Rural History*, 2nd ed. (Toronto: McGill-Queens University, 1999), 351–353.
4. Kerby Miller, "Ulster Presbyterians and the 'Two Traditions' in Ireland and America," in *Making the Irish American: History and Heritage of the Irish in the United States*, eds. J. J. Lee and Marion Casey (New York University: New York, 2006), 255–270.
5. Mary Robinson, "Imaginative Possessions," John Galway Foster Lecture, October 26, 1995 (unpublished).
6. Kerby Miller, *Ireland and Irish America: Culture, Class, and Transatlantic Migration* (Dublin: Field Day, 2003), 7.
7. James G. Leyburn, *The Scotch-Irish: A Social History* (Chapel Hill: University of North Carolina Press, 1962), x–xix; David Doyle, *Ireland, Irishmen and Revolutionary America, 1760–1820* (Dublin: Mercier, 1981), 51–76; James Webb, *Born Fighting: How the Scots-Irish Shaped America* (New York: Broadway, 2004).
8. H. W. Brands, *Andrew Jackson: His Life and Times* (New York: Anchor, 2005).
9. Randall Miller, "A Church in Cultural Captivity: Some Speculations on Catholic Identity in the Old South," in *Catholics in the Old South*, eds. Randall Miller and Jon Wakelyn (Macon, GA: Mercer University, 1983).
10. Miller, *Ireland and Irish America*, 69.

11. Hasia Diner, "Overview: 'The Most Irish City in the Union:' The Era of the Great Migration, 1844–1877," in *The New York Irish*, eds. Ronald Bayor and Timothy Meagher (Baltimore: Johns Hopkins University Press, 1996), 93.

12. Oscar Handlin, *Boston's Immigrants: A Study in Acculturation, 1790–1865*, rev. ed. (Cambridge, MA: Harvard University Press, 1991); David Emmons, *The Butte Irish: Class and Ethnicity in an American Mining Town, 1875–1925* (Champaign: University of Illinois Press, 1989); David Doyle, "The Irish and American Labor, 1880–1920," *Saothar: The Journal of the Irish Labour History Society* 1 (1975), 42–53; Dennis Clark, *The Irish in Philadelphia, Ten Generations of Urban Experience* (Philadelphia: Temple University Press, 1973); R.A. Burchell, *The San Francisco Irish, 1848–1880* (Berkeley: University of California Press, 1980).

13. Thomas N. Brown, *Irish-American Nationalism, 1870–1890* (Philadelphia: Lippincott, 1966); David Montgomery, *Beyond Equality: Labor and the Radical Republicans, 1862–1872* (New York: Knopf, 1967); Eric Foner, "Radicalism in the Gilded Age: The Land League and Irish America," *Marxist Perspective* 1 (1978), 7–55; Miller, *Emigrants and Exiles*, 544–546.

14. John Reilly to Edward Reilly, February 1841, Arnold Schrier Collection.

15. William Downes to James Shaughnessey, October 13, 1887, Kerby Miller Collection.

16. Kevin Kenny, *The American Irish* (New York: Longman, 2000), 67–71; Bryan McGovern, *John Mitchel: Irish Nationalist and Southern Secessionist* (Knoxville: University of Tennessee Press, 2009), 138–139. For arguments that the Irish chose "whiteness," see Noel Ignatiev, *How the Irish Became White* (New York: Routledge, 1995) and David Roediger, *The Wages of Whiteness: Race and the Making of the American Working Class* (New York: Verso, 1991).

17. Leon Fink, *Working Man's Democracy: Knights of Labor and American Politics* (Urbana: University of Illinois Press, 1983); Emmons, *The Butte Irish*, 13, 32; Miller, *Ireland and Irish America*, 271–280.

18. Emmett Larkin, *The Historical Dimensions of Irish Catholicism* (Washington, DC: Catholic University of America Press, 1984); Richard Shaw, *Dagger John: The Unique Life and Times of Archbishop John Hughes of New York* (New York: Paulist Press, 1977).

19. Miller, *Ireland and Irish America*, 290.

20. "Going Nowhere: Following the Emigration Trail," *Irish Times* (March 6, 2010).

21. Miller, " 'Scotch-Irish', 'Black Irish' and 'Real Irish': Emigrants and Identities in the Old South," in *The Irish Diaspora*, ed. Andy Bielenberg (New York: Longman, 2000), 143, 150–153.

9/11 Commission

Philip A. Kretsedemas

Three years after the 9/11 terrorist attacks, the Bush administration organized the 9/11 Commission in response to pressures from directly affected families. The commission members were a bipartisan selection of former and current public officials with extensive experience in matters of national security. The commission was charged with providing a thorough analysis of the circumstances that allowed the 9/11 attacks to happen. The commission's final report was published in July 2004 and quickly became a national best-seller. But despite the fact that many Americans (including some of the directly affected families) approved of the report, its analysis and recommendations have drawn criticism from many quarters. Although the report has been hailed as a plainspoken, literary triumph, it has also been criticized for being more of a public relations ploy than a serious analysis of the attacks. Much of this criticism focused on the commission's proposal to centralize all U.S. intelligence operations and the Immigration and Naturalization Service under a single national director. Other critics have argued that the report contains false information and strategic omissions that make it impossible to discern the real, underlying causes of the 9/11 attacks.

The Situation before 9/11

It is sometimes observed that targets that appear invulnerable are actually much more vulnerable than they seem, precisely because of the overconfidence that their denizens have about their invulnerability. Because it is assumed that no attacker except the most foolhardy would dare launch an assault, those attackers who are foolhardy enough to do precisely this usually have the element of surprise on their side. It has been noted that there is some evidence that U.S. intelligence agencies had succumbed to this sort of overconfidence just prior to the 9/11 attacks. Richard Posner, a former judge for the U.S. Court of Appeals, observed that, in the early months of 2001, a Defense Department report confidently stated that: "We have, in fact, solved a terrorist problem in the last 25 years. We have solved it so success-

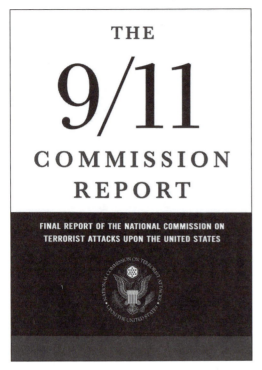

THE
9/11
COMMISSION
REPORT

FINAL REPORT OF THE NATIONAL COMMISSION ON TERRORIST ATTACKS UPON THE UNITED STATES

Cover of *The 9/11 Commission Report: Final Report of the National Commission on Terrorist Attacks upon the United States.* The report, issued on July 22, 2004, provides the findings and recommendations of a full scale investigation into the terrorist attacks on the World Trade Center and Pentagon on September 11, 2001. (National Commission on Terrorist Attacks)

fully that we have forgotten about it; and that is a threat. The problem was aircraft hijacking and bombing. We solved the problem. . . . The system is not perfect, but it is good enough. . . . We have pretty much nailed this thing."[1]

These sorts of statements do not merely highlight the dangers of overconfidence. They also draw attention to another problem raised by Posner—namely, the challenge that any large bureaucracy faces in its efforts to anticipate new threats. As other analysts have observed, it is in the nature of bureaucracies to adapt to what is known rather than to anticipate the unknown. Sociological theory and research has also shown that bureaucracies are not merely focused on adapting to the known but on creating their own insular, self-referential world of discourse that is used to the define the known. This desire to exert complete control over known reality is a positive adaptation insofar as it allows bureaucracies to increase the efficiency and regularity with which they process cases; the price, however, is increased detachment from their external environment. While a certain degree of insularity can be tolerated in institutions that process fairly mundane things (for example, driver's licenses and tax returns), it is not hard to see why this could be a fatal flaw for organizations that are charged with the task of responding to and mitigating emergency conditions (whether these are terrorists attacks, natural disasters, or severe economic downturns).

Even so, these observations do not tell the whole story about the institutional and popular culture that existed prior to the 9/11 attacks. Counterterrorism operations were actually expanded quite significantly under the 1992–2000 Clinton administration. The 1996 Antiterrorism and Effective Death Penalty Act, which was passed into law under the Clinton administration, also provided a legal framework that expanded the ability of federal agents to monitor and detain terrorist suspects. One of the most controversial aspects of this new legal framework was the power it gave federal investigators and prosecutors to try terrorist suspects on the basis of secret evidence that could never be disclosed to the public or even the defendant. The use of secret evidence was challenged by civil rights groups because of its radical departure from prior procedure and because of the danger it posed to innocent U.S. residents, native born or immigrant, who happened to fit a terrorist profile. These challenges were effective in curbing the U.S. government's use of secret evidence before 9/11. Even after 9/11, secret evidence was rarely used in terrorism-related prosecutions, though federal agents used other processes that were just as effective in expediting the detention and removal of terrorist suspects who were immigrants.

It also bears noting that—despite the 1993 World Trade Center bombings—public visibility around international terrorism and specifically Islamic fundamentalist terrorist organizations was very different prior to 9/11. This was not simply because most U.S. residents did not imagine that a terrorist attack was a serious possibility on U.S. soil. Just as important, most news coverage of terrorism was focused on bombings carried out by domestic actors (for example, the 1995 bombing of the Oklahoma federal building and the sporadic strikes of the so-called Unabomber, Ted Kaczynski, who was also apprehended in 1995). Another important factor was the controversy provoked by federal actions taken against domestic groups that were believed to have connections to terrorist outfits or were categorized as more vaguely defined security threats. Two prominent examples include the 1992 raid on a white separatist homestead in Ruby Ridge, Idaho, and the 1993 raid on the Branch Davidian compound in Waco, Texas. Both federal raids, which resulted in the killing of U.S. citizens, raised questions about the aggressiveness of federal enforcement actions.

Given this context, the popular image of the terrorist during the era of the Clinton administration was rather ambiguous. One of the most visible faces of terrorism of this era was Timothy McVeigh, the native-born U.S. citizen and former decorated army soldier who carried out the bombing of the Oklahoma City federal building. McVeigh later admitted that the bombing was retaliation for the federal raids on Ruby Ridge and the Branch Davidian compound. Even though the mainstream media denounced McVeigh's actions, they also conducted numerous interviews with McVeigh that gave his worldview a level of public exposure that was unusual for most terrorist suspects. Even among left-leaning critics there was a tendency to view McVeigh as a tragic figure whose rage was misdirected but not entirely unjustifiable. In this climate, it is not surprising that many Americans were not as likely to associate terrorism with Muslim extremists or with the same sense of imminent danger that has typified the post-9/11 era.

Proposals of the 9/11 Commission

The final report of the 9/11 Commission captured some (but not all) of the themes reviewed above. Its primary argument, however, was that the 9/11 attacks were a radical new development in terrorist strategy that caught the U.S. intelligence community off guard. As a consequence, the commission's narrative focused on the limitations of existing intelligence practices, observing that U.S. intelligence had accumulated some important clues but was unable to piece them together because of insufficient interagency cooperation or simply because of poor foresight about the significance of these clues.

In addition, the commission's analysis raised questions about the wisdom of the U.S. government's foreign-policy priorities and the problem of sending messages that work against its long-term interests (these claims were by buttressed by cautionary observations about the Bush administration's handling of the war on Iraq). The commission's report called for a more proactive counterterrorism strategy that would be more closely intertwined with U.S. foreign policy. The goal would be to increase the presence of U.S. intelligence in nations that are deemed to be breeding grounds for international terrorism and to use these operations not only to gather intelligence but to foster relations that would reduce local sympathies toward these organizations. Another of the commission's big-picture proposals was its call for a more integrated and more efficient intelligence system that would not only increase interagency cooperation but strengthen links between federal agencies and local organizations. This included removing all barriers to information sharing between intelligence agencies (in particular between the Federal Bureau of Investigation [FBI] and the Central Intelligence Agency [CIA]), reassigning more federal agents to work on counterterrorism operations, implementing more rigorous screening practices at local airports, and ensuring that all major buildings have effective evacuation plans.

All of these proposals set the stage for what became the commission's most contentious recommendation: the establishment of a new executive appointee, the director of national intelligence (DNI), who would have direct oversight over all aspects of national intelligence. The specifications for this position were not made clear in the commission's report. The details were fleshed out, however, in the Intelligence Reform Bill endorsed by the 9/11 Commission that was introduced to Congress just months after the report's publication in fall 2004. The two most controversial features of the bill were the scope of executive authority it granted to the DNI (which spanned the FBI, CIA, Department of Defense, several other intelligence agencies, the Immigration and Naturalization Service, and the Border Patrol) and the control it granted over the budget for all national intelligence agencies.

The Senate was quick to pass the bill under the terms originally endorsed by the 9/11 Commission. In contrast, Republican members of the House of Representatives were much more wary and sought to introduce alternate versions of the bill that would decrease the scope of the DNI's authority. They also tried to include other get-tough immigration enforcement provisions (such as imposing new bans on issuing driver's licenses to unauthorized immigrants) that were not part of the original proposal. The Senate rejected these get-tough proposals on the grounds that they were distractions from the main, intended goals of the bill and also because they were objectionable to civil liberties advocates. But again, the main point of contention concerned the scope of the DNI's authority.

News reports speculated that the members of Congress who were behind the resistance in the House were acting under influence of the Pentagon, which was trying to protect its turf. Statements by Secretary of Defense Donald Rumsfeld also seemed to indicate that the Department of Defense was less than enthused by the wisdom of creating an office of the DNI. This was a source of confusion for many of the bill's supporters, given that President Bush had gone on record numerous times urging Congress to pass the bill as originally drafted—despite the fact that he had initially opposed giving budgetary authority to the DNI and had even been initially resistant to the formation of the 9/11 Commission. As such, it appeared that key figures in the Bush administration were divided on their support for the bill. In the final phase of deliberations, questions were also raised about the unanimity of the 9/11 Commission's support for the bill when a former member of the 9/11 Commission issued a statement (which had not been intended for public consumption) in support of a compromise version of the bill that catered to the demands of House Republicans.

Despite all of this confusion and hand-wringing, Secretary Rumsfeld eventually gave his full endorsement for the Senate version of the bill, and President Bush signed the Intelligence Reform and Terrorism Prevention Act (IRTPA) into law in December 2004. In many respects, there is nothing unusual about the convoluted negotiation process that preceded the bill's enactment, but it bears noting that Congress and the executive office went through a similar set of debates just two years earlier in creating the Department of Homeland Security (DHS). Just like the debate over the DNI, the DHS debate was split between two factions: one that favored the creation of a new, centralized bureaucracy and another that questioned the effectiveness of adding a new layer of bureaucracy over formerly separate agencies. It is also telling that the Bush administration initially resisted the creation of the DHS, and its late conversion was explained, by some scholars, as being influenced by a strategic interest in expanding its executive authority for reasons that had little to do with counterterrorism.

Given this history, supporters of the 9/11 Commission's recommendations had some basis for questioning the integrity of the IRTPA. Some critics noted, for example, that the language of the law was fuzzy in important areas. Although it did grant budgetary authority and executive oversight of more than 15 intelligence agencies to the DNI, the language was vague enough to allow the Bush administration to define the scope of this authority in any variety of ways. Critics also noticed that the mission of the office of the DNI did not include any of the 9/11 Commission's proposals for a new approach in U.S. foreign policy toward the Middle East. On the other hand, it could be argued that the Bush administration's approach toward the DNI was informed by criticism it had suffered for the way it had handled the creation of the DHS. For example, instead of attempting to incorporate all U.S. intelligence agencies inside an entirely new bureaucracy, the IRTPA left the internal organizational structure of each of these agencies completely intact. At the same time, the executive and budgetary authority of the DNI cut through all of these agencies, allowing the DNI veto power on important decisions. In this regard, it could be argued that the IRTPA attempted to achieve a more perfect balance between the imperatives of bureaucratic centralization and organizational autonomy.

Criticism of the 9/11 Commission's Analysis and Recommendations

As already discussed, much of the criticism on the 9/11 Commission focused on its recommendation to install a director of national intelligence. Most of these critiques have been developed by Washington insiders and other individuals with a great deal of expertise on matters of national security, some being the directors of major intelligence agencies like the CIA and the National Security Administration. On one hand, it can be argued that some of these critics had a personal stake in preserving the organizational autonomy of their agencies. On the other hand, the experience of these critics added weight to their claims and gave them a certain advantage in exposing contradictions and tautologies in the commission's analysis. Judge Richard Posner argued that the commission made a serious mistake by integrating its analysis and recommendations into a single narrative. By focusing its analysis on intelligence failures, Posner observed, the commission was inevitably led to the conclusion that U.S. intelligence needed a major overhaul. As a result, the commission's recommendations were a foregone conclusion that had been determined by the very way it framed its analysis.

Douglas Jehl has observed that there is a fundamental contradiction in the commission's analysis and recommendations. The call for more bureaucracy does not seem to square with the argument, also presented by the commission, that the 9/11 attacks were a new type of terrorist strategy that could not possibly have been foreseen by the existing bureaucracy. According to Jehl, the 9/11 Commission never provided a convincing explanation of why its new bureaucratic solution was different from the old bureaucracy, especially since the commission's recommendations for increased centralization of intelligence operations merely reinforced an organizing principle that is typical of all bureaucracies. It is also possible that increased centralization could have the opposite effect—imposing a rigid chain of command and a standardized set of procedures that restrict the capacity of individual operations to respond to unexpected contingencies.[2]

Alongside these arguments, there has emerged a polemical body of criticism that is more conspiratorial in nature. In different ways, all of these critiques insist that the 9/11 Commission's report was really a cover-up that distracted attention from an even more sinister set of events. One charge is that the narrative of the 9/11 Commission deliberately obscured the role played by Saudi Arabian operatives (with government connections) in planning the attacks. Although the FBI had evidence that indicated this was a serious possibility, the 9/11 Commission avoided discussion of any of this evidence; it characterized the attacks as being organized independently by al-Qaeda members. The implication of these critiques is that the 9/11 Commission was concocting a status quo narrative that protected powerful Saudi allies of the United States.

Other critics have gone as far as arguing that U.S. government officials either planned the attacks or had advanced knowledge of the attacks and deliberately chose not to act. These arguments are similar to Pearl Harbor conspiracy theories that insist the U.S. government allowed the Japanese attack on Pearl Harbor to occur in order to tip the balance of public opinion in favor of entering World War II. In a similar fashion, some conspiracy theories suggest that the 9/11 attacks were orchestrated by Israeli operatives—perhaps working with allies in the U.S. government—who wanted to turn international opinion against the Arab world.

In his critical account, David Ray Griffin draws attention to statements by former New York mayor Rudy Guiliani, Bush White House officials, and even some New York businesses that suggest they had been given advanced warning of the attacks. Griffin also cites evidence that indicates that the 9/11 hijackers were not religious fundamentalists as commonly believed and that there is a possibility the hijackers were not Muslim at all (this claim being based on evidence that the published passenger list of the hijacked flights contained no Arab/Muslim names). Griffin, along with other conspiracy theorists, has argued that the World Trade Center towers could not possibly have been collapsed by the collisions of the hijacked airplanes. Attention is also drawn to eyewitness accounts of explosions that occurred shortly before the collapse of the towers and the collapse of a 47-story building (that was not hit by the hijacked airplanes) that took place on the same day as the attacks. All of these accounts are used to suggest that the World Trade Center towers were collapsed by strategically placed explosives that could have been planted by domestic operatives (perhaps under the auspices of a covert government operation) but not by al-Qaeda terrorists.[3]

All of the charges made by conspiracy theories have been countered by alternative explanations that are more consistent with the narrative presented by the commission. The most detailed countercriticism has been published by the editors of *Popular Mechanics*; their explanation draws on testimony from widely respected engineering and aviation experts, along with eyewitnesses.[4] Not surprisingly, conspiracy theorists have gone on to counter these alternative explanations. It should be noted, however, that much of the evidence cited by conspiracy theorists is a matter of public record (for example, the fact that relatives of President Bush had the contract for providing security to the World Trade Center). In this case, the debate does not turn on the factuality of evidence but on the interpretation of the evidence. Even so, the main thing that is lacking in 9/11 conspiracy theories is smoking-gun evidence that directly implicates specific government officials in planning the attacks either through deliberate action or deliberate inaction.

With few exceptions, there has also been no attempt to reconcile the multiplicity of alternative narratives that are suggested by 9/11 conspiracy theories. For example, the argument that there was a hidden Saudi government connection adds a new, important dimension to the 9/11 Commission's narrative, but it does not deny that al-Qaeda members were still principally involved in carrying out the attacks. On the other hand, conspiracies of U.S. government involvement tread a very fine line between suggesting that high-ranking officials in the U.S. government allowed al-Qaeda to carry out the attacks and suggesting that that no members of al-Qaeda (and no persons of Arab/Muslim heritage) were involved in any aspect of the attacks. These different narratives raise questions that carry important implications for making sense of international terrorism and its more or less tenuous connections to government operatives, but they have not been definitively answered by the evidence provided by conspiracy theorists.

Arguments for Creating a More Centralized Intelligence System

Patchwork Intelligence Gathering. According to this argument, U.S. intelligence agencies had all the information they needed to prevent the 9/11 attacks but were simply unable to put the pieces of the puzzle together fast enough. By centralizing the intelligence system under a single director, it becomes possible to better coordinate this process of putting the pieces together by creating information conduits between agencies that flow toward a single destination point. Prior to 9/11, information tended to be hoarded by different intelligence agencies, partly for reasons of protecting turf (because information is power) but also because no single individual or agency had been charged with the task of building information links between these agencies. It also stands to reason that the only way to avoid forms of centralization that allow some agencies to jockey for position over others is to create an entirely new agency that has no prior investment in these turf wars.

Institutional Barriers to Information Sharing. This argument builds on the previous one. In this case, however, barriers to information sharing are not merely political (protecting turf) or due to institutional inadequacies (the absence of collaborative practices). These barriers are also actively reinforced by the existing institutional culture of intelligence agencies that socializes its agents to focus on intra-agency projects and that provides rewards (promotions, prestigious assignments, and so on) to agents who adhere to these rules. The 9/11 Commission's report was especially critical of the institutional culture of the FBI in this regard. It also drew attention to the existence of internal policies that explicitly forbade interagency information sharing. Because the DNI sits above the internal authority structure of these agencies, this director would have the freedom and power to work with these agencies to reform their institutional practices and coordinate these reforms across agencies.

Centralization and Budgetary Control. This argument is very straightforward. In order for the DNI's authority to be meaningful, it has to have teeth. One of the easiest ways to do this is to give the national director the power to approve the budgets of all U.S. intelligence agencies. The ability to deny or provide access to vital resources is a good way to ensure that agency heads take the DNI's recommendations seriously. It also makes it possible for the DNI to better coordinate practices between agencies (e.g., reducing funding for projects that are being duplicated by too many agencies or making funding conditional on a certain level of interagency cooperation).

Standardizing Security Measures. The 9/11 Commission's report observed that major buildings and other high-risk locations across the United States did not have comprehensive security plans or even basic protocols for coordinating mass evacuations in the event of an emergency (including, but not limited to, terrorist attacks). The best way of ensuring that all of these locations meet this goal is to have the process coordinated by a single, national agency.

Arguments against Creating a More Centralized Intelligence System

Intelligence Failure Was Not the Main Problem. This argument insists that the 9/11 Commission placed too much emphasis on poor intelligence (or poorly coordinated intelligence) as the main reason for the success of the 9/11 attacks. This assumption lays the groundwork for the commission's argument in favor of more centralization. In contrast, there is plenty of evidence that the highest levels of the government had been briefed in great detail about al-Qaeda's agenda and the possibility that airplanes could be used as missiles to demolish the World Trade Center towers. Under the Clinton administration, a great deal of information was gathered on al-Qaeda (and other international terrorist groups), and this information was passed along to the Bush administration (the most obvious example being the memo "Osama Bin Laden Determined to Attack the United States" that was passed on to Secretary of State Condoleezza Rice in the early months of 2000). The problem was not that important information did not make its way up the chain of command fast enough. The problem was that people at the highest levels of this chain of command did not act on the information. There are any number of reasons why this happened—one of them being overconfidence in the control intelligence agencies thought they had over this threat. In any event, it is not clear that having even more centralized authority would have made much of a difference in how the government acted.

The Limitations of the Bureaucratic Imagination. As observed at the beginning of this chapter, bureaucracies are best at managing the known, not evaluating or anticipating the unknown. Creating new forms of centralized authority over formerly independent agencies only drags them deeper into a web of bureaucracy. The 9/11 Commission's criticism of the internal bureaucracies of pre-9/11 intelligence agencies is valid, in part. But the fundamental contradiction is that the commission believes that these problems can be fixed by even more bureaucracy.

The Benefits of Decentered Forms of Information Sharing. This argument follows up on the prior critique of bureaucracy. It points out that it is possible to enhance information sharing between agencies without creating more centralized forms of authority. In this case, intelligence agencies can be drawn into multiagency projects on an as-needed basis, which can be determined by the presidential office or an appointee of the executive office (but without creating a permanent position). It could also be possible to modify the authority and mission of the DNI so that it fit this model—acting as a facilitator for interagency collaboration. The goal should be to maximize information sharing while also preserving the operational

For more than three decades, Lee Hamilton, right, served the 9th Congressional District from Indiana, focusing mainly on foreign affairs and domestic intelligence. In the wake of the 2001 attacks, President Bush appointed Hamilton as vice-chairman of the 9/11 Commission. Its final report concluded that a "failure of imagination"—not government neglect—allowed 19 hijackers to carry out the attacks. (AP/Wide World Photos)

autonomy of each agency. As a result, the unique capacities of each agency would not be restricted, but each agency would also be able to benefit from the information gathered by others.

The Machiavellian Attraction of Centralized Authority. It has been famously observed that power corrupts and absolute power corrupts absolutely. There is a tendency for centralized authority to be used for ends other than its official purposes. It has been argued, for example, that the Bush administration used the bureaucratic structure and mission of the Department of Homeland Security to manipulate the legacy mandate of some of the agencies that were incorporated within it (notable examples being the Environmental Protection Agency and the Federal Emergency Management Agency). This was made possible by the centralized, bureaucratic structure of the DHS, which required all of the agencies that had been incorporated under it to conform to the DHS's mandate. In any event, it bears emphasizing that all forms of centralized authority in government will inevitably expand the power of the executive branch. It is also inevitable, no matter which administration is in office, that this expanded power will be used to serve the partisan, political interests of the ruling administration.

In Support of Conspiracy-Theory Arguments

Pointing out the Weakness of the Official Narrative. It is true that conspiracy theories rarely have access to smoking-gun evidence. If the people at the top of the social system (corporate leaders, government heads, and so on) are hatching conspiracies, it stands to reason that they are in the best position to hide the most damning evidence of these plots. What conspiracy theories do very effectively, however, is reveal the inadequacies of the official narrative. At the very least, they challenge people to think critically about the information they receive and to consider the political agenda of the agencies that are giving them this information. To the extent that this encourages people to become more critical consumers of information and become more involved in demanding transparency from the government and the media, this is a good thing.

Looking beyond the Framework of International Terrorism. Conspiracy theories also encourage people to situate the problem of international terrorism in a broader context. Since the attacks of 9/11, international terrorism has been presented to the U.S. public as the single most pressing danger facing the United States. The primary solution presented to the problem has been a call for more security to protect U.S. citizens from Muslim terrorists, illegal immigrants, criminal aliens, and so forth. This distracts attention from the fact that terrorism also has a domestic face (e.g., the Ku Klux Klan, the Unabomber, Timothy McVeigh). According to conspiracy theorists, this domestic face can also include government operatives. People should keep in mind that terrorism is not just something that is perpetrated by foreign-born persons and marginal groups, it can also be used to further the interests of powerful institutional actors. Conspiracy theories encourage people to explore how other governments have used this kind of violence in the past and to examine the kind of power relations that make it possible for these actions to be carried out. Ultimately, this line of reasoning connects the problem of terrorism to the problem of authoritarianism, and the solution is not more security but more democracy.

Limitations of the 9/11 Commission's Recommendations. In its own way, the 9/11 Commission's report also encourages people to put the problem of terrorism in broader context by urging a change in U.S. diplomacy toward the Middle East. However, this change is focused exclusively on the priorities of institutional actors. It does not take a serious look at the relationship between citizens and their governments (or even, for that matter, the need to support genuine movements for grassroots democracy in the Middle East and elsewhere). As a result, the broader context provided by the 9/11 Commission report is still too myopic, being focused on finding better ways of managing problem populations. Conspiracy theories, on the other hand, draw attention to the way that governments, at home and abroad, can manipulate their citizenries. Because of this, they point toward the need for wide-ranging political reforms that go far beyond the 9/11 Commission's call for a national intelligence director.

Weaknesses of Conspiracy-Theory Arguments

Overreaching Claims. What conspiracy theorists have been effective in doing is pointing out errors and omissions in the official narrative. But these errors and omissions do not necessarily prove the claims that conspiracy theorists are trying to make. For example, the fact that some or all of the 9/11 hijackers did not behave like religious fundamentalists does not necessarily mean that they were really government operatives or that they really were not members of al-Qaeda. Also, the fact that some corporations and government officials saw the 9/11 attacks as an opportunity to be exploited, does not necessarily mean that they had explicit foreknowledge of the attacks or planned the attacks. The main argument that conspiracy theorists want to make (the inside job) is built out of the inferences that are drawn from their mass of counterfactual claims. The problem, however, is that these are only inferences. The errors, retractions, and embarrassing coincidences documented by conspiracy theorists may point toward something more sinister or complex than the official narrative, but they do not provide positive, unambiguous evidence for the plot itself.

Unreconciled Narratives. Conspiracy theorists' insistence that the government is lying encourages people to fill in the vacuum created by their counterevidence with their own pet theories. As a result, conspiracy theories can easily spin off in contrary directions. Some critics have suggested that the 9/11 hijackers were really Israelis who may or may not have been working with secret operatives in the U.S. government; others think that the hijackers were really being directed by Saudi Arabian elites who are being protected by the U.S. government. Still others suspect that all of the attacks were orchestrated by the U.S. government with absolutely no involvement from international terrorist groups. So it becomes possible for conspiracy theorists to use the same evidence to insinuate very different things.

Few Concrete Recommendations. Conspiracy theories may invite people to think critically, but they rarely connect their big-picture theories of government corruption to specific recommendations for foreign policy, bureaucratic reorganization, or anything else that would make government work more effectively. For example, criticism of the government's manipulation of the war on terror can be used to suggest that international terrorism is really a nonissue, a smokescreen invented by the government. The reality, however, may be a little more complex than this. It is possible for the problem of government corruption and conspiracies to exist side by side with the problem of international terrorism (understood as a political phenomenon that exists independently of government conspiracies). It is also possible that there is a role that policy changes and institutional reforms can play in fixing these problems, as long as there are factions in government (with support from the citizenry) that are serious about addressing them. Conspiracy theories, however, do not encourage people to think on this level. Their criticism of government is so all-encompassing that little room is left for thinking about practical next steps.

Conclusion

The debate surrounding the recommendations of the 9/11 Commission officially ended with the signing of the 2004 Intelligence Reform and Terrorism Prevention Act. Since that time, the Bush administration created the Office of the Director of National Intelligence that has programmatic and budgetary authority over more than 15 federal intelligence agencies. However, most of the issues that drove the debate over the 9/11 Commission's recommendations are still very much a part of the national policy scene and the public sphere. Concerns about the new forms of bureaucratic centralization that have accompanied the post-9/11 war on terror are still very relevant, whether these concerns are focused on threats to civil liberties of the native born and immigrants, the dangers of unchecked executive authority, or government inefficiency. Since the Office of the DNI is still relatively new, it is also likely that it will face criticism in the years ahead as it tested by new developments in the international and domestic arena. Meanwhile, the amorphous and hotly debated nature of the terrorist threat facing the United States leaves many things open to speculation. Obviously, the different sides in this debate have very different definitions of terrorism, the causes of terrorism, and the likelihood that there could be future attacks as devastating as those of 9/11. It also bears noting that recent antiterrorism bills have begun to refocus on security threats within the United States, further blurring the lines between international and domestic terrorism. It is an open question as to whether the general public will see these developments as necessary protections or invasions of privacy rights (or even be aware of them at all). The occurrence (or absence) of new terrorist strikes on U.S. soil will undoubtedly play an important role in shaping public opinion on these matters, but so can high-profile cases of civil liberties violations committed against innocent citizens in the name of national security. Finally, if the popularity of John F. Kennedy assassination theories is any indication, then it is very likely that 9/11 conspiracy theories will be an entrenched feature of the U.S. political landscape for decades to come. In part, this is because they provide a provocative counternarrative to the war on terror, and as such, will remain politically relevant as long as the war on terror is a defining feature of U.S. domestic and foreign policy. Just as important, conspiracy theories thrive on the release of insider accounts and declassified information, which tends to become more easily available with the passage of time.

Notes

1. Richard Posner, "The 9/11 Report: A Dissent," *The New York Times* (August 29, 2004).
2. Douglas Jehl, "The New Magic Bullet: Bureaucratic Imagination," *The New York Times* (July 24, 2004).
3. See, for example, David Ray Griffin, *Debunking 9/11: An Answer to Popular Mechanics and Other Defenders of the Official Conspiracy Theory* (Northampton MA: Olive Branch Press, 2007); David Ray Griffin, *The 9/11 Commission Report: Omissions and Distortions* (Northampton, MA: Olive Branch Press, 2004); and David Ray Griffin and Richard Falk, *The New Pearl Harbor: Disturbing Questions about the Bush Administration and 9/11* (Northampton, MA: Olive Branch Press, 2004).
4. Popular Mechanics, *Debunking 9/11 Myths: Why Conspiracy Theories Can't Stand up to the Facts* (New York: Hearst, 2006).

Bibliography

Alexandrovna, Larisa. "FBI Documents Contradict 9/11 Commission Report." The Raw Story, February 28, 2008. http://rawstory.com/news/2008/FBI_documents_contradict_Sept._11_Commission_0228.html.
Baker, Peter, and Walter Pincus. "Bush Signs Intelligence Reform Bill." *The Washington Post*, December 18, 2004.

Center for Democracy and Technology. *Clinton Administration Counterterrorism Initiative*. http://www.cdt.org/security/usapatriot/19950427clinton.html.

Cohen, Dara Kay, Mariano-Florentino Cuellar, and Barry Weingast. "Crisis Bureaucracy: Homeland Security and the Political Design of Legal Mandates." *Stanford Law Review* 59, no. 3 (2006): 673–759.

Davis, Wendy. "The Long Arm of 'Secret' Evidence." *New Jersey Law Journal*, August 30, 1999. http://truthinjustice.org/secretevidence.htm.

Griffin, David Ray. *Debunking 9/11 Debunking: An Answer to Popular Mechanics and Other Defenders of the Official Conspiracy Theory*. Northampton MA: Olive Branch Press, 2007.

Griffin, David Ray. *The 9/11 Commission Report: Omissions and Distortions*. Northampton, MA: Olive Branch Press, 2004.

Griffin, David Ray, and Richard Falk. *The New Pearl Harbor: Disturbing Questions about the Bush Administration and 9/11*. Northampton, MA: Olive Branch Press, 2004.

Jehl, Douglas. "The New Magic Bullet: Bureaucratic Imagination." *The New York Times*, July 24, 2004.

Lipton, Eric. "Spy Chiefs Say Cooperation Should Begin at Bottom." *The New York Times*, October 14, 2004.

Marrs, Jim. *Inside Job: Unmasking the 9/11 Conspiracies*. San Rafael, CA: Origin Press, 2004.

National Commission on Terrorist Attacks. *The 9/11 Commission Report: Final Report of the Commission on Terrorist Attacks upon the United States*. New York: W. W. Norton, 2004.

Popular Mechanics. *Debunking 9/11 Myths: Why Conspiracy Theories Can't Stand up to the Facts*. New York: Hearst, 2006.

Posner, Richard. "The 9/11 Report: A Dissent." *The New York Times*, August 29, 2004.

Sheikh, Irum. "Racializing, Criminalizing and Sentencing Post 9/11 Detainees." In *Keeping out the Other: A Critical Introduction to Immigration Enforcement Today*, edited by David Brotherton and Philip Kretsedemas, 81–107. New York: Columbia University Press, 2008.

A. Mitchell Palmer (1872–1936): Red Scare

Mary Elizabeth Brown

During 1919–1920, Americans turned their attention from the end of World War I to the possibility that the Bolshevik Revolution might extend to the United States. Their focus was broad enough to include various kinds of radicals, not just the communists who overthrew czarist Russia and erected the Union of Soviet Socialist Republics but also anarchists. It narrowed, though, on one particular point: targeting foreign-born alleged radicals for deportation. The efforts to eradicate foreign radicalism led to gross violations of civil and human rights. By 1920, concern about the potential for revolution among foreign-born radicals had declined. Generations later, history texts summarized the event as a kind of spasm of national hysteria called the Red Scare. It is also summed up as the product of the personal hysteria, and ambition, of Alexander Mitchell Palmer. Without denying that Palmer had a personal interest in, and bore some responsibility for, the Red Scare, it might be possible to use this entry to place him in the context of the social, legal, and political forces of his time.

Palmer was born in Moosehead, Pennsylvania, on May 4, 1872. He was the third child and second boy, out of a total of six children, of Samuel Bernard Palmer, descendant of Quakers who had originally settled in New York, and Caroline Albert, descendant of Quakers in Luzerne County. He was named after the president of the Lehigh Valley Railroad, for whom Mr. Palmer occasionally worked building bridges (as an adult, he used the name A. Mitchell). He was educated at Stroudsburg High School, at the Moravian Parochial School, and at the Quaker's Swarthmore College. Biographers and historians often point to the irony of someone with such a thoroughly Quaker education living in a part of the country with such a mixed population as Pennsylvania had, heading up an antiradical campaign that abused people's civil liberties and sometimes threatened them physically. Although Palmer took his Quaker background seriously on some occasions, he did not see it as providing moral guidance on immigration. Nor was he influenced by the heterogeneity of his environment.

The mass arrests of accused radicals and the deportation of aliens accused of being disloyal during the Red Scare of the post–World War I years were known as the Palmer Raids, ordered by Attorney General A. Mitchell Palmer. (Library of Congress)

Upon graduation from college, Palmer laid a foundation for realizing his greater ambitions. He returned to Stroudsburg, where his family was already well known, and studied to become a court reporter. Once he had a steady job, he used his work to finance his study of the law at the offices of John B. Storm. When he became a lawyer, he used his profits to invest in local businesses. He also joined local social clubs and became known as a charismatic speaker. He became active in the Democratic Party, then not the majority party in Pennsylvania but the one with which his family affiliated. In 1898, he made an advantageous marriage. His wife, Roberta Bartlett Dixon of Maryland, belonged to a prosperous and politically active (albeit Republican) family. From such a base, Palmer developed a political career. He began by running for the House of Representatives and ultimately served three terms, being elected in 1908, 1910, and 1912.

Palmer's opposition to local captains of industry, particularly Charles Schwab of Bethlehem Steel, gave him a reputation for solicitude for the mass of voters in the working class. Palmer gravitated toward the Progressive faction of the Democratic Party. Progressive Democrats committed themselves to breaking down monopoly and to reducing the power of large social institutions so as to give individuals opportunities for advancement. Thus, rather than regulate businesses, as, say, Progressive Republicans regulated the meat and drug industries, they forced businesses to stay small and compete with each other. Their characteristic legislation included the Clayton Antitrust Act and the establishment of the Federal Trade Commission. However, it is worth noting that Progressive Democratic interest in fostering democracy and individual opportunity did not extend to their own leadership. Their leader, Woodrow Wilson, was notorious for his refusal to compromise when he thought a principle was at stake. Thus, the relationship between Palmer's adherence to the Progressive wing of the Democratic Party and his subsequent antiradical campaign is obscure. Was he a Progressive because progressivism reflected his own principled opposition to the consolidation of wealth and power in the hands of a few? Or was he a Progressive because that seemed the most expeditious way to topple, and replace, the local leadership? Or did he pick up one element of the Progressive personality, the assumption that he knew what was best for society as a whole?

In 1912, the Democrats won the presidency. Palmer's efforts did not affect the outcome. The plurality of Pennsylvanians voted for Theodore Roosevelt, who then got all of Pennsylvania's electoral votes; Pennsylvania was one of only eight states Wilson *didn't* carry. However, Palmer had supported Wilson from the start of the campaign and had made Roosevelt fight for Pennsylvania. He hoped to be rewarded for his efforts with the post of attorney general. Wilson offered to make him secretary of war, but Palmer declined, claiming it was incompatible with his Quaker faith. Palmer's 1912 election to the House meant he still had a job, though, and a position from which he could further prove his loyalty to Wilson. Until the next Congress sat, which, under the rules then in effect, meant until December 1915, Palmer helped to enact Wilsonian legislation, at the cost of his support among more conservative Democrats in Pennsylvania. In the 1914 election, he was defeated by a more conservative Democrat, Boise Penrose. In 1916, Palmer again supported Wilson for president in Pennsylvania and again failed to carry the state for him, even though this was the election in which Wilson was supposedly so popular for keeping the United States out of World War I.

Still, Palmer wanted to advance in his career, and his only hope was to convince Wilson that his services were, if not effective, at least loyal enough that he deserved a reward. And Wilson now had more offices to give. On April 2, 1917, Wilson asked Congress for a declaration of war against Germany. The government had to expand to direct the war effort. One need was for someone to take over the property that Germans—either German citizens living in the United States or investors living in Germany—had in the United States and manage it until hostilities ceased and normal relations between the two countries resumed. In October 1917, Wilson asked Palmer to be the Alien Property Custodian. In November 1918, when the war ended and the attorney general, Thomas Watt Gregory, decided to return to private life, Palmer began angling for the position he had wanted all along. On February 26, 1919, just before he left for France to negotiate the Versailles Treaty, Wilson appointed Palmer to the coveted position.

It was as attorney general that Palmer faced the full effects of the war and postwar situation. In some ways, Palmer scapegoated immigrants and made them bear the major responsibility for postwar radicalism. In some ways, history has scapegoated Palmer and placed on him blame that fell on more impersonal forces. These forces included international events, ideology, radical action, what the law permitted, what politicians proposed, and what ordinary Americans sanctioned.

Antiradicalism had a long history in the United States. Proponents of the French Revolution claimed they were imitating the American one. Americans rejected the comparison and considered the French to be not just altering their form of government but calling into question every social institution. However, the chain of cause and effect known as the Red Scare begins in 1917, at a point in World War I when the French, British, Russians, and Italians were leading an alliance against the Central Powers of Germany, Austria-Hungary, the Ottoman Empire, and Bulgaria. One reason the Central Powers had their name was that they were in the middle. The French, British, and Italians on one side, and the Russians on the other, were forcing the Central Powers to fight a multifront war.

Then one front collapsed. The Russians had not been as well prepared for the war as Czar Nicholas II thought. Soon the czar was fighting a multifront war himself. Germany attacked Russia in the summer of 1914. Other nobles, and Russia's tiny educated elite, complained that the czar was an ineffective leader. The masses resisted serving in an underequipped army and were supported in their resistance by radicals who encouraged them in their belief that World War I benefited the upper classes at the expense of the lower ones. In March 1917 (February on the Russian Gregorian calendar), Czar Nicholas II abdicated. A coalition of his elite critics under the leadership of Alexander Kerensky tried to form a "liberal" government—that is, one characterized by having the leadership elected. In other ways, the liberal government resembled the czarist one in its determination to fight World War I. In November 1917 (October by their calendar), the liberals were overthrown by the communists, who were at that time such a small part of the political spectrum that their name, Bolshevik, identified them as the minority party. In March 1918, Lenin surrendered to Germany, even giving up territory, in order to take Russia out of the war and concentrate on social revolution.

Russia's departure from the Allies had complicated consequences. On the one hand, Wilson could more easily convince Americans to enter the war, because the remaining Allies were either republics (France) or constitutional monarchies (Italy and the United Kingdom). On the other hand, Russia's collapse put more pressure on the United States to enter the war in order to shore up the remaining Allies. Instead of being an ally, revolutionary Russia became a problem for the Allies. The Allies mounted an expeditionary force to enter Soviet territory to prevent the Germans from taking advantage of the situation. There was much anger at the Soviets for taking Russia out of the war and breaking up the international coalition against the expansion of imperial Germany.

The anger was even greater because of ideological factors. Theoretically, Russia was not just changing the party in charge of government. To the communists, the real issue was class. Every other aspect of society had been constructed by the upper classes to facilitate the exploitation of the laboring classes. National boundaries were ways of keeping the working class divided. Religion was a way of pacifying them, preaching pie in the sky when you die. Education brainwashed the poor with hopes that hard work and right living would lead to personal advancement. Police removed from social circulation those who would not be brainwashed. Multiparty republics were elaborately rigged to fool people into thinking they could vote for someone who represented their interests; actually, all politicians colluded with the economic elite, selling out their constituents to enrich themselves. Also, it was not enough to overthrow czarist Russia and to create the Union of Soviet Socialist Republics, the name the government took in 1922. Some communists advocated an immediate worldwide class revolution, and all of them expected the entire international system to fall at some point. Although Wilson, in accord with his general principle of national self-government, called for permitting Russia to work out its own destiny, he had no intention of having the communist system spread to the United States. There were some in his administration who wanted to end Russia's own experiment with communism.

This was not a theoretical debate conducted in political science class. A small party of Bolsheviks had indeed changed the world. And there were activists in the United States as well. At the time of the Bolshevik Revolution, the United States had various types of radicals. To provide some short, handy definitions, socialists thought that the best economy was one controlled by society as a whole rather than one that permitted individuals to control private property. Socialists were divided on how much control society ought to have and how to go about getting it. Communists were socialists inasmuch as they agreed that the group, rather than the individual, should control the economy. However, communists departed from socialists in that they wanted not just to alter the form of government to make it more responsive to the working class; they thought *any* government would become a tool of an upper class and so advocated ultimately dismantling government in favor of community (hence the name) control over the economy. Followers of the communist theoretician Karl Marx departed from socialists in being more consistent advocates of violence; arguing that every social institution was stacked against the working class and thus could not be relied upon to protect proletarian interests and that the elite would not give up power; it must be seized from them. After Lenin led the Bolshevik Revolution, communism had two other distinguishing features. Lenin advocated party leadership—having a well-indoctrinated party that directed the proletariat in furthering the revolution. Lenin's success also made communism the most important radical movement, at least temporarily. However, there was one more category of radicals. Anarchists agreed with communists that social institutions were tools for class exploitation. However, they parted company with the communists in that they included the Communist Party as one of those tools; the party, too, could be an oppressive institution. Also, there were differences between anarchists regarding whether a violent or a pacifist approach would be the fastest way to reform society, whether to work through labor unions, or whether to eschew all groups except those of anarchists.

When the major countries of Europe entered World War I, the United States had no intention of following them. When the United States did enter the war (Wilson asked for a declaration on April 2, 1917; the Senate voted on the proposal April 4 and the House on April 6), everything had to be done at once. The United States had to raise an army, train it and ship it overseas, and provide food and manufactured goods for it. Then, 19 months later (the armistice went into effect on November 11, 1918), everything went into reverse. The United States canceled the orders for the food and equipment for the troops, demobilized the troops, and sent veterans back into a chaotic job market. There were more people in the labor market than usual, because African Americans of both sexes had been drawn out of the South and white women drawn out of traditionally female jobs to take the places of men in the military. And there was less to do than usual, because the government had just canceled its war contracts, and wartime inflation limited people's spending. There were plenty of opportunities for labor disputes in 1919. Sixty thousand workers in Seattle, Washington, went on strike starting on February 6. The entire Boston police force went on strike on September 9. Steelworkers went on strike on September 22. Coal miners walked off the job on November 1. It was a short, slippery slope from these discrete actions to rumors of a grand conspiracy orchestrated by the Bolsheviks.

On top of the strikes, which enjoyed radical support, there was a bombing campaign that was assumed from the beginning to be a radical plot. Thirty bombs were put into the mail somewhere near the New York City General Post Office, timed to reach their targets by May 1, 1919, the anniversary of the 1886 Haymarket bombing in Chicago and an annual observance of the international radical community. Several bombs did reach their destinations, and one blew the hands off the maid who opened it, but the general campaign failed because most of the bombs were held for insufficient postage. Then the bombers tried delivering the bombs to people's houses by hand. On the night of June 2, 1919, bombs went off in cities all around the Northeast, Mid-Atlantic, and Midwest regions.

The bombing campaign touched Palmer personally. One of the package bombs being held for insufficient postage was addressed to him. A bomb on his doorstep the night of June 2 damaged the front of his Washington, DC, home. It also created a grisly scenario. The bomb went off before the bomber could let go of it. The bomb blew him to pieces and scattered chunks of human remains in a blockwide radius around the Palmer household. Exactly how this affected Palmer is disputed. Franklin Delano Roosevelt, who lived across the street from Palmer and could still walk at this time, ran upstairs to check on his own son and then across the street to check on his neighbor. He recalled that Palmer was so shaken that he had regressed to the Quaker speech of his youth: "He was 'theeing' and 'thouing' me all over the place."[1]

After the bombing, Palmer requested, and received, an increase in funding for the Department of Justice. He used it to reorganize the antiradical activity he had already started. On August 1, he created a General Intelligence Division and placed it under the command of J. Edgar Hoover, who was at the beginning of a lifelong career in federal law enforcement, including being the founding director of the Federal Bureau of Investigation. Hoover began compiling an index-card file on all newspapers that espoused radicalism, all organizations that fostered it, and all individuals associated with it in any way.

It is doubtful that anyone would have tolerated Palmer using his position to conduct a personal vendetta against his attackers. Here, general public frustration enters into the picture. Leaflets mailed with the bombs, or left with them at the houses, indicated that a group of anarchists had orchestrated the bombing. The police traced the wrapping paper for bombs back to a supplier. They pieced together the person killed placing the bomb at Palmer's house. Eventually, they determined that the deceased was Carlo Valdinoci, an anarchist who lived in Stoughton, Massachusetts. But they could not figure out who his confederates were. This was worrisome because they could not predict when or where or how the anarchists might strike again.

Citizens called for action. One important incident took place at Centralia, Washington, on November 11, 1919. The town had an American Legion. The organization was open to anyone who had served the U.S. military overseas, but it also had a reputation for an intolerant brand of patriotism. It organized an Armistice Day parade that was routed to go past the hall of the International Workers of the World (IWW), a radical labor organization. Fearing an attack on their property, the IWW defended it by posting armed members along the parade route. A clash between the American Legion and the IWW ensued. Four Legionnaires were shot and killed. A mob apprehended one of those who shot a Legionnaire, IWW member Wesley Everest. The police intervened, arrested Everest for murder, and put him in jail. That night, a mob broke into the jail and carried Everest away to his death. They castrated him, tied a noose around his neck, tied the other end to a bridge, pushed him off, twice hauled him back up in order to use a longer rope, stamped on his fingers to force him to let go of the bridge, and finally riddled his hanging body with bullets.

Had Everest lived, he would have been tried for the killing of the Legionnaire, but he could not have been tried for his membership in the IWW; that was not illegal. However, had Everest not been born in the United States, he might have run afoul of numerous laws. The Immigration Act of March 3, 1903, proscribed anarchists. The Immigration Act of February 5, 1917, dropped the statute of limitation on deportations. This meant that immigrant radicals could be deported no matter how long they had been in the country. Theoretically, not only radicals who entered as radicals could be deported; those who developed radical opinions in the United States could be deported as their opinions changed. There was also an Entry and Departure Control Act of May 22, 1918, which permitted the president, in times of war or other national emergency, to proscribe or deport aliens whose presence threatened public safety. Because the United States was no longer at war, this law was not necessarily useful. However, the point is that there was more one could do to radical immigrants than one could do to native-born radicals. Thus, immigrants, rather than natives, would bear the brunt of participation in antiradical activities.

This leads to the question of which government leaders were in charge. The president of the United States at that point was Woodrow Wilson. On September 25, 1919, though, Wilson suffered a stroke. Under the Constitution at that time, he remained president, but he was so ill that Mrs. Wilson would not let him transact much business. When he was well enough, he was focused on a futile effort to get the Senate to ratify the Versailles Treaty. Leadership in domestic affairs fell to other people. The main responsibility for immigrant radicals was shared by the Department of Justice and the Department of Labor. Palmer could arrest the immigrants, but he had to depend on the Labor Department to carry out the penalties and deport them.

Presidential aspirations also figured into Palmer's calculations.[2] There was a precedent allowing presidents only two terms in office. Wilson was prepared to challenge that precedent. Generous people argue that he desperately wanted to pursue his vision of a better postwar world order and also that his mind was affected by his stroke. Cynics point to this as one more example of his messianic tendencies. Few insiders acted as if Wilson would really run again. However, one person had to: William G. McAdoo, who was not only an ambitious politician but Wilson's son-in-law. He had to wait until he got a signal from Wilson. Thus, others, such as Palmer, could get a jump on maneuvering for the Democratic nomination for the presidency in 1920.

So there *were* radicals, even if there were not as many as the public feared. There were means for deporting the aliens among them. There was a great public outcry that this be done. And there was the possibility that the one who gave the public what it wanted could ride the resulting wave of popularity all the way to the presidency. The final push into action came from the Senate. Fifty-four alien radicals had been apprehended in Seattle in the wake of the strike there and entrained for Ellis Island and deportation, amid much national praise. This had been a local initiative. On October 19, the Senate formally requested Palmer "to advise and inform the Senate whether or not the Department of Justice has taken legal proceedings, and if not, why not, and if so, to what extent."[3] On November 7, Palmer gave them their answer.

That day, Department of Justice officials assisted by local police in 12 cities went to the meeting places of an organization called the Russian Workers Union. Studies of the literature this group produced indicated that it indeed espoused the violent overthrow of all government, including that of the United States. And November 7 would be an excellent day for getting as many members as possible. It was the second anniversary of the Bolshevik Revolution, which, presumably, they would be celebrating. The raiding parties arrested everyone they could find on the premises at the time. Over the next few weeks, they worked to deport as many as possible. On December 21, an army transport ship, the *Buford*, sailed out of New York Harbor for Finland, where the 249 anarchists aboard were transferred to local transportation for passage to the Soviet Union.

Palmer followed up this performance with a second series of raids starting on January 2, 1920. Again, Justice Department officials cooperated with police in a dozen cities, although this time the targets were the Communist and Communist Labor Parties.[4] This time, the raids continued for some days, as authorities rounded up party members in smaller cities. The raids netted more than 3,000 suspects. Exactly how many is not clear, and that should be a signal alerting students to the fact that the most basic rights of citizens were not being observed. In Boston, authorities searched people's houses and papers without warrants.[5] Most raiding parties had arrest warrants but arrested more people than they had warrants for. In Boston, they arrested more people than they had room for in jail. Of 800 suspects, 400 could be accommodated in Boston. The remaining 400 were transported to windswept Deer Island in the middle of the harbor, where there was no heat and two suspects died of pneumonia before it could be determined whether they should have been detained at all. Detroit also ran out of room. Eight hundred suspects were detained in a corridor in the city's federal building, without windows or furniture; the inmates spent most of their time standing in line waiting for the lone toilet. After holding people for up to six days without informing them of the reasons for their being held and without permitting them to communicate with lawyers or family members, authorities had to release 300 of them when interrogations revealed they were not alien radicals.[6] In Philadelphia, most of the 500 people arrested had to be let go for the same reason.

This still left 3,600 people who the Justice Department thought had violated immigration laws by their advocacy of the overthrow of the U.S. government and thus should be deported.[7] Accordingly, the Justice Department prepared dossiers and sent them to the Labor Department, which had the power to draw up the actual deportation orders. Secretary of Labor William B. Wilson was ill, so from January until March 1920, Acting Secretary John B. Abercrombie presided over deportation proceedings. Then Abercrombie resigned to run for senator from Alabama. Assistant Secretary Louis F. Post became acting secretary. Post took his responsibilities seriously, carefully checking each dossier before filling out deportation forms. By April 1, he had considered 1,600 cases and dismissed 71 percent of them.[8] He began by throwing out the cases of individuals for whom there was no arrest warrant, those who had not received the benefit of a lawyer before they made incriminating statements, and those against whom evidence had been seized illegally. He differentiated between the Communist Party and Communist Labor Party, which were organizations with two different origins and ideologies, and automatically freed all those who had joined the latter. The Justice Department took membership in the Communist Party at face value; Post dismissed those cases involving individuals who belonged to groups that had affiliated with or transferred members to the Communist Party, reasoning the followers might not agree with what the leaders were doing. About the only people he deported were those who had willfully joined the Communist Party. It is likely that some alien radicals remained in the United States when he finished reviewing the cases. It is certain innocent aliens did. More than that, when the House Committee on Rules began holding impeachment hearings about Post, he appeared before the committee and defended himself convincingly. His performance went a long way to reassuring the public that competent civil servants were checking into the threat of radical aliens and would protect the country.

As May 1, 1920, approached, Palmer began to warn the public that the radicals would celebrate their Labor Day with strikes, uprisings, riots, bombings, and assassinations. When the day passed and nothing happened, Palmer began to lose credibility. Later that month, the National Popular Government League issued a 67-page pamphlet criticizing Palmer's methods in the crusade against foreign-born radicals. By June 1, the House Rules Committee was questioning Palmer as a preliminary to possibly censuring him for his conduct in office. The committee decided not to act, but by then Palmer was no longer carrying out his raids and deportation proceedings. What was left was a lingering link between immigration, radicalism, and violent terrorism that contributed to the passage of the national quota laws of the 1920s and to the anticommunist legislation of the 1950s.

Palmer never did get to be president. Although he was not in as helpless a position as McAdoo, he could not announce his candidacy until Wilson renounced his. By the time Wilson did that, James Cox, an Ohio politician who was not part of Wilson's family or cabinet and could campaign openly, was far ahead in terms of securing delegates to the Democratic National Convention. Palmer did continue to be active in politics, though, last helping to draft the Democratic platform on which Franklin Roosevelt ran in 1932. He died of a heart attack in Florida on May 11, 1936.

There are some interesting sequels to the Palmer story. Police were still trying to figure out who had tried to send Palmer a package bomb and who had conspired to plant a bomb at his house. They finally got a lead about a Brooklyn printer who produced the leaflets that came with the bombs. Justice Department officials arrested two men, Roberto Elia and Andrea Salsedo, who were indeed anarchists and printers. They held the two men at the department's New York office; Salsedo committed suicide under their watch. Word of the two men's incarceration, and their possible confession, got out to other anarchists. Some of these anarchists took steps to leave the country, to hide incriminating materials, or to protect themselves by carrying firearms. Two of those anarchists were Nicola Sacco and Bartolomeo Vanzetti of Stoughton and Plymouth, Massachusetts, respectively. When police arrested the two the night of May 5, 1920, on charges of robbing a payroll and murdering the paymaster and his assistant, they did so because they thought Sacco and Vanzetti acted as though they were guilty of something. Historian Paul Avrich argued that they probably acted that way because they were aware the police were looking for anarchists like themselves and also because they had just been moving their anarchist equipment, including dynamite, to a safe hiding place.[9] Instead of being deported as alien radicals, they were executed for a robbery and two murders that have never been successfully linked to them.

Carlo Tresca escaped the Palmer raids unscathed. Tresca would have been a prize catch. Born in Italy in 1879, he became an anarcho-syndicalist (an anarchist who advanced his cause through work with labor unions) there. When in 1904 his radicalism got him into trouble with the Italian government, he escaped to the United States and was allowed to enter despite the laws prohibiting the immigration of anarchists. He continued to proselytize and was an important figure at the IWW-sponsored textile mill strike in Lawrence, Massachusetts, in 1912 and at the Paterson, New Jersey, silk mill strike in 1913. In 1917, he refused to support the Bolshevik Revolution but also refused to support U.S. entry into World War I. In the early 1920s, he was active in the effort to free Sacco and Vanzetti, although privately he was convinced that Sacco had a hand in the robbery and murders. Tresca, though, came to a different end than Sacco and Vanzetti. When in 1922 Benito Mussolini came to power in Italy, Tresca was one of the first stalwarts of the antifascist coalition. As fascism spread, he broadened his work to include opposition to fascism in Spain and Germany. He also continued to oppose the Communist Party, which he feared might take advantage of the chaos that would wrack Italy after Mussolini left power. And he opposed the mafia. When he was assassinated in New York City on the night of January 11, 1943, he was memorialized with a grudging respect for sticking to his anarchism and for opposing the evils of fascism, communism, and organized crime.[10] Had A. Mitchell Palmer still been alive, they would have been on the same side.

Notes

1. Stanley Coben, *A. Mitchell Palmer: Politician*, Leonard W. Levy, general editor (New York: Da Capo Press, 1972), 206.
2. Ibid., 252–253.
3. *Congressional Record*, 66th Cong., 1st Sess., 6871–6872, cited in Robert K. Murray, *Red Scare: A Study in National Hysteria, 1919–1920* (Minneapolis: University of Minnesota Press, 1955; reprint, New York: McGraw-Hill, 1964), 196 (page citation is to the reprint edition).

4. The difference between these two was the members' birthplace. When the Communist Labor Party was formed, in emulation of the Bolshevik Party in the Soviet Union, American-born communists broke from their foreign-born colleagues and started the Communist Party.

5. Coben, *A. Mitchell Palmer*, 228.

6. Murray, *Red Scare*, 214–217.

7. Coben, *A. Mitchell Palmer*, 233.

8. Ibid., 232.

9. Paul Avrich, *Sacco and Vanzetti: The Anarchist Background* (Princeton, NJ: Princeton University Press, 1992).

10. Dorothy Gallagher, *All the Right Enemies: The Life and Murder of Carlo Tresca* (New Brunswick, NJ: Rutgers University Press, 1988). Officially, Tresca's murder went unsolved. Gallagher argued that Frank Garofalo, a New York Italian with connections to bootlegging, gangsters, and fascists, hired Carmine Galante to do the killing.

Bibliography

Alexander Mitchell Palmer has no collection of papers. The papers for the period during which he was attorney general are among the Papers of the Department of Justice in the National Archives and Records Administration. He does, though, have a biography: Stanley Coben, *A. Mitchell Palmer: Politician*, Da Capo Press Reprint Series, Civil Liberties in American History, Leonard W. Levy, general editor (New York: Da Capo Press, 1972). For specialized studies on the general topic of monitoring radical activity among the foreign born right after World War I, see Mark Ellis, "J. Edgar Hoover and the 'Red Summer' of 1919," *Journal of American Studies* 27, no. 1 (1994): 39–59; James J. Lorence, "Socialism in Northern Wisconsin, 1910–1920: An Ethno-Cultural Analysis," *Mid-America* 64, no. 3 (1982): 25–51; Robert K. Murray, *Red Scare: A Study in National Hysteria, 1919–1920* (Minneapolis: University of Minnesota Press, 1955; reprint, New York: McGraw-Hill, 1964); William Preston Jr., *Aliens and Dissenters: Federal Suppression of Radicals* (Cambridge, MA: Harvard University Press, 1963; reprint, New York: Harper Torchbooks, 1966); and David Williams, "The Bureau of Investigation and Its Critics, 1919–1921: The Origins of Federal Political Surveillance," *Journal of American History* 68, no. 3 (1981): 560–579.

Joseph Petrosino (1860–1909): International Criminal Conspiracies

Mary Elizabeth Brown

Joseph Petrosino was an immigrant success story, an American hero. Paradoxically, he was also involved in creating an immigrant stereotype he himself did not believe in and in pinning it firmly to his own ethnic group. Petrosino was born in Italy, and his success discredited those who saw Italians as a dangerous lot. What happened to him, though, lent weight to those who questioned the desirability of open-ended migration from Italy and who sought to limit the number of Italian immigrants on the grounds that they were criminally inclined.

Giuseppe Michele Pasquale (later Americanized to Joseph or Joe) Petrosino was born on August 30, 1860, to Prospero Petrosino and his wife, Maria Giuseppa Arato. Joe was born and grew up in Padula in the province of Salerno in the southern part of Italy. Prospero and Maria had two other children, a girl named Caterina and a boy named Vincenzo. Mrs. Petrosino died, and Mr. Petrosino subsequently married another woman named Maria Mugno. He and his new wife had three more children, Antonio, Giuseppina, and Michele. Mr. Petrosino was a tailor and made a sufficient living. He was able to send his sons to elementary school. However, long-term prospects looked better in the United States. In the summer of 1873, the Petrosinos left Padula for Naples, where they boarded an oceangoing vessel for New York City.

Had he remained in Padula, Joe would have probably entered the workforce at about age 13. It may not have seemed remarkable to him that he did the same in New York, but the fact was later incorporated into the legend of a rags-to-respectability story. At the age of 13, Joe and his friend Pietro Jorio became petty entrepreneurs. They ran a combination shoeshine and newspaper stand. They had a good spot for their little business, in front of a store at 300 Mulberry Street, which was across from police headquarters. There were a lot of men who needed to keep up their appearance by having their boots blacked and a lot of people who had a little time on their hands to kill with a newspaper. And it was a spot with a future. Across the street paraded constant examples of men who had achieved economic stability and community respect.

In the evenings, Joe attended night school. Having learned to read and write Italian, he learned English, which he would need to rise above the unskilled jobs within the Italian community and try for a job in the larger U.S. economy. Once his English was sufficient, he found an office job working for an Italian American stockbroker named DeLuca who had an office on Broome Street in the heart of the Lower East Side's Little Italy. In 1876, Mr. Petrosino became a U.S. citizen. Joe, his minor son, became a citizen when his father did.

In 1878, at age 18, Petrosino made an important economic advance. He got a full-time job as one of New York's "white wings," or street cleaners. This may sound like a fairly low-level, unskilled job, but it was steady work, with little chance of unemployment even in an economic downturn. It also turned out to have possibilities for advancement. After about a year on the job, his superiors promoted Petrosino to foreman and assigned him to supervise the loading of the garbage scows that carried the city's refuse out into the harbor and dumped it in the ocean. Cleaning the streets had the potential for an even greater kind of advancement. The street cleaners were under the control of the police department, with police inspectors checking on the street cleaners' work. When he was promoted to foreman, Petrosino came under the direct supervision of Police Inspector Aleck Williams.

Coincidentally with Petrosino's promotion, Italian migration to the United States increased. The Italian migration had some characteristics that might concern police. First, few police officers spoke Italian. Second, most of the migrants were young working-age men traveling apart from their families, hunting for low-skilled, low-paid work and making do when such work was not available—just the kind of population that might turn to crime. Third, about four-fifths of the Italians who came to the United States hailed either from the part of the mainland that lay south of Rome or from Sicily, and this was important because those parts of Italy had a reputation for criminal activity.

Italian criminal activity went by various names that originally had different meanings. The Black Hand, the most popular name during Petrosino's day, was originally an anarchist organization. The camorra was the name for extralegal organizations in the area around Naples. The mafia was the name for similar extralegal organizations on the island of Sicily. Americans used the three names as synonyms. For Americans, one important element in the history of Italian crime was the political history of southern Italy. The southern peninsula and Sicily had been owned by the Bourbon royal family of Spain, which tried to get as much money as possible from the area without providing much in the way of government protection. Into the vacuum of government authority stepped extralegal criminal organizations that established their authority over an area and engaged in kidnapping for ransom, blackmail, and extortion. To make their threats real, the criminals murdered victims who did not pay them. They also murdered gang members who betrayed the group's secrets.

Given these factors, it is natural that the New York Police Department would consider making connections with the Italians in the city. It is not clear whether Petrosino took the initiative and volunteered his services or whether Williams realized Petrosino had the necessary intelligence and character and recruited him. By the early 1880s, there was a relation between the two men. Williams used Petrosino as an informer (or "auxiliary," as Petrosino phrased it), nosing about the Italian community and reporting on possible criminal activities. In exchange, Williams promised to help Petrosino get a regular appointment to the police force. Later in his career, Petrosino became famous for his ability to go undercover, but when he was young and inexperienced, he failed to maintain sufficient secrecy. By 1883, those he was informing on knew he was an informer. At that point, Williams made good on his promise to press his superiors to hire Petrosino. It required some sus-

Lieutenant Joseph Petrosino became a New York City police officer on October 19, 1883. (Library of Congress)

pension of regulations. Police were supposed to be taller than Petrosino, who was five feet three inches tall, and if they were short, they were not supposed to weigh 200 pounds. The physical requirements were waived, and on October 19, 1883, Petrosino became a police officer.

Petrosino began his job as a patrolman, walking a beat on 13th Street. This was general police work, but Petrosino retained his interest in the connection between Italians and crime. When, on October 15, 1890, New Orleans Police Chief David Hennessey was assassinated, Petrosino speculated that the chief was right when he said "the dagoes got me"—that Hennessey had been targeted by a gang whose control of the city's produce market he had thwarted. Even without his hobbylike interest in organized crime, Petrosino was a useful and competent police officer. On July 20, 1895, then New York City Police Commissioner Theodore Roosevelt, who was devoted to the merit concept, promoted Petrosino to detective. Now Petrosino could really follow his particular interests and use his talents. Not only was he bilingual in Italian and English, he understood the spoken dialects of southern Italy. In some settings, he was able to disguise himself as a common laborer, pushcart peddler, or petty entrepreneur, at least until his distinctive short, squat physique gave him away. He also had a memorable face, scarred from a childhood bout of smallpox. He tried to fade into the crowd by wearing dark business suits and building up his height with tall derby hats and double-soled shoes.

To his competence, Petrosino added a sense of how to work with the public. He demonstrated his public relations ability during a 1901 rash of assassinations of heads of state. On July 30, 1901, Umberto I, king of the Italians, was assassinated. Italian police arrested the culprit, Gaetano Breschi. Investigation disclosed that Breschi had been living in Paterson, New Jersey, and had been part of an anarchist circle there. The anarchists had plotted the assassination and had drawn lots to choose the assassin. Breschi had sailed from Paterson to Italy to carry out the mission. Italian authorities asked the United States for assistance in tracking down Breschi's co-conspirators. The new vice president of the United States, Theodore Roosevelt, knew just the man, the Italian American he had promoted to detective in the New York Police Department. Petrosino disguised himself as a laborer, complete with a job, rented a room in a cheap boardinghouse in Paterson that was known as an anarchist meeting place, and let people think that he was sympathetic toward anarchism. He managed to sit quietly through meetings, secure introductions to prominent people within the group, and listen to them describe their exploits. Eventually, he had to get out. He had been introduced to Breschi's wife, an Irish American anarchist named Sophie Knieland, and questioned her a little too closely. (And perhaps a little too roughly; this was before the potential for police brutality was closely monitored, and Petrosino had a reputation for getting physical in the heat of interrogations.)

Rather than make his report to his superiors in New York, Petrosino traveled to Washington, DC, to speak to President McKinley and Vice President Roosevelt. He had uncovered something he thought they should know. The assassination of King Umberto I was part of a much larger plot to assassinate as many heads of state as possible, including the president of the United States. McKinley and Roosevelt thanked Petrosino for the information but did not take it seriously. Perhaps they need not have; the Paterson circle never seems to have attempted to assassinate the president. But on September 6, 1901, an anarchist unconnected to the Paterson group, a non-Italian named Leon Czolgosz, did shoot McKinley. After McKinley's September 14 death, Petrosino was talking to reporters, claiming he had warned the president about the possibility of anarchist assassination. Petrosino was stretching the truth a bit; he had not warned McKinley about Czolgosz. However, the incident became part of the legend of Petrosino, the good (skillful) detective and the good (patriotic) American.

In New York, a morbid boost to Petrosino's career came on April 14, 1903. Early that morning, a man's body was discovered stuffed into a barrel in a vacant lot on East 11th Street. The man had been stabbed to death, then mutilated, his sex organs amputated and stuffed into his mouth. The police inspector supervising the neighborhood called Petrosino. Petrosino set about solving the mystery. He used the trademark on the barrel to figure out what company had packed its original contents (which, he guessed by tasting the remnants stuck between the barrel staves, was sugar). He then had someone contact the sugar refinery to determine to whom it had shipped the barrels. When it turned out that one of the places that bought sugar from the company was a bar called the Star of Italy, he went there, took a table, sat quietly, and gathered information. Eventually, he pieced together a story. The victim was one Benedetto Maduena or Madonnia. The murderer was probably Tomasso Petto ("Petto the Ox"), a hit man for the gang that used the bar as a headquarters. Their main motive was probably to prevent Madonnia from turning informer. However, the killer had also used the corpse to send a signal to others considering the same course. Stuffing the dead man's genitals in his mouth was a way of advertising that this is what could happen to those who betrayed secrets.

Petrosino became famous for cracking the case, but it was not an entirely successful piece of detective work because he failed to obtain a conviction. As nearly as he could reconstruct it, this was because the gang was one step ahead of him. When the gang realized Petrosino had identified Petto as the killer, it sent Petto into hiding and substituted for him another man of similar physique. When Petrosino went back to the Star of Italy to arrest the murderer and conspirators, he picked up a man who looked like Petto. However, when the case came to trial, the man proved he was not, in fact, Tomasso Petto and was not connected with this murder. Without a murderer, there could be no one for the conspirators to support, and the case fell apart. Even though Petrosino could not prove it in court, he himself was convinced Petto was the killer, and, later he found at least one other person who thought so, too. At the time of Madonnia's murder, his brother-in-law, Giuseppe Di Primo, was serving a prison sentence in Sing Sing. Shortly after Di Primo's release from prison, the real Tomasso Petto, who was living under an assumed name in the mining town of Wilkes-Barre, Pennsylvania, was murdered at his own front door.

Not getting a conviction might have been fatal to Petrosino, because the case was actually more significant than the rubbing out of a potential stool pigeon. Petrosino hypothesized that Madonnia's jailed brother-in-law, Di Primo, had been part of the Star of Italy bar gang and had been sacrificed by his cohorts. He was the only member of the gang who had been caught, convicted, and imprisoned. From his prison cell, he sent his brother-in-law Madonnia to the gang's headquarters to retrieve his share of the gang's profits. The gang refused to give Madonnia Di Primo's portion, at which point Madonnia threatened them with exposure, with fatal results to himself. The murder suggested that the Star of Italy gang had important secrets to keep. Other evidence Petrosino collected pointed to gambling and counterfeiting. In short, it seems Petrosino stumbled upon racketeers at the beginning of what could have been a highly lucrative career. He was unable to end their activities through arrest. He was so sure he had the right killers that when the justice system did not convict the culprits, he undertook to do justice, as he saw it, personally. He harassed the gang with obvious police surveillance (intended to send a warning rather than to really monitor them) and with arrests for petty crimes. The gang had to disperse. But its members lived—for revenge.

The second failure connected with the barrel murder was a failure in public relations. While working on the mystery, Petrosino held press conferences and answered such questions as would not compromise the investigation. The most frequently asked was whether this was a Black Hand crime. Petrosino kept explaining that there was no such thing as an international criminal conspiracy with headquarters in Sicily and branch offices in New York. Individuals with criminal experience in Sicily and southern Italy migrated and plied their trade in New York, but they acted as individuals or as small gangs, not as part of a giant conspiracy. They confined their criminal activity to the Italian neighborhood. They posed no general threat to the United States.

The public failed to buy Petrosino's reassuring story. The number of Black Hand stories indexed in *The New York Times* increased steadily after 1903, and the *Times* even then prided itself on not being a yellow journalism scandal sheet. Similarly, the turn of the century saw an increasing number of articles on the Black Hand in English-language periodicals devoted to serious discussion of national issues, such as the *North American Review*. The Italian-language press had a different perspective on the issue and criticized Petrosino, at least partly because his efforts to arrest and prosecute gangsters reinforced the general notion that all Italians were criminals. However, it was the English-language press that concerned Petrosino and his superiors. That was the part of public opinion that had to be reassured the police were in control.

As the outcry against the Black Hand grew, Police Commissioner Theodore Bingham took action. On January 20, 1905, Detective Petrosino held the first meeting of the department's five-person Italian squad. Every member of the squad was of Italian background and bilingual. Fairly soon thereafter, the squad had its first big case. A young man named Frank Lo Cascio came stumbling out of the woods between the New York City line north of the Bronx and the adjacent City of Yonkers, alerting the first police officers he saw that he had found a body in the woods. The officers thought Lo Cascio himself had committed the murder and arrested him. Petrosino cleared Lo Cascio right away: The corpse had multiple stab wounds and bore the signs of a struggle to the death, whereas Lo Cascio was unscathed. Then Petrosino identified the corpse and tracked down the murderer. The victim was Antonio Torsiello. The perpetrator was Antonio Strollo. The motive, apparently, was money. Strollo and Torsiello worked together in the same small town in Pennsylvania. Strollo found out that Torsiello had come to the United States to track down his brother Vito but that he could not read or write. Strollo then helped Torsiello place advertisements in the papers. He then pretended to have received a written response from Vito inviting his brother to come live with him in Yonkers. Excited, Torsiello emptied his bank account in Pennsylvania. Strollo "kindly" offered to accompany him to the unfamiliar town of Yonkers and, when they reached a forsaken stretch of the route, stabbed him to death and took all his cash.

The informal Italian squad was sufficiently successful at cracking cases such as the Torsiello murder that Police Commissioner Bingham formalized it as the Italian Legion. The stolid Petrosino was becoming the talk of the town. *The New York Times* sent a reporter to interview him at Legion headquarters on Elm Street in Lower Manhattan just above city hall. Although the reporter described Petrosino as "noted for an unusual degree of taciturnity even for a member of the Secret Service branch of the Police Department of New York," the interviewee was voluble enough to provide a cohesive theory of Italian crime. He still denied the existence of a truly organized criminal syndicate and maintained that what Americans were seeing was the activity of individuals who had learned how to be criminals in Italy and who carried those techniques to the United States but who were not all part of one organization. These criminals were dangerous not so much because of what they themselves were or could do but because of circumstances. Back in Italy, the legal system was capricious and seemed to favor the rich and well connected. The average Italian assumed the same was true in the United States and did not even think of going to the police when threatened by the Black Hand:

> What they need is a teacher, someone who will make them realize that they are missing the greatest of all blessings this country affords, equal rights. If you tell them casually that anyone of them before the law of the land is as good as the richest and the proudest of the native born they will laugh at you. They must be instructed so that the humble organ grinder, the shopkeeper and even the laborer on the tracks of the Subway will know that when the Black Hand picks him out for blackmail and possible destruction, the Black Hand is not only attacking him but is also seeking to break down and destroy the laws built by Americans to protect their sacred rights, rights in which he shares equally.[1]

When Bingham announced the upgrading of the Italian Force to the status of an Italian Legion, Petrosino and some friends from the police force celebrated with dinner at Vincent Saulino's restaurant at the corner of Lafayette and Spring Street in the Lower East Side's Little Italy. Petrosino had been frequenting the restaurant for some time. Vincent Saulino had come to the United States in about 1871 from Agnoni, Campobasso; he knew how to make the dishes his southern Italian compatriots appreciated.[2] Saulino also had a daughter, Adelina. She had been married but had been left widowed and childless and had returned to her parents' house. On this night, after bolstering his courage with a couple of bottles of Chianti,

Petrosino took Adelina aside and said something to the effect that they were two lonely people who might get along together.

Adelina accepted, and the two were married on the first Sunday of April 1907, at Petrosino's parish church, Saint Patrick's Old Cathedral, between Mott and Mulberry, Prince and Houston Streets, at the northern end of Little Italy. Monsignor Michael J. Lavelle, who had been born and raised in the neighborhood when it was a predominantly Irish area and who had gone on to become the rector of Saint Patrick's new cathedral on Fifth Avenue and the archbishop of New York's liaison with Italian Catholics, presided at the wedding. The couple moved into a four-room apartment near Adelina's father's restaurant, at 233 Lafayette Street. Their only child, a daughter named Adelina Bianca Giuseppina, was born November 30, 1908, and baptized at the old cathedral.

The only thing that was not going well in Petrosino's life at this point was that he appeared to be fighting a losing battle with crime. The public was convinced there was a Black Hand, and Petrosino himself was seeing evidence that criminals in Italy and in New York had some kind of ongoing connection. It was not just a matter of individuals migrating but of groups coordinating activities. Also, the migration situation presented an easy way to evade the consequences of criminal behavior. Individuals could commit crimes in the United States, leave the country, and evade extradition proceedings. What was frustrating to Petrosino was that these people should never have been in the United States in the first place. U.S. immigration law barred the migration of persons with serious criminal records. Yet these people were slipping past Italian and U.S. authorities and becoming problems for local law enforcement.

Petrosino shared his frustrations with his superior, Police Commissioner Bingham. The commissioner went before city officials to see if he could get a secret service invested with the power to eradicate Black Hand activities. His presentation raised questions about whether the police would stick to constitutional and legal measures in their campaign against organized crime. City officials, fearing Bingham would be creating a rogue agency, refused to fund his project. Bingham then went outside city politics, outside the city's treasury, to private individuals and groups. The Italian Chamber of Commerce, eager to clear the Italian name, contributed. There were rumors that non-Italian wealthy philanthropists such as Andrew Carnegie and John D. Rockefeller also gave money. As the phrase "there were rumors" might lead one to suspect, the new agency was hardly a secret. The story was in the papers by December 1908.

What Petrosino and Bingham thought of the lack of secrecy is unknown. Both of them paid attention to the press and were aware of the newspapers' ability to create among the public the comforting feeling that something was being done about crime. For Bingham, this may have been a major consideration. His position was a highly political one; he served only as long as the mayor regarded him as a help.

Petrosino had to balance his appreciation of good public relations with another concern. Newspapers did, after all, give out news—and sometimes news criminals could use.

Sometime in January 1909, Bingham told Petrosino that the latter was going to Italy. There he was to make contact with U.S. and Italian officials but was not to rely on them for information. He was to make his own investigation into Italian police files. These were, after all, part of the public record and thus available to anyone with an interest in them. Particularly, he was to check into the criminal records of individuals known to be in the United States. With those records in hand, the New York Police Department could initiate deportation proceedings of people who had come into the United States supposedly innocent of any crimes. Petrosino was also to supplement the official records by establishing his own network of informants and gathering data from them.

Petrosino left New York at 4:00 P.M., February 9, 1909, in a first-class cabin aboard an Italian liner, the *Duca di Genova*. He immediately took seasick. When he felt better, he roamed the ship a little. Although he was traveling under an assumed identity, as an Italian Jewish merchant, a few people recognized him, and he did not feel the need to tell them to keep his identity confidential. It probably would not have mattered if he had. About the time that Petrosino left New York, two of the suspects whom he had arrested in the barrel murder case and whom he had chased out of New York after breaking up their profitable gambling and counterfeiting operation boarded another ship, the *Romanic*. Was this a coincidence, or did they know Petrosino was on his way to Italy? The timing of their trip suggests these two had some information. As of February 20, everyone had information. On that day, the *New York Herald* carried a story in which Police Commissioner Bingham described Petrosino's "secret" mission in some detail.

The *Duca di Genova* reached Genoa at 6:00 A.M. on February 21. That same day, Petrosino boarded the southbound Paris-to-Rome express at the Genoa railroad station. He got off at Rome, rented a hotel room, and settled down. The next day, he tried to see some officials but faced a barricade of holidays. At that time, the United States observed George Washington's birthday on February 22, and that year February 22 fell on the Tuesday before Ash Wednesday, and so was the last day of celebrating before Catholic Italy observed its penitential season. Petrosino turned tourist for a day, then tried again. By February 27, he had visited U.S. and Italian authorities. On that day, he boarded a southbound train out of Rome, stopped briefly to visit relatives in Padula, boarded the train again, and went to Naples. There, he took a mail boat for Palermo, the capital of the island of Sicily. The two men who had sailed on the *Romanic* were busy, too. Their ship docked in Naples, from which they went to their hometown, Partinico, on the island of Sicily. From Partinico, one sent a telegram back to the United States. Either the message was in code, or the combination of Italian and English rendered it obscure to people for whom it was not intended. However, knowing the name of the recipient was enough to arouse suspicion. He was yet another man arrested and released in the barrel murder case.

The mail boat pulled into Palermo early on February 28. Petrosino checked into the Hotel de France. Like most Italian cities, Palermo had a series of plazas, open squares around which were the facades of public buildings. The square in front of the Hotel de France was a little different. It was not completely open. In the center of the square was another square, the Garibaldi Garden. The garden had thick trees and a high iron fence around it. One could not cross the square diagonally by cutting through the garden; one had to walk around the perimeter of the iron fence. The usual plaza was reduced to a sidewalk around the garden fence. The Hotel de France was on the south side of this square. By going east to the corner and then north to the next corner, Petrosino found a good restaurant, the Cafe Oreto.

From February 28 to March 6, Petrosino followed the same routine: up and out of the hotel in the morning; to the police office of Palermo or to a police office in one of the many surrounding small towns; take notes and maybe make connections with a few informants; dinner at the Cafe Oreto in the early evening; then back to the hotel to type up the day's notes. Occasionally, Petrosino took a break from this routine to visit the post office, where he mailed letters to his wife and documents to Bingham.

On Saturday, March 6, Petrosino visited Palermo Police Commissioner Baldassare Ceola. At this meeting, he expressed his opinion that Italian police were deliberately concealing the criminal records of individuals applying for passports. Ceola tried to explain that there was no deliberate deception involved and that, under certain circumstances, Italian law rehabilitated criminals by suppressing their past records. Ceola also introduced Petrosino to one of his own subordinates, Cavalier Poli, who talked with the American detective at length about his mission. Taciturn by American standards, Petrosino talked just enough for the Italians. Comparing notes on their separate interviews with Petrosino, Ceola and Poli realized the detective's informants had access to confidential information in Italy's judicial system. Ceola asked Petrosino not to leave Palermo without letting the police know; he implied that this was for Petrosino's safety. When he was alone with his subordinate, Ceola asked that Petrosino be allowed to work undisturbed but that he should be watched. It is not clear whether Ceola's orders were followed, for Petrosino resumed his schedule of researching at the Palermo police office and visiting small towns outside the city.

On Friday, March 12, Petrosino finished another day of research, which included a trip outside Palermo to the small town of Caltanissetta and a 4:00 P.M. meeting, probably with an informant. He returned to the Hotel de France about 5:00 P.M., bought a copy of the newspaper in the lobby, and went to his room. There was a rainstorm about 6:00, but it probably did not affect Petrosino's schedule; Italians ate their last meal of the day later than that. At 7:30, Petrosino put on his derby and coat, picked up his umbrella, left the Hotel de France, and walked over to the Cafe Oreto. By 8:45 P.M., his dinner was over.

The evidence suggests that Petrosino had an appointment. He did not exit the Cafe Oreto, walk south to the end of the square, and then turn west to go back to the Hotel de France. He went the long way around the Garibaldi Garden. He walked along the north side of the garden until he had almost reached the northwest corner. Then, did he see who he expected to see? If so, he may have been surprised. He had not expected violence. He had left his police pistol back in the hotel room. But now, some persons produced guns and advanced on Petrosino until his back was to the iron fence, just as one would stand for an execution by firing squad. Then came three rapid gunshots and a slightly delayed fourth shot.

Just north of the Cafe Oreto was the terminal of one of Palermo's trolley lines. A trolley was waiting to begin its rounds, and a number of people were already seated in the trolley waiting for it to go. One of them, an Italian sailor named Alberto Cardella, jumped out of the trolley and ran west to the end of the street to see what had happened. He saw a stocky man, who had been standing against the garden fence, topple over. He saw two other men run away across the street, to an alley between two buildings, the Church of San Giuseppe dei Miracoli and the Palazzo Partanna. He heard a carriage drive away. Then he looked down and realized someone had dropped a gun.

The Palermo police arrived and took over the case. One of them searched the pockets of the victim, realized it was Petrosino, and had Commissioner Ceola summoned from his evening at the theater. The police began questioning employees working around the trolley terminal. They admitted to hearing the shots and seeing "a man and a girl" run off but could not recall anything else. The employees of the Palazzo Partanna, right across the street from the shooting, heard and saw even less. Fortunately, the deceased supplied his own list of suspects. Petrosino was carrying a notebook with a list of those whose criminal records he was checking. The police began to arrest them, and a pattern emerged. The suspects knew each other. All had at one point or another been involved in syndicate crime in Italy, had migrated to the United States, and had compiled criminal records there. Some had only recently returned from the United States—recently enough that they might have been inspired to return because they knew Petrosino was sailing to Italy. It looked as though there had been an international plot to eliminate a man seen as the scourge of the mafia.

As the police reconstructed the execution, they determined that there had been one gunman, Vito Cascio Ferro. One of the conspirators provided a detailed account of how Cascio Ferro conceived the plot, infiltrated Petrosino's informants with double agents, finally presented himself as an informant, gained Petrosino's confidence, then lured him to the northwest corner of the Garibaldi Garden and shot him. Many years later, long after it would have mattered to anyone, Cascio Ferro took credit for the crime. Usually, Cascio Ferro was not the type to kill someone. He was sufficiently high in the ranks of criminals that he sent other people to kill for him. However, he had a special animus against Petrosino. He had been one of those involved in the gambling and counterfeiting ring Petrosino had closed in on during the barrel murder investigation. Although no one had been convicted for that crime, Cascio Ferro had been one of those hounded out of New York, and, in his case, it really did close off an opportunity. Cascio Ferro was the kind of person who could have made a fortune in many honest lines of work. Having chosen crime, he still did well, directing syndicate operations in parts of Sicily. He had even been back in New York once since the barrel murder. But Petrosino had bested him once and had kept him from doing business in his city, and Cascio Ferro wanted revenge.

Police arrested Cascio Ferro in his hometown on April 3, 1909. He was held in jail while the police gathered evidence. Their case, though, began to fall apart on July 17, 1909, when Palermo's police commissioner, Baldassare Ceola, was transferred to Rome and then forcibly retired. The suspects charged with conspiracy were set free, and the investigation was closed on July 22. Cascio Ferro was never convicted of this particular crime. He seems to have died in 1943, while he was in fascist custody for his mafia activities and they were attempting to shift prisoners from a vulnerable prison to a more protected one during the Allied invasion of Italy.

The *New York Herald* broke the story in the United States, receiving information before Petrosino's wife or the New York Police Department heard anything. This was the beginning of the end for Commissioner Bingham. Although it would seem from the timing of their trips to Italy and their telegrams to each other that the conspirators had some other source of information, the publicity Bingham gave to Petrosino's work (and to his own efforts to stamp out the Black Hand) seemed to have placed the detective's life in danger. Plus, Bingham aroused other controversies regarding other ethnic groups and regarding his general handling of the city's crime. The mayor removed Bingham from office that July.

The city was concerned about the widow and infant Petrosino had left behind. At that time, there was no regular arrangement to provide for the dependents of a police officer who died in the line of duty. Assembly representative J. Oliver introduced a bill providing for a pension for Mrs. Petrosino. The bill passed the state assembly, received Mayor George B. McClellan's endorsement, and on May 30 went to Governor Charles E. Hughes for signature.[3] Friends also held at least one benefit that raised $2,500 for the family.[4]

The city also comforted the widow with a tremendous outpouring of respect for the slain detective. In Italy, Petrosino's body was kept at the morgue at the Rotoli Cemetery until Thursday, March 18, when it was moved to the Hostel for the Poor at Corso Calatafimi for embalming. On March 19, the Feast of Saint Joseph and thus Petrosino's name day, the church attached to the hostel held a funeral mass for him.[5] A funeral procession brought the body to the harbor to be sent back to New York aboard a British ship, the Cunard line's *Slavonia*. The ship left on March 23 and arrived in New York a bit behind schedule, on April 9. Monsignor Michael J. Lavelle, who had married the Petrosinos, was the homilist at a second funeral mass, held at Saint Patrick's Old Cathedral on April 12, despite threats from criminal elements that they would blow up the church.[6] Another funeral procession went a few blocks east from Saint Patrick's to Broadway; north to 23rd Street, where Broadway cuts diagonally west of Fifth Avenue; and then north on Fifth Avenue to 42nd Street, where it turned east. At the East River, the funeral party boarded a ferry for the ride to Calvary Cemetery in Queens. The procession brought the city to a halt, as 200,000 mourners lined the sidewalks and watched the casket pass by.

It did not, though, stop the presses. Through the year, the newspapers reported on efforts to track down the criminals. Both newspapers and magazines used the murder to blow apart Petrosino's long-held theory that there was no international mafia. Not only was there a mafia, but it now loomed as incredibly dangerous. Typical was the comment of the *Outlook*: "The crime should at least have one good result: it should concentrate municipal, national and international action to eradicate and crush the type of criminal conspiracy against which Petrosino fought bravely and skillfully for many years and through which he died."[7] The Petrosino murder did what Petrosino least wanted it to do: It fixed firmly in the public's mind that immigrants, particularly Italian immigrants, and criminals were one and the same.

Notes

1. "Petrosino, Detective and Sociologist," *The New York Times* (December 30, 1906): 3.
2. Arrigo Petacco, *Joe Petrosino*, trans. Charles Lam Markmann (New York: Macmillan, 1974), 70, wrote that Saulino had been in the United States 35 years as of 1906.
3. *The New York Times* (March 16, 1909): 2; *The New York Times* (April 6, 1909): 18; *The New York Times* (May 8, 1909): 6; *The New York Times* (May 30, 1909): 8.
4. *The New York Times* (March 15, 1909): 2; *The New York Times* (May 3, 1909): 6.
5. At baptism, Catholics sometimes take the names of saints. In some cultures, the saint's feast day functions as a kind of birthday, with one's friends sending good wishes on that day instead of on one's own birthday. This was the case in late-19th-century Italy.
6. *The New York Times* (April 12, 1923): 19.
7. "Blackmail and Murder," *Outlook* 91 (March 27, 1909): 656.

Bibliography

Joe Petrosino has one biography that was originally in Italian: Arrigo Petacco, *Joe Petrosino*, trans. Charles Lam Markmann (New York: Macmillan, 1974). The English translation has several small errors in its description of the New York situation, so it might be best to check any specific fact against other accounts when possible. Petrosino's death is also an element in the stories told in Thomas Monroe Pitkin with Francesco Cordasco, *The Black Hand: A Chapter in Ethnic Crime* (Totowa, NJ: Littlefield, Adams, 1977); and Humbert Nelli, *The Business of Crime: Italians and Syndicate Crime in the United States* (New York: Oxford University Press, 1976). Petrosino has no papers in the sense that others described in these biographies do. However, *The New York Times* covered the story; one can retrieve the citations to the articles through its index and then check the rival newspapers for the same dates for more details. More background is available in the articles indexed under "Black Hand" in *The Reader's Guide to Periodical Literature* for the 1900s.

Refugees at Oswego

Kathleen R. Warnes

> Mother of Exiles. From her
> beacon-hand Glows world-wide welcome
> Give me your tired, your poor,
> Your huddled masses yearning to breathe free.[1]

After decades of State Department stonewalling and indifference to the fate of the Jews in Europe under the Nazi regime, President Franklin Delano Roosevelt in 1944, "invited" 1,000 refugees to come to Fort Ontario, near Oswego, New York, to be his "guests" for the duration of the war. As a condition of circumventing the stringent immigration laws, the refugees had to sign a pledge promising to return to Europe at the end of the war, since they had no legal right to be in the United States. This seeming act of compassion rekindled hope in the hearts and minds of 982 refugees, most of whom had lost homes and families in the European Holocaust. Most of them believed they would find a haven in the United States. Instead, they foundered in a swamp of frustration, despair, and soulless bureaucracy before they could finally find solid ground and repatriation in the United States. President Roosevelt's executive order establishing the War Refugee Board that brought this first and only group of refugees into wartime America, was, in fact, not an act of compassion at all. At best, it was an act of self-interested humanitarianism and, at worst, a cynical answer to a Treasury Department report about State Department obstructive refugee policies.

When the United States contemplated the question of immigrants and refugees in the 1920s and 1930s, it did so with a restrictionist attitude. Part of this attitude stemmed from Attorney General Mitchell Palmer's "red scare" raids after World War I and the idea that unrestricted immigration admitted anarchists and communists into the United States. The Great Depression and the economic difficulties of the 1930s further restricted immigration, especially President Herbert Hoover's instructions to the State Department to stringently enforce the LPC (Likely to become a Public Charge) clause of the 1924 Immigration Act. This meant that a potential immigrant had to provide an affidavit from a sponsoring party (family member, relatives) assuming financial responsibility for him or her. The law stipulated that the affidavit could be from only one party. Corporate affidavits were not permitted. In fact, many Jewish organizations tried to sponsor refugees but could not legally do so under the immigration law.[2]

When Hitler came to power in 1933, he and his Nazi Party began to wage a campaign of terror and extortion against the Jews in Germany. At this time, Nazi policy encouraged immigration; extermination did not become policy until after the invasion of the Soviet Union in 1941. One day after Pearl Harbor—December 8, 1941—Hitler declared war on the United States, and by December 1942, American officials knew that the Nazis were systematically murdering Jews. Still, the United States did not change its immigration laws, and State Department administrative policies filled only 10 percent of immigration quota slots. By 1944, America's refugee conscience had many sins of omission staining it. Public opinion in the United States opposed increasing immigration quotas, but there was much support for the idea of free ports—the idea that, just as certain goods could be accepted in free ports as long as they were later shipped elsewhere, so could refugees be admitted if they were placed in camps until the end of the war and then sent back home or any other place in the world.

A government agency with a mandate to help Jews would contribute substantially to pressure neutral nations to accept refugees, fund escape efforts, and generally act as refugee clearinghouse. In 1944, 14 months after the U.S. government learned of the death camps, President Franklin Delano Roosevelt created the War Refugee Board by executive order.

Why did the United States decide at this 1944 late date to finally open its doors to a sizeable group of refugees? What obstacles to freedom did the refugees face after their arrival in the United States? What ironies and ambiguities were apparent in the American attitudes and treatment of the refugees? And why did it take two years and a presidential proclamation to finally award U.S. citizenship to people who had suffered so much? The answers to these questions are as complex as the questions themselves and intertwine the lives of many people, including President Roosevelt, Secretary of Treasury Henry Morgenthau Jr., Secretary of the Interior Harold Ickes, and Dr. Ruth Gruber, a noted journalist and Ickes's special assistant. Refugees Manya Hartmeyer Breuer, Walter Greenberg, and Ivo Lederer, whose stories are representative of their 979 compatriots, played central roles in the drama, and the refugees significantly impacted the lives of Oswego residents such as Geraldine Desens Rossiter and Edmund Waterbury.

Guests of FDR

President Franklin Delano Roosevelt (FDR) began the Oswego refugee story in January 1944, when he signed Executive Order 9417, creating the War Refugee

Board. His reasons for doing this were political and humanitarian. The War Refugee Board (WRB) had several purposes. One was to establish free ports or havens and bring refugees to the United States. Another was to fund overseas rescue operations, such as the one that rescued Hungarian Jews in the summer of 1944. In this operation, the WRB funded the rescue work of Raoul Wallenberg, the Swedish diplomat, who saved about 100,000 Hungarian Jews.

The antecedents of the WRB can be traced to late 1943, when Secretary of Treasury Henry Morgenthau Jr., a Jew, and some of his Treasury Department staff members, investigated the State Department's deliberate stonewalling of immigration quotas. This policy began in the 1920s with Undersecretary of State Wilbur Carr, who followed Hoover's presidential mandate to be certain that refugees were financially backed. Evidence suggests that Carr had moderate complaints against the Jews; he was not infected with the virulent anti-Semitism of his contemporary, Father Charles Coughlin, and his protégée, Undersecretary of State Breckinridge Long. Instead, Carr concerned himself more with implementing the administrative procedures that he had instituted in a badly needed State Department reform and following immigration rules and regulations to the letter.

When FDR placed Breckinridge Long in charge of the visa division of the U.S. State Department, this put the final seal on the fate of thousands of European Jews desperate to immigrate. In 1938, Long had managed to circumvent an FDR initiative to ease the immigration restrictions and instead had tightened them further.[3]

Josiah DuBois, of the Treasury Department, spent Christmas Day 1943 writing a "Report to the Secretary on the Acquiescence of this Government in the Murder of the Jews." Drawing on his 30-year close friendship with the President, Treasury Secretary Morgenthau presented this report to FDR on January 16, 1944, at a Sunday meeting at the White House. President Roosevelt immediately established the War Refugee Board.

Roosevelt's conscience did not prod him. He had known the facts of the Holocaust for years, but his acute political instincts warned him that the rescue issue would become a political flash point. He realized that the Senate would make the Treasury Department report public and Congress would probably create a refugee board. Moving to avert a scandal, he established the War Refugee Board to checkmate Congress. By creating the War Refugee Board, he addressed criticisms that the United States was not doing enough to help Jewish refugees and bypassed the restrictionist State Department. The War Refugee Board opened the shelter at Fort Ontario, an abandoned army base, in Oswego, New York, and planned to establish other camps before the war ended.[4]

Altogether, the War Refugee Board saved the lives of 200,000 Jews out of 6 million killed. Historian David Wyman affirms that "the board did prove that a few good people—Christians and Jews—could finally break through the walls of indifference. The great shame is that if Roosevelt had created the board a year earlier and if it had been truly empowered, the War Refugee Board could have saved tens of thousands, even hundreds of thousands more and, in the process, have rescued the conscience of the nation."[5]

To the 982 refugees arriving in Oswego, New York, in August 1944, the "conscience of a nation" was alive and active, even though 55,000 additional quota places for refugees remained unused that year. Emotionally and physically reeling from their European and transatlantic ordeal, the refugees literally and figuratively kissed American soil and savored the air of freedom. Manya Hartmeyer Breuer expressed what it meant to come to the United States:

> I was hiding in a convent, a Catholic convent in Rome, Italy, at the time it was liberated, in 1944, the 5th of June. After the liberation I was chosen, through a big miracle, to come to the United States. That was quite an experience, because I never dreamed that such was possible. Number one, the war was still going on. Number two, for many years my parents tried to make it to the United States, but they were not issued a visa to come here. They had an affidavit from New York, from my father's cousin, and they waited for years and years to be able to come here, but they never made it . . . I found myself alone in this convent, where I was of course, protected, but in mortal danger because even there the Germans came in. They had penetrated, they had overwhelmed Italy, Rome. It was very close, every day, to be deported. I knew that when they get me I would not come out alive.[6]

Walter Greenberg recalled his feelings in the summer of 1994, when he was recording an interview for the 50-year reunion of the refugees; he described his feelings in that summer of 1944.

> That summer of 1944 was being born again. And as with every birth, there was amazement of the miracle of new life, and also the restlessness of growth and achievement. Lake Ontario was for me an ocean, separating the Old World, the years of insanity, a time when world amnesia and a bankrupt and amoral society allowed the stench of burning human flesh, and with the death of six million Jews, ended the worst chapter in a supposedly organized, cultured, civilized society. Remember that the victim, oppressor, and yes, the spectator, are involved in the never-ending struggle between the forces of evil and goodness. And what is important for me is not really the question of whether to be or not to be, but rather how to be.[7]

Manya Hartmeyer Breuer, Walter Greenberg, and other refugees made their way to the U.S. army transport *Henry Gibbins*, anchored in the harbor on the Bay of Naples. The *Gibbins* would transport the refugees and hundreds of men wounded at Anzio and other European battles across the Atlantic Ocean to New York.

In June 1944, Secretary Ickes had appointed journalist Ruth Gruber, the daughter of Russian Jewish immigrants, his special assistant. He assigned her the duty of traveling to Italy to bring the 982 Jewish refugees to the United States. She was airlifted to the ship in a suit, white gloves, and a pair of sailor's pants and immediately began her job of expediting the 15-day Atlantic voyage for the refugees. Her duties included teaching English classes for the refugees, helping them stage musical performances to ease the monotony of shipboard life, comforting the refugees during Nazi U-boat and bomber raids, and building bridges between the wounded soldiers and the refugees. She recalled the government criteria for choosing which refugees would immigrate. The government officials making the selection chose families and survivors with skills that could help run a camp in the United States. The first priority was refugees who had been in concentration camps and escaped.

President Roosevelt also mandated that there be an ethnic and religious mix of refugees. Included in the group were Jews, Catholics, and Protestants and more than 18 different nationalities. Even at this juncture, FDR did not want to be accused of being too favorable toward Jews. There originally had been 1,000 refugees, but 18 had dropped out of the immigration process for various reasons.[8]

Secretary Ickes chose the right person to facilitate the difficult voyage. Born in Brooklyn, New York, in 1911, Ruth Gruber was one of the five children of David and Gussie Gruber, Russian Jewish immigrants. She entered college at the age of 15 and graduated with a PhD in literature at the age of 20. She won a Guggenheim Foundation Fellowship in 1935 to study women under fascism, communism, and democracy, and, while in Germany, she witnessed Hitler's rise to power and the accompanying anti-Semitism. Beginning her career as a journalist, Gruber wrote for *The New York Times* and the *New York Herald Tribune*, and she became the first foreign correspondent allowed to fly into Siberia. Here, she interviewed pioneers and prisoners, many of them Jews, in Stalin's Society Gulag and compiled the interviews in a book called *I Went to the Soviet Arctic*.[9]

For her latest assignment, Ickes gave Gruber the honorary rank of general, because if the Nazis captured her as a civilian, they could execute her as a spy. As a general, the Nazis would theoretically have to feed and shelter her as a prisoner of war. Ruth Gruber interviewed the refugees and wrote their stories as the *Henry Gibbins* made its long and dangerous voyage across the Atlantic.

In her book *Haven*, Gruber notes some of the problems and ironies that followed the refugees on their voyage to freedom. Many of the refugees were dismayed to discover that they would be put into a camp in the United States. To them, a camp meant a Nazi death camp. Early in the voyage, Gruber and the other rescue officials discovered that the wounded U.S. soldiers blamed the "damned Jews" for each enemy attack and demanded to know why they were traveling to the United States on the same ship. Gruber and her colleagues acted as liaisons between the soldiers and refugees and brought them together in musicals and plays.[10]

Ruth Gruber, second from left, laughs with New York Governor Mario Cuomo and others during an August 4, 1984, reunion of Jewish refugees marking the 40th anniversary of the day a ship carrying a thousand refugees escaping Hitler arrived in New York. (AP/Wide World Photos)

During the voyage, the refugees talked excitedly about the friends and relatives they anticipated seeing in the United States. They mulled over plans for the new lives that they intended to begin when they disembarked. Before they left Italy, all of them had to sign a statement, which read, in part:

> I declare that I have fully understood the following conditions of the offer of the United States Government and that I have accepted them: I shall be brought to a reception center in Fort Ontario in the State of New York, where I shall remain as a guest of the United States until the end of the war. Then I must return to my homeland.[11]

The refugees signed the agreement because they knew that immigration was a chance for a new life for them and their families. Some of them felt that surely they would be permitted to stay in the United States if they proved themselves to be solid, productive citizens. Some did not understand the full terms of the agreement because of language and cultural barriers. Some believed the sales pitches of officials anxious for them to immigrate. Some fully intended to be and were repatriated to their homelands after the war. And some hoped for the best in the worst of situations. Peter Ouroussoff, a Russian émigré, said, "We have signed a paper saying we would return to our homeland. But where is it? We have none. For us to go back is suicide." Carl Selan voiced their hope. "If we could stay here, America would find many of us would be assets. . . . We want only to obey the law, to have peace, liberty."[12]

The irony is that American restrictionists used the agreement the refugees signed against them to attempt to force them to return to countries and families that did not exist after the war. But Nazi prisoners of war turned out to be a greater irony than anti-Semitism and repatriation for the refugees. Two ships in the convoy with the *Henry Gibbins* carried Nazi prisoners of war (POWs). Ruth Gruber was appalled at the disproportionate numbers of Nazi POWs (some 100,000) and the refugees in her charge.

> We're bringing in Nazi soldiers who killed our boys on the beaches of France and in Italy. And no one complains, not one word. . . . We waited so long that millions died before we could get even these one thousand refugees into the U.S. And Lord only knows what the isolationists in Congress can still do to us after we land.[13]

The Guests Arrive

After two cramped, seasick, hot, and dangerous weeks, the *Henry Gibbins* glided into New York Harbor. The refugees thrilled at the sight of the Statue of Liberty. Refugee Ivo Lederer said, "If you're coming from war-time, war-damaged Europe to see this enormous sight, lower Manhattan and the Statue of Liberty, I don't think there was a dry eye on deck."[14]

The refugees soon encountered other symbols that reawakened painful memories. They had to wear tags that said, "Army Surplus Baggage." Trains, reminding them of cattle cars and death camps, carried them north to Oswego and Fort Ontario. Uniformed military police and security soldiers from the army, navy, and Coast Guard helped transport the refugees. Uniforms and their connotations terrified the refugees. Armed guards and a six-foot, chain-linked, barbed-wire fence welcomed them to their new home at Oswego. Townspeople and area residents lined up along the fence to stare at the refugees. From behind the fence, the refugees stared back. The armed soldiers kept watchful eyes on the people on both sides of the fence.[15]

On August 6, 1944, Joseph H. Smart, Director of the Emergency Refugee Shelter, greeted the refugees at Fort Ontario. He told them that the shelter was the only one in the United States and that President Roosevelt had appointed the War Relocation Authority, an agency of the United States Department of the Interior, to run it. Another irony in a situation filled with ironies is that the War Relocation Authority was the same agency that oversaw the internment of Japanese American citizens. Smart probably did not mention this fact before he introduced Dillon S. Myer, national director of the War Relocation Authority, who read a message from Secretary of the Interior Harold Ickes. Part of Ickes's message included this statement: "I hope that this haven from the intolerance, suffering, and persecution that you have undergone will in some measure ease your tragic memories."[16]

Instead of easing tragic memories, the routine delousing that the army gave its returning soldiers and now the refugees, brought them back with nightmare vividness. The parallels to the delousing process in the Nazi camps brought frightening images to the minds and senses of the refugees as they went through the process. David Hendel recalled that, "after we got our clothes back we looked like real refugees." Mrs. Fred Baum, the former Jenny Baruch, was 18 years old when she went through the delousing. She always remembered the terrified screams of the people who did not understand what was happening.[17]

Some of the 983 civilian war refugees from Europe are shown outside the mess hall buildings at Fort Ontario, Oswego, NY, August 5, 1944. (AP/Wide World Photos)

Soon the refugees met their neighbors. Oswego, population 22,962, had previously been hostile to black soldiers that the government had quartered at the fort until the soldiers had proven that they were peaceable and profitable to the town. Some townspeople groused that now they had to put up with Jews and asked what they had done to make the government angry. Others were curious about the refugees, and many wondered what they could do to help them. During the first two weeks after their arrival, crowds of townspeople gathered outside the fence to stare at the refugees. Several people passed gifts of food and clothing through the fence.

Geraldine Desens remembered that her father told her not to go to the fort because of the armed guards. Of course, she immediately rode her bicycle down to see the refugees. She organized a human pyramid and passed the bicycle over the fence so refugee children could ride it. Every day, Geraldine went to the camp, bringing what gifts she could to the refugees. She recalled:

> The people in Oswego where I worked, businessmen and lawyers, I heard them saying, "Oh, they have the best places, and the latest oven and stoves," and all this, which was absolutely untrue. They lived in the barracks. They each had two small rooms, cots to sleep on, wooden chairs to sit on, one bathroom for the whole floor, down at the end of the hall. I know Mr. Smart lived in one of the old colonels' homes. Those are nice homes. But not the refugees.[18]

The refugees were quarantined for the first month they were in camp while the government debated what to do with them and tested public opinion. Loved ones could not visit them, and they were not allowed to leave the camp. The only official visitor the refugees had during their quarantine was Ruth Gruber. Part of President Roosevelt's accommodations for his guests included restricted freedom. They could not live outside the camp or travel more than 20 miles outside it, even after the quarantine was lifted. They could obtain limited passes to Oswego and the surrounding area. These restrictions are not too different from the same strictures placed on Japanese American internees. Immediately, many camp residents wiggled under the fence to visit town, and the numbers increased to the point that there were two lines of under-the-fence traffic at most hours of the day. Several young men crawled under the fence and made secret trips to New York City to visit relatives.

Walter Greenberg described the feelings of the refugees when he said, "I felt deceived. I felt that I should have been free. I mean, I felt wonderful. I had doctors. I had nurses. I had food. I came to school. Oswegonians were very kind. . . . What good is it to have all the amenities of life if one still isn't free?"[19]

Many of the refugees had close relatives in the United States and expectations about what they would do in America. Three hundred of the refugees had already

registered for immigration, and one-third of those had affidavits of support from U.S. citizens. Fifty-one people had nonquota visas because they had American spouses or adult children, and 34 families had relatives serving in the U.S. armed forces. More than one-third of the refugees had immediate family living in the United States. Many had Americanized ambitions. They wanted to have their children enrolled in American schools or attain professional and vocational goals, and some wanted American medical care. They needed to recuperate from their European ordeals. Many had been refugees for years and had seen family members brutally murdered. Almost 100 had been in Dachau or Buchenwald and suffered hunger and disease.

Welcome to Our America

As the refugees settled into the barracks at Oswego, government agencies debated their legal status, which was ambiguous because they had entered the United States outside the usual immigration laws. The War Department wanted to register them as aliens under the Alien Registration Law. If this happened, they could be both legally and politically recognized. The Department of Justice argued that they could not be registered as aliens because they were not considered aliens. German POWs were registered as aliens and enjoyed the benefits of this status. The 982 "guests of President Roosevelt" lived in a stateless, paperless, homeless limbo.

Ruth Gruber tells the story of Manya Hartmeyer's marriage to Ernest Breuer to illustrate the refugees' difficult status. The young couple had first attempted to marry aboard the *Henry Gibbins*, but the captain could not marry them because it was a war ship. Now, Gruber had to find out whether the War Refugee Board would allow them to marry during the quarantine, whether New York State would consider them residents and issue a marriage license, and whether the WRB would allow them to leave the camp to register at city hall so they could get a license. Gruber finally managed to cut the red tape so they could marry on Thursday, August 17, 1944. Breuer reminisced about her Oswego wedding:

> I was very lucky we had wonderful friends here. We made a wonderful friend in Oswego itself, that came every week to visit me and my husband. It was a family by the name of Tompkins. Mae Tompkins became my first American friend. She came and brought me a golden wedding band that Diane (my daughter) is wearing. In fact she doesn't take it off. Mae Tompkins gave me that ring, and she gave me hope, and she gave me a lot of love. And healed a lot of wounds in my heart.[20]

Others ran into the same legal stone walls that the Breuers did. Joscph Flink, a sergeant in the army, called Gruber from New York. He had discovered that his parents were in the Oswego camp. He could talk to them, but they could not see each other until the quarantine was lifted. In Queens, New York, Mrs. Hugo Graner read the list of the 982 refugees in the paper and discovered her husband's name. She called him and discovered they would not be able to see each other until the quarantine ended.[21]

Sitting at her desk at the camp one morning, Ruth Gruber heard screams of joy. She ran to the window to see what had happened. Seventeen-year-old Miriam Weinstein was shouting to her six brothers and sisters that their mother was alive. She had read in a German-language newspaper published in New York that their mother was in Switzerland looking for them. Gruber sent the mother in Switzerland a cable telling her that her children were safe, but the family could not reunite. The children could not leave town after the quarantine lifted, because they were outside the immigration quota, and the war made it impossible to send them to Switzerland or bring their mother to the United States.[22]

A letter from Dillon Myer, War Refugee Board director, to camp director Joseph Smart at the end of August symbolized the plight of refugees wanting to live elsewhere or bring their families to camp. The letter concerned Hans Foefler, who wanted to have his father residing in camp, whom he had not seen for five and a half years, come and live with him. Myer cited President Franklin Roosevelt's cablegram of June 9, 1944, which stated that the refugees would be placed in an Emergency Refugee Shelter "where under appropriate security restrictions they will remain for the duration of the war."[23] Myer explained that no refugee could reside outside the shelter "even though their immediate family members in other communities may be in a position to receive and care for them."[24]

Word of the refugees spread across the country. *Life* magazine came to Oswego around the same time the Breuers married, and Alfred Eisenstaedt's pictures featured bewildered people lining up for towels and soap, people peering through the fence, people peering hopefully into the future. The article and pictures appearing on Monday, August 17, 1944, were so sympathetic that hundreds of letters poured into the camp from Americans wanting to help the refugees. Refugee Edith Semjen, whose partisan uniform set off her blond beauty, received marriage proposals from men from Maine to California. Soldiers wrote her that they had pinned her *Life* photo in their lockers and offered to "get her away from that fence and free her."[25]

During the month-long quarantine, newspaper stories emphasized that the refugees were deeply grateful to the United States and required little expenditure for their upkeep. On August 6, the *New York Herald Tribune* reported that the daily diets cost 43½ cents and caused incredulous comments among people who considered them "feasts." *The New York Times* described a mother explaining the use of a pillow to a puzzled child. Other refugees had survived in caves, so clean beds and a door with a key brought wonderment and joy.[26]

Mail delivery caused some temporary problems. The National Refugee Service had arranged for a list of the refugees to be published in its Special Information Bulletin, so they could correspond with friends and relatives, and it provided foreign-language newspapers, periodicals, and books for the camp library. Mail from family and friends comforted the refugees as they settled into the Fort Ontario shelter.[27]

Camp director Joseph Smart wrote a letter to WRB director Dillon Myer in Washington, DC, in late August 1944 about mail. From the camp's inception, the army's Office of Censorship had censored incoming and outgoing mail, and many people resented the practice, calling it illegal and un-American. Smart wrote:

> For the refugees, the administrative staff and myself I would like to protest in the strongest terms possible against this policy. In our view it is wholly unwarranted for reasons of security or any other reasons. It is unworkable and unenforceable since it is a simple matter to pass mail in and out of the shelter by unapproved methods even if the people were confined here as prisoners.[28]

Spirits in camp lifted in September, with the revoking of the quarantine and the mail problem improved. Eventually the War Department abolished all mail restrictions. With the lifting of the quarantine, visitors poured into the camp. Families were reunited, and some visitors created tidal waves of excitement throughout the camp. First Lady Eleanor Roosevelt and Mrs. Henry Morgenthau Jr., arrived in camp on September 20, 1944, on an unescorted, unofficial visit. Mrs. Roosevelt and her company attended a service in the Orthodox synagogue, visited all five kitchens, and toured the barracks. Refugees wanting desperately to remain in the United States took heart from her visit, because they felt that her visit meant that she was sympathetic to their cause.

The end of the quarantine and the visitors caused quite a stir in the normally quiet city of Oswego. Oswegonians reacted with mixed feelings. On one hand, the refugees seemed to be stimulating an economic boom. When the visitors rushed to Oswego, the town's two hotels quickly filled and a number of residents opened their homes to paying guests. Rumor had it that the refugees had wealthy New York relatives who would spend large amounts of money in Oswego. The flip side of the rumor machine was not as positive. Some Oswegonians accused the government of giving the refugees new electric stoves and refrigerators in the face of wartime shortages. Other Oswegonians charged that the army was drafting Oswego men to fight, while some of the "huskier" refugees were living a life of ease in the camp. Soldiers and farmers who were short of hands scowled at these rumors.[29]

The War Refugee Board decided to squelch as many rumors as it could, and with the support of Edwin Waterbury, publisher of the *Oswego Palladium Times*, camp director Joseph Smart and community leaders established a "rumor clinic."

The newspaper printed and refuted all manner of rumor. For instance, the *Palladium Times* reported that relatives of Oswego residents did not drive on rationed gas from California to the camp to visit. The car with California license plates belonged to a WRA worker.[30] Waterbury calculated that 90 percent of the population of Oswego accepted the refugees, and the remaining 10 percent did not have any real influence. But the anti-Semitism of the United States of the 1930s and 1940s had tainted some Oswegonians. To some, *refugee* meant *Jew*, and the ideas of rich New York relatives and fit men evading work and war were anti-Semitic stereotypes. Geraldine Rossiter, the bicycle pyramid organizer, remembers being called a "Jew lover." One Oswego housewife snorted, "If they're so intellectual and such a high type, I guess there won't be a chance of getting a servant among them." But for the most part, Oswegonians did not make anti-Semitic remarks to the refugees. Waterbury represented most Oswegonians when he said, "I don't think any of us expected there would be so many outstanding people at the Fort."[31]

Besides anti-Semitism and lack of freedom, labor problems, German POWs, and the weather were the most vexing issues for the refugees and their advocates. Dillon Myer wanted to establish light industry in the camp, but government regulations prohibited manufacturing goods that would compete against American products on the open market. Outside companies deluged the WRB with requests for workers, but the WRB worried that permitting outside work would sabotage its efforts to establish additional camps. The WRB permitted 50 refugees to briefly work in nearby orchards and in the local Birds Eye storage plant during the fall of 1944, because it feared that a refusal would provoke local hostility. It did not approve subsequent requests, because employees did not press the issue and the WRB preferred to generate as little adverse publicity about the refugees as possible.[32]

Despite the lack of work and the low wages, most refugees—even the most debilitated ones—wanted to support their families and contribute to the country that had rescued them. September registration for orchard and canning work drew 246 applicants, more than five times the number of workers needed. The *Oswego Palladium Times* again spoke out for the refugees. Waterbury told Ruth Gruber, "It's an outrage that they aren't permitted to help solve the difficult work problems created by the manpower shortage and that they are treated worse than German or Italian prisoners of war. We pamper the Nazi prisoners while these innocent people whom the Nazis tried to kill are treated as though they were Nazis. I just don't get it."[33]

German POWs continued to be a tragic counterpoint for the Fort Ontario refugees. The United States accepted 372,000 German POWs, out of a total of 425,000 enemy POWs. Every state except Nevada, North Dakota, and Vermont had a POW camp that helped to ease the United States' critical labor shortage. Near Oswego, 2 base camps and 11 satellite facilities housed 4,500 German POWs.

German prisoners had helped prepare Fort Ontario for the refugees and were still completing the groundwork when the refugees arrived. A poignant encounter took place between a group of refugee teenagers exploring the camp and a group of the POW workers. Finding Nazis right in their refugee camp, refugee Walter Arnstein and his friends yelled in German, "We are Jews . . . You understand, you pigs? Jews! You didn't get us all!" One of the Germans stepped up and made a wide, seeping, exaggerated bow. The others laughed wildly. Before the teenagers could do anything else, the POWs' supervisor ordered both groups to mind their own business.[34]

The refugees could not understand the German POW presence in America. Prisoners of war in the United States had more privileges and rights than the refugees did. American alien registration defined the POWs' legal status, and the Geneva Convention spelled out the government's obligation to them. American employers, the War Department, and the Roosevelt administration all welcomed the POW presence. Employers wanted to hire them, and they paid the POWs better wages than Oswego refugees earned. The Fort Ontario refugees were bewildered and angry when they discovered that the United States paid Germans to work in American orchards while American farmers fought them in Europe. The shelter residents did not know that WRB backers had promised to treat them as they did the POWs, and if this had been done, the refugees would have enjoyed the same advantages the POWs did.

After the refugees felt the initial relief of reaching the United States and seeing their children enrolled in American schools, the shock of the chain-link and barbed-wire fence and restricted movement remained. When the harsh Oswego winter came, the refugees realized that they might be facing a confinement as long and harsh as the winter. They had come from sunny Italy, and most did not have the stamina or the experience for winter weather in Oswego. Many suffered fractures from falling on the snow and ice, and camp director Smart reported that many had to rely on others to bring meals to them. Even robust people had trouble moving from building to building. When Lake Ontario winds whipped through the wooden barracks and water pipes burst, everyone became obsessed with keeping warm and dry.

Paranoia and other refugee confinement problems intensified at the camp during the winter months, to the point that the WRA sent expert counsel, Curt Bondy, chairman of the Department of Psychology at Richmond Professional Institute of William and Mary College, to investigate. Bondy said that the Fort Ontario shelter had problems similar to those of all internment camps, but it experienced some circumstantial difficulties. Many refugees suffered from loss of freedom and status, which made them feel isolated and degraded. Some changes had to be made in work, refugee representation, and discipline. He felt the camp should be closed, but if that could not be done, he wanted to introduce a visiting program, better jobs, and better camp discipline.[35]

Bondy's report got mixed reviews in Washington, DC. Interior Secretary Ickes was frustrated by his lack of complete authority over the shelter and the array of problems he had to solve. Exasperated, he wondered whether the dissatisfied refugees should return to Europe or go wherever "they would be more likely to merge into the social environment."[36]

In an April 1945 letter to William O'Dwyer, Executive Director of the War Relocation Board, Secretary Ickes urgently recommended a program of sponsored leave for the Fort Ontario refugees. Secretary Ickes saw "no justification for maintaining the refugees at Fort Ontario at public expense, when relatives and friends of the refugees and private agencies are willing and eager to assume full responsibility for their care." He recommended that the War Relocation Board reunite refugees with their relatives wherever possible, help relocate refugees, and award them sponsored leave. He also urged the Department of Justice to register the refugees so that they would be subject to the "same controls as residents of the United States," who are technically aliens of enemy nationality.[37]

Wearing Out the Welcome?

April 1945 proved to be a watershed month for the Fort Ontario shelter. Ruth Gruber visited and wrote a report of her visit for Interior Secretary Ickes. She wrote that, for most of the refugees, "the camp has meant new life." Refugees were beginning the process of Americanization, so Gruber recommended closing the camp as soon as possible. True, the refugees had signed a release in Italy promising to return at the end of the war. But now Ickes, Gruber, and many other Americans knew them well enough to realize that they were not spies or subversives. She concluded her report by stating, "We should permit those who are eligible for entry to the United States to cross the border into Canada and re-enter the United States under regular quotas on an individual basis. It is time we showed that this administration has a policy of decency, humanity, and conscience and the guts to carry that policy through."[38]

On April 12, 1945, the refugee shelter and the nation mourned the death of Franklin D. Roosevelt. The refugees wrote a full-page obituary, which was published in the camp newspaper, the *Ontario Chronicle*. The people recited the Kaddish, the prayer for the dead, and many of them cried. President Roosevelt had invited them to the United States. Now he was dead. What would become of his invited guests?[39]

At the end of April, camp director Joseph Smart answered his door one night. Three of the most distinguished refugees stood on his doorstep. Dr. Otto Lederer; Dr. Arthur Ernst, editor in chief of the camp *Ontario Chronicle*; and Dr. Edmund Landau, associate editor of the *Chronicle*, told him that they had received reliable information that all of the refugees were to be deported on June 30 and that the War Department had even committed a ship to transport them.

The men decided that they needed powerful allies to approach the new president, Harry S. Truman, and convince him to allow the refugees to remain in the

United States. Smart decided that the best course of action for him would be to resign so he could fully advocate for the refugees. He served on a committee that included Eleanor Roosevelt and Senator Robert A. Taft of Ohio, and they worked to win support to keep the refugees in America. Stories in the *New York Daily News* and the *Jewish Morning Journal* confirmed that General O'Dwyer, the new executive director of the War Refugee Board, would shut down the camp and wind up the work of the War Refugee Board by June 30, 1945. The disposition of the refugees remained up in the air. O'Dwyer suggested that perhaps the Department of the Interior would take full responsibility for the camp when the War Refugee Board shut down. The other possibilities were the State and Justice Departments.

Back at Fort Ontario, the refugees worried about deportation. The mayor of Oswego and 27 leading citizens sent a petition to President Truman and to Congress on May 27 asking that the refugees be allowed to stay. The refugees were encouraged, but Congress remained silent. Then, New York Congressman Samuel Dickstein, chairman of the House Committee on Immigration and Naturalization, announced that he planned to investigate the camp. Interior Secretary Ickes, Ruth Gruber, and a delegation from several Jewish refugee committees went to the office of Secretary of Treasury Morgenthau and presented the argument for allowing the Oswego refugees to remain in the United States. Morgenthau listened to the arguments, then he said, "You're asking that we change the instructions issued by the President. We wrote those instructions here. . . . I can't go back on my promise to the dead President. I couldn't sleep with my conscience."[40]

Morgenthau had also had trouble sleeping when his wife came back from Oswego after her visit with Eleanor Roosevelt. He said that his wife had kept him awake quizzing him about the camp. In the end, Morgenthau said that Congress held the solution to the problem. General O'Dwyer transferred the powers and responsibility for the War Refugee Board to the War Relocation Authority, which was under Harold Ickes at the Department of the Interior. Secretary Ickes sent a letter to President Truman requesting permission to close the camp in 30 days and grant the refugees sponsored leave. Before President Truman could act, Congressman Dickstein announced that, on Monday, June 25, Subcommittee VI of the House Committee on Immigration and Naturalization would begin its investigation of the camp.

A congressional delegation visited the Oswego shelter and interviewed the refugees. Edmund Waterbury, the *Oswego Palladium-Times* publisher, risked his career in Oswego when he testified, "There is more talent in this group than there is in all of Oswego together, and I am not discrediting my own hometown, but when you get painting, sculpture, music, acting, dancing, and play righting, they would do credit to a city of five hundred thousand population."[41]

The subcommittee voted unanimously to allow the refugees to remain in the United States. When the full House committee assembled in Washington, DC,

Dickstein summarized the testimony in the camp. But many of the full committee were isolationists, and the debate and politicking intensified. Dickstein read the resolution asking the government to allow the refugees at Fort Ontario to leave the camp, and it passed unanimously, but the isolationists lobbied hard and the full House committee tabled the resolution. On Friday, July 6, 1945, the House Immigration and Naturalization Committee voted that the Departments of State and Justice should investigate the possibility of returning the refugees to their homelands. If repatriation did not look feasible, then the Attorney General should institute deportation proceedings. Months passed, but on December 5, 1945, the Departments of Justice and State prepared a letter to be signed by Interior Secretary Ickes, Attorney General Tom C. Clark, and Secretary of State James F. Byrnes. The letter, recommending that the refugees leave the United States, was to be sent to the chairmen of both House and Senate committees on immigration and naturalization. Ickes refused to sign the letter. Instead, he asked Ruth Gruber to draft a letter to Undersecretary of State Dean Acheson, explaining the pro-refugee position and deliver it to him, since Secretary of State James Byrnes was out of town. In addition to her letter, Gruber prepared documents to show Acheson the character of the refugees at Fort Ontario. She included a letter from William Green, president of the American Federation of Labor, pleading that the refugees be allowed to stay. Gruber hoped that Green's letter would eliminate the argument of other labor leaders that they refugees might take jobs away from U.S. citizens.[42]

Acheson agreed to meet with Gruber and her delegation on Wednesday, December 12, 1945. The delegation consisted of Joseph Chamberlain of the National Refugee Committee; Clarence Pickett, executive secretary of the American Friends Service Committee; Judge Nathan Perlman of the American Jewish Congress; Isaiah Minkoff, director of the National Jewish Community Relations Advisory Committee; and Bruce Mohler of the National Catholic Welfare Conference, who had come as the personal representative of Archbishop Spellman of New York. The delegation walked from the Department of the Interior to the State Department and waited for Acheson in a large reception room. The meeting was postponed for three hours, and then Acheson appeared and told them he was going to see the President the next day and he would get back to them.[43]

President Truman's Christmas Present

On Saturday morning, December 22, 1945, while working at her office desk, Ruth Gruber turned on the radio to listen to the news. She heard the announcer say that President Truman would make a major statement on immigration and refugees from the White House that evening. In his speech that evening, Truman said that, to the extent that existing immigration laws permitted, everything possible should be done at once to facilitate the entrance of displaced persons and refugees from

Europe into the United States. He said that 3,900 refugees could enter the United States each month under the law, and the quotas would not change.[44] In the middle of his speech came the words that Ruth Gruber and her friends were hoping to hear. President Truman reiterated the story of President Roosevelt's decision to bring 1,000 refugees to the United States and his promise that they would be returned to their homelands after the war. The president noted:

> However, surveys have revealed that most of these people would be admissible under the immigration laws. In the circumstances, it would be inhumane and wasteful to require these people to go all the way back to Europe merely for the purpose of applying there for immigration visas and returning to the United States. Many of them have close relatives, including sons and daughters, who are citizens of the United States and who have served and are serving honorably in the armed forces of our country. I am therefore directing the Secretary of State and the Attorney General to adjust the immigration status of those members of this group who may wish to stay here, in strict accordance with existing laws and regulations.[45]

The Truman Directive broke new immigration ground because it established regular use of the corporate affidavit. In fact, many Jewish organizations tried to sponsor refugees but could not do so under existing immigration laws. His order came in time to save the Fort Ontario refugees from being deported, but the change in policy came far too late to save the lives of other Jewish refugees desperate to leave Nazi Germany and occupied Europe. Truman legalized the guarantees of responsible welfare organizations for large groups of refugees. This action disarmed State Department bureaucrats like Breckinridge Long, who used individual affidavits or the lack of them to cause delays and disqualifications to keep the immigrant quota below the legal numbers.

FDR's guests would stay permanently, but it took six weeks to process all of them. To enter the United States legally, the refugees had to travel to Canada. On January 17, 1946, three buses carrying 95 refugees left the Fort Ontario shelter at 6:00 A.M. Driving across western New York State to Buffalo, they had lunch and then traveled to Niagara Falls in Ontario, Canada. George Graves, the U.S. consul there, greeted the refugees and gave each of them a visa decorated with a red seal and a ribbon. The bus trips continued until February 6, with three buses leaving every two or three days for the four-hour ride to Niagara Falls, Canada, and the return trip across the Rainbow Bridge.[46]

An official Interior Department press release dated February 4, 1946, announced the end of the cabinet wars. The release said that the Emergency Refugee Shelter at Fort Ontario, Oswego, New York, was closed as the last group of refugees left the government-operated shelter. According to Interior Secretary Harold Ickes, the final disposition of the property and records would be completed within 45 days and the plant at the Fort returned to the War Department. Ickes cited the cooperation of several refugee and humanitarian agencies, which helped to produce President Truman's corporate immigration decision.

Ickes said that private organizations had assumed complete responsibility for the refugees. These private organizations included the National Refugee Service, the American Committee for Christian Refugees, and the Catholic Committee for Refugees. The National Refugee Service had the primary responsibility for assisting the refugees and was assisted by various other agencies throughout the United States.[47]

Ivo Lederer, who has taught Russian and East European history at Princeton, Yale, and Stanford, is the son of refugees Otto and Ruza Lederer. He spent his 15th and 16th birthdays in the Fort Ontario shelter and vividly remembers his experience.

> The refugee problem today is assuming grotesque proportions. And we don't know as a nation what to do. We want to do the right thing, but feel constrained about just opening up the doors and letting everyone who wants to come, to come to these shores. But here is one instance in which the doors did open. One thousand people, just short of 1,000 came in, worked hard, struggled, but made something of themselves. That's a story worth telling.[48]

As historian David Wyman said, a few brave, idealistic people can make a difference, and in the case of the Oswego refugees, they did.[49] The United States must constantly remind itself of its humanitarian ideals, the ones inscribed on the Statue of Liberty. Often the United States has fulfilled these ideals, often it has not. According to Wyman, the reasons the United States did not act more aggressively included anti-Semitism, indifference, and politics, including the inaction of Franklin D. Roosevelt for political reasons. Revisionists argue that FDR and the American people had limited options, limited funds, and limited capacity to support refugees. They contend that the most important objective of the United States was to help win the war and defeat the Nazis. These arguments are partially correct, but we are left haunted by the millions of lives of Jewish and other refugees who perished before 1945. No amount of money or prioritizing or revisionism will obliterate the United States' failure to follow the humanitarian path.

Notes

1. Emma Lazarus, *The New Colossus* (1883). The Statue of Liberty was an important symbol to the refugees, which underscores several political ironies. Emma Lazarus came from a prominent New York family and became a respected poet, noted for poems about her Jewish heritage. But Bartholdi, the creator of the Statue of Liberty, did not intend for his creation to become a symbol

of welcome for millions of European immigrants, including the Fort Ontario group. Bartholdi intended the statue to symbolize enlightenment for European countries still battling tyranny. The symbolism of Lazarus reverses the idea, designating the Statue of Liberty as a beacon of welcome for immigrants leaving Europe.

2. Michael Robert LeMay and Elliott Robert Barkan, eds., *U.S. Immigration and Naturalization Laws and Issues: A Documentary History* (New York: Greenwood Press, 1999), 20.

3. David Wyman, *The Abandonment of the Jews: America and the Holocaust, 1941–1945* (New York: Pantheon Books, 1984), 285.

4. Ibid., 286–287.

5. Ibid.

6. Transcript of interview with Manya Hartmeyer Breuer, conducted on August 6, 1994, as part of the 50th anniversary reunion of the Fort Ontario Emergency Refugee Shelter. Videotaped at the State University of New York at Oswego Learning Center by Safe Haven, 1994.

7. Transcript of interview with Walter Greenberg, conducted on August 6, 1994, as part of the 50th anniversary reunion of the Fort Ontario Emergency Refugee Shelter. Videotaped at the State University of New York at Oswego Learning Center by Safe Haven, 1994.

8. Ruth Gruber, *Haven: The Dramatic Story of 1000 World War Two Refugees and How They Came to America* (New York: Three Rivers Press, 2000), 83.

9. Ibid., 79.

10. Ibid., 80–82.

11. Sharon R. Lowenstein, *Token Refugee: The Story of the Jewish Refugee Shelter at Oswego, 1944–1946* (Bloomington: Indiana University Press, 1986), 46.

12. Peter Holcomb, "Oswego's Guests," *Time* (August 6, 1945): 182–183.

13. Gruber, *Haven*, 151–152.

14. Ibid., 153–154.

15. Lowenstein, *Token Refugee*, 46.

16. Ibid, 49–51.

17. Gruber, *Haven*, 76.

18. Transcript of interview with Geraldine Desens Rossiter, conducted in March 1994, in preparation for the 50th anniversary reunion of the Fort Ontario Emergency Refugee Shelter. Videotaped at the State University of New at Oswego Learning Center by Safe Haven, 1994.

19. Transcript of interview with Walter Greenberg, conducted on August 6, 1994, as part of the 50th anniversary reunion of the Fort Ontario Emergency Refugee Shelter. Videotaped at the State University of New York at Oswego Learning Center by Safe Haven, 1994.

20. Transcript of interview with Manya Hartmeyer Breuer, conducted on August 6, 1994, as part of the 50th anniversary reunion of the Fort Ontario

Emergency Refugee Shelter. Videotaped at the State University of New York at Oswego Learning Center by Safe Haven, 1994.

21. Gruber, *Haven*, 151–152.

22. Ibid.

23. Arieh Lebowitz and Gail Malmgreen, eds., *Archives of the Holocaust: An International Collection of Selected Documents*, vol. 14, Robert F. Wagner Labor Archives, New York University: The Papers of the Jewish Labor Committee (New York: Garland, 1993), 295.

24. Ibid.

25. *Life* (August 17, 1944).

26. *Oswego Palladium Times* (September 5, 1944).

27. Lowenstein, *Token Refuge*, 76.

28. Ibid.

29. Karen J. Greenberg, ed., *Archives of the Holocaust: An International Collection of Selected Documents*, vol. 5, The Fort Ontario Emergency Refugee Shelter Papers (New York: Garland, 1990), 202.

30. Ibid.

31. *Oswego Palladium Times* (September 5, 1944).

32. Lowenstein, *Token Refuge*, 77.

33. *Oswego Palladium Times* (October 4, 1944).

34. Gruber, *Haven*, 207.

35. Lowenstein, *Token Refugee*, 89–92.

36. Ibid.

37. Ibid.

38. Gruber, *Haven*, 77–82.

39. Ibid.

40. Lowenstein, *Token Refugee*, 100–106.

41. *Oswego Palladium Times*, April 10, 1945.

42. Gruber, *Haven*, 199.

43. Ibid., 200–202.

44. Lebowitz and Malmgreen, *Archives of the Holocaust*, 295.

45. Ibid.

46. Greenberg, *Archives of the Holocaust*, 272. Ickes said that WRA records showed that 69 of the original group had been repatriated or admitted to other countries, and 13 had died. Twenty-three children born in the shelter would be admitted as U.S. citizens. The rest of the group, a total of 900 persons, would be given permanent visas as they became admissible under the monthly immigration quotas of their respective countries or by temporary permits in some cases. The small number entering the country on temporary permits would be repatriated or admitted to other countries of their choice. Many of the permanent immigrants joined the households of friends or relatives already established in this country.

47. Greenberg, *Archives of the Holocaust*, 272.
48. Transcript of interview with Ivo Lederer, conducted on August 6, 1994, as part of the 50th anniversary reunion of the Fort Ontario Emergency Refugee Shelter. Videotaped at the State University of New York at Oswego Learning Center by Safe Haven, 1994..
49. David Wyman, *The Abandonment of the Jews: America and the Holocaust, 1941–1945* (New York: Pantheon Books, 1984), 282.

Bibliography

Greenberg, Karen J., ed. *Archives of the Holocaust: An International Collection of Selected Documents*, vol. 5. Fort Ontario Emergency Refugee Shelter Papers. New York: Garland, 1990.

Gruber, Ruth. *Haven: The Dramatic Story of 1000 World War Two Refugees and How They Came to America*. New York: Three Rivers Press, 2000.

Interviews with Fort Ontario Refugees. Transcript of interviews conducted on August 6, 1994, as part of the 50th anniversary reunion of the Fort Ontario Emergency Refugee Shelter. Videotaped at the State University of New York at Oswego Learning Center by Safe Haven, 1994.

Lebowitz, Arieh, and Gail Malmgreen, eds. *Archives of the Holocaust: An International Collection of Selected Documents*, vol. 14. Robert F. Wagner Labor Archives New York University: The Papers of the Jewish Labor Committee. New York: Garland, 1993.

LeMay, Robert Michael, and Robert Elliott Barkan. *U.S. Immigration and Naturalization Laws and Issues: A Documentary History*. New York: Greenwood Press, 1999.

Lowenstein, Sharon. *Token Refuge: The Story of the Jewish Refugee Shelter at Oswego, 1944–1946*. Bloomington: Indiana University Press, 1986.

Ngai, Mae. *Impossible Subjects: Illegal Aliens and the Making of Modern America*. Princeton, NJ: Princeton University Press, 2004.

Wyman, David. *The Abandonment of the Jews: America and the Holocaust, 1941–1945*. New York: Pantheon Books, 1984.

Zolberg, Aristide. *A Nation by Design: Immigration Policy in the Fashioning of America*. Cambridge, MA: Harvard University Press, 2006.

Remittances

Łukasz Albański

The International Organization for Migration defines migrant remittances as monetary transfers that a migrant makes to the country of origin. Remittances are personal, cash transfers from a migrant worker or immigrant to a relative in the country of origin. They can also be funds invested, deposited, or donated by the migrant to the country of origin.[1] According to the World Bank's definition of migrant remittances, they are considered the sum of workers' remittances, compensation of employees, and migrants' transfers. Workers' remittances are current private transfers from migrant workers who are considered residents of the host country to recipients in their country of origin. Compensation of employees comprises wages, salaries, and other benefits earned by individuals in other economies than those in which they are residents. Migrants' transfers are the net worth of migrants that are transferred from one country to another at the time of migration.[2] These three streams of monetary transfers flowing into countries are published annually by the International Monetary Fund in its *Balance of Payments Statistical Yearbook.*

Many sociologists view monetary remittances as the representation of long-distance social ties of solidarity, reciprocity, and obligation that bind migrants to their kin and friends across national borders.[3] Some scholars point out the role that social remittances play in promoting immigrant entrepreneurship, community, and family formation. Social (as opposed to monetary) remittances are the ideas, behaviors, identities, and social capital that flow from receiving to sending communities.[4]

A Brief Outline of U.S. Immigration History

Research on migration has always recognized that migrants stay in touch with members of their community through correspondence and sending remittances.[5] However, the attitude of American researchers toward immigrant issues at the turn of the 20th century, when the incorporation of millions of new immigrants presented urgent social problems, was wildly ethnocentric. A large part of early

American sociology of migration focused on the absorption of immigrants into U.S. society.[6] Moreover, in the United States, immigration history, as Dirk Hoerder points out, was basically bound to Emma Lazarus's poem about the "poor huddled masses" receiving shelter from oppression and hunger.[7] In Frank Thistlethwaite's words, there was a "salt water curtain" inhibiting understanding of European origins.[8] In Oscar Handlin's *The Uprooted*, immigrants experienced a deep feeling of alienation because they were uprooted from their original social milieu. As a result, the ghetto culture created by immigrants was not a transfer of the Old World culture but rather an effect of isolation in response to a situation not comprehended in the peasant villages of the homeland, because Handlin reduces peasants' conditions to passive and pathetic acceptance of his fortune before being uprooted on U.S. soil.[9]

The connections between immigrants and their countries of origin were especially criticized by the members of the dominant society. Early in the 20th century, the maintenance of home ties outside the United States often outraged the public opinion that immigrants should transform into productive and loyal citizens to their new country. Immigrants were expected to stay once they arrived to demonstrate their commitment to American values. Political exiles were always treated suspiciously as potential subversive elements that could spread harmful ideas in the United States. Even migrants who did not care much about building their old state, devoting their entire attention to their own material needs, inflamed popular views that they had come only for money and that they abused the United States as a noble experiment of democracy and spurned American goodwill and helping hands.[10]

Concepts such as *the uprooted* and *the melting pot* created a romantic backdrop to the migrants' experience in a new world. They reinforced the American saltwater curtain limitation rather than trying to explain a stream of migration or structural implications of building up ethnic communities. A real revolution broke out

A scene in the ghetto, ca. 1902. The ghetto culture created by immigrants was not a transfer of the Old World culture, but rather an effect of isolation in response to a situation not comprehended in the peasant villages of the homeland. (Library of Congress)

as a result of studies of chain migrations in the 1960s. Handlin's thesis on immigration was first criticized by Rudolph J. Vecoli, who conducted his research on Italian immigration to the United States and noticed that social ties linking migrants with their communities of origin provided a setting for life at the destination.[11] The research conducted by such prominent scholars as Vecoli, Bodnar, Conzen, Gerber, Kamphoefner, and Morawska on the mass migration to the United States gathered some strong evidence for the thesis that Europeans substantially migrated in chains.[12] In consequence of chain migrations, sets of migrants established contacts between their sending community and people at the destination, creating migratory networks.

Since the 1990s, some scholars have preferred to speak of networks or transnational communities.[13] Such types of migrant communities consist of, as Alejandro Portes puts it: "Dense networks across political borders created by immigrants in their quest for economic advancement and social recognition. Through these networks, an increasing number of people are able to live dual lives. Participants are often bilingual, move easily between different cultures, frequently maintain homes in two countries, and pursue economic, political and cultural interests that require their presence in both."[14]

The transnational perspective is used to shed fresh light on the past[15] as well as (even more often) to bring new insight into the study of current immigration to the United States.[16] Undoubtedly, advances in transportation and communication technologies have made it possible for immigrants to maintain more frequent and closer contact with their community of origin. Many observers see remittances as the exemplary forms of migrant transnationalism.[17] The global financial infrastructure provides immigrants with a set of network management tools in the form of money transfers. The existence of global money transfer markets facilitates reliable and efficient transfer of financial resources from migrants to their families and communities to foster better relations within. The efficiency with which contemporary migrants are able to transfer financial resources to families and communities in the country of origin facilitates reaffirmation of family and community trusts, loyalties, and interpersonal and organizational relationships. The technological and financial infrastructure has made it accessible and affordable for transnational communities to enjoy the attendant opportunities and rights of a transnational settlement. The cumulative impact of social and economic forces makes transnational migrant community life normative rather than episodic.[18]

Some scholars point out that social remittances, described as a migration driven form of cultural diffusion, play an important role in transforming sending country political and social life.[19] Remittances bring the social impact of migration to the fore. They are also a potential community development aid. In addition to reforms and positive effects on sending countries, the impact of social remittances can be negative as well. There is nothing to guarantee that what is learned in the host country can be applied to communities of origin. Of course, deliberate exchange about health, education, and business skills could encourage social change. However, social remittances will not, in and of themselves, bring about social reform. They will give an opportunity to promote better outcomes through identifiable social channels.

The intentional transmission of accurate information about working conditions and economic prospects in the Unites States might create more strategic expectations of the migrant experience on the one hand. On the other hand, understanding of contemporary migration as a network-driven process has some significant implications for a broad spectrum of U.S. policies, whether they relate to international development, trade, peacekeeping, investment, or security.

Old Paradigms, New Perspectives

The neoclassical macroeconomic perspective treats international migrations as a problem of labor market disequilibria in developed and in developing countries. The developing countries are endowed with an abundant supply of labor to capital, resulting in low wages, whereas the developed countries are endowed with an abundance of capital relative to labor, resulting in high wages. Thus, the result of migration flows is that the supply of labor decreases in developing countries and wages will rise. The supply of labor in developed countries rises in the same time and wages will fall. The conclusion is that, in the long run, when an international equilibrium is reached, it will induce return migration flows.[20] Associated with the macroeconomic approach is a microeconomic model of individual choice. The microeconomic perspective precisely emphasizes individual choice within the human capital theory. In brief, rational actors decide to migrate because a cost-benefit calculation leads them to expect better opportunities for earning money. Moreover, they will migrate to countries where they can be most productive, given their skills. However, before they consider migration as an option, they calculate and compare the higher wages associated with greater labor productivity at every potential destination with the difficulty experienced in adapting to a new labor market. Ignoring downside risk, they will emigrate if the expected benefits in a potential destination exceed the opportunities at home. Migration is thus conceptualized as a form of investment. A potential migrant goes to wherever the expected benefits are greater than the expected costs.[21]

Neoclassical economics takes the individual migrant as the unit of analysis. In contrast, a key insight of the New Economics of Migration (NELM) is that migration decisions are not made by isolated individuals, but within families or households. The NELM focuses on the strong and enduring financial ties rooted in family economics that immigrants maintain with their sending communities. Collective decision making and objectives rather than the wishes of individual migrants, determine migratory experiences and remittance flows.[22] Nonetheless, families are treated as rational actors. They allocate their different family workers over geographically dispersed and structurally diversified labor markets to reduce their income risks. As long as economic conditions are poor, households minimize risk by sending their members. Diversifying its labor portfolio allows the family to smooth consumption. Therefore, the flow of remittances is not a random by-product of migration but an integral part of the family's strategy behind migration. The family can rely on migrant remittances for support if productive activities at home fail to generate sufficient income. Migration becomes attractive as a way to accumulate funds that can be used for consumption. Some of the remittances may also be channeled into investment. Households send workers abroad to a higher wage area to accumulate savings or send them back in the form of remittances. Oded Stark argues that migrant savings and remittances can increase relative income of one household to others and hence reduce relative deprivation compared with some reference group.[23] According to the NELM, remittances are a result of three basic financial motives: family obligations and assistance, insurance (to control income risks), and investment (crucial for a migrant's successful return).

The growth of global migrant remittances represents one of the most important mechanisms through which international migrations are sustained. The inflow of migrant remittances opens up new opportunities for their community of origin. Although some sending countries are making it easier for emigrants to keep in touch with their communities in order to bolster remittances, there is a considerable lack of coordinated strategies for assisting returning migrants with economic reintegration. They often face difficulty in finding employment commensurate with the skills they have acquired abroad. They often end up running small unproductive businesses. Savings are spent on consumption rather than investment. Several studies indicate a positive role of adequate counseling both before and after return in assisting development.[24] Moreover, migrant remittances are destined to fail if government does not create an economic environment that is conducive to investments in productive activities at home.[25] In addition to migration for employment, many forms of exploitive treatment and abuses such as the trafficking of women and children appear.

Social Networks

In his historical overview of immigration into the United States, Charles Tilly emphasizes the fact that "networks migrate." He puts it, "by and large, the effective units of migration were neither individuals nor households but sets of people linked by acquaintance, kinship, and work experience."[26] Moreover, as Monica Boyd notes, "networks connect migrants across time and space. Once begun, migration flows often become self-sustaining, reflecting the establishment of networks of information, assistance and obligations which develop between migrants in the host society, friends and relatives in the sending area. These networks link populations in origin and receiving countries and ensure that movements are not necessarily limited in time, unidirectional or permanent."[27] As these networks deepen and spread, they become more institutionalized and develop into larger communities of individuals that are more loosely tied to one another.[28] The dense social networks, which immigrants' construct and actively maintain with their family, community, and country of origin, are the most important developmental resource associated with international migration.[29] Undoubtedly, migrant's social networks play a significant role in mobilizing and organizing economic and other types of resources for onward transmission to their counterpart households and communities in their country of origin. The economic impact of such networks is to be found in the flow of family and collective remittances. Migrants' communities pursue a mix of family insurance, family investment, and community welfare models. Remittances are seen as resources that help the family to make its household consumption easier in times of crisis. Remittances are also treated as an investment instrument that contributes to household assets that the migrant will inherit later in life. Remittances enable many communities to overcome capital constraints to finance public works projects such as parks, churches, electrification, road construction, and sewers. In this context, migrants' networks function as a type of international development institution. However, sometimes remittances are frittered away in personal consumption, social ceremonies, real estate, and price-escalating trading.[30]

The economic action of migrants is embedded in networks that make up social and organizational structures.[31] Granovetter's concept of *embeddedness* differentiates the ways in which economic development actions might be embedded in social networks. The *relational embeddedness* of cooperation within households includes normative roles and behavior, expectations, obligations, sanctions, the quest for mutual approval, and reciprocity of transactions. The *structural embeddedness* of cooperation deals with broader social networks involving multiple relations of vertical, horizontal, and symbiotic independence among individuals beyond those involved in relational embeddedness of cooperation. The channels through which people meet, interact, cooperate, and engage in different types of transactions to obtain desired rewards and benefits corresponds to relational and structural embeddedness of cooperation nested within social networks.[32]

Social networks shape migrants' labor market and general economic behavior by providing better economic prospects on employment and business opportunities. By improving employment search efficiency, networks enable migrants to find jobs and housing faster, more reliably, and at lower cost. In addition to providing an employment search mechanism, social networks increase the supply of labor to employers in a host country. Migratory networks can play a role in relocating migrants from labor markets in their countries to labor markets in the host country and in facilitating their adaptation in their new society. Such networks are a source of employers' information on migrant labor costs and their skill possibilities. An immigrant economic adjustment performs the action of resource-generating mechanism for their communities of origin.[33] The literature describes immigrant labor markets as the main locus of remittance generation. The timing and volume of remittances are directly connected with the overall state of the host country's economy, its unemployment ratio, and migrants' labor market activities.[34]

The emergence of immigrant entrepreneurship ventures provides access to resources to which immigrants may not otherwise have manageable access, such as the combination of business information, business knowledge, consumer market orientation, and financial resources. A high concentration of co-migrants of similar ethnic characteristics or from the same country generates business opportunities in the host country localities. The vast majority of immigrant enterprises are located within the small retail business and service sectors. They offer "ethnic" goods, imported goods, and remittance-transfer services. The core management structures of these businesses comprise the immigrant owner and the owner's personal networks (family, relatives, and friends). The immigrant entrepreneurship represents a distinct form of economic adaptation and income mobility in the context of the receiving society.[35]

A Lesson from the Past

Migration appears to be associated with costs and risks. Migrants must invest in the material costs of travel, the costs of living while moving to a new location and looking for work, and the effort involved in adapting to a new labor market. Therefore, migration decisions are usually made collectively to overcome any obstacles. Both financial resources and social capital play an important role in estimating the costs and benefits of migration. For many migrants, the initial costs can be minimized if they rely on well-established migratory networks. Otherwise, the estimated costs are subtracted to yield a potential migrant's resources to the homeland. This leads to the conclusion that migrants voluntarily leave their homelands to obtain a better position for their economic well-being. Migration becomes attractive as a strategy for generating and accumulating funds to maximize expected household income. An example of Polish peasants who migrated to the United States focuses on the process of accumulating their savings and sending them back in the form of remittances. The process of creating remittances can be understood to occur in three stages: accumulating financial resources, transferring remittances to homelands, and channeling remittances into consumption and investment.

Polish Labor Migration to the United States Prior to World War I

Since the second half of the 19th century, demographic and economic conditions pushed individuals to move from places with a surplus of population, little capital, and underemployment to areas where labor was scarce and wages were higher. International migrations followed the political and economic organization of an expanding global market. The penetration of capitalist relations into peripheral societies created a mobile population. International labor migrations between the developing and developed regions, generated by economic imbalance and social dislocations, resulted from the incorporation of the peripheries into the orbit of the Atlantic core.[36] Poland, being partitioned under three rules (Prussia, Russia, and Austria) until it regained state sovereignty in 1918, was also incorporated into the Atlantic capitalist economy during the last decades of the 19th century and the beginning of the 20th century. Between 1870 and 1914, more than 2 million Poles had permanently left the country in continental and overseas emigration.[37]

The participation in overseas migration was the result of changing old patterns of regional migration for employment into new seasonal labor migrations to Western Europe (Germany, France) and to the United States. The traditional hunger for soil and conditions of underemployment pushed peasants to leave their village for better income opportunities. Sending remittances and stories told by the first "globetrotters" affected the village and the immediate sociocultural environment in which they made their decisions to go and seek wages across the Atlantic.

Seasonal labor migrations stemmed from the process of internal economic and social diversification of the peasantry. The enfranchisement of the peasantry produced a large rural proletariat. A systematic fragmentation of peasant landholdings occurred as the land was divided and subdivided among their progeny. Furthermore, the demographic boom greatly fostered the production of the agrarian proletariat. Seasonal employment was thus needed to repair chronically insufficient domestic incomes. From the 1880s on, the Polish peasantry had become even more dependent, directly and indirectly, on economic migrations across the Atlantic.[38]

Everywhere, the beginning of a migration flow looked similar. The folk were at first skeptical about overseas travel. They were afraid of traveling on a train, and they could not even imagine a ship, because no one had even seen one before. However, one person decided to migrate to the United States and sent money back, and then others followed in his footsteps. Each act of migration altered the social context within which another decision was made, usually in ways that increased subsequent movement.[39] Krystyna Duda-Dziewierz reports that the first emigrant in Babica left the village in 1883 because he lost a lawsuit against his neighbor about a cow. He settled in Detroit and earned money quickly. After three years, he was established enough to return to Poland, and then he persuaded a group of relatives to come to Detroit with him. After that, a seed group of the local community had formed in the city. Many inhabitants of Babica eventually joined them in the company of other local people. Migrations across the Atlantic followed a pattern of network building.[40] Paradoxically, the first migrant was often a socially peripheral member of the community, who had to leave the village for bread or to pay off debts. Nonetheless, migration was generally considered a short-term circulation. The economic migrations of Poles to the United States relied on industrial employment in the growing cities. Hence, the majority of migrants would rather come back and buy a land. A few settled down after purchasing a farm in Nebraska or in Wisconsin. Others decided to start a new life in an American city.[41] However, as long as peasants had not decided to settle in the United States for good, the emigrants managed their European farms and households, either through repeated visits or through correspondence with traveling relatives or other kin. Questions (e.g., "Tell me how the weather has been, the crops, and how big the harvest"), requests for advice (e.g., "I'm writing to you for advice about what to do with this house which is for sale"), and orders (e.g., "Buy potatoes, and you may buy a pig") showed that migrants maintained strong home ties. Moreover, these sustained networks of communication played an important role of social control for both migrants and members of their community. Gossip was a powerful tool of control, and a deviant would expect to be punished or even excluded from the community. News from relatives and friends who had already settled in the United States encouraged other members of the community to accept the risk of migration, even though most of them had never left their village before.[42]

The American economy between 1860 and 1914 absorbed a large number of low-skilled immigrant labor. The rapid industrialization drew the necessary labor resources from Europe.[43] The Polish immigrants in the United States were predominantly (95 percent) employed in the factories, with three-quarters of male immigrants concentrated in three major branches of industry (coal, steel, and metal) as well as slaughtering and meatpacking.[44] They formed ethnic neighborhoods in the cities where they found employment. Poles mostly resided in seven industrial cities—Chicago, Detroit, Pittsburgh, Cleveland, Milwaukee, New York, and Buffalo—and organized their entire world there, including churches, shops, services, banks, fraternal organizations, funeral homes, and cemeteries.[45]

Although the Polish residential clusters in urban settings might look similar at first, each of the neighborhoods gradually developed and transformed in a different way as a result of the inhabitants' lifestyles. Nevertheless, the peasants had to deal with the hardship of urban life. Ludwik Krzywicki, a social activist who visited Back of the Yards in Chicago, writes about the miserable conditions of dwellers there. He mentions dirty streets, smells, and slums that he had not seen anywhere else before.[46] The *Globe Toronto* presents a negative picture of foreigners as citizens in the United States. Its correspondence claims that an average house in a Polish settlement would shelter between 30 and 40 people. They seldom

A Polish immigrant carries a trunk on his shoulder as he boards a ship, ca. 1907. (Library of Congress)

patronized an American in business, because "they spent little if any money in that country. They sent it home and followed later themselves . . . they did not want to stay there and therefore had no heart for the improvement of the country."[47] In fact, the majority of Poles migrating to the United States at the turn of century went as laborers, not as pioneers or permanent settlers. Their expected stay in the United States was to be temporary. Ewa Morawska quotes some fragmentary Polish sources that indicate that, in the first phase of labor migrations to the United States (1880s and 1890s), 60 percent to 70 percent of emigrants returned after two or three years. Moreover, many made several trips on a regular basis.[48]

The fluctuation in American labor market conditions affected the volume and direction of the migration flow. The contemporary rates of unemployment in the United States correlated with the total annual volume of Polish immigration. Especially the economic crises in the United States in 1893 to 1898 and in 1908 as well as the industrial recession of 1911 had a negative impact on the inflow of workers from Poland. Labor markets were the primary mechanism by which the flows of Polish labor were induced. Seasonal migration to Western Europe could have served as an alternative for some of those laid off from American factories.[49] Social networks constituted a social capital that migrants could draw upon to gain access to employment prospects in the United States. During times of joblessness, labor migration decelerated, because the feedback mechanisms of a network warned people in origin areas of unemployment through letters, greatly increasing the likelihood that they heard about the contemporary difficulties and went instead to seek wages elsewhere.

Accumulating Financial Resources

The process of accumulating financial resources began at home, because every migrant had to find money to cover her travel costs. The first travel abroad appeared to be associated with uncertainty, irrationality, and emotions. Many immigrants' memoirs exposed the very human nature of migration. Before gaining his first experience of overseas migration, a Galician peasant had to deal with his fear. His relatives blessed him because he could never come back. Often families would share the cost and send only one member of the family, who was then obligated to send money back or to earn money for shipping another potential migrant (a steamship ticket cost about $25 one way at the beginning of the century, and related travel expenditures were about $15 to $20).[50] Therefore, the migrant was under the pressure of paying off his debts. If he failed, he would return home with a deep sense of shame.

However, once Polish rural migrants had become incorporated into the U.S. economy and learned more about travel conditions, there were strong incentives for them and their relatives to engage in migration. If the migrant returned home with savings after a period of time, she would cover the material costs of another travel. In addition to the experience, migration sustained itself in other ways that made additional movement progressively more likely over time, because incentives for migration would spread over other members of the community attracted by the migrant's success, especially if he manifested his wealth. The community changed its perception of migration and therefore it made it easier to borrow money for migrants. In fact, the flow of remittances sent to home heightened the attractiveness of migration as a means of overcoming local production risks.

Once the number of migrants reached a critical threshold, the costs and risks of migration fell because of the expansion of social networks. Moreover, as transportation developed to support, sustain, and promote migration, the probability of movement could rise. However, village custom and local public opinion still played an important role in the process of decision-making about where to go in search of wages.[51] First, inhabitants of the village were fearful of unknown places and did not thirst for much higher earnings there. Second, even though some villagers were in the United States, the rest might head to more socially acceptable destinations in Europe. Migrations of Polish peasants at the turn of century were a collective movement.

Transferring Remittances to Homelands

When a migrant reached his destination, he faced the problem of income maximization. His main objective was to earn much money during a period of time. After that, he could come back to the village and realize his needs. The basic need of the majority of Polish rural households was survival. At the beginning of the century, a Polish peasant could buy a cow for $24 to $30, a pig for $12 to $15, and a pair of oxen for $50 to $70. The Polish peasant felt a traditional attachment to his native land; he wanted to purchase a hectare of land. Based on the quality of soil, the prices could range from $200 to $500. An unmarried peasant needed to buy a farm for $120 to $200. The custom of dowries held by the community insisted that young girls needed to pay either money or property to her husband when they got married. A well-off peasant family was obliged to give more than $400, whereas small holders offered $25 to $30. It was customary for the oldest son to buy out his siblings before he inherited lands. Depending on the value of the land, he could pay a few hundred dollars for a large farm or $25 to $30 for a small holding. There were also debts to be paid off. A migrant had to cover either a return ticket or a steamship ticket for a relative.[52]

A migrant's savings depended on how intensely she could work abroad. Previous individual experience increased the probability of employment in the destination, because she could have some basic communication skills and training. Experienced migrants often played the role of mediator between the employer and native coworkers. The migrant network lowered the costs and risks of movement, and the growth of the network facilitated employment. Once immigrants entered a job in significant numbers, they influenced the recruitment of other immigrants. Moreover, a value shift occurred among native workers, who eventually refused the "immigrant" jobs, making it even more necessary to recruit more immigrants. Polish laborers in the United States often joined an organized group to increase their job opportunities. They worked together not only for companionship but also for putting pressure on a dishonest employee. A single laborer who had a little knowledge of English could have been exploited easily.[53]

Migrants managed to save much money before returning to their villages. The costs of living for an average migrant included food and housing. To limit such costs, migrants lived in overcrowded houses. The miserable conditions of their existence could be partly explained by considering it as a temporary situation and the vision of the return home with money. The similar residential locations were generally the product of chain migrations, common occupations, and incomes.

Some unexpected events could force a migrant to stay longer than planned. A migrant knew that if he lost his savings, he would not be welcomed back. Therefore, voluntary self-help organizations and banks arose to satisfy the demand created by the possibility of experiencing an accident. Otherwise, migrants had to keep their savings themselves. It was risky because of the possibilities of robbery and fire.

The total amount of money resulted from the duration of work abroad and income. Ewa Morawska shows that, at the beginning of the century, average annual agricultural wages for three partitions of Poland were 65 percent to 70 percent lower than industrial wages obtained in the United States. Moreover, even industrial wages in Germany were, on average, only 60 percent of those received by Polish migrants in the United States. Working as low-skilled factory laborers in the United States, Polish migrants would earn $1.30 to $2.00 per day ($370 to $500 annually). If they were hired by mining and textiles industries, their wages might total $500 to $700 per year. In comparison, Polish industrial annual wages divided into three partitions were $200 (Prussian), $160 to $217 (Russian), and $100 to $170 (Austrian). Morawska estimates that a single Polish migrant in the United States would save about $200 per year.[54] However, migrant savings would be spread widely as a result of individual characteristics and social and economic conditions that increased benefits. The process of generating the migrant savings derived from earnings, employment, and a lower level of consumption abroad to decrease the cost of living.

Sending remittances involved family obligations and assistance. Transferring remittances might be hampered by either a lack of assistance in sending money or the cost of transfer, and these problems would affect the decision-making process. Polish migrants transferred remittances in three ways: First, the migrant could take money with her if she decided to return home. Second, he could pass money by asking a trustworthy person for a favor. Third, she could send money via the post office. The frequency of transferring remittances and their amount depended not only on the method of sending money and trust in their efficiency but also on information received from the sending community. The social ties that connected migrants with their relatives played a significant role in channeling, controlling, and sustaining the ventures of the village. Particularly important were networks of information about how the money would be spent. The migrants monitored their European property and family members' behavior through the circulation of correspondence with traveling relatives or other kin. An unfaithful wife would be punished by withholding financial help. On the other hand, a migrant who forgot about his family obligations rushed to send money immediately. The transplantation of village communities from Europe to U.S. cities created a transatlantic system of social control and long-distance management of family and local affairs.[55]

The impact of sending remittances is evidenced in a postal report published in 1894. At the close of the year, 5,332,966 crowns arrived in 43,365 consignments. At that time, there was no commercial exchange between the United States and Galicia. Thus, the money exclusively represented migrant remittances. Moreover, there was not a single district in Galicia that did not receive money from the United States. Furthermore, this report was produced during an economic recession in the United States.[56] One district in Galicia received 1,100,000 crowns in 1899 from North America.[57] The Association of Polish Jurists and Economists reports that some village post offices received remittances annually from the United States that ranged from 20,000 to 30,000 crowns. With those transfers, many migrant households managed to repay their debts, buy land, and improve the welfare of their rural communities.[58] Many commentators agree that the seasonal labor migrations and monetary remittances saved the country from abject poverty.[59]

The majority of Polish workers who went to the United States during the time of mass labor migration prior to World War I usually spent two to five years there.[60] The process of channeling remittances into consumption and investment had begun long before a migrant returned home. Evidence of the complex communication networks provides an argument that remittances are part of migrant households' strategy to build up their budget. While away, migrants sent home remittances in money orders and letters. When they decided to return, they brought material goods and savings. If a migrant's main aim was to collect money for purchasing land, a migrant would rather accumulate a large sum of money than send the money back to his family. The Polish seasonal workers also brought hand tools, irons, furniture and clothing, watches with chains, brimmed hats, and other material goods that were perceived as luxurious and desirable.

After her return, the migrant was supposed to fulfill her every consumption need. The pattern of consumption appeared to be associated with signaling a higher social status. She was allowed to consume more due to her current wealth. Most of the money was used for increasing consumption and better housing. The migrant usually perceived purchasing an additional hectare of land or building a new house with farm building as an investment. He could also spend money on clothing or a pair of animals for the farm to carry the family through the winter. Circular migrants, who went back and forth, needed to invest a sum of money for another steamship card to the United States and related travel expenses.

Huge amounts of money flowed into the Polish countryside from the United States during the period of mass labor migration. One commentator says, "our population is entirely the American economy."[61] Jan Stapinski reports that the migrants' remittances rescued one district suffering particularly from the flood of 1899. Other migrants also gave money for building or renovating churches.[62] Money orders from the United States to Austria-Hungary and Russia amounted to $70 million between 1902 and 1906. In 1902 alone, Polish migrants sent U.S. money orders in the sum of about $3.5 million to Galicia, and an additional $4 million was brought in by the returning migrants during the same year.[63]

Franciszek Bujak estimates that, in one village, the combined postal remittances and personal savings of 13 returning migrants from the United States, valued at $850 per capita, varied from $180 to $2,200.[64] In other villages, thanks to remittances, inhabitants purchased brick houses and farming equipment. Returning migrants brought city clothing and other material goods for household use. The people from other villages envied American gadgets. They also desired to go abroad and earn money. With its all great promise, the United States meant a small fortune. For many peasants with hope, the myth of the United States was created as a golden land.[65]

Conclusion

Luis Eduardo Guarnizo writes that monetary remittances that migrants send to their homelands have been portrayed in the literature as a subject of interest and concern, because "monetary remittances have become the most often-cited, tangible evidence and measuring stick for the ties connecting migrants with their societies of origin."[66] This does not mean, however, that there are no controversies concerning the current debate. Some scholars point out that remittances are spent on conspicuous consumption rather than investment. Therefore, remittances have less impact on the development of the sending country as one might think. Moreover, some migrants' households are affected negatively by receiving the money. Their members become addicted to the frequent transfers of remittances and thus stop their professional activity.

The sending countries manage to provide more opportunities to make productive investments. They offer counseling and assist in obtaining investment credits to facilitate the positive effects of remittances on development. The volume and stability of migrant monetary remittances become either a source of profits or a security instrument to upgrade the creditworthiness of impoverished countries to secure large-scale international loans. One of the most interesting programs is the Mexican *Tres Por Uno*. The program recognizes that the amount remitted is highly significant for the Mexican national economy. The Mexican government encourages the maximum possible inflow of worker remittances into investment and adds three pesos to each migrant's peso. Aihwa Ong describes the increased macroeconomic significance of monetary remittances for the sending countries as the post-development state strategy.

According to the authors of *the Migration and Development Brief*, as the U.S. job market continues to weaken, flows of remittances to Latin America and the Caribbean region have been falling. Especially, the slowdown in the U.S. construction sector, a major employment sector for many migrants, has badly affected remittance flows.[67] By April 2010 remittance flows were still declining, albeit at a decreased percentage from the previous two years. Fluctuations in the value of the U.S. dollar have not helped in the purchasing power of remittances. Meanwhile many migrants are forced to dip into their savings and assets back home, resulting in ever more severe economic stressors and greater poverty.

Notes

1. International Organization for Migration, Remittances: Definition, Scale and Importance of Remittances, Info Sheet, http://publications.iom.int/bookstore/free/iom_and_remittances.pdf.
2. Dilip Ratha, Sanket Mohapatra, and Ani Silwal, "Outlook for Remittances Flows 2009–2011: Remittances Expected to Fall by 7–10 Percent in 2009," *Migration and Development Brief* 10 (July 2009): 8.
3. Alejandro Portes, Luis E. Guarnizo, and Patricia Landolt, "The Study of Transnationalism: Pitfalls and Promise of an Emergent Research Field," *Ethnic and Racial Studies* 22, no. 2 (March 1999): 217–237.

4. Peggy Lewitt, "Social Remittances: Migration Driven Local-Level Forms of Cultural Diffusion," *International Migration Review* 32, no. 4 (Winter 1998): 926.

5. William I. Thomas and Florian Znaniecki, *The Polish Peasant in Europe and America*, 2 vols. (New York: Dover, 1958); Kathleen Neils Conzen, "Immigrants, Immigrant Neighborhoods and Ethnic Identity: Historical Issues," *The Journal of American History* 66, no. 3 (December 1979): 603–615; Walter D. Kamphoefner, Wolfgang Helbich, and Ulrike Sommer, *News from the Land of Freedom: German Immigrants Write Home* (Ithaca, NY: Cornell University Press 1991).

6. Herbert J. Gans, "The American Kaleidoscope, Then and Now," in *Reinventing the Melting Pot: The New Immigrants and What It Means to Be American*, ed. Tamara Jacoby (New York: Basic Books, 2004), 34–35.

7. Dirk Hoerder, "An Introduction to Labor Migration in the Atlantic Economies, 1815–1914," in *Labor Migration in the Atlantic Economics: The Europeans and North American Working Classes during the Period of Industrialization*, ed. Dirk Hoerder (Westport, CT: Greenwood Press, 1985), 8.

8. Frank Thistlethwaite, "Migration from Europe Overseas in the Nineteenth and Twentieth Centuries," in *A Century of European Migrations: 1830–1930*, eds. Rudolph J. Vecoli and Suzanne M. Sinke (Urbana: University of Illinois Press, 1991), 20.

9. Oscar Handlin, *The Uprooted: The Epic Story of the Great Migrations That Made American People* (Boston: Little, Brown, 1951).

10. Mathew Frye Jacobson, *Special Sorrows: The Diasporic Imagination of Irish, Polish, and Jewish Immigrants in the United States* (Berkeley: University of California Press, 2003) and Walter Nugent, *Crossings: The Great Transatlantic Migrations, 1870–1914* (Bloomington: Indiana University Press, 1992).

11. Rudolph J. Vecoli, "Contadini in Chicago: A Critique of the Uprooted," *Journal of American History* 52, no. 3 (December 1964): 404–417.

12. John Bodnar, *The Transplanted: A History of Immigrants in Urban America* (Bloomington: Indiana University Press, 1985); Kathleen Neils Conzen, David A. Gerber, Ewa Morawska, Goerge Pozetta, and Vecoli, J. Rudolph, "The Invention of Ethnicity: A Perspective from the U.S.A.," *Journal of American Ethnic History* 12, no. 1 (Fall 1992): 3–41; Walter D. Kamphoefner, *The Westfalians: From Germany to Missouri* (Princeton, NJ: Princeton University Press, 1987).

13. See Nina Glick Schiller, Linda Bash, and Christina Blanc-Szanton, eds., *Towards a Transnational Perspective on Migration: Race, Class, Ethnicity Nationalism Reconsidered* (New York: Academy of Science, 1992); Peggy Lewitt and Mary C. Waters, eds., *The Changing Face of Home: The Transnational Lives of the Second Generation* (New York: Russell Sage Foundation, 2002);

Michale S. Smith and Luis E. Guarnizo, eds., *Transnationalism from Below* (New Brunswick, NJ: Transaction Publishers, 1998).

14. Alejandro Portes, "Immigration Theory for a New Century: Some Problems and Opportunities," *International Migration Review* 31, no. 4 (Winter 1997): 812.

15. Nancy Foner, *In a New Land: A Comparative View of Immigration* (New York: New York University Press, 2005); Ewa Morawska, "Immigrants, Transnationalism and Ethnization: A Comparison of the Great Wave and the Last," in *E Pluribus Unum? Contemporary and Historical Perspectives on Immigrant, Political Incorporation*, eds. Gary Gertle and John Mallenkopf (New York: Russell Sage Foundation, 2001), 175–212.

16. Luis E. Guarnizo, Alejandro Portes, and William Haller, "Assimilation and Transnationalism: Determinants of Transnational Political Action among Contemporary Migrants," *American Journal of Sociology* 108, no. 6 (May 2003): 1211–1248.

17. Steven Vertovec, "Rethinking Remittances," ESRC Transnational Communities Program Working Paper WPTC-2k-15 (Oxford: Economic and Social Research Council, n.d.).

18. Alejandro Portes, Luis E. Guarnizo, and Patricia Landolt, "The Study of Transnationalism: Pitfalls and Promise of an Emergent Research Field," *Ethnic and Racial Studies* 22, no. 2 (March 1999): 217–237.

19. Peggy Lewitt, "Social Remittances: Migration Driver Local-Level Forms of Cultural Diffusion," *International Migration Review* 32, no. 4 (Winter 1998): 926–948.

20. John R Harris and Michael Todaro, "Migration, Unemployment and Development: A Two-Sector Analysis," *American Economic Review* 60, no. 1 (1970): 126–142.

21. George Borjas, "Economic Theory and International Migration," *International Migration Review* 23, no. 3 (Autumn 1989): 457–485.

22. Jacob Mincer, "Family Migration Decisions," *Journal of Politic Economy* 85, no. 5 (1978): 750.

23. Oded Stark and David E. Bloom, "The New Economics of Labor Migration," *American Economic Review* 75, no. 2 (May 1985): 173.

24. Luis E Guarnizo, "The Economics of Transnational Living," *International Migration Review* 37, no. 3 (Fall 2003): 666–699; Douglas S. Massey, Joaquin Arango, Graeme Hugo, Ali Kouaouci, Adela Pellegrino, and Edward J Taylor, "International Migration and Community Development," *Population Index* 62, no. 6 (Autumn 1996): 397–418; Oded Stark, J. Edward Taylor, and Shlomo Yitzhaki, "Remittances and Inequality," *The Economic Journal* 96 (September 1986): 722–740.

25. Massey et al., "International Migration and Community Development."

26. Charles Tilly, "Transplanted Networks," in *Immigration Reconsidered: History, Sociology, and Politics,* ed. Virginia Yans-McLaughlin (New York: Oxford University Press, 1990), 84.

27. Monica Boyd, "Family and Personal Networks in International Migration: Recent Developments and New Agendas," *International Migration Review* 23, no. 3 (Autumn 1989): 641.

28. Peggy Lewitt, *The Transnational Villagers* (Berkeley: University of California Press, 2001).

29. Boyd, "Family and Personal Networks," 641.

30. Massey et al., "International Migration and Community Development"; Guarnizo, "The Economics of Transnational Living."

31. Alejandro Portes and Julia Sensenbrenner, "Embeddedness and Immigration: Notes on the Social Determinants of Economic Action," *The American Journal of Sociology* 98, no. 6 (May 1993): 1320–1350.

32. Mark Granovetter, "Economic Action and Social Structure: The Problem of Embeddedness," *The American Journal of Sociology* 91, no. 3 (November 1985): 481–510.

33. Saskia Sassen, "Immigration and Local Labor Markets," in *The Economic Sociology of Immigration: Essays on Networks, Ethnicity and Entrepreneurship,* ed. Alejandro Portes (New York: Russell Sage Foundation, 1995), 87–127.

34. Massey et al., "International Migration and Community Development."

35. Roger Waldinger, "The Making of an Immigrant Niche," *International Migration Review* 27, no. 1 (Spring 1994): 3–30.

36. Hoerder, "An Introduction to Labor Migration," 1–31.

37. Ewa Morawska, "Labor Migrations of Poles in the Atlantic World Economy, 1880–1914," in *European Migrants: Global and Local Perspectives,* eds. Dirk Hoerder and Leslie Page Moch (Boston: Northeastern University Press, 1996), 175; Dorota Praszałowicz, "Overseas Migration from Partitioned Poland: Poznań and East Galicia as Case Studies," *Polish American Studies* 60, no. 2 (Autumn 2003): 63.

38. Andrzej Brożek, *Polonia Amerykańska, 1854–1939* (Warszawa: Interpress, 1977); James S. Pula, "Polska Diaspora w Stanach Zjednoczonych do 1914 roku," in *Polska Diaspora,* ed. Adam Walaszek (Kraków: Wydawnictwo Literackie, 2001), 63.

39. *Pamiętniki Emigrantów: Stany Zjednoczone,* 2 vols. (Warszawa: IGS, 1977).

40. Krystyna Duda-Dziewierz, *Wieś Małopolska a emigracja amerykańska. Studium Wsi Babica, Pow. Rzeszowski* (Warszawa: Polski Instytut Socjologiczny, Dział Wydawnictw, 1938), 23–28.

41. Morawska, "Labor Migrations of Poles," 184–185; Adam Walaszek, *Reemigracja ze Stanów Zjednoczonych Ameryki do Polski po I wojnie światowej (1919–1924)* (Kraków: UJ, 1983).

42. Duda-Dziewierz, *Wieś Małopolska a emigracja amerykańska.*
43. Hoerder, "An Introduction to Labor Migration," 1–31.
44. Morawska, "Labor Migrations of Poles," 184.
45. Pula, "Polska Diaspora w Stnach Zjednoczonych do 1914 roku," 51–76; Dorota Praszałowicz, "The Cultural Changes of Polish American Parochial Schools in Milwaukee, 1866–1988." *The Journal of American Ethnic History* 13, no. 4 (Summer1994): 23–45.
46. Adam Walaszek, "Wstęp," in *Polska Diaspora,* ed. Adam Walaszek (Kraków: Wydawnictwo Literackie, 2001), 16.
47. "Foreigners as Citizens," *The Globe Toronto* (October 2, 1897): 12.
48. Morawska, "Labor Migrations of Poles," 185.
49. Ibid., 183–184.
50. Ibid., 189–190.
51. Duda-Dziewierz, *Wieś Małopolska a emigracja amerykańska*, 57.
52. Morawska, "Labor Migrations of Poles," 189–190.
53. *Pamiótniki Emigrantów: Stany Zjednoczone,* 2 vols. (Warszawa: IGS, 1977).
54. Morawska, "Labor Migrations of Poles," 188.
55. Duda-Dziewierz, *Wieś Małopolska a emigracja amerykańska.*
56. The Bureau of the Mint, *The Monetary Systems of the Principal Countries of the World, 1913* (Washington DC, 1913), 4–5.
57. Wacław Kruszka, *Historja Polska w Ameryce* (Milwaukee: Kuryer, 1907), 46.
58. Józef Kleczyński, "Trzeci zjazd ekonomistów i prawników," *Przegląd Polski* (November, 1893), 396–411.
59. Ignacy Daszyński, *Pamiętniki* (Kraków, Poland: Proletarjot, 1925), 16.
60. Morawska, "Labor Migrations of Poles," 193.
61. Kleczyński, "Trzeci zjazd ekonomistów i prawników."
62. Jan Stapinski, "Kronika Galicyjska," *Biblioteka Warszawska* 221 (1896): 105–106.
63. Morawska, "Labor Migrations of Poles," 193–194.
64. Franciszek Bujak, *Maszkienice, wieś powiatu brzeskiego: stosunki gospodarcze i społeczne* (Kraków: G. Gebethner, 1901), 102–105.
65. Duda-Dziewierz, *Wieś Małopolska a emigracja amerykańska*, 79–86.
66. Luis E Guarnizo, "The Economics of Transnational Living," *International Migration Review* 37, no. 3 (Fall 2003): 666.
67. Dilip Ratha, Sanket Mohapatra, and Ani Silwal, "Outlook for Remittances Flows 2009–2011: Remittances Expected to Fall by 7–10 Percent in 2009," *Migration and Development Brief* 10 (July 2009): 8.

Bibliography

Borjas, George. "Economic Theory and International Migration," *International Migration Review* 23, no. 3 (Autumn 1989): 457–485.

Boyd, Monica. "Family and Personal Networks in International Migration: Recent Developments and New Agendas." *International Migration Review* 23, no. 3 (Autumn 1989): 638–670.

Brożek, Andrzej. *Polonia Amerykańska, 1854–1939*. Warsaw, Poland: Interpress, 1977.

Conzen Neils, Kathleen, David A Gerber, Ewa Morawska, George Pozzetta, and Rudolph J. Vecoli. "The Invention of Ethnicity: A Perspective from the U.S.A." *Journal of American Ethnic History* 12, no. 1 (Fall 1992): 3–41.

Duda-Dziewierz, Krystyna. *Wieś Małopolska a emigracja amerykańska*. Warsaw, Poland: Polski Instytut Socjologiczny, Dział Wydawnictw, 1938.

Dziembowska, Janina. *Pamiętniki Emigrantów: Stany Zjednoczone*, 2 vols. Warsaw, Poland: Instytut Gosodarstwa Społecznego/Książka i Wiedza, 1977.

Foner, Nancy. *In a New Land: A Comparative View of Immigration*. New York: New York University Press, 2005.

Gans Herbert J. "The American Kaleidoscope, Then and Now." In *Reinventing the Melting Pot: The New Immigrants and What It Means to Be American*, ed. Tamara Jacoby, 34–45. New York: Basic Books, 2004.

Granovetter, Mark. "Economic Action and Social Structure: The Problem of Embembeddedness." *American Journal of Sociology* 91, no. 3 (November 1985): 481–510.

Guarnizo, Luis E. "The Economics of Transnational Living," *International Migration Review* 37, no. 3 (Fall 2003): 666–699.

Guarnizo, Luis E., Alejandro Portes, and William Haller. "Assimilation and Transnationalism: Determinants of Transnational Political Action among Contemporary Migrants." *American Journal of Sociology* 108, no. 6 (May 2003): 1211–1248.

Handlin, Oscar. *The Uprooted: The Epic Story of the Great Migrations That Made American People*. Boston: Little, Brown, 1952.

Harris, John R., and Michael Todaro. "Migration, Unemployment and Development: A Two-Sector Analysis." *American Economic Review* 60, no. 1 (1970): 126–142.

Hoerder, Dirk. "An Introduction to Labor Migration in the Atlantic Economies, 1815–1914." In *Labor Migration in the Atlantic Economics: The Europeans and North American Working Classes during the Period of Industrialization*, ed. Dirk Hoerder, 1–31. Westport, CT: Greenwood Press, 1985.

Kamphoefner, Walter D., Wolfgang Helbich, and Ulrike Sommer. *News from the Land of Freedom: German Immigrants Write Home*. Ithaca, NY: Cornell University Press, 1991.

Lewitt, Peggy. "Social Remittances: Migration Driven Local-Level Forms of Cultural Diffusion." *International Migration Review* 32, no. 4 (Winter 1998): 926–948.

Levitt, Peggy, and Nina Glick Schiller. "Conceptualizing Simultaneity: A Transnational Social Field Perspective on Society." *International Migration Review* 38, no. 3 (2004): 1002–1039.

Massey, Douglas S., Joaquin Arango, Graeme Hugo, Ali Kouaouci, Adela Pellegrino, and Edward J. Taylor. "International Migration and Community Development." *Population Index* 62, no. 6 (Autumn 1996): 397–418.

Mincer, Jacob. "Family Migration Decision." *Journal of Political Economy* 85, no. 5 (1978): 749–773.

Morawska, Ewa. *Labor Migrations of Poles in the Atlantic World Economy, 1880–1914" European Migrants: Global and Local Perspectives,* eds. Dirk Hoerder, Leslie Page Moch. (Boston: Northeastern University Press, 1996), 170–210.

Morawska, Ewa. "Immigrants, Transnationalism and Ethnization: A Comparison of the Great Wave and the Last." In *E Pluribus Unum? Contemporary and Historical Perspectives on Immigrant, Political Incorporation*, eds. Gary Gertle and John Mallenkopf, 175–212. New York: Russell Sage Foundation, 2001.

Nugent, Walter. *Crossings: The Great Transatlantic Migration 1870–1914*. Bloomington: Indiana University Press, 1992.

Ong, Aihwa. *Flexible Citizenship: The Cultural Logic of Transnationality*. Durham, NC: Duke University Press, 1999.

Portes, Alejandro. "Immigration Theory for a New Century: Some Problems and Opportunities." *International Migration Review* 31, no. 4 (Winter 1997): 799–825.

Portes, Alejandro, Luis E. Guarnizo, and Patricia Landolt. "The Study of Transnationalism: Pitfalls and Promise of an Emergent Research Field." *Ethnic and Racial Studies* 22, no. 2 (March 1999): 217–237.

Portes, Alejandro, and Julia Sensenbrenner. "Embeddedness and Immigration: Notes on the Social Determinants of Economic Action." *American Journal of Sociology* 98, no. 6 (May 1993): 1320–1350.

Pula, James S. "Polska Diaspora w Stanach Zjednoczonych do 1914 roku." In *Polska Diaspora*, ed. Adam Walaszek, 51–76. Kraków, Poland: Wydawnictwo Literackie, 2001.

Praszałowicz, Dorota. "The Cultural Changes of Polish American Parochial Schools in Milwaukee, 1866–1988." *Journal of American Ethnic History* 13, no. 4 (Summer 1994): 23–45.

Praszałowicz, Dorota. "Overseas Migration from Partitioned Poland: Poznań and East Galicia as Case Studies." *Polish American Studies* 60, no. 2 (Autumn 2003): 59–81.

Sassen, Saskia. "Immigration and Local Labor Markets." In *The Economic Sociology of Immigration: Essays on Networks, Ethnicity and Entrepreneurship*, ed. Alejandro Portes, 87–127. New York: Russell Sage Foundation, 1995.

Stark, Oded, and David E. Bloom. "The New Economics of Labor Migration." *American Economic Review* 75, no. 2 (May 1985): 173–178.

Stark, Oded, Edward J. Taylor, and Shlomo Yitzhaki. "Remittances and Inequality." *Economic Journal* 96 (September 1986), 722–740.

Thistlethwaite, Frank. "Migration from Europe Overseas in the Nineteenth and Twentieth Centuries." In *A Century of European Migrations: 1830–1930*, eds. Rudolph J. Vecoli and Suzanne M. Sinke, 17–49. Urbana: University of Illinois Press, 1991.

Thomas, William I., and Florian Znaniecki. *The Polish Peasant in Europe and America*, 2 vols. New York: Dover, 1958.

Tilly, Charles. "Transplanted Networks." In *Immigration Reconsidered: History, Sociology, and Politics*, ed. Virginia Yans-McLaughlin, 79–95. New York: Oxford University Press, 1990.

Vecoli, Rudolph J. "Contadini in Chicago: A Critique of the Uprooted." *Journal of American History* 52, no. 3 (December 1964): 404–417.

Vertovec, Steven. "Rethinking Remittances." ESRC Transnational Communities Program Working Paper WPTC-2k-15. Oxford: Economic and Social Research Council, n.d.

Walaszek, Adam. *Reemigracja ze Stanów Zjednoczonych Ameryki do Polski po I wojnie światowej (1919–1924)*. Kraków, Poland: UJ, 1983.

Walaszek, Adam. "Wstóp." In *Polska Diaspora*, ed. Adam Walaszek, 7–29. Kraków, Poland: Wydawnictwo Literackie, 2001.

Jacob A. Riis (1849–1914):
How the Other Half Lives

Mary Elizabeth Brown

It must have been quite a show. The audience was usually composed of middle-class urbanites, some of them reformers and some of whom were drawn by their own reading or by announcements at their church. On the screen in front of them the magic lantern combined two slides, sometimes black and white and sometimes tinted, to produce a three-dimensional picture that both revolted and attracted them. They could almost step into the picture's narrow alley, squeezing between tenement house walls and lifting their skirts over the litter and garbage. From the stoops and windows, people peered back at them: men with shabby, ripped, and patched jackets, shirts, and pants and women with disheveled hair and huge aprons. Did the audience really want to get to know these people? Oh, yes, the lecturer assured them and proceeded to take them on a whirlwind tour, full of graphic details, lively anecdotes, comments about ethnic characteristics, warnings about impending class warfare, and, finally, impassioned pleas for reform, complete with detailed suggestions. And all of this delivered by an irrepressibly optimistic fair-haired man with gold wire-rim spectacles. It is unknown exactly *how* he spoke, and it is interesting that no one mentioned one detail. This group of middle-class Americans was being led on its photographic tour of immigrant slums by someone who himself might be expected to speak with a foreign accent. Jacob A. Riis was born in Denmark and immigrated to the United States as an adult.

Riis's was a show historians are still trying to analyze. Through his writings and photographs, he had a profound impact on a nation's views of immigrants, both at the time and since. He has been criticized for using, and thus perpetuating, the stereotypes of his day regarding Irish, Germans, Italians, Jews, Bohemians, Chinese, and African Americans. However, he also subverted the stereotypes, embodying and bolstering the argument that immigrant problems were due not to the immigrants themselves but to the environment in which they lived.

Riis was born on May 3, 1849, in Ribe, Denmark. As far as he was concerned, his first memorable event occurred when he was 15 years old. He caught a glimpse of nearly 13-year-old Elisabeth, the niece and foster daughter of the owner of Ri-

Jacob Riis's startling print and photographic exposés of conditions in New York City's slums in the late 19th century influenced a generation of investigative reporters and set the standard for future photojournalists. (Library of Congress)

be's only factory. Thereafter, he thought of his life story as being shaped around her. Other people might also note his father's influence. A member of the faculty of a preparatory school in Ribe, Mr. Riis may have recognized his son's talents early on, or he may have been vain enough to want someone to follow in his footsteps; either way, he wanted his boy to be a man of letters. Jacob, though, hated being stuck indoors at a desk and wanted to be a carpenter. This choice of a career brought physical proximity to Elisabeth; he helped to build a new factory for her father. However, it was not calculated to bring him into her social orbit. When he asked for her hand in marriage, her foster parents pointed out he had no steady work. Riis emphasized unrequited love rather than economics in his story of his decision to emigrate. He would make enough money to impress Elisabeth's foster parents. He arrived in New York Harbor on June 5, 1870, a month after he turned 21.

Riis had learned English in school in Denmark and so could seek work easily, but he was so anxious to get back to Elisabeth that he would not settle down. He drifted from one place to another, always returning to Manhattan. He experienced some aspects of the tramp life he later wrote about: futile searches for work followed by equally unsuccessful searches for food and for places to sleep, a stray person whose only companion was an equally stray dog. He reached a personal nadir one night when it was too cold and rainy to sleep outdoors, and he had to leave his dog outside and seek shelter at a police station lodging house. The police exercised their responsibility for New York's vagrants by opening rooms in certain station houses where the homeless might sleep. The room Riis slept in was bare of all furniture, save a platform on which planks rested. The men slept on the planks or, in other stations, on the floor, in their clothing. Most of them had not had recent opportunities for baths or laundry, and some smelled of liquor. One stole the gold locket containing a curl from Elisabeth's hair that Riis wore around his neck. When Riis complained, the sergeant on duty accused him of having stolen the locket from someone else and ordered him thrown out as a thief. When he appeared at the door, his dog rose up to greet him—only to be clubbed to death by the irate police officer. Riis shook the dust of the city from his feet and resumed his transient ways. Then he received a more severe blow. Elisabeth was engaged to a cavalry officer.

The news knocked the wind from Riis's sails. The next time he returned to Manhattan, he resolved to stay. He used his savings from his last itinerant job to take a course in telegraphy, with the idea of qualifying for a good skilled job. He dropped the course to follow what seemed a better opportunity, an entry-level position as a newspaper reporter. He had helped his father work on a newspaper in Ribe, and he liked the idea of being a reporter. It turned out the newspaper was in serious financial trouble and balanced its books on the backs of its employees, not paying them in a timely manner. Soon Riis was back on the street, homeless, hungry, reduced to peddling books on the corner by the Cooper Institute. As he told the story, his telegraphy teacher happened by, saw him, and mentioned that there was a job at a news-gathering agency. The next day, Riis showed up for it. He did well enough that, by May 1874, he could advance himself by leaving the agency and taking a better job as a reporter for the *South Brooklyn News*. He did well enough to buy the newspaper. The crowning touch was that he received another letter from home, mentioning that Elisabeth's fiancé had died.

Overlooking the morbid circumstances that permitted him to resume his persistent courtship, Riis wrote Elisabeth and received a favorable answer. He sold his newspaper for five times what he had paid for it, sailed to Copenhagen, boarded a train for Ribe, and went to visit Elisabeth's family, this time successfully. He and Elisabeth were married in Ribe's Lutheran church in March 1876. Soon thereafter, they set off for the United States. The only problem was that now Riis needed another job.

Riis returned to the newspaper he had sold, this time as editor. However, he had sold it to a group of politicians who were less reform-minded than he was. He gave up editing in favor of opening an advertising bureau. He purchased a magic lantern at a rummage sale, and he used it to develop slide shows, mixing slides of interesting scenery with those advertising consumer products. In 1877, Riis talked one of his neighbors, who was a city editor for the New York *Tribune*, into giving him a job. He moved from his starting position to a staff job at police headquarters and then, in 1890, to similar work with the New York *Sun*. His father had been correct: Riis had it in him to be a man of letters, albeit one who got outdoors a lot.

On a typical day, Riis left his Brooklyn house in the afternoon, walked or took public transportation, to the foot of Brooklyn's Fulton Street, ferried over to Manhattan's Fulton Street, and got up to the police station on Mulberry Street as quickly as possible. He checked his messages and then began nosing about the police station, alert for tips. He spent the rest of the afternoon and evening turning the tips into stories, chasing down and interviewing police officers, city officials, witnesses, and victims. During the evening, there might be some late-breaking news, in which case Riis would go along with the police to cover events firsthand and then hustle back to his desk to prepare his story. His workday wound down in the early morning. Now there was no real hurry, and so he would walk back to the ferry.

He could have gone from the police station over to the Bowery to take public transportation, but he preferred to walk. So between 2:00 and 4:00 A.M., he started down Mulberry Street, then a vast Italian neighborhood. He headed to the "Bend" or curve in the street at its southern terminus. He crossed Five Points, where several streets converged, passed City Hall, and ended up at the Fulton Ferry. During the day, when he was in the same neighborhood chasing down stories, he saw people acting tough or unconcerned or like big shots in their small circles of acquaintances. "It is a human impulse, I supposed," he mused. "We all like to be thought well of by our fellows. But at 3 A.M. the veneering is off and you see the true grain of a thing."[1]

An alley in a New York slum, as photographed by Jacob Riis ca. 1888. Riis, a police reporter who covered the Mulberry Bend neighborhood where this photograph was taken, published a book in 1890 that graphically illustrated the living conditions of the urban poor. (Library of Congress)

What he saw on Mulberry Street was disturbing enough that Riis put some distance between himself and it. In 1886, he moved his family to Richmond Hill, Long Island, where "[t]he very lights of the city were shut out. So was the slum, and I could sleep."[2] But Mulberry Street also reinforced Riis's commitment to reform: "It was not fit for Christian men and women, let alone innocent children, to live in, and therefore it had to go." The lectures on reform that Riis covered as a reporter helped him to analyze current events, and the sources he had cultivated for his newspaper stories he now began to press for assistance in understanding slum conditions. He planned a book on slums and even copyrighted the title, *How the Other Half Lives*. But he feared mere words would not convince people of what he saw nor stimulate them to action.

A solution to the inadequacy of words presented itself one morning in 1887. Riis was sitting at his breakfast and going over the newspaper when a little four-line news item caught his eye. Someone in Germany had figured out a way to make an artificial light by which one could take photographs. Riis immediately saw the implication. If he could take such photographs, he could bring the public with him to the midnight slums. This was not as easy as it sounded. Riis's first photographic outfit consisted of a box camera, a tripod on which to steady it, and a stack of glass plates, each covered with the emulsion necessary to take the pictures. To make the light, he at first used a pistol-like gadget that lit a magnesium cartridge but abandoned this in favor of a wick saturated in alcohol that he touched with a match and then used to light a thin film of magnesium he had spread across a frying pan. He did not have an easy time of it. He once set fire to the shreds of wallpaper clinging to the walls of a room in which six blind people lived, high atop a tenement building that had no fire escape. He managed to smother the flames before the situation became serious, and he was forced to try to lead the residents down the steep, rickety steps.

Riis tried to get better photographs by having someone else take them. However, few other people wanted to be in Mulberry Bend at 3:00 A.M. Perhaps also few wanted to engage in some of the tactics Riis used to get his pictures. To get a picture of overcrowding in tenement flats, he and his companions knocked on doors and then burst through, set up the camera, set off the flash, and took the picture before the sleepers could figure out what was going on. One person Riis paid to take photographs then tried to further increase his profit by selling the negatives. Occasionally, Riis could not take the photograph he wanted and so bought something similar from the Health Department or took a photograph of the photographs of criminals in the police station's rogues' gallery. For some, Riis's hiring photographers and borrowing photographs disqualifies him from being a photographer. For others, the important point is that, without his direction, the photographs would not have been taken and would not have been used for reform purposes.

Riis did not think he was a good photographer, and there is plenty of evidence in the surviving negatives to back him up. He has overexposed plates, underexposed plates, and plates with blurs on them, indicating someone moved during the exposure. Some of the technical problems would have challenged a more experienced photographer. Riis brought his camera to places that were so narrow that it was difficult for him to position himself for a good picture. The most troubling questions concern composition, or the placement of subjects in the photograph. Critics have accused Riis of posing his photographs to get what he wanted. Riis did pose his subjects. He told stories about a tramp whom he paid to sit for a photograph, only to have the tramp ask for more money when Riis wanted to include his picturesque pipe in the portrait, and about the gang that insisted on being photographed demonstrating, with wildly exaggerated gestures, its pickpocketing technique. He saw nothing wrong with posed shots. He knew what he wanted to bring out in his subjects, and sometimes he had to pose them to do it. But did he impose as well, using his photographs to communicate his ideas about the slums rather than the reality? If so, it might be important to remember one thing: Riis's ideas regarding slums may have been different from reality, but they were also different from the ideas of many of his contemporaries.

The technology of the times did not permit many photographs in newspapers. Riis therefore developed a slide show. He switched his work hours from night to day and made the rounds of churches and organizations, offering to deliver talks on tenement life and possible reforms. One evening an editor from *Scribner's* magazine was in his audience and approached him about doing a story based on the lecture and the photographs. The story, with line drawings based on the photographs instead of reproductions of the photographs themselves, appeared in the Christmas 1889 issue of the magazine. From that came an offer to write the book Riis had been planning for years, *How the Other Half Lives: Studies among the Tenements of New York*, which appeared in 1890.

How the Other Half Lives, and the photographs he took for it, made Riis's reputation. The book itself was a striking innovation. Like the *Scribner's* article, it had line drawings based on Riis's photographs, but it also had a number of the photographs themselves. They were reproduced for the book by the half-tone process, on special shiny white paper. The photographs, and the text that accompanied them, reflected Riis's immersion in his times. He knew the techniques of advertising, of newspaper journalism, and of mass-market magazines. He used them to get across a particular point of view.

It was a point of view that differed from conventional wisdom, which taught that poverty was a personal failing. Many of Riis's contemporaries argued that people were poor because they were idle, lazy, shiftless, thriftless, drunken, ignorant, and libidinous, not given to industry, punctuality, or sobriety, squandering what they had on drink, on a good time, on their vices. And they probably could not be cured of these faults. Science in the late 19th century indicated many traits were inherited. Although the phrase "gene pool" had not been coined yet, there was a sense that different groups of people had different characteristics. In a country already accustomed to racial issues and experiencing heavy immigration, it was a logical step to think that different ethnic groups had different characteristics. Given that these traits were supposed to be inherited, it was logical to keep charity to a minimum. Why do anything that encouraged the survival of the unfittest?

Riis used these stereotypes to shape *How the Other Half Lives*. The book begins with a couple of chapters on the housing problem, then turns to a long section divided into many chapters describing the various population groups. This section starts with an imaginary map of Manhattan's ethnic populations, with different colors for the Irish, Germans, Italians, Jews, Chinese, Bohemians, Arabs, and French. Riis then takes his readers into several of these neighborhoods, with chapters on Italians, Chinese, Jews, Bohemians, and Czechs and "the color line in New York."

(There is also a chapter on "street Arabs," but that was a colloquialism for home-less children.)

Riis's verbal walking tours all followed the same outline. He began on a dark note, referring to Bohemian anarchists, Chinese opium smoking, and Jewish money grubbing. Then he described the living conditions of these people and, for those who worked in the tenements, their work conditions as well. Finally, he finished with another passage on the characteristics of the ethnic group under question. Some passages fall all over themselves in an effort to sound favorable:

> With all his conspicuous faults, the swarthy Italian immigrant has his redeeming traits. He is as honest as he is hot-headed. There are no Italian burglars in the Rogues' Gallery; the ex-brigand toils peacefully with pickaxe and shovel on American ground. His boy occasionally shows, as a pick-pocket, the results of his training with the toughs of the Sixth Ward slums. The only criminal business to which the father occasionally lends his hand, outside of murder, is a bunco game, of which his confiding countrymen, returning with their hoard to their native land, are the victims. The women are faithful wives and devoted mothers. Their vivid and picturesque costumes lend a tinge of color to the otherwise dull monotony of the slums they inhabit. The Italian is gay, lighthearted and if his fur is not stroked the wrong way, inoffensive as a child. His worst offense is that he keeps the stale beer dives.[3]

How one reacts to that statement depends on how one evaluates the stereotyping behind it. Given the vicious stereotypes about the Italian mafia then circulating, Riis's assertions about Italians are pretty mild. However, any stereotype tends to obscure individuals. What about Italians who were not gay and lighthearted, who could not live up to the stereotype Riis assigned them?

Riis's chapters on Jewish and Chinese immigrants were structured differently. Instead of the upbeat conclusion about positive group characteristics, he suggested ways to help the immigrants. He had two chapters on Jews: one a general introduction to their neighborhood and the other on their work habits. Neither of these had any paragraphs praising any Jewish characteristics, and both had nasty asides about how Jews undermined their own health and oppressed their children with work beyond their years in their search for economic security. Nevertheless, none of these supposed characteristics were so ingrained that they could not be changed. The Jews, Riis wrote, "must be taught the language of the country they have chosen as their home, as the first and most necessary step."[4] He had no doubt "the people be both willing and anxious to learn" and that they could do it if they had time: "As scholars, the children of the most ignorant Polish Jews keep fairly abreast of their more favored playmates."[5] Riis did not think the Chinese were so hopeless they had to be excluded. "Rather than banish the Chinaman, I would have the door opened wider—for his wife; make it a condition of his coming or staying that he bring his wife with him. Then, at least, he might not be what he is now and remains, a homeless stranger among us."[6]

In both types of rhetoric, Riis aimed at the same conclusion: Immigrants were not naturally bad. What seemed naturally bad might be the result of their environment; the only way to find out was to change that environment. Riis definitely rejected the notion that extending charity to the poor only encouraged survival of the unfittest. In his discussion of African Americans, he saw the issues in a way not unbefitting of Booker T. Washington:

> The [color] line may not be wholly effaced while the name of the negro, alone among the world's races, is spelled with a small n. Natural selection will have more or less to do beyond a doubt in every age with dividing the races; only so, it may be, can they work out together their highest destiny. But with the despotism that deliberately assigns to the defenseless Black the lowest level for the purpose of robbing him there that has nothing to do.[7]

Another tactic Riis used further undercut the importance of heredity. He took photographs of every group he could find: Irish, Germans, Italians, Bohemians, Jews, Chinese, an English coal heaver with his wife and two daughters, a family circle of Mohawks. He put these pictures shoulder to shoulder. If one group had a particular undesirable trait, it seems everyone had it: African Americans had a gambling racket called policy, the Chinese had one called fan tan, and the Italians had their bunco games. Chinese tucked knives up the voluminous sleeves in their blouses, blacks hid razors in their boots, and Italians carried stilettos. If different races did the same things, how could these be ethnic traits? Pictured this way, it seemed doubtful ethnic background had much to do with poverty. Here were all the races of the world, all equally poor. It must have something to do with the environment in New York rather than with their heredity from the old country.

After his tour of ethnic neighborhoods established that ethnicity provided color but no substantial explanation for the horrendous conditions, Riis demolished one cornerstone of the traditional argument against the poor. His poor were anything but lazy. They worked, sometimes almost around the clock, sometimes seven days a week. Riis concentrated on those who worked in the tenements and documented the system that exploited recent immigrants, particularly Jews in the garment industry and Bohemians who worked rolling cigars. For example, coat manufacturing started in a factory, because the bolts of cloth from which the coats were cut were too expensive and heavy to move about and because cutting the pieces of cloth according to a pattern was a skilled job. However, the cut pieces went out to jobbers who promised to bring back semiassembled coats at a certain price. The jobbers either rented flats in tenements or used their own homes for tiny factories called sweatshops. They purchased sewing machines or, if they could, persuaded their employees to buy them on a kind of installment plan. Then they hired people, bearing in mind that their profit was going to be the difference between what they promised to make the coats for and what it actually cost them to have the coats made. They found it expedient to hire recent immigrants, who did not have any money, did not speak English, and thus had to find jobs fast but did not have a way to find them. The sweatshop workers basted the coats, sewed the seams, stitched the linings, added the collars, and pulled the basting threads. Then the jobber returned the coats to the factory. The coats went out again, this time to someone who worked at home; such a person was paid so much per buttonhole cut, per button sewn. The coats went back to the factory again, then to the wholesaler or retailer.

An even more complete oppression could be found in cigar making, for there the roles of real estate owner and shop owner, tenant and employee, were conflated. Cigar capitalists purchased tobacco and tenement houses. They rented out the latter to people who were willing to work in the former trade. Usually these were Bohemians, whose women learned the trade in the old country and then taught it to their immigrant husbands when language barriers prevented the men from resuming their skilled trades. The possibilities for exploitation here were almost endless, because the same person could both raise the rent and lower the piecework rates, and those who complained lost both their homes and their jobs.

The system, Riis pointed out, had many evils. Sweatshop operators paid no attention to health or safety regulations. The employees were vulnerable to sudden fires and to breathing in the lint from the cloth on which they worked. Labor was oppressed, with people working long hours for low pay, with no benefits and no job security. Children were particularly oppressed. The law said that children had to be 14 years of age to work in a factory. Riis, who had five children of his own, could tell by the little workers' growing teeth that some of these adolescents were no older than 12. He also took a sobering photograph of a woman with one baby on her lap and six more young children seated or standing at a round table, all except the baby busily assembling artificial flowers: Mom the sweatshop operator.[8]

Middle-class householder that he was, Riis was interested in what happened when the laborers turned into consumers, when these hardworking people received and spent their pay. He was appalled at what their housing money bought. There were no single-family dwellings in immigrant neighborhoods. There were houses that had once been single-family dwellings, but the families had moved to less congested neighborhoods, selling their houses to those who would live off rental income or were living off rental income themselves. Landlords increased their income by renting the house out in parts, one floor to a family or one room to a family, then letting out the cellar and the attic and building yet another rental unit in the rear. To these old houses were added modern tenements designed as multiple-unit dwellings. Whether old or new, the owners maximized their rent by neglecting their property, so that stairs sagged, plumbing leaked, and wallpaper peeled off the walls. Those who were willing to rent their houses to African Americans could increase their income by charging more than the going rate to a people who were as often shut out of decent housing by prejudice as by price.

The high rents, Riis complained, forced people to do things that worsened their housing conditions. Even the women worked, leaving no one free to do the housekeeping. If their combined income did not meet the expenses, families took in lodgers (to sleep in their flat) and boarders (to sleep and to eat). They took in work or turned their home into a sweatshop. Still, the high rents squeezed people out of their homes. Young women who could not make enough money at their work were tempted to turn to prostitution to meet their expenses. Young men had a few more options. They could become boarders or lodgers. If they could not afford that, they could stay at lodging houses for 25 cents per night, in which case they got a little partitioned area in which to sleep, with a bed and chair. Those who could afford only 15 cents got a dorm room with a row of beds, each with a locker at the foot to store clothes overnight. The 10-cent-a-night lodging house had no lockers. The 7-cent-a-night lodging house had no beds. The room had two sets of parallel wooden bars that served to anchor two tiers of hammocks. All of these were run by licensed operators. For 5 cents per night, one could crowd into an unlicensed tenement flat. For free, one could stay overnight at the police lodging house. Riis claimed to know real estate owners who cleared thousands of dollars in profit annually herding into lodging houses men who, if the rents were more reasonable, would not be homeless.

The centrifugal force of the rent pulled families apart. Children were crowded out of their households, literally, by the high numbers of people in the small space and, in an emotional sense, by the feeling that no one there noticed or cared for them. Again, boys had more options than girls. They could pick up work on the streets, blacking boots or fetching buckets of beer for construction workers. And they could reduce their expenses to almost nothing by stealing food from pushcart peddlers and by sleeping in sheltered spots. One wonders if Riis's employers were embarrassed that he photographed boys napping on the floor of the room at the *Sun* office where they would later pick up newspapers for sale.[9] Boys might fall into gangs and would thus go on to street fighting and criminal activity. Or they might grow up to be tramps, roaming the city streets, occasionally indulging in petty theft but most often begging and trying to get by.

Riis concluded his section on housing conditions and their effects with the story of a man—a husband, father, and unskilled laborer—who stood at the corner of Fifth Avenue and Fourteenth Street watching carriages full of wealthy and fashionable people roll from their uptown homes to their downtown shopping sprees. The contrast between their luxury and his penury grew too great for him to bear. He unsheathed a knife, perhaps a tool he would use for work—if he could get any.

He plunged into the traffic with the knife in his fist. "The man was arrested, of course, and locked up. To-day he is probably in a mad-house, forgotten. And the carriages roll by to and from the big stores with their gay throng of shoppers. The world forgets easily, too easily, what it does not like to remember."[10] Riis himself thought the man mad in using his knife but not in his analysis. The poor were not poor only through their own fault but through the action, and inaction, of others.

Riis then turned to describing efforts at amelioration. Balancing out his story about the man with the knife, he mentioned several wealthy individuals who were interested in alleviating poverty. He also discussed the role of religion. Riis himself was baptized into the Lutheran faith, attended a Methodist mission when he was first learning the newspaper business and before he married Elisabeth, and then settled into Episcopalianism, but he frequently mentioned the work of the Catholic clergy. Catholicism was set up on a territorial basis, with clergy responsible for particular areas, so some of them did live among the poor and knew how to help them. Riis also described institutions: the New York Foundling Asylum for babies; the Five Points Mission, Five Points House of Industry and Children's Aid Society for youngsters; the Newsboys' Lodging House on Duane Street; and agencies devoted to the concerns of working women. Yet these were not quite enough, as he noted when he told the story of the mother and her adult daughter who were found "sewing and starving" in an Elizabeth Street attic. Benevolent folk found the two women a job in New Jersey and a place to live there. Three weeks after being settled in their new home, the two were back in their wretched neighborhood. Another example of the ungrateful poor, who did not know what was good for them? Not at all. Riis was listening when the younger woman said, "We do get so kind o' downhearted living this way, that we have to be where something is going on, or we just can't stand it." And he answered those who argued that the poor were different from the middle class: "[T]here was sadder pathos to me in her words than in the whole long story of their struggle with poverty; for unconsciously she voiced the sufferings of thousands misjudged by a happier world, deemed vicious because they are human and unfortunate."[11]

New York was, in Riis's phrase, "a city of a thousand charities where justice goes begging." It needed fewer people to rescue the unfortunate and more to exercise ordinary humanity in their everyday dealings. In fact, the final point of *How the Other Half Lives* was that New York needed people who would not attempt to make a killing in the real estate market but would accept a reasonable profit and in turn provide reasonable housing. Riis closed the book with a few chapters describing model tenements, complete with maps showing how the buildings were laid out and how they were surrounded by gardens.

To reinforce his point that model tenements would find model tenants, Riis photographed tenement dwellers. The photographs were a good example of how he got people to see beyond the standard image of the slum. Some of the photographs showed the kind of nuclear family in which Riis himself lived: husband, wife, children. Photographs of people living alone showed how they made their dwellings homelike. Mrs. Benoir, a Mohawk woman, sat in her tiny dormer room braiding rugs, with just enough space to put her chair between her bed and her stove.[12] A Jewish man celebrated the Sabbath in a cellar with a single loaf of challah on a table devoid of even a cloth.[13] An Italian woman posed amidst the paraphernalia of the rag picker's trade, a swaddled baby on her lap, a Madonna of the slums.[14]

Riis did well by doing good. He remained in demand as a writer and lecturer the rest of his life. He turned out numerous magazine articles, more books on the need for reform, still more books on his native Denmark, and a campaign biography of Theodore Roosevelt. (His family published a collection of his Christmas stories posthumously.) He did well enough that he could afford to quit his job at the newspaper and to devote himself to freelance writing and to lectures.

Riis did more than just write. He wanted to enact some of the reforms he wrote about. After *How the Other Half Lives* came out, then-Police Commissioner Theodore Roosevelt left his calling card, and the two struck up a friendship. Riis told Roosevelt the story of his miserable night at the police lodging house; Roosevelt had the power to order the entire system shut down, which he did in 1896. He and Riis were more impassioned than thoughtful, as this action meant there was then no place at all for homeless people to stay. Riis succeeded in getting the block of tenements on the western side of Mulberry Bend condemned and then in getting the City of New York to turn the vacant lot into Columbus Park. This was another action that was more impassioned than thoughtful, as there were no plans to build replacements for the houses thus demolished.

Riis went on to become the chief advocate of small parks for neighborhood use, even serving as secretary of the Small Parks Commission. He helped to add to the modern notion of park use. Traditionally, a park was a green space where city dwellers renewed themselves by contact with nature. Riis championed the erection of children's playgrounds where youngsters could indulge what people at the time thought was their natural propensity for activity. He was so supportive of the charitable work of an Episcopalian women's group, the King's Daughters, that they named their settlement house after him. Riis's reporting on tenement house conditions influenced housing reform in New York in the 1890s. His enjoyment of the Christmas holidays made him a promoter of Christmas events: setting up a Christmas tree at Madison Square, holding a community carol sing (to give one more example of Riis's command of the technology of his time, the words to the songs were projected on big screens around the park), and selling Christmas seals to raise funds for research into tuberculosis.

By 1901, Riis had been married to Elisabeth for 25 years. Their family had grown to include grandchildren. Theodore Roosevelt had succeeded to the presidency upon the assassination of William McKinley, raising the possibility that the

Progressive urban reforms the two had championed locally in New York could now become national policy. It was a propitious time for an autobiography. *The Making of an American* became, after *How the Other Half Lives*, Riis's most popular work.

The Making of an American provides another perspective on Riis's attitude toward immigration. He and Elisabeth, who wrote half a chapter on their courtship from her perspective, freely extolled the beauties of their native Denmark. For Riis, the transition to American life was difficult primarily because he missed Elisabeth and because he had trouble holding a job. Any problems he might have had with English or American customs were reduced to a story typical of the kind he told about himself; he heard a mother tease her daughter about the latter having "set her cap" for him, but he did not know what that meant, and he sought to find out by asking the girl herself. He reported that Elisabeth was homesick on first coming to the United States. They remained attached to Denmark. The last chapter of the autobiography describes how Riis visited Denmark and lunched with the king. Riis summed up his attitude toward his own immigration with a familiar metaphor. The home country was his mother, the United States his wife. His love for one did not reduce his love for the other. Why did he not express similar sentiments in *How the Other Half Lives*? Perhaps because that was not his point. *The Other Half* was not about the importance of immigration and ethnicity; it took those for granted and went on to examine the American environment in which these people lived.

Riis also identified other crusades: eradicating child labor, designing better school buildings and placing those buildings in playgrounds, and setting up reformatories so that wayward boys were not mixed in with the hardened criminals of the city's penal system. But he had to leave these crusades to others. He was busy meeting the demand for his writings and lecturing and thereby meeting the financial demands of his family. Of the four children who had reached adulthood at the time of his death, three were still dependent on him financially, at least occasionally. He also suffered from personal tragedies. Elisabeth died on May 18, 1905. In 1907, Riis took a second wife, his longtime secretary Mary Phillips. He had one more child by her, a son who died soon after birth. Then Riis's own heart began to falter. On May 26, 1914, just weeks after his 65th birthday, his heart condition took his life.

Although Riis had been ill for some time, his death was unexpected and untimely. He and his second wife had planned his estate to the point of leaving it to his children. She had a small settlement that she used to build a long career as an entrepreneur on Wall Street. Most of his children were grown and living far away; his youngest son was still in school and too young to take responsibility for his father's legacy. They did not even attend to his collection of glass negatives. When another immigrant photographer, Alexander Alland, inquired about them, no one knew where they were. Riis's youngest son, Roger William, uncovered a box of lantern slides at the Barre, Massachusetts, farm his father had bought after his second marriage. When they were preparing to tear down Riis's former house in Richmond Hill, the new owners found the rest of Riis's materials under the eaves: 412 glass negatives, 161 lantern slides, and 193 prints.

The family donated the recovered material to the Museum of the City of New York. They have been used in exhibits and reproduced in photography books, new editions of *How the Other Half Lives*, and a variety of texts and monographs on the urban, ethnic working class at the turn of the century. Along with the photographs of the younger Lewis Hine, Riis's photographs have become the pictures of immigrant neighborhoods that people carry in their heads: ethnic groups with different costumes and customs, suffering under the same harsh living and working conditions, and striving toward the same goals of familial and economic stability.

Notes

1. Jacob A. Riis, *The Making of an American* (New York: Macmillan, 1901), 235–236.
2. Ibid., 287.
3. Jacob A. Riis, *How the Other Half Lives: Studies among the Tenements of New York*, with a new preface by Charles A. Madison (New York: Dover, 1971), 47.
4. Ibid., 106–107.
5. Ibid., 99–100.
6. Ibid., 83.
7. Ibid., 115.
8. Ibid., 123.
9. Ibid., 155.
10. Ibid., 233.
11. Ibid., 133.
12. Ibid., 190.
13. Ibid., 105.
14. Ibid., 45.

Bibliography

Most of Riis's photographic negatives are at the Museum of the City of New York. They have been published in two editions of *How the Other Half Lives: Studies among the Tenements of New York* (New York: Charles Scribner's Sons, 1890; reprinted with a new preface by Charles A. Madison, New York: Dover, 1971); a second is edited with an introduction by David Leviatin (Boston: St. Martin's [Bedford Press], 1996). They are also in Alexander Alland Sr., *Jacob A. Riis: Photographer and Citizen* (New York: Aperture, 1973). Two more recent critical editions include those edited by Hasia R. Diner, *How the Other Half Lives: Authoritative Texts, Contexts, Criticism* (New York: W. W. Norton, 2010) and Sam Bass Warner, *How the Other Half Lives: Studies among the Tenements of New York* (Cambridge, MA: Harvard University Press, 2010). There is no published collection of Riis's papers or anthology of his books. Besides *How the Other Half Lives*, Riis's books include the following studies of immigration, its impact on urban neighborhoods, and the possibilities for reform: *Out of Mulberry Street* (1898; reprint, Upper Saddle River, NJ: Literature House, 1970); *A Ten Years' War: An Account of the Battle with the Slum in New York* (1900; reprint, Freeport, NY: Books for Libraries Press, 1969); *The Battle with the Slum* (New York: Macmillan, 1902; reprint, Montclair, NJ: Patterson Smith, 1969); *The Children of the Poor* (New York: Charles Scribner's Sons, 1902; reprint, New York: Arno, 1971); *Children of the Tenements* (1903; reprint, Upper Saddle River, NJ: Literature House, 1970); *The Peril and Preservation of the Home* (New York: Macmillan, 1903); *Theodore Roosevelt, the Citizen* (New York: Outlook, 1904); and *Neighbors: The Life Stories of the Other Half* (New York: Macmillan, 1914). This was only part of his literary output, which also included magazine articles, Christmas tales, and accounts of Denmark. Riis also published an autobiography, *The Making of an American* (New York: Macmillan, 1901). Besides the biographical information in the reprints of *How the Other Half Lives* and in Alland, there is a good young reader's biography, Edith Patterson Meyer, *"Not Charity but Justice": The Story of Jacob A. Riis* (New York: Vanguard Press, 1974). A more recent journalistic biography is by Tom Buk-Swienty, *The Other Half: The Life of Jacob Riis and the World of Immigrant America*, translated from the Danish by Annette Buk-Swienty (New York: W. W. Norton, 2008).

Theodore Roosevelt (1858–1919): Race Suicide

Mary Elizabeth Brown

Theodore Roosevelt was a man of many accomplishments. Born in New York City on October 27, 1858, he entered public life in 1882 with his election to the New York State Assembly. He then held many and diverse offices, including police commissioner of the City of New York, assistant secretary of the navy, colonel in a volunteer regiment in the Spanish-American War, vice president of the United States, and, from 1901 to 1909, president of the United States. He was also the first presidential candidate of an important third party, the Progressive Party.

His achievements as president were equally diverse. He prevented the powerful banker J. P. Morgan from acquiring a monopoly over the nation's railroads, made the Panama Canal possible, promulgated the Roosevelt Corollary to the Monroe Doctrine, won the Nobel Peace Prize for his mediation of the Russo-Japanese War, supported the passage of the Pure Food and Drug Act and the Hepburn Act to regulate railroads, promoted conservation of natural resources, and sent U.S. naval ships on a round-the-world cruise to display U.S. military might. In private life, his activities included the hands-on management of a ranch he owned in the Dakotas, authorship of books and articles about historical and contemporary events, big-game hunting in Africa, and the exploration of previously unknown areas in Brazil, which named one of its rivers after him. Ironically, his adventurous life ended when he died quietly in his sleep at his estate on Oyster Bay, Long Island, on January 6, 1919.

Roosevelt's presidential administration could have been a turning point in the debate over U.S. immigration. His personal contacts put him in touch with the leading theoreticians of his day, the people whose ideas had implications for national immigration policy. His political clout gave him the power to press for laws. Yet he took the ideas of the intellectual leadership of his time in a wholly different direction, one that ended up putting off immigration restriction for a generation. How that happened is a story that encompasses the intellectual history of the day, politics, and Roosevelt's own personality.

The story starts with the research of Francis Amasa Walker, an economist and sometime president of the Massachusetts Institute of Technology and the person

Portrait of Theodore Roosevelt, ca. 1904. (Library of Congress)

who supervised the taking of the 1870 federal census. Walker was comparing that census's results with those of later censuses when he noticed that immigrants had higher birthrates than did native-born Americans. He explained this phenomenon in terms that came readily to an economist. By the late 19th century, industry was replacing agriculture, and urban living replacing rural. The shift to industry and urbanization increased the cost of living for several reasons. People were now paying for consumer goods, such as food, which they used to raise on the farms. They were paying more for consumer goods they had bought even when they did live on the farm; their city houses were on more expensive real estate than their farm homesteads. There were more things they could buy: No one needed to buy light bulbs until there was electricity, but once the house was wired, one might as well buy not only light bulbs but books and magazines to read under the new lights. Finally, there was more to want in the city, and large retail stores were happy to oblige. This, in turn, gave rise to the spectacle of store windows, posters, and newspaper advertising, all leading to the desire to be like other people with their stylish clothes. And it cost more to pass one's social status on to the next generation. Each child had to be carefully educated to find his or her place in the urban economy. The native born realized they had to limit the number of children they had and to spend more on each child's education in order to maintain their place in society.

By contrast, Walker continued, immigrants made different economic calculations. They clung to economic strategies developed in rural agricultural societies, where more children meant more hands for farm work. Even after they transferred from farm to factory and from country to city, they continued to take their children out of school early and to put them to work, preferring the pittance children brought in to the prospect of better future income from well-educated young adults. They either did not understand or did not care that they were undermining their own position by increasing the pool of cheap labor and lowering the overall wage rate.

Why did the immigrants have a different strategy than the natives? Walker argued that the immigrants were "beaten men from beaten races."[1] They were inherently, genetically, "racially," as Walker said, different from the natives. They were incapable of the kind of moral thought that would lead the natives to care so much for their children as to provide the best future for them. They were also incapable of rational economic calculations, of reasoning that if they temporarily forswore the earnings of their unskilled children, they could later count on greater earnings from highly educated children. Given that this is what Walker and other economists thought, it is no wonder immigration restriction had some support.

Another pioneer economist, John Rogers Commons, took Walker's analysis a step further. Commons was a paradoxical figure. He was interested in economic reform and particularly in making sure that economic prosperity reached the farm population and the industrial working class. However, he also thought that immigrants were incapable of reform, that they were racially different from native whites, further down on the evolutionary scale. However, Commons pointed out, this primitive nature meant the immigrants actually had the better survival plan. The native strategy sounded better in that it produced higher family income through education and in that it avoided the moral evil of child labor. However, the natives were still going to lose population. They were producing fewer children, while the immigrants were producing more. Eventually, the natives would lower their birthrate below the point of replacing themselves. They would then die out, leaving the country to the more numerous sons and daughters of immigrants. This replacement of native offspring by immigrant offspring was called "race suicide."

Here, the characterization of immigrants as members of primitive races came into play again, this time with disastrous consequences for U.S. history. Walker, Commons, and other social scientists and natural scientists argued that all the good characteristics of the United States were inherited. They denied that immigrants could assimilate—that is, acquire these characteristics through schooling or exposure to U.S. society. They further denied that immigrants could acquire these traits through intermarriage and the production of children of mixed parentage, for, they argued, mixing advanced people and primitive ones would dilute the traits of the advanced people. When the natives died out, then, all the good qualities of U.S. life would disappear with them, and the immigrants' invidious traits would take over. Thus, there was a second reason for restricting immigration. Not only were the immigrants themselves considered undesirable; their offspring could not be brought up to U.S. standards, and so the whole group should be barred at the outset.

Roosevelt knew about the economists and natural scientists. He had a lifelong interest in natural history. As a child, he terrorized the household servants by using the kitchen ice box to store the corpses of birds and small animals until he could mount them. He received his early education at home but entered Harvard College in 1876, came in contact with scientists there, and for a time seriously considered a scientific career for himself. As an adult he retained an interest in natural science. He knew one leading advocate of immigration restriction, Madison Grant, from their work together at the Boone and Crockett Club in Manhattan and from their mutual interest in the American Museum of Natural History. Roosevelt had fewer connections with the social scientists. He preferred history and politics to sociology and economics. However, he did know some restrictionists among the historians and politicians. The only reason he was not on a first-name basis with biographer, editor, politician, and restrictionist Henry Cabot Lodge was because Lodge used his middle name, which linked him to an old New England family. Lodge referred to Roosevelt as "Roosevelt," and Roosevelt referred to Lodge as "Cabot."

Roosevelt could have brought the social scientists' and natural scientists' racist notions to the presidency. He could have used the "bully pulpit" of the presidency, a phrase he coined, to push for immigration restriction. He was popular with the public, and he had what politicians call long coattails, the ability to get everyone else running on his party ticket elected. He could have led the way to restricted immigration. Instead, his record regarding immigration and race was mixed.

In one instance, Roosevelt refused to press for a racially restrictive immigration law. Roosevelt had been vice president for seven months when, on September 6, 1909, an anarchist shot William McKinley while the latter shook hands in a receiving line at an exposition in Buffalo, New York. Although the anarchist was native born, he had a foreign-sounding name, Leon Czolgosz. Congress drafted a bill prohibiting the migration of anarchists.

The bill included a number of other immigration-related provisions. It continued the prohibition on the importation of contract labor, extended to three years the grace period during which authorities could double-check to see that each immigrant had been properly admitted to the United States, provided for the deportation of those improperly admitted, and permitted deportation of those who became public charges (went on welfare) within two years of their arrival. Most important, the bill required each immigrant (or one person in a family) to be able to read a 50-word passage in a modern language of the immigrant's choice. This last provision was a Trojan horse. The places that scientists thought sent undesirable immigrants also had low literacy rates. Requiring literacy would thus exclude the racially undesirable.

Immigrants and immigration advocates realized the literacy test was being used to sneak racial restrictions into immigration law. They demanded that the proposal be dropped from the bill. Even though one of the literacy test's supporters was Roosevelt's good friend and political colleague Henry Cabot Lodge, Roosevelt advocated compromise, and the literacy test was dropped from the final version of the law, which Roosevelt signed in 1903. There was no literacy test, and thus no racial restriction of Europeans, until 1917, 14 years after Roosevelt signed the law and 8 years after he left office.

Although Roosevelt did not support a literacy test for incoming immigrants, he did support raising the standards for naturalized citizens. In 1906, Roosevelt signed a law regulating the naturalization process. The law created a Bureau of Immigration and Naturalization, the predecessor of the Immigration and Naturalization Service. It set up a standard process for applying for citizenship, with forms used throughout all the states and with fixed fees for processing those forms. Included in the requirements for naturalization was one that all candidates for citizenship who were between childhood and old age have some ability to speak English.

Other Roosevelt actions recognized the role of immigrants in U.S. political life. In 1906, newspaper entrepreneur William Randolph Hearst ran for governor of the state of New York on the Democratic ticket. In his campaign, Hearst called for generous immigration laws. Hearst could not have carried out this particular campaign promise. Even if he had been elected, immigration law was a federal, not a state, affair. Nevertheless, he seemed to be on his way to winning—and in Roosevelt's home state. Roosevelt did the Republicans back home a favor. He called on Jacob Schiff, a German Jewish immigrant, entrepreneur, and philanthropist, and asked him for suggestions for candidates for a new office, secretary of the Department of Commerce and Labor. On Schiff's recommendation, he gave the job to Oscar Straus. Roosevelt's act undermined Hearst's claim that the Democrats were the immigrants' best friend and helped to defeat Hearst. It also may have been of real help to immigrants, as Straus headed the cabinet department charged with supervising immigration. It definitely broke new ground in patronage. Previous presidents had balanced their cabinets by selecting members based on their geographical background. By appointing Straus, a Jew, Roosevelt pushed the idea to include balancing the cabinet with representatives from various ethnic and religious groups.

In another instance, Roosevelt did make a racial exclusion, but he did so in order to halt racism at another level of government. In 1906, the state of California began to segregate Asian children into separate classrooms in its public schools. The government of the Empire of Japan protested this treatment of its citizens and their offspring. Roosevelt explained to imperial diplomats the difference between federal and state government, hoping to buy some time. In February 1907, he brought the Californians to a meeting in Washington, DC, and bought some time from them, too, convincing them to desegregate their schools in exchange for his promise to work toward federal legislation limiting Japanese migration. That October, Roosevelt sent William Howard Taft to Japan to work out the details of the "Gentlemen's Agreement," whereby the United States would not issue passports to citizens bound for Japan whom the Japanese would find objectionable, and Japan would not issue passports to subjects bound for the United States whom the Americans would find objectionable. This diplomatic agreement was intended to limit Japanese immigration. It was backed up by legislation. Roosevelt again sacrificed a clause for a literacy test in order to get through Congress a 1907 bill containing a provision preventing the Japanese who had gone to the U.S. possession of Hawaii to work in the sugar fields from coming to the United States.

The most support Roosevelt gave those who wanted to restrict European immigration on racial grounds came in 1907, when he signed an omnibus immigration law. The law concretized the 1907 Gentlemen's Agreement with Japan, prohibited the immigration of people with various sorts of mental handicaps (the exact wording of the law referred to "imbeciles," the "feeble-minded," and the "mentally defective," each of which had a precise meaning to the mental health professionals of the day). The law also established a commission to study immigration. Under the care of William Paul Dillingham, the commission produced a multivolume study rigged to prove that immigrants coming from Southern and Eastern Europe were inferior to those coming from Northern and Western Europe, which strengthened the restrictionists' cause and contributed to the passage of restrictive laws in 1917 and in the 1920s.

Roosevelt did not do as much as he could have done to promote immigration restriction. None of his work on immigration mentions race suicide or the ideas associated with it. Perhaps Roosevelt was simply a shrewd politician, unwilling to risk immigrant votes by coming out openly against immigration. However, Roosevelt's published writings suggest another reason why he did not urge immigration restriction. He had a different solution to the perceived problem of race suicide. He called not for fewer immigrants but for more American babies.

Shortly after his second inauguration, on March 13, 1905, Roosevelt addressed the National Congress of Mothers. He laid out ideas that he would return to again. The first was the relationship between the individual and the state. Individuals, he claimed, had responsibilities to the state. (This was very different from the idea expressed in the Declaration of Independence that "governments are instituted among men, deriving their just powers from the consent of the governed," meaning the people did not owe the government as much as the government owed the people.) Women, Roosevelt told his audience, had a responsibility specific to their sex. Only women could bear and rear children. On them, then, population increase depended, and on population increase depended settlers for the frontier, the labor force for the economy, and the soldiers for the army. Thus, it was women's responsibility to have as many children as possible.

The problem was, women were not having many children. Roosevelt asserted, correctly, that the birthrate was declining. He also asserted, correctly, that it was declining fastest among the well educated and well off. He further asserted that this was because women preferred to do other things rather than to have children.

In this case, Roosevelt made a break with other theorists of race suicide. Walker and Commons thought of the lowered birthrate as a *family* strategy, done to better provide for each child. Roosevelt saw it as a *woman's* strategy, something that gave women more options in life than motherhood.[2]

Roosevelt also differed from Walker and Commons in his solution to the problem of the declining birthrate. Rather than advocate immigration restriction, he urged women to have more children. Throughout his presidency, *The Ladies' Home Journal*, a leading women's monthly magazine of the day, carried short essays from Roosevelt on the importance of motherhood. One might argue that Roosevelt's writings for *The Ladies' Home Journal* were public relations pieces. Mrs. Roosevelt was of the opinion that a lady's name should appear in the press only at birth, marriage, and death. Since the women's magazines could not get much out of her, they had to content themselves with the material her more voluble husband was always eager to supply.[3] There is other evidence, though, that Roosevelt was really interested in boosting the U.S. birthrate. In April 1907, he was reading an article about "The Doctor in the Public School," another idea Progressive reformers championed, in the *Review of Reviews*. The article concluded that the physician's experience showed the importance of maintaining a low birthrate so that people could have fewer children and take better care of them. Roosevelt called the editor, long-distance, with a rebuttal that appeared in the next issue:

> There are countries which, and people in all countries, who, need to be warned against a rabbit-like indifference to consequences in raising families. The ordinary American, whether of the old native stock or the self-respecting son or daughter of immigrants, needs no such warning. He or she needs to have impressed upon his or her mind the vital lesson that all schemes about having "doctors in public schools," about kindergartens, civic associations, women's clubs, and training families up in this way or that are preposterous nonsense if there are to be no families to train.[4]

After leaving the White House, Roosevelt continued to advocate parenthood. In 1917, he published a collection of essays entitled *The Foes of Our Own Household*. Among the essays were "The Parasite Woman; the Only Indispensable Citizen" and "Birth Reform from the Positive, Not the Negative, Side." Roosevelt used these later essays to answer objections to his theory that had been raised in the eight years since he first voiced it. One of the most serious was the complaint that he was urging women to have children only in order to have cannon fodder. This was especially problematic by 1917, when the United States entered World War I. Roosevelt stuck to his guns, writing, "If we now had war, these four boys [his sons] would all go. We think it entirely right that they should go if their country needs them."[5] They did go, and they, and Roosevelt, paid a high price. Roosevelt was devastated when, on July 20, 1918, he received word that his son Quentin had died when his airplane went down behind German lines. (Roosevelt would lose two other sons to war. His son Kermit died while on duty in Alaska in 1943 and another son, also named Theodore, died on July 12, 1944, of a heart attack while serving as military governor of Cherbourg, recaptured from the Nazis shortly after the D-day invasion.)

Urging women to have large families may make Roosevelt sound as retrograde regarding sex as Commons, Walker, and other restrictionists were regarding race. Actually, Roosevelt was ahead of his time in some matters related to women's place. While physicians argued that too much education drained a woman's energy toward her brain and away from her reproductive organs, leaving her unfit for childbearing, Roosevelt declared "the woman is entitled to just as much education as the man, and it will not hurt her one particle more than it hurts the man."[6] When law and custom barred women from traditional male professions, Roosevelt proclaimed, "any woman should be allowed to make any career for herself of which she is capable, whether or not it is a career followed by a man."[7] When other people argued that if women were allowed to vote, they would forsake their homes for politics, Roosevelt wrote, "The right to vote no more implies that a woman will neglect her home than that a man will neglect his business."[8] When he bolted the Republican Party and fostered the development of a third party, the Progressive Party, it was a woman, Jane Addams, who seconded his nomination as the party's candidate for the presidency in 1912, eight years before women got the right to vote nationwide. Regarding more intimate forms of male domination, Roosevelt was a Victorian gentleman. He opposed men siring large families simply to show off their virility: "[T]he imposition on any woman of excessive childbearing is a brutal wrong; and of all human beings a husband should be most considerate of his wife."[9] In an age that practiced a sexual double standard, Roosevelt held himself to the higher standard usually considered appropriate for women. He was very proud that he had not engaged in sex before marriage and therefore had nothing to hide from his wife.

Roosevelt's vehement attitude toward women's role in race suicide might have stemmed not from any ideas about competition between natives and immigrants, or from any ideas about women, but from personal experience. Biographers make much of two events of Roosevelt's childhood. Roosevelt was born shortly before Lincoln's election. His father, also Theodore, did not fight in the Civil War. He was married to Martha Bulloch, a native of Georgia, and he did not want to upset her by going to war against her home state and her relatives. Their son, by contrast, went out of his way to involve himself in the Spanish-American War. When World War I broke out, President Woodrow Wilson had to find a tactful way to turn down the 59-year-old Roosevelt's offers to resume command.

Besides a father who did not fight in the war, the young Roosevelt had precarious health. He always had poor eyesight and wore thick spectacles. (Years later, when he was drawing pictures of himself for his preliterate children, he always made sure to draw the eyeglasses.) During his youth, he had asthma attacks. His father turned the back of their house on East 20th Street into a home gymnasium so the youth could build himself up. Some of his body-building exercises included learning how to box. In adult life, he sought out physical challenges. Biographers argue that Roosevelt's father's lack of a military record and his own sickly childhood gave him obstacles to overcome. These incidents gave him an early start in the belligerence that one can see in many incidents of his life.

Insofar as race suicide is concerned, the pertinent experiences seem to be those of adulthood. Early in 1879, when he was in the second semester of his junior year at Harvard, Roosevelt met 17-year-old Alice Hathaway Lee and fell for her completely. He spent eight months energetically campaigning for her to marry him. He was so involved with her that his friends worried about what might happen to him if she turned him down. She agreed to marry him on January 25, 1880. They announced their engagement on Saint Valentine's Day, and then Roosevelt launched an equally vigorous campaign directed at her parents to permit them to marry as soon as possible. Their wedding took place on his 22nd birthday (she was 18), October 27, 1880. Shortly thereafter, the young Roosevelts bought property on Long Island on which to build a big house for the large family they both hoped to have. Theodore wanted to name it Leeholm, in honor of Alice's family.

There was some problem starting that large family. Alice had to consult doctors and even undergo surgery to improve her prospects for becoming a mother. However, plans for a family seemed well under way on February 13, 1884. Roosevelt was at work in the capitol building in Albany when a telegram reached him notifying him that Alice had given birth to a daughter. At that time, there was no reason for him to be at her bedside. Women of Alice's class were attended by physicians and nurses, and women who could not afford or did not want a male doctor could still get a midwife and some women friends. Later that day came news that Alice was ill, and Roosevelt took the train south from Albany to New York City. He found not only that Alice was dying of Bright's disease but that his mother was also dying of typhoid fever. Martha Bulloch passed away first, in the early hours of February 14. Alice died that afternoon.

In those days, it was not unusual for someone who had suffered the loss of a close family member to withdraw for a period of time. Roosevelt, though, withdrew all the way to the Dakotas. After the end of the legislative session and the Republican convention, Roosevelt used his inheritance (his father had died while he was at Harvard) to purchase a ranch in the Dakotas, which he managed himself from 1884 until 1886. His ranching came to an end when the blizzard of 1886 wiped out his ranch.

Roosevelt did make trips back east, though, and it was on one of those trips that he found a second wife. During his adolescence, Roosevelt had become acquainted with his sister Corinne's best friend, Edith Carow, and they may have become close. At some point after Alice's death, Roosevelt resumed his friendship with her. They became engaged on November 17, 1885. On December 2, 1886, the two married in a quiet ceremony in London.

Alice's daughter, whom Roosevelt had named Alice Lee in her mother's honor, joined Theodore and Edith at the Long Island estate, which Theodore renamed Sagamore Hill. Edith and Theodore had five more children: Theodore Jr. (born 1887), Kermit (1889), Ethel (1891), Archibald (1894), and Quentin (1897). Roosevelt's move to the White House brought his family to public attention. At that point, his six children were, respectively, in their 17th, 14th, 12th, 10th, 7th, and 4th years. They brought to the White House a stable of horses and a menagerie of pets. They tried out all their toys; the stilts were particularly well suited to the high ceilings in the formal rooms. They livened up the White House in a way not seen since Abraham and Mary Todd Lincoln brought their boys there and not seen again until John F. Kennedy and Jacqueline Bouvier Kennedy brought Caroline and John-John. And they were not alone. Roosevelt's letters to them indicate that he was, in some ways, one of them. When he went on trips, he wrote them letters. If they were too young to read, he drew them pictures. Upon his return, he brought them animals for their menagerie. He played with them and through play guided them to adult skills such as horseback riding.[10] Edith's poise and distant, detached demeanor reinforced the general perception that her lively, playful husband was in some ways another one of her children.[11]

It is difficult to read Roosevelt's oft-repeated line that "the pangs of motherhood put all men in women's debt" and not hear the voice of a husband whose wife died shortly after childbirth. When reading his praise of good mothers, the image of Edith comes to mind: a woman who raised several children and spent her time on caring for them, her household, and her husband. Altogether, there is something autobiographical about Roosevelt's writings on race suicide, a sense that Roosevelt was preaching about what he was practicing. Perhaps that is what makes his writing more compelling than the scientific treatises or the anti-immigrant rantings of people who made race suicide part of the debate on immigration.

Ironically, it was that same passion that brought the issue of race suicide to the public. During Roosevelt's presidency, there was a burst of interest in his argument that the lowered birthrate was a problem and that it stemmed from women's reluctance to have children. The issues Roosevelt raised continue to be of concern to those interested in women's issues.

However, during Roosevelt's presidency, this shifting of the debate over race suicide to a focus on women was a diversion. After Roosevelt left the presidency, leadership in the discussion of race suicide returned to the social scientists and natural scientists who regarded it as a problem only insofar as immigrants tended to increase faster than natives. Therefore, they saw it as a problem that could be solved through immigration restriction.

Notes

1. Francis A. Walker, "The Tide of Economic Thought," *Publications of the American Economic Association* 6 (January–March 1891): 37.
2. Linda Gordon, *Woman's Body, Woman's Right: Birth Control in America*, rev. and updated (New York: Penguin, 1990), 136–158.
3. Betty Boyd Caroli, *First Ladies*, exposition edition (New York: Oxford University Press, 1995), 120–121.
4. "A Letter from the President on Race Suicide," *Review of Reviews* 35 (May 1907): 550–551.
5. Ibid., 551.
6. Theodore Roosevelt, *The Foes of Our Own Household*, vol. 19 of *The Works of Theodore Roosevelt* (New York: Charles Scribner's Sons [National Edition], 1926), 143.
7. Ibid., 141.
8. Ibid., 145.
9. Ibid., 165.
10. Theodore Roosevelt, *Letters to His Children*, vol. 19 of *The Works of Theodore Roosevelt*, ed. Hermann Hagedorn (New York: Charles Scribner's Sons [National Edition], 1926).
11. Caroli, *First Ladies*, 118–124.

Bibliography

Elting E. Morison and John M. Blum, eds., *The Letters of Theodore Roosevelt*, 8 vols. (Cambridge, MA: Harvard University Press, 1951–1954) and Hermann Hagedorn, ed., *The Works of Theodore Roosevelt*, 20 vols. (New York: Charles Scribner's Sons, 1926) bring together Roosevelt's writings. Among these, the most useful are volume 19 of the National Edition set, which contains a reprint of *The Foes of Our Own Household* (1917), chapters 11 and 12 of which are on women and birth control. Another useful volume is Willis Fletcher Johnson, ed., *Theodore Roosevelt: Addresses and Papers* (New York: Sun Dial Classics, 1908). One can also consult Roosevelt's pieces in the periodical press, specifically: "A Letter from the President on Race Suicide," *Review of Reviews* 35 (May 1907): 550–551, and essays in *The Ladies' Home Journal* 20 (July 1905): 3–4; 23 (February 1906): 21; and 24 (June 1908). For useful one-volume biographies, see William H. Harbaugh, *The Life and Times of Theodore Roosevelt,* new rev. ed. (New York: Oxford University Press, 1975) and Nathan Miller, *Theodore Roosevelt: A Life* (New York: William Morrow, 1992). Regarding the effect of the race suicide debate on U.S. women's history, see Linda Gordon, *Woman's Body, Woman's Right: Birth Control in America*, rev. and updated (New York: Penguin, 1990), esp. chapter 7, 136–158. For context on the national character, see Leroy G. Dorsey, *We Are All Americans, Pure and Simple: Theodore Roosevelt and the Myth of Americanism* (Tuscaloosa: University of Alabama Press, 2007); Laura L. Lovett, *Conceiving the Future: Pronatalism, Reproduction, and the Family in the United States, 1890–1938* (Chapel Hill: University of North Carolina Press, 2007); Delber McKee, *Chinese Exclusion versus the Open Door Policy, 1900–1906: Clashes over China Policy in the Roosevelt Era* (Detroit: Wayne State University Press, 1977); Hans P. Vought, *The Bully Pulpit and the Melting Pot: American Presidents and the Immigrant, 1897–1933* (Macon, GA: Mercer University Press, 2005).

Sanctuary Movement

Nicholas Rademacher

Sanctuary, in relation to immigration into the United States, refers to a social movement that was started in the 1980s to provide aid to undocumented persons in the United States by assisting them with their applications for asylum or citizenship; providing aid in the form of food, clothing, and shelter, among other social services; and advocating for change in U.S. immigration policy. The history of the sanctuary movement from its foundation to the present day is characterized by tension between sanctuary workers and agents of the government, both at the federal and local level, who are intent on enforcing immigration laws that require the deportation of people who are in this country illegally and that restrict the extent of assistance U.S. citizens can provide to those who are here without documentation.

The conflict between sanctuary members and the federal government arises from both political and religious differences. The political dimension of the conflict has to do with a fundamental disagreement over U.S. immigration policy, with particular emphasis on how best to respond to the various political and economic crises faced by people from all parts of the world but with special attention paid to people from Mexico, Central America, and South America who come to the United States for political and/or economic reasons. Agents of the federal government see the presence of undocumented persons strictly in terms of legal justice and thereby seek to have them removed because their presence violates state or federal law. Additionally, under certain circumstances, individuals or groups of people who harbor undocumented persons may be in violation of the law and subject to prosecution. Sanctuary workers, on the other hand, have challenged government policy both on legal grounds, through the lens of international treaties to which the United States is a signatory, and on religious grounds according to biblical justice. The appeal to biblical justice reflects the religious dimension of the conflict. Sanctuary workers are motivated in large part by their faith commitments, which are rooted in scripture and tradition. Given this religious dimension, the sanctuary movement may be described in terms of a church-state conflict.

This essay provides an overview of the history of the sanctuary movement in the United States from its beginnings in the 1980s; a discussion of the political and religious dimensions of the conflict; and a consideration of the contemporary status of the sanctuary movement. The history of the sanctuary movement reveals the role that civil society can play in shaping U.S. immigration policy. Confronted by the human face of immigration and inspired by their religious convictions, sanctuary workers have challenged a bureaucratic approach to the movement of peoples across the southern U.S. border that appears to reduce the immigrant to a faceless "illegal alien" who is subject to hasty deportation and who possesses minimal to no rights.

A Long History of Sanctuary

The word *sanctuary* is derived from the Late Latin *sanctuarium*, a derivative of *sanctus*, meaning holy, sacred, and refers to a place that is set apart and distinct from the everyday for the worship of a deity or deities. The term sanctuary also refers to the role of a religious building as a safe haven for people seeking refuge from state-administered law. The notion of sanctuary in the Western world dates back to Hebrew Scriptures and undergoes significant development within the Christian tradition, especially through its encounter with Roman law and the eventual emergence of Western European nation-states.

In the Hebrew Scriptures, specifically in Exodus, Numbers, Deuteronomy, and the first book of Kings, sanctuary was available to people who accidentally committed murder. Intentional killing was punishable by immediate death; thus, a claim of sanctuary provided an opportunity for a trial by an assembly in order to potentially obviate any further loss of innocent life.

Sanctuary was not relevant in the Christian tradition until the persecution of Christians abated in the decades after Constantine's conversion when Christianity was legalized. The first official reference to sanctuary in a Christian context appears in the Theodosian Code of 392, which discussed asylum for Christian fugitives in the area surrounding a church. Because Christianity was, by this time, the official religion of the Roman Empire, Jewish people and other people outside of the Christian religion were not granted asylum under any circumstances. As the concept and practice of sanctuary developed, the local church authority—bishop, abbot, or other clergy, depending on the circumstances—acquired the jurisdiction to investigate the status of the fugitive's claim over and against claims made against the accused by the state when an accused person declared sanctuary according to prevailing norms. Disputes between imperial and ecclesiastical officials on this matter reflected the ongoing tension between the jurisdiction of church and state in the temporal order as each party attempted to establish authority over its counterpart. Church leaders were able to retain vestiges of authority in this area until the Reformation and the emergence of nation-states, well into the 18th century in England and Continental Europe.

Since 1996, when Congress suppressed all sanctuary policies (Pub. L. No. 104-193, 110 Stat. 2105 [1996] and Pub. L. No. 104-208, Division C, 110 Stat. 3009, 546 [1996]), there is no legal standing for sanctuary as such in the United States. The term, however, has been invoked in instances of civil disobedience both before and after the 1996 congressional action. Civil disobedience refers to nonviolent resistance to the laws of a ruling government or occupying authority in an attempt to expose and overturn injustice in the established order but not necessarily to overthrow the entire system. Refusal to obey the laws of the state can be rooted in adherence to divine law. Civil disobedience has a long history in the United States, but, in connection to the claims of sanctuary, numerous Christian ministers most famously employed it during the abolition movement through the Underground Railroad, when they flouted the Fugitive Slave Act of 1850 by harboring runaway slaves, and during the Vietnam War, when they harbored draft resistors.

The U.S. government does not abide sanctuary claims because they have no legal standing. During the Vietnam War, for example, the federal government did not respect the draft resisters' claims to sanctuary and routinely arrested violators of conscription whether they were in a church building or elsewhere. Nevertheless, in the 1980s, less than 10 years after the draft was repealed in 1973, the anti-Vietnam war rhetoric provided the background and theoretical framework for the sanctuary movement in the United States. In forming the sanctuary movement, many individuals felt compelled by conscience to disobey U.S. immigration law in order to adhere to their interpretation of God's law as interpreted according to Scripture and theological tradition. In doing so, they opened their churches and homes to people fleeing their homelands for safer habitats.

Sources of the Sanctuary Movement in the United States, 1980–1990

Several events made front-page news in the United States in 1980 that raised many Americans' awareness to the plight of the people in Central America. They simultaneously served to galvanize the efforts of those Americans who wanted to show solidarity with the region. First, the assassination of Oscar Romero, Archbishop of San Salvador, El Salvador, on March 24, 1980; second, on July 7, 1980, the discovery of a group of distinctively middle-class refugees who had been abandoned in an Arizona desert by their trafficker; and, third, the rape and murder of three American religious women and one lay woman missioner on December 2, 1980.

The assassination of Archbishop Oscar Romero was particularly significant for the United States, because he consistently and vociferously criticized the arms trade of the United States government, which was providing weapons to the repressive regime that held power in El Salvador. When Romero became archbishop

The violently repressive actions of the Salvadoran government against its citizens and clergy transformed Archbishop Oscar Romero into a crusader against human rights violations and a critic of U.S. military aid to El Salvador. The flight of so many Salvadorans to the U.S. prompted the sanctuary movement among many American Christians. (Leif Skoogfors/Corbis)

of San Salvador, he was not conscientized to the plight of the Salvadoran people, but, over time, through direct contact with their suffering, he became immersed in their struggle and denounced the violence on both sides of the conflict, including the role of the United States. As a result of his protest, Romero was assassinated while saying Mass on March 24, 1980.

Closer to home, the death of middle-class Salvadorans in an Arizona desert received widespread media coverage, because it revealed that people were not fleeing that country for solely economic reasons. Instead, people with financial means were fleeing their homeland to escape rampant political violence. Middle- and upper-class Americans were able to identify with these victims of the punishing wilderness. Finally, the rape and murder of the religious women from the United States made front-page news. Suddenly the victims of the violence in El Salvador were not exclusively Salvadorans, but the casualties now included humanitarian workers from the United States.

The Story behind the Stories: Crises in Central America

Media coverage of the events of 1980 prompted the uncovering of significant and compelling human rights abuses happening across several countries in Central America. The civil wars in El Salvador and Guatemala were the impetus for a significant spike in immigration from those countries to the United States. Salvadorans and Guatemalans were not fleeing their homelands simply to discover better economic opportunities elsewhere but to escape the horrific conditions arising from the civil war.

A handful of families in El Salvador held the vast majority of land while the majority of Salvadorans lived in poverty. There were numerous revolts against the ruling class from the time El Salvador gained independence in 1842, but none were successful in democratizing the government or the economy. Revolts against military dictatorships in the 1960s and 1970s were met with government repression. Frente Farabundo Martí para la Liberación Nacional, a coalition of left-wing revolutionary groups, was the main opposition to the government that was run by the Partido de Conciliación Nacional (PCN). PCN ruled over a country that was growing increasingly dissatisfied with the status quo, as evidenced by a rising number of strikes and demonstrations against the government. Even members of the Roman Catholic clergy in the country, who otherwise could be relied upon to support the government, were voicing opposition. In 1979, PCN was deposed by a military coup, and a 12-year civil war ensued. Human rights abuses that had been characteristic of the military dictatorships continued during the civil war. Both government agents and the guerrillas were responsible for roving death squads that killed or disappeared combatants and noncombatants alike. The civil war did not end until 1992. Over the course of the war, approximately 75,000 Salvadorans were killed with an additional 8,000 disappeared. The atrocities of the civil war forced thousands of Salvadorans to flee their homeland.

The civil war in Guatemala lasted from 1960 to 1996, with little respite. Right-wing military dictatorships controlled the government and the majority of land in Guatemala. Their policies led to a severe imbalance in economic and political participation and opportunity. Death squads terrorized the nation by kidnapping and killing suspected left-wing dissidents. Political terror, inflation, and unemployment took a heavy toll on the poor in the country, leading to the unification of various leftist rebel groups against the government under the banner Unidad Revolucionario Nacional Guatemalteco. Liberation theology gained a foothold in the country as Roman Catholic clergy made a preferential option for the poor rather than support the tyrannical government. More than 200,000 people were killed or disappeared during the war. Numerous Guatemalans chose to flee the barbarity of the situation in their homeland; many of them came to the United States.

Responding to the Central American Crisis: From Legal Remedies to Civil Disobedience

The border of the United States and Mexico was the first place of personal contact between U.S. citizens and the immigrants from El Salvador and Guatemala during the time of their respective civil wars. Individuals in border towns saw the human face of immigration as immigrants arrived in the United States having traveled all the way through Mexico. A number of U.S. citizens sought to help the immigrants by providing water, food, shelter, and clothing. They helped them to complete applications for refugee status when they heard the stories of atrocities in their homeland.

The origin of the sanctuary movement in the United States is complex, but histories of the movement trace it to the border city of Tucson, Arizona, and the response of three faith-inspired individuals and their fellow believers: Jim Corbett, a Quaker; John Fife, pastor of Southside Presbyterian Church; and Rev. Ricardo

Elford, a Roman Catholic priest and member of the Congregation of the Most Holy Redeemer. Fife and Elford were part of the Tucson Ecumenical Council (TEC), which mobilized its shared resources in response to the emerging crisis. Members of TEC eventually formed a subcommittee called the Tucson Ecumenical Task Force on Central America. These men and other members of their communities provided multifaceted assistance to the immigrants: they enabled some of the immigrants to cross the border; helped them to complete their applications to qualify as political refugees; provided money for bail bond to immigrants who had been arrested by the U.S. Immigration and Naturalization Service (INS); and they supplied all of the people in their care with food, shelter, and clothing, among other social services.

These efforts went unrewarded, however, because the INS, following official U.S. policy, rejected the vast majority of asylum applications submitted by the Central American immigrants. Once the applications were denied, the immigrants from Central America were deported.

The disagreement between sanctuary members and the U.S. government centered around whether to designate the Central American persons who were flowing into the United States as "refugees" or "economic migrants." The sanctuary workers became increasingly convinced of these immigrants' refugee status as they heard firsthand accounts of the human rights abuses occurring in El Salvador and Guatemala. Contrarily, the INS was denying the applications, because the U.S. government took the position that these people were not refugees but economic migrants who were traveling north to find work. The administration of President Ronald Reagan (1981–1989) argued that, since safe and plentiful destination points for the migrants existed in Mexico and Honduras, better jobs and higher income were the only reasons for them to move further north.

Declaring Sanctuary

The disagreement over the status of Central American people in the United States between the federal government and advocates for migrants was unyielding. The members of this ecumenical immigrant support network became increasingly frustrated by the futility of their efforts to protect the people seeking safe haven in the United States and fundamentally disagreed with the refusal of the federal government to designate this population of immigrants as refugees. Since they felt that they had exhausted the legal means to protect these immigrants, they turned to the tactics of civil disobedience under the banner of sanctuary.

The first significant turn in this direction occurred on March 24, 1982, the second anniversary of Oscar Romero's assassination, when John Fife at Southside Presbyterian Church in Tucson and five churches in Berkeley, California, declared themselves to be sanctuaries for refugees from Central America. In other words, these churches openly declared that they were willing to harbor Central American immigrants who were in the United States without proper documentation. They did so in direct defiance of U.S. policy. In the same year, the movement expanded to the Midwest with the creation of the Chicago Religious Task Force on Central America (CRTFCA). The CRTFCA consisted of concerned people from Christian and Jewish faith backgrounds who wanted to help the refugees from Central America. As months and years passed, hundreds of faith groups from all around the country joined the sanctuary movement by declaring their congregations to be safe havens for people fleeing violence in Central America.

Members of various congregations assisted in their own way. Some provided temporary, midrange, or long-term hospitality to Central Americans who arrived in their community. Others helped the Central Americans move further north to Canada, where more lenient refugee laws provided them with a better chance of avoiding deportation. Still others were engaged in efforts to educate the public about the situation of the people from Central America in order to effect change in U.S. immigration policy toward them. Not only would they tell the story of the violence and terror that plagued countries like El Salvador and Guatemala, they attempted to expose what they considered an unjust U.S. immigration policy.

Political Disagreement over U.S. Immigration Policy

Members of the sanctuary movement argued that the United States was violating not only international law but its own law when officials routinely deported Salvadorans and Guatemalans. The sanctuary workers believed that, by protecting the Central Americans, they were upholding the law. They based their protest of U.S. policy on international law emanating from the United Nations (UN) and domestic law as articulated in the 1980 Refugee Act of the United States. The sanctuary workers argued that the status of Central American immigrants was due in large part to fear of political persecution, which meant that the United States was legally required to grant them asylum.

At the international level, protestors argued, the United States was beholden, as a signatory, to uphold the 1967 United Nations Protocol Relating to the Status of Refugees, which defined a refugee as a person with "well-founded fear of being persecuted for reasons of race, religion, nationality, membership of a particular social group or political opinion, is outside the country of his nationality and is unable or, owing to such fear, is unwilling to avail himself of the protection of that country; or who, not having a nationality and being outside the country of his former habitual residence as a result of such events, is unable or unwilling to return to it" (Article 1 (A)(2)). Congress adopted this definition in the Refugee Act of 1980, which led protestors to argue that deportation of Salvadorans and Guatemalans violated U.S. law as well.

The Refugee Act of 1980, however, had language that made it possible for the U.S. government to discriminate among those who applied. Namely, the law distinguished those people who are "of special humanitarian concern to the United States." The burden was on individual applicants for asylum to prove that if they returned to their native land, they personally would be subject to persecution for any of the reasons presented in the UN protocol.

The sanctuary workers accused the Reagan administration of refusing asylum status to people from El Salvador and Guatemala because of its support for the governments that were forcing people to flee in the first place. The Reagan administration was, in fact, funding the wars being waged by those governments on the grounds that they were keeping communism in check. If the U.S. government provided asylum for the people fleeing those governments, the administration would, in effect, be admitting that the United States was supporting regimes that were causing widespread human rights violations.

In defense of their defiance of immigration policy, the sanctuary workers were quick to point out that the UN High Commissioner on Human Rights determined that U.S. policy to refuse asylum to large numbers of Salvadorans "represent[ed] a negation of its responsibility assumed upon its adherence to the Protocol [of 1967]."[1] The Reagan administration ignored the UNCHR's judgment of their policy and continued to deport Salvadorans en masse. In turn, sanctuary members continued to harbor and assist Central American immigrants.

Religious Convictions as Basis of Protest

The sanctuary protest was firmly rooted in religious convictions and drew on the history of sanctuary explained above. Frequent reference and comparison was made to the sanctuary tradition in Christian and European history and its application in the United States during the period of the Underground Railroad and, more recently, during the Vietnam War.

Both primary and secondary sources give witness to the faith dimension of the sanctuary workers' efforts. The text *Sanctuary: A Resource Guide for Understanding and Participating in the Central American Refugees' Struggle* is worthy of particular note as an artifact from the period and because it contains writings from many of the key players in the sanctuary movement of the time. The book emerged out of the Inter-American Symposium on Sanctuary held in January 1985 that was sponsored by the Tucson Ecumenical Council for Central America.[2] The planning committee for the symposium included, among others, Corbett, Fife, and Elford. The articles included in this resource guide have theological themes woven through them. An entire section, "Theological and Biblical Perspectives on Sanctuary," is dedicated to the faith dimensions of the movement.[3] The preface of the book, written by Herb Schmidt, a member of the planning committee, reveals the religious dimension of the struggle. "It [the book] is, rather, a passionate, involved, soul-searching, intellectually challenging, theologically penetrating, personal expression by scholars, refugees, and sanctuary workers reflecting on the existential struggle to be faithful to our visions of faith with committed action that challenges the oppressive 'principalities and powers' of our day."[4] In other words, sanctuary was an organic movement rooted in both action on behalf of the immigrant and theological reflection on that action. Theological reflection helped members to understand and calibrate their action in light of the faith that motivated them to act in the first place. Additionally, their faith commitment enabled them to persevere in the face of fierce opposition from the federal government.

Church and State Conflict: Sanctuary in the Court of Law

The government did not tolerate the sanctuary movement for very long. It used undercover agents to infiltrate the movement in Tucson and to acquire evidence against the members in order to stop their illegal activities. Sixteen people were indicted on January 14, 1985, less than three years after sanctuary was originally declared. Among the defendants were Roman Catholics, Methodists, Quakers, and a Presbyterian. The charges included, among other things, helping immigrants cross the border and transporting and harboring them once they were on U.S. soil.

Trials are important moments in any civil disobedience strategy because they provide a platform for protesters to articulate their case before an audience. In the case of the sanctuary trial, the defendants had the privilege of national media attention, which made it possible for them to broadcast across the country their disagreement with U.S. immigration policy.

The closing arguments encapsulate the fundamental disagreement between the prosecution and the defense. The prosecution focused on the fact that the defendants explicitly broke the law. It is important to note how the prosecution framed its argument. As anthropologist Hilary Cunningham points out, "the prosecution called on the jury to 'have the courage' to decide, as the framers of the Constitution would have wished them to, that there is 'no higher law than that passed by Congress.'"[5] The reference to "no higher law" was made to undercut claims that the defense made to its religious motivation. Indeed, as Cunningham explains, the defense argued, "the jury was deciding 'for America' whether or not U.S. citizens would be able to pursue humanitarian and religious values without state interference."[6] Sociocultural anthropologist Susan Bibler Coutin refers directly to defense attorney James Brosnahan's argument that "the allegedly conspiratorial interest that motivated the defendants was nothing more than the biblical verse, 'For I was hungry and you gave me meat, I was thirsty and you have me drink, I was a stranger and you took me in, naked and you clothed me, I was sick and you visited me, I was in prison and you came unto me.'"[7] Rather than focus on the rule of law as enacted by Congress, the defense focused on common sense, namely doing good for people in need, and the religious basis of the commitment to help others that can be found in Christian scripture.

The defendants were found guilty on various charges and sentenced to corresponding jail time. The sanctuary movement had drawn such widespread and indeed favorable attention that the judge, under significant pressure from concerned onlookers ranging from ordinary citizens to U.S. senators, suspended their sentences and placed the defendants on probation. Additionally, interest in and commitment to the sanctuary movement rose in the period following the trial. The government's attempt to end illegal activities on behalf of Central American immigrants had backfired.

In 1985, the same year that the Tucson case opened, more than 80 religious and refugee assistance groups filed a class action lawsuit against the U.S. government, specifically against U.S. Attorney General Edwin Meese III and INS Commissioner Alan Nelson. The lawsuit was referred to as the "ABC case" for short: *American Baptist Churches in the USA, et al., v. Thornburgh.* The plaintiffs in the case argued that the sanctuary workers should be free from government interference based upon their constitutional right to free exercise of religion, which in this case related to their protection of Central American refugees. Furthermore, they argued that the government was derelict in its duty to protect the people from El Salvador and Guatemala based upon the Refugee Act of 1980 and the UN Convention and Protocol Relating to Refugees.

The ABC case was settled out of court in 1990, when the U.S. government realized that it was not going to receive a favorable ruling. As part of the settlement, scores of refugees who had been denied asylum were allowed new asylum hearings under officers who had been recently trained; the applicants were permitted to work while they awaited determination of their status; and U.S. foreign policy was no longer permitted to influence decisions on asylum claims. Hilary Cunningham explains how sanctuary members interpreted the settlement. "Sanctuary workers seized upon the settlement as a vindication of the movement, but more importantly as an indication that progressive religious groups could effect positive change in the political realm. The *ABC* decision asserted that churches had a legitimate right (as well as responsibility) to influence government policies, and encouraged churches to take governments to task (even to the point of a court suit) for violating moral/religious values."[8]

To underscore the success of sanctuary members to influence U.S. immigration law and policy, historian María Cristina García has noted that, "as a parallel development, Congress passed the omnibus Immigration Act of 1990, which included the statutory basis for safe haven through a *temporary protected status*" (emphasis in original) for which "over two hundred thousand Salvadorans living in the United States registered."[9] The tireless efforts of the sanctuary workers had led to significant gains on behalf of the immigrants from Central America, who now had hope of safe refuge from the terror in their homeland.

The sanctuary movement started as a single act of protest on March 24, 1982; in less than 10 years, it had blossomed into a national movement that had effected significant legal and political changes in favor of immigrants to the United States from not only Central America but from all over the world.

The United States and Immigration in a New Era, 1993–2010

The passage of the 1990 immigration bill closed one chapter of U.S. immigration history as a new one was beginning. If the sanctuary movement arose as a response to U.S. foreign policy and its impact on immigration policy in the context of the Cold War, the new sanctuary movement has arisen as a response to U.S. immigration policy in the era of the "war on terror." The fall of the Berlin wall in 1989, occurring just two years before the 1991 collapse of the Soviet Union, symbolized the end of the Cold War. The jubilation and apparent victory for the United States was not long lasting, as new challenges emerged almost immediately.

The detonation of a car bomb on February 26, 1993, in the north tower of the World Trade Center in New York City and the detonation of a truck bomb on April 19, 1995, at the Alfred P. Murrah building in Oklahoma City led to legal changes that had a significant impact on immigration. First, in 1994, Congress passed legislation that would make it easier to deport aliens with a criminal record. Second, in 1996, Congress enacted the Antiterrorism and Effective Death Penalty Act, the Personal Responsibility and Work Opportunity Reconciliation Act, and the Illegal Immigration Reform and Immigrant Responsibility Act. These three items had serious implications for the immigrant community and their allies by expanding the grounds upon which federal agents could obtain information on illegal immigrants, whether federal agents could detain people, lengthening the period of time that they can hold detainees, and increasing the list of deportable offenses, including the allowance of retroactive deportation of individuals for minor criminal offenses committed years prior.

The new millennium brought more challenges to U.S. immigration policy. The attack on the World Trade Center in New York City and the Pentagon in Washington, DC, on September 11, 2001, led to new legislation and significant changes in the structure of the U.S. bureaucracy related to enforcement of immigration laws. The Uniting and Strengthening America by Providing Appropriate Tools Required to Intercept and Obstruct Terrorism Act, more commonly known as the Patriot Act, has had enormous impact on the immigrant population and on those who harbor undocumented persons in the United States.

The Department of Homeland Security (DHS) was established on November 25, 2002, to "secure the nation from the many threats we face" by preventing acts of terrorism, securing the border, enforcing immigration laws, and preparing to respond to and assist in the recovery from natural disasters.[10] The Immigration and Naturalization Service was folded into DHS and officially dissolved in 2003.

Three offices were created to take over the various functions of the INS: United States Citizenship and Immigration Services deals with, among many other functions, the process of becoming a U.S. citizen through naturalization and the process of acquiring refugee status or asylum;[11] United States Customs and Border Protection includes, among many other branches, Border Patrol, whose job it is to prevent illegal immigration at U.S. borders;[12] and United States Immigration and Customs Enforcement (ICE), which is "the largest investigative agency in the Department of Homeland Security," with the stated mission "to protect the security of the American people and homeland by vigilantly enforcing the nation's immigration and customs laws."[13] ICE partners with willing local law enforcement agencies to enforce immigration law; thus, ICE's reach is exponentially expanded because local law enforcement officers can execute the duties of immigration officers.

Toward the end of his first term in 2004 and at the start of his second term in 2005, President George W. Bush promoted a plan for immigration reform that included a guest worker program to allow undocumented immigrants with jobs to keep those jobs for up to six years with a temporary visa and to provide those immigrants who are in the workforce with corresponding workers' rights, including a minimum wage and legal recourse should their rights be violated. Many members of Congress opposed his proposal by arguing that it failed to protect U.S. workers from the impact of cheap labor in the marketplace, and, they contended, it weakened national security. The House of Representatives passed HR 4437, the Border Protection, Anti-Terrorism, and Illegal Immigration Control Act, on December 16, 2005, which would make it a felony to illegally enter the United States. Additionally, the bill would make it a crime to help someone who has arrived in the country illegally. The measure stalled, however, because the Senate was not able to reach agreement on it. Controversy surrounded the measure while its status remained unknown.

U.S. Department of Homeland Security national operations center. (U.S. Department of Homeland Security)

Response to passage of the bill was swift. On December 30, 2005, Cardinal Roger Mahony, the archbishop of Los Angeles, wrote a letter to President Bush in which he denounced what, in his view, was an attempt by the federal government to "stifle our spiritual and pastoral outreach to the poor, and to impose penalties for doing what our faith demands of us." He urged the president to "speak out clearly and forcefully in opposition to these repressive—and impossible—aspects of any immigration reform efforts." He went further in his protest by addressing the legislation during his Ash Wednesday sermon on March 1, 2006. He instructed the employees of Catholic social service agencies in Los Angeles to continue serving those in need regardless of their immigration status, thus ordering everyone in his diocese, in effect, to break the law through civil disobedience.

Also on March 1, 2006, in Washington, DC, an interfaith gathering of Christian and Jewish leaders met to denounce the bill. Cardinal Theodore E. McCarrick, then the Catholic Archbishop of Washington, DC, was among those attending. He explained that religious and moral principles motivated their response. He said, "We are here today, representing our individual faith communities, because we believe that immigration is not just a theoretical policy issue, but ultimately a humanitarian issue that impacts the basic dignity and life of the person, created in the image and likeness of God." In his own Ash Wednesday admonition, McCarrick urged Christians to pray and fast for immigrants and those who serve them.

The reaction of these religious leaders helped to initiate widespread protests across the nation. Cardinal Mahony's reaction spurred massive demonstrations in Los Angeles, including one of the largest in the city's history on March 25, 2006.[14] Two days later, a series of demonstrations against the legislation occurred across the country, including a theatrical protest that involved leaders from a number of religious groups who gathered outside the capitol building in Washington, DC. A *New York Times* article reported that "about 100 of the clerics bound themselves with plastic handcuffs" and "marched to the Senate office building and chanted, 'Let our people stay!'"[15]

Washington, DC, New York City, Chicago, Phoenix, and Los Angeles saw massive protests on April 10, 2006, which was dubbed the National Day of Action for Immigrant Justice. Civic leaders, including Senator Edward M. Kennedy of Massachusetts, and religious leaders, including Cardinal McCarrick, addressed the crowds in Washington, DC. Protests were not limited to major urban centers; they occurred in all corners of the nation, including Fort Wayne, Indiana, and Eugene, Oregon.

The Emergence of the New Sanctuary Movement

Cardinal Mahony's 2006 Ash Wednesday homily was the inspiration for the development of the new sanctuary movement.[16] Additionally, an increase in raids and deportations of immigrants catalyzed the formation of the movement. In 2006, ICE was active in its pursuit of immigrants who were in the United States illegally. ICE reported its success noting, in particular, its improvement on the work of the INS, the previous agency responsible for enforcing immigration laws: "More than 4,300 arrests were made in ICE worksite enforcement cases, more than seven times the arrests in 2002, the last full year of operations for U.S. Immigration and Naturalization Service."[17] ICE reported its record-breaking success in its deportation work as well, noting that it removed "a record 189,670 illegal aliens from the country . . . a twelve percent increase" over the previous year. Additionally, the agency enlarged its capacity for enforcement. ICE "increased its detention bed space by 6,300 . . . for a total of 27,700 beds" and "nearly tripled the number of fugitive operation teams deployed nationwide from 18 to 50."[18] This increased enforcement put pressure on both U.S. business owners who were employing undocumented immigrants and the workers and their families.

The threat that HR 4437 posed to religious groups' ability to provide aid legally to undocumented workers and the increased arrests and deportations of these immigrants led faith leaders to discuss the creation of a coalition designed to protect their rights. On January 29, 2007, in Washington, DC, Christian, Jewish, and Muslim leaders strategized about how they might organize themselves to support immigrants. A few months later, on May 9, 2007, they publicly declared their commitment to the new sanctuary movement in several cities across the United States, including New York City, Chicago, Los Angeles, and San Diego.

The new movement is coordinated by several organizations: Clergy and Laity United for Economic Justice; Interfaith Worker Justice; and the New York Sanctuary Movement.[19] It is intentionally interfaith. Religious groups of Christian, Jewish, and Muslim background are involved. They have opened their faith communities to people from all corners of the globe, including Latin America, Africa, and Asia. Like the earlier iteration of the sanctuary movement, the new sanctuary movement works at both the level of charity, by providing immediate assistance to those in need, and systemic reform, by seeking change in the current legal framework of immigration in the United States. The charity comes in the form of "prophetic hospitality," including food, clothing, shelter, and spiritual support in addition to pro bono legal assistance. The members of the new sanctuary movement also advocate on behalf of the immigrants and seek to influence comprehensive immigration reform.

The principal protest of the movement against current immigration laws, detention, and deportation emerges from the fact that enforcement of current legislation separates families and disrupts the lives of otherwise law-abiding workers. As sanctuary members state in their pledge, "We stand together in our faith that everyone, regardless of national origin, has basic common rights, including but not limited to: 1) livelihood; 2) family unity; and 3) physical and emotional safety."[20]

According to supporters, immigration reform is a human rights issue rooted in family, labor, and holistic human well-being.

ICE spokespersons responded to the sanctuary declarations by reiterating that the agency will continue to enforce the law. As reported in *The New York Times*, a spokesman for ICE said, "We certainly understand, as does everybody, that nobody is above the law and that removal orders are issued by a federal judge, and they are something that should be complied with."[21] If they were to break the law, participants in the new sanctuary movement would not be exempted from enforcement on the grounds that they are affiliated with a religious organization, church, synagogue, or mosque.

Although they find current legislation ineffective and unjust, there is no intent to break the law in the new sanctuary movement. The contemporary strategy is to "provide a public witness" by sheltering "a limited number of immigrant families whose legal cases clearly reveal the contradictions and moral injustice of our current immigration system while working to support legislation that would change their situation."[22] Their legal case must be "viable under current law." Congregations who undertake this service would not be breaking the law, "because the family's identity will be public."[23] The family under protection, therefore, must have children who are legal U.S. citizens, and at least one of the parents must have a "good work record." The host family must be available to appear with the protected family for press conferences. The goal of this strategy is to challenge the current legal system that leads to the breakup of families through the deportation of responsible contributors to the U.S. economy and civil society.

The new sanctuary movement is explicitly interfaith. Members view their respective religious traditions as valuable resources that can enable them to serve as a prophetic voice for the articulation of a just immigration policy.[24] The movement is rooted in a spirituality that values prayer and fasting as necessary components of a sustained commitment for immigrant justice.

A key resource from the new movement is entitled *For You Were Once a Stranger: Immigration to the U.S. through the Lens of Faith,* published by Interfaith Worker Justice in 2007. This resource includes prayers from various traditions along with references from holy texts in the Jewish, Christian, Muslim, Hindu, and Sikh traditions that speak to the immigration issue. The Scriptural passages provide insight into the faith reasons for helping immigrants. Many books in the Hebrew Scriptures, including Genesis, Exodus, Deuteronomy, and Leviticus, discuss this topic with reference to rendering justice unto the stranger and sojourner. For example, Leviticus 19 reads, "you shall love them [the strangers who sojourn with you] as yourself." The Gospel of Matthew is cited as a relevant source from Christian Scripture, because, in it, Jesus says, "I was a stranger and you welcomed me." From Islam, the Qur'an instructs the reader to "serve God . . . and do good to . . . strangers." Additionally, a passage from Hindu Scripture explains, "The guest is a representative of God." These spiritual resources are meant not only to provide a theological justification for the movement but also to serve as a resource for movement members, who are on a very long and potentially costly journey to change U.S. immigration policy.

Conclusion

At present, the legal issues surrounding immigration are as complicated and contentious as ever before. On April 23, 2010, Arizona Governor Jan Brewer signed legislation that empowers law enforcement officials to detain anyone who is suspected of being in the country illegally. A nationwide debate erupted around the legislation even before it was passed. Critics fear that the law will encourage racial profiling of Latino/as. The legislation, according to Brewer, "represents another tool for our state to use as we work to solve a crisis we did not create and the federal government has refused to fix—the crisis caused by illegal immigration and Arizona's porous border."[25] She cited security concerns such as increases in violence and kidnappings along the border as her primary reason for signing the bill.

President Barak Obama (2009–), who supports comprehensive immigration reform, asked members of his administration to investigate the legality of the legislation, which he criticized as irresponsible and misguided.[26] The Justice Department and the Department of Homeland Security are determining whether a lawsuit can be brought against the bill.

Religious leaders have been vocal in opposition to the bill, as well. The fundamental injustice, as perceived by supporters of comprehensive immigration reform, is summed up by Cardinal Mahony's response to the Arizona legislation: "We have built a huge wall along our southern border, and have posted in effect two signs next to each other. One reads, 'No Trespassing,' and the other reads 'Help Wanted.'"[27]

As the United States enters into the second decade of the 21st century, the struggle for immigrant justice carried on by the sanctuary movement remains as relevant today as it was 30 years ago. From the Cold War to the war on terror, members of the sanctuary movement represent an important voice in the civic discourse about immigration. Under the banner of sanctuary, people inspired by a faith that is rooted in Scripture and tradition continue to advocate for change in local and national immigration policy. Current members of the movement hope to repeat the success of their activist forebears as they lead, by example, their fellow Americans toward a compassionate response to the human dimension of immigration.

Notes

1. *Report of the United Nations High Commissioner for Refugees Mission to Monitor INS Asylum Processing of Salvadoran Illegal Entrants—September 13–18, 1981*, reprinted in *Congressional Record*, February 11, 1982, S827–831.

2. Gary MacEoin, ed., *Sanctuary: A Resource Guide for Understanding and Participating in the Central American Refugees' Struggle* (San Francisco: Harper & Row, 1985).

3. Ibid., 33–72.

4. Herb Schmidt, "Preface," in *Sanctuary*, ed. Gary MacEoin (San Francisco: Harper & Row, 1985), 1.

5. Hilary Cunningham, *God and Caesar at the Rio Grande: Sanctuary and the Politics of Religion* (Minneapolis: University of Minnesota Press, 1995), 59.

6. Ibid.

7. Susan Bibler Coutin, *The Culture of Protest: Religious Activism and the U.S. Sanctuary Movement*, Conflict and Social Change Series (Boulder, CO: Westview Press, 1993), 139.

8. Cunningham, *God and Caesar*, 206. All parenthetical remarks are Cunningham's.

9. María Cristina García, *Seeking Refuge: Central American Migration to Mexico, the United States, and Canada* (Berkeley: University of California Press, 2006), 112.

10. See "Our Responsibilities," Department of Homeland Security, http://www.dhs.gov/xabout/responsibilities.shtm.

11. See "What We Do," U.S. Citizenship and Immigration Services, http://www.uscis.gov/portal/site/uscis/menuitem.eb1d4c2a3e5b9ac89243c6a7543f6d1a/?vgnextoid=fb89520b9f9a3210VgnVCM100000b92ca60aRCRD&vgnextchannel=fb89520b9f9a3210VgnVCM100000b92ca60aRCRD.

12. See the U.S. Customs and Border Protection website, http://www.cbp.gov/.

13. See "About," U.S. Immigrations and Customs Enforcement, http://www.ice.gov/about/index.htm.

14. John Pomfret, "Cardinal Puts Church in Fight for Immigration Rights," *The Washington Post* (April 2, 2006), http://www.washingtonpost.com/wp-dyn/content/article/2006/04/01/AR2006040101206_pf.html.

15. "Protests Go On in Several Cities as Panel Acts," *The New York Times* (March 28, 2006), http://www.nytimes.com/2006/03/28/national/28protests.html?scp=25&sq=immigration++protest&st=nyt.

16. See "Why Now?" New Sanctuary Movement, http://www.newsanctuarymovement.org/why-now.htm.

17. See "Fact Sheet: Select Homeland Security Accomplishments for 2006," available through the online archive of the U.S. Department of Homeland Security, http://www.dhs.gov/xnews/releases/pr_1167404984182.shtm.

18. Ibid.

19. See "About the Coordinating Organizations," New Sanctuary Movement, http://www.newsanctuarymovement.org/organizations.htm.

20. See "New Sanctuary Movement Pledge," New Sanctuary Movement, http://www.newsanctuarymovement.org/pledge.htm.

21. James Barron, "Congregation to Give Haven to Immigrants," *The New York Times* (May 9, 2007), http://www.nytimes.com/2007/05/09/nyregion/09sanctuary.html.
22. See "Prophetic Hospitality: Strategy for a New Movement," New Sanctuary Movement, http://www.newsanctuarymovement.org/hospitality.htm.
23. Ibid.
24. See especially Jessica Vazquez Torres and Hollen Reischer, "The Prophetic Voice: The Religious Community Responds," chapter 7 in *For You Were Once a Stranger: Immigration to the U.S. through the Lens of Faith* (Chicago: Interfaith Worker Justice, 2007), http://www.newsanctuarymovement.org/resources.htm.
25. "Statement by Governor Jan Brewer on Senate Bill 1070," April 23, 2010, http://www.governor.state.az.us/.
26. President Barack Obama, "Remarks by the President at Naturalization Ceremony for Active-Duty Service Members," April 23, 2010. http://www.whitehouse.gov/the-press-office/remarks-president-naturalization-ceremony-active-duty-service-members.
27. Cardinal Roger Mahony, "Arizona's Dreadful Anti-Immigrant Law," April 18, 2010. Available on *Cardinal Mahony Blogs L.A.: Personal Reflections and Experiences from the Roman Catholic Archbishop of Los Angeles.* http://cardinalrogermahonyblogsla.blogspot.com/2010/04/arizonas-new-anti-immigrant-law.html.

Bibliography

Bau, Ignatius. *This Ground Is Holy: Church Sanctuary and Central American Refugees.* New York: Paulist Press, 1985.

Corbett, Jim. *Goatwalking.* New York: Viking, 1991.

Coutin, Susan Bibler. *The Culture of Protest: Religious Activism and the U.S. Sanctuary Movement.* Conflict and Social Change Series. Boulder, CO: Westview Press, 1993.

Crittenden, Ann. *Sanctuary: A Story of American Conscience and the Law in Collision.* New York: Weidenfeld & Nicholson, 1988.

Cunningham, Hilary. *God and Caesar at the Rio Grande: Sanctuary and the Politics of Religion.* Minneapolis: University of Minnesota Press, 1995.

Davidson, Miriam. *Convictions of the Heart: Jim Corbett and the Sanctuary Movement.* Tucson: University of Arizona Press, 1988.

García, María Cristina. *Seeking Refuge: Central American Migration to Mexico, the United States, and Canada.* Berkeley: University of California Press, 2006.

Hagan, Jacqueline Maria. *Migration Miracle: Faith, Hope, and Meaning on the Undocumented Journey.* Cambridge, MA: Harvard University Press, 2008.

Hondagneu-Sotelo, Pierrette. *Religion and Social Justice for Immigrants.* New Brunswick, NJ: Rutgers University Press, 2007.

Lorentzen, Robin. *Women in the Sanctuary Movement*. Philadelphia: Temple University Press, 1991.

MacEoin, Gary, ed. *Sanctuary: A Resource Guide for Understanding and Participating in the Central American Refugees' Struggle*. San Francisco, Harper & Row, 1985.

Report of the United Nations High Commissioner for Refugees Mission to Monitor INS Asylum Processing of Salvadoran Illegal Entrants—September 13–18, 1981, reprinted in *Congressional Record*, February 11, 1982.

Slater, Nelle G., ed. *Tensions Between Citizens and Discipleship: A Case Study*. New York: Pilgrim Press, 1989.

Alan K. Simpson (1931–): "There Can Be No Perfect Immigration Reform Bill"

Mary Elizabeth Brown

"Folksy and witty, Alan Simpson was once lauded as the Senate's Will Rogers," *Newsweek* columnist Eleanor Clift observed. Then he changed. Simpson himself identified at least one reason for that change. Maneuvering two major reforms of immigration law from bill to signed legislation in a four-year period was like "giving dry birth to a porcupine."[1] His work on immigration law revealed Simpson as a more complex man than his colleagues had first thought. In turn, Simpson helped to make Americans realize that immigration law was inherently more complex than a focus on anyone argument for or against immigration.

Simpson was not one to be easily frustrated by political processes. His family long provided political leadership to Wyoming. One great-grandfather, Finn Burnett, advised a Shoshone chief. Another, John Simpson, founded the first store and post office in the vicinity of Jackson, Wyoming. His father, Milward Lee Simpson, was governor of the state from 1955 to 1959 and senator from 1962 to 1967. His older brother, Peter, was in the state legislature from 1980 to 1984 and an unsuccessful candidate for governor in 1986.

Alan Kooi Simpson (the middle name was the maiden name of his mother, Lorna) was born on September 2, 1931, and grew up in Cody, Wyoming. He attended the public schools, graduating from Cody High School in 1949 and the University of Wyoming in 1954. Upon graduation, he married Ann Scholl, who had already started a career in real estate. From 1954 to 1956, Simpson was in the United States Army with the Fifth Infantry Division and Second Armored Division, part of the occupation forces of post–World War II Germany. He graduated from the University of Wyoming's law school in 1958 and opened a law practice that he maintained until 1978. Besides practicing law, he moved ahead in ever-widening political circles. In 1959, he was appointed assistant attorney general for Wyoming and later city attorney for Cody. In 1964, despite Lyndon Johnson's Democratic coattails, the young Republican won election to the state legislature. By 1975, he was the majority floor leader and, by 1977, the speaker pro tempore of the House. The next year, Wyoming senator Clifford Hansen retired, and Simpson defeated other Republicans in the primary and then his Democratic opponent in order to succeed Hansen. He won reelection in 1984 and 1990. Senate Republicans elected him whip in 1985.

Wyoming became a state in 1869, when the Republicans dominated national politics. The early Simpsons allied with that party, and Alan maintained that allegiance. As new issues came up, he helped to formulate Republican policy on them. An example is his work on land-use laws while in the Wyoming state legislature. Since Theodore Roosevelt, the Republicans have had a reputation for seeing the environment as part of the whole of human society. It was important for humans to preserve the natural environment, but that could be done only by considering social needs, economic demands, and what was politically possible. Simpson continued that tradition while in the state legislature. During the 1960s and early 1970s, colleagues, entrepreneurs, and conservationists respected Simpson's work on Wyoming land-use laws.

A different example of how Simpson helped to form contemporary Republican policy was with the issue of abortion. During his high school days, Simpson knew schoolmates who endured illegal abortions in Wyoming or who spent a great deal of money to go to the state of Washington, where abortion was legal.[2] By the time Simpson became a lawyer, abortion was an important issue in other states, although it does not seem to have been significant for his work in Wyoming. In 1973, the Supreme Court made a decision, *Roe v. Wade*, binding on all 50 states. *Roe v. Wade* ruled that, during the first three months of a woman's pregnancy, an abortion was a matter between her and her physician. Simpson agreed with *Roe v. Wade* and carried that opinion with him into national politics.

The Republicans offered mixed guidance regarding immigration. An immigration policy with a minimum of rules and regulations was consistent with some Republicans' idea that government ought to govern as lightly as possible. For business-oriented Republicans, high immigration was desirable because it created a steady stream of labor, improving the employers' chances of hiring people they wanted and keeping wages low. On the other hand, there were some ways in which immigration might be bad for business. It might cost money to take care of the immigrants in the U.S. population, in which case taxes went up. Immigrants might bring subversive, anticapitalist ideas into the United States. There were also some Republicans who put other considerations ahead of business and argued that too many people of different racial backgrounds and different cultures were entering the United States; the Republican tradition included advocacy of the restrictive national quotas of the 1920s. Simpson had to decide what elements of the Republican past he wished to use to develop new immigration laws.

By the time Simpson entered the federal legislature, the 1965 law had come under heavy criticism. Backers of the 1965 law convinced colleagues to vote for it with the argument that the law itself had no effect on immigration rates, because there were few reasons for people to leave their homelands and to seek their fortunes in the United States. Proponents were unrealistically optimistic. In 1969, the United States commenced a period of budget deficits, annually spending more than it took in via taxes. To cover these deficits, the U.S. government borrowed money. Having such a powerful competitor for loans exerted inflationary pressure on U.S. interest rates. Given that U.S. banks lent to the world, inflation soon affected the global economy. In the early 1970s, Richard Nixon altered U.S. Cold War policy, achieving agreements with the Soviet Union and the People's Republic of China. When it was no longer necessary to build a grand alliance of many nations opposed to communism, Nixon ceased to attend to certain allies and to provide economic support. Nixon's neglect caused developing nations' economies to slow down even further. At the same time, the new Cold War policy meant that the United States concentrated on relations with the two other major atomic powers, the Soviet Union and China, and delegated to medium-sized nations the work of neutralizing local radicals. Countries such as Argentina and Chile entered periods of repression. Finally, the new Cold War policy meant the United States had to withdraw from Vietnam, because its presence there was threatening to China, which in turn meant that, by 1975, communist forces in Vietnam dominated the entire country and refugees tried to escape to safer places. Altogether, after 1965, economic decline and political disaster meant that many more people now wanted to migrate to the United States.

The 1965 law may not have created the conditions for migration, but once people wanted to migrate, it did create the conditions that let them into the United States. Since the 1920s, U.S. law permitted legal residents of the United States to sponsor their spouses and their offspring for migration without regard to whether such migration raised total migration above the annual limit. The 1965 law expanded the family reunification program. In theory, if the United States admitted X number of immigrants in one year, five years later, when those immigrants were sworn in as citizens, the United States would admit not only X, the total number permitted by law, but X1, a number equal to X and representing the spouses of the new citizens admitted five years earlier, and Y, a number of unknown quantity representing the new citizens' offspring. Family reunification outside of the annual limits drove up the total number. The 1965 law also permitted U.S. citizens to sponsor more distant relatives. These relatives also had to comply with the annual ceiling requirements, so their admission did not swell annual totals above those ceilings. But once admitted and once sworn in as citizens, they brought their spouses and children, thus adding to the extra limit admissions. Soon potential immigrants were complaining that it was impossible to get an immigration visa unless one already had a close family member—usually a post-1965 immigrant—already in the United States.

Further issues arose over illegal immigration. In 1964, the United States terminated its bracero agreement with Mexico, intending to replace the ad hoc agreements with laws. The 1965 law introduced the first legal limits on migration from the Western Hemisphere. Some people already had established the pattern of living in Mexico but traveling through the United States in search of seasonal labor. These people had to weigh the fact that what they had been used to doing was now illegal against the fact that this was the only way they had to make a living. As the economies of Spanish-speaking Western Hemisphere countries worsened, more people chose to break U.S. law.

In 1978, Congress mandated the appointment of a 16-member Select Commission on Immigration and Refugee Policy (SCIRP) to gather facts and to make recommendations regarding U.S. immigration policy. When he first arrived in Congress in January 1979, Simpson received appointment to the Senate Judiciary Committee, its subcommittee on immigration, and to SCIRP. Originally, President Jimmy Carter appointed Reubin D. Askew, a Florida attorney and politician, to chair the committee. The Rev. Theodore Hesburgh, C.S.C., then president of Notre Dame University and long active in federal-level public service, replaced Askew. President Carter appointed three other citizen-members, drawn from the different ethnic groups affected by immigration law, from the legal profession, and from labor. Four cabinet members whose portfolios were affected by immigration also served ex officia: the secretary of state: the attorney general: the secretary of labor: and the secretary of health, education, and welfare. The speaker of the House appointed four members. Robert McClory (R-IL) was the ranking, or senior, member of the minority, or Republican, party on the House Judiciary Committee. McClory helped to represent Republican interests and also the interests of a state that received numerous immigrants. The three other representatives were Hamilton Fish Jr. (R-NY), Elizabeth Holtzman (D-NY), and Peter W. Rodino Jr. (D-NJ). All had been on the House's immigration subcommittee, and Holtzman was the House sponsor of an important refugee bill. The president pro tem of the Senate also appointed four people. Edward M. Kennedy (D-MA) had been in the Senate since 1962 and had already been influential in immigration legislation. Charles McC. Mathias Jr. (R-MD), had been in the Senate since 1969, and Dennis DeConcini (D-AZ) since 1977. When Zero Population Growth prepared a flyer to introduce the SCIRP to its members, all it put next to a photograph of Alan Simpson was "new member of Senate in 1979, a state representative in Wyoming from 1964 to 1978."

While the SCIRP held hearings, studied data, and formulated proposals, the executive branch of the U.S. government changed hands. In 1980, Ronald Reagan was elected president. Reagan was reelected in 1984 and continued to hold office until 1989. Not only was Reagan a Republican, but, although born in Illinois, he was a longtime resident of California and had served as governor of that state. His vice president, George H. W. Bush, had roots in Connecticut (which state his father served as senator) and a vacation home in Kennebunkport, Maine, but resided in Texas. Western Republicans were doing well. The Republicans held a majority in the Senate, so that instead of being a young senator in the minority party, Simpson found himself warming Senator Edward M. Kennedy's former chair as the head of the subcommittee on immigration. In 1981, Simpson took responsibility for turning SCIRP findings into legislation.

During 1982 and 1983, Simpson looked for the narrowest possible issue on which to focus, to get the widest possible congressional support for action. He settled on the issue of undocumented immigrants. Even that issue had possibilities for conflict, as one might be able to tell from the varied names for them; they were also called illegal immigrants. Undocumented immigrants were those who had not been admitted to the United States as immigrants. About half of them were admitted in some other capacity, as tourists or students. The half that really grabbed the public imagination, though, were those who intended to enter the United States with no visa of any kind, such as people crossing the border under cover of darkness or stowing away on ships. Punishing these people for illegal entry was not a straightforward matter. First, the United States had not enforced such laws for years and might not even have enough personnel in the Border Patrol and Coast Guard to do it properly. Second, in cases involving undocumented immigrants who worked, the immigrants were not the only culprits. The people who hired them broke even more laws. They failed to provide Social Security, unemployment, workers' compensation, or even, in some cases, the minimum wages, maximum hours, and right to unionize guaranteed in U.S. law. Third, the public image of the undocumented alien was of Spanish-speaking people. The Hispanic Caucus in Congress raised the question of whether employers would refuse to hire any Hispanics for fear of hiring undocumented ones.

Sticking to the narrow agreement that something ought to be done "about" (not necessarily "for" or "against") undocumented aliens, Simpson proposed a three-point plan. The Carter administration that had formed the SCIRP had also drafted a proposed immigration bill. The bill proposed granting amnesty, or freedom from prosecution, for undocumented aliens already in the United States by a specific date—the date to be determined when the law was passed. Undocumented immigrants coming after that date were subject to penalties, usually deportation. To prevent undocumented aliens from getting jobs and to prevent employers from taking advantage of their workers, employers were forbidden to knowingly hire undocumented workers. To prevent the employers from discriminating against foreign-looking people, Simpson proposed a national, forgery-proof worker's identification card, which all Americans, citizens by birth or by choice, presented when seeking employment.

Simpson spoke in support of wiping the slate clean for past undocumented workers and then starting a more stringent policy. As he explained to the Senate:

Illegal immigration continues to depress wages and working conditions for American workers, especially low-income, low-skilled Americans who are most likely to face direct competition. Illegal immigrants continue to remain a fearful, exploitable subclass in American society, and I believe that widespread flouting of our Nation's immigration laws still leads to a disrespect for our laws and institutions in general.[3]

Simpson realized he was asking for compromise and that some of his colleagues desperately wanted to go home to their constituents able to claim they had adhered to their original positions. Simpson warned such colleagues that steadfastness could also be interpreted as stubbornness. "This will be the test: Is U.S. politics increasingly controlled by narrow and wholly selfish special interests rather than being representative of the broad public will?"

The narrowest possible basis for agreement turned out to be too broad. The proposal for a national identification card bought into the debate on immigration a new voice, that of civil libertarians. They wanted the government to be as small and unobtrusive as possible. Forgery-proof right-to-work cards issued by the federal government did not fit with their vision. Ethnic political leaders dismissed the idea that the national identification cards would prevent hiring discrimination.

Nonetheless, Simpson got the bill through the Senate in 1982. The bill's cosponsor, Romano Mazzoli (R-KY) was unable to get it through the House. In January 1983, the Congress elected in November 1982 sat. Simpson got the immigration bill through the Senate again, but Mazzoli still could not get it through the House. House Speaker Thomas "Tip" O'Neill managed to avoid giving any reason for the delay until October, and then said he did not think President Reagan would sign the bill. Simpson was the one who convinced O'Neill that the bill had administrative support. O'Neill then scheduled the bill for debate, but for 1984. By the time debate started, House members wanted to go home and start their biennial campaigns.

When the new Congress sat in 1985, Simpson picked up an important House ally in Representative Peter Rodino (R-NJ). Rodino did not support the Simpson-Mazzoli bill because one version eliminated the fifth level of family reunification preferences, the one permitting U.S. citizens to sponsor siblings. Simpson himself thought the elimination of the sibling preference reasonable. One could easily see the economic and emotional ties between immigrants and their spouses, children, and aging parents, but brothers and sisters were another matter. Also, eliminating the sibling preference was a crucial step in breaking the chains of family migration that filled the ranks of those admitted under the quotas and added to the numbers admitted outside quotas. However, Simpson compromised and restored the sibling preference. In return, he made a solid ally with the ability to advance the legislation through the House.

Simpson also compromised on another matter. He dropped his request that the federal government issue forgery-proof identification cards to people eligible to work in the United States. He accepted a proposal that employers determine legal status using documents governments already issued. Issuing national worker-identification cards might have been a straightforward way to solve the problem, but if it did not seem so straightforward to others, Simpson was willing to try to see their viewpoint and to modify his own.

Most important, Simpson provided philosophical support for his modifications. He reminded the Senate, "There can be no perfect immigration reform bill."[4] He worked to balance competing special interests in the hope that everyone would agree the final result was in the national interest. And he and Mazzoli got the bill through the House, through the Senate, across President Reagan's desk, and into law as the Immigration Reform and Control Act (IRCA) of 1986. Simpson's colleagues told the press, "Everyone loves the guy."[5] Simpson basked in public approval as a competent, effective senator with a down-to-earth brand of humor and a willingness to work with his colleagues toward a common good. Storm clouds, though, were already gathering.

One of the checks and balances in the Constitution is that presidential nominations to the Supreme Court are subject to Senate approval. Reagan had campaigned on the argument that the Supreme Court was too liberal and promised to appoint justices who were more conservative, especially on the issue of abortion. Charging that Reagan was politicizing the Supreme Court, Democrats on the Senate Judiciary Committee politicized the approval process as well. The stage was set for a series of confrontations between liberal Democrats and conservative Republicans. Simpson was ranked as one of the most conservative Republicans around when it came to economic issues but not abortion.[6]

In 1987, Chief Justice Warren Burger retired. Reagan nominated Associate Justice William Rehnquist for a promotion. Although Rehnquist was already on the Court, Judiciary Committee Democrats made him spend a long time in nomination hearings in order to air their ideological differences with Reagan. After the Senate confirmed Rehnquist for the chief justice position, Reagan nominated Antonin Scalia to replace Rehnquist as associate justice. As liberal opposition to Scalia hardened, Simpson let his colleagues know he had had enough ideological fighting: "Three sitting members, though, of this United States Senate, right now, voted against the sweeping Civil Rights Act of 1964. Do we keep score on them? Do we let them know we will never forgive? They changed, they listened, they adopted, they adapted, and they learned. Don't others get the leeway in this particular arena?"[7]

Simpson did not confine his criticism to liberal Democrats. The National Organization for Women (NOW) was dedicated to allowing women the widest possible leeway in deciding for or against abortions for themselves. Molly Yard and Eleanor Smeal, president and president emeritus, respectively, of NOW, complained that the Supreme Court was being loaded with people who did not support their viewpoint. Simpson, whose position on abortion was similar to theirs, told them not to push their own interests to the exclusion of other considerations.[8]

Besides the carping over Supreme Court nominations, there were other causes for criticism. For example, people who had favored the 1965 law began to see disadvantages in that law and to argue that new laws should remedy their situation. IRCA created a program that made available 5,000 visas per year for two years to people who could not get visas under the regular national ceilings because those visas had already gone to people who could meet family reunification requirements. The program had been inspired by the Irish, who felt as though they were at a special disadvantage under the new system. (Irish immigration had been at a low point for the generation before the passage of the 1965 reforms; when it picked up again in the 1980s, the Irish were unable to get visas because they were squeezed out by other potential immigrants favored by various family reunification programs.) Representative Brian Donnelly, backed by Senator Edward M. Kennedy, had developed a pilot program that they now wanted to continue past its two-year trial period.[9]

Similarly, people who previously used braceros complained that after 1965 it was difficult to find workers. Accordingly, IRCA had a special program for legalizing undocumented aliens who were special agricultural workers (SAWs). Three million people applied for legalization. Even people who did not complain much about immigrants complained about fraud in the SAW legalization program.

Employers checking documents had a number of problems with IRCA. Native Americans did not carry documents that the law specified they needed to prove they were eligible for jobs.[10] Along with illegal immigrants there sprung up an illegal business forging documents. Employers did not have to verify the documents, merely to prove that they had seen them, and so had no real incentive to turn down job applicants whose documents were not too obviously forged. IRCA did nothing about the political and economic conditions that compelled Hispanics and Asians to migrate, and events after IRCA's passage seemed conducive to more immigrants. In 1989, the Berlin Wall fell, and former Soviet satellites slipped from their orbits. With freer governments, migration from Eastern Europe increased. In 1991, the Soviet Union collapsed. Migration became a strategy for coping with the new Russia's social and economic insecurity.

In 1988, Simpson girded himself to revisit the field of immigration. He made another significant alliance. He worked with Senator Ted Kennedy. Kennedy was allied with the opposite ideological camp, he was a member of the opposite party, and he came from the opposite part of the country. However, he and Simpson shared a similar approach to politics. Simpson praised Kennedy's trustworthiness. When Kennedy said he would support a colleague, he indeed extended support. When it was time to negotiate, he listed the issues on which he could not compromise and cooperatively conceded the rest. For his part, Kennedy acknowledged,

"We do not always vote together, but we have learned to work well together, especially in this area of . . . immigration matters."[11]

Simpson and Kennedy got a bill through the Senate in 1988, but the House delayed consideration until the bill died for lack of action. In 1989, Kennedy and Simpson again got a proposal through the Senate, only to have the House again delay. House members who had constituents who wanted the law passed were hamstrung by other members who had constituents who did not want the law passed. The House's window of opportunity came in November 1990. The 1990 elections were over—and with them the danger of being voted out of office by dissatisfied constituents. The 1992 elections were still too far away to worry about. The House hurriedly passed the bill, and it became law on November 29, 1990.

The bill Simpson and Kennedy sponsored increased the total number of immigrants to 700,000 per year for the years 1992 to 1994. In 1994, the level decreased to 675,000. The 675,000 slots were divided in a new way: 480,000 people were to be admitted in order to reunite them with their families; 140,000 were to be admitted on the basis of their contributions to the economy; and 55,000 were to be admitted on a point basis.

It was hardest to alter the distribution of the family reunification visas. Simpson still wanted to reduce the number of people admitted as siblings of U.S. citizens, but Asians, especially, found chain migration useful for rescuing family members from persecution and poverty. The bill was able to divide the 140,000 visas given on the basis of economic contribution into different categories, including a new one for immigrants who invested $1 million in the U.S. economy and created 10 jobs. The remaining 55,000 visas were available through application. Each application was awarded points according to the candidate's education level and job skills. The visas went to the candidates receiving the highest scores.

Like IRCA, the 1990 law was a compromise, addressing the most pressing questions while leaving enough unsolved issues to guarantee future legislation. The problem with that approach was that each time the subject of immigration came up, the lines were more firmly drawn, it took more effort to achieve compromise, and Simpson had to give more and more to see any results at all. The 1990 law had been set to operate for five years. Thus, immigration came up again in 1995, at which point, new developments complicated discussion of the subject. As part of its efforts to balance the budget, the government was seeking to cut spending and was taking a hard look at spending for welfare benefits. It was possible to trim the budget by denying benefits to legal immigrants, but it might not save enough to justify the economic and political cost of doing so. To this discussion was appended discussion on other questions related to immigrant use of public services, particularly those used by illegal immigrants. Also, 1996 was an election year. The Democratic nominee, Bill Clinton, had been elected president in 1992, but the Republicans thought he could be ousted from office as he had ousted George Bush.

Republican Senator Alan Simpson of Wyoming discusses illegal immigration on Capitol Hill, March 21, 1996. (AP/Wide World Photos)

When consideration of a new immigration bill began, Simpson hoped to make the discussion as comprehensive as possible, so the bill included sections on both legal and illegal immigration, but the two issues had to be divided into two separate bills before the rest of the Senate would agree to proceed. Because Simpson had thought the majority of people were concerned about immigrant competition with natives for jobs, the original proposal for curbing illegal immigration included a revamping of the procedure whereby employers established whether job applicants were eligible to work in the United States. It turned out that there was also a widespread perception among employers that it was unfair to expect business to act as police and to check into job applicant eligibility. The proposal got nowhere until Simpson agreed to remove language that would make it difficult for employers to offer positions to job candidates abroad without violating legislation regarding illegal immigration.[12]

The bill reached a vote in the House first, where it was accepted only after significant modification. The majority of representatives voted to permit individual states to deny access to public schools to the children of illegal immigrants. The House agreed business should not be asked to assume the work of the police; instead of mandatory changes in the employee verification program, they voted only for a voluntary pilot program. On the other hand, the House did not want to give entrepreneurs an endless supply of inexpensive labor; it rejected an amendment to grant temporary work visas to a maximum of 250,000 foreign farm workers.[13]

When the bill went to the Senate floor, Simpson's colleague on the 1990 law, Ted Kennedy, announced he would vote against it because of its welfare provisions: It would have denied legal immigrants access to Medicaid and to college grants and loans.[14] Senator Spencer Abraham from Michigan, Simpson's Republican colleague, also opposed the bill, mostly on the grounds that it would limit family reunification.[15] Senate Majority Leader Robert Dole, who was hoping to secure the Republican presidential nomination for himself, complained the Democrats were trying to force votes on the bill just to embarrass the Republicans, and he pulled the bill from the floor.[16] When Dole rereleased the bill, the senators modified it, eliminating Simpson's plan to reduce overall immigration by suspending some categories of relatives that could be sponsored by legal residents.[17] Simpson accepted the loss and stayed out of the intraparty fight that followed. House Republicans wanted to deny the children of illegal immigrants access to public schools. Dole was willing to go along with the House Republicans, but another Senate Republican leader, Henry Hyde of Illinois, opposed both Senate and House Republicans.[18] The Republicans eventually agreed not to follow the House on the school issue and to leave most questions of immigrants and welfare to the welfare reform law. New immigration legislation was approved and signed on September 30, 1996.[19] At first, it seemed the August 22 law reforming welfare would be as significant as that reforming immigration; it reinforced the standing law to the effect that illegal immigrants were ineligible for most benefits, it made immigrants ineligible for some of them, and it imposed a time limit on refugees' eligibility.[20] However, legal immigrants' access to particular welfare benefits, such as food stamps, was restored early in 1997.

This was Simpson's last immigration law. Events were already eroding his power in the Senate and changing the political environment in which he had done his best work. Almost immediately upon getting the 1990 law through Congress, Simpson had returned to the work of the Supreme Court. Thurgood Marshall retired from the Supreme Court in 1991. President Bush, who in 1988 had been elected to succeed Reagan, nominated Clarence Thomas to succeed Marshall. As a member of the Judiciary Committee, Simpson had to be on hand for the hearings. As in the Rehnquist and Scalia hearings, there were some ideological differences between the conservative Thomas and liberals in the Senate. This, time, though, it was not the confrontation between liberals and conservatives that shaped the hearings. National Public Radio reporter Nina Totenberg broke the story that one of Thomas's former coworkers, a lawyer and law professor named Anita Hill, had given the Judiciary Committee material that she said proved that in his office Thomas created a highly sexualized climate that demeaned women. The Judiciary Committee called on Hill to testify, then approved Thomas's nomination despite her testimony.

Simpson came in for criticism because he claimed he had evidence that Hill was not a credible witness but then failed to produce it. Simpson's reputation as a genial senator willing to cooperate to get legislation passed dissipated. Newspaper columnists offered amateur psychoanalyses, remarking pointedly on the use of humor as a mask for anger.[21] The press stopped praising Simpson's wit and began to comment on how often he denounced the media. Profiles and character sketches of Simpson written years after the event were careful to include his more famous criticisms: how when in 1986 the press condemned Reagan for his participation in the Iran-Contra affair, Simpson complained that the press was trying to "stick it" to Reagan in the "gazoo"; or how when in 1991 television reporter Peter Arnett criticized President Bush's conduct of Desert Storm, Simpson made unsubstantiated charges that Arnett's Vietnamese brother-in-law had worked for the Viet Cong.

Simpson was also hurt by the changing political climate within the Republican Party. Throughout the 1980s, Simpson was not quite a Reagan Republican. Reagan did little to restrict abortions but supported restriction vocally; Simpson thought abortion was for the woman involved to decide. Reagan raised the Veterans Administration to cabinet status. Simpson faulted veterans for looking out for their own interests at the expense of other groups. In the Wyoming legislature, Simpson had worked with different groups to forge land-use laws. Reagan Republicans backed the entrepreneurs who wanted to use natural resources and ridiculed environmentalists as Luddites who thought that plants and animals were the equals of humans.

The situation worsened as Bush succeeded Reagan, and then, in 1992, Bill Clinton succeeded Bush. Off-year elections usually favor the party that does not control the presidency, so it was not unusual that when the Democrat Clinton was elected president, the Republicans would pick up a few seats in Congress in the next biennial election. However, in 1994, Republicans gained enough seats to get a majority in the House. These were not Simpson's Republicans, though. Although he and they claimed to be conservatives, they defined conservatism differently. Simpson's conservatism was of a kind traditional to the Republican Party nationally in that it tended to favor the capitalist system and traditional to the Republican Party in the West in that it tended to favor small government and wide scope for individual action. Younger conservatives were also conservative in the moral realm, especially about abortion. Simpson's younger colleagues also disagreed with Simpson's leadership style and methods. Trent Lott, a young Mississippi Republican, ran against Simpson for the post of Senate whip and won. For his part, Simpson explained his differences with the young conservative Republicans to an interviewer in 1996, after he announced he would not stand for reelection that fall. The new Republicans, Simpson said, did not understand how to "compromise an issue without compromising yourself."[22]

When Simpson retired from the Senate, he left a substantial record of immigration law, but the debate over immigration remained very much alive. In 1987, Simpson sponsored a law that granted amnesty to illegal immigrants; the 1996 law tossed out that precedent and required illegals seeking to legalize to go home and reimmigrate (a requirement subsequently modified). His predecessors drafted laws that emphasized racial hegemony or family reunification; he divided his legislative priorities among families, jobs, refugees, and answering the claims of various groups that the new immigration laws placed them at a disadvantage. Altogether, Simpson's was a record of compromise.

Perhaps Simpson developed his record because he had to. His successor, Trent Lott, came into office as Senate majority leader allied with the more unbending Republicans and then, like Simpson, developed a reputation for crafting legislative deals. However, Simpson's rhetoric elevated compromise from a strategy to a principle. Politics is an exercise in humility, in the most profound sense of that phrase. To engage in politics is to admit that one's colleagues are different but equal people with viewpoints and priorities that are just as valid as one's own and that must be respected. Among equals, a compromise in which no one gets everything but everyone gets something is an honorable way of collaborating. It was not only immigration that admitted of no perfect bill.

Notes

1. Eleanor Clift, "Taking the Low Road," *Newsweek* (October 28, 1991): 30.
2. Claudia Dreifus, "Exit Reasonable Right," *The New York Times Magazine* (June 2, 1996): 24–27.
3. *Congressional Digest* 62 (August–September 1983), 214, 216, 218.
4. *Congressional Digest* 65 (March 1986), 86, 88, 90, 92.
5. Douglas A. Harbrecht, "Nice Guys Do Finish First—Just Ask Al Simpson," *Business Week* (November 9, 1987): 94.
6. "Employers May Pay If They Hire Illegals," *Business Week* (June 21, 1982): 38.
7. "In the Pit," *National Review* (April 10, 1987): 80.
8. John Newhouse, "Taking It Personally," *The New Yorker* (March 16, 1992): 56ff.
9. "A Deserved Honor for Kennedy," *Irish Voice* 7, no. 39 (September 18, 1993): 10.
10. The evidence is purely anecdotal. In 1987, the author had to prove citizenship to be hired for a new job. "May I see your Social Security card, please?" The employment officer set it aside to photocopy for the record. "Now I need a second piece of evidence. May I see your passport?" I had never been outside the United States. "Your driver's license?" Did not have that, either; this was the era when it was uncommon for students to have cars. "A voter registration card?" I had discarded the one issued in my old address and had not received

one for the new address. I was on the verge of being deported to my native Massachusetts. This really *is* a free country.

11. Deborah Levy, "Irish Eyes Are Smiling; Immigration Bill: Who Needs It?" *Legal Times* (April 4, 1988): 14.

12. *The New York Times* (March 8, 1996), 20.

13. *The New York Times* (March 24, 1996), 47.

14. Edward M. Kennedy, "Statement by Sen. Kennedy on the Adoption of the Immigration Act," Congressional Press Release, March 21, 1996. This was provided through the kindness of Senator Edward M. Kennedy's office.

15. "Angst v. Optimism," *The Economist* (May 11, 1996): 30.

16. *The New York Times* (April 16, 1996), 1.

17. *The New York Times* (May 5, 1996), 42.

18. *The New York* Times (June 20, 1996), 16; (June 20, 1996), 8.

19. *The New York* Times (September 24, 1996), 1; October 1, 1996, 1.

20. Joyce C. Vialet and Larry M. Eig, "Alien Eligibility for Benefits under the New Welfare and Immigration Laws," *Migration World* 25, no. 3 (1997): 32–34.

21. Clift, "Taking the Low Road," 30.

22. Dreifus, "Exit Reasonable Right," 25.

Bibliography

Simpson has published a specialized memoir focusing on one aspect of his public career, *Right in the Old Gazoo: A Lifetime of Scrapping with the Press* (New York: William Morrow, 1997). Far more material (some 750 boxes) is housed at the University of Wyoming, which maintains the Alan K. Simpson Papers. As a contemporary public figure, he is well served by directories such as *Who's Who* and *Current Biography* and by the periodical press. The most useful source for quotes from Simpson regarding immigration law are transcripts of Senate speeches that appeared in the *Congressional Digest* 62 (August–September 1983), 214, 216, 218; 65 (March 1986), 86, 88, 90, 92; and 68 (1989), 240, 242, 244. For articles about Simpson, see "Angst v. Optimism," *The Economist* (May 11, 1996): 30; Eleanor Clift, "Taking the Low Road," *Newsweek* (October 28, 1991): 30; Claudia Dreifus, "Exit Reasonable Right," *The New York Times Magazine* (June 2, 1996): 24–27; Douglas A. Harbrecht, "Nice Guys Do Finish First—Just Ask Al Simpson," *Business Week* (November 9, 1987): 94; and John Newhouse, "Taking It Personally," *The New Yorker* (March 16, 1992): 56ff. For analysis of the process of immigration legislation, see Rosanna Peroni, "IRCA Antidiscrimination Provisions: What Went Wrong?" *International Migration Review* 26, no. 3 (Fall 1992): 732–753.

John Tanton (1934–): Of Grass and Grassroots

Mary Elizabeth Brown

The play on words in the chapter title is deliberate. John Tanton first became interested in immigration questions through a lifelong interest in the natural environment. When he determined that immigration was a significant danger to U.S. natural resources, he also found that there were no mechanisms in the political system for getting his views across and for affecting legislation. Hence, he turned to a grassroots effort combining mass appeal, leadership by a few dedicated individuals, and attempts to influence officials at the highest levels of the federal government.

Tanton's ancestors were immigrants. His father was born in Canada, served in the Canadian Expeditionary Forces in World War I, and graduated from the University of Toronto. He left Canada after the Great Depression, which started with the 1929 crash of the New York Stock Exchange and then spread around the world, affecting employment, wages, and prices globally. He immigrated to Detroit. Tanton's mother was of German ancestry but born and raised in rural Michigan. She had come to Detroit to study for her nursing diploma. Tanton valued a number of aspects of his family life. His parents were moderately religious; his mother had been raised in the Lutheran faith, and the family attended the Evangelical United Brethren Church. His parents encouraged reading. During his adult life, Tanton thought his own sense of responsibility to the common good came from his family training.

Best of all, his parents gave him a rural upbringing. John was born on February 23, 1934, in Detroit, the first of three children. When he turned 11, his family relocated to the part of Michigan where his mother had been raised. They took over a failing farm from a maternal uncle and made it succeed, mostly by having every member of the family participate in the hard work. John liked the land, and so when he won a scholarship to Michigan State University, he enrolled in the School of Agriculture with the intention of becoming an agronomist.

However, John had two paternal uncles who were physicians. When he did extremely well in college, he decided that he could learn what was necessary to become a physician, too, and switched to become a chemistry major. He received his

Bachelor of Arts degree in 1956, his medical degree in 1960, and a degree in his medical specialty, ophthalmology, in 1964. In 1966, he was admitted to the American Board of Ophthalmology, the last step toward becoming a well-qualified physician.

Meanwhile, Tanton had started a family. He met Mary Lou Brown at a get-together planned by his fraternity and her sorority; the first thing they found they had in common was boredom at these events. They married in 1958. They had two daughters, Laura in 1961, and Jane in 1965. In 1964, the Tantons decided to relocate to Petoskey, a small town in northern Michigan. They wanted to live in a rural area. This particular area also offered advantages for Tanton's career. He wanted to work with a group of physicians and found such a group at the Burns Clinic, where several specialists combined their talent and training to provide comprehensive medical care. The ophthalmologist on the Burns Clinic staff was getting older and did not want to perform surgery anymore. Tanton soon achieved economic security in two senses. While never fabulously wealthy, he had enough for his family. Also, he was safe from possible boycotts and other forms of economic retaliation against him for any unpopular opinions he might hold. Thus, he was able to engage in volunteer work, even controversial volunteer work.

Tanton's early volunteer efforts stemmed from two interests: medicine and conservation. Historians such as Linda Gordon have documented the long interest American women have had in birth control. About the time Tanton entered medicine, birth control options for women expanded to include contraceptive pills. John and Mary Lou Tanton helped to open a Planned Parenthood Clinic for northern Michigan. Tanton was also involved in conservation activities. By the early 1970s, the two types of volunteer efforts were beginning to come together in his mind:

When the first Earth Week occurred in April 1970, I spent a whole week on the road. In the course of a week I gave thirty talks on population growth as part of the conservation problem. It had long been my inclination, when talking about problems, not just to complain about them but to suggest ways in which they might be addressed. So I felt that in my talks I had to examine where population growth came from. I concluded that there were, for instance, women who were having children they didn't want to have—unwanted children. Maybe that problem could be addressed, as we had tried to do through Planned Parenthood. That would be a help. And then there were women who already had large families and who perhaps still wanted more children, but who could be convinced that two, or three, or four was enough, rather than five or six. So that was another group. Then I began to notice the question of immigration as part of population growth, so I did some studies and found that in the late 1960s, immigration counted for 10–15% of U.S. population growth. I began to wonder about that as a possible category to be looked at to reduce the rate of population growth.[1]

Tanton found support for his linkage of population increase and environmental degradation in books such as Paul Ehrlich's *The Population Bomb*. In 1968, Tanton joined Zero Population Growth (ZPG), an organization created to take practical action to stem population increase and thus to ward off the possibility that there might be more humans than the environment could support. In 1973, he was elected to a seat on the national board of ZPG, and from 1975 to 1977, he served as national president of the organization. However, when Tanton raised the issue of ZPG's stemming population increase by working to reduce immigration, he found a fundamental difference between himself and other members of ZPG. For most members of ZPG, *where* people were was irrelevant; the main issue was to maintain a level of population that the planet Earth could support. They were interested in reducing birthrates, and with the U.S. birthrate under control, they expanded their horizons to controlling birthrates in other countries. Tanton argued that just because the U.S. birthrate was down did not mean U.S. population growth was under control; immigration also caused population growth, and thus immigration had to be reduced to fully stabilize the U.S. population.

In his conservation activities, Tanton was reaching a similar impasse. While in medical school, he joined the Michigan Natural Areas Council, a conservation group. The Michigan Natural Areas Council introduced him to politics; one of its projects was preventing the construction of a road that threatened the environment in the north shore of Michigan's Upper Peninsula, along Lake Superior. When Tanton moved to Petoskey, he organized a project to reclaim the Bear River for conservation-minded community use. In 1964, as part of the larger Great Society program, the federal government enacted the Wilderness Preservation Act. To take advantage of federal funds and other provisions of that law, the state government formed a new Michigan Wilderness and Natural Areas Council. Aware of Tanton's experience in conservation, the governor appointed him to the council. In 1969, Tanton organized a population committee for the Mackinac chapter of the national Sierra Club. In 1970, he organized the Petoskey Regional Group of the Sierra Club. The Sierra Club's leadership, though, divided over whether to urge immigration restriction as part of a general program of environmental protection. Some club members thought that immigration restriction was too far afield from the Sierra Club's main interests in environmental preservation. (Immigration continued to be a controversial issue for the Sierra Club. In 1998, club members who wished to expand club conservation efforts to include immigration restriction convinced the club's board to organize a referendum. In a general vote, members defeated the proposal in favor of maintaining the Sierra Club's tradition of not having a policy on immigration.)

Tanton argued that controlling immigration was a legitimate part of conservation. By 1977, he had concluded that he would have to organize a new group that focused on his analysis of the situation and would work to save the U.S. environment by restricting immigration.

Tanton already had considerable experience with organization and administration. During college, he joined a fraternity, Delta Upsilon. He learned how to set agendas, run meetings, and take minutes. He developed an appreciation for organizational history and got the records of his chapter of Delta Upsilon in order, compiling a list of all past members. He made Delta Upsilon financially sound by placing a portion of each member's initiation fee into an endowment fund. During medical school, he joined a combination honor-and-service society called Galens, where he gained further experience in organizational work. Shortly after moving to Petoskey, he helped to establish a Planned Parenthood Clinic and to compile a directory of social services for the needy. His work in conservation led him to increasingly prominent leadership roles. He was the lead plaintiff in *Tanton v. Department of Natural Resources Board* (1972), a suit designed to stop the relevant state agency from granting a permit to a developer who wanted to dam a trout stream called the Monroe Creek. He helped to organize the Little Traverse Group, which purchased land and set it aside for preservation and filed additional lawsuits in an effort to protect the environment. Between 1977 and 1979, Tanton put his previous experience to work in developing his new organization.

Tanton called his organization the Federation for American Immigration Reform (FAIR). The name had several advantages. Its initials spelled the word *fair*, which signaled Tanton's conviction that the 1965 legislation that governed immigration at the time was *unfair* and should be replaced. The full title conveyed concisely what FAIR was about. It wanted to change U.S. immigration law. There was only one semantic problem. A "federation" is an organization composed of groups that in turn have their own independent existence, as the states in the Union combine to form the United States, with power divided between states and the United States. No independent groups combined to form FAIR. Tanton organized a board of directors to determine policy and priorities. Later, he organized a separate national board of advisers to provide a broad background for the board of directors' decisions. He hoped to attract a large number of members, but these would be individuals, not groups with their own agendas. The members would all support the main FAIR office, which was in Washington, DC. The members were not encouraged to do much about immigration issues in their local areas, because FAIR was mostly interested in changing the federal law, and that could only be done in Washington. In his memoirs, Tanton did not say why he chose the name, or why he chose the word *federation*, but he needed a word that began with *F* so that he could get the proper acronym.

Volunteer efforts are like any other business in that they need start-up capital. When Tanton realized that not all of his associates in conservation and population control agreed with him on the importance of reducing immigration, he began to watch carefully for those who did. One who seemed to agree with him was Jay Harris, a philanthropist who had been Tanton's predecessor as president of ZPG.

After he had finished his own term as president of ZPG, Tanton spent about one year making plans. Then he contacted Harris. He outlined his proposal for FAIR and asked Harris to provide seed money. In 1978, Harris promised to give $25,000 for the first and second years of FAIR's existence and then gave $5,000 less each year for the next five years.[2] By then, FAIR would have been in existence for seven years, long enough to develop a group of supporters.

Even though Tanton hoped to build an organization with numerous supporters, he had to start with the leadership. To that end, he contacted Roger Conner. Conner was a lawyer whom Tanton had met in 1970, when they both worked to organize the first Earth Week celebration. Conner had then gone on to work for the West Michigan Environmental Action Council. By the late 1970s, he had reached the top of that field and was looking for new challenges. He agreed to start FAIR's Washington, DC, headquarters.

After the leaders were in place, Tanton concentrated on increasing the number of followers. FAIR started a newsletter in 1979, but who to mail it to? Until 1983, FAIR relied on direct mail. It purchased mailing lists of names and addresses from organizations that had similar interests. It then hired a consultant to draft a letter soliciting interest in FAIR, printed up enough letters to match the number of names and addresses, and mailed the letters out. People who engaged in direct mail were satisfied if 1 percent of the people who got mail showed any interest. FAIR improved the results of its direct-mail campaign by borrowing a tactic from another organization, the Prison Fellowship led by Chuck Colson, that of putting a return envelope in the mailing. This made it easy for people to respond, and soon the direct-mail contributions were measured in the thousands of dollars.[3]

FAIR intended not to lead mass protests but to lobby Congress directly. However, it was necessary to lobby for public support, too. Tanton thought that placing advertisements in newspapers was expensive, but it did attract attention and donors. Under Dan Stein, who succeeded Roger Connor as executive director, FAIR conducted another sort of public relations campaign. Stein regularly wrote letters to the editors of newspapers, and some of them did get printed. He was especially successful in getting letters to the editor accepted by the *Wall Street Journal*, which is worth noting, because that newspaper, in accord with its interests in reduced government regulation and in having as large and inexpensive a labor market as possible, favored a minimum of immigration restrictions.[4] Stein's numerous print appearances gave FAIR opportunities to influence not only Congress but the public, and it was easier to get Congress to do something if it seemed that much of the public, not just one lobbying group, favored it.

Tanton's interest in immigration soon broadened. The more he thought about immigration, the more he thought about issues that had little to do with the relation between immigration, population, and the environment. When he began thinking about issues such as job competition and language, he found books and articles that supported conclusions he was already reaching in his own mind. "We set FAIR up specifically to deal with *all* aspects of immigration policy, not just those dealing with population numbers."[5] Instead of identifying one reason to limit immigration that many could agree with, Tanton provided a number of reasons to join FAIR, some of which could also be perceived as reasons *not* to join FAIR.

The same year that FAIR began its work, 1979, a bill to set U.S. policy for admitting refugees was introduced into Congress. FAIR tried to limit the total number of refugees to be admitted. The law that was passed, though, permitted the president, in consultation with Congress, to exceed the annual limit. Soon FAIR got another chance to influence immigration legislation beyond the question of refugees. In 1979, President Jimmy Carter appointed his Select Commission on Immigration and Refugee Policy (SCIRP). In 1981, when SCIRP finished its work, Wyoming Republican senator Alan K. Simpson took up the task of getting new immigration legislation through Congress. FAIR emerged as a critic, and supporter, of the legislation.

FAIR managed to get some of what it wanted written into law. Tanton had observed that U.S. immigration law tended to be written as if it were permanent. Perhaps laws ought to have time limits or to be subject to congressional reapproval every so often. What he was asking for was what was colloquially known as a "sunset" provision, and such a clause, calling for a study of the working of the immigration law after a certain period of time, was written into the bill. FAIR also asked for a commission to study practical ways, such as ditch digging, fence building, or increasing the U.S. border patrol, to control immigration at the Mexican border, and such a commission was established by the legislation. However, FAIR soon learned that legislation needs to be enforced. The study of the working of the 1986 law did not appear on time. (The study of how to reinforce the border did appear on time. FAIR claimed it was inadequate and funded its own study.)

FAIR opposed a key element in Simpson's bill—amnesty for illegal immigrants—but finally decided it had to compromise. Tanton recalled:

> We were, of course, concerned about the multiplier effect of amnesty. If you let some people in, their relatives will eventually come—one way or another. We were also concerned about the legitimacy of it. Here we had people standing in line around the world following the rules, waiting for a chance to migrate, and we were about to give special status to those who broke the rules, cut the line, came ahead. That rankled. And we were concerned about the precedent, because we knew that other countries around the world had declared amnesties and subsequently declared other amnesties. We had debates back and forth. Then there was the political realism, of course, to the whole thing. We had all these migrants here. They were probably not all going to be sent back home, so how should we deal with them? Then there was Senator

Simpson's firm commitment to the idea of amnesty. We had worked well with him, so that also moderates what you might do and how hard you might want to knock heads on this one issue.[6]

Commitment to Senator Simpson was so firm that it resulted in a slight rewriting of history. The bill that raised so many questions for FAIR passed in 1986. It in turn came up for reform in 1990. FAIR found the 1990 law disturbing: It not only raised the limit of the total number of people admitted to the United States; it also permitted people to bring in certain family members without regard to limits, thus swelling the totals. Dan Stein included the 1990 law in a bill of indictment against Massachusetts Democrat Edward M. Kennedy, whom Stein referred to as the "Godfather of the Immigration Mess."[7] However, Simpson co-sponsored the bill in the Senate and supported it on the floor of the Senate and in the media.

Even while FAIR was organizing itself to lobby for immigration restriction in what became the 1986 law, Tanton was reconceptualizing the immigration debate. Work on immigration had introduced him to other reasons to oppose it than its contribution to population increase and environmental degradation. In 1979, at the same time that he did the legal paperwork for FAIR, Tanton did the paperwork for a second not-for-profit, politically active corporation, which would serve as an umbrella organization to sponsor any new projects he might come up with. He called the corporation U.S. Over the decade of the 1980s, under the umbrella of U.S., he organized two other agencies that concerned themselves with particular angles on the immigration issue.

Tanton also organized a procedure by which he brought together influential people whom he could influence to think about the most important issues in the broadest possible way. To name the organization, he borrowed from 15th-century English a word, *witenagemot*, for a body of councilors that advised the crown on matters of state, and called his group WITAN. He held the first WITAN meetings in 1984. Richard Lamm, an advocate of immigration reduction and at that time governor of Colorado, lent the prestige of his office to the movement by hosting two of the early meetings in his governor's mansion.[8] WITAN's history later intersected with that of another organization Tanton had founded.

This second organization was U.S. English. Tanton himself was no monolinguist. Describing his many interests in Petoskey, he commented, "I became interested in trying to refurbish the German that I had taken in college. My mother spoke German. I'm a great believer in the discipline of learning a language."[9] However, Tanton became convinced that there had to be only one language for the United States, that that language had to be English, that recent immigrants were insufficiently committed to learning it, and that legislation was necessary to enforce the use of English.

Influencing legislation regarding use of the English language was a more complicated procedure than legislation to reduce immigration. Thanks to an 1875 Supreme Court decision, it was clear that immigration counted as interstate commerce and thus as a matter for federal regulation. Did the federal government also have the sole right to legislate regarding English? Senator Samuel Ichiye Hayakawa of California had introduced to Congress a constitutional amendment making English the official language of the United States and requiring that it alone be used for official purposes. When Hayakawa was about to retire, his amendment had not even passed Congress, let alone been released for states to consider ratifying. Hayakawa agreed to let Tanton have his mailing lists. Tanton suggested to the FAIR board of directors that FAIR use Hayakawa's mailing list to jump-start its own efforts to lobby for legislation requiring the use of English. The FAIR board turned down the suggestion; Tanton thought it was because FAIR had enough to do. In 1983, Tanton organized a new agency, U.S. English, to lobby for this new cause.

By 1986, both WITAN and U.S. English seemed to be going well. That year, the state of California put on the fall ballot a referendum question regarding whether English ought to be the official language of the state.

U.S. English promoted the referendum, and the voters favored it. The same year, Tanton scheduled a WITAN meeting for Middleburg, a town in rural Virginia near Washington, DC. As usual, he prepared a memorandum to stimulate the WITAN participants so that they would come prepared to talk. As he later remembered it:

> When I wrote this memo, I was not trying to be particularly cautious or definitive. Following my usual practice, I included everything that might remotely pertain to the topic, including some speculations that would have been better left out! . . . My memo was written for a group of people who were already initiated into immigration, population, and language issues. It was not written for people off the street who'd never heard any of these ideas before and had no background in them. It assumed a good deal of knowledge of the subject.[10]

These two separate events—U.S. English's success and WITAN's discussions for the initiated—came together in 1988. That year, U.S. English succeeded in placing referendums regarding whether English ought to be the official state language on the ballots for Arizona, Colorado, and Florida. Opponents to English as the official language for Arizona campaigned for a nay vote by linking the movements to make English official and to reduce immigration. They did this by publishing Tanton's 1986 preparatory memorandum for the WITAN meeting. When U.S. English executive director Linda Chavez read the memorandum Tanton had prepared for those who were "initiated" into the discussion of "immigration, population, and language issues," she pronounced it anti-immigrant and anti-Hispanic and resigned her position rather than continue to work with Tanton. Her pronouncement and resignation created a stir that Tanton feared would lead to the defeat of the official-English referendum in Arizona. Therefore, Tanton also resigned his position with U.S. English so that the referendum question could be judged on its merits rather than by association with him. He took comfort from election-day results, which favored making English an official language.

Referendums to make English the official language of one state had no effect on the federal government. Other states whose citizens spoke various languages took another path; in New York State, public service campaigns are conducted in many languages, and voting information is published in Chinese, English, and Spanish. The official-English movement did have a long-term side effect: It was a stage in altering the debate over immigration into a debate over the motives of the different participants in that debate.

Tanton began to study his pro-immigrant opponents and to develop a hypothesis regarding their motives. He identified two possible explanations for pro-immigrant action. One was political expedience. For example, during the debate over the 1986 law, FAIR's lobbyists noticed that the Hispanic congressional representatives claimed they opposed the bill on behalf of the larger Hispanic community. On the other hand, historic events such as the efforts of Cesar Chavez among farm workers indicated the Hispanic community was split into various groups. FAIR commissioned a survey that revealed there was no one Hispanic position on the 1986 bill; findings helped solidify support for the bill. Another example of how immigration could be used as part of a plan to advance a political cause was the sanctuary movement of the early 1980s. People fleeing violence in Guatemala and El Salvador found it difficult to obtain immigration visas. They tried to apply as refugees, but the United States would not accept their applications, because the United States was allied with the governments in power in Guatemala and El Salvador and did not want to admit its allies were at best unable to control their own countries and at worst were dictatorships violently suppressing opposition. U.S. citizens who wanted to challenge U.S. policy in Central America encouraged Guatemalans and Salvadorans to enter the United States anyway, promising to offer them sanctuary in churches, knowing it would be acutely embarrassing for the federal officials to raid houses of worship to remove impoverished refugees. Tanton thought sanctuary advocates exploited immigrants to score foreign policy points.

Tanton further hypothesized that his opponents were inspired not by the issue of immigration but by the broader questions immigration raised. He identified five areas besides immigration in which he and his opponents had substantial differences of opinion. First, Tanton thought the world had set limits and fixed boundaries. Although he was not exactly sure what the number was, there was some limited number of people the U.S. environment could support, and the country had to be sure not to exceed it. He contrasted that to the view of human capital economists who stressed human ability to solve human problems and pointed to a past record of eradicating particular diseases and reducing world hunger. Past performance, though, does not guarantee future prospects.

Second, Tanton emphasized the importance of the nation-state. He agreed that the United Nations could solve some worldwide problems, including some having to do with the environment. However, he did not think it realistic to suppose many nations, especially many new nations just emerging from colonial status into independence, would cede their authority to a higher level of government. He thought that his opponents wanted to create a one-world system into which everyone would fit.

Third, Tanton believed in emphasizing the common ground among the people of a particular nation-state. "I *do* hold to the metaphor of 'the melting pot,'" he declared to interviewer Otis Graham during an oral history. "I hold that as a country we should be trying to efface, or at least to minimize, our differences and accentuate our similarities so that in the face of all the diversity we have, we can get along better with one another."[11] Tanton thought his opponents emphasized that diversity to the point where the country was "just an address for disparate groups that happen to live in North America, and who live out their separate lives with little interaction with one another."[12]

Fourth, Tanton identified language as an especially important unifier. He argued his case on practical grounds. Just as a country had one currency or one system of weights and measures, so it ought to have one language to facilitate communication between its residents. He also argued that language had tremendous symbolic importance. Around the world, would-be separatists rallied their forces around the flag of a distinct language. Discouraging different languages would make it harder to emphasize differences and easier to emphasize commonalities.

Fifth and finally, Tanton thought there was a distinct U.S. culture. He characterized his opponents as hewing to a particular sort of hyphenated Americanism. In this definition, the modifier carried all the cultural connotations. To say that one was Mexican American or Chinese American or German American was to say that one drew one's whole culture from the Mexican, Chinese, or German part of the phrase. On the contrary, Tanton argued, the American part of the phrase connoted a specific culture. It was possible not to be a hyphenated American and still to have a culture worth preserving. In fact, that was the culture Tanton was particularly interested in preserving.

Viewed this way, Tanton's opponents in the immigration debate were as threatening to public life as the immigrants themselves. Gradually, Tanton expanded his work to include a critique of the pro-immigrant forces. This brought Tanton to a new field, controversial writing. Tanton considered himself a slow starter when it came to writing. "During four years of high school I wrote only one paper, of five or six hundred words, and that was on farm tiling!"—a drainage method he knew from having seen it practiced on his family's farm.[13] However, years of taking minutes and drafting material for meetings, plus reading Jacques Barzun's *Simple and Direct*, honed Tanton's style. In 1975, he entered an essay in a competition in which all participants wrote on the topic "Limits to Growth." He won third prize, $3,000. One of the other contestants was the editor of a journal called the *Ecologist*. He liked Tanton's essay so well that he published it as a cover article. To accompany the founding of FAIR, Tanton published *Rethinking Immigration Policy*. Over the years, he published opinion articles and letters to the editor in the *Christian Science Monitor*, the *Houston Chronicle*, and the *Wall Street Journal*. He also published at least one article, "Immigration and Criminality in the U.S.A.," in a research-oriented periodical.[14] Tanton's writing career became more central to him in 1990, when he founded *The Social Contract*. The quarterly ran articles on immigration but also broadened its scope to discuss the underlying philosophy that led to support or rejection of particular political positions.

Tanton also produced two books in the early and mid-1990s, and they are significant for understanding the direction of the debate on immigration. In 1993, he and Wayne Lutton coauthored a book entitled *The Immigration Invasion*, published by Tanton's Social Contract Press. Even favorable reviewers regarded *The Immigration Invasion* as "a handbook, almost a work in progress in its frantic pack-rat compilation of press clippings, the assimilation and accuracy of which" left even supporters uneasy.[15] However, even critics admitted that the issues it raised deserved consideration.[16] *The Immigration Invasion* was interesting for three other reasons. First, it was part of a spurt of books specifically on the perils of U.S. immigration policy. It was preceded in print by one year by Virginia D. Abernathy's *Population Politics: The Choices That Shape Our Destiny*.[17] The year after *Immigration Invasion* came out saw the publication of Brent A. Nelson's *America Balkanized: Immigration's Challenge to Government*, Peter Brimelow's *Alien Nation: Some Common Sense about America's Immigration Disaster,* and Roy Beck's *The Case against Immigration: The Moral, Economic, Social, and Environmental Reasons for Reducing U.S. Immigration Back to Traditional Levels*.[18] Second, the spurt of books moved steadily toward the mainstream: *Immigration Invasion* was self-published, but Brimelow's book was published by Random House and Beck's by W. W. Norton, the former a commercial press that published many items of general interest and the latter a press with a good reputation for scholarly works on U.S. history. For commercial publishers to produce books frankly opposing immigration indicated a faith that this was a subject of widespread interest. Finally, the appearance of the reviews reinforced Tanton's observation that the immigration debate had created two camps. Reviewers generally agreed that Tanton wrote about important topics. They also agreed that his subjects needed more careful research. They divided into friends and foes regarding his conclusions.[19]

Tanton's second book of the 1990s came in 1996, when he co-edited a volume of essays from *The Social Contract* that were then published as *Immigration and the*

Social Contract: The Implosion of Western Societies.[20] Compared to *Immigrant Invasion*, this anthology was a much neater and more organized compendium of anti-immigrant arguments, with specialists writing on issues such as labor competition. It was also much more focused in that it looked beyond immigration to what Tanton was coming to consider the central issue: "the implosion of Western society." The title *The Social Contract* called to mind not only Tanton's quarterly but, more important, John Locke's theory of the origin of government. In his 1691 *Two Treatises on Civil Government*, Locke explained that individuals, realizing their vulnerability to outside forces, banded together in a social contract designed to protect and promote the interests of those who created it. Tanton then brought the social contract to bear on immigration. The world, he pointed out, was a limited place, with finite resources and a ceiling on its capacity for growth. Ultimately, the only way for one population group to expand was at the expense of another. Equally important, there was no global social contract. Only like-minded people, those who wanted to protect and preserve a shared culture, joined the social contract. It is worth noting that Tanton's two co-editors hailed from Australia. Denis McCormack was the Australian liaison for *The Social Contract* quarterly, and Joseph Wayne Smith was a college professor. It was not just immigration to the United States that Tanton was concerned about. It was immigration to anywhere that Western civilization had established a foothold.[21] For their part, Tanton's opponents agreed that there were profound differences between their values and his. For both sides, immigration ceased to be the focus of the debate. Whether or not one favored reducing immigration became, as Tanton himself observed when he titled his memoirs, "A Skirmish in a Wider War."

It would be difficult to deny that the most important issues of life are the questions of what one values and why. However, a debate over immigration that yields to a debate over values leaves questions about immigration still to be settled. It also leaves the questions less likely to be settled if all the two sides can agree on is that they have such disparate value systems that they cannot agree.

Notes

1. "A Skirmish in a Wider War: An Oral History of John H. Tanton, Founder of FAIR, The Federation for American Immigration Reform," interview with Otis L. Graham Jr., Captiva Island, FL, April 20–21, 1989, 10–11.
2. Ibid., 22.
3. Ibid., 43.
4. For example, see "Illegal-Alien Law: Your Stance Is a Riot," *The Wall Street Journal* (June 20, 1991), 15; "Deep Denial on the Immigration Issue," *The Wall Street Journal* (September 10, 1993), 19; "Immigrants and Rose Colored Myths," *The Wall Street Journal* (August 4, 1994), 13; and "Coming to America," *The Wall Street Journal* (March 19, 1996), 19.

5. Tanton and Graham, "A Skirmish in a Wider War," 31.
6. Ibid., 41.
7. Dan Stein, "Godfather of the Immigration Mess," *National Review* (November 7, 1994): 48.
8. Ibid., 62.
9. Tanton and Graham, "A Skirmish in a Wider War," 23.
10. Ibid., 71.
11. Ibid., 66.
12. Ibid., 67.
13. Ibid., 2.
14. John Tanton, "Immigration and Criminality in the U.S.A.," *Journal of Social, Political and Economic Studies* 18, no. 2 (Summer 1993): 217–234.
15. Peter Brimelow, "The Immigration Invasion," *National Review* (October 24, 1994): 64–67.
16. Lawrence Fuchs, "Four False Alarms and Two Beams of Light," *International Migration Review* 30 (Summer 1996): 591–600.
17. Virginia D. Abernathy, *Population Politics: The Choices That Shape Our Destiny* (New York: Insight Books, 1993).
18. Brent A. Nelson, *America Balkanized: Immigration's Challenge to Government* (Monterey, VA: American Immigration Control Foundation, 1994); Peter Brimelow, *Alien Nation: Some Common Sense about America's Immigration Disaster* (New York: Random House, 1995); and Roy Beck, *The Case against Immigration: The Moral, Economic, Social, and Environmental Reasons for Reducing U.S. Immigration Back to Traditional Levels* (New York: W. W. Norton, 1995).
19. See, for example, Fuchs, "Four False Alarms"; and Eileen Mulhare, "Are Immigrants 'Invaders'? A Response to Lutton and Tanton," *International Migration Review* 30 (Spring 1996): 348–350.
20. John Tanton, Denis McCormack, and Joseph Wayne Smith, eds., *Immigration and the Social Contract: The Implosion of Western Societies* (Aldershot, UK, and Brookfield, VT: Avebury, 1996).
21. To further buttress the argument that the real issue is the clash of cultures, Peter Brimelow, author of *Alien Nation*, might qualify as an alien, at least in the sense of having been born in Great Britain. However, Brimelow's argument against immigration is based on the idea that, after 1965, U.S. immigration law admitted mostly people from outside the traditional U.S. culture background.

Bibliography

The papers of Tanton's chief vehicle for influencing the debate on immigration, the Federation for American Immigration Reform (FAIR), are at the Department of Special Collections at the Melvin Gelman Library at George Washington University. Historian and FAIR activist Otis L. Graham Jr. conducted an oral-history interview with Tanton during a stay at Captiva Island, Florida, on April 20–21, 1989. For a quick sense of FAIR's legislative agenda, see Stephen Moore, "New Year's Resolutions," *National Review* (January 29, 1996): 46–48. Tanton's own book-length publications include *Rethinking Immigration Policy* (Washington, DC: Federation for American Immigration Reform, 1979). He and Wayne Lutton coauthored *The Immigration Invasion* (Petoskey, MI: The Social Contract, 1994). Tanton, Denis McCormack, and Joseph Wayne Smith edited *Immigration and the Social Contract: The Implosion of Western Societies* (Aldershot, UK, and Brookfield, VT: Aveburg, 1996). Tanton is the publisher of *The Social Contract*, for which he has written numerous pieces. He has published articles in other periodicals, an example being "Immigration and Criminality in the U.S.A.," *Journal of Social, Political and Economic Studies* 18, no. 2 (Summer 1993): 217–234. Items by Tanton appeared in the *Christian Science Monitor*, January 27, 1982, August 11, 1986, and April 17, 1992; and in the *Houston Chronicle*, May 30, 1988. This entry mentions the titles of various books that provide support for specific portions of Tanton's argument. Mention should also be made of Juan F. Perea, *Immigrants Out! The New Nativism and the Anti-Immigrant Impulse in the United States*, Critic America Series, eds. Richard Delgado and Jean Stefancic (New York and London: New York University Press, 1997), which summarizes opposition to Tanton's positions but also provides a good example of how both sides of the debate share some of the same assumptions and some of the same debate methods.

U.S.-Mexico Border Violence

Judith Ann Warner and Patrick J. Hayes

The vast southern border with Mexico presents a unique set of problems in the history of immigration in the United States. From the time it was erected, the border with Mexico has been a sieve and an almost arbitrary and artificial barrier to those who would cross it. Migration flows from the southern border such that policy makers are continuously playing catch-up to the movements of immigrants, many of whom skirt the required paperwork. Students of the border have focused on a number of sociological, economic, and political determinants of what seems to them in the national interest, and anthropologists have been investigating the motivations and effects of migration over fences, through deserts, and by way of "coyotes" eager to capitalize on human trafficking and frequently with tragic results. Assassination and intimidation of residents and officials on both sides of the border have been among the latest problems, often as a result of illegal drug activity, where immigrants themselves find that they are pawns used by cartels to further the export of narcotics. How did we get to this point? This article aims to survey several major subject areas related to the United States' border policies, as well as to provide some further analysis of the broader context of how the southern influx has shaped national identity. These subjects include the nation's border deterrence strategy—including the unilateral imposition of a border fence by the United States and the use of border patrol guards, the utilization of which has been considered an unnecessary and imprudent challenge to human rights. The presence of border security has led to a culture of militarization on the border and has fostered the notion of threat or attack upon the homeland along border states. Additionally, we remark on recent border violence, migrant deaths, the undocumented as such, and, lastly, we give an overall assessment of U.S.-Mexico border relations.

The Boarder Deterrence Strategy

The U.S. Border Patrol relies on a strategy of prevention through deterrence in urban regions. Having officers deployed along the border, in view, is thought to make temporary economic migrants and potential permanent immigrants stop and think twice. In this high-stakes border game, the migrants have taken their business elsewhere—on their own or with the help of organized smugglers who help them travel through remote desert and mountainous regions, sometimes making transporting drugs a part of the price. The number of U.S. Border Patrol apprehensions continues at a high level—a possible indicator of enforcement success—but unauthorized entrance and drug smuggling continues unabated.

The U.S. Border Patrol is a part of Immigration and Customs Enforcement (formerly the Immigration and Naturalization Service) in the Department of Homeland Security. The Border Patrol has a history dating back to the 1920s and has received constant budget upgrades since the early 1970s. Since the 1970s, the American public has consistently made stopping undocumented immigration an issue. Politicians have repeatedly campaigned with the conservative theme of strengthening border enforcement. In the 1990s, Congress responded with a series of new initiatives to change the pattern of undocumented immigration. Intensive enforcement began with Operation Hold the Line in El Paso (1993) and the construction of fencing. Currently, these operations have been extended with Operation Gatekeeper in San Diego (1994); Operation Rio Grande (1997) in McAllen, Texas, and Laredo, Texas; and Operation Border Safeguard (2003) in Tucson, Arizona. Together, all of these intensified enforcement efforts in and around urban centers have been referred to as the Gatekeeper Complex.

The U.S. Border Patrol is the enforcement arm of the southern border enforcement strategy. It uses active patrols, checkpoints and high technology, including infrared heat-seeking thermal cameras, to detect individuals trying to enter without inspection and visas or other documents. Traditionally, U.S. Border Patrol enforcement has been spread out along the entire border, with various sectors targeted to be strengthened. This resulted in fluctuation in the ability to apprehend undocumented crossers. In 1994 to 1995, Attorney General Janet Reno and Immigration and Naturalization Service Commissioner Doris Meissner introduced the Southwest Border Strategy. They proposed targeting the areas of the southwest border most often penetrated and increased personnel and high-technology infrastructure. In Arizona, for instance, the Southwest Border Strategy apprehended 384,942 individuals in 2004, an increase of 42 percent over the previous year.

Such high numbers have prompted a mushrooming of vigilante groups, most notoriously that of the Minutemen, a civilian group that patrols the border and alerts the U.S. Border Patrol to the presence of undocumented border crossers.

In 1994, Operation Gatekeeper in San Diego, California, initiated a prevention-through-deterrence strategy. A five-mile zone along Imperial Beach was estimated to account for 25 percent of all unauthorized crossings nationwide. After enforcement was tightened at Imperial Beach, a 66-mile area in the San Diego sector was included and apprehensions in 2001 dropped dramatically for a corridor that had accounted for an estimated 45 percent of all illegal entries. Operation Gatekeeper was then extended into the Imperial Valley and El Centro, California, as human smugglers attempted to find ways around the U.S. Border Patrol. In 1998, the additional staffing of 140 agents in El Centro resulted in 226,580 apprehensions, a 55 percent increase over the prior year, in part due to the fact that the checkpoints were staffed at all hours. In 1999, 78 more agents were deployed, and apprehension dropped to a very low level as individuals were deterred from trying to cross there.

In 1993, Operation Hold the Line was initiated in El Paso, Texas, located across from Ciudad Juarez, Mexico. In the 1990s, the Rio Grande in El Paso was contained in concrete conduits and surrounded with fencing and U.S. Border Patrol agents. After 1993, intensified enforcement reduced apprehensions by 50 percent. As a result of that success, Operation Rio Grande was begun in McAllen, Texas, located across from the city of Reynosa, Mexico. Two hundred and sixty new U.S. Border Patrol officers were added in McAllen, and 205 positions were added in the Laredo, Texas, sector. Laredo is located across from Nuevo Laredo, Mexico. In this region, infrared scopes, night-vision goggles, underground sensors, and the IDENT biometric fingerprint system were introduced. Because the border in this area is identified as the U.S. side of the Rio Grande, all-weather roads were built. This involved bulldozing and destroying much of the natural ecosystem vegetation on the American side and creating an eyesore view. In some areas, the scenery was further impacted by the construction of fences, almost none of which were uniform or served as an impenetrable barrier.

In 1995, Operation Safeguard was directed at undocumented entry between Nogales, Mexico, and its sister city, Nogales, Arizona. The U.S. Border Patrol presented this strategy as directing potential unauthorized entrants to more open regions where they could be more easily detected. In each of these cases, deterrence was directed at decreasing unauthorized entrance into cities and local communities where it was thought individuals could gain cover to enter U.S. territory. In 2002, Arizona had 1,000 agents, compared to fewer than 300 in 1994. That number has grown steadily ever since. The impact of increased enforcement is first seen in an increased number of apprehensions, but, as a deterrence effect occurs, a drop in apprehensions begins as individuals realize there is poor possibility of getting through. In 2006, Operation Jump Start deployed 6,000 National Guard troops to the major southern border corridors. This effort was meant to supplement the U.S. Border Patrol while 6,000 additional U.S. Border Patrol agents were trained, but it has also had the effect of militarizing the border. The U.S. Border Patrol has arrested over 1 million unauthorized entrants annually. In the past, this figure has included individuals who have been arrested on more than one occasion and deported to the home country through the catch-and-release program that ended in 2007.

The policies of border enforcement, combined with a guest worker program leading toward proper legalization of immigrants, President Obama has advocated for easier pathways to citizenship and more efficient ways to process individuals who seek temporary resident status for work. Already in 2004, President Bush had advocated against unauthorized entrance by promoting legal means to obtain work. He urged Congress to pass comprehensive immigration reform, impelled by what he described as the risk of loss of life in "dangerous desert crossings" and the problem of trusting one's life to "brutal rings of heartless smugglers." While both presidents appear contradictory in both promoting legal entrance and increasing enforcement to keep people out, it is apparent that the national policy of controlling migration by allowing temporary guest workers is motivated in part to reduce the death rate.

The southern border deterrence strategy resulted in decreased apprehensions in areas of intensified enforcement, presenting the image of successful deterrence. An image of reduced apprehension statistics is not the same as preventing human smugglers and undocumented entrants from finding other methods to cross. One major consequence of the southern border strategy has been an increase in the sophistication of human trafficking. In the past, individual smugglers would accept a small payment to transit people across the border and into the interior. Today, smuggling is carried out by organized criminal organizations that charge much higher prices and even extort funds or labor from individuals after a successful crossing. A common response has been for migrants to find riskier ways of entering, even at the cost of their lives, and to become permanent undocumented immigrants.

Militarization of the Border

As a hedge against immigrant deaths in desert regions along the border, an increased militaristic presence has been put in place. The term *militarization of the border* is controversial, because it refers to the use of (para)military techniques against the citizens of friendly nations who attempt to cross the border without papers as well as criminals such as drug traffickers and human smugglers. The U.S. Border Patrol is receiving increased assistance by the U.S. military, including deployment of thousands of National Guard soldiers. Consequently, this has developed a culture of suspicion, concomitant intensification of paramilitary activity by drug cartels, and human rights violations. Beginning with and subsequent to the Reagan administration, the use of low-intensity conflict tactics to control unauthorized immigration, combat drug smuggling, and detect terrorist incursion has cost the nation billions of dollars and produced an uncertain outcome that is still being debated in Congress. U.S. Border Patrol administration, agents, and resources have been repeatedly increased. In the 1980s, a multiagency federal task force called the Alien Border Control Committee developed plans for a mass sweep targeting undocumented immigrants; the intended result was a sealed border. There have been attempts to merge the activities of the military and the police by modifying legal restrictions, particularly for antidrug trafficking operations. In 1986, Operation Alliance joined federal and state law enforcement agencies and the military to counter drug-smuggling operations. Since the 1980s, the military has provided the U.S. Border Patrol with training in intelligence gathering and small-unit tactics. Drug enforcement has involved the military in repeated off-base operational missions along the border. The emphasis on securitization of the U.S.-Mexico border led to the development of the Southwest Border Intelligence Task Force, which was originally focused on drug trafficking enforcement but now includes counterterrorism. This securitization was augmented by the extensive adoption of military equipment and technology for use by the U.S. Border Patrol and the Drug Enforcement Agency. The specific elements of militarization include both ground and high-technology response operations. On the ground, checkpoints stop all traffic, intelligence-driven special operations occur, and patrols are sent to specific target areas through rapid response that includes technology originally developed for military use, including night-vision equipment, high-intensity stadium lighting, electronic and magnetic intrusion ground detection sensing systems, remote-controlled 24-hour video surveillance and sensing cameras, unmanned video towers, helicopters, air support, and unmanned aerial vehicles.

Increased militarization involves a level of cooperation between the U.S. Border Patrol and the military in which the distinction between the two is sometimes blurred. An example of this level of militarization of the border is when marines at the Barry M. Goldwater Range located in the desert near Yuma, Arizona, deploys a ground surveillance system that tracks movement and locates vehicles, relaying Global Positioning System coordinates to the U.S. Border Patrol. This type of technology is considered more effective than building fences and is referred to as a virtual wall. Some would allow the secretary of defense to place army, navy, air force, and marine corps personnel to assist the U.S. Border Patrol, essentially flouting the Posse Comitatus Act that prevents the military from enforcing civilian law without an act of Congress. National Guard troops are not subject to this act unless they are federalized. The United States Senate has repeatedly voted down measures that would, in effect, complete the militarization of the border.

Two factors drive the increase in lethal firepower along the southern border. First, drug smugglers have adapted paramilitary tactics, including use of high-tech weaponry to move their loads. Second, drug cartels vie for control of territories, including the very profitable I-35 interstate highway that runs from Laredo, Texas, on the Rio Grande to Chicago, Illinois. In 2005 to 2006, a conflict between the Gulf cartel and the Sinaloa cartel resulted in shootouts and deaths in Nuevo Laredo, Mexico, the twin city of Laredo, Texas. Violence in Nuevo Laredo was extreme, and former Mexican President Vincente Fox (2000–2006) called in Mexican troops. In 2006, a substantial cache of weaponry was seized near Laredo, including two bombs and enough material to assemble dozens more. The coup de grace came in July 2010, when 12 people were assassinated in Nuevo Laredo and 21 wounded, including several children.

Along the U.S.-Mexico border, considered the back door for terrorists, there has been limited activity, but any activity is of concern because 9/11 demonstrated that the actions of a very few can result in massive damage. The Department of Homeland Security announced that by December 2005, 51 nationals from countries known to harbor terrorists had been arrested by the U.S. Border Patrol and other organizations in the Joint Terrorism Task Force. They came from Egypt, Lebanon, Iran, Iraq, Syria, and Pakistan. These suspected terrorists were arrested for crimes ranging from weapons smuggling to wiring large sums of money. In November 2005, an Iraqi al-Qaeda operative was arrested and detained at the border. In 2006, Robert Mueller Jr. indicated that Hezbollah had sent operatives across the U.S.-Mexico border for purposes of terrorism and that the Federal Bureau of Investigation had arrested and broken up a ring.

An extremely negative consequence of border militarization is civilians caught in the crossfire. In May 1997, a U.S. Marine corporal, Clemente Banuelos, deployed in a clandestine joint U.S. Border Patrol/military surveillance operation shot and killed 18-year-old Esequiel Hernandez Jr. while he was herding goats in Redford, Texas, near the southern border. This sad incident is related to how the military is trained. Troops are trained to seek out and destroy an enemy, while law enforcement is trained to capture a suspect, observing due process in order to detain the suspect and bring his or her case to the attention of the legal system. A grand jury declined to bring charges for the death of Hernandez, and the Pentagon defended the action as reflecting the duty of engagement.

The Border Fence

To prevent unauthorized entrants from crossing the U.S.-Mexico border, the construction of partial or complete fencing has been passed in Congress, though there is no uniformity to the plan, still less to its execution. Both Americans and Mexicans residing on the border view it as offensive; no similar action has been proposed for Canada. Economic migrants from Mexico, Central, and South America have been forced to cross in ever-more remote and hazardous regions. The solution for preventing these deaths could be legalizing increased immigration rather than fencing the border. While fencing could prevent some criminal activity along the border, it might promote more human smuggling. Border fencing was first installed in urban locations along the California-Mexico border and in Arizona, New Mexico, and southeast Texas. In 2008, 670 additional miles in south Texas was under construction. The degree of security offered by the fence varies. Often rural fencing is no more than a railing to deter vehicles. Other sections of the border fence located near cities and communities are comprised of a steel plate wall or two fences that are 15 feet high and run parallel to each other with a track for motor vehicles in between. Individuals or groups crossing the border without authorization trigger motion sensors and alert the U.S. Border Patrol. On one side of each of the two parallel fences is eight feet of coiled barbed wire, and before the barbed wire are ditches to prevent sport utility vehicles and trucks used by human and drug smugglers from crossing. In more remote areas, rail fences have been installed to prevent vehicle crossing.

The U.S.-Mexico border is 1,951 miles long and crosses urban areas, desert, and mountainous regions. Historically, the highest rates of unauthorized entrance have been through the San Diego, California, and El Paso, Texas, urban areas, which suffered increased crime due to the unlawful measures taken to cross migrants and attempts to assault and rob them during their passage. These are the sites at which the first border fences have been built. Fencing began with the installation of 14 miles of steel wall as a part of Operation Gatekeeper in the Tijuana–San Diego undocumented immigration corridor. It was made with steel plates that served as makeshift aircraft runways during the first Iraq War. These walls have been tunneled under. At Otay Mesa, San Diego, a half-mile, 75-foot-deep tunnel with electricity and ventilation was discovered with ground-penetrating radar. The tunnel

A U.S. serviceman welds together border-fence panels along the U.S.-Mexican border in Yuma, Arizona, April 24, 2007. (USAF Photo/Senior Airman John Hughel, Jr.)

connected to a Tijuana industrial park and contained bales of marijuana. U.S. Border Patrol officials indicate that the San Diego wall was never meant to stop unauthorized entrance, but to slow people down. A fence that caused injury would render the United States subject to liability lawsuits.

Although Operation Gatekeeper and Operation Safeguard were intended to be temporary, they became permanent. The result was diversion of unauthorized entrants and human smugglers to more remote areas and an almost complete drop in apprehensions in the urban areas that were fenced. Instead of stopping unauthorized immigration, crossers choose different and more difficult rural desert areas that are hazardous. Border crossers have been diverted to the Sonora Desert and Baboquivari Mountains in Arizona. Since the inauguration of Operation Gatekeeper, more than 1,200 have died within Arizona alone as a result of trying to cross in this region. Additionally, fences encouraged traffickers to use ever-more sophisticated methods. Since 2001, 21 cross-border tunnels have been discovered in California and Arizona.

The Senate confirmed the U.S. House of Representatives Secure Border Fence Bill of 2006 to authorize and partially fund construction of 700 miles of double-walled fencing along the U.S.-Mexico border. The sites include two spots in California, most of the Arizona border, and heavily populated areas of Texas and New Mexico. Fourteen known drug-smuggling corridors are included. Protests and lawsuits over proposed border walls in south Texas occurred, but in 2008, the Supreme Court turned down hearing a case against border fencing.

On the Mexican side of the border, the former President Vincente Fox (2000–2006), ministers of several Latin American countries, and Mexican intellectuals have considered the construction of a border wall to be "shameful." The Mexican press condemned the wall project as a xenophobic and racist act. A wall implies that the United States is superior to Mexico and that social problems originate on the Mexican side, not the American side. The United States is protected from Mexico, not vice versa. Mexicans regard the fence as a negative response to individuals who work hard and contribute to the North American economy and are concerned that it will impact ties between Mexicans and family members located in the United States. President Fox vowed to start an international campaign to stop the fence.

Others contend that the border-wall mindset has weakened the ties between the United States and Mexico. There is a sense of separation that undermines cross-border social ties and makes it difficult to negotiate binational solutions to problems like unauthorized immigration. Today, border residents are less likely to visit together, and twin cities on the U.S. and Mexico side are more socially, if not geographically, distant. Texas governor Rick Perry (2000–present) opposes the fence, because it undermines trade; he suggests that technology should be used to promote safe and legal migration and cross-border contact.

Environmentalists are also opposed to border fencing. The ecology of desert regions and river systems will be disrupted. The San Diego border fence constructed as a part of Operation Gatekeeper is in a three-and-a-half-mile area of marsh. In 2005, a federal judge ruled against a lawsuit brought by the Sierra Club and other environmental groups to protect the sensitive ecological balance of the Tijuana River marshes. It is one of the few intact estuaries and coastal lagoon systems in Southern California. A more general objection to fencing at most rural points of the border is that it hampers wild animal migration.

In south Texas, many lawsuits were brought against the border fence. The fence disrupts the use of private property, placing a barrier between animals and water or ranchers and their own land. It has had social consequences such as dividing the campus of the University of Texas at Brownsville into U.S. and Mexican areas. A coalition of Texas mayors and other public officials sought to stop the fence, but their effort to bring the issue before the Supreme Court was unsuccessful. To facilitate fencing, the secretary of the Department of Homeland Security issued 30 waivers of laws protecting endangered species, migratory birds, deserts or forests, antiquities, Native American graves, and rancher's property rights.

Migrant Deaths on the U.S.-Mexico Border

A mixture of reaction has accompanied American sentiments over undocumented migrants crossing the southern border. One reaction is to spare no expense to close off the entire border. Another reaction is to express compassion for successful crossers and sorrow for the dead. Humanitarian rescue efforts such as providing water stations in deserts have been misunderstood and condemned. The U.S. Border Patrol is involved in harm-reduction strategies for migrant death prevention. It has joined a bilateral Border Safety Initiative with Mexico and established the Search Trauma and Rescue (BORSTAR) team. The Mexican government is now circulating a guide to migrants warning that *polleros* (smugglers) may lead them into hazardous situations.

Raquel Rubio-Goldsmith, a Bi-national Migration Institute researcher at the University of Arizona, and her colleagues have referred to the impact of relative closure of urban crossings as a funnel effect because migrants are increasingly crossing in riskier areas, particularly the Arizona desert, where thousands have died. Rubio-Goldsmith and her colleagues, Wayne Cornelius (a sociologist at the University of San Diego), and the Government Accountability Office (GAO) all agree that intensified border enforcement has caused an unprecedented series of migrant deaths. Since 1995, it is estimated that between 2,000 and 3,000 men, women, and children have died trying to cross the U.S.-Mexico border and/or make their way into the interior[1] Wayne Cornelius estimates that, from 1994 to 2004, 2,978 border migrants died attempting to cross the border or make their way into the interior. Cornelius states, "To put this death toll in perspective, the forti-fied U.S. border with Mexico has been more than ten times deadlier to migrants from Mexico during the last nine years than the Berlin Wall was to East Germans throughout its twenty-eight year existence."[2]

Approximately 1,000 migrants are estimated to have died in Arizona. Raquel Rubio-Goldsmith and her research associates studied all cases of unauthorized border-crosser deaths examined by the Pima County Medical Examiner's Office from 1990 to 2005. During this time, 927 bodies were examined. GAO estimates are that Arizona accounted for 78 percent of the increase in all U.S.-Mexico bor-der deaths from 1990 to 2003. Over 80 percent of deaths were individuals under age 40, but there was an upward trend in deaths of individuals under age 18. Fur-thering concern over this issue, the U.S. Border Patrol has criteria for being in-cluded in the death estimate that result in an undercount. For example, deaths on the Tohono O'odham reservation are not handled by the U.S. Border Patrol or in-cluded in the count.

Criticism has come from the GAO in testimony before the House Subcommittee on Immigration, Border Security and Claims of the Committee of the Judiciary.[3] GAO research indicates that intensified enforcement is the reason for a massive increase in migrant deaths. Using Border Safety Initiative migrant-death data, the GAO found that, from 1985 to the early 1990s, migrant deaths declined. In the late 1990s through 2005, the number of deaths approximately doubled. In 1999, there were 241 deaths, while 476 were recorded in 2005. National Center for Health Statistics data indicate that three-quarters of 1990–2003 increases in migrant death were primarily confined to the Tucson, Arizona, Border Patrol Sector. Deaths due to heat exposure increased, while traffic fatalities, the major cause of death in the 1990s, declined. The GAO concluded that, after the 1994 implementation of the Southwest Border Strategy, migrant border crossing shifted from urban San Diego and El Paso into the Arizona desert.

The Border Safety Initiative has emphasized the role of the smuggler in guiding migrants into high-risk regions. By shifting the blame to the smuggler, migrants can be viewed as victims. This has been done in situations involving criminal ac-tivities in which one party has greater responsibility. For example, the primary re-sponsibility for drug abuse can be viewed as belonging with the dealer rather than the physically addicted. Representing the migrant as a victim allows a change in perspective that valorizes saving human life while situating the smuggler as the primary offender. U.S. Border Patrol involvement in preservation of human life is a standard principle found in all public service agencies.

Since implementation of the Border Safety Initiative, the U.S. Border Patrol has trained officers in rescue and life-saving techniques. BORSTAR is a special-ized unit for search and rescue under hazardous conditions, including swift water and mountain and desert rescue. A study compared the impact of response by a

BORSTAR team to a regular U.S. Border Patrol officer in the Tucson, Arizona, sector where BORSTAR was implemented. The results showed that, in 2003, BORSTAR agents effected a 93 percent (260 people) success rate and that 7 percent (18 people) died when BORSTAR was involved. In contrast, only 53 percent (76 people) of U.S. Border Patrol officers were successful at rescue. Statistical analysis showed that the likelihood of death was reduced 84 percent when a BORSTAR agent responded.

In 2003, the U.S. Border Patrol began the Lateral Repatriation Program (LRP), which involved releasing migrant detainees from the west desert area of the Tucson sector into the south Texas sector. Prior to the end of the catch-and-release policy in 2006, migrants were immediately returned to Mexico in the sector from which they had tried to cross. LRP, a $1,352,080 program, operated for 23 days and relocated 6,200 migrants. It was periodically enacted at times of high risk in hot, arid crossing regions. Claudia Smith, the border project director of the California Rural Legal Assistance Foundation, has criticized the LRP for moving migrants away from the risks of a desert crossing only to face the risks of a south Texas crossing. She notes that the U.S. Border Patrol only enumerates deaths within its sectors near the line and does not count suffocation deaths.

Among the most notorious cases where this is in evidence is that of the deaths of 19 migrants on the humid night of May 13, 2003, from asphyxiation, heat exposure, and dehydration while crowded into the back of a tractor trailer in Victoria, Texas. When the truck was opened, 73 migrants were found, but there may have been more who escaped into the night. The known migrants were from Mexico (48), Honduras (15), El Salvador (8), Nicaragua (1), and the Dominican Republic (1). From the time the migrants entered the truck in Harlingen, they were sweating, and many of them became dizzy and nauseous from the heat. The humidity was 93 percent on that night. The elderly and children were among the first to succumb to heat exposure, and Marco Antonio Villasenor, a five year old boy, was taken to the back of the truck by his father. The migrants were scared, and many began to hyperventilate. Some people lost consciousness and others began to vomit. Driving slowly to avoid attention, the driver had not reached the U.S. Border Patrol checkpoint. The migrants began to discuss crying out for help to be let out versus staying quiet in the hopes of getting through to the U.S. interior. At the Sarita checkpoint, no one noticed the broken taillights on the back of the truck. The driver of the truck, Tyrone Williams, thought that he was being paid to take them through the Sarita checkpoint and to the Kingsville/Robstown area, not the Victoria/Houston destination. Tyrone was promised $3,500 for taking them to the original destination, but the smugglers called and offered him an additional $2,500 to go all the way to Houston. During the third hour of their captivity, some people began to die of heat exposure and suffocation. There was no water in the back of the truck. The migrants beat against the driver's cab and called out with no response. Finally, the truck air conditioner was turned on, but it takes several hours for people to recover from heat exposure. This was not enough. In Victoria, Williams finally noticed a problem with the taillight and stopped the truck at a gas station. Williams heard the shouting and opened the doors. He and his companion, Fatima Holloway, went into the gas station and bought water, which they distributed to the migrants. Williams then panicked and fled after detaching the semi from the cargo carrier. It was too late for 19 victims. The five-year-old child and his father died in each other's arms.

Williams was found guilty of transporting undocumented migrants and then fleeing without seeking aid. The Justice Department sought the death penalty for Williams. He admitted that he heard the migrants being loaded onto the truck but not that he heard the migrants crying out in distress. Williams pled guilty in exchange for a reduced sentence. Karla Chavez was identified as connected to a trafficking operation and, after being tracked down in Central America, was brought to the United States and indicted on 56 counts, including the death of 19 migrants. Fourteen other traffickers were identified during the investigation due to linkages with Karla Chavez, but none were assigned the death penalty because of insufficient evidence as to how the operation had been organized. Karla had 55 charges dismissed and was given a lighter sentence in return for testifying against other trafficking defendants.

Migrants face drowning or suffocation and accidental injury or death in high-speed motor chases in the LRP receiving zones. In addition, women have been repatriated without contacts to Ciudad Juarez, Mexico, where hundreds of women have been raped and murdered in unsolved cases in recent years. In 2003, 82 percent of deceased migrants were male; 76 percent were from the bordering country of Mexico, and 64 percent were under 30. The youth of the deceased implies that they died under very harsh conditions. In 2003, out of 122 incidents, 74 percent of people died of heat exposure and dehydration. In 8 percent of the incidents, another migrant went for help that did not arrive in time. In 9 percent of incidents, the U.S. Border Patrol did not arrive prior to death. Seventy-four percent of heat exposure deaths occurred when temperatures were above 105 degrees Fahrenheit. Guerette controlled for a variety of situational variables (age, nationality, size of the group of migrants, and level of U.S. Border Patrol activity) and found that women were 29 percent more likely to die of heat and dehydration than men. Others drown, with nearly two-thirds of these incidences occurring outside of flooding situations. In 88 percent of drowning deaths, a U.S. Border Patrol officer was not present to assist the victim. Bodies are found floating in the river. Five percent of the time, a U.S. Border Patrol officer is present and too distant to get there in time or unable to come to help. Finally, motor vehicle collisions account for a large percentage of migrant deaths. About 44 percent of the 32 incidents in 2003 involved migrants in high-speed collisions when the U.S. Border Patrol was present.[4]

Although the Minutemen and other citizen volunteer groups seek to locate and apprehend migrants, there are humanitarian groups in opposition to this practice who seek to help migrants. Border Angels maintains 340 water stations in the El Centro, California, Border Patrol sector. *Paisanos al Rescate* (Countrymen to the Rescue) looks for migrants in distress by air. Humane Borders maintains 65-gallon water stations with flags that fly 20 feet in the air. These humanitarian activities are not conducted in secret. Links to humanitarian groups aiding migrants can be found at http://www.nomoredeaths.org.

Border Patrol and Human Rights Violations

A critical human rights issue is whether undocumented migrants from Mexico and Central America are deliberately mistreated by the U.S. Border Patrol. In the 1990s, arrangements such as the North American Free Trade Agreement increased the transfer of goods across borders and aided in the softening of political boundaries. In turn, levels of undocumented immigration increased and created intense conflict along the U.S.-Mexico border. The tension in the U.S.-Mexico border region makes it difficult to determine when the use of force or deadly force is justified. What is clear is that changes in U.S. border security policy could reduce the potential for human rights abuses. Mexican immigration was of little concern in the early history of the Border Patrol. In fact, it was encouraged by the bracero program from World War II (1942) to 1964 due to labor shortages. Following the war, attitudes altered. From the late 1940s to the 1970s, the U.S. Border Patrol was focused on stopping illegal Mexican immigrants from crossing the border. In the 1980s, the U.S. government's war on drugs added another element to border security. Agents were no longer only concerned with people crossing the border but with illegal substances as well. Now the stakes are higher. In 2006, the Department of Homeland Security secretary, Michael Chertoff, ordered an end to the catch and release of foreign nationals who were other than Mexican. Such persons were released into the United States and ordered to attend a hearing before an immigration judge, but they seldom did and often became part of the undocumented population. This release policy was due to lack of jail space. In 2007 and 2008, President Bush mandated an end to the catch and release of Mexican nationals, who had previously been immediately deported back to Mexico, and took steps to expand detention facilities. The detention of Mexican nationals is being expanded by Operation Streamline to many border-enforcement sectors. A first-time attempted entry can result in mandatory detention from 15 to 180 days. Attempting to enter more than once without inspection is a felony, carrying a federal prison term of up to two years.

It could be argued that the U.S. Border Patrol tries to prevent both migrant abuse and deaths while performing its basic job of trying to keep unauthorized persons out. Situational crime-prevention techniques attempt to deter undocumented cross-ers from hazardous situations. The U.S. Border Patrol has undertaken initiatives to warn migrants of risks in Spanish and English so that they will be aware of haz-ards prior to crossing. The U.S. Border Patrol's Search Trauma and Rescue team attempts to find and locate victims before they succumb to such problems as de-hydration, heat stroke, and extreme cold. Humanitarian groups have been active in assisting migrants in life-threatening situations as well.

However, human rights advocates argue that international law and the U.S. Con-stitution protect people regardless of citizenship. They believe human-rights vi-olations frequently occur on the U.S.-Mexico border. People and their property are illegally searched. Verbal, psychological, and physical abuse are committed against adults and children. There are documented instances involving the depri-vation of food and water, withholding of medical attention, torture, and excessive force, including assault, battery, and murder. Human-rights advocates argue that interrogations regularly involve shouting and threats. At processing centers, Mexi-cans and other foreign nationals are humiliated and intimidated.

Immigration Policy and the Undocumented

The United States is embroiled in a debate surrounding what to do about unauthor-ized immigrants and how to stop undeclared entrance. One of the social factors affecting the debate concerns variance in the estimates of the size of the undocu-mented population. Another concern is that, although many Americans view these immigrants as Mexican, because they make up about 50 percent of unauthorized entrants, many people do not realize the range of national origins of people who cross land, sea, and air borders with no papers or fraudulent documents. Because the United States wants to control its borders to prevent terrorists from entering, the sheer estimated size of the unauthorized population, 12 million, and all of the ways of access that would need to be controlled has frightened the public.

Demographers in the field of sociology define an unauthorized immigrant as an individual who crossed into the United States without official government paper-work and remained in residency. The Department of Homeland Security has com-plicated the meaning of being unauthorized by including any person who is not a legal resident. This includes individuals who enter with visas and overstay their time limit as well as those who are applying for legal residence under the Immigra-tion and Nationality Act of 1965 section 245 (i), who may even hold a green card. American citizens believe that the vast majority of unauthorized entrants cross the U.S.-Mexico border without paperwork and inspection. This is not true, although it is taken for granted because of the constant focus the media has on the southern border. To counter that belief, it is necessary to combine two very different esti-mates: (1) entry without inspection and (2) visa overstay. As shown in Table 1,

Table 1 Pew Estimates of Modes of Entry for the Unauthorized Immigrant Population

Entered Legally with Inspection	
Nonimmigrant Visa Overstayers	4 million to 5.5 million
Border Crossing Card Violators	250,000 to 500,000
Subtotal Legal Entries	4.5 million to 6 million
Entered Illegally without Inspection	
Evaded Immigration Inspectors and Border Patrol	6 million to 7 million
Estimated Total Unauthorized Population in 2006	11.5 million to 12 million

Source: Pew Hispanic Center. Modes of Entry for the Unauthorized Migrant Population Fact Sheet. Washington, DC: Pew Hispanic Center, 2006. For these estimates, the Center used information from a March 2005 population survey and Department of Homeland Security reports.

the Pew Hispanic Center found that from 45 percent to 50 percent (4.5 million to 6 million) of the unauthorized population had entered legally with a nonimmigrant visa or border crossing card and inspection.

Six million to seven million, more than 50 percent, are thought to have entered without inspection. This can be done by evading the U.S. Border Patrol at the U.S.-Mexico border or by a variety of means, including evading inspectors through entrance at the Canadian border or sea and air borders. This implies that, to control the flow of people in and out of the United States, it is necessary to track international visitors and focus on more regions than just along the U.S.-Mexico border. This is a reasonable assumption based on estimates, but because the estimates are not hard fact, it is important to consider that there is insufficient numerical evidence for dealing with both issues.

Tourists and business visitors make up the vast majority of visa overstayers. In recent years, 250,000 to 350,000 people who entered with permission have overstayed. This is 1 percent to 1.5 percent of visitors, and this group is becoming a significant component of the unauthorized population. This is supplemented by individuals entering from Canada or Mexico with border crossing cards who then do not return. It is apparent that keeping track of immigration is not just a matter of focusing on the U.S.-Mexico border. Along the Canadian and U.S.-Mexico borders, many citizens use border crossing cards. The number of entries by people who cross, sometimes on a daily basis, was estimated at 148 million in 2004. The Pew Hispanic Center stated that, even if only a small percentage of this number overstayed, they would significantly increase the number in the undocumented population. Once again, this is only an estimate because an accurate count is not kept to begin with.[5]

In 1998, the federal government began to issue credit card-like crossing identification cards to Mexicans with a biometric marker: a fingerprint. The year 2001 was the deadline for replacing the cards, and the Department of State issued 4 million. A U.S.-Mexico border crossing card authorized a visit of no more than 30 days inside a zone of 25 miles in California, Texas, and New Mexico and 75 miles in Arizona. It is necessary to apply for a visa for a longer stay and to fill out an I-94 form. Many such visa requests are refused by U.S. consulates if the individuals cannot demonstrate financial means in an attempt to prevent undocumented immigration, which is especially targeted at Mexicans.

Mexico, which accounts for 57 percent of all undocumented immigrants, is the primary sending country and the focus of media attention (see Table 1). As of March 2004, Mexicans have predominated among all undocumented immigrants since 1990. This results in political concern about control of the southern U.S. border. The Central American countries of El Salvador, Guatemala, and Honduras, estimated to be the source of 12 percent of the undocumented immigrants, also contribute to the group most likely to gain entrance over the southern border. Additional undocumented immigrants from Asia arrive from India, Korea, China, and Vietnam through various means much less likely than crossing the southern border. The Philippines and Brazil are increasingly significant as sending countries. It is estimated that 2,410,000 have arrived from a wide variety of countries and the people from these countries, unlike Mexicans and Central Americans, are not likely to enter at the U.S.-Mexico border—the primary focus of concern.

What is to be done with these individuals? The Illegal Immigration Reform and Immigrant Responsibility Act of 1996 greatly increased the number of people that U.S. Immigration and Customs Enforcement must detain. From 1996, the number of immigrants and refugees detained on any given day increased from 8,279 to more than 20,000. Annually, the figure is more than 200,000. In an attempt to cope with this, in 2004, federal legislation authorized the creation of 40,000 new beds in detention centers by 2010. Detaining and removing immigrants costs more than $1 billion annually. The average detention cost is $65.61 per bed, per day. In addition to detention, the United States also practices deportation. According to the *Yearbook of Immigration Statistics*, published by the Department of Homeland Security, in 2006, 1,206,457 individuals were deported.[6] The vast majority (1,179,601) came from North America, and 1,057,253 were returned to Mexico. The remainder of those who were deported were from Asia (9,967), South America (9,004), Africa (3,507), Europe (3,255), Oceania (218), and an unknown country of origin (905).

The Mexican Migration Project is located at the Center for Comparative Immigration Studies, University of California, San Diego. Its research monitors the reactions of border crossers from sending communities in Mexico. Seidy Gaytan, Evelyn Lucio, Fawad Shaiq, and Anjanette Urdaniva interviewed past and potential Mexican migrants.[7] In their study, the four primary reasons given by returning migrants and new migrants were economic: (1) financial necessity; (2) return to a prior job in the United States; (3) a better wage in the United States; and (4) lack of work in Mexico. Approximately three-quarters of those seeking to cross without inspection had financial reasons; 9.5 percent of recent migrants came back to see their families; and 12.2 percent of prospective migrants wanted to leave for the United States for family reunification.

Since the 1980s, Douglas Massey, a sociologist at Princeton University, has been active in the study of undocumented immigration. His statistical estimates are that migrants and immigrants who crossed at San Diego or El Paso now seek new and remote locations that lead 55 percent to seek work in new geographical destinations. Massey referred to this as the nationalization of undocumented immigration as the three traditional destinations (California, Texas, and Illinois) are receiving fewer new immigrants as they disperse to new receiving states. This partially explains the new pattern of geographic dispersion being described by the U.S. Census estimates, and it implies that employers are breaking the law in new rural and emerging gateway city destinations.

U.S.-Mexico Border Violence

How much harm, if any, is caused by temporary migrant transit and immigrant settlement in the immediate U.S.-Mexico border region? While both legal and undocumented individual migrants can have an impact upon the crime rate in border cities and outlying rural regions, research indicates that it is minimal. While undocumented entrance into the United States is illegal, it is a civil offense, not a crime, until it is committed more than once, at which point it may be treated as a felony. An increasing number of immigrants without documents are being placed in detention. Although crossing the border is not the same as committing a property crime or homicide, the public believes that these immigrants are conventional criminals once they cross the border, and keeping them in detention fortifies this image.

In an address to the nation, President George Bush stated: "Illegal immigration puts pressure on public schools and hospitals; it strains state and local budgets *and brings crime to our communities*" (emphasis added). However, Mathew T. Lee, an academician specializing in criminal justice, has studied the relationship between immigration and homicide in El Paso and San Diego. El Paso has primarily Hispanic immigrants, while San Diego has Hispanic and Asian immigrant populations. Lee used a statistical method called multiple linear regression and found no relation between immigrant concentration in neighborhoods and homicide. He found that socioeconomic factors were primarily related to homicide. Economic deprivation, problems with the availability of jobs, and neighborhood instability (the rate at which people move in and out) strongly correlate with homicide. Typically, U.S. Census data show that immigrants to the United States have a much lower crime rate than the U.S.-born.

According to Pablo Villa, an ethnographer, the public always views the criminal as originating from the other side. Villa interviewed residents from the twin border cities of El Paso and Ciudad Juarez. When Operation Blockade was instituted by the U.S. Border Patrol, El Paso residents supported it because they associated Mexicans with poverty, crime, and other social problems. Many El Paso residents said that they felt safer because they did not worry as much about having their homes broken into. In El Paso, Mexicans from Ciudad Juarez were viewed as a major factor in crime. *Juarenses* (residents of Ciudad Juarez) did not think the same way. They view themselves as residents of Ciudad Juarez. According to them, any undocumented entry or border crime is attributed to "Southern Mexicans." Thus, crime is always displaced and blamed on another "outsider" group. This could be interpreted as a trend in which an in-group typically stereotypes an out-group as the cause of problems. This displacement of blame for crime upon outsider groups mirrors how U.S. citizens view the cause of crime at the national level.

In the 1980s, after drug routes shifted from the Florida coast to the U.S.-Mexico border, Mexicans developed cooperative ties with Colombian cartels providing cocaine and continued to ship Mexican-grown marijuana. Seizures of cocaine and marijuana at the U.S.-Mexico border have increased over time, which suggests that the flow of illegal drugs northward massively increased. The conflict between the Gulf cartel and the Sinaloa cartel has occurred because Gulf cartel leader Osiel Cardenas was arrested, under pressure from the United States, and sent to La Palma, a Mexican prison from which, until his extradition to the United States, he is believed to have continued running his drug operation. This created an opportunity for the Sinaloa cartel to try and take over his drug smuggling routes by force.

Mexico has suffered serious violence due to competition between the Gulf and Sinaloa drug cartels and its government's attempts to stop the trafficking. Mexico has experienced increased shoot-outs, decapitations, and execution-style killings. In Nuevo Laredo, Mexico, many civilians, police, politicians, and journalists were killed during 2005 due to the cartel's battle for control of territory. Former Mexican President Vincente Fox (2000–2006) had to send the Mexican army to Nuevo Laredo to restore order. The reason for the cartel conflict in Nuevo Laredo concerns access to Laredo, Texas—a major North American Free Trade Agreement truck transport route and the most lucrative drug smuggling route along the border. This intercartel violence has increased to a point where it is now referred to as the "Mexican Drug War," a three-way conflict between fighting cartels and the Mexican government.

In 2006, Homeland Security Secretary Michael Chertoff signed an agreement with the Mexican administration to facilitate transborder policing. These actions are directed at drug trafficking smugglers and gunmen involved in smuggling or cartel battles over territory. Mexico has detained more than 1,000 suspects. Nevertheless, given the inequalities in policing resources between the two nations, there is no certainty that sufficient assistance across national jurisdictions can disrupt transborder corruption. Mexican President Felipe Calderon (2007–present) cooperated by extraditing Sinaloa cartel leader Osiel Cardenas to the United States on January 20, 2007. Since taking office, Calderon's activities to curb the drug trade have included deploying 25,000 Mexican troops armed with American M-16 automatic rifles at the border and at sites in Mexico linked to the cartels. He has spent an unprecedented $7 billion combating the drug trade. The U.S. Congress has approved the Merida Initiative, which will provide Mexico and Central American nations with $1.6 billion in law enforcement training and equipment to combat drug trafficking.

Chris Simcox, cofounder of the vigilante Minutemen, referred to undocumented immigrants as a "throng of insects."[8] Members of these groups are generally armed, and most incidents involving migrants involve shots being fired, dog bites, assault with flashlights, kicking, and taunting migrants who are then informally imprisoned, which is illegal. Increasingly, ranchers are supporting vigilante groups. Roger Barnett is a rancher who has stated that he will kill any Mexican migrant crossing his ranch and carries an assault rifle with a hunting scope. Ranchers have shot at migrants. Near Sasabe, Arizona, five migrants were ambushed and fired upon by Anglo ranchers. One was shot in the face by a high-powered hunting rifle and lost half of his face. He survived by dragging himself back to the Mexican border. In another incident, a Texas rancher shot one of two migrants who were searching for water. The injured man was held on the ground by the rancher until he bled to death. In 2006, the Border Action Network petitioned the Organization of American States' Inter-American Commission on Human Rights for not prosecuting vigilante groups. Migrant victims have been asked to pursue legal cases in the U.S. court system, which is difficult for foreign nationals with low income and no documents. There is a history of violent vigilante confrontation in San Diego. In 1967, white supremacists used AK-47s to shoot from the back of pickup trucks and killed a group of four migrants. This group was convicted and sentenced to life in prison. Presumably, the disproportionate level of aggression shown by the group against unarmed migrants led to a conviction. In recent years, the U.S.-Mexico border has experienced recurrent hate crimes, including harsh beatings, lynching, and murders. This forces migrants to take more and more remote and life-threatening routes through the deserts and mountains of the Southwest.

Conclusion

The foregoing overview of the historical developments of the last 30 years of U.S.-Mexico border relations suggests that there are serious shortcomings in various the approaches to border security and immigrant passage. The joint efforts of the United States and Mexico to resolve the difficulties that face each nation are overshadowed by a routinely ruthless and unconscionable criminal element that kills with impunity, even large numbers of police officers, prosecutors, government officials, and journalists. The safety of innocents on each side of the border has become so imperiled as to lead some to question who is in charge, with the result that many either form vigilante-type groups—assuming the responsibilities of the authorities—or attempt to deal directly with those who would terrorize communities, bypassing local officials, as in the case of the editor of *El Diario* in Ciudad Juarez, the site of scores of killings over the last several years. The legacy of bloodshed is in the fore, at least since Mexican President Felipe Calderon assumed office in 2006. He has ratcheted up the military presence along the border, resulting in more than 28,000 deaths. The United States' effort to assist Mexico, as well as other Central American and Caribbean governments, has been led by the Merida Initiative begun in 2008. With $775 million invested and another $550 million requested from Congress in 2010, there is an increasing sense of desperation on the part of border governments to deal with the crisis. The intimate links between narco- and human trafficking, of risk and economic gain, is symptomatic of a dangerously complex alchemy of greed and hope for a better life. The problems are daunting, and immigrants continue to face separation from their families, jail time, and even death in their quest to enter the land of the free.

Notes

1. Sanjeeb Sapkota, Harold W. Kohl III, Julie Gilchrist, Jay McAuliffe, Bruce Parks, Bob England, Tim Flood, Mark Sewell, Dennis Perrota, Miguel Escobedo, Corrine E. Stern, David Zane, and Kurt B. Nolte, "Unauthorized Border Crossings and Migrant Deaths: Arizona, New Mexico, and El Paso, Texas, 2002–2003," *American Journal of Public Health* 96, no. 7 (2006): 1282–1287.
2. Wayne A. Cornelius, "Controlling 'Unwanted Immigration:' Lessons from the United States. 1993–2004," *Journal of Ethnic and Migration Studies* 31, no. 4 (2006): 775–794, 784.
3. House Subcommittee on Immigration, Border Security and Claims of the Committee of the Judiciary, *Hearing on Deadly Consequences of Alien Smuggling* (Washington, DC: U.S. Government Printing Office, 2003).
4. Rob T. Guerette, *Migrant Death: Border Safety and Situational Crime Prevention on the U.S.-Mexico Divide* (New York: LFB Scholarly Publishing, 2007).
5. Pew Hispanic Center, *Modes of Entry for the Unauthorized Migrant Population Fact Sheet* (Washington, DC: Pew Hispanic Center, 2006).
6. Office of Immigration Statistics, Department of Homeland Security, *Yearbook of Immigration Statistics, 2006* (Washington DC: Department of Homeland Security, 2007).

7. S. Gaytan, Evelyn Lucio, F. Shaiq, and A. Urdanivia, "The Contemporary Migration Process," in *Impacts of Border Enforcement on Mexican Migration: The View from Sending Communities*, eds. Wayne A. Cornelius and J. M. Lewis (San Diego: University of California at San Diego, Center for Comparative Immigration Studies, 2007), 53–75.
8. Chris Reel, "Men with Guns," *Sojourners Magazine* (2003), http://www.sojo.net/index.cfm?action=magazine.article&issue=soj0307&article=030720.

Bibliography
Border Deterrence
Nevins, Joseph. *Operation Gatekeeper: The Rise of the "Illegal Alien" and the Making of the US-Mexico Boundary*. New York: Routlege, 2002.

Office of the Border Patrol. *National Border Patrol Strategy*. Washington, DC: U.S. Customs and Border Protection, U.S. Department of Homeland Security, 2006.

Border Fence
Buchanan, Patrick. *State of Emergency: The Third World Invasion and Conquest of America*. New York: Thomas Dunn Books/St. Martin's Press, 2006.

Downies, Lawrence. "The Not-So-Great-Wall of Mexico." *The New York Times*, April 20, 2008. http://www.nytimes.com/2008/04/20/opinion/20sun4.html.

Liptak, Adam. "Power to Build U.S. Border Fence Is Above U.S. Law." *The New York Times*, April 8, 2008. http://www.nytimes.com/2008/04/08/us/08bar.html.

Payan, Tony. *The Three U.S.-Mexico Border Wars: Drugs, Immigration and Homeland Security*. Westport, CT: Praeger Security International, 2006.

Border Patrol
Brinkley, Douglas. *The Great Deluge: Hurricane Katrina, New Orleans, and the Mississippi Gulf Coast*. New York: Harper Perennial, 2007.

Cornelius, Wayne. "Death at the Border: Efficacy and Unintended Consequences of U.S. Immigration Control Policy." *Population and Development Review* 27, no. 4 (2001): 661–685.

Guerette, Rob T. *Migrant Death: Border Safety and Situational Crime Prevention on the U.S.-Mexico Divide*. New York: LFB Scholarly Publishing, 2007.

Kean, Thomas, and Lee Hamilton. *The 9/11 Commission Report—Final Report of the National Commission on Terrorist Attacks upon the United States*. Washington, DC: National Commission on Terrorist Attacks upon the United States, 2004.

Krauss, Erich, and Alex Pacheco. *On the Line: Inside the U.S. Border Patrol*. New York: Citadel Press, 2004.

Maril, Robert. *Patrolling Chaos: The U.S. Border Patrol in Deep South Texas*. Lubbock: Texas Tech University Press, 2004.

Massey, Douglas. "Beyond the Border Buildup: Towards a New Approach to Mexico-U.S. Migration." *Immigration Policy in Focus* 4, no. 7 (2005):1–11.

Nunez-Neto, Blas. *Border Security: The Role of the U.S. Border Patrol*. Washington, DC: Congressional Research Service, 2006.

Ulsperger, Jason S. "U.S. Border Patrol." In *The Encyclopedia of Police Science*, edited by Jack R. Greene, 1315–1318. New York: Routledge, 2006.

U.S. Department of Justice. *IDENT/IAFIS The Batres Case and the Status of the Integration Project*. Washington, DC: U.S. Department of Justice, Office of the Inspector General, 2004.

Border Patrol and Human Rights Violations

Eschbach, Karl, Jacqueline Hagan, Nestor Rodriguez, Ruben Hernandez-Leon, and Stanley Bailey. "Death at the Border." *International Migration Review* 33, no. 2 (1999): 430–454.

Guerette, Rob T. "Immigration Policy, Border Security, and Migrant Deaths: An Impact Evaluation of Life-Saving Efforts under the Border Safety Initiative." *Criminology and Public Policy* 6, no. 2 (2007): 245–266.

Guerette, Rob T. *Migrant Death: Border Safety and Situational Crime Prevention on the U.S.-Mexico Divide*. New York: LFB Scholarly Publishing, 2007.

Huspek, Michael, Roberto Martinez, and Leticia Jimenez. "Violations of Human and Civil Rights on the U.S.-Mexico Border, 1995–1997: A Report." *Social Justice* 25, no. 2 (1998): 110–130.

Border Violence

American Civil Liberties Union. "Creating the Minutemen: A Small Extremist Group's Campaign Fueled by Misinformation." Joint report, ACLU of Arizona, New Mexico, and Texas, 2006. http://www.ilw.com/articles/2006,0619-ybarra.pdf.

Associated Press. "Daily Tally of Dead Soars in Mexico as Drug Cartels Lash Back at Crackdown." May 15, 2007. http://www.azstar.net.com/sn/border/183324.

Associated Press. "Napolitano-Richardson Letter Rips U.S. about Border Violence." May 16, 2007. http://www.azstar.net.com/sn/border/183324.

Bean, Frank D., Roland Chanove, Robert G. Cushing, Rodolfo de la Garza, Gary P. Freeman, Charles W. Haynes, and David Spener. *Illegal Mexican Migration and the United States/Mexico Border: The Effects of Operation Hold the Line on El Paso/Juarez*. Research Paper presented at the U.S. Commission on Immigration Reform, Population Research Center, University of Texas at Austin, 1994.

Border Action Network and Border Network for Human Rights. *U.S.-Mexico Border Policy Report: Effective Border Policy: Security, Responsibility and Human Rights at the U.S.-Mexico Border*. Washington, DC: Border Action Network and Border Network for Human Rights, 2008. http://www.utexas.edu/law/centers/humanrights/borderwall/communities/municipalities-US-Mexico-Border-Policy-Report.pdf.

Ellingwood, Ken. *Hard Line: Life and Death on the U.S.-Mexico Border*. New York: Pantheon Books, 2004.

Hagan, John, and Alberto Pallioni. "Sociological Criminology and the Mythology of Hispanic Immigration and Crime." *Social Problems* 46 (1999): 617–632.

Jamieson, Ruth, Nigel South, and Ian Taylor. "Economic Liberalization and Cross-Border Crime: The North American Free Trade Area and Canada's Border with the U.S.A." *International Journal of the Sociology of Law* 26 (1998): 245–272.

Kil, Sang Hea, and Cecilia Menjivar. "The War on the Border: Criminalizing Immigrants and Militarizing the U.S.-Mexico Border." In *Immigration and Crime: Race, Ethnicity and Violence*, edited by Ramiro Martinez Jr. and Abel Valenzuela Jr., 164–188. New York: New York University Press, 2006.

Lacey, Marc. "Drug Violence Alters the Flow of Life in Mexico. *The New York Times*, August 30, 2008. http://www.nytimes.com/pages/world/americas/index.hteml.

Lee, Matthew T. *Crime on the Border: Immigration and Homicide in Urban Communities*. New York: LFB Scholarly Publishing, 2003.

Reel, Chris. "Men with Guns." *Sojourners Magazine*. 2003. http://www.sojo.net/index.cfm?action=magazine.article&issue=soj0307&article=030720.

Rumbaut, Ruben G., Roberto D. Gonzalez, Golnaz Komaie, Charlie V. Morgan, and Rosaura Tafoya-Estrada. "Immigration and Incarceration: Patterns and Predictors of Imprisonment among First and Second Generation Young Adults." In *Immigration and Crime: Race, Ethnicity and Violence*, edited by Ramiro Martinez Jr. and Abel Valenzuela Jr., 64–89. New York: New York University Press, 2006.

Militarization of the U.S.-Mexico Border

Dunn, Timothy. "Border Militarization through Drug and Immigration Enforcement: Human Rights Implications," *Social Justice* 28, no. 2 (2001): 7–30.

Dunn, Timothy. *The Militarization of the Border, 1978–1992: Low Intensity Conflict Doctrine Comes Home*. Austin: CMAS Books, Center for Mexican American Studies, University of Texas, 1996.

Hayworth, J.D., and Joseph J. Eule. *Whatever It Takes: Illegal Immigration, Border Security, and the War on Terror*. Washington, DC: Regnery, 2006.

Payson, Tony. *The Three U.S.-Mexico Border Wars: Drugs, Immigration and Homeland Security*. Westport, CT: Praeger Security International, 2006.

Tancredo, Tom. *In Mortal Danger: The Battle for America's Border and Security*. Nashville, TN: WND, 2006.

Migrant Deaths on the U.S.–Mexico Border

Andreas, Peter. *Border Games: Policing the U.S.-Mexico Divide*. Ithaca, NY: Cornell University Press, 2001.

Cornelius, Wayne A. "Controlling 'Unwanted Immigration': Lessons from the United States. 1993–2004." *Journal of Ethnic and Migration Studies* 31, no. 4 (2006): 775–794.

Cornelius, Wayne. "Death at the Border: Efficacy and Unintended Consequences of U.S. Immigration Control Policy." *Population and Development Review* 27, no. 4 (2001): 661–685.

Echsbach, Karl, Jacqueline Hagan, and Nestor Rodriguez. *Causes and Trends in Migrant Deaths along the U.S.-Mexico Border, 1985–1988*. Houston: University of Houston Center for Immigration Research, 2001.

Echsbach, Karl, Jacqueline Hagan, and Nestor Rodriguez. "Death at the Border." *International Migration Review* 33, no. 2 (1999): 430–454.

Government Accountability Office. *Border Crossing Deaths Have Doubled since* 1995: *Border Patrol's Efforts to Prevent Deaths Have Not Been Fully Evaluated*. Washington, DC: U.S. Government Printing Office, 2006.

Guerette, Rob T. *Migrant Death and the Border Safety Initiative: An Application of Situational Crime Prevention to Inform Policy and Practice*. Doctoral dissertation, Rutgers University, 2004.

Guerette, Rob T, and Ronald V. Clarke. "Border Enforcement, Organized Crime, and Deaths of Smuggled Immigrants on the United States-Mexico Border." *European Journal on Criminal Policy and Research* 11 (2005): 159–174.

House Subcommittee on Immigration, Border Security and Claims of the Committee of the Judiciary. *Hearing on Deadly Consequences of Alien Smuggling*. Washington, DC: U.S. Government Printing Office, 2003.

Kirkorian, Mark. "Long Hot Summer: Border Enforcement and the Deaths of Illegal Immigrants." *National Review Online*, June 6, 2006. http://www.cis.org/articles/2006/mskoped060906.html.

Lumpkin, Mary F., Dan Judkins, John M. Porter, Rifat Latifi, and Mark D. Williams. "Overcrowded Motor Vehicle Trauma from the Smuggling of Illegal Immigrants in the Desert of the Southwest." *American Surgeon* 70 (2004): 1078–1082.

Nevens, Joseph. *Operation Gatekeeper: The Rise of the "Illegal Alien" and the Remaking of the U.S.-Mexico Boundary*. New York: Routledge, 2001.

Palafox, Jose. "Opening Up Borderland Studies: A Review of U.S.-Mexico Border Discourse." *Social Justice* 27, no. 3 (2000): 56–72.

Ramos, Jorge. *Dying to Cross: The Worst Immigrant Tragedy in American History*. New York: Harper, 2005.

Reyes, Belinda I., Hans P. Johnson, and Richard Van Swearingen. *Holding the Line? The Effect of the Recent Border Buildup on Unauthorized Immigration*. San Francisco: Public Policy Institute of California, 2002. http://www.ppic.org/content/pubs/report/R_702BRR.pdf.

Rubio-Goldsmith, Raquel, M. Melissa McCormick, Daniel Martinez, and Inez Magdelena Duarte. *The "Funnel Effect" and Recovered Bodies of Unauthorized Immigrants Processed by the Pima County Office of the Medical Examiner, 1990–2005*. Report Submitted to the Pima County Board of Supervisors. Tucson: Binational Immigration Institute, Mexican American Research and Studies Center, University of Arizona, 2006.

Rubio-Goldsmith, Raquel, M. Melissa McCormick, Daniel Martinez, and Inez Magdelena Duarte. *A Humanitarian Crisis at the Border: New Estimates of Deaths among Undocumented Immigrants*. Washington, DC: Immigration Policy Center, 2007.

Scharf, David A. "For Humane Borders: Two Decades of Death and Illegal Activity in the Sonoran Desert." *Case Western Reserve Journal of International Law* 38 (2006): 141–172.

Smith, Claudia. "Border Enforcement: Deadlier Than Ever and Ineffective as Always." *Latino Studies* 2 (2004): 111–114.

Sapkota, Sanjeeb, Harold W. Kohl III, Julie Gilchrist, Jay McAuliffe, Bruce Parks, Bob England, Tim Flood, Mark Sewell, Dennis Perrota, Miguel Escobedo, Corrine E. Stern,

David Zane, and Kurt B. Nolte. "Unauthorized Border Crossings and Migrant Deaths: Arizona, New Mexico, and El Paso, Texas, 2002–2003." *American Journal of Public Health* 96, no. 7 (2006): 1282–1287.

Stone, David. "Sealing the Border with Mexico: A Military Option." *USAWC Strategy Research Projects*. Carlisle Barracks, PN: U.S. Army War College, 2004.

Undocumented Immigrants

Bean, Frank D., and B. Lindsey Lowell. "Unauthorized Immigration." In *The New Americans: A Guide to Immigration since 1965*, edited by Mary C. Waters and Reed Ueda, 70–82. Cambridge, MA: Harvard University Press, 2007.

Chacon, Justin Akers, and Mike Davis. *No One Is Illegal: Fighting Racism and State Violence on the U.S.-Mexico Border*. Chicago: Haymarket Press, 2006.

Frequently Asked Questions on the State Alien Criminal Assistance Program: Congressional Research Service Report for Congress. Washington, DC: Congressional Research Service, 2007. http://www.ilw.com/immigdaily/news2007,0906-crs.pdf.

Fuentes, Jezmin, Henry L'Esperance, Raul Perez, and Caitlin White. "Impacts of U.S. Migration Policies on Migration Behavior." In *Impacts of Border Enforcement on Mexican Migration: The View From Sending Communities*, edited by Wayne A. Cornelius and Jessa M. Lewis, 53–75. San Diego: University of California at San Diego, Center for Comparative Immigration Studies, 2007.

Gaytan, S., Evelyn Lucio, F. Shaiq, and A. Urdanivia. "The Contemporary Migration Process." In *Impacts of Border Enforcement on Mexican Migration: The View from Sending Communities*, edited by Wayne A. Cornelius and Jessa M. Lewis, 33–52. San Diego: University of California at San Diego, Center for Comparative Immigration Studies, 2007.

Government Accounting Office. *Over-Stay Tracking: A Key Component of Homeland Security and a Layered Defense: A Report to the Chairman, Committee on the Judiciary, House of Representatives*. Washington, DC: U.S. Government Printing Office, 2004. http://www.gao.gov/new.items/D0482.pdf.

Hoeffer, Michael, Nancy Rytina, and Christopher Campbell. *Estimates of the Unauthorized Immigrant Population Residing in the United States, January, 2006*. Washington, DC: Department of Homeland Security, Office of Immigration Statistics Policy Directorate, 2007. http://www.dhs.gov/xlibrary/assets/statistics/publications/ill_pe_2006.pdf.

Huntington, Samuel. *Who Are We? The Challenges to America's National Identity*. New York: Simon & Schuster, 2004.

Massey, Douglas. "When Less Is More: Border Enforcement and Undocumented Immigration: Testimony of Douglas Massey before the Subcommittee on Immigration, Refugees, Border Security and International Law, Commission on the Judiciary, U.S. House of Representatives." 2007. http://www.judiciary.house.gov/media/pdfs//Masset070420.pdf.

Office of Immigration Statistics, Department of Homeland Security. *Yearbook of Immigration Statistics, 2006*. Washington, DC: Department of Homeland Security, 2007.

Passel, Jeffrey S. *Estimates of the Size and Characteristics of the Undocumented Population. 2005*. Washington, DC: Pew Hispanic Center, 2005.

Pew Hispanic Center. *Modes of Entry for the Unauthorized Migrant Population Fact Sheet*. Washington, DC: Pew Hispanic Center, 2006.

Booker T. Washington (1856–1915): "Cast Down Your Buckets Where You Are"

Mary Elizabeth Brown

African American leader Booker T. Washington approached immigration with his own priorities firmly in mind. When immigration could be made good for blacks, as in the case of not forbidding migration from Africa, he was all for it. When it seemed harmful to blacks, as in the case of job competition, he watched it warily. It was the African American that was important to him, not immigration per se. However, Washington's commitment to African Americans could also make him a fascinating commentator on immigration.

Washington's views have become more important in the past generation. The 1970s saw a rise in interest in white ethnicity. This white ethnic revival took place in the context of the civil rights movement. In some ways, white ethnic leaders were reacting to the civil rights movement, and in other ways they were borrowing from it. Thus, there has long been scholarly interest in white immigrant and white ethnic perceptions of African Americans. To get a complete picture, it is important to do similar research into African American perceptions of white immigrants and ethnic groups.

Since 1965, the United States has had many immigrants coming from new sources. Unlike 19th-century and early 20th-century immigrants, the newcomers are less likely to be of European background. Some are African Asian; people from the Caribbean, Latin America, and South America often have ancestors from more than one race. There are several possible scenarios for the integration of new immigrants. They could follow the pattern established by previous generations of immigrants, or they could follow the pattern set by indigenous racial minorities. One force determining the pattern of integration that new immigrants will follow is the reception they receive from all Americans, of every race. Thus, the particular history of the African American response to immigration becomes more important than ever. How have African Americans seen immigrants? In terms of economic competition? As people from another culture, whose culture would change in the U.S. environment? Or as people from another race, whose racial traits would not change even after generations in the United States? This essay cannot answer these

Born a slave in 1856, Booker T. Washington became a staunch civil rights activist and one of the most influential educators in American history. (Library of Congress)

questions for all African Americans, but it can introduce the subject by focusing on the thought of Booker T. Washington.

Booker Taliaferro Washington was born into slavery on April 5, 1856, the son of a white man whose identity he never learned and of a slave woman named Jane Burroughs, who had a husband who was a slave on another plantation and also another son, also by a white man. Washington was nine years old when slavery ended in 1865. He experienced emancipation as moving from one kind of poverty to another. His family moved from his parents' slave cabins to Malden, West Virginia, where his stepfather took a job in a salt mine. Young Washington worked full-time in a mine and then as a houseboy. In 1872, at 16, he worked his way diagonally across West Virginia and Virginia to the Hampton Normal and Agricultural Institute, and thereafter education was his life. He completed the program at Hampton, then briefly taught there and served as a dormitory supervisor. On July 4, 1881, at age 25, he became president of the new Tuskegee Institute in northern Alabama. He built Tuskegee into an institution offering black men and women a basic education and vocational training or preparation for teaching. He pushed himself to the limit to ensure Tuskegee's survival, to the point where he took fatally ill while on a fund-raising trip. Informed of the hopelessness of his condition, he insisted on going home to Tuskegee, where he died on November 15, 1915. Tuskegee built upon the firm foundation he laid and has grown into a university.

Washington's work at Tuskegee led to an invitation to give a speech at the Cotton States and International Exposition held at Atlanta, Georgia, in 1895. His speech, given on September 18, is sometimes known as the Atlanta Compromise because in it Washington claimed that "[i]n all things that are purely social we can be as separate as the fingers yet one as the hand in all things essential to mutual progress," effectively rejecting the notion of immediate legal, political, and social equality between blacks and whites in favor of an emphasis on opportunity for blacks in the Southern economy. Other prominent blacks, such as William Monroe Trotter and W.E.B. DuBois, have since become more attractive examples of black thought in the Progressive Era, but in his day, Booker T. Washington was the most important African American leader.

His role as a black spokesperson supplemented Washington's role as a political insider. Washington connected white Northern and Southern entrepreneurs, philanthropists, and politicians. He identified black institutions to which philanthropists might donate their money, and blacks who might be the beneficiaries of political patronage. To black rivals, he seemed a powerful machine politician. But Washington knew how limited his power was. He had to pick his priorities, husband his strength, and not squander his ammunition shooting at unimportant targets.

Washington dealt with the issue of black migration on several occasions. The most highly publicized occurred near the end of his life. In January 1915, Senator James A. Reed, a Democrat from Mississippi, secured an amendment to a general immigration bill that would have barred African immigration. Had it passed, Africans would have been excluded by congressional action solely on account of their ethnic origin. The bill would also have had more far-reaching consequences than the word *African* might suggest. It was drafted in such a way that every person of African descent was excluded, no matter where the person was born—thus also excluding much migration from the Caribbean and South America. It also contributed to the generally negative attitude toward blacks born of several generations of Americans.

Washington swung into action. On this issue, he joined forces with DuBois and with Trotter, two African American leaders who questioned Washington's leadership and his goals. The three of them used whatever influence they had, and Washington was the one with the most political connections at the federal level. He even planned a personal appeal to President Woodrow Wilson. Washington also wrote editorials and newspaper articles under his own name and sent information to others, urging them to write. He pointed out that African exclusion was unnecessary, because few people emigrated from any predominantly black nations. More to the point, he claimed it was unfair. Characteristically, he based his accusation of injustice not on the abstract notion of equal rights but on the idea that blacks had done so much for the United States that they deserved better treatment. In this case, Caribbean blacks had performed most of the labor of building the Panama Canal, a 10-year project that had been completed in 1914. Surely, the United States could not turn around and forbid former canal construction workers and their conationals from migration. The bill was defeated.

Throughout most of his career, though, Washington was not so concerned that blacks might want to come from Africa as he was that U.S. blacks might want to go to that continent. Historically, U.S. migration to Africa has been small, but Washington was in no position to see the big historical picture. What he did know was that before he was born, white Americans had thought to end slavery by sending even U.S.-born blacks "back" to Africa and had founded Liberia as a place to which U.S.

blacks should relocate. In Washington's day, people such as Henry McNeal Turner, a bishop of the African Methodist Episcopal Church, preached that racism made black life impossible in the United States and promoted black migration to Africa. (In 1916, after Washington's death, the Jamaican-born Marcus Garvey came to New York to revive interest in black migration to Africa.) In 1913, a missionary named Joseph Booth wrote to Washington regarding a plan to raise money to assist U.S. blacks who wished to relocate to South Africa. Washington replied with a reference to the one part of Africa that had seen substantial white immigration. His words sounded like deadpan humor: "For my part, I cannot help feeling that any funds that were raised to assist Negro emigration to Africa might better be used in sending back home the class of white people in South Africa who are making the most trouble."[1]

Washington also worried that U.S. blacks might try to move around the United States. The late 1870s and early 1880s saw an internal migration known as the Exoduster movement, in which Southern blacks who could do so tried to escape Southern racism and poverty by moving to the frontier to claim their own farms and to live in communities that had not yet passed segregation ordinances. During the late 19th century, African Americans participated in the worldwide movement from country to city. At the end of Washington's life, in World War I, Southern blacks moved north to take jobs that would normally go to white immigrants, had not the war cut off European immigration. Washington tried to discourage this black migration. He opened his Atlanta speech with a story about a ship becalmed at sea. Upon sighting another vessel, it sent a signal for water. The answer came back: "Cast down your buckets where you are." The message had to be transmitted twice more before the captain actually did it—only to find that all this time his ship had been stuck in a stream of fresh, clean, potable water pouring into the ocean from the nearby Amazon. From this parable, Washington drew a moral: black Americans should cast down their buckets where they were, in the rural South.

Regarding black migration, Washington seems inconsistent. He worked to make it possible for blacks to migrate from Africa, but he also worked to discourage blacks from moving out of, or around, the United States. Yet both positions were consistent with Washington's priorities. An advocate for black people, he did not want the humiliation of having black migration barred. His discouragement of internal migration was another sort of advocacy for blacks, this time mixed with self-protection. Whites might have objected to a black spokesperson who urged blacks to migrate, depriving the South of labor and raising the specter of racial mixing elsewhere. Washington had built Tuskegee on the idea that blacks' best opportunity was to stay in the South; to suggest blacks could also better their condition by leaving the South would undermine his work at Tuskegee. Finally, whether one agrees with Washington on this point or not (and historians generally have not), he did sincerely reject immigration in favor of Southern blacks building an economic community that was integrated into the economy of the South.

Similarly, Washington dealt with white migration from Europe on several occasions. The most public was probably the Atlanta Compromise, in which he urged Southern whites also to cast down their buckets: "[A]mong my people, helping and encouraging them as you are doing on these grounds, and to education of head, hand, and heart, you will find that they will buy your surplus land, make blossom the waste places in your fields, and run your factories."[2] In other words, do not bring in white immigrants to supplant native blacks.

When asked directly about immigration, Washington responded politely. In 1915, the *Jewish Immigration Bulletin* solicited his thoughts and received a response that said, in part:

> While I do not claim to be a special student of this subject it appears to me that the immigrants of today as well as those of yesterday are contributing much to American life. While I write there comes to mind the great work which Jacob Riis did, the splendid lessons which Mary Antin is teaching us. The European peasant and the Negro, however, I believe are at present contributing most to American life by teaching the lessons of helpfulness, patience, tolerance, forbearance, brotherliness, in fact all those things which are comprehended under what is characterized as the broader humanity.[3]

It was so brief and bland that one cannot blame the *Jewish Immigration Bulletin* for not printing it. Washington was equally opaque when a student who was associate editor of a University of Alabama student publication asked him for his opinion:

> I am not at all opposed to European immigrants coming to the South. What I have said from time to time in advising the colored people [is] to see to it that they must take advantage of their opportunities in the South or else they will be crowded to the wall by others who will come in and get more out of the soil than they get out of it. I have some personal feeling, however, as to how well European emigrants and our native Southern people will get on together, but this has nothing to do with the direct matter of European emigrants coming to the South.[4]

Occasionally, the mask slipped. Washington once wrote about education in the Austro-Hungarian Empire, which, in the early 20th century, was engaged in a project of teaching all children in the languages they used in their homes and small villages. The result was that the Austrian side of the empire had some 8,000 German schools, 5,578 Czech schools, 645 Italian schools, 162 Romanian schools, 5 Magyar schools, and 6,632 schools teaching various Slavic languages. Even then, Washington confined himself to widely held sentiments, claiming that if each of these groups migrated to the United States and attempted to preserve its distinctive language and culture, "we might have a racial problem in the South more difficult and more dangerous than that which is caused by the presence of the Negro."[5]

Washington's approach to the connection between immigration and criminality was similarly commonplace. He noted that, of 112 unsolved murders committed in and around New York City between 1906 and 1909, 54 involved Italian victims. He claimed that the victims either were objects of extortion rackets who had failed to pay their protection money, or they were people whom someone else feared might go to the police. Their murders were unsolved because other Italians observed the code of *omerta* rather than identify the killers to the police. They avenged the murders themselves, producing another round of unsolved cases. The preponderance of Italians "suggests, at least, the manner in which our own country is affected by the conditions of the masses in southern Italy and Sicily."[6]

In private, Washington was more interested in certain aspects of immigration. One of these, job competition, was a widespread concern. Washington received letters from people who thought that, as a leading black spokesperson, he should know how immigration affected African Americans. One correspondent informed him that "ten years ago all the barbers in Richmond were Negroes, and they were good ones, too. Now nine tenths of them are Italians. The Richmond Locomotive Works is supplanting its Negro laborers with Italians."[7] Washington's friends also kept him informed. Belton Gilreath, a Birmingham coal executive and Tuskegee trustee, had his secretary send Washington's secretary a clipping showing that Italians remitted $400 million to their home country in 1907. "[S]uch figures show the importance of encouraging and developing our own people here to the highest extent, who are investing all of their earnings here among us, as your race do."[8]

Washington made use of such information. He ran a redoubtable public relations effort and was always placing news where it would be used, as in this letter to Oswald Garrison Villard, son of the abolitionist William Lloyd Garrison, a reformer himself, and also editor of the *New York Post*.

> You may recall there has been considerable talk from time to time in the South about securing Italians to take the place of the Negro as a cotton farmer. You may also recall that Mr. Alfred Holt Stone in his book [*Studies in the American Race Problem*] and in all of his lectures on the subject has laid considerable emphasis upon what the Italians have done on a certain farm in Arkansas in replacing the Negro. Because of all Mr. Stone has said, I thought perhaps you could make some use of the enclosed marked article from the Daily Graphic of Pine Bluff, Arks., which shows that Mr. John M. Gracie, the man who employed the Italians to which Mr. Stone refers, has gotten rid of the Italians and replaced them by Negro labor.[9]

Again, Washington acted inconsistently, even deviously, professing to have no opinion while showing his disapproval of white migrants taking plantation jobs. Again, the two seemingly opposite actions were consistent with Washington's own priorities. He wanted to make sure no one stole black jobs, but he did not dare say so openly, for fear of jeopardizing his work at Tuskegee and his position as the black leader to whom whites listened.

One can see where Washington's heart really lay in two other statements he made regarding immigration. One was in a private letter in which he made another deadpan-sounding comment:

> There are reasons—I shall not venture to say how valid they are—why some restrictions should be put upon all forms of immigration to this country. There are, perhaps, other reasons in the case of the Japanese and other oriental [*sic*] people, why immigration should be even more restricted. One of these is the very fact that there is a prejudice, in some parts of this country, against people who are not white.[10]

The other communication, also private, came in the course of a project Washington participated in for *The Outlook*, a monthly magazine with which he was affiliated. (It serialized the chapters of the biography that became his best-known book, *Up from Slavery*.) *The Outlook* opposed unrestricted immigration. However, it was also a magazine of integrity, and it tried to provide a forum for differing views, at one point soliciting writers who would contribute articles questioning its position on immigration. Washington notified an acquaintance that the latter had been accepted as a contributor to that forum, and then he passed along what he considered the really important news: "I have gotten *The Outlook* thoroughly committed to use the capital 'N' for Negro in the future."[11]

Did Washington ever look at immigration itself, without trying to determine whether it was good or bad for blacks? He did have one opportunity to do so. From August 20 to October 9, 1910, Washington and a companion, Robert Ezra Park (who later became a pioneering sociologist at the University of Chicago), traveled through Europe. The board of trustees of Tuskegee had insisted that Washington get some rest and relaxation and had offered to pay for the trip. Washington agreed to go, but only on the condition that he be allowed to study the people whose social, economic, and political status most closely resembled that of African Americans.

The itinerary of Park and Washington began in England, with a side trip to Scotland to visit Andrew Carnegie, one of Tuskegee's major benefactors, at Skibo Castle. They went across Europe by rail, seeing Berlin, Prague, Vienna, Budapest, Belgrade, Sofia, and Constantinople; they even crossed the border to see a village in the Russian empire. Then they sailed through the Greek islands to Sicily and to

Naples. At Naples, they switched back to the train and rode up through Rome and northern Italy to France, Berlin, and Copenhagen. They boarded a ship for England and there boarded another for the United States. Through it all, Washington studiously avoided cathedrals, museums, art galleries, palaces, historic ruins, and other tourist sites and went out of his way to see the most oppressed and exploited workers he could find.

During long train rides, Park and Washington discussed what they saw. Washington then thought over their conversations and formed a text in his head. When they reached major cities, Washington dictated his thoughts to a stenographer while Park gathered the books and official papers that supplied supporting documentation and expanded their observations. On their return to the United States, Park edited Washington's dictation into a book-length manuscript. The two published their observations in a series of articles in *The Outlook* in 1911 and in a book titled *The Man Farthest Down* in 1912.

Parts of *The Man Farthest Down* indicated that Washington did not take full advantage of his opportunity to study immigration firsthand, because he was still trying to be a black who pleased U.S. whites. Nearly everything he saw in Europe reminded him of the advantages U.S. blacks had. For example, he toured a new kind of establishment in England, an ancestor of the modern laundromat, where the urban poor could wash their clothes. He mused that Southern blacks could wash their clothes at home, which was true enough, except that it involved making soap, building a fire, heating the water, pounding the dirty clothes against rocks or washboards, rinsing them by hand in cold water, wringing them in a mechanical wringer, drying them outdoors on fences or branches, and ironing them with heavy irons (more like weights with handles) heated on top of stoves—tasks so time-consuming and arduous they seldom got done.

Other parts of *The Man Farthest Down* indicated that even when he was not conscious of how whites might interpret his writings, Washington was still unable to take full advantage of his opportunities, because he himself shared some of the stereotypes of other Americans. When they visited Palermo, Washington temporarily turned into the thrill-seeking tourist. He saw the exact spot where New York police detective Lieutenant Joseph Petrosino was gunned down. He wove together the influence of the Catholic Church and the mafia in order to create a system that produced impoverished, and degraded, peasants.

However, *The Man Farthest Down* also showed how Washington's own preconceptions and experiences could help him to make sensitive observations regarding the people who became immigrants. Consider his conclusion that, in Europe, "the man farthest down is woman ... men have profited by the use of machinery more than women. The machines have taken away from the women the occupations they had in the homes, and this has driven them to take up other forms of labour, of more or less temporary character, in which they are overworked and underpaid."[12] Immigration increased women's burdens, driving them into the fields to replace the absent men, while not offering them relief from cooking, cleaning, and child care, the traditional women's jobs of their respective cultures.

Washington was also sensitive to the working class and particularly to child laborers. When he heard there were mines in Sicily, he went out of his way to find them, pushing his carriage driver into unfamiliar territory high in the hills. Once there, he headed down hundreds of feet beneath the earth, where he observed the relative temperatures and took meticulous notes of how the work was done and who was doing it. His description of little boys staggering as they lifted their loads, reeling to maintain their balance under the weight, clambering to carry their packs to the surface—and his comparison of how machinery made this a relatively light task in West Virginia—makes for harrowing reading.

In many of the places Washington visited, it seemed that no person or institution with any power was making any effort to improve the life of the working class. When the upper classes or government officials did benefit the poor, it was an unintended side effect. He told the story of the agricultural college in Hungary that did indeed attract a number of students and train them to be more productive farmers. However, the agricultural college had to be closed because it was too close to a liberal arts college that served the aristocracy; the authorities feared that such close contact with the upper class would unfit the lower one for its position. The tartness of Washington's comment comes through his efforts to frame his thoughts as a visitor's humble opinion: "In short, I think I might sum up the situation by saying that Hungary is trying the doubtful experiment of attempting to increase the efficiency of the people without giving them freedom." He pointed out the obvious response to a government that feared the rise of its own citizens: "[T]he masses of the people are emigrating to America in order to better their condition."[13]

In places where the government was not actively frustrating people with its efforts to improve them, neglect functioned as another kind of oppression. Italy, for example, had laws against child labor, but they were seldom enforced. The government ran in a traditional manner, including the collection of many regressive taxes on consumer goods. "[T]he only way the poor Italian can get free is by going to America, and that is why thousands sail from Palermo every year for this country."[14]

In general, Washington judged immigration by the standards of black welfare. He treated it warily, because he knew that employers would hire almost anyone before they hired blacks. However, he was also wary about criticizing migration, because a crusade to prevent immigrants from entering the United States would probably turn to exclusion on racial grounds, and any more racism would also be bad for blacks. Only occasionally, as in *The Man Farthest Down*, did Washington let his guard down a little, to indicate that he knew that not everyone could cast down their bucket where they were.

Notes

1. Booker T. Washington to Joseph Booth, Tuskegee, November 13, 1913, in Louis R. Harlan, ed., *The Booker T. Washington Papers*, 14 vols. (Urbana: University of Illinois Press, 1974), 12:330.
2. Booker T. Washington, *Up from Slavery* (1901), reprinted in John Hope Franklin, *Three Negro Classics* (New York: Avon, 1965), 148.
3. Harlan, *Booker T. Washington Papers*, 13:369–370.
4. Washington to Wyatt Rushton, Tuskegee, January 14, 1915, in Harlan, *Booker T. Washington Papers*, 13:222.
5. Booker T. Washington and Robert E. Park, *The Man Farthest Down* (Garden City, NY: Doubleday, 1912; reprinted with a new introduction by St. Clair Drake, New Brunswick, NJ: Transaction Books, 1984), 83–84 (page citations are to the reprint edition).
6. Ibid., 180.
7. W. B. Watkins to Washington, Richmond, April 24, 1908, in Harlan, *Booker T. Washington Papers*, 9:508–510.
8. George A. McQueen to Emmett Jay Scott, Birmingham, June 12, 1908, in Harlan, *Booker T. Washington Papers*, 9:571.
9. Washington to Oswald Garrison Villard, Huntington, New York, August 7, 1910, in Harlan, *Booker T. Washington Papers*, 10:363–364.
10. Washington to J. Harada, Tuskegee, November 10, 1913, in Harlan, *Booker T. Washington Papers*, 12:329.
11. Washington to Kelly Miller, New York City, February 1, 1911, in Harlan, *Booker T. Washington Papers*, 10:572.
12. Washington and Park, *The Man Farthest Down*, 316–317.
13. Ibid., 221–222.
14. Ibid., 145.

Bibliography

Washington wrote several books; the two most helpful here were *Up from Slavery* (1901), reprinted in *Three Negro Classics*, with an introduction by John Hope Franklin (New York: Avon [Discus Books], 1965), xxv–205); and with Robert E. Park, *The Man Farthest Down* (Garden City, NY: Doubleday, 1912; reprinted with a new introduction by St. Clair Drake, New Brunswick, NJ: Transaction Books [Black Classics of Social Science], 1984). Washington's other writings are in *The Booker T. Washington Papers*, edited by Louis R. Harlan, 14 vols. (Urbana: University of Illinois Press, 1974). Harlan also has a comprehensive two-volume biography of Washington: *The Making of a Black Leader, 1856–1901* (New York: Oxford University Press, 1972), and *The Wizard of Tuskegee, 1901–1915* (New York: Oxford University Press, 1983). For more on the subject, see D. J. Hellwig, "Black Leaders and United States Immigration Policy, 1917–1929," *Negro History Bulletin* 65 (July–September 1982): 65; Arnold M. Shankman, *Ambivalent Friends: Afro-Americans View the Immigrant* (Westport, CT: Greenwood Press, 1982); Silvia Pedraza and Ruben G. Rumbaut, eds., *Origins and Destinies: Immigration, Race, and Ethnicity in America* (Belmont, CA: Wadsworth, 1996); and Jeff Diamond, "African American Attitudes Towards United States Immigration Policy," *International Migration Review* 32, no. 2 (Summer 1998): 451–470.

Yellow Peril: The Chinese Exclusion Act (1882) to the Johnson-Reed Act of 1924

Ariane Knuesel

The first Chinese immigrants arrived on the East Coast of the United States in the mid-18th century. Their numbers in the United States remained small until 1848, when news of gold discoveries in California resulted in an increase in Chinese immigration to the West Coast. Many Chinese also traveled across the Pacific Ocean to escape civil war in China. In the mid-19th century, China was defeated twice by Western powers in the Opium Wars (1839–1842 and 1856–1860). Most of the Chinese immigrants to the United States arrived from southern China, which was greatly affected by these conflicts. The Chinese city of Canton, for example, lost its monopoly on Chinese trade with foreign powers, which had a devastating effect on the economy of the area. At the same time, the Chinese government imposed huge taxes on the population in order to pay for the indemnities demanded by the foreign powers after the Opium Wars. The ruling Qing Dynasty was also troubled with various uprisings and rebellions, and the population suffered from the destruction of fields and crops by Chinese soldiers and rebels. Suffering from poverty and hunger, many Chinese men decided to leave their families and search for a better life elsewhere in order to support their families.[1]

The Formation of the Anti-Chinese Movement in the United States

When Chinese immigrants began arriving on the West Coast of the United States, however, Americans were not happy. Press reports on the Opium Wars had portrayed the Chinese in unflattering ways, and letters reaching the United States from U.S. diplomats, merchants, and missionaries in China were full of negative stereotypes of the Chinese. Consequently, many Americans held a negative predisposition toward the Chinese before they actually met any of them. Chinese immigrants on the West Coast also quickly became a target of racism, because they looked different from European immigrants and were considered racially inferior to white Americans or immigrants from Europe. Thus, even though far more Britons, Irish, and Germans immigrated to the United States between 1850 and 1885

Table 2 Number of Chinese, British, Irish, and German Immigrants Entering the United States, 1850–1885

Year	Chinese	British	Irish	German
1850	3	51,085	164,004	78,896
1855	3,526	47,572	49,627	71,918
1860	5,467	29,737	48,637	54,491
1865	2,942	82,465	29,772	83,424
1870	15,740	103,677	56,996	118,225
1875	16,437	47,905	37,957	47,769
1880	5,802	73,273	71,603	84,638
1885	22	57,713	51,795	124,443

Source: U.S. Department of Commerce, Bureau of the Census, *Historical Statistics of the United States: Colonial Times to 1970,* part 1 (White Plains, NY: Kraus, 1989), 106 and 108.

(see Table 2), Chinese immigrants were seen as a particular problem because they were not white.[2]

Another reason for the quick formation of the anti-Chinese movement was that most Chinese immigrants settled in states around California, where they worked in mines. Many also built railroad tracks and tunnels, cleared forests, worked on farms, or became farmers themselves. Their willingness to work for little money caused white Americans as well as European immigrants to view them as a threat and accuse them of forcing down the wages of white workers. Because the majority of the Chinese immigrants in the United States settled in California, the anti-Chinese agitation was strongest there and soon resulted in demands for an end to Chinese immigration. Particularly, white miners were hostile toward the Chinese arrivals, because mining was no longer lucrative and so the Chinese were regarded as competition that reduced the chances of white miners striking gold.[3]

Although the U.S. society that Chinese immigrants encountered in the 1850s thought of itself as committed to equality and liberty, it was clearly defined along color lines: African Americans and Native Americans had no political say, and racism had been institutionalized in 1790 with the Naturalization Act, which stipulated that only whites were eligible for citizenship. For the Chinese, this meant that they could only become U.S. citizens if they were perceived as white, which they were usually not. In fact, various legal measures were introduced that sought to define the Chinese as nonwhite and, therefore, as undesirable for U.S. society. In 1854, for example, the U.S. Supreme Court ruled in *People v. Hall* that Chinese were banned from giving testimony against whites. This not only defined the Chinese as nonwhite and put them on the same level as African Americans, who had already been barred from testifying in court cases, it also turned the Chinese into an easy target for anti-Chinese mobs who wanted to drive them away because they could not testify against their white attackers. As a result, violence against Chinese immigrants increased, ranging from beatings and the burning of buildings to murder and the destruction of Chinatowns.[4]

Legal Discrimination of the Chinese

When working conditions for miners became difficult in 1854, white miners took their anger out on Chinese and blamed them for their diminished incomes. They argued that hordes of Chinese were invading the West Coast and that the Chinese would destroy American civilization unless they were stopped, and they demanded their exclusion. California's legislative houses reacted by setting up committees with the task of analyzing the situation. Both committees came to the conclusion that Asian immigrants indeed threatened American workers.[5] As a result, in 1855, California introduced the Act to Discourage the Immigration to This State of Persons Who Cannot Become Citizens Thereof, which stipulated that non-European immigrants had to pay a head tax of $50. Opponents of Chinese immigration hoped that this would deter Chinese from coming to California. The act was declared void in 1857, but the California legislature continued to introduce various anti-Chinese legal measures, including a Chinese exclusion bill in 1858, which was entitled An Act to Prevent the Further Immigration of Chinese or Mongolians to This State. Like its predecessors, the bill was declared unconstitutional by California's state supreme court, and Chinese immigrants were allowed to enter the United States so that, by 1860, more than 9 percent of California's population was Chinese. Given that almost 40 percent of California's population was foreign born at that time, it is clear that the Chinese were singled out for discrimination.

In 1862, the California legislature passed the Capitation Tax (An Act to Protect Free White Labor against Competition with Chinese Coolie Labor, and to Discourage the Immigration of the Chinese into the State of California). This tax required $2.50 per month from most Chinese laborers who resided in California. However, the California state supreme court eventually ruled that the capitation tax violated the Constitution, because Congress was in charge of immigration, not individual states.[6]

Nevertheless, ongoing anti-Chinese agitation and laws that discriminated against Chinese miners caused many Chinese to find work in other professions where they posed no threat to white workers—for example, in laundry businesses, domestic service, textile and cigarette factories, agriculture, and the fishing industry. Yet, for opponents of Chinese immigration, this was not enough, because they claimed that the Chinese were invading the United States and had to be stopped or else they would take over the country. Tensions increased when the Chinese moved away from mining towns into cities. Although the Chinese tended to take up trades where they did not pose competition for whites, the anti-Chinese movement quickly spread, culminating in the foundation of the Pacific Coast Anti-Coolie Association in 1867, which lobbied for the exclusion of Chinese. California introduced various measures aimed at curbing Chinese immigration, including An Act to Prevent the Importation of Chinese Criminals, and to Prevent the Establishment of Chinese Slavery and An Act to Prevent the Kidnaping [*sic*] and Importation of Mongolian, Chinese and Japanese Females, for Criminal and Demoralizing Purposes. There were also laws that were blatantly directed at the Chinese; one law, for example, prohibited people from walking on the sidewalks with baskets hung from a pole that rested on their shoulders, which was the typical way Chinese carried goods. The Laundry Ordinance stipulated that laundries using horse-drawn vehicles to deliver laundry paid a much lower tax than laundries that relied on people to carry laundry to the customers. Because Chinese laundries did not use vehicles, the law clearly targeted them. The Chinese did not suffer such discrimination passively; on various occasions they took legal action, and in many cases they succeeded in having the laws declared void.[7]

Sometimes the Chinese resorted to other means of subverting efforts to expel them. For example, in 1870, the San Francisco Board of Supervisors introduced the Cubic Air Ordinance, which made it mandatory for lodging houses in San Francisco to provide every inhabitant with at least 500 cubic feet of air. Violators were punished with a penalty of either a fine or imprisonment. The law was enforced particularly in Chinese lodging houses to make Chinese pay so many fines until they left San Francisco. However, most Chinese opted for a jail sentence, causing the plan to backfire and causing overcrowded prisons instead. To force the Chinese to pay the fine, the Board of Supervisors retaliated in 1873 with the Queue-Cutting Ordinance, which required all men prisoners to cut their hair down to one inch. Because Chinese men wore their hair in a queue, this would have been extremely humiliating for them. Thankfully for them, the Queue-Cutting Ordinance was vetoed by San Francisco's mayor, and the Cubic Air Ordinance was not enforced for three years.[8]

The 1870s and 1880s saw the formation of a white U.S. working class. This affected the position of Chinese workers, who tended to be described by their opponents as "coolies," meaning contract laborers who had been brought to the United States against their will. Although Chinese contract laborers were used in various countries, Chinese laborers in the United States were not coolies and were only under a contract until they had paid back their debt for the passage from China to the United States. After that, they were free workers. However, Chinese continued to be referred to as coolies by their opponents, and the invocation of coolie labor put them on a similar level as African American slaves in the antebellum period. At the same time, the Chinese coolie was used as an image to describe the Chinese workers as cheap, inferior labor that threatened free, white labor.[9]

The anti-Chinese movement not only established the Chinese as racial others who did not belong in American society, it also served to turn Irish immigrants into what were perceived as "real" Americans. Prior to the arrival of the Chinese, Irish immigrants had been viewed as inherently different from the white Anglo-Saxon Protestant American society due to their Catholic faith and Celtic origin. The Irish reacted to their hostile reception by many Americans by attacking African Americans, and later Chinese immigrants, in an effort to reposition themselves as part of the white settler community in the United States. This was done by applying stereotypes associated with African Americans to Chinese.[10]

The Exclusion of Chinese Laborers

Because the United States was generally presented as a nation of immigrants, anti-Chinese organizations claimed that the Chinese were incapable of assimilating with U.S. society in order to justify their demands for Chinese exclusion. Chinese immigrants were also often accused of being sojourners, even though it was quite common for immigrants of any ethnicity to return to their country after working in the United States for a period of time. Like other ethnic groups, Chinese immigrants tended to settle down in areas with other Chinese. Although this was not seen as a problem with other immigrants, the establishment of Chinese neighborhoods was used as an example of the inability of Chinese to become American. Chinatowns also quickly became targets of anti-Chinese stereotypes that described the Chinese as filthy criminals, prostitutes, or opium addicts. The Chinese as immoral and uncivilized people were, so the argument went, unfit for American society.[11]

The discrimination of Chinese was not limited to Chinese adults. In San Francisco, Chinese children were not allowed to go to school with white children. In 1854, a school for African American children was opened in San Francisco. A school for Chinese children was opened five years later, but because there were not enough Chinese children to keep it running, it was closed again. This meant that Chinese or Chinese American children had to be privately educated or go to missionary schools until a new "Oriental" School was founded in 1885, after Joseph and Mary Tape went to court in 1884, successfully arguing that the San Francisco School Board denied their Asian American daughter the right to public education. As the Tapes' example shows, Chinese immigrants did not simply acquiesce to discrimination but successfully challenged many anti-Chinese statutes and laws.[12]

Most Chinese immigrants were men, yet anti-Chinese legislation was also used to ensure that Chinese women could not join their husbands in the United States. This also served to keep Chinese communities from growing and to avoid children of Chinese immigrants becoming American citizens (any child born in the United States automatically becomes an American citizen). Few Chinese women emigrated to the United States, and many of those who did were prostitutes.

Although many others were wives of merchants, opponents of Chinese immigration were quick to claim that Chinese women immigrants were mostly prostitutes and therefore had to be kept from entering the United States. This argument found widespread support and led to the Page Law of 1875, which allowed the exclusion of any Chinese woman who was a prostitute. The Page Law further strengthened the stereotypes of Chinese women as a menace to white men, because they had the power to lure them away from righteousness. Ironically, measures like the Page Law had the effect that prostitution became even more widespread in Chinese communities, because few Chinese women were allowed to enter the United States and join their husbands or get married and thereby even out the very uneven balance of Chinese men and women in the United States (see Table 3).[13]

Because the Chinese presence was largest in California, politicians and political parties in California and on the West Coast increasingly resorted to anti-Chinese sentiment to gain votes in the 1860s and 1870s. Since the 1850s, laws had been issued that targeted Chinese immigrants or that banned the immigration of Chinese, although the latter were declared unconstitutional because only the federal government could regulate matters regarding immigration. Nevertheless, demands for Chinese exclusion increased, and after Chinese workers were used as strike breakers in North Adams, Massachusetts, in 1870, the anti-Chinese movement became a nationwide phenomenon.[14]

Between 1849 and 1882, more than 250,000 Chinese immigrants arrived in the United States.[15] While they were immediately regarded with suspicion and hostility, the anti-Chinese movement gained particular popularity when labor conditions worsened. It is, therefore, no wonder that when an economic crisis hit the United States in 1873, the anti-Chinese movement intensified and increased

Table 3 Percentage of Chinese Men to Women in the Entire United States, 1860–1920

Year	Chinese Women (%)	Chinese Men (%)
1860	5.1	94.9
1870	7.2	92.8
1880	4.5	95.5
1890	3.6	96.4
1900	5.0	95.0
1910	6.5	93.5
1920	12.6	87.4

Source: U.S. Bureau of the Census, *Historical Statistics of the United States: Colonial Times to 1970, Bicentennial Edition* (Washington, DC: U.S. Census Bureau, 1975).

fears that the Chinese were taking the jobs of whites. Demands for an end to Chinese immigration were accompanied by numerous references to the Chinese as the "yellow peril," which described them as a social, racial, moral, and political threat to American society. In 1875, for example, legislative committees from Congress and from the California Senate supported Chinese exclusion, adhering to the usual arguments of opponents to Chinese immigration by warning of a Chinese invasion of the United States, which would be devastating for U.S. society because the Chinese were morally degraded, culturally inferior, and generally unfit for democracy. In 1877, the Workingman's Party of California was founded and adopted as its slogan "The Chinese Must Go!" Two years later, a plebiscite on Chinese exclusion met with the approval of 96 percent of California voters, and the legislature promptly issued various anti-Chinese measures, including a law prohibiting the employment of Chinese laborers; all of the measures were later deemed unconstitutional.[16]

Yellow peril fears existed not only in California. In 1873, President Ulysses S. Grant began referring to the Chinese with yellow peril stereotypes, paving the way for national measures against Chinese immigration. As more and more workers lost their jobs, the continuing immigration of Chinese led to various anti-Chinese demonstrations and a general anti-Chinese hysteria that centered on the image of Chinese hordes invading the country, taking white men's jobs, and destroying the moral basis of the United States. In 1879, Congress passed the Fifteen Passenger Bill, which allowed no more than 15 Chinese on ships entering the United States. The bill was vetoed by President Rutherford B. Hayes, because it violated the Burlingame Treaty of 1868, which stipulated that Chinese and Americans had a reciprocal right of migration and that the Chinese enjoyed the same rights and privileges as other nationalities in the United States. This meant that the U.S. government was legally bound to admit Chinese immigrants and was not allowed to impose laws that affected only Chinese immigration. Although Hayes sympathized with proponents of Chinese exclusion, he felt that diplomatic efforts between China and the United States had to precede unilateral measures such as a Chinese exclusion law.[17]

In 1880, China and the United States signed a treaty that allowed the United States to limit or suspend the immigration of Chinese laborers but not that of Chinese students, merchants, teachers, or tourists. After it was ratified in 1881, Congress was flooded with petitions against Chinese immigration, and eventually a bill was passed that suspended the immigration of Chinese laborers for 20 years. President Chester A. Arthur vetoed the bill, explaining that he would prefer a shorter period than 20 years. Congress then passed the Chinese Exclusion Act (An Act to Execute Certain Treaty Stipulations Relating to Chinese), which suspended the immigration of Chinese laborers for 10 years. This time, President Arthur did not object and signed the bill into law on May 6, 1882. Chinese laborers would not be able to enter the United States freely again until 1943.[18]

Enforcing Chinese Exclusion

Chinese exclusion was enforced by the U.S. Customs Service, but initially there were no clear rules on how this was to be done. All that was clear was that when ships with Chinese immigrants arrived in the United States, the Chinese inspector, a U.S. customs official, had to judge which passengers were allowed to enter the country.[19] The Exclusion Act from 1882 did not prevent the immigration of Chinese laborers if they had been in the United States before November 17, 1880. In order for those laborers to leave the United States and be allowed to return, customs officials issued return certificates to Chinese workers who left the United States for China and planned to come back. Upon their return, the certificates were compared to the identification record of the laborer that the customs official had created. Those Chinese who were not returning laborers had to bring a certificate from the Chinese government that stated that they belonged to one of the exempt classes (merchants, students, tourists, or diplomats). Chinese who were denied entry had a right to challenge their detention with a writ of habeas corpus. Because many Chinese laborers successfully claimed that they had left the United States before return certificates became required for reentering the country, in 1884, an amendment to the Exclusion Act stated that all Chinese laborers had to have a certificate to be able to return to the United States. This led to widespread fraud with the issuance or sale of return certificates by Chinese and customs officials. Moreover, by appealing for a writ of habeas corpus, thousands of Chinese were granted the right to enter the United States even if customs officials had denied them entry. As a result, various newspapers claimed that the Chinese undermined the Exclusion Act and that the invasion of Chinese hordes continued. The press and the public also blamed the judicial system for creating loopholes for Chinese immigrants.[20]

Even though, between 1882 and 1887, 25,000 more Chinese left the United States than entered it, fears of Chinese cunning and deception caused Congress to pass the Scott Act in 1888, which prohibited all Chinese laborers from returning to the United States, even if they had certificates as required by the 1884 amendment. This meant that more than 20,000 Chinese who had left for China before 1888 were no longer allowed to enter the United States Yet, instead of stopping once and for all Chinese attempts at outwitting the law, the Scott Act simply encouraged them to find new ways of doing so. Because the Scott Act made it impossible for Chinese laborers to immigrate to the U.S., most Chinese arriving after 1888 claimed that they were either merchants or had been born in the United States and were, therefore, American citizens.[21]

Through a writ of habeas corpus, a petitioner could force the person detaining him or her to demonstrate that the confinement was lawful. As a result, Chinese resorted to writs of habeas corpus after they had been refused entry by immigration officials. The large majority of such petitions were granted by federal courts, because the judges tended to require less evidence than the immigration officials and because Chinese petitioners had the right to counsel. Chinese petitioners were also sometimes coached by their lawyers and friends or relatives who sent coaching letters that explained how they had to testify in order to be admitted to the United States Between 1882 and 1891, Chinese immigrants who had been denied entry to the United States had filed 7,080 petitions for writs of habeas corpus in San Francisco alone. Of these, over 85 percent were granted and the collector's decision was overturned. Needless to say, this was not popular with anti-Chinese groups and increased anxieties about continuing Chinese immigration.[22]

As a result of continuing fears of the yellow peril, particularly on the West Coast, the mid-1880s witnessed widespread anti-Chinese agitation. Chinese were killed or forcibly expelled from various towns and their buildings set on fire. As in the previous decades, anti-Chinese agitation was worst in California, but anti-Chinese massacres, riots, and forcible expulsions of Chinese also took place in Idaho, Colorado, Oregon, Wyoming, and Washington. In September 1885, for example, the infamous Rock Springs Massacre took place at a coal mining factory in Rock Springs, Wyoming, where more than 600 Chinese workers were employed. When the Chinese workers refused to join a strike with European American workers for higher wages, a mob of white workers set the shacks of the Chinese workers on fire, killing 28 Chinese and wounding 15. The remaining 550 Chinese workers eventually returned to Rock Springs under the protection of federal troops. In Seattle, anti-Chinese agitation occurred between October 1885 and February 1886. In November 1885, Chinese residents of Tacoma were expelled by whites, and the town's Chinatown was set on fire. In February 1886, a mob in Seattle brought 350 Chinese immigrants to the docks and wanted to put them on a ship and force them to leave. The governor intervened, and federal troops were called to protect the Chinese.[23]

One explanation for the continuing hostility, hatred, and brutality shown toward Chinese immigrants by many Americans is that the exclusion of Chinese and the portrayal of Chinese immigrants as non-American contributed to U.S. nationalism. Because nationalism establishes unity through exclusion, the exclusion of Chinese immigrants contributed to the definition of what it meant to be American, and thereby to the discursive formation of American nationhood. By excluding Chinese (and later all Asians) from the United States, American national identity was increasingly defined as white (and, to a lesser degree, white Anglo-Saxon Protestant).[24] Thus, while Chinese immigration was denied, Western European immigration was encouraged, resulting in a far higher percentage of Western Europeans than Chinese among the immigrant population of the United States (see Table 4).[25]

Moreover, since the Chinese constituted only 0.2 percent of the U.S. population in 1880 and less still by 1920, they were not a real threat to white workers. Never-

White miners massacre Chinese workers in a racially motivated attack in Rock Springs, Wyoming, in 1885. Twenty-eight Chinese were killed and 15 were wounded. (Library of Congress)

Table 4 Percentage of Chinese, Irish, and German Immigrants among the U.S. Population, 1870–1900

Year	Chinese (%)	Irish (%)	German (%)
1870	1.13	33.33	30.37
1880	1.56	27.76	29.44
1890	1.15	20.23	30.11
1900	0.79	15.62	25.76

Source: U.S. Census Bureau, Population Division, *Table 4: Region and Country or Area of Birth of the Foreign-Born Population, With Geographic Detail Shown in Decennial Census Publications of 1930 or Earlier: 1850 to 1930 and 1960 to 1990* (Washington, DC: U.S. Census Bureau, 2008), http://www.census.gov/population/www/documentation/twps0029/tab04.html.

theless, the image of Chinese hordes invading the United States and taking away the jobs of (white) men proved an effective tool to resolve class tensions during economic crises or times of high unemployment, and so the Chinese continued to be used as scapegoats even after their exclusion. The extent of the dehumanization of Chinese immigrants even went so far that advertisements portrayed them as vermin that had to be exterminated.[26]

The Immigration of Women and Children

In 1890, there was an uproar when a federal court in Oregon decided that Chinese merchants were allowed to bring their wives and children to the United States. As has already been mentioned, a widespread stereotype of Chinese women was that they were prostitutes. Prostitution was indeed a huge problem for Chinese women in the United States, because many had been sold into prostitution or kidnapped. As a result, immigration officials suspected all Chinese women of being prostitutes and not only interrogated the husband and wife separately and compared their statements for divergence, but many also required testimonies of white witnesses (they did not trust Chinese witnesses) or a legal documentation of the marriage before they would believe that a couple was indeed married.[27] In 1900, the Supreme Court stated that wives and children automatically assumed the status of the husband or father. Thus, wives and children of laborers were not allowed to enter, while those of merchants could. Consequently, Chinese women also had to prove that their character was proper and that they were really part of the merchant class. They did so via testimonies of Americans (preferably whites) and affidavits. Proof of belonging to the merchant class was achieved by wearing expensive clothes and traveling from China to the United States in first-class accommodations. Even bound feet were argued to be a sign of a respectable woman.[28]

The fact that Chinese merchants or Chinese who were born in the United States were allowed to bring their family led to the "paper son" phenomenon. Paper son refers to the fact that son and father were related only on paper. Because few Chinese women traveled to the United States, there were far more paper sons than paper daughters. Paper sons were created in the following way: A Chinese merchant who lived in the United States would travel to China and, upon his return to the United States, claim that his wife had given birth to a son. The merchant would then sell the slot position of his son to a Chinese who would come to the United States using fake certificates to pass as the son of the merchant.[29] To pass off as son and father, both men had to invent and memorize their family's history and additional information. Paper sons had to change their birthdays so that it fit the father's story. Detailed crib sheets and maps were used that contained information about the village and the extended family (including the occupation, physical appearance, birthdays, and so on), because inspectors questioned both the applicant (the son) and the father and then compared the statements to see if there were any inconsistencies. The questions were extremely detailed, asking such things as the number of windows in the room on the third floor of the house, the number of steps leading to the back door, the number of vacant spaces in the village's rows of houses, and the applicant's seat in the school room. The questions became more difficult and longer over the years, so that sometimes even real relatives had to have coaching in order to pass the interrogation.[30]

Additional problems with the immigration procedure included that officials distrusted Chinese interpreters who were present at the interrogations (most immigrants could not speak English). As a result, in 1896, the Treasury Department decided to fire all Chinese interpreters who worked for immigration officials and replaced them with whites who were not affiliated with Chinese in any way. However, there were not enough such interpreters available, and even the few who could speak Chinese could not speak the various dialects spoken by the immigrants.[31]

In 1891, anti-Chinese judges took over California's federal and district courts, and hopes grew that the federal courts would stop supporting the majority of Chinese who filed petitions against their deportation. Nevertheless, the courts continued to overturn negative decisions by the immigration officials. Part of the reason for the success of Chinese petitions lay with the support Chinese immigrants received from the Chinese American community. Arriving Chinese immigrants could rely on people from their village who already lived in the United States, family organizations, and the Chinese Six Companies to help them. The Chinese Six Companies' official name was Chinese Consolidated Benevolent Association. Founded in 1862, it represented Chinese interests and fought against discriminatory measures by hiring attorneys to contest anti-Chinese legislation.[32]

In 1892, the 10-year period of the original Chinese Exclusion Act of 1882 was over. As a result, Congress passed the Geary Act (An Act to Prohibit the Coming of Chinese Persons into the United States), which renewed the exclusion of Chinese laborers until 1902. The Geary Act stipulated that all Chinese laborers in the United States had to obtain a certificate that stated that they resided legally in the United States. Chinese residents without such a certificate were imprisoned, forced to hard labor for 60 days, and deported unless they had a white witness who would testify that they had in fact lived in the United States before 1880. The certificates of residence included photos and personal information, and they were precursors to the green card. Despite strong objections and legal action from the Chinese community against the Geary Act, it was declared constitutional by the Supreme Court, and Chinese who did not register were deported. Until 1928, Chinese were the only immigrants who were required to have such certificates.[33]

Even children of Chinese parents who were born in the United States were sometimes refused entry by immigration officials who claimed that they were not U.S. citizens. Wong Kim Ark was one of them. After Wong went to China in 1894, he was refused entry upon his return in 1895 on the grounds that he was not a U.S. citizen because his parents were Chinese. Wong took his case to the U.S. Supreme Court, arguing that he was a U.S. citizen because he had been born in the United States, despite his parents being Chinese—and therefore exempt from naturalization—and not living in the United States anymore. The Supreme Court ruled in favor of Wong, stating that any person born in the United States was entitled to U.S. citizenship, regardless of whether his or her parents were U.S. citizens.[34]

The Supreme Court's ruling sparked a flurry of petitions from Chinese claiming that they had been born in the United States, but they faced long interrogations, and from 1892 they had to provide testimonies of white witnesses to prove that they had been born in the United States. This was problematic because the Chinese tended to live in segregated communities (usually because they were not allowed to live in non-Chinese neighborhoods). Of course, there were whites who were willing to lie in return for money, but in 1902 the Bureau of Immigration changed its requirement to that of a Chinese witness. However, immigration officials also conducted other tests to determine whether Chinese immigrants had in fact grown up in the United States, as they had claimed. Supposed citizens were tested in American history, geography, and English-language skills, which was difficult for Chinese, because most had grown up in Chinese neighborhoods speaking Chinese, not English. The treatment of Chinese born in the United States as non-American also shows how Chinese immigrants and their children continued to be viewed as not being part of American society.[35]

Further Measures to Curb Chinese Immigration

In 1902, the Geary Act expired, causing supporters of Chinese exclusion to demand a new, more restrictive law. The law passed by Congress extended Chinese exclusion indefinitely but also respected the existing treaty between the United States and China, which was due to expire in 1904. Additionally, the 1902 law excluded Chinese laborers from all American territories, including Hawaii and later also the Philippines.[36] Angered by the treatment of its subjects in the United States, China refused in 1904 to renew its treaty with the United States. Congress retaliated by introducing another Chinese exclusion law, again without a time limit and including all American territories. However, opponents of Chinese immigration had been complaining for years that the Chinese used federal courts to enter the United States through loopholes and deception of judges, and so, in 1905, the U.S. Supreme Court ruled that Chinese who had been denied entry to the United States by immigration officials could no longer appeal to federal district courts. The federal district courts had indeed allowed thousands of Chinese to enter the United States. Between 1891 and 1905, 2,657 habeas corpus cases from Chinese immigrants were heard in the San Francisco courts alone, and many of them eventually were ruled in favor of the Chinese petitioners. The fact that these courts were no longer allowed to hear Chinese admission cases, therefore, drastically limited the chances of Chinese immigrants being admitted to the United States.[37] Moreover, in 1903, the Bureau of Immigration had taken control of all matters relating to Chinese immigration. Many of the bureau's officials were anti-Chinese and strictly interpreted the Chinese exclusion laws to keep out as many Chinese immigrants as possible.[38]

Chinese resentment and outrage over the extension of the Exclusion Act in 1904 and the impossibility of challenging the decisions of immigration officials led to a boycott of American goods in China beginning in May 1905 and lasting until 1906. The boycott was also supported by Chinese communities in San Francisco and Los Angeles. In the fall of 1905, the Chinese government began to suppress the boycott, but it, nevertheless, affected American businesses in the United States and in China and caused them to demand new policies on Chinese immigration to the United States. Although some American newspapers criticized the way Chinese merchants, students, and travelers had been treated by U.S. immigration officials, there was no such sympathy for Chinese laborers, and opposition to their immigration continued.[39] Worried about the effects of the boycott on the U.S. economy, President Theodore Roosevelt suggested a new law that allowed the immigration of all Chinese except for laborers. While this bill never made it through Congress, the government stated that the exclusion law had to be enforced without restricting the freedom of Chinese who were part of the exempt classes. While the exclusion laws, thus, remained intact, some aspects of the immigration process, particularly humiliating procedures, were changed, and from 1907, Chinese immigrants were allowed to have attorneys with them during the hearings.[40]

In 1910, a new immigration station on Angel Island opened. Before that, Chinese immigrants had been held at the Pacific Mail Steamship Company detention shed on San Francisco's Pier 40 until they received a decision on their immigration petition. The conditions in the shed were horrifying. Constantly overcrowded, the detention shed usually housed about 400 immigrants, even though it had originally been built for 200. It had only one room with six windows and poor ventilation, resulting in illness and death among Chinese immigrants. Some inmates were detained in what they described as an iron cage or a jail for several months. With the opening of Angel Island, things only marginally improved for Chinese immigrants. The sanitary conditions remained appalling, rooms were overcrowded, and detainees rarely got to leave their quarters. Moreover, admission rates of Chinese immigrants dropped sharply while application procedures became increasingly difficult to pass.[41]

Built on an island in San Francisco Bay, Angel Island not only kept Chinese immigrants geographically separated from American society and Chinese settlers in the United States (it was feared that Chinese applicants for immigration were coached by relatives and friends on how to pass the interrogation process), it also made escape from detention impossible. Although immigrants of various nationalities were held at Angel Island, by far the majority were Chinese. After their arrival in San Francisco, the Chinese were singled out, and husbands and wives were separated until they had passed the immigration procedures. Those without satisfactory papers for immigration (i.e., most of the passengers) were sent to Angel Island, where they had to undergo interrogations, cross-examinations, and medical examinations. During this process, Chinese immigrants were measured, described,

Chinese and Japanese women and children wait to be processed as they sit in a wire mesh enclosure at the Angel Island internment barracks in San Francisco Bay in the late 1920s. (AP/ Wide World Photos)

and photographed in a very humiliating way; their luggage was searched; and applicants as well as their witnesses had to testify separately to the inspectors in order to expose lies. Those Chinese who claimed they were merchants had to pass a literacy test and testify that they had not performed physical labor (they were also checked in the medical examination for physical marks of labor).[42]

Newly arriving Chinese immigrants usually relied on friends and relatives in the United States for financial and moral support. Many of these also served as witnesses during long and often hostile immigration hearings. Because affidavits and testimonies from whites were judged more important than those of Chinese, many Chinese immigrants or returning immigrants ensured that they had supporting letters from white Americans. More and more immigrants also resorted to hiring lawyers to process papers and represent them before the immigration authorities.[43]

The Chinese exclusion marked the beginning of American exclusion of those classified as "undesirable" immigrants. Arguments that were used against the Chinese—for example, that they were racially inferior, that their cheap labor posed a threat to (white) American workers, and that they were arriving in such large numbers that they were invading the United States—were used in a similar form against other immigrant groups, including those from Southern and Eastern Europe and Asia in the following decades, particularly between 1891 and 1924, the high tide of the nativist movement. Nativists differentiated between old and new immigrants and viewed the former as the native stock of Americans, while the latter were regarded as a threat to American society, culture, and race. Old immigrants were defined as people who arrived from Western European countries, including Scandinavia, because—so it was argued—these were the countries of origin of most immigrants before 1880. By defining only Western Europeans as old immigrants, American society could be presented as being based on a core ethnicity of Germans, Swedes, English, Irish, and Scots—that is, white Western European. From 1890, nativists increasingly demanded immigration limitations on or the exclusion of immigrants from Asia as well as Southern and Eastern Europe, because Southern and Eastern Europeans were not perceived to be as white as Western Europeans.[44] Yet, while anti-immigration feeling spread, the focus did not so much shift away from the Chinese as widen to include additional ethnicities. As a result, Chinese immigration and the yellow peril remained in the spotlight of the press and public. Moreover, although immigration procedures for all nationalities contained various examinations, those for Chinese included much more detailed investigation.[45]

Illegal Immigration

To evade the immigration proceedings, many Chinese immigrated illegally by paying guides hefty fees to be led safely across the Mexican or Canadian border into the United States. It is estimated that, between 1880 and 1920, more than 17,000 Chinese entered the States this way from Mexico to San Diego, El Paso, and San Antonio and from Canada to Seattle and Buffalo. Canada was popular among Chinese immigrants as a departing location for the United States, because there was no exclusion law for Chinese immigrants in Canada until 1923. Moreover, the U.S.-Canada border was unguarded in some locations. Thus, thousands of Chinese made the journey from Canada to the United States following the enactment of the Exclusion Act in 1882. Of those who were caught, many claimed successfully that they had been born in the United States and were therefore U.S. citizens. Immigration officials along the northern border were accused of being corrupt and admitting Chinese immigrants in return for bribes. Mexico was another starting point for illegal Chinese immigration to the United States, because, as in Canada, there were no Chinese exclusion laws. In fact, Mexico supported foreign immigration, because it was regarded as contributing to the development of the country. The majority of Chinese immigrants arriving in Mexico made their way to the United States with the help of smugglers who acted as guides across the border. Some Chinese also tried their luck on their own and walked across the border or hid in railcars.[46]

Many Chinese who crossed the border illegally disguised themselves as Native Americans, Mexicans, or African Americans in order to either pass as U.S. citizens or as Mexicans, who were allowed to enter the United States. The ethnicity the Chinese took on depended on the region in which they crossed the border, because their chances of not getting caught were higher if they looked as if they belonged to an ethnic minority that was common in the area. Thus, in the Southwest, Chinese would often disguise themselves as Mexicans or Native Americans; in the South, they pretended to be African Americans; and in the North, they posed as Native Americans or Canadian Indians. The changing of ethnicity was achieved by wearing traditional ethnic costume or dress, changing the hair by cutting off queues (queues were a clear indication of being Chinese), and painting or darkening skin. Interestingly, U.S. immigration officials found it very difficult to distinguish between Mexicans and Chinese.[47]

Chinese were not the only immigrants who came to the United States illegally. Many Eastern and Southern Europeans who had been denied entry on the East Coast tried their luck at the Canadian border. In the early 1900s, there were thousands of illegal border crossings each year from Canada alone, and by the end of the decade, immigration from Canada and Mexico amounted to a larger number than any legal point of entry with the exception of New York. Nevertheless, despite an increasing international variety of illegal immigrants, Chinese immigrants were the least desired and continued to represent illegal immigration for most Americans. Although illegal immigrants from Southern and Eastern Europe were not as desirable as those from Britain, Ireland, or Germany, they were perceived to be more like Western Europeans than the Chinese. Even Mexican immigrants were preferred to Chinese, because the American Southwest economy depended on cheap Mexican labor following the exclusion of the Chinese. Mexican immigration was not restricted until 1917, when the Immigration Act required Mexicans to pay a head tax and pass a literacy test in order to be allowed to enter the United States.[48]

There were other means of Chinese entering the United States than illegally across the northern and southern borders. In 1906, San Francisco was hit by an earthquake and a fire that destroyed all Chinese public records. Because anyone who was born in the United States automatically became a U.S. citizen, many Chinese forged certificates that stated that they had been born in the United States. With no documents that proved otherwise, it was difficult for immigration officials to argue against such claims when witnesses could be presented that swore that the person in question had been born in the United States. Once they had officially been given citizenship status, many claimed that they had sons in China who they wanted to bring to the United States. Because the documents that stated the number of children of Chinese immigrants had also been destroyed by the earthquake, immigration services had to accept such claims. The Chinese Americans who had been granted their request to bring their sons to the United States in turn sold the slots for their sons to Chinese in China who wanted to come to the United States. As a result, Chinese paper sons arrived in much greater numbers after 1906.[49]

In the early 20th century, opponents of Chinese immigration became increasingly worried about other Asian immigrants, and so in 1917, the Asiatic Barred Zone was established, which excluded Indians, Burmese, Siamese, and other Asians from entering the United States.[50] Five years later, the Cable Act stipulated that Americans marrying aliens ineligible for citizenship lost their citizenship. Thus, any Chinese American woman who married a Chinese man was stripped of her American citizenship.[51] Antimiscegenation laws had existed in the United States since the days of slavery, and between 1880 and 1910, various Western states imposed laws that banned marriages between whites and Chinese, because this was where most Chinese lived. As more and more Chinese immigrants settled down in other states, many of them also introduced similar laws, but until 1922, no federal law existed that prohibited marriages between Americans and Chinese.[52]

The Cable Act symbolizes the growing obsession about miscegenation and the racial purity of U.S. society. In 1924, another immigration act was passed that further sought to alleviate such anxieties and classified immigrants according to race and nationality. Known as the Johnson-Reed Act, the legislation advocated preferential treatment of people from Northern and Western Europe, while those from other areas of the world became classified as nonwhite and undesirable. By denying entry to aliens ineligible for citizenship and stating that all people from Asian nations were nonwhite, the act also prevented Japanese, Indians, and Nepalese from entering the United States.[53] With its quota system, Johnson-Reed established the legality of supplying immigration visas to 2 percent of the total number of people of each nationality already in the United States. These numbers were determined based on the 1890 census. Of all the Asian countries affected, Japan was the most incensed by this action. Among the most forthright interpretations of this legislation is that from the U.S. Department of State's Office of the Historian, who has noted that the Congress "had decided that preserving the racial composition of the country was more important than promoting good ties with the Japanese empire."[54] The quota system would remain in place until the Johnson administration abolished it.

Conclusion

The history of the anti-Chinese movement in the United States between 1850 and 1924 shows how racial, social, economic, and cultural anxieties contributed to the perception of the yellow peril and led to the Chinese Exclusion Act as the first instance of immigration restriction along the lines of nationality. However, it is important to remember that the Chinese did not suffer passively, but often resorted to legal action to fight discrimination. Many Chinese also used legal loopholes to enter the United States, while others crossed the borders illegally, leading to the creation of a federal immigration bureaucracy. As Erika Lee points out:

The American gate keeping ideologies, policies, and practices that originated in Chinese exclusion were at the center of the reshaping of America, and especially the growth of the federal government at the turn of the twentieth century. . . . State mechanisms used to regulate immigration, enforce national borders, and distinguish U.S. citizens, legal immigrants, and illegal immigration, such as the U.S. Immigration and Naturalization Service, U.S. passports, "green cards," and illegal immigration and deportation policies, can all be traced back to the Chinese exclusion era.[55]

Although Chinese exclusion ended in 1943, the stereotypes used to legitimize Chinese exclusion have not disappeared. Particularly the yellow peril with its image of hordes of Chinese remains an integral part of American culture and continues to live on in American films, novels, and newspapers.

Notes

1. Sucheng Chan, *Asian Americans: An Interpretive History* (Boston: Twayne, 1991), 5–8; Gary Y. Okihiro, *The Columbia Guide to Asian American History* (New York: Columbia University Press), 2001, xiii and 9–11; Dorothy Hoobler and Thomas Hoobler, *The Chinese American Family Album* (New York: Oxford University Press, 1994), 9–19 and 52–53.
2. Chan, *Asian Americans*, 28 and 45–46; Roger Daniels, *Asian America: Chinese and Japanese in the United States since 1850* (Seattle and London: University of Washington Press, 1995), 72; Stuart Creighton Miller, *The Unwelcome Immigrant: The American Image of the Chinese, 1785–1882* (Berkeley and Los Angeles: University of California Press, 1969).
3. Chan, *Asian Americans,* 3, 25–32, and 81–83; Ronald Takaki, *Strangers from a Different Shore: A History of Asian Americans* (Boston, Toronto, and London: Little, Brown, 1989), 84–87, 94–99, and 104–105; Najia Aarim-Heriot, *Chinese Immigrants, African Americans, and Racial Anxiety in the United States, 1848–1882* (Urbana: University of Illinois Press, 2003); Miller, *The Unwelcome Immigrant*, 146–151 and 186–190; Erika Lee, *At America's Gates: Chinese Immigration during the Exclusion Era, 1882–1943* (Chapel Hill and London: University of North Carolina Press, 2003), 112; Daniels, *Asian America*, 19; Isabella Black, "American Labour and Chinese Immigration," *Past and Present* 25 (1963): 65; Robert G. Lee, *Orientals: Asian Americans in Popular Culture* (Philadelphia: Temple University Press, 1999), 58–61.
4. Roger Daniels, *Not Like Us: Immigrants and Minorities in America, 1890–1924* (Chicago: Ivan R. Dee, 1997), 7–8; Chan, *Asian Americans*, 48–49; Takaki, *Strangers from a Different Shore*, 14; Lee, *Orientals*, 106–108; Aarim-Heriot, *Chinese Immigrants*, 7–10, 15, 25, 35, and 44–45.

5. Aarim-Heriot, *Chinese Immigrants*, 45–46.

6. Charles J. McClain and Laurene Wu McClain, "The Chinese Contribution to the Development of American Law," in *Entry Denied: Exclusion and the Chinese Community in America, 1882–1943*, ed. Sucheng Chan (Philadelphia: Temple University Press, 1991), 4–7; Christian G. Fritz, "Due Process, Treaty Rights, and Chinese Exclusion, 1882–1891," in Chan, *Entry Denied*, 27; Aarim-Heriot, *Chinese Immigrants*, 45–59 and 66–67.

7. McClain and Wu McClain, "The Chinese Contribution," 12–16; Aarim-Heriot, *Chinese Immigrants*; Chan, *Asian Americans*, 32–34 and 54–56; Takaki, *Strangers from a Different Shore*, 82, 88–94, and 240–245; Daniels, *Asian America*, 19–22 and 32–39; Hoobler and Hoobler, *Chinese American Family Album*, 54–56 and 92–96; Daniels, *Not Like Us*, 11.

8. McClain and Wu McClain, "The Chinese Contribution," 4–11; Aarim-Heriot, *Chinese Immigrants*, 159–160 and 165–166; Estelle T. Lau, *Paper Families: Identity, Immigration Administration, and Chinese Exclusion* (Durham, NC, and London: Duke University Press, 2006); Lucy E. Salyer, *Laws Harsh as Tigers: Chinese Immigrants and the Shaping of Modern Immigration Law* (Chapel Hill: University of North Carolina Press, 1995), 13.

9. Aarim-Heriot, *Chinese Immigrants*, 11 and 30–35.

10. Matthew Pratt Guterl, "The New Race Consciousness: Race, Nation, and Empire in American Culture, 1910–1925," *Journal of World History* 10, no. 2 (1999): 315–317; Daniels, *Asian America*, 31–32; Aarim-Heriot, *Chinese Immigrants*, 45–46 and 10; John Kuo Wei Tchen, *New York before Chinatown: Orientalism and the Shaping of American Culture 1776–1882* (Baltimore and London: Johns Hopkins University Press, 2001), 221–224; Lee, *Orientals*, 9, 32–43, and 61–72; Krystyn R. Moon, *Yellowface: Creating the Chinese in American Popular Music and Performance, 1850s–1920s* (New Brunswick, NJ, and London: Rutgers University Press, 2005).

11. Aarim-Heriot, *Chinese Immigrants*, 60, 68–69, and 159–160; Miller, *The Unwelcome Immigrant*, 146–166; Chan, *Asian Americans*, 54–57; Lee, *At America's Gates*, 23–36; K. Scott Wong, *Americans First: Chinese Americans and the Second World War* (Cambridge, MA, and London: Harvard University Press, 2005), 7; Tchen, *New York before Chinatown*, 260–278; Takaki, *Strangers from a Different Shore*, 11 and 116; Daniels, *Not Like Us*, 42.

12. Chan, *Asian Americans*, 57–58; Fritz, "Due Process," 27.

13. Okihiro, *Columbia Guide*, 13 and 141; Aarim-Heriot, *Chinese Immigrants*, 62, 168–171; Chan, *Asian Americans*, 57–61, 104–107, and 115; Ruthanne Lum McCunn, *Chinese American Portraits: Personal Histories 1828–1988* (San Francisco: Chronicle Books, 1998), 41–45; Takaki, *Strangers from a Different Shore*, 121–123 and 235; Lee, *Orientals*, 72–82; Daniels, *Not Like Us*, 12.

14. Daniels, *Asian America*, 36–43; Aarim-Heriot, *Chinese Immigrants*, 126–136 and 178–182; Chan, *Asian Americans*, 54; Miller, *The Unwelcome Immigrant*, 160 and 191–204; Daniels, *Not Like Us*, 7–8; Tchen, *New York before Chinatown*, 175–180.

15. Daniels, *Not Like Us*, 5.

16. Aarim-Heriot, *Chinese Immigrants*, 172 and 179–193; Salyer, *Laws Harsh as Tigers*, 9–13.

17. Aarim-Heriot, *Chinese Immigrants*, 172–179 and 197–204; Fritz, "Due Process," 25–26; Daniels, *Asian America*, 45–54; Lee, *At America's Gates*, 165–167; Daniels, *Not Like Us*, 11–13; Salyer, *Laws Harsh as Tigers*, 14.

18. Aarim-Heriot, *Chinese Immigrants*, 204–214; Fritz, "Due Process," 26–27 and 31; Daniels, *Asian America*, 55–56; Black, "American Labour," 64–65; Daniels, *Not Like Us*, 13–14; Salyer, *Laws Harsh as Tigers*, 14–17.

19. Lee, *At America's Gates*, 49; Salyer, *Laws Harsh as Tigers*, 38.

20. Fritz, "Due Process," 27–40; McClain and Wu McClain, "The Chinese Contribution," 17; Salyer, *Laws Harsh as Tigers*, 17–21 and 72–81; Lau, *Paper Families*, 34–36.

21. McClain and Wu McClain, "The Chinese Contribution," 17; Fritz, "Due Process," 47–49; Lee, *At America's Gates*, 45 and 153; Salyer, *Laws Harsh as Tigers*, 20–23.

22. Fritz, "Due Process," 49–50; Salyer, *Laws Harsh as Tigers*, 72–85; Lau, *Paper Families*, 29–31.

23. Chan, *Asian Americans*, 49–53; Okihiro, *Columbia Guide*, 15–16; Aarim-Heriot, *Chinese Immigrants*, 164; McCunn, *Chinese American Portraits*, 48–53; Daniels, *Asian America*, 59–64, Black, "American Labour," 67–69.

24. See Etienne Balibar, "Racism and Nationalism," in *Race, Nation, Class: Ambiguous Identities*, ed. Etienne Balibar and Immanuel Wallerstein (London and New York: Verso, 1991), 49; David Leiwei Li, *Imagining the Nation: Asian American Literature and Cultural Consent* (Stanford, CA: Stanford University Press, 1998), 3.

25. Daniels, *Not Like Us*, 31.

26. U.S. Bureau of Immigration, *Laws, Treaty, and Regulations Relating to the Exclusion of Chinese from the United States* (Washington, DC: U.S. Government Printing Office, 1903); Yuko Matskuawa, "Representing the Oriental in Nineteenth-Century Trade Cards," in *Re/collecting Early Asian America: Essays in Cultural History*, eds. Josephine Lee, Imogene L. Lim, and Yuko Matsukawa (Philadelphia: Temple University Press, 2002), 204–206; Aarim-Heriot, *Chinese Immigrants*, 208–215; Daniels, *Not Like Us*, 13–14; Takaki, *Strangers from a Different Shore*, 110–112.

27. Lee, *At America's Gates*, 93–96; Salyer, *Laws Harsh as Tigers*, 44–45.

28. Lee, *At America's Gates*, 134–135; Salyer, *Laws Harsh as Tigers*, 43.

29. Lau, *Paper Families*; Salyer, *Laws Harsh as Tigers*, 44.

30. Lau, *Paper Families*; Salyer, *Laws Harsh as Tigers*, 59–62.

31. Lee, *At America's Gates*, 58–63; Salyer, *Laws Harsh as Tigers*, 62.

32. Salyer, *Laws Harsh as Tigers*, 33–35 and 40–41; Lau, *Paper Families*, 25.

33. Lee, *At America's Gates,* 42 and 45; McClain and Wu McClain, "The Chinese Contribution," 18–19; Salyer, *Laws Harsh as Tigers*, 46–57; Lau, *Paper Families*, 16–17.

34. Lee, *At America's Gates*, 103–105; McClain and Wu McClain, "The Chinese Contribution," 20–21; Salyer, *Laws Harsh as Tigers*, 99.

35. Salyer, *Laws Harsh as Tigers*, 59 and 99–100; Lee, *At America's Gates*, 105–108; Lau, *Paper Families*, 86–87.

36. Salyer, *Laws Harsh as Tigers*, 102–106.

37. Lee, *At America's Gates*, 46–48 and 125; Salyer, *Laws Harsh as Tigers*, 111–114.

38. Lee, *At America's Gates,* 49–57 and 68; Salyer, *Laws Harsh as Tigers*, 38.

39. Guanhua Wang, *In Search of Justice: The 1905–1906 Chinese Anti-American Boycott* (Cambridge, MA, and London: Harvard University Press, 2001), 1–2 and 193–195; Shih-sham Ts'ai, "Reaction to Exclusion: The Boycott of 1905 and Chinese National Awakening," *Historian* 29, no. 1 (1976): 95–110; Sin-Kiong Wong, "Die for the Boycott and Nation: Martyrdom and the 1905 Anti-American Movement in China," *Modern Asian Studies* 35, no. 3 (2001): 565–567, 572–573, and 585; Delber L. McKee, "The Chinese Boycott of 1905–1906 Reconsidered: The Role of Chinese Americans," *Pacific Historical Review* 55, no. 2 (1986): 171–178 and 183–184; Mira Wilkins, "The Impact of American Multinational Enterprise on American-Chinese Economic Relations, 1786–1949," in *America's China Trade in Historical Perspective*, eds. Ernest R. May and John F. Fairbank (Cambridge, MA: Harvard University Press, 1986), 264–271; James J. Lorence, "Organized Business and the Myth of the China Market: The American Asiatic Association, 1898–1937," *Transactions of the American Philosophical Society* 71, no. 4 (1981): 49–55; Sherman Cochran, "Commercial Penetration and Economic Imperialism in China: An American Cigarette Company's Entrance into the Market," in *America's China Trade in Historical Perspective*, eds. Ernest R. May and John F. Fairbank (Cambridge, MA: Harvard University Press, 1986), 190–196.

40. McKee, "The Chinese Boycott," 178–189; *Atlanta Constitution,* June 15, 1905; Ralph Eldin Minger, *William Howard Taft and United States Foreign Policy: The Apprenticeship Years 1900–1908* (Urbana, Chicago, and London: University of Illinois Press, 1975, 166; Lee, *At America's Gates*, 125–126.

41. Lee, *At America's Gates*, 124–128; Salyer, *Laws Harsh as Tigers*, 63.

42. Lee, *At America's Gates*, 68, 81–85, and 89–91.

43. Lee, *At America's Gates*, 131–141; Salyer, *Laws Harsh as Tigers*, 70.

44. Salyer, *Laws Harsh as Tigers*, 23–26 and 121–135; Daniels, *Not Like Us*, 39–41, and 60–63; Lee, *At America's Gates*, 21 and 30–38.
45. Salyer, *Laws Harsh as Tigers*, 140–149.
46. Lee, *At America's Gates*, 148, 151–161, and 179; Lau, *Paper Families*, 33.
47. Lee, *At America's Gates*, 161–164.
48. Ibid., 169–172.
49. Daniels, *Not Like Us*, 16–17; Lau, *Paper Families*, 37.
50. Lau, *Paper Families*, 6.
51. Lee, *At America's Gates*, 100.
52. Lau, *Paper Families*, 21.
53. Mae M. Ngai, "The Architecture of Race in American Immigration Law: A Reexamination of the Immigration Act of 1924," *Journal of American History* 86, no. 1 (1999): 67–92; Takaki, *Strangers from a Different Shore*, 209–212.
54. See U.S. Department of State, Office of the Historian, "Milestones: 1921–1936, The Immigration Act of 1924 (The Johnson-Reed Act)," http://history.state.gov/milestones/1921-1936/ImmigrationAct.
55. Lee, *At America's Gates*, 10.

Bibliography

Aarim-Heriot, Najia. *Chinese Immigrants, African Americans, and Racial Anxiety in the United States, 1848–1882*. Urbana: University of Illinois Press, 2003.

Balibar, Etienne. "Racism and Nationalism." In *Race, Nation, Class: Ambiguous Identities*, edited by Etienne Balibar and Immanuel Wallerstein, 37–67. London and New York: Verso, 1991.

Black, Isabella. "American Labour and Chinese Immigration." *Past and Present* 25 (1963): 59–76.

Chan, Sucheng. *Asian Americans: An Interpretive History*. Boston: Twayne, 1991.

Cochran, Sherman. "Commercial Penetration and Economic Imperialism in China: An American Cigarette Company's Entrance into the Market." In *America's China Trade in Historical Perspective*, edited by Ernest R. May and John F. Fairbank, 151–203. Cambridge, MA: Harvard University Press, 1986.

Daniels, Roger. *Asian America: Chinese and Japanese in the United States since 1850*. Seattle and London: University of Washington Press, 1995.

Daniels, Roger. *Not Like Us: Immigrants and Minorities in America, 1890–1924*. Chicago: Ivan R. Dee, 1997.

Fritz, Christian G. "Due Process, Treaty Rights, and Chinese Exclusion, 1882–1891." In *Entry Denied: Exclusion and the Chinese Community in America, 1882–1943*, edited by Sucheng Chan, 25–56. Philadelphia: Temple University Press, 1991.

Guterl, Matthew Pratt. "The New Race Consciousness: Race, Nation, and Empire in American Culture, 1910–1925." *Journal of World History* 10, no. 2 (1999): 307–352.

Hoobler, Dorothy, and Thomas Hoobler. *The Chinese American Family Album*. New York: Oxford University Press, 1994.

Lau, Estelle T. *Paper Families: Identity, Immigration Administration, and Chinese Exclusion.* Durham, NC, and London: Duke University Press, 2006.

Lee, Erika. *At America's Gates: Chinese Immigration during the Exclusion Era, 1882–1943.* Chapel Hill and London: University of North Carolina Press, 2003.

Lee, Robert G. *Orientals: Asian Americans in Popular Culture.* Philadelphia: Temple University Press, 1999.

Li, David Leiwei. *Imagining the Nation: Asian American Literature and Cultural Consent.* Stanford, CA: Stanford University Press, 1998.

Lorence, James J. "Organized Business and the Myth of the China Market: The American Asiatic Association, 1898–1937." *Transactions of the American Philosophical Society* 71, no. 4 (1981): 1–112.

Matsukawa, Yuko. "Representing the Oriental in Nineteenth-Century Trade Cards." In *Re/collecting Early Asian America: Essays in Cultural History*, edited by Josephine Lee, Imogene L. Lim, and Yuko Matsukawa, 200–217. Philadelphia: Temple University Press, 2002.

McClain, Charles J., and Laurene Wu McClain. "The Chinese Contribution to the Development of American Law." In *Entry Denied: Exclusion and the Chinese Community in America, 1882–1943*, edited by Sucheng Chan, 3–24. Philadelphia: Temple University Press, 1991.

McCunn, Ruthanne Lum. *Chinese American Portraits: Personal Histories 1828–1988.* San Francisco: Chronicle Books, 1998.

McKee, Delber L. "The Chinese Boycott of 1905–1906 Reconsidered: The Role of Chinese Americans." *Pacific Historical Review* 55, no. 2 (1986): 165–191.

Miller, Stuart Creighton. *The Unwelcome Immigrant: The American Image of the Chinese, 1785–1882.* Berkeley and Los Angeles: University of California Press, 1969.

Minger, Ralph Eldin. *William Howard Taft and United States Foreign Policy: The Apprenticeship Years 1900–1908.* Urbana, Chicago, and London: University of Illinois Press, 1975.

Moon, Krystyn R. *Yellowface: Creating the Chinese in American Popular Music and Performance, 1850s–1920s.* New Brunswick, NJ, and London: Rutgers University Press, 2005.

Ngai, Mae M. "The Architecture of Race in American Immigration Law: A Reexamination of the Immigration Act of 1924." *Journal of American History* 86, no. 1 (1999): 67–92.

Okihiro, Gary Y. *The Columbia Guide to Asian American History.* New York: Columbia University Press, 2001.

Salyer, Lucy E. *Laws Harsh as Tigers: Chinese Immigrants and the Shaping of Modern Immigration Law.* Chapel Hill: University of North Carolina Press, 1995.

Takaki, Ronald. *Strangers from a Different Shore: A History of Asian Americans.* Boston, Toronto, and London: Little, Brown, 1989.

Tchen, John Kuo Wei. *New York before Chinatown: Orientalism and the Shaping of American Culture 1776–1882.* Baltimore and London: Johns Hopkins University Press, 2001.

Ts'ai, Shih-sham. "Reaction to Exclusion: The Boycott of 1905 and Chinese National Awakening." *Historian* 29, no. 1 (1976): 95–110.

U.S. Bureau of Immigration. *Laws, Treaty, and Regulations Relating to the Exclusion of Chinese from the United States.* Washington, DC: U.S. Government Printing Office, 1903.

U.S. Census Bureau, Population Division. *Table 4: Region and Country or Area of Birth of the Foreign-Born Population, With Geographic Detail Shown in Decennial Census Publications of 1930 or Earlier: 1850 to 1930 and 1960 to 1990.* Washington, DC: U.S. Census Bureau, 2008. http://www.census.gov/population/www/documentation/twps0029/tab04.html.

U.S. Department of Commerce, Bureau of the Census. *Historical Statistics of the United States: Colonial Times to 1970.* Part 1. White Plains, NY: Kraus, 1989.

Wang, Guanhua. *In Search of Justice: The 1905–1906 Chinese Anti-American Boycott.* Cambridge, MA, and London: Harvard University Press, 2001.

Wilkins, Mira. "The Impact of American Multinational Enterprise on American-Chinese Economic Relations, 1786–1949." In *America's China Trade in Historical Perspective*, edited by Ernest R. May and John F. Fairbank, 259–292. Cambridge, MA: Harvard University Press, 1986.

Wong, K. Scott. *Americans First: Chinese Americans and the Second World War.* Cambridge, MA, and London: Harvard University Press, 2005.

Wong, Sin-Kiong Wong. "Die for the Boycott and Nation: Martyrdom and the 1905 Anti-American Movement in China." *Modern Asian Studies* 35, no. 3 (2001): 565–588.

An Immigration Timeline of the United States

The three periods with the largest immigrant influx are indicated in **bold**.

1502   Africans are brought as slaves to the island of Hispaniola (present-day Dominican Republic and Haiti) by the Spanish, with 10 million enslaved Africans to follow and arrive on U.S. shores.

1619   First Africans arrive at Jamestown, Virginia, as indentured servants.

1700–1776   First big wave of immigration: Europeans, mostly English, arrive in large numbers.

1790   U.S. population reaches almost 4 million.

1790   As of March 26, the federal government requires two years of residency for naturalization, per Article 1, Section 8 of the U.S. Constitution.

1795   The Naturalization Act of 1795 raises the period required for citizenship from two years to five.

1798   Alien Enemy Act, commonly known as the Alien and Sedition Acts is comprised of four laws: the Naturalization Act, the Alien Act, the Alien Enemies Act, and the Sedition Act. The bar was raised higher for residency status from 5 to 14 years, and the Alien Act gave the president the power to arrest and deport aliens considered dangerous. The aim was mainly to keep out Irish immigrants and French refugees who had previously been critical of the Adams administration. The Alien Enemies Act permitted the arrest and deportation of subjects of foreign powers at war with the United States. The Sedition Act made it a criminal offense to print or publish false, malicious, or scandalous statements directed against the U.S. government, the president, or Congress; to foster opposition to the lawful acts of Congress; or to aid a foreign power in plotting against the United States.

1800	The Alien Act, one of the four Alien and Sedition Acts, expires.
1802	The Naturalization Act, one of the four Alien and Sedition Acts, is repealed.
1808	Congress makes it illegal to bring slaves to the United States.
1816	The American Colonization Society forms, assisting in the repatriation of free African Americans to a Liberian colony on the west coast of Africa.
1819	On March 2, the first federal law passes requiring ports of entry to count incoming travelers.
1820–1870	**Second big wave of immigration: About 7.5 million arrive, mainly from northern and western Europe (especially Great Britain, Ireland, and western Germany).**
1840–1845	Wave of Irish immigrants arrives, escaping famine because of potato crop failure. The famine kills nearly 1 million and prompts almost 500,000 to immigrate to the United States over the next five years.
1848	Discovery of gold results in Chinese and Latin American immigrants coming to the West Coast. Some 4,000 Germans flee to the United States due to civil unrest in Central Europe.
1855	On March 3, Congress streamlines the counting of immigrants by separating them into temporary and permanent resident aliens.
1860	Poland's religious and economic conditions prompt immigration of approximately 2 million Poles by 1914.
1862	The American Homestead Act allows any man over the age of 21 and the head of a family to claim up to 160 acres of land and improve it within five years or to purchase the land at a small fee. Scandinavian farmers take advantage of the opportunity and help populate Minnesota and Wisconsin. Congress also passes the first law restricting immigration by Chinese immigrants by forbidding American ships to transport them.
1864	Congress legalizes the importation of contract laborers. Thousands of Navajo Indians endure the "Long Walk," a 300-mile forced march from a Southwest Indian territory to Fort Sumner, New Mexico.
1868	Japanese laborers arrive in Hawaii to work in sugar cane fields. Additionally, the Fourteenth Amendment to the U.S. Constitution takes effect, virtually assuring that all persons born within U.S. borders, regardless of parentage, will be considered American citizens.

1870s   Chinese immigrants increase competition for jobs and their presence lowers wages among unskilled laborers. The Naturalization Act of 1870, passed in post-Emancipation United States, naturalizes whites and all those of African descent, but continues to exclude Asians and Native Americans from citizenship. Moreover, given the harsh treatment that former slaves continue to endure, the act becomes merely a symbolic gesture with no real teeth.

1875   In *Henderson v. Mayor of New York*, the Supreme Court decides that immigrants crossing state lines are a form of interstate commerce and so subject to federal, not merely state, regulation. Page Act of 1875 passes and becomes the first legislative act to exclude particular groups of people ("undesirables") from entering the United States.

1876   California Senate committee investigates the "social, moral, and political effect of Chinese immigration."

1877   United States Congress investigates the criminal influence of Chinese immigrants.

1879   Advocates of immigration restriction succeed in passing legislation in Congress to limit the number of Chinese arriving to 15 per ship or vessel. President Rutherford B. Hayes vetoes the legislation because it violates a treaty with China, but he renegotiates with the Chinese to limit immigration to the United States.

1880   Italy's troubled economy, crop failures, and political climate begin the start of mass immigration, with nearly 4 million Italian immigrants arriving in the United States.

1881–1920   Third big wave of immigration: Nearly 23.5 million arrive, mainly from Southern and Eastern Europe (especially Austro-Hungary, Italy, and Russia).

1882   On May 8, the Chinese Exclusion Act is signed by President Chester Arthur to prevent Chinese workers from immigrating to the United States. This is the first act in U.S. history to place broad immigration restrictions on a particular nationality. Russia's May Laws severely restrict the ability of Jewish citizens to live and work in Russia. The country's instability prompts more than 3 million Russians to immigrate to the United States over three decades. As of August 3, with the passage of the Immigrant Act, immigrants likely to become public charges could become subject to exclusion; the act bars convicts, "lunatics," "idiots," and others and established a head tax (50 cents) on immigrants.

1885   With passage of the Alien Contract Labor Act, Congress bans the admission of contract laborers.

1886   Statue of Liberty is unveiled.

1888   Extension of Chinese Exclusion Act by the Scott Act, which makes reentry to the United States after a visit to China impossible, even for those with extensive legal residency.

1891   On March 3, the Immigration Act creates a federal immigration bureaucracy, placing immigration affairs in the hands of the Treasury Department; admission of people with communicable diseases ends, as well as those with criminal backgrounds and polygamists; deportation of illegal aliens begins.

1892   Ellis Island opens. The Geary Act of 1892 continues the country's Chinese exclusionary policies. In the case of *Holy Trinity Church v. United States*, the Supreme Court judged that the 1885 act on foreign labor did not apply to a Christian English preacher.

1900   The U.S. population reaches 76 million. Congress establishes a civil government in Puerto Rico, and the Jones Act grants U.S. citizenship to island inhabitants. U.S. citizens can travel freely between the mainland and the island without a passport.

1902   The Geary Act of 1892 is expanded to exclude Chinese from immigrating to Hawaii and the Philippines. Congress later extended the exclusionary policy indefinitely.

1903   On March 3, a law is passed that excludes immigrants who hold certain political opinions, including anarchism and other antidemocratic ideologies.

1906   The Naturalization Act of 1906 standardizes naturalization procedures, makes some knowledge of English a requirement for citizenship, and establishes the Bureau of Immigration and Naturalization.

1907   On February 20, restrictions are placed on the numbers of immigrants from Japan; the president is given powers to refuse admittance of so-called undesirables, who could mean those who would be detrimental to labor. Additionally, those with mental disabilities, tuberculosis, unaccompanied minors, those formerly convicted of moral crimes, and women coming or being brought to the United States for prostitution are all excluded. This last regulation was reinforced by the Mann Act of June 25, 1910. In 1907, for the first time, 1 million immigrants pass through Ellis Island in one year. The United States and Japan form a "Gentleman's Agreement" in which

Japan ends issuance of passports to laborers and the United States agrees not to prohibit Japanese immigration. The Dillingham Commission is created.

1911   The Dillingham Commission identifies Mexican laborers as the best solution to the Southwest labor shortage. Mexicans are exempted from immigrant head taxes set in 1903 and 1907.

1913   California's Alien Land Law rules that aliens "ineligible to citizenship" are ineligible to own agricultural property.

1917   People who are illiterate are excluded from immigrating to the United States. End of the era of restriction of certain groups and beginning of the era of quotas, though the Immigration Act of 1917 (Barred Zone Act) restricted immigration from Asia by creating an Asiatic Barred Zone. The United States enters World War I, and anti-German sentiment swells. The names of schools, foods, streets, towns, and even some families, are changed to sound less Germanic.

1921   May 19 passage of the Alien Land Act or the Johnson Quota Act places limitations on the number of entrants to the United States based upon the percentage of the U.S. population of individuals from a particular country. The National Quota Law limits immigration of each nationality to 3 percent of the number of foreign born of that nationality living in the United States in 1910.

1922   The Supreme Court rules in *Ozawa v. United States* that first-generation Japanese immigrants are ineligible for citizenship and cannot apply for naturalization. The Cable Act of 1922 passes and remains in force until 1936. Sometimes called the Married Women's Independent Nationalities Act, it provided citizenship rights to women who chose to marry an alien "eligible for naturalization." However, this excluded Asian males, so that any woman who married one automatically forfeited her citizenship. Additionally, Congress extended quotas put in place in 1921 until 1924.

1924   Congress limits number of immigrants by nationality, including Southern and Eastern Europe. Quotas are based upon the numbers represented in the 1890 census. Immigration Act of 1924 (Johnson-Reed Act) establishes fixed quotas of national origin of those of Eastern Europe and eliminates Far East immigration. The act sets annual quotas for each nationality at 2 percent of the number of persons of that nationality in the United States as determined by the 1890 census. The National Origins Formula is established with the Immigration Act of 1924. Total annual immigration is capped at

150,000. Immigrants fit into two categories: those from quota nations and those from nonquota nations. Immigrant visas from quota nations are restricted to the same ratio of residents from the country of origin out of 150,000 as the ratio of foreign-born nationals in the United States. The percentage out of 150,000 is the relative number of visas a particular nation receives. Nonquota nations, notably those contiguous to the United States, only have to prove an immigrant's residence in that country of origin for at least two years prior to emigration to the United States. Laborers from Asiatic nations are excluded, but exceptions exist for professionals, clergy, and students to obtain visas. The U.S. Supreme Court decides the case of *Chung Fook v. White* and rules that a man does not have the automatic right to bring his wife to the United States if he married her after entering the United States. The ruling hinges on an exception for spouses that is not given explicit mention in the law.

1927   A third quota is put in place. Each country is allowed to send a percentage of up to 150,000 total immigrants to the United States every year. The percentage is based upon the nationalities reported in the 1920 census. Each nation's quota corresponds to the collective number of individuals from that nation currently residing in the United States.

1929   Congress makes annual immigration quotas permanent. National Quota Law apportions annual quotas of 1924 for each country according to each nationality's percentage of the 1920 census.

1934   The Tydings-McDuffie Act (Philippine Independence Act) is issued on March 24 launching a 10-year transition period leading toward Philippine sovereignty. It declared all Filipinos living in the United States to be aliens and limited immigration quotas to 50 Filipinos each year.

1940   Alien Registration Act; Smith Act of 1940. Immigration and Naturalization Service is transferred from the Labor Department to the Department of Justice as a national security measure.

1942   Congress allows for importation of agricultural workers from within North, Central, and South America. Beginning in August, the Bracero Program allows Mexican laborers to work in the United States and continues through 1964.

1943   The Magnuson Act of December 17, 1943, repeals the Chinese Exclusion Act of 1882; establishes quotas for Chinese immigrants; and makes them eligible for U.S. citizenship.

1945   Puerto Ricans begin to arrive in large numbers. The War Bride Act and the G.I. Fiancées Act allow immigration of foreign-born wives, fiancé(e)s, husbands, and children of U.S. armed forces personnel. The United States Senate passes the United Nations Participation Act and becomes an early member of that body.

1946   Luce-Celler Act permits Indian Americans and Filipino Americans to naturalize.

1948   The United States admits persons fleeing persecution in their native lands, allowing 205,000 refugees to enter within two years, mostly from Europe.

1950   Internal Security Act expands grounds for both exclusion and deportation; establishes alien registry. Irrespective of race, the Alien Spouses and Children Act admits foreign-born spouses and unmarried children of members of the U.S. armed forces.

1952   The McCarran-Walter Immigration and Nationality Act reaffirms national origins quota system and adds new grounds for exclusion based on political activities (such as having communist sympathies), ideology, and sexual preference. The Immigration and Nationality Act allows individuals of all races to be eligible for naturalization. The act also reaffirms national origins quota system, limits immigration from the Eastern Hemisphere while leaving the Western Hemisphere unrestricted, establishes preferences for skilled workers and relatives of U.S. citizens and permanent resident aliens, and tightens security and screening standards and procedures.

1953   In the Refugee Relief Act, Congress amends the 1948 refugee policy to allow for the admission of 214,000 more European refugees.

1954   Operation Wetback begins as a project of the Immigration and Naturalization Service to remove about 1.2 million illegal immigrants from the southwestern United States, with a focus on Mexican nationals. Since the 1920s, the term *wetback* has been a slur referring to Mexicans in general. Ellis Island closes, marking an end to mass immigration.

1957   Refugee-Escapee Act grants special status for refugees fleeing communist regimes.

1959   Fidel Castro's Cuban revolution prompts mass exodus of more than 200,000 people within three years.

1960   The Cuban Refugee Program handles an influx of immigrants to Miami, with 300,000 immigrants relocated across the United States during the next two decades.

1963   Refugee Assistance Act extends cash, medical, and educational support to refugees.

1964   The Bracero Reauthorization terminates the Bracero Program and establishes short-term guest worker visas primarily for seasonal labor from Mexico.

1965   Hart-Celler Act dismantles origins quotas; begins seven-category preference system with an emphasis on family reunification. Senator Edward M. Kennedy sponsors legislation to ease immigration restrictions by ending quotas (number limit) based on nationality. Immigration from Asia and West Indies increases.

1968   Visas begin to be issued to a limit of 120,000 immigrants annually from the Western Hemisphere on a first-come, first-served basis.

1975   Indochina Refugee Act begins the Indochinese resettlement program.

1976   The Immigration and Nationality Act Amendments set per-country limits at 20,000 for both the Eastern and Western Hemispheres.

1977   The Indochinese Refugee Act admits 174,988 refugees from Indochina.

1978   The Immigration and Nationality Act Amendments establish a worldwide ceiling of 290,000 on annual immigrant admissions.

1980   Refugee Act adopts the United Nations definition of a refugee (those fleeing from persecution because of their race, religion, nationality, or political opinions) and expands annual refugee admissions, extending this status, for instance, to those who hand over any U.S. prisoner of war or U.S. citizen considered missing in action. It excludes those refugee admissions who have been convicted of murder or fomenting political hostilities toward the United States.

1986   Immigration Reform and Control Act (IRCA) forbids hiring of illegal immigrants; helps them become legal immigrants; grants amnesty/permanent residence to 3 million undocumented aliens; imposes watered-down employer sanctions; establishes immigrant antidiscrimination agency in Justice Department; initiates special agricultural worker program.

1990   The Immigration Act increases the annual immigration cap to 700,000 for the next three years and 675,000 thereafter; reaffirms family reunification preferences but adds employment-based and diversity visas.

1992   Chinese Student Protection Act, sponsored by U.S. Representative Nancy Pelosi, granted permanent residency status to Chinese nationals living in the United States and extended an amnesty to all potential Chinese deportees.

1996   Personal Responsibility Act limits immigrant access of noncitizens to public welfare benefits. The Illegal Immigration Reform and Individual Responsibility Act (a different act) strengthens border enforcement and employer sanctions; expedites the deportation process, in part through new detention regulations; and establishes exceptions for noncitizen access to public benefits. The Anti-Terrorism and Effective Death Penalty Act rounded out this legislative troika by ordering the disclosure to investigative officials of confidential information from immigrant application files.

2000   On October 30, the Child Citizenship Act was made law. It amended the Immigration and Nationality Act to permit foreign-born children—including adopted children—to acquire citizenship automatically under certain conditions. It took effect on February 27, 2001.

2002   Congress begins discussions leading to the adoption of the Patriot Act, which seeks to restrict immigration and reduce the risk of allowing terrorists entrance to the United States.

2003   The Department of Homeland Security replaces the Immigration and Naturalization Service.

2005   The REAL ID Act creates more restrictions on political asylum, curtails the use of habeas corpus writs of relief for immigrants, increases immigration enforcement mechanisms, alters judicial review, and imposes federal restrictions on the issuance of state driver's licenses to immigrants and others.

2006   Congress begins a yearly process of large-scale funding for the building and future enhancements of border security, including the erection of a fence along the Mexican border.

2007   Congress pushes for immigration reform and focuses on integrating new Americans. According to the Department of Homeland Security, the number of illegal immigrants dwelling within the United States was nearly 12 million—up from 8.5 million in 2000.

2008   In January it is reported that there is a small decline in the number of unauthorized immigrants living in the United States.

2010   In April a controversial measure was signed into law by Arizona Governor Jan Brewer making it a state crime to be an unauthorized immigrant in the United States and granting broad power to law enforcement to stop and question people on the suspicion that they are present in Arizona illegally. In July Federal Judge Susan Bolton grants an Obama administration request for a temporary stay against the Arizona law and blocks a provision in the law that requested immigrants of whatever kind to have documentation on their person testifying to their status. By September a large dip in the rates of unauthorized immigration are in evidence, owing largely to the economic downturn.

2011   On May 26 the U.S. Supreme Court decided in favor of an Arizona law that would sanction employers hiring illegal immigrants, paving the way for other states to enact similar legislation. Appellants had argued that the Immigration and Reform Control Act of 1986 had made it impermissible for states to impose sanctions on those businesses that do hire illegal immigrants, but the Court's decision abrogates this. Within the legislative and executive branches of government, comprehensive immigration reform remains largely a dead letter and despite the complaints of states in the southern tier, churches, and advocacy groups, the plight of immigrants remains off the wider public's radar.

Selected Bibliography

Abraham, M. *Speaking the Unspeakable: Marital Violence among South Asian Immigrants in the United States*. New Brunswick, NJ: Rutgers University Press, 2000.

Alba, Richard, and Victor Nee. *Remaking the American Mainstream: Assimilation and Contemporary Immigration*. Cambridge, MA: Harvard University Press, 2005.

Alden, Edward. *The Closing of the American Border: Terrorism, Immigration, and Security since 9/11*. New York: Harper Collins, 2008.

Aleinikoff, T., & D. Klusmeyer, eds. *From Migrants to Citizens: Membership in a Changing World*. Washington, DC: Brookings Institution Press, 2000.

Andreas, Peter. *Border Games: Policing the U.S.-Mexico Divide*. Ithaca, NY: Cornell University Press, 2000.

Bailyn, Bernard. *Voyagers to the West: Emigration from Britain to America on the Eve of the Revolution*. New York: Knopf, 1986.

Balin, Bryan. *State Immigration Legislation and Immigrant Flows: An Analysis*. Baltimore: Johns Hopkins University Press, 2008.

Bammer, A., ed. *Displacements: Cultural Identities in Question*. Bloomington: Indiana University Press, 1994.

Barkin, E., and M. Shelton, eds. *Borders, Exiles, Diasporas*. Stanford, CA: Stanford University Press, 1998.

Basch, L., N. Schiller, and C. Blanc. *Nations Unbound: Transnationalism Projects, Postcolonial Predicaments, and Deterritorialized Nation-States*. London: Gordon and Breach Science Publishers, 1994.

Bauböck, R., and J. Rundell, eds. *Blurred Boundaries: Migration, Ethnicity, Citizenship*. Burlington, VT: Ashgate, 1998.

Bauder, Harald. *Labor Movement: How Migration Regulates Labor Markets*. New York: Oxford University Press, 2006.

Bayor, Ronald. *Neighbors in Conflict: The Irish, Germans, Jews, and Italians of New York City, 1929–1941*. Baltimore: Johns Hopkins University Press, 1996.

Bean, F., R. de la Garza, B. Roberts, and S. Weintraub, eds. *At the Crossroads: Mexico and U.S. Immigration Policy*. Lanham, MD: Rowman & Littlefield, 1997.

Bean, Frank, Barry Edmonston, and Jeffrey Passel, eds. *Undocumented Migration to the United States: IRCA and the Experience of the 1980s.* Washington, DC: Urban Institute; Santa Monica, CA: RAND Corporation, 1990.

Bender, B., and M. Winer, eds. *Contested Landscapes: Movement, Exile, and Place.* Oxford, UK: Berg, 2001.

Bodnar, John. *The Transplanted: A History of Immigrants in Urban America.* Bloomington: Indiana University Press, 1987.

Bonus, R. *Locating Filipino Americans: Ethnicity and the Cultural Politics of Space.* Philadelphia: Temple University Press. 2000.

Briggs, V. *Immigration and American Unionism.* Ithaca, NY: Cornell University Press, 2001.

Buff, R. *Immigration and the Political Economy of Home: West Indian Brooklyn and American Indian Minneapolis, 1945–1992.* Berkeley: University of California Press, 2001.

Burns, J., E. Skerrett, and J. White, eds. *Keeping Faith: European and Asian Catholic Immigrants.* Maryknoll, NY: Orbis Books, 2000.

Calavita, Kitty. *U.S. Immigration Law and the Control of Labor: 1820–1924.* London: Academic Press, 1984.

Calavita, Kitty. *Inside the State: The Bracero Program, Immigration, and the I.N.S.* New York: Routledge, 1992.

Cannato, Vincent J. *American Passage: The History of Ellis Island.* New York: Harper Collins, 2009.

Canter, L., M. Siegel, and R. Boswell, *U.S. Immigration Made Easy.* Berkeley, CA: Nolo. com, 2000.

Castles, S., and A. Davidson, A. Citizenship and Migration: Globalization and the Politics of Belonging. New York: Routledge, 2000.

Castles, S., and M. Miller. *The Age of Migration: International Population Movements in the Modern World.* New York: Guilford Press, 1998.

Chan, S. *Asian Californians.* San Francisco: MTL/Boyd & Fraser, 1991.

Chavez, L. *Shadowed Lives: Undocumented Immigrants in American Society.* Fort Worth, TX: Harcourt Brace College Publishers, 1998.

Chen, Y. *Chinese San Francisco 1850–1943: A Trans-pacific Community.* Stanford, CA: Stanford University Press, 2000.

Chin, K. *Smuggled Chinese: Clandestine Immigration to the United States.* Philadelphia: Temple University Press, 1999.

Clark, W. *The California Cauldron: Immigration and the Fortunes of Local Communities.* New York: Guilford Press, 1998.

Cordero-Guzman, H., R. Smith, and R. Grosfoguel, eds. *Migration, Transnationalization, and Race in a Changing New York.* Philadelphia: Temple University Press, 2001.

Cornelius, Wayne A. "Reforming the Management of Migration Flows from Latin America to the United States." Working Paper 170. San Diego: Center for Comparative Immigration Studies, University of San Diego, and Washington, DC, Brookings Institution, 2008.

Cornelius, Wayne A., David Fitzgerald, and Pedro Lewin, eds. *Mexican Migration and the US Economic Crisis: A Transnational Perspective.* San Diego: Center for Comparative Immigration, 2010.

Daniels, Roger. *American Immigration: A Student Companion*. New York: Oxford University Press, 2001.

Daniels, Roger. *Coming to America: A History of Immigration and Ethnicity in American Life*, 2nd ed. New York: Harper Perennial, 2002.

Daniels, Roger. *Guarding the Golden Door: American Immigration Policy and Immigrants since 1882*. New York: Hill and Wang, 2004.

Daniels, Roger. *Not Like Us: Immigrants and Minorities in America, 1890–1924*. Lanham, MD: Ivan R. Dee, 1998.

Daniels, Roger, and Otis L. Graham. *Debating American Immigration, 1882–Present*. Lanham, MD: Rowan & Littlefield, 2001.

Davis, M. *Magical Urbanism: Latinos Reinvent the US City*. London: Verso, 2000.

DeLaet, Debra L. *U.S. Immigration Policy in an Age of Rights*. Westport, CT: Praeger, 2001.

De La Torre, Miguel A. *Trails of Hope and Terror: Testimonies on Immigration*. Maryknoll, NY: Orbis Books, 2009.

Diner, Hasia R. "History and the Study of Immigration," in *Migration Theory: Talking Across Disciplines*, eds. Caroline B. Brettell and James F. Hollifield, eds., 27–42. New York: Routledge, 2000.

Diner, Hasia R., Alan Kraut, and Elliott Barkan, eds. *From Arrival to Incorporation: Migrants to the U.S. in a Global Era*. New York: New York University Press, 2007.

Dinnerstein, Leonard, Roger L. Nichols, and David M. Reimers. *Natives and Strangers: A History of Ethnic Americans*, 5th ed. New York: Oxford University Press, 2009.

DiSipio, Louis, and Rudolfo O. de la Garza. *Making Americans, Remaking America: Immigration and Immigrant Policy*. Boulder, CO: Westview Press, 1996.

Do, H. *The Vietnamese Americans*. Westport, CT: Greenwood Press, 1999.

Dolan, Jay P., and Allan Figueroa Deck, eds. *Hispanic Catholic Culture in the U.S.: Issues and Concerns*. Notre Dame, IN, and London: University of Notre Dame Press, 1997.

Dreby, Joana. *Divided by Borders: Mexican Migrants and Their Children*. Berkeley: University of California Press, 2010.

Ebaugh, H., and J. Chafetz. *Religion and the New Immigrants: Continuities and Adaptations in Immigrant Congregations*. Walnut Creek, CA: AltaMira Press, 2000.

Eck, D. *A New Religious America: How a "Christian Country" Has Become the World's Most Religiously Diverse Nation*. San Francisco: Harper Collins, 2001.

Esbenshade, Jill. *Division and Dislocation: Regulating Immigration through Local Housing Ordinances*. Washington, DC: Immigration Policy Center, American Immigration Law Foundation, Summer 2007.

Espin, O. *Women Crossing Boundaries: A Psychology of Immigration and Transformations of Sexuality*. New York: Routledge, 1999.

Espiritu, Y. *Filipino American Lives*. Philadelphia: Temple University Press, 1995.

Ewen, Elizabeth. *Immigrant Women in the Land of Dollars: Life and Culture on the Lower East Side 1890–1925*. New York: Monthly Review Press, 1985.

Ewing, Walter A. *Border Insecurity: U.S. Border-Enforcement Policies and National Security*. Washington, DC: Immigration Policy Center, American Immigration Law Foundation, Spring 2006.

Fitzgerald, D. *Negotiating Extra-territorial Citizenship: Mexican Migration and the Transnational Politics of Community*. San Diego: Center for Comparative Immigration Studies at the University of California, 2000.

Foley, Michael W., and Dean Hoge. *Religion and the New Immigrants: How Faith Communities Form Our Newest Citizens*. New York: Oxford University Press, 2007.

Fox, C. *The Fence and the River: Culture and Politics at the U.S.-Mexican Border*. Minneapolis: University of Minnesota Press, 1999.

Gardner, Martha. *The Qualities of a Citizen: Women, Immigration, and Citizenship, 1870–1965*. Princeton, NJ: Princeton University Press, 2005.

Goldin, L., ed. *Identities on the Move: Transnational Processes in North America and the Caribbean Basin*. Albany, NY: Institute for Mesoamerican Studies, and Austin, TX: University of Texas Press, 1999.

Gonzalez, J. *Harvest of Empire: A History of Latinos in America*. New York: Viking, 2000.

Gordon, E. *Disparate Diasporas: Identity and Politics in an African-Nicaraguan Community*. Austin: University of Texas Press, 1998.

Goulbourne, Harry, John Solomos, Tracey Reynolds, and Elisabetta Zontoni. *Transnational Families: Ethnicities, Identities and Social Capital*. New York: Routledge, 2010.

Gracia, J., and P. De Greiff, eds. *Hispanics/Latinos in the United States: Ethnicity, Race, and Rights*. New York: Routledge, 2000.

Guterl, Matthew Pratt. *The Color of Race in America, 1900–1940*. Cambridge, MA: Harvard University Press, 2001.

Gutierrez, D. *Walls and Mirrors: Mexican Americans, Mexican Immigrants, and the Politics of Ethnicity*. Berkeley: University of California Press, 1995.

Gutierrez, D. *Between Two Worlds: Mexican Immigrants in the United States*. Wilmington, DE: SR Books, 1996.

Hahn, C. *Becoming Political: Comparative Perspectives on Citizenship Education*. New York: State University of New York Press, 1998.

Haines, Michael R., and Richard H. Steckel. *A Population History of North America*. New York: Cambridge University Press, 2000.

Handlin, Oscar. *A Pictorial History of Immigration*. New York: Crown Publishers, 1972.

Haour-Knipe, M. *Moving Families: Expatriation, Stress and Coping*. New York: Routledge, 2001.

Hart, D. *Undocumented in L.A.: An Immigrant's Story*. Wilmington, DE: Scholarly Resources, 1997.

Hart, J., ed. *Border Crossings: Mexican and Mexican-American Workers*. Wilmington, DE: Scholarly Resources, 1998.

Herman, Richard T., and Robert L. Smith. *Immigrant, Inc.: Why Immigrant Entrepreneurs Are Driving the New Economy (and How They Will Save the American Worker)*. Malden, MA: Wiley, 2009.

Heyck, D. *Barrios and Borderlands: Cultures of Latinos and Latinas in the United States*. New York and London: Routledge, 1994.

Higham, John. *Send These To Me: Patterns of American Nativism, 1860–1925*. New Brunswick, NJ: Rutgers University Press, 1988.

Hing, B. *Making and Remaking Asian America through Immigration Policy, 1850–1990.* Stanford, CA: Stanford University Press, 1993.

Hirschman, C., P. Kasinitz, and J. DeWind, eds. *The Handbook of International Migration: The American Experience.* New York: Russell Sage Foundation, 1999.

Hondagneu-Sotelo, P. *Gendered Transitions: Mexican Experiences of Immigration.* Berkeley: University of California Press, 1994.

Hondagneu-Sotelo, P. *Domestica: Immigrant Workers Cleaning and Caring in the Shadows of Affluence.* Berkeley: University of California Press, 2001.

Horton, J. *The Politics of Diversity: Immigration, Resistance, and Change in Monterey Park, California.* Philadelphia: Temple University Press, 1995.

Immigration Policy Center. *Economic Growth and Immigration: Bridging the Demographic Divide.* Washington, DC: Immigration Policy Center, American Immigration Law Foundation, November 2005.

Indra, D., ed. *Engendering Forced Migration.* New York and Oxford, UK: Berghahn Books, 1999.

Isbister, J. *The Immigration Debate: Remaking America.* Hartford, CT: Kumarian Press, 1996.

Jacobson, David. *Rights across Borders: Immigration and the Decline of Citizenship.* Baltimore: Johns Hopkins University Press, 1996.

Jacobson, Matthew Frye. *Whiteness of a Different Color: European Immigrants and the Alchemy of Race.* Cambridge, MA: Harvard University Press, 1998.

Jacobson, Matthew Frye. *Special Sorrows: The Diasporic Imagination of Irish, Polish, and Jewish Immigrants in the United States.* Berkeley: University of California Press, 2002.

Jonas, S., and S. Thomas, eds. *Immigration: A Civil Rights Issue for the Americas.* Wilmington, DE: SR Books, 1999.

Joselit, J. *Immigration and American Religion.* New York: Oxford University Press, 2001.

Joselit, Jenna Weissman. *A Parade of Faiths: Immigration and American Religion.* New York: Oxford University Press, 2007.

Kerwin, Donald, and Serena Yi-Yang Lin. *Immigrant Detention: Can ICE Meet Its Legal Imperatives and Case Management Responsibilities?* Washington, DC: Migration Policy Institute, 2009.

Kim, Hyung-Chan. *Asian Americans and the Supreme Court: A Documentary History.* New York: Greenwood Press, 1992.

Kolb, Eva. *The Evolution of New York City's Multiculturalism: Melting Pot or Salad Bowl? Immigrants in New York from the 19th Century until the End of the Gilded Age.* Norderstedt, Germany: Books on Demand, 2009.

Kraut, Alan M. *The Huddled Masses: The Immigrant in American Society, 1880–1921,* 2nd ed. Arlington Heights, IL: Harlan Davidson, 2001.

Kraut, Alan M. *Silent Travelers: Germs, Genes, and the Immigrant Menace.* Baltimore: Johns Hopkins University Press, 2007.

Laham, Nicholas. *Ronald Reagan and the Politics of Immigration Reform.* New York: Praeger, 2000.

Lamphere, L., ed. *Structuring Diversity: Ethnographic Perspectives on the New Immigration.* Chicago and London: Chicago University Press, 1992.

Lamphere, L., A. Stepick, and G. Grenier, eds. *Newcomers in the Workplace: Immigrants and the Restructuring of the U.S. Economy.* Philadelphia: Temple University Press, 1994.

Lavie, S., and T. Swedenburg, eds. *Displacement, Diaspora, and Geographies of Identity.* Durham, NC: Duke University Press, 1996.

Lee, Erika, and Judy Yung. *Angel Island.* New York: Oxford University Press, 2010.

Lee, J., I. Lim, and Y. Matsukawa,, eds. Re-collecting Early Asian America: Essays in Cultural History. Philadelphia: Temple University Press, 2002.

Legrain, Philippe. *Immigrants: Your Country Needs Them.* Boston: Little, Brown, 2007.

LeMay, Michael. *Anatomy of a Public Policy: The Reform of Contemporary American Immigration Law.* New York: Praeger, 1994.

LeMay, Michael, and Elliott Robert Barkan, eds. *U.S. Immigration and Naturalization Laws and Issues: A Documentary History.* New York: Greenwood Press, 1999.

Lopez-Garza, M., and D. Diaz, eds. *Asian and Latino Immigrants in a Restructuring Economy: The Metamorphosis of Southern California.* Stanford, CA: Stanford University Press, 2001.

Lowe, L. *Immigrant Acts.* Durham, NC: Duke University Press, 1999.

Lowell, B. Lindsay. *Foreign Temporary Workers in America: Policies That Benefit the U.S. Economy.* New York: Praeger, 1999.

Lowenthal, A., and K. Burgess, eds. *The California-Mexico Connection.* Stanford, CA: Stanford University Press, 1993.

Mahler, S. (1995). *American Dreaming: Immigrant Life on the Margins.* Princeton, NJ: Princeton University Press, 1995.

Marrus, Michael, and Aristide Zolberg. *The Unwanted: European Refugees from the First World War to the Cold War.* 2nd ed. Philadelphia: Temple University Press, 2001.

Martin, Philip L. *Trade and Migration: NAFTA and Agriculture* (Washington, DC: Institute for International Economics, October 1993.

Martin, Philip L., and Elizabeth Midgely. "Immigration to the United States," *Population Bulletin: A Publication of the Population Reference Bureau* 54, no. 2 (June 1999): 1–48.

Massey, Douglas S. *Beyond Smoke and Mirrors: Mexican Immigration in an Era of Economic Integration.* New York: Russell Sage Foundation, 2003.

Massey, Douglas S. *Beyond the Border Buildup: Towards a New Approach to Mexico-U.S. Migration.* Washington, DC: Immigration Policy Center, American Immigration Law Foundation, September 2005.

Massey, Douglas S., Joaquín Arango, Hugo Graeme, Ali Kouaouci, Adela Pellegrino, and J. Edward Taylor. *Worlds in Motion: Understanding International Migration at the End of the Millennium.* New York: Oxford University Press, 2005.

Matovina, T., and G. Poyo, eds. *Presente! U.S. Latino Catholics from Colonial Origins to the Present.* Maryknoll, NY: Orbis Books, 2000.

Meilander, Peter C. *Towards a Theory of Immigration.* New York: Palgrave/Macmillan, 2001.

Menchaca, M. *The Mexican Outsiders: A Community History of Marginalization and Discrimination in California.* Austin: University of Texas Press, 1995.

Menjivar, C. *Fragmented Ties: Salvadoran Immigrant Networks in America.* Berkeley: University of California Press, 2000.

Menjivar, Cecilia. "Immigrants, Immigration, and Sociology: Reflecting on the State of the Discipline." *Sociological Inquiry* 80, no. 1 (2010): 3–27.

Milkman, R., ed. *Organizing Immigrants: The Challenge for Unions in Contemporary California*. Ithaca, NY: ILR Press, 2000.

Molina, Natalia. *Fit to Be Citizens? Public Health and Race in Los Angeles, 1879–1940*. Berkeley: University of California Press, 2006.

Motomura, Hiroshi. *Americans in Waiting: The Lost Story of Immigration and Citizenship in the United States*. New York: Oxford University Press, 2007.

Myers, Dowell. *Immigrants and Boomers: Forging a New Social Contract for the Future of America*. New York: Russell Sage Foundation, 2007.

Nevins, J. *Operation Gatekeeper: The Rise of the "Illegal Alien" and the Making of the US-Mexico Boundary*. New York: Routledge, 2002.

Ngai, Mae. *Impossible Subjects: Illegal Aliens and the Making of Modern America*. Princeton, NJ: Princeton University Press, 2005.

Ong, A. *Flexible Citizenship: The Cultural Logics of Transnationality*. Durham, NC: Duke University Press, 1999.

Ong, P., E. Bonacich, and L. Cheng, eds. *The New Asian Immigration in Los Angeles and Global Restructuring*. Philadelphia: Temple University Press, 1994.

Orrenius, Pia M. *Beside the Golden Door: U.S. Immigration Reform in a New Era of Globalization*. Washington, DC: American Enterprise Institute, 2010.

Passel, Jeffrey S. *Estimates of the Size and Characteristics of the Undocumented Population*. Washington, DC: Pew Hispanic Center, March 2005.

Passel, Jeffrey S. *Growing Share of Immigrants Choosing Naturalization*. Washington, DC: Pew Hispanic Center, March 2007.

Passel, Jeffrey S., and Roberto Suro. *Rise, Peak and Decline: Trends in U.S. Immigration*. Washington, DC: Pew Hispanic Center, September 2005.

Pearce, Susan C. *Immigrant Women in the United States: A Demographic Portrait*. Washington, DC: Immigration Policy Center, American Immigration Law Foundation, Summer 2006.

Perea, Juan, ed. *Immigrants Out: The New Nativism and the Anti-Immigrant Impulse in the United States*. New York: New York University Press, 1996.

Portes, A., ed. *The Economic Sociology of Immigration: Essays on Networks, Ethnicity, and Entrepreneurship*. New York: Russell Sage Foundation, 1995.

Portes, A., and R. Bach. *Latin Journey: Cuban and Mexican Immigrants in the United States*. Berkeley: University of California Press, 1985.

Portes, Alejandro, Donald Light, and Patricia Fernández-Kelly. "The American Health System and Immigration: An Institutional Interpretation." Working Paper 09-02. Princeton, NJ: Center for Migration and Development, Princeton University, 2009.

Portes, A., and R. Rumbaut. *Immigrant America: A Portrait*. Berkeley: University of California Press, 1996.

Portes, Alejandro, and Ruben Rumbaut. *Immigrant America: A Portrait*, 3rd ed. Berkeley: University of California Press, 2006.

Portes, A., and R. Rumbaut. *Legacies: The Story of the Immigrant Second Generation*. Berkeley: University of California Press, 2001.

Reimers, David. *Unwelcome Strangers: American Identity and the Turn against Immigration*. New York: Columbia University Press, 1999.

Rubin, Rachel, and Jeffrey Melnick. *Immigration and Popular Culture: An Introduction*. New York: New York University Press, 2007.

Rumbaut, R., and W. Cornelius, eds. *California's Immigrant Children: Theory, Research, and Implications for Educational Policy*. San Diego: Center for U.S.-Mexican Studies, 1995.

Rumbaut, R., and A. Portes, eds. *Ethnicities: Children of Immigrants in America*. Berkeley: University of California Press, 2001.

Rumbaut, Ruben, and Walter Ewing. *The Myth of Immigrant Criminality and the Paradox of Assimilation: Incarceration Rates among Native and Foreign-Born Men*. Washington, DC: Immigration Policy Center, Spring 2007.

Salyer, Lucy. *Laws Harsh as Tigers: Chinese Immigrants and the Shaping of Modern Immigration Law*. Durham, NC: University of North Carolina Press, 1995.

San Juan, E. *From Exile to Diaspora: Versions of the Filipino Experience in the United States*. Boulder, CO: Westview Press, 1998.

Sandoval, M. *On the Move: A History of the Hispanic Church in the United States*. Maryknoll, NY: Orbis Books, 1993.

Sassen, S. *Guests and Aliens*. New York: New Press, 1999.

Schrag, Peter. *Not Fit for Our Society: Immigration and Nativism in America*. Berkeley: University of California Press, 2010.

Schuck, Peter H. *Citizens, Strangers, and In-Betweens: Essays on Immigration and Citizenship*. Boulder, CO: Westview Press, 1998.

Schuck, Peter H. "Demography, Human Rights, and Diversity Management, American-Style," *Journal of Law and Ethics of Human Rights* 2 (2008): 87–127.

Schuck, Peter H. "The Disconnect between Public Attitudes and Policy Outcomes in Immigration." In *The Politics of Immigration Reform*, edited by Carol Swain, 17–31, New York: Cambridge University Press, 2007.

Schuck, Peter H. "Immigrants' Political and Legal Incorporation in the United States after 9/11: Two Steps Forward, One Step Back." In *Bringing Outsiders In: Transatlantic Perspectives on Immigrant Political Incorporation*, edited by J. Hochschild and J. Mollenkopf, 158–175. Ithaca, NY: Cornell University Press, 2009.

Schuck, Peter H. "U.S. Citizenship: Contemporary Challenges and Future Directions." In *Beyond Exceptionalism: Immigration in Postwar Germany and the United States*, edited by J. Hollifield and D. Thraenhardt, New York: Palgrave, forthcoming.

Simon, J. *The Economic Consequences of Immigration*. Ann Arbor: University of Michigan Press, 1999.

Suarez-Orozco, M., ed. *Crossings: Mexican Immigration in Interdisciplinary Perspectives*. Cambridge, MA: Harvard University Press, 1998.

Takaki, Ronald. *A Different Mirror. A History of Multicultural America*. Boston: Little, Brown, 1993.

Takaki, Ronald. *Iron Cages: Race and Culture in Nineteenth-Century America*. New York: Knopf, 1979.

Tanaka, Hiroyuki, Rocco Bellanova, Susan Ginsburg, and Paul De Hert. *Transatlantic Information Sharing: At a Crossroads*. Washington, DC: Migration Policy Institute, 2010.

Tichenor, Daniel J. *Dividing Lines: The Politics of Immigration Control in America*. Princeton, NJ: Princeton University Press, 2002.

Tien, H., and H. Ngoc. *Female Labour Migration: Rural–Urban*. Hanoi, Vietnam: Women's Publishing House, 2001.

Trueba, E., and L. Bartolome, eds. *Immigrant Voices: In Search of Educational Equity*. Lanham, MD: Rowman & Littlefield, 2000.

Tywoniak, F., and M. Garcia. *Migrant Daughter: Coming of Age as a Mexican American Woman*. Berkeley: University of California Press, 2000.

Ungar, Sanford J. *Fresh Blood: The New American Immigrants*. New York: Simon & Schuster, 1995.

Vickerman, Milton. *Crosscurrents: West Indian Immigrants and Race*. New York: Oxford University Press, 1998.

Villa, P. *Crossing Borders, Reinforcing Borders: Social Categories, Metaphors, and Narrative Identities on the U.S.-Mexico Frontier*. Austin: University of Texas Press, 2000.

Waldinger, R. *Still the Promised City? African-Americans and New Immigrants in Postindustrial New York*. Cambridge, MA: Harvard University Press, 1996.

Waldinger, R., ed. *Strangers at the Gates: New Immigrants in Urban America*. Berkeley: University of California Press, 2001.

Weissbrodt, David S., and Laura Danielson. *Immigration Law and Procedure in a Nutshell*. 5th ed. Eagan, MN: West Publishing, 2005.

Welchman, J., ed. *Rethinking Borders*. Minneapolis: University of Minnesota Press, 1996.

Westwood, S., and A. Phizacklea. *Trans-nationalism and the Politics of Belonging*. London: Routledge, 2000.

Wong, Carolyn. *Lobbying for Inclusion: Rights Politics and the Making of Immigration Policy*. Stanford, CA: Stanford University Press, 2006.

Yang, Y. *Chinese Christians in America: Conversion, Assimilation, and Adhesive Identities*. University Park: Pennsylvania State University Press, 1999.

Yans-McLaughlin, Virginia. *Immigration Reconsidered: History, Sociology, and Politics*. New York: Oxford University Press, 1990.

Yazbeck, Y., and J. Smith, eds. *Muslim Minorities in the West: Visible and Invisible*. Walnut Creek, CA: AltaMira Press, 2002.

Yoo, D., ed. *New Spiritual Homes: Religion and Asian Americans*. Honolulu: University of Hawaii Press, 1999.

Yung, J. *Unbound Feet: A Social History of Chinese Women in San Francisco*. Berkeley: University of California Press, 1995.

Zhao, X. *Remaking Chinese America: Immigration, Family, and Community, 1940–1965*. New Brunswick, NJ: Rutgers University Press, 2002.

Zolberg, Aristide. "Contemporary Transnational Migrations in Historical Perspective: Patterns and Dilemmas." In *U.S. Immigration and Refugee Policy*, edited by Mary M. Kritz, 15–51. Lexington, MA: Lexington Books, 1983.

Zolberg, Aristide. *A Nation by Design: Immigration Policy in the Fashioning of America*. Cambridge, MA: Harvard University Press, 2006.

Index

Boldface indicates page numbers for main entries.

About the Editor and Contributors

Editor

Patrick J. Hayes, PhD, has taught theology and religious studies in colleges and universities around the United States and in 2010 was a visiting scholar in theology at the University of Makeni, Sierra Leone. He is the author of *A Catholic Brain Trust: The History of the Catholic Commission on Intellectual and Cultural Affairs, 1945–1965* (2011). Hayes is presently the Archivist for the Baltimore Province of the Redemptorists based in Brooklyn, New York.

Contributors

Łukasz Albański, Jagiellonian University, Kraków, Poland

Sofya Aptekar, Department of Sociology, Princeton University

John H. Barnhill, Independent Scholar

Douglas C. Baynton, Department of History and Communication Studies, University of Iowa

Mary Elizabeth Brown, Archives, Marymount Manhattan College, Center for Migration Studies

Jean-Paul R. deGuzman, Department of History, University of California, Los Angeles

Carmen DeMichele, Department of Economics, Ludwig-Maximilians University, Munich, Germany

Jeffrey Scott Demsky, Department of History, San Bernardino Valley College

Cristina Ioana Dragomir, Department of Political Science, New School for Social Research

Ariane Knuesel, Department of History, University of Zurich

Philip A. Kretsedemas, Department of Sociology, University of Massachusetts Boston

Maddalena Marinari, Department of History, American University

Bryan McGovern, Department of History, Kennesaw State University

Joanna L. Mosser, Department of Politics, Drake University

Matthew Peterson, Department of History, University of Pittsburgh

David Pieper, Department of International and Area Studies, University of California, Berkeley

Nicholas Rademacher, Department of Religious Studies, Cabrini College

Utku Sezgin, Graduate Center and New York Dominican Studies Institute, City University of New York

Julia C. Skinner, School of Library and Information Studies, Florida State University

Alexander I. Stingl, Independent Scholar

Judith Ann Warner, Department of Sociology, Texas A&M International University

Kathleen R. Warnes, Independent Scholar

Christina Anne Ziegler-McPherson, Independent Scholar

Aristide R. Zolberg, Department of Political Science, New School for Social Research

Rochelle Raineri Zuck, Department of English, University of Minnesota Duluth

ARTISTS UNDER VICHY

ARTISTS UNDER VICHY

―――――

A Case of Prejudice and Persecution

―――――

Michèle C. Cone

PRINCETON UNIVERSITY PRESS
PRINCETON, NEW JERSEY

Library of Congress Cataloging-in-Publication Data
Cone, Michèle C., 1932–
Artists under Vichy: A case of prejudice and persecution/
Michèle C. Cone.
p. cm.
Includes bibliographical references and index.
ISBN 0-691-04088-5
1. Art and state—France.   2. Art—Political aspects—
France—History—20th century.   3. France—History—German
occupation, 1940–1945. I. Title.
N6848.C66 1992
701'.03—dc20   91-17011

This book has been composed in Adobe Times Roman

Princeton University Press books are printed on
acid-free paper, and meet the guidelines for permanence
and durability of the Committee on Production
Guidelines for Book Longevity of the
Council on Library Resources

Printed in the United States of America

2 4 6 8 10 9 7 5 3 1

FOR ROSALIE

CONTENTS

CONTENTS

ILLUSTRATIONS

ILLUSTRATIONS

ILLUSTRATIONS

ILLUSTRATIONS

Color plates can be found following page 88.

ACKNOWLEDGMENTS

I would like to thank the Institute of French Studies of New York University, and Prof. Nicholas Wahl in particular, for enabling me to resume graduate studies with a university fellowship. I would like to thank the Cultural Services of the French Embassy in New York for granting me a Chateaubriand Fellowship to conduct research in France for ten months in 1984.

In the past two years, I have been given several opportunities to speak about my research and to have it discussed in ways that have been extremely useful to the final draft of this book. I therefore thank Klaus Herding for including me in his section at the Congrès International d'Histoire de l'Art held in Strasbourg in September 1989; Otto-Karl Werckmeister for including me in the symposium on German artists in exile, 1933–1945, held at Northwestern University in Chicago in November 1989; Stephen Polcari for inviting me to speak at the College Art Association meeting in New York in 1990; Steven Ungar for asking me to speak at the International Colloquium on Twentieth-Century French Studies at the University of Iowa in April 1990; Jeff Halley for making it possible for me to address the Artistic Reception section of the World Congress of Sociology in Madrid in July 1990; David Halle who invited me to speak at the 1990 Institute for Cultural Analysis Conference at SUNY, Stony Brook, and of course the financing institutions: the Institute for Advanced Study in Princeton, Northwestern University, the School of Visual Arts, and the National Science Foundation.

My thanks go to the following persons for their help and ideas in the course of research: Jean Philippe Antoine, Michel Beaujour, Juan Manuel Bonnet, Maurice Cézard, Claudine Cohen-Naar, Cécile Coutin, Christian Dérouet, Laurent Gervereau, Romy Golan, Maurice Jardot, Gérard Loiseaux, Edda Maillet, Jean-Hubert Martin, Pascal Ory, Robert O. Paxton, Robert Pincus-Witten, Rona Roob, Robert Rosenblum, Margit Rowell, John Shepley, Kenneth Silver, Kirk Varnedoe, Nicole Villa, Nicholas Wahl, and Sarah Wilson.

I am grateful to the persons who agreed to speak to me about the Occupation years and to all those who gave me access to precious archival materials; whenever possible, their names appear in the bibliography. I have included reproductions of certain documents despite their poor condition because of the important part they play in the story.

ACKNOWLEDGMENTS

I thank Elizabeth Powers of Princeton University Press for her judicious editorial remarks; and also Tim Wardell for his assistance in the production of this book. For her sensitive copyediting, I am grateful to Jane Lincoln Taylor. Last but not least, my husband, Terry Cone, deserves thanks for his patience and interest.

PREFACE

For all the interest in various facets of French life and culture during World War II, little was known until recently about the work of artists who lived in France during the period bounded by the June 1940 armistice and the liberation of Paris in late August 1944—a period when France was essentially out of touch with the West. One assumption that may have inhibited research is that, due to the exile of major art personalities, the period must have been completely fallow. Recent exhibitions such as Paris-Paris, 1937–1957 at the Centre Georges Pompidou in Paris in 1981, La Planète Affolée: Surréalisme, Dispersion, Influence, 1938–1947 at the Centre de la Vieille Charité in Marseilles in 1986, and El Surrealismo entre Viejo y Nuevo Mundo at the Centro Atlantico de Arte Moderno of Las Palmas in the Canary Islands in 1989–90 have begun to change this view. While confirming the idea that the departure for New York of important figures in the Surrealist movement marked a "before" and an "after" for the state of the visual arts in France, they have broken the silence about the intervening period.

It is true that the New World benefited enormously from this influx, but the number of emigrating artists compared with those who did not or could not leave remains minute. Furthermore, most of those who did leave had lived through the early days of the new regime. This important though brief moment in their lives needs a closer look.

The inevitable question remains: How in a country turned in on itself, with the most antiliberal forces at the helm of the French government, could art help being controlled by these new voices? A recent publication by Laurence Bertrand Dorléac[1] shows how Vichy ideology seeped into the culture. In this interesting text, the focus is on the artistic policies of the new regime and on the art forms produced during that time that best demonstrate the traditionalism embedded in Vichy ideology. For all its usefulness, this point of view offers only one facet of the situation. What characterized the Vichy regime as much as its traditionalism—the return to "community, métier, humanism, roots," analyzed by Bertrand Dorléac—was its racism. During those four years, France, a country that had acquired the reputation of being a haven—or *terre d'accueil*—for the talented and the persecuted, reached a peak of xenophobia, anti-Semitism, and sectarianism that caused drastic changes in the art world. The uniqueness of the visual arts

during Vichy goes far beyond the traditionalist values it revived. Nazi Germany was not the only place where the onus of decadence served as an alibi that empowered certain groups while punishing others. It was also the case in France, where avengers of decadence from Vichyite and collaborationist factions of the French art world proposed various artistic norms against decadence ("art between the Jew and the *pompier*," "bleu-blanc-rouge painting," "the return to Classicism," "the revival of decorative arts") from which artist scapegoats were to be totally excluded. That, at least, is the premise of this text, which, in part 1, looks at the esthetics of these avengers of decadence and, in part 2, reveals the fate of their scapegoats.

Encouraged by the discovery of a series of hitherto unnoticed monthly reports by observers of the art world stationed at the Paris office of the German Propaganda-Abteilung[2] (see appendix 1) that repeatedly mention exhibitions being subjected to "previews," articles being "censored," galleries being "Aryanized," and artists "willing to work with us," I have hypothesized a far more complex network of French and German interests behind the art seen in Vichy France during those years than is found in Bertrand Dorléac's text. Neither collaboration nor the devastating impact of combined Vichy and Nazi policies on former participants in the French art world receives special attention in her work.

Compared to what we know of the situation of the visual arts in Nazi Germany, the period 1940–44 for the visual arts in France was, as Bertrand Dorléac also observes, surprisingly lively in spite of the witch-hunt against decadent art undertaken by the Nazis, and of the position against decadence taken in official Vichy circles. In Paris, only a few months after the Nazi occupation the art world reorganized itself and the normal rhythm of activities began again. Salons functioned, and galleries held regular one-person and group shows. Theme shows were organized by museums and private galleries; the new press had its art columns. Artistic controversies were aired and good art was seen. The situation in the visual arts paralleled that of the cinema industry—abundant and lively[3]—and contrasted with the quality of the new literature that passed censorship.[4]

Explanations for this strange situation vary. Some see it in an economic context; according to Raymonde Moulin, since civilian goods and diversions were in short supply and much new money was floating around, art acquired entertainment value as well as investment value.[5] The presence at the helm of the fine arts department of the Ministry of Education and Youth (until March 1944) of Prof. Louis Hautecoeur, an enterprising bureaucrat (albeit one with archconservative tastes), and his success in wrenching considerable sums for artists from the government, may also have been contributing factors.

There is also the hypothesis, proposed by Helmut Lehmann-Haupt in his *Art under a Dictatorship*,[6] that, throughout the twentieth century, new regimes have tended to attract a broad spectrum of members of the art world, including its avant-gardes. Since this rallying is always based on a misconception of the goals of the regimes in question, the coexistence of revolutionary new governments and the avant-gardes that claim to represent them is usually short-lived. In the French case, shifts in the military advantage confused the situation; hence, what would have happened to the new art born of the war, had the war lasted longer, becomes moot.

More recent instances of art thriving under political censorship—in the Eastern Europe described by Miklos Haraszti—have given rise to the idea that freedom may not be a prerequisite for creativity even for Modernist art. Only "the optimist outsider imagines that power and art are spheres which intersect only in front of the firing squad," Haraszti writes.[7] Speaking of artists in the days before the recent demise of Hungarian state socialism, Haraszti remarks:

> Few, of course, would openly confess that they and their friends are accomplices in their own oppression and exploitation. But in reality our artists, despite their worries, gratefully accept society's attention and revel in their own effectiveness. Just as dignitaries of the Middle Ages believed their faith to be the same as that of the Crucified, so too do these artists consider themselves, even as state employees, to be apostles of freedom.[8]

Certainly, undivided attention was attractive to artists who, in the years before the Occupation, had been given a secondary place in the public's mind and now thrived in the limelight. A "velvet prison" was for them infinitely more comfortable than either neglect or the threat of a real jail.

As for Haraszti's judgment on those who think they are identifying with the "crucified" when in fact they are serving the state—an example during World War II was the use and positive reception by Vichy and by the Nazis of formally vanguard art produced by a few painters "in the French Tradition"—this ambivalence brings up an important issue. What are the moral options open to artists under authoritarian regimes, given that a policy of silence signifying disaffection with the state and sympathy with the outcasts is financially disastrous, while exile is practicable only in a few exceptional cases?

The only possibility, it seems to me, is to avoid being used by one's enemy. So I will be harsher toward the formally vanguard art approved by French and German censors than is Bertrand Dorléac, who argues that its ambiguity was a true reflection of "l'état des choses." Through the simulacrum of freedom that

the display of this art in official Vichy contexts provided, a sense of normality was being artificially maintained. The German occupiers also took advantage of it and used it as a diversionary tactic and a strategy of seduction, as a metaphorical smoke screen for the Holocaust, and for the illegal secret seizure of museum pieces and Jewish art collections on behalf of Nazi officials and of Hitler's museum in Linz.

If concern with work was fervent among the artists willing to exhibit under the vigilant eye of the occupying forces, it was no less so for persecuted artists. They went on making art in improvised surroundings, most frequently in the unoccupied area of France (they remain a distant though sympathetic presence in Bertrand Dorléac's text, whose main concern is art history then being made in Paris), despite their reduced circumstances and the hounding they endured from the French police and the Gestapo. In their case, the need to create art transcended issues of public response and, for the less well known among them, posthumous fame, as the chances of their art surviving them were as slim as their own chances for survival. Unlike the artists exhibiting in Paris whose vanguardism was acceptable to the censors, the persecuted artists whose art was vanguard enough to be considered "Judeo-Marxist-decadent" by the Nazis put their lives in jeopardy by continuing to paint and to sculpt as they had done before the war.

Yet these were productive times for the artists who remained in Vichy France, including Victor Brauner, Hans Bellmer, Wols, Sonia Delaunay, and Otto Freundlich, and also for those who were to stay only a few months in the unoccupied zone before emigrating, such as Marc Chagall, André Masson, and Max Ernst, or those who left after two years, as did Hans Arp and Sophie Taeuber-Arp. It was also a productive time for Pablo Picasso in occupied Paris.

One may well ask what kind of art emerges when the possibilities of showing in a public arena no longer exist, when society ignores the work, when only a few friends and admirers get to look at it—conditions that escape the velvet-prison state defined by Miklos Haraszti—even if in both cases the attentiveness of the police must be taken into account. Is it more "free," more oppositional, and if so what language does it use? Does it seek to communicate a subversive message? If so, how does it do it?

Although it may be risky to apply to the visual arts strategies that have been used in writing, two (some might say three) models of self-expression from the viewpoint of resister-writers may be worth examining in relation to these questions.[9] The first is the classical model, whereby the "truth" is uttered between the lines more or less furtively but *un*ambiguously—at least for those sympathetic to

the views expressed in disguise. The second model, whereby an official message is resisted and garbled by an internal modification of its material parts that renders its meaning totally opaque yet has the appearance of a typographical error, has been used in Eastern Europe under communism. The third model (which I do not find believable) is one in which the official views expressed in the writing can be interpreted in conflicting ways.

The first model is the Leo Strauss model (examined in *Persecution and the Art of Writing*) typical of the discourse of the Enlightenment;[10] the second is the Miloszian model, in *The Captive Mind*, of Ketman—"which is an old Arabic word for evading and disrupting the conditions of cultural repression."[11] The third is Derrida's "double edge,"[12] which, applied to the wartime writings of Paul de Man, would make it possible—at least for Derrida—to read irony in the voice that spells out the official view. As will be seen, although subversive messages make furtive appearances, particularly in Picasso's oeuvre, the most striking feature of the art of the persecuted is the autobiographical motif.

In order to account for the rise of certain artists and the disappearance of others from the Parisian art world during the Vichy regime (what Stanley Hoffmann and Robert O. Paxton after him have called, in a general political context, "the revenge of the minorities"),[13] one must return to the 1930s and to the artistic policies of the Popular Front. The reorganization of the art world under Marshal Pétain responded to contradictions and tensions that had developed under the Popular Front government of Léon Blum, particularly at the time of the 1937 World's Fair and its attendant building and art programs. There were contradictions in the cultural policies of the government, and there was competition between French and "foreign" artists (often a euphemism for Jewish artists—hence the quotation marks).

Even the pro-German feelings of certain well-known artists during the Occupation can be ascribed to the positive reception of an exhibition of *French* art in Berlin sent there under official French auspices in 1937. Although a reaction clearly began immediately after the 1937 World's Fair, not only did the backlash effect under Pétain become magnified but, with government by decree, the desired results were inevitable. By law, Jews and Freemasons, as well as "dangerous" foreigners and stateless persons, would be excluded from the national life of the country. In *L'Ecole des cadavres*, dated 1938, Céline offers a hint of the realignments about to take place under Vichy.

Who, I'd like to know, benefited from the Popular Front? Strictly the Jews and the [Free]masons (synthetic Jews). The Aryans, they got it in the

knuckle. Bourgeois, workers, peasants, small shopkeepers, artists, small bureaucrats? Done for [bulldozed over]!

But at last all of that is going to end. Adjournments cannot continue forever.[14]

These realignments have led me to divide my text into two sections, one devoted to avengers of decadence and the other to scapegoats of decadence. This division means that, geographically speaking, part 1 deals with Paris, where the avengers of decadence received acclaim, and part 2 deals primarily with the situation in the unoccupied zone of France, where all varieties of "foreign" artists could be found, in total isolation from the new Paris mainstream. Although the "foreigner" Picasso spent the war years in Paris, he is discussed in part 2.

The 1937 Paris World's Fair as a paradigm of tensions resolved in a specific way during the Pétain regime is not by itself sufficient to explain the turnabout of French culture during World War II. In France, the rampage against decadence and the connection between decadence and Jewishness antedate not only Léon Blum's Popular Front but even the Dreyfus affair, as Michel Winnock, in his study of Edouard Drumont's *La France juive* (1885), has shown: "His [Drumont's] role . . . consisted in designating the Jew as the universal principle of the disorders and misfortunes of France since the Revolution."[15] Winnock goes on to cite a rich assortment of nineteenth-century authors, including Simonini, Bonald, Gougenot des Mousseaux, Veuillot, Michelet, Fourier, Proudhon, Renan, and especially Toussenel in his *Juifs rois de l'époque* (1845) and Tridon in *Du Molochisme juif* (1884), as Drumont's principal mentors on the Catholic right and the Socialist left.[16]

This study of art and artists under Vichy must also necessarily take into account the specific conditions in France between 1940 and 1944. The Vichy vision of culture, the ubiquitous interference of Germans in the decisions of French policymakers, and the censorship of the public and private art sectors are key elements. So are changes in the international balance of power, such as the Allies' invasion of North Africa and the German occupation of all of France that followed immediately in November 1942; these are turning points that Bertrand Dorléac's more abstract, structuralist approach overlooks. It is also important to keep in mind that throughout the Occupation, the Germans had the upper hand and could arrest, confiscate, and kill (or merely threaten to do these things to) people then living in France.

As the period of the Occupation recedes into the past, revisionist history is threatening the demarcation between villains and heroes, between collaborators

and Resistance activists during Vichy. Such intellectualization is intolerable to the memory of the victims, those who suffered torture in silence, those who died at the hands of Nazis. Notions of individual responsibility have come into question, but Resistance activists knew the difference between what Sartre in another context called "resignation" and "revolution."[17] Without presuming to lift the final veil from the imponderable factors that undoubtedly affected individual choices, I have dedicated an epilogue to collaboration and to resistance in artists' ranks.

Methodology—what limits to set to my "corpus"—was a major hurdle. The usual fragmentation of the art world was compounded by geographic factors: in Paris, several groups of "racially pure" French artists vied for recognition in exhibitions reserved for those who could prove they were French and not Jewish, while towns and villages in the free zone of France witnessed the arrival in their midst of small groups of refugee artists, brought there by the exodus, who, though unwilling or unable to return to the French capital, resumed work. Not even confinement in French internment camps stopped artists from working, although small, often anonymous drawings and murals became substitutes for easel painting and sculpture.

The notion of network, analyzed by Howard S. Becker in his *Art Worlds* and by Lawrence Alloway in his *Network: Art and the Complex Present*, offered a convenient means of getting around the geographic spread and the diverse situations of participants in the French art world.

"What does the vague term art world cover?" asks Alloway, as a way of introducing the notion of network. "It includes," he answers, "original works of art and reproductions; critical, historical, and informative writing; galleries, museums, and private collections. It is a sum of persons, objects, resources, messages, and ideas."[18] Or, in Becker's words, "Whatever the artist . . . does not do must be done by someone else. The artist thus works in the center of a network of cooperating people, all of whose work is essential to the final outcome."[19]

The advantage of approaching the art world as a system is that it invites the identification of subsystems involving not only specific groups of artworks but also the clusters of attention that tend to focus on them, in the forms of critical reception and of commercially and culturally inspired activities concerning them. For my particular subject, this notion extended to "survival networks," exceptional communities born of the political situation of refugee artists who were more or less in hiding during the Occupation years.

I thus investigated a spectrum of art networks ranging from the quasi-institutionalized arrangement between the faculty of the Ecole des Beaux Arts, the

Salon de la Société des Artistes Français, and the fine arts section of the French government, to the most exceptional and fragile form of networking—the bartering of art for favors, a practice to which certain eminent international Modernists of the prewar period were forced to resort.

In general, I have tended to give a sociopolitical reading to the artistic forms and themes of the period. I do not claim that such a reading is exhaustive, nor that it should be a substitute for other types of readings. But for the sake of future researchers who will have to rediscover a past I experienced firsthand as a child, I have chosen to test the hypothetical role of context in the creation and reception of art.

As this approach suggests, my aim has not been primarily to find new names to inscribe in the pantheon of twentieth-century art. "Art history," Jauss writes, "which is most frequently considered as a poor relation and as dependent upon general history, was it not once a fecunding element, and could it not become again an eventual paradigm of historic knowledge?"[20] I hope this study of the visual arts under Pétain will help fill the gap between two cultural epochs, the one that ended in 1940 and the one that began with the liberation of Paris in late August 1944. I also hope this study will be read as a testimony to what happens when prejudice becomes embedded in the law and extermination policies find official apologists.

(The translations are mine unless otherwise attributed.)

PART I

AVENGERS OF DECADENCE

1

An Epoch Ends in Disarray

In order to go from one room to the other, one had
to step on his canvases. Delaunay encouraged us
to do as he was doing, saying that it did not matter if
we stepped on them.
A. Magnelli

When the Germans entered Paris on 13–14 June 1940, the city was a ghost town and a cultural desert. Stranded during the German blitzkrieg were French soldiers and Foreign Legionnaires about to be taken prisoner. The painter Jean Hélion reports in *They Shall Not Have Me*:

> They [the German troops] arrived in armored cars, roaring so that the trees shook. It was five o'clock, the 19th of June. . . . From all the cars, German soldiers jumped down and lined up. They carried hand grenades ready to throw. . . . I was gathering my most important belongings when a German hit me with the rifle I had just laid in the bushes. He pushed me in the open, made me take off my helmet, my leather belt, my equipment, and hurried me towards the road. There I joined the rest of my group. . . . Nobody could speak to us anymore. We were prisoners of war.[1]

Much of its civilian population was away from Paris as well. The art dealer Daniel-Henry Kahnweiler, a Jew, had left Paris in the nick of time, as he later told Francis Crémieux in an interview:

> I myself left on the very last day, June 12, 1940. I left with my wife and the older of my sisters-in-law, who was living with us. We went by car, taking with us everything we could.
>
> *Did you leave all the paintings in Paris?*
>
> Of course, what else could I do? I should tell you, though, that I had already sent a certain number of paintings to Repaire-l'Abbaye, the country place where I went later. This was a small house I had rented, three kilometers from Saint-Léonard-de-Noblat, twenty-three kilometers from Limoges.[2]

Chaim Soutine could be found in Civry near Avallon (Yonne). In 1941, he was to spend some time in Paris before moving to the Touraine, whose woodsy, moody landscape he memorialized frequently in his last paintings. (He died from ulcers in 1943.)[3] No one knows for sure whether Otto Freundlich and the critic Walter Benjamin were still interned in French camps or whether they had been released by 15 June 1940. Marc Chagall had recently moved to Gordes in Provence. Louis Marcoussis and his wife, Alice Halicka, had gone to Cusset, near Vichy, where the artist died on 22 October 1941. All of them were Jews.

For Robert Delaunay (whose wife, the painter Sonia Delaunay, was a Jew) the end was also in sight. Ill with cancer, he was then on the road with Sonia, headed toward Cannes on the Côte d'Azur. While passing through the town of Cannes (their car loaded with rolled-up canvases), they were hailed by their friend Alberto Magnelli and his wife, Susi, who saw them from a sidewalk café. They took an apartment in nearby Mougins. On 24 October 1941, Delaunay died in a Montpellier hospital.

Surrealists and former Dadaists had also left Paris. André Masson and his family (his wife was Jewish) were in the Auvergne. Max Ernst was probably on a train full of foreign refugees shuttling between Bayonne and Marseilles.[4] The Arps were either in the Dordogne (Nérac) with Gabrielle Buffet-Picabia or with the Jewish heiress Peggy Guggenheim near Lake Annecy.[5] Francis Picabia was on his way from Switzerland to Golfe Juan near Cannes on the Côte d'Azur with his third wife, Olga. André Breton, who had served in the army, was about to rejoin his wife and daughter at Martigues in the South.[6] The Marseilles area was teeming with refugee Surrealists. In Carcassonne, a contingent of Belgian Surrealists, including René Magritte, had descended on Joe Bousquet, a paraplegic poet and collector.[7] Another contingent of Surrealists—Victor Brauner, Jacques Hérold (both Jews), Oscar Dominguez, and Dr. Pierre Mabille—stopped in Perpignan as guests of the poet Robert Rius. Joan Miró was on his way to Barcelona and Majorca.

It would thus appear that the fear that had led millions to take to the roads ahead of the German army had not spared the artists. Hard as it is to make light of the exodus, Marcel Duchamp's *Boite en valise* (1938–41), a briefcase containing diminutive versions of his major works, and Alberto Giacometti's matchbox size sculpture from 1942–43 (the artist moved to Switzerland in December 1941) humorously render the drastic paring-down of earthly belongings that characterized these last-minute escapes. Other artists whose whereabouts can be traced include Matisse, ensconced in St.-Jean-de-Luz, Picasso, who had moved to Royan, and Duchamp, who with Mary Reynolds and the Crottis was staying in

the resort of Arcachon, near Biarritz.[8] Wassily Kandinsky was in Cauterets in the Pyrénées, near the Spanish border, while Georges Braque had with André Derain found a haven in the village of Gaujac (Ariège), also near the Spanish border. Fernand Léger was on his way to Marseilles to catch a ship headed for New York.

On 17 June 1940, Marshal Philippe Pétain announced over the French radio that he had asked the Germans for an armistice. On 22 June, an armistice was declared, and on 25 June it was signed by Pétain and Hitler at Rhetondes. The division of France into two parts caught a number of refugees in what turned out to be the occupied zone, as the entire Atlantic coast fell on the German side of the armistice line. Braque, Derain, and Kandinsky, although in the free zone, eventually returned to the occupied French capital. Matisse in St.-Jean-de-Luz, Duchamp in Arcachon, and Picasso in Royan found themselves in the occupied zone, facing the choice of moving again to avoid meeting the German occupiers, or trying to leave France before the frontiers closed.

Fig. 1

Matisse made his way to Nice after a long and tiring trip from southwestern to southeastern France. He turned in his ticket for Rio de Janeiro and also declined the invitation of Mills College to teach there. Duchamp opted for Paris and took nearly two years to make up his mind to leave France. Meanwhile, he commuted between occupied Paris and Marseilles, the only major French port in the free zone, in the guise of a cheese buyer.[9]

Picasso stayed in Royan long enough to watch the Germans take over the French resort. "Our anguish was overwhelming," Picasso's friend and secretary Jaime Sabartès writes of the artist's first sight of the German army in Royan. "Picasso watched them [German troops] file past his studio because the Commissariat was behind it and the Kommandantur had been installed a short distance from Les Voiliers. The neighboring Hotel de Paris was taken over by the officers and soon there was a constant movement of cars, trucks, motorcycles, cannons and all the rest."[10]

Picasso's was the "anguish" of all those who, for one reason or another, risked falling under the Judeo-Marxist-decadent label that the chancellor of the Third Reich had coined for those his regime wanted to get rid of, including numbers of nonconformist artists.

To judge by the Entartete Kunst exhibition (the exhibition of "degenerate art") held in Munich in 1937, in Nazi Germany the profile of the typical creator of decadent paintings or sculpture was frighteningly inconsistent. On the one hand, Hitler refused to make a distinction between decadent individuals and decadent art. As Henry Grosshans observes, "Hitler extended his animosity from the paint-

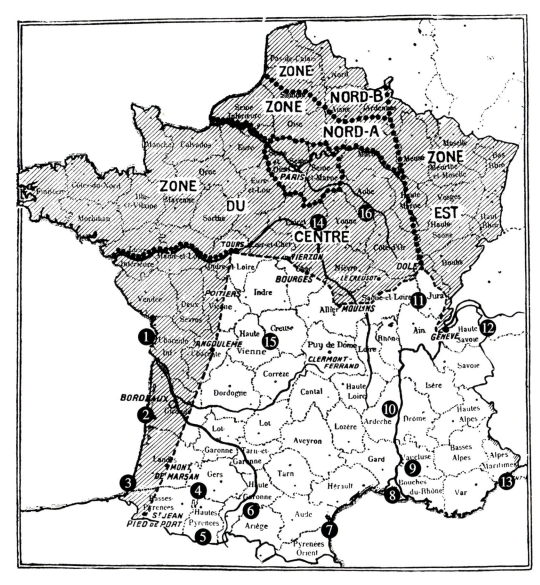

1. Locations of some figures of the prewar Paris art world after the signing of the armistice.

1. Pablo Picasso
2. Marcel Duchamp
3. Henri Matisse
4. Walter Benjamin
5. Vassily Kandinsky
6. André Derain, Georges Braque
7. Otto Freundlich
8. Wifredo Lam, Victor Brauner, Jacques Hérold, André Breton, Jacqueline Lamba, others

9. Marc Chagall
10. Max Ernst
11. Gertrude Stein
12. Peggy Guggenheim
13. Jean Arp, Sophie Taeuber-Arp, Sonia Delaunay, Robert Delaunay, others
14. Max Jacob
15. Daniel-Henry Kahnweiler, André Masson
16. Chaim Soutine

ing to the painter. For him art was the expression of the moral character of the artist (as he declared, 'stunted men have the philosophy of stunted men'), and what he regarded as perversion in a work of art indicated the diseased mind of its creator."[11] On the other hand, an artist with non-Aryan blood was decadent whatever style he or she practiced and, if the art had been fertilized by alien African or Oceanic "primitivist" cultures, even if the artist was pro-Nazi (as was the case with party member Emil Nolde) the art remained Judeo-Marxist-decadent.

As attested by the presence on the cover of the Entartete Kunst show catalogue of Otto Freundlich's *Cubist Head* with negroid features, one could be sure of a featured place in the register of Judeo-Marxist-decadent art if one's blood and one's art were both impure. Inclusion was also guaranteed by eclecticism in art and by having the wrong politics, as shown by the illustration in the same catalogue of Ernst's collage, *The Beautiful Gardener* (a work formerly in the collection of the Museum of Dusseldorf and subsequently destroyed).[12] Rarely noticed is the fact that Fauve painting was not included in the show.[13]

Sinister as was Hitler's hatred of Judeo-Marxist-decadent art, of liberal politics, and of individuals who did not match Aryan physical specifications, it was by no means unique to the chancellor of the Third Reich. Hildegard Brenner has shown that racism, fear of bolshevism, and the refusal to accept changes in an alleged ideal canon of art were not uncommon in Germany even before Hitler came to power.[14] What made Hitler particularly dangerous was the way he acted on his hatred. "If some self-styled artist submits trash for the Munich exhibition, then he is either a swindler, in which case he should be put in prison; or he is a madman, in which case he should be in an asylum; or he is a degenerate, in which case he must be sent to a concentration camp to be 'reeducated' and taught the dignity of honest labor," Hitler reportedly said in private conversations with Bormann.[15]

In Nazi Germany, beginning in 1933, museums were emptied of modern art, museum staffs were fired, and a Chamber of Culture made up of loyal party members tightly controlled the nation's artistic life, including the education of artists. By 1936, the Chamber of Culture had become an arm of the Ministry of Propaganda.[16] Meanwhile, prisons, insane asylums, and concentration camps became filled with those Hitler called swindlers, lunatics, and degenerates—artists and nonartists alike.

Small wonder that the sight of German soldiers consolidating their victory within sight of Picasso's studio in newly occupied Royan filled the artist with anguish—an anguish captured in the scraggly lines of his frontal self-portrait

2. Pablo Picasso. *Self-Portrait*, 11 August 1940.

drawings from August 1940. Insofar as the Entartete Kunst selection of art and   Fig. 2
artists defined Judeo-Marxist decadence, Picasso was a likely candidate for
"reeducation." Although that show had been an assemblage of paintings and
sculpture mostly by German artists then living in Germany, it had also included
works by a small but notable contingent of artists who then lived in France:
Freundlich and Ernst; Chagall, a Jew and recently naturalized French citizen;
Gert Wollheim, a German refugee; Kandinsky, who had fourteen works in the
show although he was neither a Jew nor staunchly antifascist (see "Le Second
Futurisme et l'appel de l'Italie," in *Kandinsky*, Centre Georges Pompidou, cata-

logue by Christian Dérouet and Jessica Boissel); and Picasso, the "infamous" creator of *Guernica*.[17]

Even so, as Hitler went on a whirlwind tour of a deserted Paris three days after the armistice, his intentions toward French artistic life were something of a mystery in French circles. On the one hand, as Sarah Wilson points out in "Collaboration in the Fine Arts,"[18] the policies against degenerate art and artists in Nazi Germany had been publicized in Paris thanks to Christian Zervos's "Réflexions sur la tentative d'esthétique dirigée du Troisième Reich," which appeared in *Cahiers d'art* in 1936 and 1937. "The Reich Chamber of Culture (or RKK)," one could have read in the 1936 issue, "has installed a severe and stringent legislation which forbids elements who claim allegiance to Expressionism, Cubism, and Dadaism to participate, under any guise whatsoever, in the artistic life of contemporary Germany."[19] On the other hand, the Prussian Academy in Berlin had in 1937 hosted a show of French artists, a small number of whom might have been taken to be Judeo-Marxist-decadent by Nazi standards.[20]

That the latter exhibition polarized the artistic milieu in prophetic ways is suggested by an unsigned notice in the 1937 issue of *Cahiers d'art* on the subject of the Berlin show: "The attitude of Paris modernists, Picasso above all, and of all the painters and sculptors who are discussed in these *Cahiers* has not changed. Out of solidarity with their German confrères whom National Socialism has banned from the society of artists, they have refused to participate in the Berlin exhibition."[21]

One of the first acts of the German occupiers after the June armistice was to set up in Paris a branch of Goebbels's Propaganda Ministry, the Propaganda-Abteilung, which had the duty, among other tasks, of keeping the French press and art worlds under surveillance. At the German Embassy under Otto Abetz and at the German Institute headed by Karl Epting, social events designed to attract a "certain" French and pro-German literary and artistic intelligentsia were planned.

The relation of the newly installed French government at Vichy to the country's cultural elite was also unpredictable. Many people were relieved: "Well anyway there was the armistice Pétain made it and we were all glad in a way and completely sad in a way and we had so many opinions," was how Gertrude Stein greeted the news of the armistice from the village in Bilignin (Ain), not far from the Swiss border, to which she and Alice B. Toklas retreated until February 1943, when they moved to nearby Culoz. "I did not like his way of saying I Philippe Pétain, that bothered me and we were in the unoccupied area and that

was a comfort," she went on in *Wars I Have Seen*, a memoir.[22] As legislation detrimental to many of those who had sought refuge in Vichy France was being prepared, the marshal was telling the French, "I summon you to an intellectual and moral redressing."[23] The onslaught against decadence on French terms was underway.

As René Rémond, among others, has pointed out, "The Vichy experiment was not homogeneous: the phrase conceals several realities."[24] Not only was Vichy "not entirely right wing . . . but it was not the same throughout its career."[25] It had a Pétain phase, a Laval phase, and toward the end a Darnand phase. Likewise, it borrowed its ideology from a variety of sources. The monarchist Right, "the earliest Right, the only absolute Right, the counter-revolutionary Right of the Ultras as carried on by the school of Maurras"[26] was influential, Rémond observes, but a younger figure, the corporatist-minded Gustave Thibon, "whose thought is typical of traditionalist organicism,"[27] was also important. As for remedies against social, moral, and political decadence, they were inspired equally by La Tour du Pin's school of social Catholicism and by Frédéric Le Play's counterrevolutionary attitudes.

If the political, social, and economic aspects of the Révolution Nationale were shaped by a variety of points of view, the fear of decadence loomed large in its artistic program,[28] which was also univocally antiforeigner.[29] Romy Golan, in her essay "The Ecole Française vs. the Ecole de Paris," shows how the stage for the Occupation period was made ready by such critics in the twenties and thirties as Camille Mauclair and Waldemar George, who not only complained of the false esthetics and dishonest underside of the so-called Ecole de Paris, those regulars of Montparnasse cafés, many of them émigré Jewish artists from central Europe, but hinted at an alleged "conspiracy on the part of foreign Jews against the French heritage."[30]

What new names were to be championed by avengers of decadence clamoring in the press of occupied Paris, and what arguments in support of these new favorites, aside from their Frenchness, were going to be proffered?

2

Middle-of-the-Road Romantic Realists
Nab the Light

PROFILE OF A "JUDENREIN" ART WORLD

The first winter of the Occupation was the coldest France had known for years. It was the winter when Picasso composed *Desire Caught by the Tail*, a play of sorts with references to chilblains and frozen fingers. It was also the time when many of those who had fled Paris with the exodus returned to the French capital and began reorganizing their lives.

Momentous changes, some visible and some not, had meanwhile taken place there. Nazi flags flapped in the wind above the entrances to famous hotels now used as headquarters by the newly installed German occupiers. Cars transporting mostly German officers, since gasoline had been rationed to French citizens, circulated on the city's nearly deserted streets. German soldiers were a common sight at sidewalk cafés, while the best seats at the Opéra were reserved for them. Warnings posted in conspicuous places recommended compliance with Nazi orders. Periodically, lists of hostages killed in reprisal for some act of resistance would appear on public walls.

The French Assembly, the heart of political life during the three French republics, was now deserted. The French government, ruling without a consultative body, operated from Vichy, a town mostly renowned for its curative waters on the south side of the armistice line that now divided the country into two parts—the occupied and free zones. Ministers in the newly created French government who needed to consult with their administrative subordinates left behind in Paris had to ask the Germans for permits to cross the armistice line. Such trips back and forth were strictly limited and, by order of the Germans, Jews were not allowed back into the occupied zone. Neither, for that matter, were Alsatians who had fled their province during the exodus.

In a drastically changed atmosphere, rendered suspect by the ubiquitous presence of the Germans, Parisians learned to cope with the new circumstances.

– 11 –

Within the art world, authorization for a gallery or salon to function again required a visit to the German Propaganda-Abteilung (52, avenue des Champs Elysées). No poster advertising an exhibition could be hung without first being approved by that office. No show could open without first being visited by a German *referat* (spy or observer).

These handicaps notwithstanding, by the end of 1941, the Orangerie, the Musée des Arts Décoratifs, and the Musée Galliéra had already held exhibitions;[1] the Salon des Artistes Français, the Salon des Tuileries, the Salon d'Automne, and the Salon des Indépendants had made their annual presentations at the Palais de Tokyo, and gallery activity had resumed. "Old galleries rival each other in activity.... All over the place new galleries arise," the critic writing for *Les Beaux Arts* noted in his 6 February 1942 survey. "In all corners of Paris the appearance of new galleries that plan to dedicate themselves to artists whose reputation is not yet established has been announced."[2] Between 8 May 1941, the day the show called Jeunes Peintres de Tradition Française opened, and the fall of 1943, when Jean Fautrier had his retrospective at the Galerie Drouin, the number of galleries had practically doubled (see appendixes 2 and 3).

No art exhibition held in a locale belonging to the French administration could include Jewish exhibitors;[3] in fact, Jews were forbidden by the Germans to exhibit anywhere. French artists who had left France were blacklisted by Vichy, and Picasso was prevented from showing his work under pressure from Franco's Spain. For other artists, silence and abstention were far from the rule during the four years when these limitations applied.

Among established members of the art world, Jean Cocteau, Aristide Maillol, Georges Rouault, Raoul Dufy, and Henri Matisse had solo exhibits at Galerie Carré: Cocteau in May, Matisse in November, Maillol in December 1941, Rouault in 1942, and Dufy in June 1943. Pierre Bonnard had shows at Pétridès in 1941 and in 1943, Maurice Utrillo in 1942, Othon Friesz in March 1943, and the naïf painter Bombois in February 1944. Georges Braque was the featured artist at the Salon d'Automne of 1943, and had an exhibition at the Galerie de France that year. Maurice de Vlaminck was on constant display in several galleries, including the new Galerie de l'Elysée. Utrillo, Vlaminck, André Derain, Maillol, and Charles Despiau showed in the group exhibitions of the Galerie Charpentier, which reopened in December 1941, revamped under the direction of M. Nasenta. Even Joan Miró, then living in Majorca, and Wassily Kandinsky, who lived in Paris, were on view at the Galerie Jeanne Bucher:[4] Kandinsky in 1942 (21 July–4 August 1942) and again in a group show with Domela and Nicolas de Stael in 1944 (January–February 1944), Miró in 1943 (19 October–15 November 1943).

As for younger artists, non-Jewish French artists whose stars had just begun to rise in the 1930s, a good number simply moved in to fill the void created by the persecution of former colleagues (and rivals). In order to exhibit at the Salon d'Automne, a showplace for moderate vanguardism, artists routinely signed the

Fig. 3   humiliating register, stating that they were French and not Jewish. A similar procedure applied in all French administrations. Simone de Beauvoir, a lycée teacher at the time, later remarked: "I found it repugnant to sign, but no one refused: for most of my colleagues as well as for me, there was no alternative."[5]

Overall, art critics covering the Paris art scene had more to report than might have been expected. Although no attention was paid to the activities of the Galerie Jeanne Bucher and its small shows of international modernists, Jean Paulhan, a well-known literary figure in prewar Paris, championed the French modernist Fautrier in the pages of *Comoedia*, the most prestigious weekly of the Occupation period, [6] when a historical survey of Fautrier's work to date was held at the Galerie Drouin in November and December 1943.[7] In July 1944, Georges Limbour wrote about Jean Dubuffet in the same publication when a landscape show at Drouin included a work by Dubuffet. The painter Jean Bazaine contributed to *La Nouvelle Revue française* articles on the newest developments in painting. In *Le Rouge et le bleu*,[8] a small-circulation Socialist publication in favor of collaboration with Nazi Germany, Roger Lesbats[9] also wrote on Fautrier as well as on Henri Michaux, better known then as a poet than as a painter, and Jacques Villon. This same publication, and the new dailies *Aujourd'hui* and *Les Nouveaux Temps*, championed various strands of the painters in the "French Tradition" group. All this occurred in an unusual context, since the Paris press was under German censorship, subsidized by secret German funds and, by 1944, 50 percent German-owned.[10]

Although lively, the Paris art world hardly looked as it did before the war. The gallery run by Yvonne Zervos, a haven for young artists from abroad, disappeared as the Zervoses retired to Vézelay and worked with the Resistance there. Among galleries owned by Jews, Galerie Pierre—which had been the showcase for the Surrealists—closed and Pierre Loeb emigrated to Cuba. Paul Rosenberg went to New York. René Gimpel, soon to be a victim of the Holocaust, became inactive and joined a Resistance network. Léonce Rosenberg kept a low profile in Paris. Josse Bernheim moved to Lyons, where he died in 1941. Daniel-Henry Kahnweiler, whose Galerie Simon was known for its Picassos and who represented André Masson, "sold" the gallery to Louise Leiris, his non-Jewish sister-in-law, in order to avoid "Aryanization."

"Aryanization"—meaning expropriation—was the fate of all businesses (and homes) owned by Jews, including art galleries. "Provisional administrators"

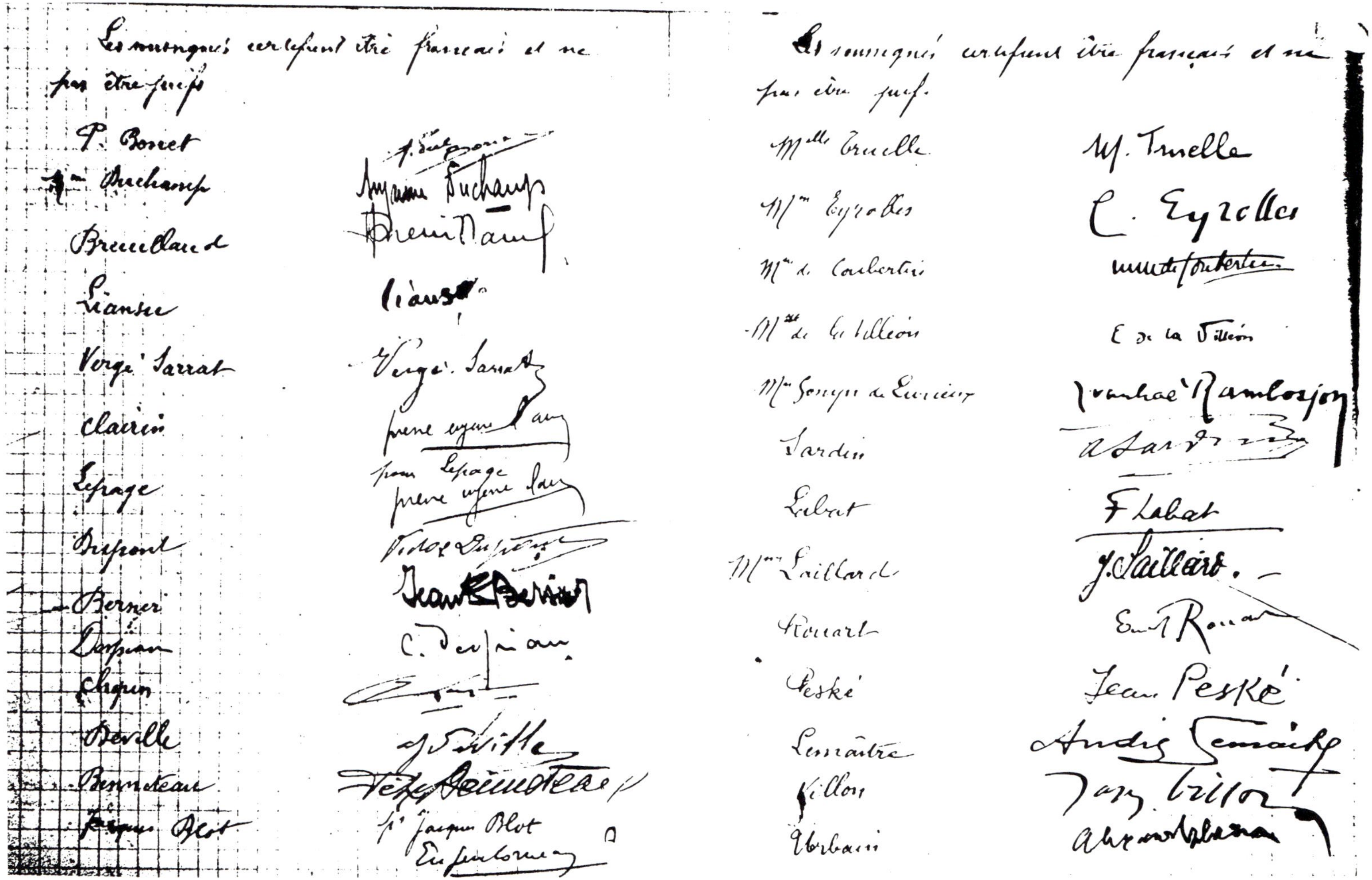
Les soussignés certifient être français et ne pas être juifs

P. Bonnet
Mme Duchamp
Breuillaud
Vergé Sarrat
Clairin
Lepage
Dupont
Berner
Despiau
Chapin
Deville
Jacques Blot

Les soussignés certifient être français et ne pas être juifs

Mlle Truelle
Mme Eyrolles
Mme de La Villéon
Labat
Mme Gaillard
Rouart
Peské
Lemaître
Villon
Urbain

3. Signatures on the register, Salon d'Automne, 1941.

were installed. Then, for a fraction of the businesses' value, French people sympathetic to German interests could buy them. In some cases, a fictitious sale of the business was arranged before the expropriation had occurred. In that case, a relative, an employee, or a non-Jewish partner, rather than a provisional administrator, ran the business. Georges Wildenstein's Galerie des Beaux Arts, where the International Exhibition of Surrealism had taken place in 1938, was "sold." A similar arrangement was concluded between Louis Carré and the Jewish dealer André Weill. Bernheim Jeune was "Aryanized" and became the Galerie Saint-Honoré Matignon, serving German interests.

As far as publications were concerned, *Minotaure*, the platform for Surrealist sympathizers, folded after the thirteenth number, dated 12 May 1939; *Cahiers d'art*, run by Christian Zervos, stopped publication with volume 15 in 1940. *La Gazette des beaux arts* was "Aryanized" and reappeared with a new staff as *Les Beaux Arts: Journal des arts*, while a new glossy periodical named *Atalante*, representing the viewpoint of the Salon de la Société des Artistes Français (the stronghold of academic artists), came out four times between December 1941 and the summer of 1943. Changes due to the banning of Jews from the press by article 5 of the Statut des Juifs[11] transformed yet another aspect of the Paris art world. Art critics with Jewish names were now silent.

As for the art on view, one need only consult the monthly calendar of galleries, particularly during the first months after artistic activity had resumed, to note that the offerings were overwhelmingly middle-of-the-road.

MIDDLE-OF-THE-ROAD ART

Middle-of-the-roadism had represented the path of the majority of artists ever since the notion of the avant-garde had emerged in opposition to the Académie, a phenomenon whose dating is as controversial as the very idea of Modernism.[12] But the focus of attention on the two extremes, battling each other, meant that the existence of a third voice had been overlooked, if not forgotten.

In nineteenth-century France, middle-of-the-roadism had been an art movement called *juste milieu*, with a political agenda of social reconciliation. Highly appreciated by Louis-Philippe and his entourage, according to Albert Boime, it had included Camille Corot and nearly all the young Barbizon artists (Narcisse Virgile Diaz, Jules Dupré, Théodore Rousseau, and Paul Huet), while "occupying a point midway between the entrenched academic and the innovative Romantic styles."[13] Then, during World War I, artistic moderation was encouraged for its capacity "to contribute to the national cause" and, according to Kenneth Silver, "the painters, sculptors, critics and theorists within avant-garde circles had

to navigate a course. . . . through the Scylla and Charybdis of 'treasonous' decadent esthetics on the one hand and complete capitulation to the forces of reaction on the other."[14]

After World War I, middle-of-the-road art made major incursions in Parisian salons (the Salon des Indépendants, the Salon d'Automne, the newly founded Salon des Tuileries), and a critical apparatus on its behalf was installed,[15] while at the same time, as pointed out by Romy Golan, an increasing variety of styles went under the heading "middle-of-the-road," ranging from the Neoclassicism of Picasso, Derain, Matisse, Maillol, and Despiau to a naturalistic style in landscape (Dunoyer de Segonzac, Vlaminck), to a hybrid of Cubism and Naturalism (André Lhote). Indeed, most living figures of the pre–World War I vanguard art world—Bonnard, the Fauves, Maillol, and even the Section d'Or Cubists, whose avant-garde activities in the early years of the century had been superseded by newer avant-gardes (Surrealism, Geometric Abstraction)—were forced into this position, as were the heirs of the Douannier Rousseau, instinctive painters and naïf painters such as Utrillo and Bombois.[16] In Golan's thesis and in Silver's *Esprit de Corps*, a parallel is made between the rise of conservatism in French political life right after World War I (with an accent on national values, celebration of rusticity, backlash against industrialization) and the abandonment of avant-gardism by its very practitioners, a theme also examined by a number of French historians under the general term "return to order."[17]

For the new generation of artists that came of age during the 1930s, the times were not favorable to formal innovation either. Even the new wave of Surrealists—Magritte, Dali, Pierre Roy—was figurative. In the words of Bernard Ceysson, writing on French art in the 1930s, "the collapse of markets able to absorb production does not predispose toward ruptures, does not incite toward experimentation with new formulas."[18] It is a time when Ecole des Arts Décoratifs graduates Raymond Legueult (b. 1898), Roland Oudot (b. 1897), Maurice Brianchon (b. 1899), and Marguerite Louppe (b. 1902), and Maillol's followers, the sculptors Hubert Yencesse (b. 1900) and Belmondo (b. 1898)—all of them inclined neither toward formal audacity nor toward rigorous Classicism—found themselves on the cusp. Bernard Ceysson speaks of "an entire fringe of painting losing itself . . . in the escapism of 'poetic reality.'"[19]

Typical of this mode are portraits like Raymond Legueult's *Figure with a Rose* (1938–41), acquired by the French state in 1941, in which the interior, the sitter, and the manner of painting refer respectively to a middle ground of wealth, class, and artistic ambition. In a bourgeois interior sketchily rendered, a youngish woman is seated. The contrived pose of her left arm lacks natural elegance. Resignation can be guessed from her inward glance. Her pretty yet matronly face is

Fig. 4

unmarred by wrinkles. The feathery strokes that here and there animate the smooth surfaces in greys and rose, the Cézannean shifts of perspective, give the Bonnard-derived painting an informality that does not transgress tasteful banality. On Legueult's art, and on the pensive face of his female sitter, world events seem to intrude only slightly. If anything, art is for this artist a refuge from world events (Matisse's art as a view from a comfortable armchair). The same thing might be said of austere female portraits by the middle-of-the-road sculptor

Fig. 5 Charles Despiau. Ceysson explains that such art "exorcises the convulsions of the real in the exaltation of an unchanging image of the everyday quality of the French soil," and he speaks of this revival of Bonnard-like "intimisme" as "dear to French culture, expressive of the enjoyment of the slow passing of days and hours in the sunlit peace of warm and quiet bourgeois interiors."[20]

At the pro–Popular Front Galerie Billiet-Worms, another middle-of-the-road attitude is seen in classical paintings by Forces Nouvelles painters Georges Rohner (b. 1913), Robert Humblot (b. 1907), and Henri Jannot (b. 1909). "Their most stringent geometric orthodoxies [are] strangely reinflected by disquieting Chiricoesque perspectives and blanched by the ashen stamp of the *Scuola Metafisica*," Linda Nochlin observes of Rohner's *Drowned Man* (1939), a painting exhibiting the airless atmosphere, sharp outlines, and earth tones favored by these painters.[21]

Fig. 6 In *Lili with Objects in Disarray* (1935 or 1936), a rare example of Jean Dubuffet's early and unknown production in the Forces Nouvelles style, the young model in the artist's studio, cut off from view at an odd angle by the right margin, has an expression of mysterious eroticism as she poses among ordinary things— a picture frame, an egg on a table, an umbrella, a crumpled piece of cloth, a hat, a chair. Even in this immature Classical work, immobility is pregnant with drama, like an exaggerated calm before the storm.

In a climate more propitious to theorizing than to artistic practice, important forces on the far left were also questioning the meaning of vanguardism, and the relationship between formal vanguardism in art and progressivism in politics (as in the "Formalism" controversy in Soviet Russia under Stalin). Evoking the passionate debates that took place in the spring of 1936 at the Maison de la Culture in Paris (remembered as *La Querelle du réalisme*)[22] between the leftist Fernand Léger, Le Corbusier, Jean Lurçat, and the Surrealist poet Louis Aragon, a recent convert to communism and to Stalinist-style Social Realism, Ceysson points out that "there are also all the [artists] who . . . search for an answer in the real relationship of their work as painters to the reality they are living."[23] In *The Dead Worker* (1936) by Edouard Pignon (b. 1905), or *Starving to Death, Spain* (1937)

Fig. 7 by André Fougeron (b. 1913), both Communist artists, a legible, somewhat

4. Raymond Legueult. *Figure with a Rose*, 1938–41.

5. Charles Despiau. *Madame Henraux*, n.d.

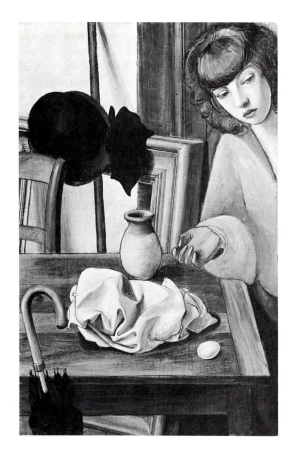

6. Jean Dubuffet. *Lili with Objects in Disarray*, 1935 or 1936.

7. Edouard Pignon. *The Dead Worker*, 1936.

Cubist angular style translates themes derived from real life into moralistic allegorical paintings.

One might conclude from this overview that middle-of-the-roadism always had an extra-artistic agenda: reconciliation of social classes under Louis-Philippe, patriotic consensus during World War I, a rallying to conservative values in the 1920s, and in the 1930s various attitudes concerning a social role for art.

During the Occupation years, middle-of-the-roadism, particularly the escapism of "poetic reality," was to have an extra-artistic agenda again. This time, it was taken up by a Fascist art critic whose nonartistic agenda was intended to exclude from the artistic life of France "the Jew and the *pompier*." His name was Lucien Rebatet, probably a Nazi plant at the fiercely collaborationist paper *Je suis partout*.[24] What follows is an investigation of the arguments Rebatet invoked to justify ridding France of *pompier* art (the word for "fireman" in French is also a vulgar way of labeling the academic milieu, the most conservative group among living artists) and "Jewish" art (art by the artists this particular critic loathed), in the context of a desire—typical of the time—to weed decadence out of modern art.

THE SCAPEGOATS OF LUCIEN REBATET

Je suis partout, a right-wing journal of the 1930s, is better known for its extremist politics than for its columns on cultural events, and the name Lucien Rebatet immediately brings to mind violent anti-Semitic diatribes in this and other right-wing publications, although in the 1930s Rebatet was also making a name for himself as a film and music critic. Little, if any, notice has been paid to his role as the art critic for *Je suis partout*, a position he held throughout the Occupation years; he replaced François Fosca, a Jew, who returned to his native Switzerland for the duration of the war. A French Fascist and pro-Nazi connoisseur of art, Rebatet represents a highly unusual critical voice. Since his verve has been compared to Céline's,[25] he clearly deserves a close reading and, as *Je suis partout* claimed a readership of two hundred thousand during the Occupation years,[26] one has to assume that Rebatet's views were widely read, if not shared.

In his first column, "Between the Jew and the Pompier," Rebatet stated that, in order to rid French art of decadence, a struggle had to be waged against both Jewish art and academic (pompier) art: "From the spot previously occupied by [François Fosca], I expect to present a chronicle in which combat will be the most important feature for as long as will be necessary." He went on to

declare that degenerate art was a cruel reality, and compared French art to a tree whose trunk is still vigorous but whose branches need pruning. "It is essential to chop off the rotten branches. We must Aryanize our fine arts." However, he continued, "the purification of our art must not bring about the return of academicism."[27]

As Rebatet prowled through salons and art galleries, he used his influence to validate the tradition started by Corot in painting and by Maillol in sculpture by demonstrating that the art of these two masters coincided with truly French taste, and that it communicated empathy for the most natural of feelings, the love of French soil and the love of healthy female bodies. He would pour Célinean venom on all art that transgressed such notions, on pompier art that echoed the vulgarity of the bourgeoisie, and on what he lumped together as "Jewish" art.

Who was Lucien Rebatet?

"I have never had a single drop of democratic blood in my veins," he proudly announces at the beginning of his memoirs.[28] Even his close friend Robert Brasillach, his colleague at *Je suis partout*, always considered him "the most violent among us."[29] Born in 1903, Rebatet had come of age too late to participate in the carnage of World War I. He received his first impressions of Germany and its people on a walking tour during the summer of 1934, a year after Hitler came to power. In his memoirs, *Les Décombres*, first published in 1942, he describes his observations of Fascism in action, tells how he discovered in Hitler a master of mise-en-scène, and admits that "the images of Hitlerism exerted a powerful attraction for him."[30] As for the smiles and hospitality of the people, they indicated to him a nation that was joyously celebrating its return to political health.[31] France, by contrast, appeared to him to be exceedingly sick.

From the insight provided by his widow in an interview with David Pryce-Jones, in which she noted that her husband "thought France might have to be conquered before it could pull itself up,"[32] one glimpses the sense of mission with which he set out after the debacle had fulfilled his secret and ardent hopes. He read his own perverse patriotism in a painting by one of his favorite painters, Utrillo, who—Rebatet noted with some glee—at a bleak time in French history, in June 1940, had painted (according to Rebatet) one of the most joyous landscapes of his career, the *View of Sainte-Maure de Touraine*.[33]

Having served in the French army until the defeat, Rebatet briefly became a radio commentator at Vichy. He worked under his friend Georges Hilaire, who, in March 1944, was to replace Louis Hautecoeur as head of the fine arts department in the Vichy government. Dismissed by Pétain after two months for the fanaticism of his reporting and apparently for opting for Laval's rather than

Pétain's version of collaboration,[34] he regrouped the *Je suis partout* fraternity in Paris and became an art critic.

Between Rebatet's first appearance as "L'Encadreur" (the Framer) in *Je suis partout*—which began publishing again on 6 February 1941, the anniversary of the day in 1934 when a right-wing march toward the Paris Chamber of Deputies threatened the Third Republic and nearly started civil war—and his last review of the Salon de la Société des Artistes Français in the spring of 1944, his pro-Nazi activism and his between-the-Jew-and-the-pompier esthetics never faltered. In July 1944, Rebatet fled France in a military truck put at his disposal by the Germans. He was condemned to death by the Liberation tribunals but his sentence was commuted and he lived a free man in France from 1953 until his death in 1973.

Prone to outbursts of vulgar and abusive language when anything remotely Jewish was involved, and to lapses into affected epithets on the subject of his favorite artists, he was the epitome of the committed critic, a vile and despicable figure in the annals of art criticism, even if Robert Brasillach could refer to him as a first-rate polemicist. The point of view of one who "dissent[s] from the traditional nationalism of Maurras, and lean[s] rather toward an organic nationalism, totalitarian in essence"[35] was to pervade Rebatet's art columns.

To Rebatet, pompier art embodied the worst traits of democracy and of bourgeois capitalism. Speaking of the Salon de la Société des Artistes Français, whose "daubs" could be seen yearly, he wrote: "It is an assemblage of the ugliest imaginable stuff that an industrial civilization can produce in a democratic country."[36] He added, "It is the perfect expression of a bourgeoisie that has reached the last degree of decadence, is petrified in its foolishness and bad taste, but still pretends to occupy a place of which it is no longer worthy."[37] In other words, the yearly Salon simultaneously manifested an unwillingness and an inability to eradicate deadwood from its midst; it mirrored the functioning of Third Republic governments and the mentality of the bourgeoisie it had served.

In 1943, in his Salon review titled "Obscène Bourgeoisie," he identified this mentality as materialistic, money grubbing, and overly respectful of old age (academicians were a notoriously elderly lot). The Salon, he told his readers, epitomized the self-destructive dynamism of this bourgeois mentality: "[Salon art will leave behind] a prodigious documentation on the spiritual vacuum of a caste, the worship of money, and the monstrous triumph of old age that led the French bourgeoisie to its grave."[38]

More appalling still, as he observed in "Between the Jew and the Pompier," had it not been for the academic instruction given at the Ecole des Beaux Arts, the "Jewish virus" would not have taken hold.[39] From 1941 in "L'Offensive des

pompiers" (12 March 1941), when Rebatet exhorted his readers to prevent an academic comeback, ("we cannot allow *pompier* art to develop its new enterprise,")[40] to the spring of 1944, when his career as an art critic was coming to a close, he never changed his tune. If anything, in May 1944 the tone became more violent: "Why can't Jewish bombs [American bombs were allegedly destroying the art treasures of Italy] fall on the Salon, for heaven's sake, clearing away container and contained?"[41]

As much as pompier art, what provoked the most abusive response from Rebatet and other virulent anti-Semites was art that somehow suggested Jewishness. His colleague Ralph Soupault dismissed Chagall in these words: "From a purely artistic point of view, Chagall's art is totally indefensible. We don't want to have anything to do with these Jewish morbidities, these women who walk upside down, these palavers of rabbis."[42] On the one hand, any image that could be interpreted as metaphorically representing disequilibrum, disorder, decay—

Fig. 8   not only Soutine's images and the upside-down figures of Chagall, but paintings, as Rebatet noted, with "purplish colors reminiscent of Jewish putrescence"[43]—suggested Jewishness. And under this label Rebatet had to include Expressionist artworks by non-Jews, such as the images with crusty surfaces, indeterminate drawing, and off-key colors by Fautrier (see fig. 26). "If you want an aperçu of dementia precox, go see the mauve landscape, the yellow and pink ones [by Fautrier]. What debauchery, for God's sake. What a waste of canvas which could have been more usefully employed for making sheets or baby diapers."[44] Here an amalgam was made of Jewishness, "debauchery," and the look of decaying matter (dirty diapers).

Every single work of art made by a Jew was to be condemned: "The public presentation in any form whatsoever, concert, theater, cinema, books, radio, exhibition, of a Jewish or half-Jewish work of art must be forbidden, and this without nuance or reservation," Rebatet wrote in *Les Décombres*. (This passage is deleted in the later edition of his memoirs.)[45] Thus even if an artist fitted his

Fig. 9   esthetics—as did Moishe Kogan,[46] the middle-of-the-road sculptor admired by Maillol—his religion sufficed to keep him out of Rebatet's canon.

A horror of formulas learned at the Ecole des Beaux Arts, scorn for bourgeois democracy, a visceral distaste for certain colors, textures, and images, and a virulent anti-Semitism were amalgamated in Rebatet's artistic judgments. Although negative feelings toward Pompierism *and* Expressionism denote a paradoxical viewpoint, they can be explained. Signs of what Rebatet called "decadence," namely the depiction of a condition of decay, are detectable in the productions of both late Classicism and Expressionism. Morbidity has often been read into the cold, "lifeless" rendering of the nude in late Classical art (particularly noticeable

8. Chaim Soutine. *Pigs*, 1939–40.

9. Moishe Kogan. *Nude*, n.d.

in the violet skin tones of William Bouguereau) and into what Jean Michel Palmier has called "the macabre visions of Expressionism."[47]

The struggle against decadence in French art would then have to do not only with the suppression of the academic and Jewish artistic networks, but with the removal from view of art showing any sign that could be taken to contain overt or covert references to the morbid, to the very principle of life, as pointed out by Michel Foucault, for whom "degeneration lies at the very principle of life, [so that] the necessity of death is indissociably bound up with life."[48]

AVENGERS OF DECADENCE

Despite its authoritarian connotations and its appropriation by artists in Nazi Germany, slick representational painting did not coincide with Rebatet's notion of art "between the Jew and the pompier." Not even the Mantegnesque realism of Rohner (see fig. 19) and other Neoclassical painters was to Rebatet's taste. In his review of the show Woman in Contemporary Painting and Sculpture, held at the Galerie Charpentier, Rebatet indicted Rohner for "coldness" vis-à-vis the female nude and complained: "There is a kind of infirmity, a refusal in front of the most natural sensations, which very much resembles impotence."[49]

Not even academic genre painting of the 1930s, with its "moralizing esthetics," characterized by Christian Dérouet as "right-wing and emulating that practiced among Axis countries and the Stalinist order,"[50] met with Rebatet's approval. Reviewing a show also held at the Charpentier on the subject of family life, the typical moralizing theme of authoritarian regimes, he found the exhibition boring and disparaged the eighteenth century, when genre had triumphed.[51]

Rebatet saw himself as a blasé connoisseur of prewar avant-gardes (at least of Cubism and abstract art) who could dismiss the current revival of Cubism and Fauvism, not out of ignorance or lack of appreciation but from a sense of déjà vu:

> There are two ways to consider a Jacques Villon or a Pignon: That of the stupid bourgeois or old fuddy-duddy, and that of the art lover who was twenty in 1910 or 1925, who never overlooked anything, who always nourished a favorable bias toward everything around him that was new or appeared to be new, and who stuck his neck out for those all-too-often questionable Impressionists and Cubists. This art lover, if he acts in good faith, cannot contest the fact that all of the problems that today's Subjectives pose for themselves had already been dealt with in every possible way between 1880 and the end of the First World War. . . . The abstractions of Cubism in particular have long exhausted their contribution to painting—a meager one at that.[52]

In painting, Rebatet prized poetic reality: he admired artists who could "finish" work without being heavy-handed and who rendered landscape with the artificiality of a stage set.[53] *Les Deux Hangars* (1943) by Derain, now in the Levy collection at the Musée d'Art Moderne de Troyes, examplifies this mode. With its curtainlike background and the bizarre illumination on the miniature protagonist, the work conveys an operatic atmosphere and at the same time succeeds in evoking a stretch of French countryside in strange weather—stormy skies and lightning.

Fig. 10

In sculpture Rebatet praised Maillol and Yencesse for their depictions of energetic female types, and admired the idealized portraiture practiced by Despiau and his epigone Belmondo. "Harmony"—the name Maillol gave to his last, unfinished, and not particularly strong sculpture—was to be one of Rebatet's major qualifiers of acceptable art. Making his way through the Salon des Tuileries in 1941, he decided that "nearly all French artists are instinctual harmonists."[54]

Fig. 11

Freshness was another criterion in Rebatet's esthetics. "Freshness" was usu-

10. André Derain. *Les Deux Hangars*, n.d.

La Sculpture

par Pierre du COLOMBIER

AVANT de quitter Paris pour retourner dans sa studieuse retraite, Maillol a donné une preuve de l'estime où il tient le Salon des Tuileries, en prescrivant d'y envoyer son célèbre groupe des « Trois Grâces » qui unit, dans une souple architecture, la pureté antique aux rondeurs charnelles. Cependant, Despiau, qui a assumé la direction effective du placement, montre, pour sa part, deux de ses plus beaux bustes anciens, un buste de femme âgée et celui du peintre André Dunoyer de Segonzac, dont il a dégagé une noblesse romaine que la jovialité de l'artiste dissimule souvent, sans compter une statue assise, de formes paysannes et bloquées, dont un sculpteur, près de moi, disait qu'elle se transposerait aisément en une « Jeanne d'Arc écoutant les voix ».

Avec de pareils patrons, le programme est tout tracé. Y a-t-il donc un esprit collectif de la sculpture, aux Tuileries? Je serais tenté de le croire, il est fait de la croyance que le style ne saurait se séparer de l'expression de la vie, et qu'il est vain de le rechercher, comme il le fut de mode de le faire voici quelques années, dans des imitations, qui deviennent vite exaspérantes, des arts archaïques. La prédilection des sculpteurs pour les formes à la fois les plus jeunes et les plus naturelles, se manifeste partout, même chez les maîtres chevronnés.

On la distingue singulièrement dans les statues qui, à vrai dire, pour des raisons évidentes, ne sont pas très nombreuses. Celle que présente Dejean attire naturellement l'attention tant par l'effort dont elle témoigne que par le mérite de son auteur. Avouerai-je pourtant que ce n'est point, parmi ses œuvres, celle que je préfère? Certes, dans le torse et dans le ventre se retrouve le subtil modeleur de morceaux qu'est Dejean. Mais l'ensemble ne va pas sans quelque froideur, due surtout, semble-t-il, à la tête qui ne doit pas avoir été conçue en même temps que le corps et pour lui. Entre les jeunes, Bouret et Martin prennent la tête. Du premier, une statue de pierre : « Jeunesse », que l'on a déjà vue mais dont on ne se lasse point. L'originalité de la pose n'en compromet pas la stabilité. Le torse, dont les formes ont la délicatesse sans indécision de l'adolescence, s'étire avec une élégance tendue. Quant à Martin, on doit lui faire un très grand mérite d'avoir toujours travaillé en demeurant lui-même, d'obéir au penchant qui l'entraîne vers le mouvement et vers la grâce. Son fragment, « Sapho », développe une esquisse particulièrement séduisante que nous avions déjà vue. Le modelé brille par une sensibilité aussi vive que celle des dessins que le même

artiste a eu la bonne inspiration d'exposer aussi. On ne saurait manquer de rendre justice à Damboise, l'un des plus doués parmi les jeunes, qui n'avait guère abordé encore de figures aussi considérables. Je ne suis pas certain cependant — mais peut-être est-ce l'effet d'un plâtre médiocrement patiné, matière assez pauvre — qu'on ressente devant cette « Vénus des Sports », puisque c'est le nom qu'elle porte (est-il bien choisi, Vénus n'ayant guère passé pour une déesse sportive?) le plaisir complet que causaient les anciennes statuettes. Car il existe un charme propre à la statuette, qu'on goûtera dans l'« Accordée » de Mme Vénard, dont l'intelligente ampleur fait penser aux Bacchantes de Deluol, ou dans la petite étude de Watkin. La statue de Max Barneaud offre des mérites certains, mais a peut-être souffert d'un excès de travail qui l'a refroidie. L'artiste aurait avantage à la laisser de côté quelque temps pour la reprendre plus tard dans la matière.

Après ces figures nues, l'« Adolescente » habillée de Cornet apporte une note différente. Cornet, qui suit de très près la nature, s'est laissé entraîner par son modèle loin de la lourdeur où il se plaît volontiers, pour donner à cette petite fille la souplesse d'une ligne presque serpentine, la vivacité de son âge. Yencesse, avec une demi-figure, fait la transition avec les bustes. Cet artiste mérite d'être loué pour s'être remis à un travail serré. Des commandes trop nombreuses risquaient de lui gâter la main. Le voici en train de redevenir le beau sculpteur dont nous avions salué les débuts.

La qualité des bustes est peut-être ce qui mérite le plus d'être mis en valeur cette année. École admirable quand on s'y adonne sans rechigner, et Wlérick donne l'exemple. Encore qu'il ne soit plus d'un âge où l'on exige d'un artiste qu'il se renouvelle, il nous surprend par son buste de Mme Corbin, à la fois femme du monde et déesse, d'un style châtié mais qui garde la chaleur de la vie. Belmondo a modelé une tête de jeune fille d'un type curieux, semi-asiatique, aux traits nettement écrits. Saupique, qui avait quelque peu déserté les expositions, y revient avec une savante effigie, fortement construite. Coutin, Chauvenet, Mme Bruneton méritent des éloges. Et quelle invasion d'enfance! C'est à croire que les sculpteurs se font les propagandistes de la famille. L'enfant de Pommier a l'autorité simple que l'on attendait chez ce maître. Celui de Rivière est tout en passages subtils, en finesses. Mais, pour l'expression, je donnerais la palme au jeune Corbin dont la petite fille, un peu maigrichonne, respire une tendre malice.

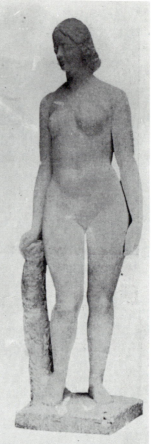

Dejean — Femme nue
(Photo B.-M. Bernand)

Joseph Rivière — Jean Loup
(Photo Marc Vaux)

Paul Belmondo — Buste de jeune fille
(Photo B.-M. Bernand)

M. Lavrillier-Cossaceanu
Buste du Dr Truffert (Marbre)

11. A review of the sculpture section at the Salon des Tuileries in *Les Beaux Arts*, 10 June 1942.

ally linked with words like "joyous" and "lively," as in Touchague's "fresh and joyous panels,"[55] Dignimont's landscapes, "so fresh, so luminous, so lively,"[56] or Utrillo's latest canvases, in which "we have the joyous surprise of tasting its fruits in their full freshness."[57] "Authenticity," connoted by the word "freshness," was also conveyed by the word "honesty," a trait Rebatet particularly observed in naïf painting. Kléophas Bogailei (one of the first victims of postwar purges),[58] "whose fantasy is indebted to Breughel, has the frankness of his truculence." Fig. 12 Honesty, in this context, suggested medieval craftsmanship, the instinctive approach of both the medieval craftsman and allegedly the modern-day, naïf painter.

Anti-intellectual in his tastes, Rebatet logically tended to praise paintings whose value he could translate by sense-related analogies. Harmony is a musical term, and great masters were often called "tenors." But it was through the senses of smell and taste that Rebatet expressed himself most rapturously: "The epoch

12. Kléophas Bogailei. *Untitled*, n.d.

of cheap bistros is over; that of cooks is not abolished but today they concoct far more honest ragouts,"[59] he wrote of the 1941 Salon des Tuileries. One is reminded here of a saying by Vlaminck, a Rebatet favorite: "Painting is like cooking—it cannot be explained, only tasted."[60] Brianchon, Legueult, and Oudot, three painters of poetic reality, were praised by Rebatet as "discreet talents who prolong the savory and honest tradition."[61]

The reference to taste would hardly seem accidental. Whereas what constitutes harmony in sound and sight is a highly subjective matter and includes compositions that some might find totally disharmonious, what the palate, especially a French palate, tells of food or wine has something authoritative and irrefutable. By applying gustatory metaphors to art, Rebatet may have sensed that he could persuade viewers of the uncontested value of his judgments while in fact validating banalities, particularly in painting.

Harmony not only characterized modern French art; according to Rebatet, it was observable in the evolution of French art over the previous hundred years. During the Occupation, to Rebatet's delight, several exhibitions took place in which the selection of modern art was intended to show the harmonious continuity of French art since the era of Romanticism. The Galerie Charpentier was the main purveyor of such revisionist art history.

"The Charpentier is the most beautiful, the most lively, and the most intelligently run gallery in all of Paris," he told his readers.[62] Displays of the good life Fig. 13 were routine at the Charpentier. Music recitals were held there privately, and on the occasion of a show with the theme of French gardens (1943), the front room of the gallery was turned into a seventeenth-century garden by the landscape designers Villemorin and Andrieu.[63] *Fontaine* (November–December 1942), a Resistance publication, insinuated that Germans attended the elegant openings with champagne flowing and well-stocked buffets: "Van Dongen is exhibiting at the Galerie Charpentier. The vernissage was a very elegant affair—we cannot go so far as to call it very Parisian," it was observed.

The exhibitions were accompanied by catalogues signed by Cocteau, Colette, and Louise de Vilmorin. They usually included the moderate academic painters Montézin and d'Espagnat, the trio of painters of poetic reality, Legueult, Oudot, and Brianchon, and a sprinkling of recent masters, from Matisse and Braque to Bonnard, Rouault, Vlaminck, Derain, Segonzac, and van Dongen. In sculpture, one would routinely find Maillol, Despiau (who became known as the van Dongen of sculpture, so numerous were his busts of the affluent), and their epigones, and on occasion Arno Breker, Hitler's official sculptor. There were no Cubist works, no Kandinskys, no traces of Surrealism in the art on display.

13. Buffet and guests at Un Siècle d'Aquarelles, Galerie Charpentier, Paris, 1942.

Two shows of French watercolors took place there, one in 1942, Un Siècle d'aquarelle, and one in 1944, L'Aquarelle romantique et contemporaine. Watercolor was favored because, as Rebatet remarked of those by Segonzac, "it is the perfect means of translating the most direct and acute sensations."[64] Watercolor also made reference to a nineteenth-century tradition that had renewed French painting without incurring a loss of métier. "Watercolor," wrote Prof. Louis Réau, in his introduction to the show Un Siècle d'Aquarelle, "became for the Romantics not only a very precious process of color notation but the principle for the renewal of oil painting at a time when it was poisoned by the *goudronnage des bitumes*, dear to Prud'hon, Théodore Rousseau, and Courbet, who were its victims."[65]

Charpentier presented a major exhibition of Spanish art, La Quinzaine d'Art Espagnol, in 1942. It honored van Dongen, Chas Laborde, Dignimont, Constantin Guys, Paul Poiret, and Emile Bernard with retrospectives; it organized group shows of painting and sculpture—La Femme, les Peintres, et les Sculpteurs Contemporains, its inaugural show, in December 1941; Treize Peintres, Sculpteurs Contemporains in 1943; La Jeune Sculpture Française in 1943—

and it organized theme shows in which old and new artworks were juxtaposed: Le Paysage de Corot à Nos Jours in 1942; Les Fleurs et les Fruits depuis le Romantisme, La Vie Parisienne, L'Automne, and Jardins de France in 1943; La Vie Familiale in 1944.

The two exhibitions that most indulged Rebatet's predilections were Le Paysage de Corot à Nos Jours and Les Fleurs et les Fruits depuis le Romantisme, with a catalogue containing an introduction by Colette. Concerning the landscapists, Rebatet wrote: "Corot takes us from the historicist landscape of Lorrain and Poussin all the way to Impressionism." In his review he also pointed out, "Painters seem to hold hands. Georges Michel in 1800 foreshadows our Vlaminck. . . . Where can one place the demarcation between light painting and the other when contemplating Daubigny's village, such a modern composition!"[66] Commenting on the Fleurs et Fruits show, he said "the contemporary rooms demonstrate, as happened in the landscape show, that the continuity of French painting remains assured."[67]

Rebatet's emphasis on continuity from Corot and the Barbizon school painters onward, and his appropriation of these nineteenth-century artists for the "modern" camp, were not accidental. In rehabilitating the Barbizon school, safely premodernist in outlook without being pompier, Rebatet had found for painting the origins of the tradition in art he wanted to see preserved and continued: Louis-Philippe's *juste milieu*. It had once signified social reconciliation, its origins were French, and it had not been bastardized by any "foreign" influences.

From the point of view of content, the tradition of art that began with Corot and the Barbizon school also established legitimacy for what Rebatet saw as a constant in the French artistic tradition—a harmonious relationship between man and nature. "One notices," he wrote, "that direct contact with nature has remained a living tradition here, even in the most rigid epoch of our art."[68] He larded his own language with nature-inspired metaphors. Art was compared to a tree; the unwanted tradition was called the Jewish "weed." The current scene made him exclaim, "No one can say that our pictorial sap has run dry."[69]

Only the strictest formalist would deny that the relationship of man to some aspect of the world is a constant of art. However, Rebatet interpreted this relationship in a restrictive way. Nature meant the country as opposed to the city. Direct contact with nature meant contact with the ancestral land. Since in the stereotype of Jewishness, Jews are nomads and city dwellers par excellence who need the hubbub of the city, either for capitalist pursuits or as a place to work, they cannot partake of this harmony between man and nature.

"The visage of France is without blemishes, without scar. It is pure," wrote Roger Lannes about the Landscape from Corot to Today show, in *Fontaine*, the

Resistance publication. "When at every road corner . . . at every street corner, signals of death are aimed at us, it may be off-key to say so, but that's what's being said."[70] What the Barbizon school tradition offered from the perspective of 1941 was a nostalgic vision of the relation of man to "nature," a world where "nature" was depicted as pristine and misleadingly reassuring.

It is all too easy to dismiss Lucien Rebatet the art critic. But Rebatet's choices make sense if one considers not only the public of nouveaux riches that Rebatet hoped to seduce but also the biography, politics, and artistic styles of artists with a poetic-reality sensibility in painting. (The cases of Maillol and Despiau will be addressed in the epilogue on collaboration in the artists' milieu.) Legueult had gone to the Ecole des Arts Décoratifs, a more open art school than the Ecole des Beaux Arts, but one from which a bureaucratic career could also be launched if one did remarkably well there. Both Oudot and Legueult had earned the Blumenthal Prize, founded in 1924 to reward the elite from that school,[71] and they taught there. This bureaucratic mentality (shared by the sculptors Belmondo and Yencesse) would lead Oudot and Legueult to agree to participate in the German trip organized for French artists by the German Ministry for Propaganda in November 1941. (The other nonacademic artists who participated in the German propaganda trip—Vlaminck, Derain, de Segonzac, Othon Friesz, Belmondo, and Despiau—were also championed by Rebatet.)

Brianchon, Oudot, and Legueult had worked for the French state as set designers before the war,[72] and continued to do so during and after the war. Sets and costumes for the ballets *Sylvia* and *Les Animaux modèles* (choreographed by Serge Lifar) were designed by Brianchon and Oudot; Dignimont, also a Rebatet favorite, did sets and costumes for two other Opéra productions, *Guignol et Pandore* (Lifar) and *La Tragédie de Salomé* (Aveline).[73] Oudot and Brianchon also collaborated on sets and costumes for productions of *Andromaque* by Racine and of *La Reine morte* by Montherlant at the state-run Comédie-Française.

From any government's point of view, the theater is an important tool of propaganda, used as a diversionary tactic by authoritarian regimes of the left and the right. Derain, himself a stage and costume designer in the 1920s and 1930s, formulated this notion in an interview with Pierre Lagarde in 1941: "To shake up the country's apathy, there is only the theater. The rest, painting, sculpture, is something more closed, private. The theater is current, immediate; what a way to galvanize people and unite them."[74]

In plastic terms, poetic realism was sufficiently uncontroversial not to offend popular taste, and, unlike Modernist art, it was legible and required no particular guidance. Its pleasing theatricality was its strong point. Although art by Oudot, Fig. 14

14. Roland Oudot. Color
lithograph, illustration for
the play *Sodomme and
Gomorrhe* by Jean
Giraudoux, 1945.

Legueult, Brianchon, Dignimont, Touchagues, and other painter–stage designers
favored by Rebatet hardly resembled that seen at the Munich House of German
Art (with its obviously rhetorical approach and its celebration of the new German
man, healthy family life, hard work, and the newly won might of the Third
Reich), it too celebrated a sensibility that concealed signs of violence and hid
evidence of the traumatic present.

If ranting against the decadence of pompier art on the part of a pro-Nazi art
critic seems odd in light of the look of National Socialist painting with which we
are familiar, it has to be placed in its proper context: Rebatet was on the lookout
for the images of National Socialist art in French terms. Furthermore, even in
Nazi Germany, according to reports of private conversations between Hitler and
his colleagues, the Führer complained bitterly of the German Academy's misguided teachings, emphatically telling his dinner guests on 30 June 1942:

Most of the Academy's professors lack both the insight and the judgment
necessary to bring real talent to the fore. Recall if you please, how the beau-

tiful seascapes of von Bock were refused by the Prussian Academy, although in their wonderful sweeps they alone of current paintings gave a true picture of the northern seas. The same Prussian Academy which rejected these pictures was, however, not ashamed to adorn its walls with absolute muck. Even in my exhibition in the House of German Art, they always try to gain acceptance for the daubs of their protégés. But when it comes to flinging these confections out, I seem exceptionally obstinate! My views on the value of the Academies are well known.[75]

The professed admiration of Hitler for "seascapes" is interesting in light of Rebatet's predilection for landscape painting. It should be recalled that the art student Adolf Hitler had been rejected by the Akademie, further suggesting that Rebatet's criticism was finely tuned to Hitler's tastes and prejudices.

The popularity of return-to-the-soil motifs in the years after World War I has been ascribed to a rebellion against the technological world and to a desire on the part of certain artists to reclaim their French roots in an agrarian past. In the early forties, the escapism of poetic reality in Corot-style landscape, in fantasy naïf painting, and in the eternally youthful nude peasant types shaped by Maillol imprisoned both artists and viewers in the kind of false, nostalgic worldview that the Nazi occupiers particularly desired. As Edith Thomas, a Resistance worker, pointed out "Our role, as writers, was to 'scream out the truth,' the yellow stars on the chests of Jews, the brutal separation of children from their mothers, the deportation toward unknown locations. . . . That was the truth at a time when attempts were being made to enclose writers in a world of dream, fantasy, irresponsibility, childishness, and puerility."[76]

As had happened during World War I, the values of French moderation were being invoked against decadence. This time there was not much artistic extremism within the young generation to give up, and the motive of the critic who advocated moderation was antipatriotic and pro-German. Middle-of-the-road practice, that had in the 1930s become associated with the search for a social purpose for art, had been sidetracked by Rebatet's rhetoric. Thus it seemed appropriate that artists who did not share Rebatet's fanatical pro-Nazi outlook react against his views. A formal effervescence was going to take place in Paris during the very same period, 1940 to 1944. Postwar French art historians called it pro-France and patriotic, although its nationalist agenda remained pro-Pétain, at least in the beginning.

3

Converts to "Patriotic" Abstraction

Where are the wooden floors—the light bulbs—the
cigarette smoke? Where is what we feel—without
notions—ideas—good intentions? No, ... give
everyone the soothing lullaby of "art."
Philip Guston

AWKWARD AUSPICES FOR PAINTING IN THE FRENCH TRADITION

On 6 August 1942, the Musée National d'Art Moderne, a national institution run by Vichy's Ministry of Education and Youth, was hurriedly inaugurated in its new premises, a wing at the barely completed Palais de Tokyo.[1] The word had gone around that the Germans were about to seize it for storage, as they had already done the Musée du Jeu de Paume, where they kept art confiscated from Jews prior to its shipment to Germany.[2] Improvised remarks by Abel Bonnard, head of the Ministry of Education and Youth, and a speech by Louis Hautecoeur, the head of the fine arts department in the Vichy Ministry of Education and Youth, preceded the official opening. The latter explained that only one-third of the paintings were put on view, due to the dispersal of the collections.[3]

According to the catalogue (Musée National d'Art Moderne, *Exposition permanente*) that was hurriedly prepared for this event, there were no Picassos and no paintings by Pascin, Soutine, Modigliani, and other Ecole de Paris Jewish artists; there was no abstract art to be seen either. Although Neoimpressionism, Symbolism, French-style Cubism, and particularly Fauvism were well represented (a lone Tanguy stood for French Surrealism), the untutored person might be led to believe these movements had been accidents, aberrations in a history of modern art still looking to the nineteenth century and earlier for guidance (see the list in appendix 4).

Six major pieces by Maillol greeted visitors in the entrance hall. The Salon sculptor Henry (Henri) Bouchard had two works (*L'Architecte* and *Le Sculpteur*) on the landing of the stairs leading down to the sculpture rooms. Conventional

Fig. 15

INAUGURATION

DU

MUSÉE   NATIONAL
D'ART   MODERNE

PAR

M. Abel BONNARD,
Ministre de l'Education Nationale
(6 août 1942).

(Clichés Diffusion Nationale Photographique.)

15. Top, Abel Bonnard and Louis Hautecoeur; bottom, sculpture hall, inaugural exhibition,
Musée National d'Art Moderne, Paris, 1942.

portraits, still lifes, and landscape paintings hung modernistically low on high-ceilinged walls, and were shown next to equally conventional sculptured busts such as *Madame Faure, Madame Henraux* (see fig. 5), and *A. Meyer* by Despiau.

Two other exhibitions of contemporary French art organized during the war by a branch of the Ministry of Foreign Affairs, known as L'Action Artistique à l'Etranger,[4] showed a similar profile. One of them, Jeunes Peintres Français et Leurs Maitres, traveled through Switzerland (Geneva, Zurich, Bern, Lucerne, and Basel) between September 1942 and March 1943. The other one, Artistas Franceses Contemporaneos, went to the Museo Nacional de Arte Moderno in Madrid in 1943, with an introduction to the catalogue by Louis Hautecoeur, head of the fine arts department in the Vichy government.

Revisionist as these three exhibitions under Vichy sponsorship were, they included artists who had participated in a group show at the Galerie Braun in Paris in May 1941, hailed by postwar French art historians as the reassembling of "all the live revolutionary forces, those most relentlessly opposed to intellectual compromise." [5]

Although the exhibition, entitled Jeunes Peintres de Tradition Française, has left few traces, and the number of participants remains something of a mystery, the artists known to have been contacted hardly represented a complete roster of "revolutionary forces," and they were not especially revolutionary at that point. The most trustworthy list is that provided by Jean Bazaine at the time of the exhibition in the *Nouvelle Revue française* of August 1941. The artists named were Jean Bazaine (b. 1904), André Beaudin (b. 1895), Paul Berçot (b. 1898), Jean Bertholle (b. 1909), Francesco Borès (b. 1898), Lucien Coutaud (b. 1904), François Desnoyer (b. 1894), Maurice Estève (b. 1904), Léon Gischia (b. 1904), Charles Lapicque (b. 1898), Jean Lasne (1911–1940), Lucien Lautrec (b. 1909), Raymond Legueult (b. 1898), Jean Le Moal (b. 1909), Alfred Manessier (b. 1911), André Marchand (b. 1907), Edouard Pignon (b. 1905), Suzanne Roger (b. 1899), Gustave Singier (b. 1909), Tal Coat (b. 1905), and François Walch (b. 1898).[6] What can be said is that not one of them had completed the curriculum of the conservative Ecole des Beaux Arts or competed for a Prix de Rome.

The August 1942 Musée National d'Art Moderne inaugural exhibition had included Coutaud, Desnoyer, Lapicque, Lautrec, Legueult, Pignon, and Walch. In the traveling Swiss show, Bazaine, Desnoyer, Estève, Lapicque, Lautrec, Legueult, Manessier, Marchand, Pignon, Singier, and Tal Coat could be found; Bazaine, Coutaud, Desnoyer, Estève, Gischia, Lapicque, Lautrec, Legueult, Marchand, and Pignon had participated in the exhibition sent to Spain in 1943.

Conspicuously absent was Jean Fautrier, although he too belonged in the French Tradition, and Jean Dubuffet, although this was not a surprise as he was better known then as a wine merchant than as an artist. No Jew was included in this "Ecole Française" offering. If Sarah Wilson is correct, the exhibition of May 1941 was "mostly comprised of landscapes and still lifes painted before the war,"[7] a description that aptly describes 1930s middle-of-the-roadism. On the list, one recognizes the poetic realist Raymond Legueult, three Neoclassical Forces Nouvelles painters, Lasne, Lautrec, and Tal Coat, and Pignon, the Communist author of *L'Ouvrier mort*.

What made this show singular from the standpoint of content was, according to Wilson, the fact that "one could discern a religious strain among some of the painters."[8] This was attributable to the presence of artists such as Bertholle, Le Moal, and Manessier, who had belonged in the 1930s to the group Témoignage, a Lyons-based Catholic movement,[9] or who, like Beaudin and Suzanne Roger, had been involved in artistic discussions held in the milieu of Esprit, the 1930s "Personalist" movement led by Emmanuel Mounier. Inspired by St. Thomas Aquinas, Mounier separated *la personne* from *l'individu*, and claimed that the person—what is noblest and most perfect in all of nature—must be salvaged in life and in art through some sort of spiritual purification.[10]

One of the participants in the show, the painter and theorist Jean Bazaine, had in the 1930s been a contributor to *Esprit*, Mounier's publication. To judge by Bazaine's *Glassware* (1937), this purification may have been expressed by the Fig. 16 metaphysical quality of simple objects observed from a variety of viewpoints, and nonchalantly grouped à la Morandi on a tabletop painted in pale violet, a color associated with spirituality.

In retrospect, the intention of the organizers of the Braun show may well have been to reconcile—through a corporatist-style *union sacrée*—artists of varying political affiliations (with the painter Edouard Pignon at the extreme left of the roster), the Témoignage and Esprit elements inflecting it toward some form of spiritual cleansing and away from social and artistic decadence.

According to Gino Severini, a participant in the discussions that took place in the *Esprit* milieu in the 1930s, the group then stood against "the exploitation of spiritual values by the money world (dealers, businessmen), by the social regime (politicians), by government . . . and by the press."[11] To the question of what kind of art would emerge now that the Cubist battle had been won, Marcel Michaud, the spokesperson for Témoignage and the author of a Témoignage manifesto dated 19 April 1939, had answered: "In the first place [we claim] a return to the spirit of the past, a distant past; also a definite break from the Renaissance and—naturally—a difficult ascent from substance to essence."[12]

16. Jean Bazaine. *Glassware*, 1937.

The Jeunes Peintres de Tradition Française exhibition had been organized by the visual arts section of Jeune France, a Vichy association for culture very much inspired by the review *Esprit*. Started in January 1941 with subsidies from the French Ministry of Education and Youth, Jeune France counted four Vichy officials on its board of twelve persons, and among its participants were Pierre Schaeffer, the music expert, Maurice Blanchot, the essayist, and Emmanuel Mounier, the editor of *Esprit*. The painter Jean Bazaine, head of the visual arts section of Jeune France in the occupied zone, was responsible, with André Lejard, for the art in the Braun show.[13]

For Michel Winock, Jeune France was "a cultural movement launched with subsidies from the government . . . that aimed to provide a popular theater for the nation, aid popular dance, launch companies, enliven places deserted by culture, and eventually set up Maisons de la Culture."[14] Here the connection with the Popular Front is stressed. Jean Louis Loubet del Bayle called Jeune France a cultural association that would "work at promoting the arts and remaking men."[15] A more fascistic interpretation emerges from such ambitions. Finally, P. de Senarclens emphasized Mounier's antidecadent aims for Jeune France: "Jeune

France is a cultural association founded under the aegis of the Ministry for Youth. Its ambition, in Mounier's words, is 'to reshape the cultural equipment of the country from the bottom up, beginning with its youth.'"[16]

Emmanuel Mounier himself shared with his 1930s collaborators at *Esprit* a politically tortuous profile, redeemed by his joining a Resistance network in 1942–43. In his writings in *Esprit* during the thirties, one finds a number of Pétainist motifs—lamentations on the subject of French decadence, on the rottenness of parliamentary democracy, on the shortcomings of internationalism. In the words of Zeev Sternhell, "Mounier rejects Fascism, but wouldn't deny that his violent critique of "instilled disorder" [*désordre établi*] rejoins that of the Fascists."[17] Mounier was apparently quite ambivalent toward the Popular Front; he refused to sign the Manifesto of the Comité de Vigilance des Intellectuels Anti-Fascistes.[18] He had resumed his editorship of *Esprit* under Vichy censorship until he was ordered to close it down in August 1942.

Jeune France was disbanded by law on 20 March 1942 (*Le Journal officiel*, 11 July 1942), accused of squandering its funds, of having too many individuals in its employ, and of "evolving politically in a direction that was not the one wanted by the Ministry for Youth,"[19] and Emmanuel Mounier's review *Esprit* was forced to stop publication shortly thereafter, but this does not mitigate the initial affiliation with Vichy. It simply shows one of many instances of the evolution of individuals and associations from pro- to anti-Vichy between the years from 1940 to 1944.

As disaffection from the Pétain regime occurred, and the balance of power on the military front changed, a pictorial effervescence stimulated by the revival of Fauvism did manifest itself. But Jeune France's sponsorship of the 1941 Braun show, the positive reception the new art received in some of the censored press, and the German leniency toward the new work put a damper on claims that its practitioners were against intellectual compromise. T. J. Clark's remark, "is not all art of real complexity fated to be used, recruited, and misread?"[20] does not resolve the issue of "guilt by association" raised by the political, social, and esthetic context in which this art was seen and discussed.

OPPORTUNE CONVERSIONS

On 11 January 1943, an article entitled "La Peinture bleu-blanc-rouge" and signed by Jean Bazaine came out in *Comoedia*. The artist who in May 1941 had gathered the eclectic group of painters in the French Tradition seen at the Galerie Braun thus explained the homogeneity of the new exhibition in whose name he

now spoke: "Yes, a nation does not choose its flag by chance.... And there would be a lot to say concerning this sort of colored crystallization of the deep instincts of a people. To conclude that all of French painting participates in this choice in the organization of color would be a bit hazardous but not totally false."[21] The paintings he was alluding to were about to be seen together for the first time at Galerie de France, with sculpture by Chauvin in a show that opened on 6 February 1943 under the name Douze Peintres d'Aujourd'hui.

Having opened on 8 February 1942, the Galerie de France had made its mark during its first year not only with an exhibition of early Fauve paintings and a retrospective of Jacques Villon but with a show of Odilon Redon black pastels (28 April–22 May 1942), and one of Neoimpressionism (12 December–15 January 1943). In 1942, the gallery had shown the work of Marcel Duchamp's brother-in-law Jean Crotti, and of the sculptor Raymond Duchamp-Villon, a victim of World War I. When it came to supporting new talent, the Galerie de France opted for the painters of the Galerie Braun exhibition who worked in a coloristic vein: Bazaine, Estève, Lapicque, Pignon, Borès, Beaudin, Villon, Singier, Manessier, Le Moal, and Gischia. The twelfth, André Fougeron, was a new recruit.

To claim—as Bazaine did—that all these painters worked in the tricolor of the French flag is an exaggeration. Estève's palette then was dominated by a golden yellow plus purple, red, and white. Pignon's palette contained orange, blue, green, violet, white, and red. Gischia used mostly violet, red, pale and dark blues, yellow, and black. Only Lapicque and Bazaine favored the dominance of red and blue. But whatever color scheme they chose, they did push it to the saturation of colors found in the French flag—or, one might also say, in early Fauve painting.

As for the formal traits of these vivid works, Bazaine would later offer Viveca Bosson a sense of his intentions at that time. He evoked "a certain moment in 1942 when with objects in front of the window, a violent coloristic transposition upsets and recreates the space of the picture; forms and colors from the outside landscape invade the room, penetrate objects."[22] It is certainly the case in his *Still Life in Front of the Window* (1942), where an all-over pattern in red and blue
Fig. 17   flattens chair and table and spills over to the landscape and the window frame. Such treatment of outside and inside space as a continuous flow of light and color also applies to the work of the other tricolor painters. Using recognizable subject matter, mostly still lifes or figures in an interior, often with a window view in the background as Matisse liked to show landscape, their paintings at that time do
Fig. 18   tend to glow with a strange all-over light.

17. Jean Bazaine. *Still Life in Front of the Window*, 1942.

18. Edouard Pignon. *Seated Woman at a Table*, 1942. (Color Plate 1)

As they moved toward intense color and shallow space, how much encouragement did these painters derive from the fact that the Germans had allowed shows of the Fauves and of Jacques Villon at the Galerie de France during the first half of 1942? We do not know. Asked what made him change, the tricolor painter Edouard Pignon would only say: "I had an admirable tool against all of that filth, it was painting. . . . During the war, our painting was a highly coloristic painting, in opposition to the sadness of the times. A painting of optimism like a cry of revolt and of hope."[23]

The critic Gaston Diehl,[24] who wrote the catalogue essay for the show Douze Peintres d'Aujourd'hui, began with a mea culpa: He admitted that he had underrated these artists when he first saw them at the exhibition at the Galerie Braun and had not sensed, as he did now, that they represented a "liberating force."[25]

Indeed, when Diehl, pursuing the path opened by the Braun show, had brought together at the Galerie Berri Raspail some eighty-five artists during the winter of 1941–1942 under the heading Les Etapes du Nouvel Art Contemporain (24 October 1941–26 February 1942), his catalogue essay hardly showed confidence in the group he now endorsed. Speaking of those he had grouped together under the label "organizers of a plastic conscience," Bazaine, Estève, Gischia, Lapicque, Pignon, Manessier, Desnoyer, Singier, and Fougeron (an early resister, he did not participate in the Braun show nor in any officially sponsored exhibitions), he had noticed their spiritual affinity but had expressed his doubts: "Their patient and tenacious investigations . . . have not always been successful," he had written in the accompanying catalogue.[26]

His doubts had been shared by the critic Jean Marc Campagne, a Rebatet acolyte writing in *Les Nouveaux Temps*, who titled his art column of 19 February 1942 "Spirit, Are You There?"[27] and felt that spirit was hardly the word befitting this particular group. Campagne favored the Forces Nouvelles Classicists and other figurative painters grouped by Diehl under the label "les enlumineurs de rêve," consisting of Alfred Courmes (b. 1898), Pierre Ino (b. 1909), Jean Marembert (b. 1900), and Jean Janin (b. 1898), post-Surrealists without the anti-Fascist zeal of the Breton group.

In March 1943, the Galerie Friedland, an art gallery of singular importance, which had come to life in the early stages of the Occupation, closed after thirteen months of activity. It had been Jean Bazaine's idea that a gallery dedicated to showing art by the artists he had gathered at Galerie Braun in 1941 should open, and to that end he contacted his cousin Jacques. Jacques Bazaine, an advertising man during the 1930s, finding himself without his major client after his release from the army—his agency had represented Peugeot cars, which were no longer

being built—listened to Jean Bazaine's advice and decided to show the artists his cousin recommended. The decorator Jean Charles Moreu did the interior decor for the new Galerie Friedland, which opened on 18 January 1942 on Avenue de Friedland with a group show.[28] On view was the Forces Nouvelles painter Jannot, the painters of poetic reality Legueult, Oudot, and Brianchon, and Pignon, Estève, and Francis Gruber (b. 1912).[29]

Jacques Bazaine organized nine shows in thirteen months (the Magritte exhibition that was on his calendar had to be cancelled, as the artist apparently changed his mind)[30] and then "lost interest" and closed the gallery. Still, during its thirteen months of existence, the gallery had organized one-artist and group shows, and presented imaginative theme shows, Hommage aux Anciens, in which the participants named their artistic lineage,[31] and a show of self-portraits, Peints par Eux-Mêmes, an important motif of that epoch.

One reason Bazaine could not continue, he says, is that a more powerful dealer was forever stealing his artists and giving them contracts. First Estève, then Pignon, then Legueult all left him for the Galerie Louis Carré, where Jean Bazaine and Lapicque were already established. He continued privately to support Francis Gruber (a leader in the Resistance artists' front), and still owns many of his works. That he did not continue with Neoclassical painters (who had the backing of Jean Marc Campagne) and the painters of poetic reality in his stable (favored by Lucien Rebatet) may have had something to do with the turn international events had taken during the thirteen months the gallery functioned.

All accounts of the Occupation period concur in the judgment that at first the French expected the Vichy regime and the Occupation to last a long time and had organized their professional lives accordingly. "Attentisme," Robert Paxton's expression, was de rigueur. Movies were being made, plays produced, books published—mindful of censorship. What precisely alerted this or that group living in France of a likely victory for the Allies depended on a variety of factors. Since literature on this subject abounds,[32] let it just be said as a reminder that the invasion of the Soviet Union by Hitler's troops in June 1941 is often mentioned as having been an occasion for the Communists of Europe to regroup and prepare their resistance.[33] Nazi victories in Russia and the Pearl Harbor disaster on 7 December 1941 kept many members of other social and political groups waiting until the November 1942 landings of the Allies in North Africa and the occupation of all of France by the Nazis. Robert Paxton puts it this way:

In retrospect, the winter of 1942–43 was the war's turning point. On 23 October 1942 the great tank battle began at El Alamein, hardly two hundred miles from the Suez Canal, which turned back Rommel's deepest advance

in North Africa. During the night of November 7–8, Allied forces landed on the south shore of the Mediterranean in Morocco and Algeria. Rommel was now taken from behind, and the dream of some German strategists . . . was at an end. Although the Germans quickly occupied the rest of France, fortress Europe was now vulnerable from the south. On the eastern front, General Paulus' Sixth Army . . . was encircled and cut off by a Soviet counterattack at Stalingrad in the days after November 20. Paulus surrendered on 31 January 1943.[34]

Events in the art world appear to confirm that the winter of 1942–43 was a watershed. For the Galerie Friedland and other galleries, institutions, and individuals, the changing international situation demanded drastic decisions.

Nineteen forty-three was also a turning point at the Salon d'Automne: "Where are masters such as Derain, Pierre Roy, where are Humblot, Rohner, Jannot, Venard, Chapelain Midy, Pierre Devaux, Courmes, Robert Grange, Claude Marquis? Nowhere in these rooms,"[35] complained the *Nouveaux Temps* critic Campagne about the absence of Neoclassical painters from the 1943 Salon d'Automne. (He even promised to vindicate them by organizing a show that he would call "Objectivism," but it never materialized.)

The yearly Salon d'Automne—a venerable institution known for its early championship of the Fauves and for its cosmopolitanism—had not missed a beat. No sooner had the armistice been signed than the directing committee, largely composed of men over the draft age, had begun looking for space since its habitual locale, the Grand Palais, had been requisitioned by the Germans. A wing of the Palais de Tokyo was made available to them. The Germans had been informed and, except for ordering that art by Jewish artists be removed, they had allowed the salon to open. Thereafter, the salon had functioned normally, if conservatively.

In 1943, however, the Salon d'Automne had apparently changed its image under the stewardship of Montagnac, its new vice president, an artist who had become involved in the Resistance network of artists, and who had decided to jettison the artists supported by Jean Marc Campagne, who was tainted as a collaborator. To the horror of Rebatet, who bitterly complained in his column in *Je suis partout* about the "all-too-generous space given over to the decadent . . . typical of the old Judaic anarchy in all of its contortions,"[36] the 1943 Salon d'Automne featured bleu-blanc-rouge painting.

The year 1943 was in many ways the worst year of the Occupation on the domestic front. All of France was now occupied; deportations of Jews drastically increased; young Frenchmen were being sent to Germany by force to work in

German factories. Food shortages were acute, and the Resistance suffered losses.[37] However, "by this point Vichy had irrevocably lost its mass base of acceptance."[38] Starting in 1943, Resistance-inspired meanings began to crop up everywhere; there was a new kind of patriotism in the air and a need on the part of those who had bet on the "wrong" side to redress their images. Nationalism, which had been a key Pétain value, now became associated with the idea of de Gaulle and of liberation. Just as in 1944 French city halls decked out with tricolor flags were to signal the recent liberation of a French village or town, in 1943 bleu-blanc-rouge painting was becoming a secret code for the coming liberation. In this way, the artists who had changed the atmosphere of the 1943 Salon d'Automne with their brightly colored paintings became the stars at the first Salon d'Automne after the liberation of Paris the following year.

The emergence of bleu-blanc-rouge painting not only could be traced through the decisions of galleries, the commentaries of critics, and the presentations at the Salon d'Automne between 1941 and 1944; it also surfaced in Vichy acquisitions of art during the same period (appendix 5). In 1941, works by Legueult and his friends Oudot and Brianchon were purchased. In 1942, and even in 1943, Neoclassical painters did well. After 1943, purchases from Neoclassical artists and "peintres de la réalité poétique" tapered off while purchases of coloristic painting increased. *Fighting Roosters* by Manessier (1944) was one of them. Not only does the work reach a new high of subjectivity and abstraction in the all-over treatment of forms, but the subject matter, a cockfight, is a reminder of the fact that for nearly four years two "roosters" had fought in the name of France: Pétain and de Gaulle.

Fig. 19

Fig. 20

Put in the context of shifts in military developments and the sure victory of the Allies, these developments made sense. Tricolor abstract art connoting individualism was endowed with the attributes of freedom and of avant-gardism in artistic terms, as against Neoclassicism and the "peintres de la réalité poétique." From the point of view of its reception, this new-born French painting had been sufficiently apolitical to serve all sorts of causes: first Vichy, then de Gaulle, and, surprisingly enough, the Nazi cause.[39]

GERMAN LENIENCY TOWARD FRENCH "DECADENT" PAINTING

The revulsion of certain artists toward National Socialist art may well have been a factor in the adoption of a vivid palette. Presenting art that the Germans considered degenerate was no doubt an act of courage. But the fact that artistic activity

19. Georges Rohner. *Still Life with Skull*, 1942.

20. Alfred Manessier. *Fighting Roosters*, 1944.

and exhibitions of one's art depended on German leniency puts "paintings of optimism and hope" (Pignon) in a more ambiguous perspective.

The leniency of German censorship toward the Fauves is easy to document. At the inaugural exhibition of the Musée National d'Art Moderne in August 1942, attended by German censors, paintings by the Fauves were very much in evidence—even though they were relegated to the farthest reaches of the museum. According to the catalogue, room 210 contained three Dufys, four Marquets, one Camoin, one Puy, one Manguin, four Vlamincks, five Frieszes, two Rouaults, four Derains, and two Matisses (an *Odalisque* and a *Tête de Femme*). There was another Matisse *Odalisque* in room 214. Six Matisses were on display in room 212 (mostly drawings): *L'Espagnole, Musique, Le Repos, Tête de femme, Les Amies,* and *Portrait de Rouveyre*.[40]

A show of early Fauve painting, Les Fauves, 1903–1908, took place between 11 June and 13 July 1942 at the Galerie de France. *Les Fauves*, a book on early Fauve works of Braque, Derain, Dufy, Friesz, Albert Marquet, Matisse, van Dongen, and Vlaminck, in the series by Editions du Chêne, came out with a text by Gaston Diehl in 1943; *Peintres d'aujourd'hui*, a collection of interviews with artists, most of whom were old Fauves—Braque, Denis, Derain, Dufy, Friesz, Matisse, Rouault, Dunoyer de Segonzac, and Vlaminck—also by Diehl, came out in 1943 (published by Comoedia Charpentier).

Explaining the revival of interest in early Fauvism, Gaston Diehl proposed the following argument in his introduction to the exhibition at the Galerie de France in 1942: "Fauvism is a beginning, a birth, a profound renewal that opens to painting an era full of promise. . . . The Fauves had understood the dangers of a long decadence. . . . They were going to forget everything and to start anew, on the basis of their own means, the genesis of art. . . . Powerful, aggressive, violent, the Fauves have defied time and are still capable of answering point by point the need for color, for joy, and for ardor that manifests itself these days among the new generations."[41]

With expressions such as "ardent joyous blood," "primitive virility," "the pagan drunkenness of the creative impulse"—words Diehl used in his book *Les Fauves 42*—the critic was making of Fauvism not only a poetic response to the art movement called Decadence, but—naively—a dynamic fascistic force against world decadence.

That the old Fauves (or in many cases the former Fauves) welcomed the opportunity to be heard from again can also be documented by their frequent interventions in the authorized press: "Naissance du fauvisme," by Friesz, Vlaminck, Braque, and Rouault appeared in *Comoedia*, 25 July 1942. Matisse had three

interviews with Diehl, two of them published in *Comoedia* and one in *Peintres d'aujourd'hui*; he had one with André Lhote, "Matisse et la pureté," which appeared in the *Nouvelle Revue française* in 1941, and one with M. Bouvier, "A Cimiez avec Henri Matisse," in *Les Beaux Arts* in 1942. Matisse even gave radio interviews—an exclusive during these years—which were transcribed and published in *Le Rouge et le bleu*.[43]

In fact, Matisse was a vivid if distant presence in Paris during that epoch. He lived in the hills of Nice, away from the Paris hubbub, its grey uniforms, its resounding boots and curfew. Like the other Fauves, he showed at the Salon d'Automne, at the Salon des Tuileries, in the group shows of Galerie Charpentier, and was in the Galerie de France Fauves show. Louis Carré exhibited his most recent drawings in November 1941 (from which the French government bought *Nature morte au magnolia* and *Portrait*). Fabiani (who succeeded Vollard) stocked and sold his recent paintings.[44] In Cannes, on the Côte d'Azur, the

Fig. 21

21. Henri Matisse. *Portrait*, 1941.

Galerie Serguy exhibited his works with those of Bonnard and with Picabia's hyperrealist portraits (10–30 April 1943) (see fig. 59).

His work was also available in reproduction. In conjunction with the drawing show at Louis Carré in December 1941, an illustrated catalogue came out with Matisse's "notes on drawing." In 1943, Editions du Chêne published an album with sixteen color reproductions of recent paintings and a text by André Lejard (*Matisse: Seize peintures*). Also in 1943, Fabiani published *Henri Matisse: Thêmes et variations*, preceded by a text by Aragon, "Matisse en France," with reproductions of two hundred drawings dating from 1941 and 1942. For *Pasiphaé*, a prose poem by Montherlant published by Fabiani in 1944, Matisse contributed a series of eighteen engravings.

In the reports of Matisse's visitors, the notion of art as a quasi-mystical activity carried on by a magician with special privileges is buttressed by descriptions of a setting of books, primitive objects, and Egyptian funerary masks that "set a tone suitable to the fairy-tale kingdom inhabited by this master magician."[45] The image of the artist as an erstwhile primitive is what the interviewers unwittingly convey in their descriptions of Matisse's way of life. The exotic birds, the tropical plants in the studio, the pretty female models posing for Matisse are the details that repeatedly get noted; completing the illusion of an island paradise is the blue sky seen through the window. "Out of the wide open window—an immense blue sky puts the finishing touches to the radiant quietude that emanates from his abode."[46]

Sheltered by an aura of respect and the innocence of Defoe's Friday, the artist pursues his intended task: to enrich civilization with art. Work and problems associated with work dominate the interviews. Asked by Diehl to answer the question "What matters most to you?" a rather loaded question at a time when human suffering was visible all around, Matisse answered as follows: "What matters most to me? To work from my model until I have it sufficiently within me to be able to let my hand run while managing to respect the greatness and sacred character of all living things."[47]

In the exchanges of notes between Matisse and Bonnard, who then lived above Cannes at Villa du Bosquet in Le Cannet, far more space is devoted to work, and to the difficulties of working under less than ideal general circumstances, than to concern for these circumstances: "Work fortunately is going fairly well," wrote Bonnard to Matisse from Le Cannet on 4 July 1940, after telling his friend that shortages—particularly of gasoline—were making themselves felt in the area.[48]

"I immediately went back to work so as to recover my equilibrium," replied Matisse from Nice on 7 September 1940, just ten days after the conclusion of his arduous trek from the southwestern to the southeastern tip of France.[49]

Not that work always went well. Threats to peace of mind made concentration difficult. Matisse, for one, admitted in a letter dated 7 November 1940 that he was unable to finish and would ceaselessly begin again. "It is certain that constant worrying is harmful to the unconscious work that generally stays with us when we are not in front of our easel,"[50] he told Bonnard. For Bonnard, problems of physical survival such as shopping for food (which meant queuing up for essentials) consumed working time. "Near famine is making itself felt at Le Cannet: twelve days with neither meat nor cheese. . . . Work of course takes its toll. It is not a matter of painting but of eating,"[51] he wrote Matisse on 14 January 1941.

As in the letters dating from these years, the issues raised in the wartime interviews focus exclusively on plastic problems and on his book projects.[52] Between the two interviews with Diehl published in *Comoedia*, the invasion of the free zone by German troops in November 1942 had taken place, bringing Matisse closer to the war. In the February 1942 interview, Matisse talks of the way drawing can generate light: "To modify the diverse parts of the white paper, it's enough to play on factors of proximity."[53]

In June 1943, speaking of the lino engravings for the *Pasiphaé* book, he says: "Three elements interplay, the linoleum, the gouge, the fellow himself (*bonhomme*). All that is necessary is to reach an accord among them, that is to say to express oneself according to the materials, to live with them." On the *Thêmes et variations* project, he says "I have the feeling that all those drawings result from a sort of fusion of my experiences, of my work, of my need for knowledge. They are the result of a prodigious sum of acquired knowledge that takes shape inside me subconsciously. I feel it erupt from my interior being like a great outburst of laughter."[54]

Current events find no place in Matisse's comments, with the exception of the transfer from Rome to Nice of the Villa Medicis, the headquarters for the Prix de Rome winners. In Matisse's opinion, the Prix de Rome should have been done away with.[55] Curiously, the gestation of *Jazz*, thought to be a major breakthrough in Matisse's art (because with colored paper and scissors he resolved the conflict between drawing and painting that had been gnawing at him), is not brought up in these interviews.[56]

Matisse's often quoted statement in a letter to his son "if everyone who has any value leaves France, what remains of France?"[57] provides another plausible answer to why Matisse made his presence felt during the Occupation years. It suggests that, for Matisse, devotion to France meant devotion to some abstract symbol, French soil, a symbol to which Matisse's name was attached. On the basis of this abstraction, the continued prestige of France depended on native

sons like himself making themselves heard, irrespective of who held power in France and what causes those in power espoused.

There is also the possibility that Matisse (unlike his wife and his daughter, both of them active in the French Resistance) sided with the nationalism of the current Vichy regime. In 1924, he is reported to have told a Danish critic, "I do not consider it to be desirable in all respects that so many foreign artists come to Paris. The result is frequently that these painters carry a cosmopolitan imprint which many people consider to be French. French painters are not cosmopolites." The same source also points out that in his teachings, Matisse always underscored the importance of relying on a national heritage, "something I have done myself."[58] Overall, however, it seems to me that Matisse's "life as usual" attitude reflected a belief imbedded in the collective psyche of the French bourgeoisie concerning the apolitical nature of art and the political naïveté of artists.

I do not suggest that Braque received in Paris during the Occupation an acclaim comparable to that of the Fauves, nor that he particularly went after the kind of recognition some of the old Fauves sought. In fact, one has to wait until 1943 for early paintings by Braque to become visible at the Galerie de France and for some recent works, including small pieces of sculpture, to be shown at the Salon d'Automne. From 1940 to 1943, Braque did not exhibit. His dealer, Rosenberg, had left for New York. Nevertheless, Braque's apolitical paintings (with the exception of *La Patience*, 1942) were much appreciated during the Occupation by a coterie of French and German intellectuals.

The German novelist Ernst Jünger, stationed in Paris much of the time during the Occupation years, noted in his diary: "Paris, 4 October 1943. This afternoon with Jouhandeau [I went] to see Braque, who owns near the Parc Montsouris a small, pleasant, and warm atelier exposed to the South. The walls were covered Fig. 22 with paintings. I was particularly seduced by the image of a black table, the surface of which rather than reflecting, 'spiritualized' the cups and the glasses that rested on it."[59] The German censor of French literature, Gerhard Heller, reports in his memoirs: "With Braque, guided by Paulhan, I penetrate a world superficially simple and fluid, yet open to the very mystery of things, transforming our vision and our sensibility."[60]

Nor can it be said that the bleu-blanc-rouge painters sought the approval of the German occupiers. Yet one of the most judicious reviews of their work at the Salon d'Automne of 1943 is to be found in the *Pariser Zeitung*, a German newspaper for German and French consumption published in Paris. In the 24 October Fig. 23 1943 issue, the German painter Paul Strecker observed:

22. Georges Braque. *Le Salon*, 1944.

French art having become national through necessity, obliged to produce by its own means, independently of the contributions and of the efforts of foreigners, has recovered some of its substance and mobilized autochthonous sources. One has put aside foreign influences hurriedly; one stays at home and need no longer elbow one's way. In all quietness . . . one has found an infinity of somnolent reserves, and one has begun to exploit them rationally. It turns out that the first years of this century overflowed with currents of ideas that had not been allowed to mature, because of the constant search for novelty.

After that Surrealism . . . mosty flaunted by foreigners, had been set aside due to the departure of its creators . . . it became possible to move toward regions more suitable to art and to search more flourishing plants. Fauvism, abandoned too soon by its founders, seemed like a favorable terrain on which to build. . . . One understands why Fauvism is currently being re-

VISAGE FRANÇAIS

considérations sur le
Salon d'Automne

L'ART français étant devenu national par nécessité, devant produire par ses propres moyens, indépendamment des contributions et des efforts des étrangers, il a repris de la substance et a mobilisé les sources autochtones. On a écarté les influences étrangères à la hâte ; on restait chez soi, on n'avait plus besoin de jouer des coudes. En toute tranquillité, le bilan une fois dressé, on a trouvé une infinité de réserves qui sommeillaient et on a commencé à les exploiter rationnellement. Il s'est avéré que les premières années de ce siècle débordaient de courants d'idées qui n'avaient pu mûrir dans la recherche constante de la nouveauté. A peu d'intervalle, on a vu se succéder l'impressionnisme, le néo-impressionnisme, le symbolisme, le fauvisme, le cubisme, l'expressionnisme et le surréalisme. C'était là un grand capital inexploité.

Après que le surréalisme, dernier des grands mouvements artistiques, prôné surtout par des étrangers, fut écarté par le départ de ses créateurs et qu'on n'eut plus besoin de le suivre, on a pu passer à des régions plus propres à l'art et y rechercher des plantes plus florissantes. Le fauvisme, abandonné trop tôt autrefois par ses fondateurs, parut un terrain favorable sur lequel on pouvait construire. En arrière, il se reliait à Gauguin, Van Gogh et les symbolistes ; en avant, il se liait facilement au cubisme et à l'art abstrait. De tous côtés, les voies étaient ouvertes.

On comprend ainsi comment le fauvisme est repris actuellement par le groupe principal des jeunes peintres français d'après des principes modernes. Même Matisse, un des premiers fauves, âgé de 73 ans, revient dans ses derniers

CONSTANT LE BRETON : LA JEUNE FILLE ENDORMIE
Photo Marc Vaux.

tableaux, dont on voit quatre au Salon d'Automne, aux problèmes de sa jeunesse. Il manie son répertoire avec virtuosité et les qualités qu'on voyait dans ses tableaux antérieurs reparaissent peu modifiées par le temps. Comme nouveauté, on voit l'utilisation fréquente du noir pur, qui avait été écartée au temps des fauves. Les peintres reviennent à la recherche des problèmes purement formels. Il n'y a plus le pathétique des sujets, proclamé il y a quelques années. Ils construisent leurs tableaux tridimentionnellement par des taches violemment colorées, rappelant quelque peu la puissance de couleur des anciens vitraux. Leurs efforts ne donnent un résultat que dans les natures mortes. Il faut nommer, à cette occasion, Legueult, Desnoyer et Gromaire. Cet art dispose dans la toile des nappes multicolores, de la vaisselle et des fruits. La violence disparaît. Mais, sitôt qu'il faut construire un sujet, le principe n'est plus valable. Les personnages des tableaux, surtout des femmes, par suite des possibilités des étoffes multicolores, se changent également en nature morte et ne sont jamais représentés autrement qu'au repos car tout mouvement équivaudrait à l'abandon du système. On songe involontairement, avec admiration, aux maîtres anciens, par exemple les Siennois qui savaient résoudre ce problème en exprimant le mouve-

ment d'une façon presque abstraite. Actuellement, les efforts des jeunes Français sont encore au stade de l'évolution. Leur goût est souvent fatal. Des peintres comme Brianchon conçoivent leurs tableaux du point de vue décoratif et non de celui de la couleur ou de la puissance évocatrice des objets. Avec Marchand, on a l'impression d'une lutte pour la couleur et l'expression. Son grand crucifiement comporte des parties puissamment senties et doit être noté comme un effort pour sortir du domaine des natures mortes.

La sensation du Salon d'Automne est sans nul doute la salle comportant vingt-cinq tableaux de Braque, surtout des œuvres de ces dernières années. On peut remarquer chez l'artiste la suite d'une évolution continue qui procède comme le lent mûrissement d'un fruit. Sur ces toiles, on voit revenir éternellement les mêmes sujets, comme certains airs de musique chez les compositeurs ; mais leur valeur et leur répartition sont constamment modifiées d'une façon imperceptible, en sorte que chaque tableau donne la surprise d'un nouvel aspect et crée des émotions nouvelles. Il semble que, jamais avant Braque, une table de cuisine, un pot de grès et une vaisselle bon marché n'aient eu autant d'importance. Mais, s'il s'agit d'y ajouter un visage humain ou un corps féminin, l'art disparaît et on ne suit plus.

Au milieu de la salle se trouve une vitrine avec des sculptures de Braque. Un cheval de bronze rappellent les fouilles de Chaldée et une amphore avec des têtes d'animaux complètent logiquement les tableaux et représentent les conceptions du peintre sur un autre plan.

Paul Strecker.

PIERRE POISSON : FEMME ASSISE
Photo Marc Vaux.

23. Page from *Pariser Zeitung*,
24 October 1943.

trieved by the principal group of young French painters, according to modern principles. Even Matisse, one of the early Fauves, aged seventy-three, is going back to problems from his youth in his latest pictures, four of which are at the Salon d'Automne.... Artists are returning to purely formal problems. The pathetic element, acclaimed a few years ago, is gone from their subject matter. They build their paintings' third-dimension by means of violently colored touches, evoking in some respects the power of color in old stained glass.[61]

It is not known whether this review, written by a German whose loyalty to the Third Reich is undisputable (the critic Gaston Diehl, who had known Strecker before the war, expressed his surprise at seeing him in occupied Paris wearing an SS uniform), came after Hitler's quip to Speer on the presence of "degenerate" art at the Salon d'Automne: "Are we to be concerned with the intellectual soundness of the French people? Let them degenerate if they want to! All the better for us."[62] What the German response brings to mind is yet another way of understanding what Hitler meant by degenerate art—decorative formalist art, which the Führer judged worthless as anti-Nazi propaganda.[63]

PRIMITIVISM AND POLITICS

In 1952, the critic Michel Tapié de Céleyran, whose artistic career had begun shortly before World War II in the Dadaist milieu of *Réverbères*, called attention to two French artists who also went through major transformations during World War II, Fautrier and Dubuffet, both of them figurative artists before the war. Fautrier's painting had shown an occasional affinity with Soutine, while Dubuffet had been more consistently Neoclassical. According to Tapié, for them and their American counterparts, the New York Abstract Expressionists, what had been set afoot by World War II was the need for a cultural tabula rasa, a complete break with Western art traditions and the formal referents of high art. "I believe," he wrote, "that there is something truly new, it is the consciousness . . . that 'isms' are impossible. It is also on the part of a few artists a certain reticence in the handling of form, this stupid form in the name of which so many researches were justified, to the detriment of all meanings." [64]

Starting in 1942–43, Dubuffet had begun to look to the primitivism of children's art. Dubuffet's 1943 drawings and paintings of city dwellers riding the subway (the *Métro* series), and his farming scenes (the series of cows and horses in a pasture), exhibited at the Galerie Drouin in November 1944, shared with

children's creations not only an absence of modeling and a bright palette, but also the way children instinctively suggest depth by piling on top of one another nontouching forms of equal size. (Could he have seen a highly publicized show of children's drawings in homage to Pétain held at the Musée Galliéra in January 1942 and reviewed in a glossy weekly, *L'Illustration*, the same month?)

Fig. 24

Fig. 25

Quite different from Dubuffet's use of children's art was the use by Fautrier of the "savage" primitivism of the cave artist. In 1942, Fautrier paid homage to prehistoric primitivism in a series of lithographs entitled *Lespugue* (after a statuette of the Aurignacian period on view at the Musée de l'Homme), which was accompanied by a long Resistance poem by Robert Ganzo.[65] Fautrier's 1942 landscape paintings, with their awkward markings seemingly haphazardly placed over rugged surfaces (shown at Drouin in 1943), evoked the plasticity of cave art. (In October 1940 l'Abbé Breuil had discovered paintings in the Lascaux caves, examples of which were then reproduced in *L'Illustration*, and, during World War II, the caves were used to store arms for the Resistance.)

24. Jean Dubuffet. *Cinq Vaches*, 1943.

25. "The Marshal Speaks in Front of a Microphone." From *Hommage au Maréchal*, a show of children's drawings at Musée Galliéra, Paris, 1942.

Fig. 26

The globs of layered matter picturing disfigured and flattened heads of victims of Nazi savagery in his *Hostage* series begun in 1943 (seen at the Galerie Drouin in 1945) resembled the rugged, rocky surfaces on which the cave artist worked, and his palette has their washed-out drabness. Thoughts of victims of Nazi barbarism shot as hostages within hearing of Fautrier's refuge bore heavily on these works.

Jean Bazaine and the other tricolor painters were not attracted to the kind of cultural tabula rasa with which Dubuffet and Fautrier identified, but rather to the primitivism of the French Catholic Romanesque and to Gothic stained glass. *Woman with Shopping Basket* (1942) by Estève is a case in point. Done in yellows, oranges, and blues, it combined the planar treatment of form found in

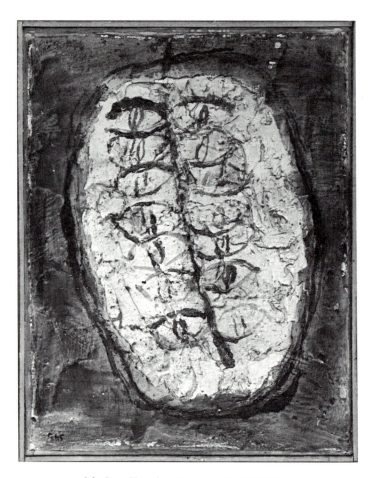

26. Jean Fautrier. *Hostage Head*, 1945.

Cézanne, the audacity of color of Fauve painting, and the religious mood of Ro-   Fig. 27
manesque church murals. So full of resigned dignity is the simplified image of
the young woman reading a letter, seated by a jumble of inedible kitchen stuff
within sight of an empty shopping basket, that a title such as *The Madonna of the
Shopping Basket* readily suggests itself. The delicacy of the naively rendered
body and surrounding objects encourages this reading.

Why the Romanesque and the early Gothic meant so much to the tricolor   Fig. 28
painters has found a variety of explanations. At a time when many museum collections were in storage, the recently opened museum of historic monuments on
Place du Trocadéro, with its replicas of provincial church murals and sculpture,
was one of the few places one could look at art.[66] Alfred Manessier, who was the
most religious of the group—he spent several weeks in a Trappist monastery
during the Occupation—explained to an interviewer that for him painting was an
act of faith: "Did you think that if your canvases were saved, man and events
would be too?" he was asked. He replied, "That's quite a statement, but it's a bit
the sensation I have."[67]

Jean Bazaine appropriates not so much the imagery of medieval frescoes as the
feeling and colors of the stained glass at Chartres Cathedral. *Mass for an Armed
Man*, 1944 (the reference is to the mass attended by medieval knights prior to   Fig. 29
going into battle) shows a man in armor emerging from the jumble of brittle red
and blue forms through which light mysteriously shines. In an article in 1942, he
suggested that disaffection from Renaissance art had to do with something very
immediate: "The Primitives are fashionable because they respond to profound
needs and anxieties," he wrote. Empathy for "the spirit of the Primitives, this
nudity in front of a virgin world, this purity and simplicity of intentions and of
means, this honesty and this freedom of attack that some would call maladroit,"
was particularly timely, he went on to say.[68]

As to why the primitivism of the Middle Ages was more appropriate than what
he called the primitivism of the savage, Bazaine explained: "In the Middle Ages,
man and nature, possessed with a single God, are still united in their destiny. But
man is no longer lost in the 'cosmos,' he has become the center of the world,"[69]
whereas in the plastic universe of the primitive, "reality is a confused weight of
sensations, a heavy charge of poorly disentangled forms, sources of pleasure or
of disquiet [comparable to] bovine reality."[70] Catholicism, in this view, had introduced more than a single God. It had introduced a new sense of order and
hierarchy in man's ability to deal with, to recreate, to represent the world.

Furthermore, it was because of difficulties in finding one's path when so many
choices were possible that Bazaine advocated being as "open and naked as a

27. Maurice Estève. *Woman with Shopping Basket*, 1942. (Color Plate 2)

28. *Woman and Dragon*. Mural painting of the porch at Saint Savin sur Gartempe (detail)

29. Jean Bazaine. *Mass for an Armed Man*, 1944. (Color Plate 3)

primitive." He explained: "It is not a matter of adding up known things or of accumulating problems, but of going to the very bottom of one's essential exigencies. Let's not cheat with our instinct or our lucidity, as uncertain as may be the world which our discoveries lead us to. It is far more an invitation to risk-taking, to an intransigent honesty, than any helpful memento to our certitude or a wise, safe recipe."[71]

Reminiscent of the Gottlieb-Newman-Rothko manifesto of June 1943 and its notion that "to us art is an adventure into an unknown world, which can be explored only by those willing to take risks,"[72] Bazaine's text compared the working process to a risky adventure into the unknown. Bazaine, however, proposed that instinct and lucidity were forever in dialectic confrontation, whereas the Americans were willing to leave lucidity behind and allow the irrational full play: "This world of the imagination is fancy-free and violently opposed to common sense."[73] Note also that it was by listening to one's "instinct" rather than to one's "unconscious" that discoveries were made according to Bazaine. Bergson (who died in Paris on 4 January 1941), not Freud, provided Bazaine's subtext.[74]

As for the discoveries made through this form of abandon, this laying of one's soul "bare and open as a primitive," they did not reveal a world "fancy-free and violently opposed to common sense" but—Bazaine ventured—an "uncertain" world, a world of uncanny family resemblances. "True sensibility begins," Bazaine explained, "when the painter discovers that the ripples (*les remous*) on a tree and the bark (*l'écorce*) on water are kin."[75]

At a time when self-censorship was the recommended strategy for survival, Surrealist abandon to the voice of the unconscious was out of the question for this artist and for most of his peers. From the start, Jean Bazaine, an intellectual as well as an artist (he had exhibited with Fautrier in 1937 within the context of the Paris World Fair,[76] and written philosophical essays for *Esprit*), adopted the point of view of Emmanuel Mounier, the editor of *Esprit*, that submitting your writing—or your art—to censorship was not reason enough to abstain from publishing or from exhibiting. "I do not believe in a policy of absence, of waiting, of prudence," Bazaine wrote in the August 1941 issue of the *Nouvelle Revue française*, his platform during these years.[77] His choice of a French, Christian primitivizing lineage, his exclusion of Surrealism, the bête noire of avengers of decadence, confirmed this position. Seen through the philosophy of *Esprit*, and of Vichy's nationalist ideology, the outcome was a French style of painting that sought to be both avant-garde and against decadence. In the eyes of the enemy, this formalistic avant-gardism remained decadent art, but Hitler was apparently not afraid of blue-white-and-red painting.

It would appear that, contrary to the backtracking of vanguardism in French art that accompanied World War I and lingered on throughout the interim between the two world wars, a spurt of energy inspired by primitivist referents could be observed in the period 1940–44. The élan noted by Huyghe and other French art historians was evident during World War II, although the painters in the French Tradition singled out in French art histories were not all involved in this pictorial breakthrough, nor were they exclusively those who realized it. On their own, Dubuffet and Fautrier also went through a radical change of outlook, attuned to the primitivism of children's and prehistoric art, rather than to the French Catholic Middle Ages.

It is generally assumed that conventional art forms are best suited for propaganda purposes and that conventional artists rally to governments that treat art as propaganda. This was certainly the point of view of the conservative network of the Salon de la Société des Artistes Français, whose ambitions are questioned next. If, however, nonconformist artistic energies did rally to the Vichy cause at first, it would hardly be the first time that a new regime had attracted certain types of art revolutionaries.

The case of revolutionary Russia and its avant-garde is amply documented, as is that of the Futurists in Mussolini's Italy. Even in Nazi Germany, as is slowly becoming clear, not only was Emil Nolde a member of the Nazi party but more artists than are suspected wished that there might be a place for them and for their art in the new regime. Oskar Schlemmer wrote in a letter to Goebbels dated 25 April 1933, "Artists are fundamentally apolitical,"[78] and he submitted a design to the competition for the decoration of the Congress Hall in the Deutsches Museum in Munich, which was rejected.[79] Possibly by 1943 Hitler was ready to take advantage of such errors in judgment.

4

No Victory for Salon Artists

SALON ARTISTS COURT VICHY

"From now on artists must express our sense of life, not that which the Révolution Nationale condemns but that which it approves, that which will triumph over all resistance because it will be the only possible one, the only admissible one," the unsigned editorial of *Atalante*,[1] a new glossy art magazine devoted to the promotion of art by the Salon de la Société des Artistes Français and its companion, the Société Nationale des Beaux Arts,[2] announced in its first issue in 1941. When Lucien Rebatet forewarned that the elimination of the Jew must not bring about the triumph of pompier art, he was pointing a finger at this very milieu, an ultraconservative group of painters and sculptors, generally overlooked in analyses of twentieth-century art.

"The days of unhealthy conceptions of art, of a mercantile apologia for overrated talents and easy daring, are over. From now on, *Atalante* will fight for a healthy and vigorous art, for art rid of pernicious influences,"[3] another unsigned proclamation read, brandishing the health and purity of Aryan and Greco-Roman classical roots as an antidote to decadence in art. Meanwhile, the sculptor Henri Bouchard, speaking as the newly chosen president of the Salon on "A Retrospective View of Salons," also insisted on the need to combat decadence in art: "It is necessary to combat by all possible means the decadence of our plastic arts."[4] Tightness of form, harmony of tones, rightness of values, balanced composition, and respect for knowledge should not be disregarded as they had been in modern times, he declared.[5]

What seems to have occurred in France under Vichy was a phenomenon that Berthold Hinz also observed in his study of artists under the Third Reich: "Traditionalist art rooted in the nineteenth century was making use of the National Socialist assumption of power—not only in terms of form and content but also in terms of cultural policy—to insure its own position of dominance in the art world."[6] Concerned since its beginnings with the moral purpose of art, the Salon

coterie saw as its agenda the fulfillment of the new government's own agenda: to deliver the nation from decadence or, in their words, from "social decomposition, . . . moral and intellectual anarchy."[7]

Who made up this neglected group of artists, associated with the Salon de la Société des Artistes Français, though not necessarily with the politics of its president (the painter Maurice Denis and the sculptor Louis Leygue, a winner of the Prix de Rome in 1931, were both enrolled in Resistance networks, and Leygue was in fact deported)? Essentially, this group was made up of professors at the Ecole des Beaux Arts, former winners of the Prix de Rome,[8] members of the elite corps of the Académie des Beaux Arts,[9] and other guardians of a tradition handed down with minimal changes from generation to generation through the teachings of the Ecole des Beaux Arts. By 1939, it also included a few outsiders such as Maurice Denis and Edouard Vuillard, who were voted into the Académie des Beaux Arts in 1932 and 1938 respectively.

Neither Vuillard nor Denis had won the Prix de Rome, nor completed the Ecole des Beaux Arts curriculum, nor risen through the ranks via the usual route;[10] the profile of Bouchard, on the other hand, was typical for this milieu. The son of a carpenter and a seamstress, Bouchard (1875–1960) was from Dijon. With a small scholarship he was able to move to Paris, eventually entering the atelier of Barrias (who, according to Bouchard's biographer, Louis Vauxcelles, writing under the assumed name of Thérèse Vallier in 1943, greeted him "not without grumbling a bit at first)."[11] After five tries, according to his daughter-in-law,[12] he finally was awarded the Prix de Rome in sculpture. In Rome he became friendly with a student also there on a prestigious scholarship, the future art and architectural historian Louis Hautecoeur, who rose through bureaucratic ranks from museum curator and instructor at the Ecole du Louvre to head of artistic services for the Paris World's Fair to Secretary General of the fine arts department of the Ministry of Education and Youth under Pétain.

Bouchard first taught sculpture at the Académie Julian, the independent art school that had the best reputation for preparing students for the Ecole des Beaux Arts itself. A well-received report on how to improve the teaching of sculpture at the Ecole des Beaux Arts—done as part of an inspection assignment—led to his nomination as *chef d'atelier* there in 1929 on the death of Injalbert. He was elected in 1933 to Injalbert's seat at the Académie des Beaux Arts. In 1939, his name appeared twice in the Salon de la Société des Artistes Français hierarchy: once as president of the sculpture section and once as president of the jury for sculpture. In 1941, he was elected president of all the Salon sections. Over the years, Bouchard had also benefited from commissions from the French state

(monuments to the war dead throughout the French provinces, a fifteen-foot-tall *Apollo*, 1937–38, in bronze for the Palais de Chaillot in Paris), rewards that former Prix de Rome winners and recipients of medals at the Salon de la Société des Artistes Français obtained with steady regularity.

As can be seen from this succinct biography of Bouchard, working-class parents, rewarded tenacity, a steady climb in the teaching hierarchy, stepping into the shoes of an established elder, Injalbert, friendship with Louis Hautecoeur (himself on the way up the bureaucratic ladder), and election to the presidency of the Salon epitomized the stages of a career and the rise into the establishment made possible by a Republican government for one with humble origins.

That it was a career built on social acumen as well as on talent was something Lucien Rebatet was not the only one to find objectionable. "Starting at the beginning of this century," writes Raymonde Moulin, "budget reporters were denouncing the dangerous and anonymous influence of ... academies, which formed a sort of state within the state, aimed at the predominance of a coterie of special interests, a grouping of students one pushes, of friends one favors, of flatterers to be rewarded."[13]

Even during Léon Blum's Popular Front government, when the French government opened its purse to painters and sculptors outside its usual constituency for the large building and arts program connected with the 1937 Paris World's Fair,[14] *copinage*—the French equivalent of old-boy networking—still functioned between traditional artists and functionaries of the French state. Mady Menier has pointed out how exceptional the Delaunays' presence was, and she reminds us that while the artworks commissioned from Modernists for the Paris World's Fair of 1937 were most frequently placed in temporary structures and have disappeared (including the Lipchitz *Prometheus*), the more traditional artists' contributions are still there in the permanent buildings that went up in the 1930s.[15]

Copinage between art bureaucrats and Salon artists may also have influenced the mysterious selections made for the Maitres de l'Art Indépendant show held at the Petit Palais in Paris in 1937. According to research by Bernadette Contensu, the painter Fautrier was not included, although he received eight votes. Neither was Duchamp, who received four votes, while there were several traditionalist artists who received one or two votes and yet were included. She asks, "Did the moral rigor that must preside over such operations succumb to the friendly relations of certain members of the committee?"[16]

As for Bouchard, he had been among those selected for the Palais de Chaillot *Apollo* although he sat on the board responsible for the choice of art there,[17] and had been awarded the commission—for which he received 224,000 francs[18]—

thanks to the intervention of Louis Hautecoeur, who was then head of artistic services for the Paris World's Fair. Hautecoeur had acted to override the architects' choice of Jacques Swobada.[19]

The Blum breezes had been light indeed and there were reasons why the arrival of Marshal Pétain, a benevolent dictator and himself an academician, was enthusiastically welcomed by Salon artists. *Copinage*, as a way of life between the Salon de la Société des Artistes Français and the state, had a good chance of recovering after a partial eclipse during the Popular Front. Although, as has been pointed out by Albert Boime, "contrary to general thought, these terms (official and academic) are neither synonymous nor mutually reinforcing,"[20] throughout the history of the Salon, such an amalgam had been sought. The nomination of Louis Hautecoeur to a key post in the fine arts department added to Bouchard's personal prospects.

What did the Salon propose against social, moral, intellectual, and esthetic decadence, and how did the Vichy regime respond to its offers of service? Much as the Salon's offerings aimed to please the new French government at Vichy, the Salon milieu failed to achieve its goal. The aim of the new government was a prosperous, classless nation, economically dependent on all its productive forces, especially its arts and crafts. An eclectic range of French traditions and French values was necessary to the fulfillment of this program.

SALON IMAGES AGAINST DECADENCE

The disappearance of much of the work, and the need to rely on incomplete catalogue illustrations and reproductions in art periodicals, make the following analysis tentative. At first glance, Berthold Hinz's observation on the exhibition of German art held in Munich in 1937 "that landscapes, nudes, and pictures of farmers dominated the exhibit, followed by portraits, still lifes, and paintings of animals"[21] would seem to apply to Salon painting in Paris. Yet Salon artists appear to have been immune to the racist rhetoric typical of Nazi art. For example, one does not find among Salon sculptors anyone who "not only models the muscle of a male body to recapture the classic Greek image but also shapes each part so as to express a paroxysm of wrath and vengeance," to quote Helmut Lehmann-Haupt on Hitler's favorite sculptor, Arno Breker.[22]

One should remember that the new art of the Third Reich was not necessarily by artists trained as the French Salon artist was. Arno Breker (b. 1900) had an artistic background closer to that of Maillol and Despiau than to the Prix de Rome winner Henri Bouchard. Hitler's disgust with the "Academy" has already

been mentioned. Furthermore, it took more than a thorough classical grounding in art to receive acclaim as an artist in the Third Reich. As reported by Hildegarde Brenner, "Goebbels . . . had the ambition of transforming the arts into a modern instrument of political stewardship."[23] There is little evidence that Goebbels had a counterpart at Vichy. In *Vichy et le fascisme*, Michèle Cointet-Labrousse evokes the continuing infighting between Pétain and his prime ministers over control of the Office of Information and Propaganda; she mentions Paul Marion as someone who would have liked to play that role "had he been given the means to do so."[24]

This does not mean Pétain neglected his public image. Under the direction of the ceramicist Robert Lallemant, an artistic office was organized whose aim was "to create over the long term an *Art Maréchal* that paid homage to his person but also, in line with his own wishes, celebrated eternal verities on the theme of the country, the family, and work."[25] (The Musée d'Histoire Contemporaine—formerly the Musée des Deux Guerres Mondiales—in Paris has a collection of these cult objects, plates, ashtrays, vases, small plaster busts by the Salon artist Cogné, medals by various authors, all of them intended as gift souvenirs.)[26] An Atelier Maréchal opened near Aubusson (Creuse) for the realization of tapestries on themes dear to the marshal. "L'Imagerie Maréchal" circulated deep into the French provinces through the services of youth movements, charity events, and the post office. Even "matchboxes, cigarette packs, cigar boxes, railroad advertising . . . [carry] official slogans."[27]

An official bust of the marshal was commissioned from Léon Drivier, a student of Auguste Rodin and a friend of Despiau, to replace that of Marianne in French city halls and schools. (The marshal's official portrait was painted by Constantin Le Breton, after Bonnard declined the honor.) Even a new public park bearing the name Philippe Pétain was in the planning stage.[28] But, measured by its influence on public opinion, Vichy propaganda never achieved the kind of "annihilation of memory and its constant recreation in response to the ideological and political imperatives [of the National Socialist party state]"[29] that was taking place in Nazi Germany.

To return to Salon offerings: whereas in 1939 the sculpture section of the Salon had included a bust of General Franco by Maxime Real del Sarte (1888–1954),[30] and one of Colonel de la Roque, whose followers had participated in the right-wing demonstrations of February 1934, by Madame Chapaud-Letulle,[31] now it frequently featured effigies of Pétain. (Hardly the Republican milieu despised by Rebatet, the Salon group appears to have been a hotbed of Maurras admirers.) Reviewing the 1942 Salon in *L'Illustration*, a glossy periodical with

Fig. 30

Fig. 31
a marked bias in favor of Salon offerings, Louis Baschet favorably mentioned busts of Pétain by Pierre Traverse (b. 1892) and Robert Busnel (1881–1957), and the full-length effigy of the marshal by François Cogné (1870–1945),[32] apparently destined for the courtyard of the Chancellery of the Legion of Honor. Concerning Bouchard's dignified though colossal *Philippe le Bon*, the comment was: "It's a great work in the grand style."[33] Not only did the Duke of Burgundy, Philip III "the Good" (1396–1467), share with Pétain the name Philippe, but he had become one of the most powerful sovereigns in Europe.

New to the Salon were religious images of Christ, the Virgin Mary, Saint John the Baptist, and religious motifs in general. Joan of Arc, as a Catholic, anti-English heroine, "savior" of France, and anointed saint, was a favorite symbol. Maxime Real del Sarte, a personal friend of the marshal's, was commissioned to do a considerable number of statues of Joan of Arc for the provinces. (Religious painting also saw a comeback in art schools.)

Interiors, still lifes, and portraiture continued to abound. But while in 1939 an eminently Parisian chic predominated, with many views of Paris, Parisian interiors, men and women dressed for a Parisian evening, and the kind of bibelots and flower arrangements found in fashionable Parisian interiors, now a "return to the soil" was manifest in interiors that featured rustic furniture and objects, and bouquets of simple flowers; the dress code was that of the gentleman farmer, of the provincial housewife. Even Bouchard's *Philippe le Bon* in medieval costume evoked a glorious rural past. Landscapes typical of this or that region and pictures of farm animals continued to be popular subjects.

Fig. 32
The theme of work, as in the Pétainist motto "Travail, Famille, Patrie," focused exclusively on farm work, on the various phases of harvesting hay, wheat, and grapes. *Harvest*, by Montézin (1874–1946), shown at the Salon of 1942, with its farm workers in conversation in the left foreground, was noted for its "explosion of pale hues invading the foreground of the picture so as to bring out near the top of the picture the chalky whites, raw greens, and deep blues of a nearby village in unexpected alliance."[34] Clearly, Bouchard's demand for tightness of form and harmony of tones was not enforced, although one could read in *L'Illustration*, "The work [of Montézin] is of an evolved Impressionism. [It is] a personal art, direct and cleaned of the imprecision of Monet's disciples."[35]

Hardly new to Salon visitors was the abundance of paintings of female nudes. Despite the official promotion of prudishness, at the 1942 Salon *Sleep* showed a nude female on a couch, and *Rest* was portrayed by a young woman in frilly underwear, her panties off, her stockings half pulled down, lying on a satin-

30. The sculptor François Cogné with maquette of statue (of Pétain) about to be exhibited at the Salon de la Société des Artistes Français, Paris, 1942.

31. *Philippe le Bon* by Bouchard at the 1942 Salon de la Société des Artistes Français. From right to left: Bouchard, Lejeune, Montezin, Garnier, and Bernier.

covered bed. (A formalist description in the catalogue next to the reproduction of the work muted the salacious qualities of the painting.)

Effigies of women in a wide variety of roles now supplanted those of men. Women predominated in interior scenes, a reality of the times when so many women were becoming de facto heads of households. Giess, a 1930s Prix de Rome winner whose *Interior* is typical of these lopsided family scenes, received praise from *L'Illustration* as a rare example of "conscientiousness and hard work."[36] Exhibited at the 1942 Salon, *Le Génie de la musique*, by another 1930s Prix de Rome winner, Albert Bouquillon,[37] was symbolized by a tall Wagnerian heroine with broad shoulders, small breasts, and stern stance, towering immobile over her viewers, her body covered with a long tunic, her head turned slightly upward and eyes fixed on a distant point.

In both sculpture and painting, youth tended to be signified by the bodies of preadolescent girls. Paul Dupuy used a naked little girl holding a flowering branch like a jump rope above her head in his painting *Spring Flower*, an allusion to the purity of beginnings present equally in spring and in youth. Meanwhile, his nymphet, staring unabashedly at the viewer, hardly offered the healthy conception of art said to be taking the place of decadent modernist images. Bouchard produced a *Bacchante* and an *Atalante*, both of which depicted athletic young girls gracefully gesturing.

In 1942, the subject of the Prix de Rome for sculpture, "The Apparition of a Young Eve at Dawn," was won by Gambier, a student of Bouchard. The naked yet sanctimonious pose—knees close together—of the young Eve was typical of the double standards of the Salon milieu. Through the depiction of female nudes and virgins in alluring poses, Salon artists were unloading their consciences in relation to the value set on youth by the Pétainists, while indulging in subjects of prurient interest to themselves and, they hoped, to the marshal and his entourage.

However, there was also an antianecdotal trend in Salon art, particularly in the look of sculpture destined for public places. An absence of expression, a minimum of gesturing, a quiet stillness of attitude characterize the composed, inward-turned *Pasteur* by Niclausse, clothed in a Roman toga, and his companion piece, a *Berthelot* by Crouzat, rendered in magisterial robes, two of the statues in white marble commissioned during the Vichy regime and installed on the stairway of the Paris Faculté de Pharmacie. Bouchard's *Philippe le Bon* of 1942 belongs with them. We are reminded here of Louis Hautecoeur, writing in *Considératons sur l'art d'aujourd'hui* (1929), a text dating from his days as instructor at the Ecole du Louvre: "Sculpture is important in itself outside of subject matter. No more anecdotes, no more symbols, no more little stories. No more sentiment nor

32. Pierre Montézin. *Harvest*, 1942.

33. Giess. *Interior*, 1942.

34. Paul Dupuy. *Spring Flower*, 1942.

smiles. They [women in sculpture] remain expressionless. The body is no longer agitated. Standing, seated, or lying down, figures simply pose with clothes falling straight down."[38]

In light of the cliché image of the regime as "traditionalist," one would expect Vichy to have responded positively to the Academy's overtures. Indeed, Vichy took advantage of the friendly disposition of this group to fulfill its collaborationist goals. I will discuss in the epilogue the visit paid to Germany by thirteeen

artists (including several Salon artists) at the behest of the German Office for Propaganda. Other collaborationist tasks entrusted to members of this milieu include the participation of Albert Bouquillon in the 1941 exhibition *Le Juif et la France*, organized by the Institut des Questions Juives, whose inauguration was attended by delegates of the Vichy government,[39] the involvement of Henri Bouchard in the creation of an artists' organization modeled after German Chambers of Culture, and the role played by Bouchard in fulfilling a demand made by the occupiers for bronze metal at the cost of vandalizing the French patrimony of numerous examples of public sculpture.[40]

But although Salon artists exploited motifs presumed to be in harmony with the marshal's public and private yearnings, they failed as a group to persuade the government that its agenda and theirs were identical.

THE VICHY AGENDA: A REVIVAL OF FOLK AND DECORATIVE ART

Marshal Pétain did not produce a *Mein Kampf.* Nor did he emulate the Führer, who, in 1937, had used the opening of the new House of German Art in Munich to rant against decadent art.[41] Abel Bonnard, the sixth and last Minister for Education, was the spokesperson when the opportunity to speak on art arose, in August 1942, with the inauguration of the Musée National d'Art Moderne in its new locale in Paris. Although the marshal was friendly with the Salon sculptor and Action Française activist Maxime Real del Sarte—when Pétain was ambassador to Spain, the sculptor obtained for him an advance copy of the speech that Maurras was to deliver at the Madrid Academy[42]—and while he sat for the "sculptor of marshals," the Salon artist Cogné, no record remains of his conversations with these artists. The account of an exchange with Arno Breker, the official sculptor of the Third Reich who offered to make a bust of the marshal for his birthday, suggests through Pétain's answer—"I'd rather own one of your Venuses"[43]—the crudeness of the military man's approach to art.

The acquisitive attitude of Hitler and his acolytes toward art had no counterpart at Vichy.[44] Negating two years of effort at keeping art treasures out of German hands,[45] the line that divided France into an occupied and a free zone ran just south of the chateaux on the Loire river where the bulk of the art had been transported, leaving it in German hands in the southernmost part of the occupied zone.[46] By contrast, when the Rosenberg staff[47] at the Jeu de Paume museum began sorting out art collections plundered from Jews, apportioning them to various Nazi leaders, bartering the modern art for older works, allegedly destroying

some by fire, and shipping millions of francs worth of art out of France,[48] Pétain's government argued in its complaints to the Armistice Commission that this was French property and ought to be sold according to the law of 23 July 1940 for the benefit of the Secours National, a French charity.[49]

As part of his strategy to keep Spain out of the war, Marshal Pétain would sign into law on 19 July 1941 an art exchange in which France was the clear loser, ignoring the French law under which artworks cannot be traded or sold once they have entered the national art patrimony. For good measure, the marshal also surrendered "everything that was in France from the Spanish National Archives of Simancas." [50] As for Vice President Darlan, in March 1941 he tried to persuade the French Minister of Education and Youth to surrender to Ribbentrop a Boucher nude from the Louvre, *La Diane au bain*, "whose thighs the German minister had fallen madly in love with,"[51] hoping to obtain the return of French war prisoners in exchange. (The painting was returned after two months for unknown reasons. Some prisoners were freed.)

One should not deduce from such gestures that the visual arts were ignored by Vichy and that artists were not expected to play an important role in the ambition of the Pétain regime to uproot decadence in society. We have already mentioned the artistic service of the marshal, *l'art maréchal*, the *imagerie maréchal*, the *atelier maréchal*; all of them made use of artists. The Galliéra museum, a municipal Parisian museum, seems to have specialized in art exhibitions on themes reflecting Pétainist ideology; the cult of youth (Le Sport dans l'Art, March 1941, March 1943; Fêtes de Jeunesse dans la France de Demain, April 1942; children's drawings glorifying the marshal, January 1942), the return to the soil and to provincial values (the Salon des Provinces Françaises, January 1944); and yearly Salons of popular imagery. A Salon des Prisonniers for art by French prisoners of war was also held there. The Pétain government supported a variety of associations wholly or partially involved in the visual arts such as Jeune France, L'Entr'aide aux Artistes, and Les Chantiers Artistiques, aimed at helping the young and the unemployed.[52]

Measures for the protection of the French patrimony, better care of art objects entrusted to museums resulting from a Statut des Musées de France, upgrading the qualifications of curators of provincial museums,[53] simplification of the acquisitions and commissioning policy of the state,[54] reforms at the Ecole des Beaux Arts, and the creation of a graduate school for architectural training and of an architects' corporation were among the innumerable decrees, statutes, and laws concerning the fine arts that one finds reprinted in *Beaux Arts de France*. They were juxtaposed with less savory ones: decrees instituting a restrictive cor-

porative organization for graphic and plastic arts and for arts and crafts, laws and decrees announcing student quotas for universities, the expulsion of Jews from teaching and administrative posts, and laws ordering the collection and melting down of bronze statuary.[55] Outwardly those measures were about "a 'crusade' against bad taste and for the rationalization of social activity in favor of artists,"[56] while also creating new ways to control and exclude the regime's alleged enemies.

Under the stewardship of Louis Hautecoeur, Pétain's choice for the post previously held by a Jew, Georges Huisman, as Directeur des Beaux Arts,[57] credits for painting and sculpture increased [58] and a group of paintings from the estate of Edouard Vuillard was obtained.[59] Drawings by Matisse were added to the nation's art collections.[60] Existing schools (Conservatoire de Musique, Collège de France), post offices, churches in Paris (Eglise St.-Esprit) and in the French provinces were to be adorned with murals, reliefs, and sculpture decorations. Work at the Orangerie de Meudon and on the Autoroute de l'Ouest (the Paris-to-Normandy highway) was going to prompt sculptural decorations.[61]

But, to the not-so-divine surprise of Salon artists, these projects did not benefit them exclusively. According to a tabulation of sculpture commissions approved in 1941, twenty went to Salon exhibitors and twenty-one to others (see appendix 6). These "others" were middle-of-the-road artists. Belmondo, for example, had been a student of Despiau rather than a pure product of the Ecole des Beaux Arts, and showed at the Salon des Tuileries rather than at the Salon de la Sociéte des Artistes Français. His art was figurative, but in addition to rejecting anecdote and expression, he smoothed out physical defects and signs of age.

Painting commissions during the same period reveal a more pronounced slant in favor of determinedly non-Salon art. For example, at the Faculté de Pharmacie, a painting commission (worth 32,000 francs) went to Alfred Courmes, and another commission (worth 32,000 francs) to Coutaud, both of them pseudo-Surrealists. At the Conservatoire de la Musique, a set of three decorative panels (worth 75,000 francs) went to Maurice Brianchon and his wife Marguerite Louppe. At a school in a Paris suburb, the Ecole Professionelle de Creil, one notes among the recipients of commissions the name of Edouard Pignon, a tricolor painter.[62]

Of the 244 paintings approved during the years 1942, 1943, and 1944, 98 came from the Salon and the Société Nationale combined, 112 had been bought from the Salon des Tuileries and Salon d'Automne combined, and 34 came from independent artists, according to Georges Hilaire, Hautecoeur's successor from March to late August 1944.[63] For the year 1941, the French state spent 85,900

francs on Salon artists (the Salon de la Société des Artistes Français, Société Coloniale, and Société Nationale des Beaux Arts combined), 88,800 francs at the Salon des Tuileries and Indépendants combined, and 158,400 francs at the Salon d'Automne.[64]

Neither Drivier, the sculptor who made the official bust of Pétain, nor Le Breton, the author of the official painted portrait of the marshal, was a Salon exhibitor. Thus, the Salon failed to become the image maker of the new regime despite the allegiance of its president to the Révolution Nationale and his avowed desire to cement officially the relationship between the Salon and the state. The Salon agenda on art and Vichy's did not mesh.

It is not my intention here to argue with the commonly held view that the marshal's priority was to "artisans [who]—to quote from the 1 May 1941 Commentry speech—had been the first to understand this great truth [corporatism], and to put it into practice."[65] It can easily be shown that the country's artisans, not its artists, were the creators the marshal sought out in his frequent travels through the French provinces. As announced in *Le Figaro*, during the four days (16–20 June 1941) that the marshal planned to travel through the province of Limousin, he was scheduled to congratulate a group of young workers at St.-Leonard for refurbishing an abandoned farm; at Ambazac, he was going to attend a lunch, the high point of which was *clafoutis aux cerises*, a local specialty. In Limoges, he would pay a visit to the Beaublanc ateliers "where 130 young men and 150 young women are currently initiating themselves to working with wood, iron, leather and porcelain"; at the tapestry center of Aubusson, where renowned artists (Jean Lurçat, Marcel Gromaire, Saint-Saens, and others) were producing cartoons for weavers to translate into tapestries, the *Figaro* reports the marshal's intention to see the center "where young workers are learning the difficult technique of tapestry weaving."[66]

The marshal told an audience at Thiers, a town reputed for its cutlery, on 1 May 1942: "It is to you, artisans, that I address myself from this town of Thiers, which draws its fame from high quality articles forged by your own hands. . . . France is first of all an agricultural country. The renaissance of our farms can only take place if the artisan brings the farmer . . . the assistance of his industrious activity."[67]

But with all the attention paid to the agrarian features of Pétainist ideology, the revival of the decorative arts achieved by Vichy has been overlooked. Yet in the Thiers speech, the marshal made a point of addressing not only country artisans such as village cobblers, but more sophisticated types: "The artisan is also the auxiliary of the industrialist. He accomplishes certain phases of the fabrica-

CHAPTER 4

tion."[68] Avowal of decadence in decorative arts is a leitmotif in *Métiers de France*, a publication dedicated to arts and crafts: "We must frankly admit that quite often, crafts products do not combine quality and good taste."[69] Blaming the artisan and the artist, the author proposes that better technical training be imposed on those with taste, and a better sense of taste on those with know-how. "Under such conditions," the author concluded, "France will be able to ship outside its frontiers products whose price will not be measured by mathematical calculation alone."[70]

The discourse on decadence in the decorative arts was consistent with that condemning lack of craftsmanship in certain forms of art, but the emphasis on commercial appeal precluded stylistic uniformity. In fact, Robert Lallemant, who headed the service responsible for projecting the proper image of the new leader, was a ceramicist whose objects, many of them vases, were on occasion inspired   Fig. 35 by Cubism. Among the tapestries commissioned by Lallemant's artistic services, *National Renovation*, by Paul Charlemagne, shows Pétain on horseback headed toward fragmentary (Cubism-inspired) idyllic images of France at work. It   Fig. 36 should be noted here that Louis Hautecoeur, the closest to an Albert Speer that can be found in Pétain's entourage, placed revival of know-how ahead of esthetics in *Considérations sur l'art d'aujourd'hui* (1929) and, while not concealing his classical taste for painting and sculpture destined to adorn architecture, he allowed that in the decorative arts, Cubism was an acceptable mode: "The best Cubist pictures are probably today's rugs and book bindings."[71]

In the private sector, when the Orfèvrerie Cristofle, a firm famous for its silver-plated dinnerware, responded to the challenge of a revival in decorative arts by inviting artists to adorn ceramic plates, metal platters, and other luxury objects, the roster included Bonnard, Cocteau, Vlaminck, Delluol, Yencesse, and Marie Laurencin.   Fig. 37

As for the cult objects—*l'art maréchal*, objects that the marshal gave as souvenirs—their aim was not to respond to more or less conservative tastes but to appeal to a populist or an elitist identity. A Baccarat crystal vase (author unknown) illustrates the elitist style. Here the marshal's francisque, an emblem   Fig. 38 shaped like a double hatchet,[72] is incised in the center of the symmetrical V-shaped vase and the words "offered by Marshal Pétain" are printed below. Cult objects with a "rural" code were more anecdotal and more didactic. A dinner plate (there is irony in the recurring use of dinner plates as gift objects, considering the food shortage in France during the Pétain era) bordered with naively rendered blue, white, and red field flowers on a white background alluded to the   Fig. 39 importance of hard work for all classes of people through a message handwritten

35. Robert Lallemant. Polychrome vase
with cubist decoration (cubist-guitar
series no.3), n.d.

37. Marie Laurencin. Engraving on a Cristofle plate.

36. Paul Charlemagne. *National Renovation*, 1942.

38. Baccarat vase with the Marshal's emblem.

39. Dinner plate.

in the center: "Work is shared by all men on earth and is enforced by an ineluctable necessity," signed "Maréchal Pétain."

On a hexagonal ashtray (possibly by Lallemant) showing a field of blue, white, and red flowers, a rising sun, and church bells, one could read on a calling card pictured in one corner: "Une France nouvelle est née, Maréchal Pétain." The message "a new France is born" was conveyed not only by the written message but also by means of "pure" primary colors and an allegedly "pure" naive style. In short, the cult objects were created according to their appeal to disparate social classes.

This principle also applied in the commercial realm. While in Paris a store opened on the fashionable rue de la Paix, where for the first time Gobelins and Beauvais tapestries, enamelware from Limoges, Sèvres porcelain, Louvre chalcography, and reproductions of artworks from the national museums, all produced by state-run "manufactures," could be purchased,[73] in Vichy a shop-cum-atelier where several artists and artisans created l'imagerie maréchal, ranging from popular prints to blotters, children's coloring and pop-up books, and calendars, also offered its wares for sale.[74] Thus, different "families" of artisans produced for different groups of consumers. As in the heyday of the Central Union of the Decorative Arts, the aim was to revitalize the decorative arts under government sponsorship, but whereas in the 1890s, to quote Deborah Silverman, "government efforts had facilited the discovery of a quintessentially French style moderne,"[75] a certain eclecticism was now de rigueur.

The Vichy agenda for culture has tended to be seen in terms of paradox: continuity with and breaks with the past (Bertrand Dorléac, Ory, Rioux); regionalist focus with a centralist subtext (Fauré). From the previous analysis another paradox emerges: in this allegedly classless society of artisan workers, the revival of decorative arts, far from developing in an egalitarian manner, seemed destined to cater to populist tastes and means, on the one hand, and to a refined and moneyed public, on the other. Ironically, in plans being made for a rational division of labor in a Europe dominated by Nazi Germany,[76] France was to keep its luxury trade, including fashion,[77] while heavy industry would be entirely in German hands.

In the history of French decorative arts, the debate concerning the blurring of the separation between applied and free art has been a passionate and often violent one. On the one hand, when the Royal Academy first flowered under Louis XIV, an artist like Charles Lebrun crossed the line from fine arts to applied arts without demurring; in the nineteenth century, as pointed out by Patricia

CHAPTER 4

Mainardi, the Salon milieu (which after the French Revolution inherited the privileges of the Royal Academy and monopolized the teaching of art students) repeatedly attacked as crass and vulgar (but also as threatening to its prestige) the phenomenon of Universal Exhibitions, where a nation's industrial and handicrafts were shown side by side with painting and sculpture.[78] An exhibition entitled Art Décoratif Contemporain at the Paris Musée des Arts Decoratifs (March–April 1941), displaying—in the fashion of nineteenth-century Expositions Universelles—lighting fixtures, jewelry, ceramics, and tapestries together with modern painting and sculpture, prefigured the defeat of the Salon viewpoint during the remaining years of Vichy.

Had the meaning of decadence been a stylistic issue alone, Salon art, by disallowing departure from the Classical canon, might have been guaranteed an exclusive place. If decadence meant the loss of moral content in art, the Salon hardly offered a viable alternative. But either way, Vichy's method of fighting decadence, the pragmatic view of the artist as an artisan collaborating with other artisans in the creation of beautiful, salable objects prevented any artistic network from gaining exclusive recognition as the artistic image maker of Vichy France.[79]

However, the pragmatism that blurred certain distinctions between high and low stopped short of validating as art the machine-made object. At stake was the repudiation not only of excessive industrialization but of the Marxist view developed by Fernand Léger in the 1920s to the effect that not criteria of quality but capitalist motives—"the increase in the artistic and commercial value of the object"[80]—artificially maintained a hierarchy between the handmade "luxury" and the machine-made object. This viewpoint was reformulated by Walter Benjamin with respect to photography in his article on art at the end of the mechanical age.

Indeed, unlike Léger, who had predicted the phasing-out of the métier of artist, Louis Hautecoeur saw artists gaining in importance, as the decorative arts capitalized on artists' know-how and fame. Said Hautecoeur, "Nothing ought to prevent the decoration of a piece of furniture with a bronze medal, with a precious inlay or a sculpted motif. For this purpose, one can have recourse to well-known artists whose very signature will increase the value of the piece of furniture."[81]

Both traditionalist and eclectic, elitist and demagogical, the program for art—or rather, for decorative arts—sponsored by Vichy was also going to be viciously and profoundly antiforeigner, bringing to a climax the nationalism already appar-

ent in the Central Union's program in the mid-1880s to "restore our French genius . . . [and] help our French artworks to triumph."[82]

One should observe that in the 1890s, when decadence was genuinely attached to an artistic style, the nationalist forces in decorative arts used the unhealthy [decadent] argument against internationalism as a subtext for their anti-Semitism. When M. Bing, who was a Jew, opened his Maison de l'Art Nouveau with an assembly of decorative arts to which artists from all over the world had contributed, Arsene Alexandre commented in *Le Figaro* on the show in these words: "All this is confused, incoherent, almost unhealthy. It all smacks of the vicious Englishman, the Jewess addicted to morphine, or the Belgian spiv, or a good mixture of these three poisons."[83]

Time and again, talk of the unhealthy, the bizarre, and the decadent in art was going to be the guise for talk against foreign (and frequently Jewish) influences. Although a French artist, Marcel Duchamp, had first sensitized society to the possibility of art without craftsmanship, foreigners were accused of lowering the standards of art by attracting attention to "what is strange and new" rather than (by implication) to the beautifully crafted. In 1929, the future head bureaucrat in charge of the arts during Vichy, Louis Hautecoeur, thus expressed his views on the influence of "foreigners" in the art life of France:

At the time of Romanticism, the English crossed the Channel, visited France, and exhibited in the salons. Today, Czechs, Poles, Romanians, Russians, Yugoslavs, Americans, Spaniards, Portuguese, Belgians, and Dutch artists participate in our artistic life. But this pacific invasion is not without its drawbacks. We are overly friendly toward foreigners. We tend to praise in them what is strange and new. Since they are anxious to achieve Parisian recognition, they show an ardor, and sometimes, one must admit, a sense of publicity that is lacking among our compatriots. Solicited art critics praise them to the skies so that this foreign colony plays a role in our midst that their production does not always justify.[84]

What had merely been the expression of a point of view in 1929 changed into public policy when Louis Hautecoeur became a Vichy official. In the catalogue of the 1943 Madrid exhibition of modern art organized by the Action Artistique à l'Etranger, Hautecoeur claimed that "French painting has always manifested its taste for moderation, for harmony, and for nature." He complained that for twenty years, Paris salons and art magazines had boastfully expressed that the opposite was true, because numerous foreigners who exhibited there—"most of

them Jews coming from Russia, Lithuania, Poland, and the Balkans—[practiced] an art that was different from ours." And he hoped that the Madrid exhibition of purely French art would show "the continuity of a living tradition capable of adapting to all variations of taste."[85]

Translated into concrete effects, such xenophobia had turned the tables on several major figures of the prewar Paris art world and made Jewish artists into marginal figures and hunted prey.

PART II

SCAPEGOATS OF DECADENCE

5

"Resistancialism" and the
French Art World

Shortly after the surrender of Paris to the Allies, signed by General von Choltitz at the Gare Montparnasse (25 August 1944), liberated Paris offered an unexpected spectacle to its first visitors from the West: "Actual damage to the face of the capital was skin deep," Lincoln Kirstein wrote in his first report from France. "In the general enthusiasm of the street insurrection, a number of plane trees which are part of the marvellous rational decorations of the boulevards were tossed into barricades," he noted. "Naturally the gardens have not been kept up, although nothing looked really poor or forgotten. Certain important things escaped damage entirely: the equestrian statue of Louis XIV in the Place des Victoires, the Vendôme Column. . . . In the Place des Pyramides, Frémiet's Jeanne d'Arc was coated with a dazzling skin of gilt to greet the big parades."[1]

The normality observable in the physical appearance of Paris extended to the look of its people, despite years of food shortages. Sartre was compelled to address an open letter to the English—who had lived those same years under constant alerts and bombings—explaining the nature of the pain endured by Parisian intellectuals like himself during the Occupation years.[2]

Also to their surprise, American art aficionados in uniform were able to observe that somehow culture had not stopped dead in its tracks during the four years France had been cut off from the Western world. "During all the closed years Picasso has never ceased to work in this studio," noted John Pudney after his visit to the artist.[3] On 29 October 1944, the Sunday magazine section of the *New York Times* reproduced eight Picassos painted during the war, to accompany an article on Picasso.[4]

In the *Art Digest* of December 1944, John Groth, an artist-reporter, told of his visits to artists' studios in these words: "In Paris, I found the studios and galleries full of new and exciting works. . . . In both Montmartre and Montparnasse, I saw

paintings in galleries, new paintings as well as paintings by Utrillo, Vlaminck, and other well-known names." He also noted his surprise that art books had been published: "I was astounded at the great number of art publications of the last four years. Books of color reproductions of the paintings of the old masters . . . and of the modern masters. . . . There is a series of the familiar 5″ × 7″ books of contemporary painters selling for twenty francs."[5]

In 1945, the new names in French art began to receive critical analysis in the American art press. The Paris correspondent for the *Magazine of Art*, Gladys Delmas,[6] wrote "A New Group of French Painters,"[7] discussing, among others, Bazaine, Estève, Fougeron, Gischia, Lapicque, Le Moal, Manessier, and Pignon. René Huyghe in his "Letter from Paris," also in the *Magazine of Art*,[8] mentioned the same group of artists.

After years of isolation, curiosity concerning the artistic situation in Paris was indeed intense. Those queried were eager to establish their version of recent events, and particularly emphasized the role played by artists in the Resistance movement. Not only was Picasso safe but his wartime behavior had been exemplary: "Picasso Is Safe—the artist was neither a traitor to his painting nor his country," the *San Francisco Chronicle* headlined its 3 September 1944 article by Peter D. Whitney.[9] In January 1945, there appeared in the *Museum of Modern Art Bulletin* (New York) a "digest with notes" on the war record of Picasso, written by Alfred H. Barr, Jr.: "Reports from Paris suggest that, while Picasso's art is meeting with some hostile prejudice in liberated France [the exhibition of his paintings at the Salon d'Automne had stirred some violence], his position in the Resistance movement is of unique importance."[10]

The American painter Emlen Etting was apparently told that "most of the younger artists were active members of the resistance."[11] Amid unbridled enthusiasm, quietly, revisionist history was congealing.

Henry Rousso, who has analyzed the evolution in the historiography of the Vichy regime since 1944, refers to such an emendation of history as "Resistancialism" and, although Rousso sees the Resistancialist myth manifesting itself most acutely in the mid-nineteen-sixties—"it takes hold officially only after the return of de Gaulle and finds its apogee between the Algerian war and May '68"—he does acknowledge that it "tentatively started at the time of the Liberation."[12]

Resistancialism is explained as follows:

It describes a process that sought first the marginalization of what the Vichy regime was and a systematic diminution of its imprint on French society, including its most negative aspects; second, the construction of an *Objet de mémoire*, the "Resistance," far larger than the algebraic sum of the acting

minorities who were resisters . . . ; three, the assimilation of this "Resistance" into the entirety of the nation, typical of Gaullist Resistancialism.[13]

In the days and weeks following the liberation of Paris, Resistancialism meant silence on the rampage against decadence that had enabled the new art to flourish, no mention of the Aryan Frenchness of this new Ecole de Paris, no questions asked about the absent ones, no mention of collaboration in the artistic avant-gardes. For postwar French art historians, the strategy of Resistancialism proved useful in two ways. Thanks to de Gaulle, the substitution of an *objet de mémoire*—Resistance—for a name signifying a group of individual "resisters" resulted in whitewashing the behavior of an entire nation. Likewise, the Resistance activities of a few artists became typical of the French vanguards. In his 1945 "Letter from Paris," René Huyghe could say "The art of experimentation and boldness thus naturally found itself allied to the Resistance."[14]

But the substitution of an abstract objet de mémoire for specific individuals accomplished yet another goal. In Huyghe's history of modern French art dating from 1949, the substitution of abstract "isms"—Surrealism and Expressionism—for the individuals in these movements enabled him silently to glide over what certain human beings in these very movements had gone through during the Vichy regime:

So Surrealism, whose sensationalism and scandalmongering character was no doubt going to the head of the American rubberneck, had found a new youth on American shores; in France . . . it seemed to have exhausted its sap.

In Paris, the situation was simplified. Having gotten rid of Surrealism . . . the French school confronted the two traditional currents of modern art, the expressive and the plastic tendency. One could assume that by the normal play of reaction, the second tendency, neglected in favor of the first one during the prewar era, would become preeminent. As a matter of fact, it [this second tendency] was the one that was going to benefit from the most novel input of energy and investigation.[15]

Arguments can be marshaled against the view that Surrealism had died a natural death. A case-by-case review of the treatment by Vichy of leading Surrealist personalities, many of them refugees in the free zone of France in the aftermath of the debacle (such as Hans Arp, André Masson, Max Ernst, André Breton, Jacqueline Lamba, Victor Brauner, Hans Bellmer, and others), will reveal a different story.

As for the natural "play of reaction" that brought formal tendencies forward, this view overlooks the fact that between 1940 and 1944, not only was the expressive tendency viewed as foreign to the French sensibility and typical of the way foreign Jews painted—"Expressionism," wrote Vichy's chief art bureaucrat, Louis Hautecoeur, in 1942, "found a favorable terrain among Jewish painters who in the aftermath of 1918 gathered in Paris from the four corners of Europe. They brought to us their anxiety and the habits their parents had picked up in the countries they had roamed through"[16]—but Expressionism indicated a state of decadence that could only be cured by ostracizing Jews and foreignness. As observed earlier in this text, the gallicization of the Ecole de Paris engaged the energies of all the factions claiming to fight artistic decadence, whether they represented the views of someone with a Fascist, a Personalist, and an academic outlook, or the interests of the Vichy government.

So the changes, thanks to which "new and exciting works" were encountered by the liberators of Paris in the fall of 1944, were not so natural as the "pendulum" image might make them seem. Not only a normal change of taste but a rhetoric against decadence aimed at "foreigners" and Jewish artists lay behind this transformation. I have exposed the varieties of critical approaches used to foreground purely French art; I will now address, as another way of redressing the rosy image of the Paris art world described by its liberators in 1944, what happened to the artists who were pushed into the background.

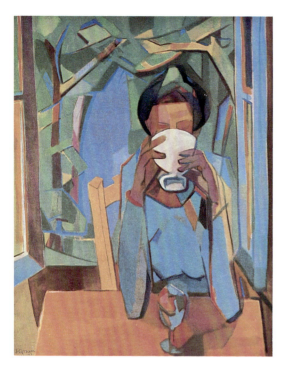

Plate 1. Edouard Pignon. *Seated Woman at a Table*, 1942

Plate 2. Maurice Estève. *Woman with Shopping Basket*, 1942

Plate 3. Jean Bazaine. *Mass for an Armed Man*, 1944

Plate 4. Hans Reichel. *Cahier de Gurs*, 14 July 1942

Plate 5. Francis Gruber. *Hommage à Jacques Callot, ca. 1942*

6

An Uncanny "Return to the Soil"

NESTLING IN THE FREE ZONE

Fig. 40

During his stay in the Savoy after Pétain's armistice, Balthus (half-Jewish, he fled to Switzerland in 1941) painted *The Cherry Tree*. A rural landscape bathed in the late afternoon light of early fall, the work not only captures the specificity of Savoy, a region of contrasts between sun-filled valleys and darker mountain slopes, but the languid light, the lightest of breezes in the foliage, the arrested pose of the little girl perched on her ladder connote the profound longing for calm shared by all who had endured the exodus.

Among those who had reason to believe that they figured on a list of Judeo-Marxist-decadent artists, many were choosing to stay in the free zone of France where their flight ahead of German troops had landed them. Jews and Alsatians, it has been said before, had no choice in the matter, as the Germans refused to allow them to return to their homes in the occupied zone. The changes undergone by art-world figures who had once lived comfortable and sometimes even elegant lives are hardly imaginable. Yet their adjustment proved remarkable.

"Well, anyhow, for the time being, we are living in this beautiful country," Kahnweiler told Gertrude Stein in a letter of 8 August 1940, written from Le Repaire, his refuge near St.-Léonard (Haute Vienne). "I am not nervous at all," he told her. "We are walking a lot, and our place is very nice. So at least this 'holiday,' which we did not want, is perhaps doing some good for our health. We have a big garden too."[1] Both Stein's and Kahnweiler's "holiday" would be fruitful for their writing. While Stein wrote her memoirs,[2] Kahnweiler worked on his book on Juan Gris, as he told Stein in a letter of 21 December 1940.

> I am trying to write my book about Juan. I can't write his life here, having no documents. But I am writing what is to be the second part of this book, his work, and hope to manage it. I have a few books, I bought some more at Limoges, and there is a small public library at St.-Léonard where I find

40. Balthus. *The Cherry Tree*, 1940.

good historians of the 19th century. Michelet, Macaulay . . . Taine, etc. Time passes away.[3]

By December 1941, Kahnweiler was telling Stein: "I have finished now the second part—L'oeuvre de Juan Gris—about 180 pages. I am writing now the first part—La vie de Juan Gris—there is a third part—Les Ecrits de Juan Gris—a bibliography, list of museums, collections and exhibitions, etc. . . . Time passes away, one doesn't know how."[4]

For his part, Hans Arp (because of his Alsatian origins, he faced the obligations of a German now that Alsace had been annexed), who with his Swiss wife Sophie and the recently widowed Sonia Delaunay had found peace near Fig. 41

41. Sophie Taeuber-Arp, Nelly van Doesburg, Hans Arp, and Sonia
Delaunay at Château Folie, Grasse, 1941–42.

Grâsse on the Côte d'Azur, evoked his wife's utter delight at her new surroundings in these words:

> Sophie Taeuber spent the last two years of her life with me in Grâsse, a
> town in southern France. She was in love with the land. It was her paradise
> on earth. She always pressed me to go on new explorations. Her eyes never
> let go of the silvery green of the olive trees, the meditative silhouettes of the
> shepherds amidst their herd, the villages pressed hard against the moun-
> tains, the scintillating, blinding snow cover. We lived between a spring, a
> cemetery, an echo, and a bell. In our garden there grew palm trees and olive
> trees. When the foliage of the palm trees started whispering we would have
> rain. The olive trees constantly were animated by an imperceptible shiver.
> Each day brought with it a new richness of light and of happiness and So-
> phie revelled in it.[5]

Another artist who "dug in his heels" in a village of rural France was Chagall. He bought a former Catholic girls' school at Gordes, a village in Provence, in the spring of 1940, hired a truck to fetch the pictures he had left at St.-Dyé, and moved in, expecting to work there in peace. According to Franz Meyer, "the scenery captivated him at first sight."[6] (He had been told about Gordes by André Lhote.) The story of the visit of Varian Fry, the head of the American Rescue Committee in Marseilles,[7] who came with the American consul in Marseilles to tell Chagall he was in danger and must leave for America, is well known, including Chagall's question "Are there trees and cows in America too?"[8] But the anecdote says as much about the ignorance of the artist concerning America and of his reluctance to move as it does about his attachment to a rural way of life. Chagall heeded the warning and left France.

The German Jewish refugee Wols,[9] destitute and insecure as he was during those years, also reacted to the beauty of his refuge, the fishing village of Cassis, in a particularly lyrical way. Throughout his oeuvre as a draftsman, he would lovingly depict the old town enmeshed in sails and hulls: "At Cassis, the stones, the fish, the rocks, the salt of the sea and the sky seen through a magnifying glass made me forget human relevance, invited me to turn my back on the chaos of our acts, showed me eternity in the small waves of the port repeating themselves without repeating themselves."[10]

The depictions of Air Bel, the villa in a suburb of Marseilles rented for the staff of the American Emergency Rescue Committee, but better known for its guests, including the André Breton family and their Surrealist visitor-friends, are less haloed, but a mysterious mood emanates from the memories left by tenants and visitors. Varian Fry writes: "The first time I saw Villa Air Bel it was closed as tight as a fortress. The walks and gardens were overgrown with weeds, the hedges had not been trimmed in years. But the view across the valley to the Mediterranean was enchanting and I was impressed by the terrace with its enormous plane trees and by the double flight of steps which led down left and right to a formal garden and a fishpond."[11]

"Whenever I recall the Air Bel days," the Surrealist painter from Roumania Jacques Hérold (a Jew) was to say to an interviewer, "their strangeness still haunts me."[12]

Consuelo de Saint-Exupéry recalled in her memoirs the strong scent that exuded from the garden—hyacinths, mimosas, violets, and jasmine, and the peculiarities of its interior: "One came in through a vast hall with worn carpets and tall, half-broken urns, pale old engravings. On the ground floor a music room with two old pianos and Louis XV chairs, a great dining room furnished in Provencal style."[13]

The library on the second floor was apparently notable for its wallpaper, which had mythological scenes. The owner of the house, an old doctor and ornithologist whose stinginess Breton never forgot, lived nearby with his sister: "He used to lie in wait outdoors even in the worst of cold weather for fear someone might rob him of a dead branch."[14]

Few of the refugees in the free zone were as naive as Gertrude Stein, who admired Pétain enough to volunteer to translate his speeches;[15] but, as the Russian revolutionary Victor Serge, one of the residents of Air Bel,[16] reports in his memoirs, a wait-and-see attitude could be observed in the period immediately following the signing of the armistice, caused in no small measure by faith in the old marshal: "Prisoners of habit, they do not 'realize' the extent of the disaster, they vaguely hope for a bearable solution. General tendency to adapt among intellectuals. . . . Undeniably, the 'Révolution Nationale' and the personal prestige of the Verdun soldier . . . duped a great many in the initial disarray."[17]

At Air Bel, the refuge not only of the families of Breton and Victor Serge and of the American Rescue Committee hierarchy, but also on occasion of some of their exhausted and despairing clients, a typical conversation around the dining room table went as follows, according to Consuelo de Saint-Exupéry, in transit there on her way to the United States:

Why leave, said I, in a tired voice. If we all leave, where will France be?

Where is France now? asked the little professor. They have killed my wife and my parents.

Of course, you don't have anything to fear here, said Maurice. . . . You are a woman. You have no political activity. You will not be persecuted. For us, it's different, the only question is to know where we can *work* best.[18]

The Arps in their refuge at Chateau Folie near Grasse were also among those who hesitated between leaving and staying put, worried by the time their papers had finally come through that they would not be able to resume life normally now that America was at war:

As for us [Sophie Taeuber-Arp writes to an unknown correspondent in a letter dated 17 April 1942], we are very tormented. We have all the papers for America and we must decide in a few days. There is some hope that in New York we may little by little rebuild our lives. If America were not in the war, we would not hesitate, but in these circumstances we have in no way any certainty that we will succeed, but we hope to be able to have an artistic activity. Here for years to come any activity will be impossible, that is to say sales, exhibitions, etc.[19]

The Masson case is also revealing. Masson had received offers to emigrate in 1938 from Ernest Hemingway and later from Tanguy, yet he said "I preferred to wait, to swarm in the fatal earthquake."[20] Not until the first anti-Jewish decrees were made public in early October 1940 (Masson's wife was a Jew) did he contemplate emigration. At the suggestion of Breton, he moved his family from their refuge at Freluc in the Auvergne to the estate of the Comtesse Pastré (Montredon) near Marseilles, their likely port of departure. There he apparently also basked in the unreality of his new surroundings and was "enjoying a rare state of bliss in his retreat, where the singing of the wind in the pine trees incited him to work,"[21] according to Jean Ballard,[22] the editor of *Cahiers du sud* who paid Masson a visit at the hunting lodge in the pine woods where he stayed from December 1940 to 31 March 1941.

Of the portraits of Breton attributable to Masson's stay at Montredon, one of them—a double portrait—may have been intended to evoke the conflicting desires between wanting to stay and hoping to leave that candidates for emigration apparently experienced. It shows the poet's two profiles, one looking aft and the other looking forward, eyes open in one and eyes closed in the other, the two heads strangely cemented in the back like Siamese twins.[23]

Fig. 42

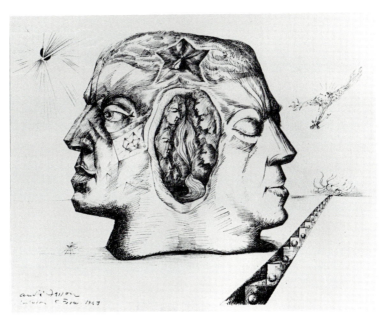

42. André Masson. *Double Portrait of André Breton*, 1941.

Even Freundlich, the Judeo-Marxist-decadent artist par excellence—he had made Cubist and abstract art, he had been something of an anarchist in Germany in his youth, he was Jewish, he was stateless, and one of his works had been chosen for the cover of the Entartete Kunst show brochure—hesitated about emigrating. Writing from a hotel room in St.-Paul-de-Fenouillet in the Pyrénées to his companion Kosnick Kloss, who was to rejoin him later, he worried that she, not being officially his wife, might not be able to leave with him (only married couples could leave on the same visa).[24]

Speaking of Jewish refugees who, unlike the independent-minded Hannah Arendt, obeyed the orders of the new regime to register at the local prefecture, Arendt's biographer comments, "The gravity of the situation was not apparent to people an ocean removed from it, and it was not always apparent to those caught by the conditions of Europe."[25]

At Oppède in the Luberon, in an almost-abandoned village perched high up, the French architect and recent Prix de Rome winner Bernard Zehrfuss settled down after his release from the army (he was a Jew, and hence was also among those who could not return to their Paris homes) and invited an assortment of artists, including Surrealists Jacques Hérold, Zelman, Consuelo de Saint-Exupéry, a young sculptor named Etienne Martin, the Forces Nouvelles painter Georges Humblot, and also artisans and architects to live communally and rebuild the village.[26] Inspired by the eagles who lived in the ruins,[27] Hérold painted *The Reader of Eagles* while at Oppède.[28]

In an article titled "Oppède essai de renaissance," Zehrfuss outlined the group's intentions. They reflected the views of Jeune France, the sponsor of the Oppède experiment:

> Without returning to old methods or antiquated conceptions, we must lean on traditions, on the sequence of efforts that have made our country the most civilized and the most radiating, by tying them closely to new techniques.
>
> The role of architects in the moral and material rebuilding of our country is proving to be an immense task. Collective efforts, a team spirit . . . that is what we want to do at Oppède. Out of this abandoned village, we wish to create an immense atelier, a great community of the arts in a first stage and a professional community of builders. . . . We wish to animate lifeless regions by attracting artists, workmen, artisans, and making sure that they have adequate material living conditions.[29]

Zehrfuss explains that this idea was born after three architects, demobilized and out of jobs, came to the area as farm workers and, with the support of their

CHAPTER 6

"patron" in Marseilles, the chief government architect E. Beaudoin, had studied the possibility of having an Ecole des Beaux Arts annex at Oppède. "We are now seventeen, and sixty architects from the Marseilles atelier are going to join us."[30]

Oppède was to be the first of several centers that, under the Zehrfuss plan, were to experience a renaissance by taking advantage of their own natural resources. Essential to his plan was the use of the region's natural and human resources. The Oppède region was rich in stone quarries and benefited from the presence of experienced quarrymen. Zehrfuss explained: "At Apt, thanks to its ochre, there are glassblowers, stained-glass makers, mosaic specialists to work with; at Gordes, painters, poster artists, costume makers and decorators; at Vaucluse, miniaturists and engravers, and at l'Isle sur Sorgues, there is a river with remarkable properties for metiers requiring work in iron and steel."[31]

In addition to the places mentioned in the Zehrfuss article, there is evidence that Wols, after spending time in Cassis,[32] rejoined in 1943 a group in Dieulefit (Drome) of potters and artists, including Etienne Martin, who had previously been at Oppède. In Aubusson and St.-Céré (Lot), tapestry makers regrouped around Lurçat.

Decentralization, national reconstruction, regionalism, recourse to uniquely national resources, the revival of landscape painting prompted, as Kenneth Silver observes, by the "bucolic experience,"[33] and arts and crafts activities, key aspects of Pétain's program against decadence, were finding converts among the refugees whose "return to the soil" was forced by events. The sculptor François Stahly—who sold his handmade buckles to designers of fancy clothes in Cannes—would go so far as to write, "If it had not been for the threats and the incertitudes of the war, this return to the soil would remain in my memory like a single long luminous day."[34]

The way life was lived is symbolized in an anecdote repeated to me by Susi Magnelli, the German-Jewish refugee wife of Alberto Magnelli, himself a refugee from Fascist Italy. Alarmed that she was going to be alone in her house during a looming thunderstorm, friendly neighbors invited her to spend the night with their family. In the middle of the night, the Gestapo came to arrest the head of the household, who belonged to a Resistance network, and would have taken her along as a Jew, had she accepted their offer.[35]

AN ART OF EXCEPTIONAL
CIRCUMSTANCE EMERGES

"In this sort of semi-tranquillity we all worked on our artistic problems," writes Magnelli, who had persuaded the Arps and Sonia Delaunay to join them. "Each of us pursued the realization of his ideas." He continued to paint as long as he

Fig. 43

had canvas and oil; "later I went in for papiers-collés and gouache, of which I made a large series."[36] He used music paper as a background for his collages and, according to Susi Magnelli,[37] even painted on embroidered linen sheets from his wife's trousseau.

Indeed, while refugee artists produced art even in the most difficult circumstances, they frequently had to resort to improvised materials. In some cases, linen was beaten to a pulp in order to expand the amount of available canvas; ink and watercolors were diluted.[38] Wood and cardboard were substitutes for canvas and fine paper, and in sculpture most of the work was done in plaster and only later cast in bronze.

Fig. 44

For the Surrealists, these shortages acted as stimulants to the discovery of new techniques. Arp used ordinary paper, which he crinkled and then mixed with gouache, ink, or oil for his "papiers froissés," black-and-white works with ragged edges and rough textures.[39] The decalcomania technique invented by Dominguez in 1935 spread to Bellmer (*Self-Portrait*, 1942) and to Max Ernst (*Europe after the Rain II*, 1940–42). For Victor Brauner (a Jew from Romania) who moved from place to place and eventually settled on an abandoned farm in the Alps, the lack of traditional art materials led to a particularly interesting turn in his art and brought him into the orbit of *l'art brut* (which he abandoned after the war). He began using candle wax instead of oil, and sticklike forms appear scrawled on the surfaces. As described by Marcel Jean, the technique involved "spreading a thin base of melted candle grease on canvas or cardboard, and engraving on this surface a design accentuated afterwards by means of smoke black, the shapes themselves being colored by lightly glazed hues."[40]

Gouache was a favorite medium during those years. Magnelli describes some done by Sonia Delaunay: "She made quantities of gouaches which, although of small format, exuded a magnificent rigor and luminosity."[41] Otto Freundlich, who lived in poverty and isolation at St.-Paul-de-Fenouillet, continued working in the abstract patchwork vein for which he was known, but now the paintings were most frequently gouaches on cardboard or, occasionally, on wood.

Chagall found in gouache a means of renewal for his work. Says Werner Haftmann, "In these and all the years that followed, the gouache was Chagall's most sensitive medium, and it became more frequent in all contexts. In *The Village in the Snow*, which may have been done in the winter 1940–41 . . . the paint is applied in numerous superimposed coatings to produce a translucent enamel-like solidity in the film of color."[42] Masson has also acknowledged the importance of gouaches for him at that time, saying of *Matriarchal Landscape* that "it reveals many things to me."[43] Decalcomania gouaches also form a significant part of Bellmer's work during the 1940s, according to his biographer.[44]

43. Alberto Magnelli. *Untitled*, 1941.

44. Hans Arp. *Fleur*, 1942.

Whether done in gouache, watercolor, ink, pencil, or oil, the works of some usually unconventional artists often included conventionally rendered landscape, still life, and portrait motifs during their sojourn "close to the soil." Chagall made a number of studio still lifes inspired by the gifts of food that friendly peasants would bring him. Franz Meyer writes:

> A rich, almost "fluid" light flickers on the rounded forms of berries and fruit, on the leaves and pelts. The morning glow that pervades the pictures gives them a curious, happy resonance. One can also sense an autumnal note attuned to the season of the year. But one is inclined to construe it as a note of farewell to the natural happiness of the prewar period on the threshhold of years of misery for Europe and of exile for Chagall.[45]

Fig. 45 In *Bella at Gordes*, a drawing in a normative vein by Chagall showing his wife Bella seated with the village of Gordes behind her, in a watercolor by Sophie Taeuber-Arp of farmhouses near Grasse framed by rustling trees, in sketches of the mountains around St.-Paul-de-Fenouillet by Freundlich, and in the last works of the old Cubist Marcoussis,[46] nostalgia and a sense of impending loss may have motivated the reference to natural surroundings.

A surprising amount of portraiture in the most traditional manner was made by normally unconventional artists. The Surrealist Hans Bellmer drew normative or quasi-normative portraits of "friends" (inmates, guards) while at the internment camp of Les Milles, including one of Max Ernst, and continued to do so right through the war. The abstract painter and sculptor Otto Freundlich portrayed an Fig. 46 internee in winter garb moving what the title describes as manure at the unseen end of his pitchfork. The normative mode served a practical purpose, since artists not only exchanged their art with each other but also bartered it for favors from people who knew nothing about art but were being helpful (guards in internment camps; suppliers of art materials and of food and drink).[47]

Self-portraiture is also a recurring theme in refugee art during these years.
Fig. 47 Bellmer and the poet Max Jacob[48] are among those who drew their faces, as if to
Fig. 48 reassure themselves of some continuity in their own self-images at a time when
Fig. 49 society was treating them as though they were "the scum of the earth." Of his mimetic self-portrait in ink (*Après la défaite*), André Masson would say, "I put myself in front of a mirror so as to analyze my torment."[49] During the time he spent as a refugee in Vichy France, Masson made drawings of labyrinthine architectural structures, desert landscapes, ladders leading nowhere, and impregnable walls, which he grouped under the title *Anatomy of My Universe*, a less direct, more psychoanalytical form of self-portraiture.

45. Sophie Taeuber-Arp. *Landscape*, 1942.

46. Otto Freundlich. *Male Figure Holding a Pitchfork for Moving Manure*, 1939.

HANS BELLMER

47

48

49

47. Hans Bellmer. *Self-Portrait in the Camp des Milles*, 1940.

48. André Masson. *Self-Portrait*, 1940.

49. Max Jacob. *Self-Portrait*, n.d.

Chagall, while in Gordes, made several self-portraits, including some as Christ holding a palette. A sense of impending death—as in the self-portrait made by Marcoussis during his last illness—may also have motivated an unusual amount of self-portraiture among artists whose health was good yet whose lives were equally in jeopardy, such as those men and women who were detained in French internment camps after the armistice.

According to Francis V. O'Connor who has analyzed self-portraits by Dürer, Rembrandt, Mondrian, Kahlo, Pollock, Schoenberg, Picasso, and others, frontal self-portraiture marks "points of transition and crisis in the life course of its creator which engender especially powerful compensatory images of concentricity."[50] These crisis moments would seem to happen at seven-year intervals, starting with the third cycle, "when the young artist begins to reject influence and to present a personal, self-centered vision of the world."[51]

O'Connor also claims that self-portraiture serves "a . . . therapeutic purpose at moments when the artist must find a center,"[52] when life's future course is very much in doubt, as was certainly the case for the artist refugees in Vichy France. Investigating the rhythms of self-portraiture in the case of Arnold Schoenberg, the atonal composer and occasional painter, O'Connor found that Schoenberg's last concentration of frontal self-portraits "occurred when Schoenberg defiantly asserted his Jewishness in the face of the threat of Nazism and, turning his back on a hostile Europe, fled to the United States." He notes, "The first dated sheet . . . occurred in 1933, when the composer left Vienna for Paris, lost his academic position because of his religion, and, with the painter Marc Chagall standing witness, reconverted to the Jewish faith he had rejected in his youth."[53]

Of course, the diarist mode, with its transparent transcriptions of nature and of people's faces, made no more than an occasional—albeit unexpected—appearance. Parallel to their conventional productions, artists continued to work in a personal manner, sometimes finding new modes of expression: Freundlich, for one, left a small group of drawings that suggest a series of catastrophic apocalyptic eclipses. An exceptional series in his overall production, they depict black suns ringed in black; in some cases, pale oblong shapes seem to pass over them. André Masson's exegesis of one of his own works from that time, the *Dream of a Future Desert*, also speaks of "a black sun [that] oscillates [on the horizon] for the last time; an eye veiled by a scythe which destroys the landscape of a world's end."[54]

Fig. 50

In the 1930s, the Surrealists had integrated the Spanish civil war into their work; now, in an atmosphere of fear and uncertainty about their future, and in a mental climate of dependency on signs and omens, esoteric knowledge and her-

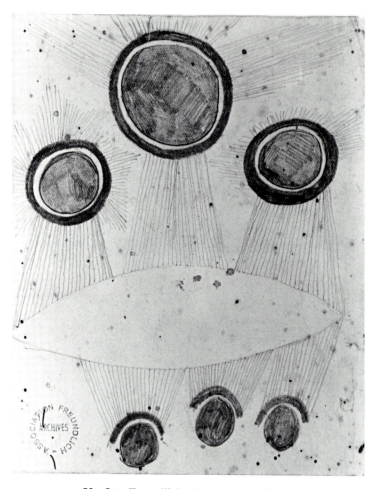

50. Otto Freundlich. *Composition*, 1943.

meticism reached a peak. Numbers become magical. Jacques Hérold's painting entitled *The Reader of Eagles* refers to the prognostic powers said to exist in patterns of the entrails of eagles. Brauner believed that the number seven and the day of freedom were intertwined. On his *Tableau Optimiste* of 1943 he inscribed a few lines that spoke of the "secret of the number seven," of the "seven openings among cosmic, fluid, biological, social, and economic correspondences," and of the "seventh and total revolution, that of definite liberation." He also made a series of seven paintings entitled *Lion, Light, and Liberty*. For Masson, it would seem that the number five—as in the five-pointed star visible in the double portrait of André Breton (see fig. 42)—was a magic number.

CHAPTER 6

"*Anatomy of My Universe*," remarks Carolyn Lanchner, "is Masson's *summa theologica*, an often brilliant and highly individual potpourri of ideas adopted from occultism, alchemy, astrology, Neo-Platonism, the Cabala, Scholasticism, and as said the King of Siam, 'etcetera.'"[55] Victor Brauner's new phase during the Occupation years has already been noted as far as technique is concerned, but his themes evolved as well. Dominique Bozo evokes Brauner's initiation into the Cabala and brings up the "objets d'envoûtement et de contre envoûtement[56] that Brauner concocted as a desperate resort to keep evil—namely the Gestapo—away from him. Speaking of work done between 1941 and 1945, Sarane Alexandrian has observed: "After having read Paracelsus, Cornelius Agrippa, Saint-Martin, and Fabre d'Olivet, Brauner became fascinated with the idea that there were magical forces in the universe and proposed in his painting to take them into account by depicting them in the form of myths and symbols. In particular, he is influenced by the Tarot."[57] (See below, the collaborative creation of a deck of Tarot cards done in Marseilles in 1940 by the Surrealists, including Brauner, who coincidentally was responsible for the card representing the twentieth-century seer Helen Smith.)

Collaborative works and collective activities, which had been common among prewar Surrealists, resumed, but with a different purpose. They brought together artists of different reputations and generations; the anonymity of the projects was caused by fear that the authors would suffer if their art was recognized. Arp, who collaborated with Sonia Delaunay, Taeuber-Arp, and Magnelli on an album of lithographs, explains his reasoning: "1941. We found ourselves in Grasse. The constellations that had brought together these four artists were especially favorable to the realization of collective work, for the tragic hours during which these lithographs were conceived compelled modesty, the sacrifice of all vanity, the effacement of any overly individual expression."[58]

According to Susi Magnelli, "the original gouaches were either made together or each artist made a drawing and passed it to the other. Nothing was rejected, and the entire project took one or two months."[59]

This album did not in fact come out until 1950. A first batch of gouaches was taken to a local printer. The project was in proof form when the printer, André Kalin, was arrested for Resistance activities by Gestapo agents, who destroyed the proofs. Sonia Delaunay managed to retrieve the original gouaches and saw the project to its conclusion after the war. In 1950, the suite of ten lithographs was pulled by Editions Nourritures Terrestres, a name associated with André Gide, coincidentally a neighbor of the Grasse group during the war.[60]

Collaborative efforts were also common at Air Bel, albeit in a different atmosphere. "Every Sunday, it's holiday time at Air Bel. André has reconstituted a

circle of Surrealists and one can see, arriving as a flock, by tramway, the painters who since the debacle have transferred their headquarters from the Deux Magots to the Brûleur de Loups, a café in the old port."[61]

Breton has left a singularly sexist list of those who "rejoin or cross each other's path at Air Bel"—namely Arthur Adamov, Brauner, Breton, René Char, René Daumal, Frédéric Delanglade, Dominguez, Duchamp, Ernst, Hérold, Silvain Itkine, Wifredo Lam, Masson, Benjamin Péret, and Tristan Tzara.[62] To this list must be added Jacqueline Lamba, Consuelo de Saint-Exupéry, Henriette Gomez, Rémédios Varo, Peggy Guggenheim, and several other women, wives, and friends whose presence around Air Bel is not clearly documented.[63]

Barrels of wine would be consumed and then, suddenly, interrupting all conversations, Breton would say "So shall we play?"[64] at which point the poet would ply his friends with old magazines, pencils, scissors, color tubes, and glue and they would play the old game of Exquisite Corpse,[65] making collective drawings in which the sheet of paper would be divided into a grid within which different contributors made their marks and drew rebuslike symbolic portraits of well-known persons. "For example, one would draw a symbol and the others had to figure out what character was being evoked."[66] One such portrait, a collage entitled *Ce sacré crétin de Pétain*, showing crossed spoon and fork (cut from a catalogue for Cristofle silverware) atop an officer's kepi, made trouble for the Air Bel group when the French police descended on them shortly before the marshal was scheduled to visit Marseilles.[67]

Related to the symbolic portraits was another collaborative project, the invention of a totally new deck of cards called the *Tarot de Marseille*. "Do not say King of Spades but Genius of Dream, do not announce Queen of Diamonds but Siren of Revolution; the trump is not Club but Knowledge," was how the doctor-poet Pierre Mabille evoked the new card game.[68]

Indeed, after Breton found out that playing cards had military connotations,[69] he decided to rename the suites and give to the Joker the features of Jarry's Ubu. The group came up with Love, Dream, Revolution, and Knowledge. They then drew new effigies for the newly named suits depicting mythical or historical persons. To mask the participants' individual styles, Delanglade redrew the set.[70]

To the reproach of frivolity that these games entailed, Breton would answer by saying that on the one hand, they were intended to distract him and his friends if only for a brief moment from the "anxieties of the times," and on the other, whatever the material circumstances might be, it was essential to show that the debacle was not a debacle of the spirit: "What appears to me as the task of intellectuals is not to let this purely military defeat, for which intellectuals are not responsible, attempt to carry with it the debacle of the spirit."[71] Like the album

of lithographs collectively done by the Groupe de Grasse, the *Tarot de Marseille* did not see publication at that time.

One project that did come to light was the redecoration of a Marseilles café by three members of the Oppède group, Zehrfuss, Zelman,[72] and Hérold. In a letter to the author, Zehrfuss described this project: "Outside, frescoes by Zelman. Inside, I had conceived a play of mirrors on the walls and ceilings, the effect of which was to reproduce the image of visitors a thousand times. The surface of tabletops represented Newton's disk, hence a highly coloristic effect. On the walls and under the glass top of the bar there were all sorts of strange insects created by Hérold."[73] To this description, Hérold added in an interview, "The café was called L'Eden. Through the glass top of the bar, fish could be seen circulating underneath."[74]

There is nothing left of this collaborative effort except the site of the café, and there is even less evidence of other "little things" collaboratively done in the climate of insecurity induced by events. A number of projects for sets and costume designs, started in the context of a theatrical revival in Marseilles under the aegis of Jeune France, were aborted in their initial stages. Masson was working on stage and costume designs for *L'Escurial*, a play directed by Sylvain Itkine, a young director-playwright (he had staged *Ubu Roi* in Paris with sets by Ernst in 1937), but Itkine, a Jew, had to abandon it while it was still in rehearsal.[75]

Another play put into rehearsal by Itkine with sets and costumes by Hérold (*Les Barbes nobles* by André Roussin) met an identical fate.[76] Itkine's friend Léo Sauvage had better luck with his company, Compagnons de Basoche, which undertook a revival of medieval French farces.[77] Among those successfully produced were *Conrad le maudit*, with sets and costumes conceived by Hérold and executed by Brauner, and *La Pipée*, a sixteenth-century anonymous play for which the cartoonist Jean Effel designed "a poetic universe of little birds and daisies."[78]

At Montredon, an active center of underground musical life because of the Comtesse Pastré's love of music and generous welcome to Jewish musicians, the ballet *Midsummer Night's Dream*, with music by Jacques Ibert, an orchestra conducted by Manuel Rosenthal, and choreography by Boris Kochno, was staged in June of 1942 in the park of the château. "The representation left an unforgettable impression, like an end-of-the-world spectacle. Due to the lack of materials, in order to make the costumes, designed by Christian Berard, it was necessary to pull down and use the drapes and curtains of the chateau windows. It was an exceptional evening, in the park surrounded by woods, bathed in magnificent moonlight."[79]

Collaborative work even went on in French internment camps. At the camp of St.-Sulpice, an internment camp for political prisoners, murals were done under the direction of Taslitzky, a Communist painter and an early resister.[80] At the internment camp of Les Milles, near Aix-en-Provence, an internment camp for German refugees that in 1942 became a way station to deportation, traces of a mural on the walls of the internees' dining hall, probably done under the guidance of Max Lingner, have recently been uncovered.[81] While interned together at Les Milles, Ernst and Bellmer combined their talents in drawings such as *Les Créations, les créatures de l'imagination*.[82]

Fig. 51

Access to well-known artists on a casual basis was indeed a bonus of these moments. A German refugee named Ferdinand Springer attributes the move toward abstraction in his work to that time and gives credit to Arp for the change: "In spite of his irrational and poetic side, he lived in the present, which he liked to analyze with humor and common sense. Thanks to his friendly advice, and that of Magnelli and Sonia Delaunay, I found the courage to transpose my plastic language on a plane that seemed to me then better adapted to our time."[83]

François Stahly, a young sculptor who lived near the Arps in Grasse, also speaks of the "kind way in which Arp encouraged me in my rare sculptural efforts."[84]

According to Jacques Hérold, it was while participating in the Surrealist games of Air Bel that Picasso's protégé, Wifredo Lam, "discovered himself." His

51. Mural in the dining hall at the internment camp at les Milles, artist unknown.

illustrations for the poem "Fata Morgana," written by Breton while at Air Bel, Fig. 52 reveal indeed the seed of the personal cosmogony characteristic of his later work.[85] The positive impact of changed circumstances on the development of artists also applies to Wols, who apparently began his artistic career while an internee during the Phony War in an atmosphere bleak in all ways except for the companionship of talented intellectuals and artists in the same straits. A drawing by Wols titled *All Prisoners*, showing various species of humanity together in- Fig. 53 side barrels, symbolically reveals this rich mix.

Explaining the abundance of work created during these difficult days, and re- calling in particular Arp's bedroom lined from floor to ceiling with papiers froissés, Alberto Magnelli would say, "There was nothing else to do but work and see each other."[86] Taeuber-Arp, writing to an unknown correspondent in 1942, confided, "Arp is working very well and is much less nervous."[87]

Arp, for his part, tenderly recalled the energy with which Taeuber-Arp worked during her last two years (she died of asphyxiation in Switzerland in January 1943): "In the small tower where her bedroom is, she works with ardor. Her fine approving profile goes up and down in front of the distant sea. She distills an admirable clarity into her canvases. . . . She draws lines, long curves, spirals, roads that snake through reality and dream. She paints the last of the singing circles."[88]

The recently widowed Sonia Delaunay thus evoked the little group of friends gathered at Grasse: "With his [Arp's] wife, Sophie Taeuber, Susi and Alberto Magnelli, our little group formed an island of peace and friendship . . . that cre- ated an atmosphere favorable to work."[89]

Transported right after the armistice to unlikely though fittingly poetic-sound- ing places deep in the *France profonde* from which Pétain expected so much, artists had found an urge to work in their new surroundings.

SURVIVAL NETWORKS IN ACTION

The work done by artist refugees hibernating in Vichy France stood no chance of receiving sympathy from the new art hierarchy. Louis Hautecoeur, the head of the fine arts department of the Ministry of Education and Youth under Pétain, was conservative in his tastes and xenophobic in outlook, as noted earlier. Although in his memoirs Hautecoeur claims that he carried out a vigorous acquisitions policy by arguing for the importance of art in lifting morale and spiritual values,[90] and proudly notes that his ideas were endorsed by the Ministry of Finance—about ten million francs per year were used for purchases and

52. Wifredo Lam. Illustration page from *Fata Morgana* by André Breton, 1940.

53. Wols. *All Prisoners*, 1939.

commissions during his tenure at the Beaux Arts—his successes never benefited refugee artists.[91]

While "philanthropy" is invoked by Hautecoeur to defend the mixed quality of the acquisitions, it did not go where most needed, namely toward isolated refugee artists in the free zone, as far as one can tell from acquisition records for the period 1940–44. There is no reason to doubt that Hautecoeur intensely disliked Surrealism and left-wing politics and that he shared the anti-Semitism of the typical Vichy official, even if—as his memoirs reveal—he refused to fire his Jewish secretary.[92] As for André Dézarroi, whose Musée du Jeu de Paume had been dedicated before the war to "foreign schools," he had no role left there. During that period, the Musée du Jeu de Paume was used by the Nazis to store and display art seized from Jewish collections prior to their transfer to Germany. Jean Cassou, whose book on Picasso came out in 1939, and who was interested in these "foreign schools," had no official post then either.

In her own chatty way, Peggy Guggenheim provides precious testimony of the negative attitude of Vichy toward the international Modernists she herself had collected while living in France, many of whom were now refugees in the free zone. Recalling her sojourn in the Savoy region of Vichy France, where the exodus had landed her, her children, and her friend Nelly van Doesburg, she noted:

Nelly was a friend of M. André Farcy, the director of the Musée de Grenoble. He liked modern art, so I sent her to see him and asked for his help. She came back with no definite promise, but with an invitation to me to send the pictures to the museum at Grenoble, where he would at least shelter them. We immediately dispatched them, and Nelly and I followed and settled in Grenoble.

Farcy was in a very bad jam himself at this time. Because of the Vichy government he nearly lost his museum directorship and finally ended up in prison. He couldn't do much for me. Though he did want to exhibit my collection, he was too frightened. As he was expecting Pétain to visit Grenoble, he had hidden the museum's modern pictures in the cellar. He gave me perfect freedom in the museum to do anything with my pictures except to hang them. I had a beautiful room where I placed them along the wall and could show them to my friends, photograph them and catalogue them. But he would never fix a date for the show, claiming he must pave the way with the Vichy government first. . . . He did not want me to remove the paintings either, and after six months in Grenoble, I lost my patience and told him that I was going back to America, but I knew I would never leave without it.[93]

The situation evoked by Peggy Guggenheim shows that the government back-lash, which had begun after the inroads of international Modernists at the 1937 Paris World's Fair,[94] had gained sufficient momentum to intimidate the most pro-gressive museum director in France at that time.

Prewar international Modernists, however, were accustomed to enduring xen-ophobia and lack of understanding from the art bureaucracy, which in France runs national museums, including those for modern art. They had managed with-out official support so long as there were galleries and sympathetic salons to show them and sympathetic publications and critics supporting their art. Now, as artist refugees in the free zone, they were isolated from their networks by the impenetrable border separating them from Paris in the occupied zone, and the networks themselves were greatly disrupted.

Cannes on the Côte d'Azur and Lyons in the center of France inherited some of the energies that Paris had lost. There was a lot of private dealing in Cannes due to the presence of refugee dealers. Fredo Sides, Solomon Guggenheim's former Paris contact, was among them.[95] Peggy Guggenheim, now in the free zone of France, was solicited by both Surrealist and nonobjective painters stranded in France until her departure for New York in the spring of 1941. In Lyons, the support network of the prewar group Témoignage continued to func-tion, and Gleizes, François Stahly, Etienne Martin, and Zelman were present at manifestations organized by Galerie Folklore and the Académie Minotaure.[96] In Marseilles, however, hopes for shows by refugee Surrealists were nil, as Breton found out when he looked around for a gallery to exhibit his Surrealist friends.[97]

The only Surrealist publication of the war years was *La Main à plume* (which became a writing platform for Hérold, Dominguez, and Brauner).[98] Printed under clandestine conditions, it hardly had the prestige, format, or audience of *Cahiers d'art* and *Minotaure*. *Fontaine* did what it could to maintain independent think-ing from Algiers, where it was published. *Cahiers du sud* and *Confluences*, pub-lished officially in Marseilles and Lyons respectively—hence subject to Vichy censorship[99]—were cautious in their art coverage.

In October 1940, *Cahiers du sud* did publish Breton's poem "Pleine Marge," and its March 1941 number contained "Peindre est une gageure," an article on painting by André Masson notable for introducing into Surrealism the question of consciousness and rational understanding in Surrealist representations. He concluded: "Rational understanding and consciousness must go hand in hand with intuition and the unconscious."[100] In later issues, *Cahiers du sud* dedicated itself to esoteric subjects.

Fortunately for some of the refugee artists, private individuals came to the rescue: Peggy Guggenheim visited Air Bel twice, leaving money each time and buying art.[101] Some refugee artists were on occasion visited by a Paris dealer. Susi Magnelli says that Louis Carré came once and bought something from Arp.[102] Support was also found locally: the poet Joe Bousquet bought from Ernst and Hans Bellmer; a doctor began collecting Brauner;[103] a couple of refugee collectors briefly paid for Freundlich's hotel room in exchange for his art,[104] and it is likely that in the French provinces there is still today, not yet accounted for, refugee art that was once bartered for favors.

Artists sometimes received stipends from collectors. A letter from Arp to Mr. and Mrs. Sacher in Switzerland explains: "Life is especially hard for us because we have no relatives with nice farms. . . . We are beginning to suffer from hunger. I am not saying this in jest. Dear friends, could you please increase my monthly allowance?"[105]

The Emergency Rescue Committee apparently also sent stipends. A letter of appreciation from Freundlich reveals the degree of poverty reached by this prewar modernist:

Dear Sir,

Allow me to express my appreciation of the help you have accorded us, for without it our situation would be still more desperate. And because here in France you are the only ones to whom I can address myself, permit me to describe the conditions under which my wife and I are obliged to survive. We do not have the means to buy wood for the approaching winter and we have lost the credit accorded us by our hotel.[106]

When Breton failed to persuade a gallery in Marseilles to show the work of the Surrealist refugees there, he arranged auctions at Air Bel of artworks done by the refugee artists. In May 1941, an exhibition of Max Ernst's work was held in the gardens of Air Bel: "All the artists from Marseilles came to look at the canvases and the engravings exhibited in the hothouse or, better still, hanging from tree trunks or from the main branches of the plane trees," says Daniel Bénédite. "A   Fig. 54 few days before his departure for the United States, Max is at the peak of his success, to which Peggy Guggenheim has contributed by coming to preside over the ceremony (the inauguration of a swimming pool in the garden of Air Bel) and lending a few works from her collection."[107] No list survives of the paintings Ernst showed at Air Bel, but from a photograph it seems that *The Attirement of the Bride* (1940), bought by Peggy Guggenheim, who exhibited it at the Art of This Century Gallery in New York in 1942, was among them. Bénédite does not say whether any works were sold.

54. Jacques Hérold helps Daniel Bénédite and Max Ernst (?) hang
Ernst's show at Air Bel in Marseilles, 1941.

At Montredon, the music-loving Comtesse Pastré started an *association d'en-traide* called Pour que l'Esprit Vive, which distributed to needy refugees the proceeds of the musical afternoons held there. "There was music at all times at the Montredon chateau, concerts every afternoon, with Madeleine Grey and Eliane Magnan among the regulars. The cellist, Pablo Casals, came to give a recital without accepting a fee. The pianist Clara Haskil performed in a Mozart festival . . . and Francis Poulenc accompanied himself on the piano for songs that he had composed on poems by Paul Eluard."[108]

Even with all these efforts, for many refugees an alternative way of survival had to be found. In Marseilles proper, the actor and stage director Itkine, after Vichy laws against Jews in the theater had deprived him of his livelihood, created a cooperative venture called Croque Fruit (or Croquefruits), and staffed it with needy artists and intellectuals who lived in the Marseilles area. They made a sweet consisting of dates, almonds, and walnut paste, true delicacies at a time

of nothing but ersatz sweets; "it was a poet's solution," writes the Paris publisher Jose Corti in his memoirs. "Everyone did his hours at Croque Fruit; each one would give it a morning or an afternoon, for work was organized in brigades like the post office and, in exchange, the cooperative provided a daily salary of seventy francs, raised, once prosperity had come, to eighty francs."[109]

An atmosphere of goodwill and cheer apparently reigned in the loft on rue des Trois Escaliers where the painters Dominguez and Hérold, the writers Benjamin Perret and Prévert, and others of "great, medium, or small reputation" rolled the dough.[110]

During its two years of operation, from December 1940 to December 1942, Croque Fruit prospered, relying for its advertising on the same fluid population of local refugee poets and artists. Breton wrote slogans for it. The most notable poster was the work of the cartoonist Jean Effel, for the food fair in Marseilles in September 1941. "Above the Croque Fruit stand was his large poster representing the paradise of temptation. Eve in her primitive nudity receiving this gift from the heavens in spite of restrictions."[111]

In the milieu of *La Main à plume*, the making and disposal of fake paintings was a common pursuit not only to keep the clandestine publication going but to attend to the needs of persons with a heavy past (particularly Spanish Loyalists) who had to survive in total secrecy lest their whereabouts become known to the French police or to the Gestapo.[112]

The artists at work in the free zone were for the most part a déclassé lot. The crisis for material survival was acute for most artists of prewar renown and worse for less well known refugees. The Stahlys and the Magnellis were forced to try their hands at farming on their land in the outskirts of Grasse.[113] Wols's companion became a cleaning woman.[114]

Works made by artist refugees in the free zone of France came into public view for the first time in the United States in 1941. The Baltimore Museum of Art, which held a small retrospective of Masson from 31 October to 22 November 1941, was the first institution to display art made in France by an artist who lived and produced work through the early stages of the Vichy regime. The Pierre Matisse Gallery gave Chagall a small retrospective between 25 November and 13 December 1941, which included several paintings done at Gordes. Peggy Guggenheim exhibited at the Art of This Century Gallery the collection she had assembled while living in France, which included works done during the first months of the Vichy regime. The First Papers of Surrealism exhibition, organized by the Coordinating Council of French Societies between 14 October and 7 November 1942, also included works done in Vichy France.

While it is true that a move away from the French capital on the part of artists antedates the World War II years,[115] the prewar movement was one of choice, unlike the one considered here. Ignored by the official art establishment, bypassed by the art market, the artist refugees in the unoccupied area were now returned to the bohemian conditions of their youth, albeit in a far-from-optimistic mood, and the unknown artists among them were confronted with unimaginable hardships. One by one, these rural communities disbanded and dispersed, particularly when there ceased to be a free Vichy zone.

Even so, it would appear that for many artist refugees in Vichy France, to exercise their talent was a means of keeping the anxieties of the day at bay. Sometimes the diarist mode prevailed; sometimes new expressions were invented in response to the intense state of tension, or due to lack of ordinary artistic materials, and the need for bricolage. What changed the most was the artists' lives and the destination of the art—frequently collaboratively made, it circulated mainly among friends. The "return to the soil" of prewar stars of the Parisian art world and of lesser-known figures of the Ecole de Paris whose names have come up in this chapter is more than a case study. It poses the question of how art is made under the fear of persecution.

7

Victims and Survivors

Unlike Nazi Germany, where "a number of artists and scholars were imprisoned in hurriedly constructed concentration camps that many would never leave again,"[1] in the part of France under Pétain rule, Judeo-Marxist-decadent artists who had sought refuge there were not harassed because of their art. They risked arrest by belonging to broader categories of targeted individuals: stateless persons considered to be a drain on the national economy, recently nationalized French Jews, political refugees wanted by the Third Reich, persons in various categories distrusted by the Pétain regime (Jews, Freemasons, Communists, anarchists, and anti-Nazis). Frequently they were potential victims on more than one of these grounds.

From the start, life was far from easy for refugees in Vichy France. All persons residing in France had to have identity papers in order to qualify for ration coupons and, in the event of a police roundup, had to be able to show that their papers were in line with the latest decree; at the same time, proper identification could cause their arrest and internment. Furthermore, since the information filed at the prefectures concerning refugees was routinely shared with the most dreaded branch of the Nazi police, the Gestapo, refugees daily faced the possibility of arrest, unless they tried to survive in total clandestinity.

Even before Pétain, the administrative response of French governments to foreign refugees from Hitler's Germany and from Spain had become harsh in the late 1930s, as pointed out by Marrus and Paxton.[2] To give one example, all foreign refugees had to make regular appearances at the French prefecture to get their temporary identity cards renewed and, if something in their dossiers seemed out of order, they could be deported back to their country of birth, or "sent by the Ministry of the Interior to some assigned residence . . . where they

could easily be watched"[3] or put in jail. The German refugee painter Max Lingner (not a Jew but an active Communist), who worked as a cartoonist for the French Communist press, was arrested as a dangerous international Communist agitator and almost deported to Germany in September 1939. He was placed in solitary confinement in one jail after another, before his internment as a German national.[4]

At the onset of the Phony War, in early September 1939, foreigners from countries with which France was at war had been isolated from the rest of the population. This is why Max Ernst and Hans Bellmer, who happened to be in Provence at that time, came to be interned together at Les Milles near Aix-en-Provence. A former brick factory, it consisted of a series of Kafkaesque spaces better suited to giant termites than to humans, with low-ceilinged, poorly lit tunnels (the old brick ovens) where the inmates lived and slept; the courtyard was notable for mountains of blowing dust and piles of decomposing bricks, which became an obsessive theme in Bellmer's art of these years.

In Paris, Freundlich and the critic Walter Benjamin were among those sent to Colombes, a sports stadium on the outskirts of Paris. There inmates lived under the stars and slept on benches. After ten days, they were transferred to smaller camps, often on farms in the French provinces.[5] Benjamin ended up at Clos St.-Joseph near Nevers (Nièvre).[6] Freundlich was sent to the Camp de Rassemblement at Francillon par Villebaron (Loir et Cher).[7]

As the Phony War dragged on, the better-known internees used influence and obtained their liberation. Ernst was liberated in December 1939, thanks to the intervention of Paul Eluard at the Ministry of Interior,[8] Freundlich in February of 1940 thanks to the then-president of the Société des Artistes Indépendants and of the poet Jean Gacon.[9] Benjamin was released in November 1939 through the intervention of Paul Valéry, Jules Romains, Paul Desjardins, Adrienne Monnier, and Jean Ballard, his editor at *Cahiers du sud*.[10] The younger internees were pressured to join the Foreign Legion or to become *prestataires*—assigned, among other duties, to the building of fortifications for the regular military.[11] Hans Bellmer became a *prestataire*.

After the 10 May breakthrough of German troops, foreign men and women over the age of sixteen were interned, including those who had been interned previously. Max Ernst, Freundlich, and Benjamin were no exceptions. Those who were interned in the northern half of France were transferred to the south by train. The French briefly entertained the idea of shipping a group of internees, including Max Ernst, to North Africa. Instead, his group was shuttled back and forth along the Pyrénées mountains by train, and finally marched from Nimes to

the camp of St.-Nicolas.[12] A drawing by Ernst, *Stateless*, showing two paper-thin   Fig. 55
creatures tottering on compass points in the midst of a barren landscape, captures
in a symbolic way the disorientation and nonidentity of stateless persons barely
hanging on in a desert of indifference.

All over France, confusion reigned regarding these thousands of Germans and
other foreign nationals, hated by the Third Reich, unwanted by the French, and
in a limbo of national identity. *Maimed and Stateless* is what Arp called a news-   Fig. 56
paper relief he made at that time, showing the torso of what must be the remains
of a foreign legionnaire or *prestataire*—his head bandaged, one arm in a sling
and hands missing. Legionnaires and *prestataires* stranded in the exodus were
throwing away their identity papers to avoid execution by the Germans for
having fought on the enemy's side. Bellmer was in that category.

As the head of the convoy of refugees carrying Ernst back and forth along the
Pyrénées said to his contingent, "Your situation is desperate: on one side the
Nazis, on the other the Falangists, and between them the French gendarmes, but
you are free to choose among these three possible ways of losing your life."[13]

In the days following the armistice, many internees were liberated, especially
if they could show they had a home in the free zone and sufficient means of
subsistence. Susi Magnelli returned to her home in Grasse.[14] Ernst fled to his
house at St.-Martin-des-Ardèches;[15] Freundlich landed at St.-Paul-de-Feno-
uillet.[16] Benjamin found himself in Lourdes, a town in the Pyrénées.[17]

But the respite was short-lived as Pétain put into place his antiforeigner legislation. Starting on 27 September 1940, pursuant to the law regarding foreigners
as a burden on the national economy, penniless refugees under the age of forty
were ordered incorporated into work companies and sent to build the Trans-
Sahara railroad in Africa.[18] The German painters Hans Hartung and Hans Escher
and the novelist Arthur Koestler were among those deported to Africa. All three
escaped and survived.

Other foreign refugees between the ages of seventeen and sixty-five, including
those who had been liberated in June, could be interned again for indeterminate
periods of detention at the discretion of French prefects, who were granted this
power by the law of 4 October 1940.[19] Refugee foreigners who could afford it
could live outside in a *résidence surveillée* (under house arrest), but they were
forbidden to travel and watched by the police. Freundlich remained under house
arrest in St.-Paul-de-Fenouillet. Ernst, after a third internment, escaped and returned to his country house, staying there until the last days of 1940.[20] Beginning
in November 1940 the internment camps would be run not by the fairly indiffer-
ent military but by *gardes mobiles*,[21] a special unit of the French police known
to cooperate with the German police.

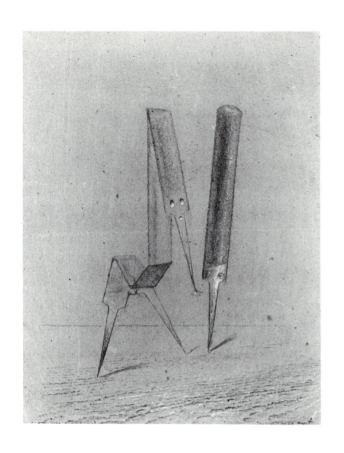

55. Max Ernst. *Les Milles-Apatrides*
(Stateless), 1939.

56. Hans Arp. *Maimed and Stateless*,
1939.

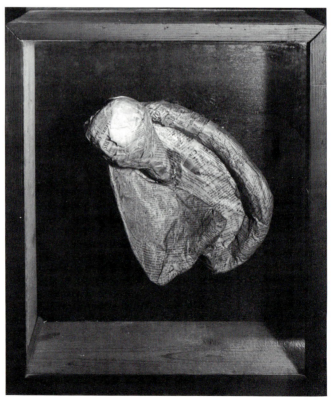

Worst of all, the Vichy government agreed to surrender to the German authorities anyone specifically designated by the Reich government as *fauteur de guerre*. This agreement, contained in article 19 of the armistice treaty, not only was in total contradiction to France's tradition of giving the right of asylum to political refugees,[22] but its application meant deportation and death to any German refugee thus surrendered on demand.

Vichy is seen in an even harsher light when one learns that the Germans had no lists of fauteurs de guerre to start with and needed the cooperation of the French police to obtain as complete a list of refugees as possible, from which a contingent of fauteurs de guerre would be selected to be turned over.[23] Lists of refugee inmates in thirty-one internment camps, sixteen prisons, and ten hospitals were provided to a deputation of Gestapo and military personnel known as the Kundt Commission,[24] which visited internment camps in the unoccupied zone during the autumn of 1940. Other names obtained by the Germans were those of refugees who had registered at the prefecture nearest them.

Furthermore, not only did the French government refuse to issue exit visas to German refugees during the time the Nazis were compiling their lists,[25] but, according to Varian Fry, the names of visa applicants were passed on to the German authorities.[26] Ernst and Benjamin, two well-known antifascists who had started formalities for emigration after their first internments, were no doubt among those whose names were seen by the Gestapo, giving them a good chance of being picked as fauteurs de guerre.

Without an exit visa, the only way to leave France was illegally, usually by crossing the Pyrénées. During the months when the Germans were gathering their information on refugees, the border with Spain was closely watched and those caught on the French or Spanish side—unless they met understanding patrols—were turned back and sent to French internment camps, where the conditions were appalling. Daniel Bénédite, Fry's right-hand man, who visited such camps, writes:

A miserable humanity, in rags, filthy, vermin-ridden, people these immense   Fig.57
bare spaces from which no vegetation emerges. Food is notoriously insufficient, based on vegetable debris. Hygiene is nonexistent (water which serves for external as well as internal use is pumped on the beach). . . . Sanitary facilities are deplorable. With warm clothes on, I am ashamed of venturing into other sectors where most of the internees, men, women, and childen, sleep directly on the ground underneath cloth tents torn by the wind.[27]

57. Internment camp, Gurs, France.

They were the camps that became way stations to the gas chambers.

By the time the Germans had finished making their lists—no example of which has yet been found—and the borders were temporarily reopened (January to May 1941), Benjamin and the art historian Carl Einstein had committed suicide. Benjamin was one of those caught crossing into Spain illegally; fearing repatriation to a French internment camp, he killed himself with morphia tablets the night of 26–27 September 1940. It is believed that Carl Einstein threw himself into a torrent in the vicinity of Bayonne for fear of falling into the hands of the Gestapo.[28] Ernst left France stealthily in June 1941 after a last brush with the French police at the border.[29] Bellmer lived in hiding in the south of France.

What motivated the cruelty of the new Vichy government toward "foreign" refugees can only be surmised. According to Marrus and Paxton, "the Vichy regime would have greatly preferred the repatriation or the expulsion of these refugees. Since wartime conditions made either impossible, the regime could at least keep them under guard and isolated from the normal labor market."[30]

But, as the authors point out, economic factors do not tell the entire story, particularly when one realizes that the great majority of persecuted foreign refugees were Jews, and as one notices that simultaneously with policies against foreigners came the first Vichy decrees against Jews both foreign and French (the Statut des Juifs). "In this inward-turning, inhospitable, even xenophobic climate of the summer of 1940, we can perceive," Marrus and Paxton observe, "the impact of the defeat.... We believe that the Vichy racial laws of 1940–41 are inconceivable without that seismic shock of June 1940."[31]

After the fall roundups and internment of foreign Jews, the first police arrests of recently naturalized French Jews came in the spring of 1941. In Marseilles, roundups were frequent because of the presence there of so many refugees in all categories. Chagall, a recently naturalized French citizen and a Jew, was among those arrested. He had gone to Marseilles to pick up visas for himself and his family and was seized at the hotel where he was staying.

Fry, the head of the American Emergency Rescue Committee, who had friends at the prefecture, intervened and got him released. The Chagalls left for New York in May 1941. "Others were not so lucky," writes Varian Fry. "They were expelled from the district, placed in *residence forcée* or, if they they had no means, in concentration camps or sent into forced labor."[32]

While the camps were still under the jurisdiction of Vichy before all of France came to be occupied, the first deportations from these camps took place. Between 7 August and 5 September 1942, the first loads of internees from Les Milles, Gurs, and other camps in the free zone were herded into trains headed for Drancy and deportation to Auschwitz.[33] Among them, according to André Fontaine, were "a certain number of naturalized French citizens who had lost their nationality thanks to Pétain, some 4,500 Germans and 1,100 Austrians, other refugees from the Reich, and persons who had been deported from Germany in the Burckel operation of October 1940."[34] The painter Felix Nussbaum was one of the deportees. He escaped from the train and fled to Belgium, where he was eventually caught, deported, and killed.[35]

During that same period, the painter Hans Reichel, an internee at Gurs who was not sent to Drancy, made a series of miniature works in watercolor called *Cahiers de Gurs*. All of them use the enigmatic, indirect, pictorial language of works by Paul Klee. One watercolor, marked Gurs, 14 July 1942, depicts human-like fish in all sizes, ages, and shapes, obviously out of the water and standing in a huddle, with stunned, resigned, or upturned open eyes. Fig. 58

Nor did the Pétain government deal gently with those—whatever their nationality or "race"—who did not agree with its policies (foreigners in spirit, one

might call them), as the inhabitants of Air Bel found out shortly before and during the visit of Marshal Pétain to Marseilles in December 1940. Air Bel was searched by the police on the suspicion that the place harbored Communists and anarchists who might try to blow up the train in which the marshal was riding when it passed through the environs of the property.

Following the search, which uncovered the symbolic collective portrait captioned *Ce sacré crétin de Pétain*, and the interrogations, the entire male contingent, including Breton, Victor Serge, Fry, Bénédite, and Ghemaling, plus the financial angel of the Emergency Rescue Committee in Marseilles, Mary Jayne Gold, the only childless female in the group, were rounded up and taken to a ship where they were kept in close quarters with hundreds of other imagined or real enemies of the Vichy regime who had been collected in a similar manner by the Marseilles police.[36]

"Marseilles has given to Maréchal Pétain the most vibrant proof of its absolute trust—Everywhere on his passage the Chief of State was welcomed with immense ovations,"[37] the headline of *Figaro* on 4 December 1940 unashamedly proclaimed, while a floating jail filled to capacity with innocent inmates bobbed silently in the old port.

Although the Air Bel group was liberated after three days in jail, thanks to the intervention of the American consul, Breton deduced from his experiences that

58. Hans Reichel. *Cahier de Gurs*, July 1942. (Color Plate 4)

emigration was his solution. "It was clear that, until things got better, I was deprived of the right to express myself," Breton would say in defense of his decision to leave France.[38] Breton, Jacqueline Lamba, and their daughter, Wifredo Lam, the Victor Serges, and Claude Levi-Strauss set out for Martinique on 25 March 1941 on the *Capitaine Lemerle*. The André Masson family departed on the *Carimare* on 31 March, also headed for Martinique.

From this French island on the Caribbean, the Bretons and Massons were to go on to New York; Lam headed for Cuba, and the Serges for Mexico. On 24 June 1941, Jacqueline Breton addressed a letter to Fry with the Bretons' first impressions of New York: "What is for sure, is that America is the Christmas tree of the world," she told him.[39]

In September 1941, Fry, who had successfully plucked from the Gestapo's clutches some of its most wanted persons, was taken to the French border by the Sureté Nationale and duly expelled for his illegal activities in favor of "political enemies" of France.[40]

LEFT BEHIND: OTTO FREUNDLICH, A VICTIM OF THE HOLOCAUST

In Lisbon, his stopover on the way home, Fry received the following news of Air Bel via a letter from Brauner, dated 3 October 1941: "It is raining at Air Bel and we are regretting your departure. No more clandestine beef nor roses in our shoes and now with the approach of Winter, a lingering boredom has invaded the area, which does not augur well."[41]

There is thus reason to believe that after commuting to Air Bel from hiding places in the eastern Pyrénées, Brauner, who was among those Jews attempting to survive in total clandestinity, made lengthier visits to Air Bel when a vacancy occurred due to Fry's departure in September 1941. Unable to get him emigration papers, the Emergency Rescue Committee supplied him with an allowance.[42] In the spring of 1942, as Air Bel was on its way to becoming a center for Alsatian refugees, the staff of the committee began making plans to abandon Air Bel, and so did Brauner. He spent the remainder of the war concealed as a shepherd on farms near Gap at Rémollon, the Plaine de Theus, and Celliers de Rousset. He survived.

It seems that the Emergency Rescue Committee also had something to do with the financing of Croque Fruit, which continued functioning until the occupation of Marseilles by the Germans.[43] In December 1942, the enterprise closed down for fear of a Gestapo raid. Itkine, who had joined the Resistance, was arrested on

1 August 1944, tortured by the Gestapo, and either executed right there or deported and gassed in a concentration camp.[44]

Hérold, also a Jew, and one of the artists who had worked at Croque Fruit, began a nomadic life of hiding and changes of identity. Disguised as a rag picker,[45] he attempted to escape to Switzerland and was repeatedly turned back. He and Dominguez reappeared in Paris in early 1943 after the free zone ceased to exist. Meanwhile, Hérold had made contact with a Resistance network and with the Surrealist group La Main à Plume.[46] He became a specialist in forged papers. Dominguez also became associated with La Main à Plume. Not a Jew, he was able to have an exhibition in Paris in 1943 at the Galerie Louis Carré, for which Eluard wrote an introduction. Both Hérold and Dominguez survived the war.

Switzerland was the refuge of the Arps, and of Leo Maillet, Chana Orloff, and Lipsi, the latter three of whom were Jewish artists. The Arps did not leave until the very day the Germans invaded the unoccupied zone. The Magnellis, thinking a big city might now be safer, especially if they lived there with false papers, returned to Paris. Magnelli participated in a group show of abstract artists with Kandinsky, Domela, and de Stael at the Galerie l'Esquisse (7 April 1944). This gallery, unbeknownst to them, was a front for Resistance activities. The show closed immediately for fear of a Nazi raid, but no one was arrested. Sonia Delaunay remained in Grasse until the Liberation.[47] Michel Kikoine, Léon Zack, and Marevna were other artists hiding in the south of France.[48] They survived.

After the dismantling of Oppède, Zehrfuss went to Spain and was able to rejoin the Allied armies. Zelman died of tuberculosis. Etienne Martin moved to Dieulefit and remained active in the Resistance. He and Zehrfuss survived.

Kahnweiler survived, as did Gertrude Stein and Alice B. Toklas. Although a friendly Vichy official told Stein and her companion in February 1943 (when all of France had become occupied) "that they must leave at once for Switzerland, tomorrow, if possible, otherwise they'll be put into a concentration camp," they decided against it, as it meant going across the border by fraud. "No I am not going, it is better to go regularly wherever we are sent than go irregularly where nobody can help us if we are in trouble, no, I said, they are always trying to get us to leave France but here we are and here we stay."[49]

Their artist friend Picabia survived too, but he spent the first four months after the Liberation of his area in a prison hospital, accused of collaboration by a purge tribunal. Gabrielle Buffet-Picabia, a Resistance worker, came to his rescue and, after a month in Cannes trying to find out why he was in jail, obtained his release.[50] To this day, the Picabia case remains shrouded in mystery. A gambler, he

constantly needed money; that is well known. That a quantity of kitschy photo-inspired portraits and double portraits mimicking National Socialist paintings were created and sold during that time is also beyond demonstrating. Gertrude Stein, in her catalogue essay for the 1941 Picabia show in Cannes, evokes this prolific output: one, sometimes two paintings per day. "He is the only one who, most of his life, has made so many paintings," she writes.[51]

Still, the perverse subtext of some of his subjects, in contrast to the uplifting tone of the alleged Nazi model—in *Women with Bulldog*, a nude blonde beauty is shown playing sexual games with her canine "friend"—gives a parodistic edge to the conservative, polished, figurative style. Perhaps it was his article in *L'Opinion* (1 March 1941) that landed him in jail for collaboration. Entitled

Fig. 59

59. Francis Picabia. *Women with Bulldog*, 1940–42.

"Jeunesse," it concluded: "Marshal Pétain is a young man, younger than all of our deputies and ministers, unfortunate creatures, who for the most part were ignoble egoists and thieves, effortlessly exploiting . . . France, which only wanted to believe, to love, and to live in freedom."[52]

The abstract painter Otto Freundlich did not survive. He was among the victims of the Holocaust. After the June armistice, Jeanne Kosnik Kloss (who was not a Jew) was able to rejoin Freundlich, as the latter tells Picasso in a letter dated 13 May 1941, asking the artist please to pay five months' rent on his Paris studio so that he does not lose it.

> My dear friend:
>
> I have been here since June 1940, and my wife rejoined me in September. We continue living and working as best we can. A few friends in Paris have taken care of the studio in our absence, but they just warned us that the landlord of the house is asking for back payment owed on the rent. . . .
>
> You would really help me a lot if you could send the 200 francs of monthly rent from May to September. It would amount to 1,000 francs for the five months. Jeanne will certainly talk to you, I hope, if she is in Paris. I thank you, and I salute you with much friendship, dear Picasso, and Jeanne also.
>
> Otto Freundlich.[53]

From the beginning of his sojourn at St.-Paul-de-Fenouillet, Freundlich's financial situation was precarious and he was often close to starving, as he tells a collector who apparently is paying for his hotel room in a letter of 11 July 1940: "Thanks to your great sweetness, I am in the pretty room. . . . I was able to withstand o.k. until now the deprivations to which I was subjected after our liberation from the camp in Bordeaux. But it is especially the nights that become terrible if the body has not taken a minimum of nourishment."[54]

Searching for financial support, he apparently made contact with Nelly van Doesburg, who wrote him of her own difficulties (letter of 29 August 1940) and told him that she would ask Peggy Guggenheim, with whom she was traveling, to help. A few months later (letter in French, dated 18 January 1941?), he heard from Guggenheim that she had sent him a thousand francs.

> Thank you very much for sending me your biography. I am very happy to have it from now on. Here things are not going too well. I am beginning to lose patience. I hope that you will be able to have canvas so that you can

continue to work. I sent you 1,000 francs for that, the day before yesterday. Kindly let me know the title of your painting in black and white that was in London.

Peggy Guggenheim.[55]

Bank transfers suggest that he received money through the French correspondent of a Swiss bank (the donor was probably E. Musch, a teacher in Switzerland and an admirer of his work). As noted earlier, it seems that for a while, in 1941, Fry's committee also assisted him financially.[56]

Although Freundlich hesitated to emigrate, a friend named Jiri Fischer apparently "made efforts to have your name and that of Jeanne placed on that list" (Fry's list of persons in danger needing an American visa), according to a letter in German from Fischer, dated 16 August 1940:

> The biggest difficulty is not with the American visas, but with the permission to leave the country, which is not easily given, and with the permission to travel through Spain and Portugal; and another matter is the question how this will be financed, which seems to be of no possible solution. So don't get your hopes up too high. But you should be aware that you haven't been completely abandoned.[57]

Freundlich attempted to contact friends and relatives in America, but mail got lost and nothing came of it, although his plight was known not only by Fry's committee but by other organizations as well. The Comité d'Assistance aux Refugiés, the American Friends Service Committee, and the Union Générale des Israelites de France all tried to help him.[58] In fact, as late as August 1942 he received a letter from the Union Générale des Israelites de France, inviting him to come to Perpignan "to consult an occulist," obviously a means for Freundlich to get permission to travel there for other purposes. But in the midst of these attempts to get away, Freundlich made the mistake of answering a letter from the prefecture asking him to state his religion, with an admission of his Jewish roots:

> Monsieur le Préfet
>
> Allow me to tell you that I am of the Jewish race, that my parents and grandparents were also [Jews]. I have no wealth. Being a painter, and a sculptor, having made mosaics and stained glass, I have lived modestly and honestly from the sale of my paintings to foreign collectors. I have been in France since 1924, and I have been closely tied to French art since my

youth. One of my paintings is in a French state museum, the Musée du Jeu de Paume, in Paris. It was offered to that museum by a subscription of personalities, artists, and well-known writers on the occasion of my 60th birthday, three years ago.[59]

By Christmas 1942, the Germans occupied all of France. Freundlich left St.-Paul-de-Fenouillet and moved to an abandoned tower nearby at St.-Martin-de-Fenouillet. There, Gestapo men finally found their target in early February 1943. Freundlich was taken to the camp of Gurs, then to Drancy and deported. He died either en route or shortly after his arrival.[60] His last writings, with their utopian, messianic ring, are reminiscent of Malevich writing under the stresses of the Russian Revolution: "It would seem that cosmic laws themselves represent a symbol for a higher plane of being, and that their geometric application to corporeal things might be but the preparation for a broader and deeper solution."[61] Breaking away from the totally abstract mode that he had practiced all his life, Freundlich painted a black, tall, "doorlike" rectangle (passage into the unknown, intuition of death, mounting anxiety?) on what is believed to be his last and unfinished work with patchwork forms.

Fig. 60

60. Otto Freundlich. *Composition* (unfinished), 1943.

CHAPTER 7

Within the group studied in this chapter there were more survivors than victims, and it is true that the arrest of Freundlich took place after the free zone of France had ceased to exist. Even so, it would appear that the muses fled not only Hitler but also Pétain in the aftermath of the French armistice. The Vichy government, by denying a minimum of security to those who placed themselves under its protection in the free zone, revealed its own methods of attack on "decadent" art. The internments of Ernst, the jailing of Breton during the marshal's visit to Marseilles, the arrest of Chagall, the eviction from France of Fry, the protector of these men, and Freundlich's *résidence surveillée* before his arrest hardly do credit to Vichy.[62]

In a postwar talk, the former Dadaist Tristan Tzara, who apparently tried unsuccessfully to emigrate and, when that attempt failed, went underground in Vichy France and worked with a Resistance network, spoke harshly of the Surrealists who had abandoned ship. He particularly indicted those who, from across the ocean, had criticized the militant poetry being written by Resistance poets "for defending France ... in a litany like old-fashioned form."[63]

The issue raised by the Tzara talk is not only the relationship between militancy and creativity during periods of curtailed freedom, but the difficulty of understanding from afar the dilemmas faced by those who live under these circumstances. Time has not served to clarify these dilemmas. First there was Hannah Arendt, accusing Jews of having complied too easily with Vichy orders and thus becoming sitting ducks for the Nazis. Would Freundlich have been saved had he not sent the letter quoted above to the prefecture? Nothing is less sure. Denunciations were all too common, and paid well. Questions have also been raised about whether Picasso did his share for the cause of freedom.

8

Picasso's War in Occupied Paris

The man who sees sharply from where he is and from
elsewhere at the same time is like a twinned person in
whom contradictory natures concur.
Leo Steinberg

Picasso's Gamble

Picasso produced between three and four hundred paintings, plus large numbers
of drawings, prints, and sculpture, during the Occupation years.[1] Since he was
not allowed to exhibit his art, he worked in relative freedom in the privacy of his
studio. Furthermore, his wealth insulated him from the physical hardships endured by most artist refugees in the free zone, and the fame attached to his name
gave him a certain amount of immunity.

Even so, not being a French citizen, he risked arrest if his papers happened not
to be in order during a police roundup. Since he had been dubbed by Hitler a
Judeo-Marxist-decadent artist—Paul Ortwin Rave mentions a Picasso "watercolor" in his list of works seen at the Entartete Kunst exhibition of 1937—his
freedom hung by a thread. On several occasions, Germans in various guises—
including threatening Gestapo men—came to his studio on spying missions. Indeed, connected to the Spanish loyalist cause in the 1930s, his friends, most of
them active in a Resistance network, and his visitors, especially the Spanish
Communist ones, were suspect. (It is not known whether the Germans were
aware that his companion Dora Maar was half-Jewish.)

Thus the atmosphere in which Picasso worked in occupied Paris and the tensions experienced by many people then trying to survive in Vichy France had
much in common: life was most of the time a roller coaster of emotional states
in which a modicum of freedom and the fear of its loss were continually in the
balance. That is what makes of Picasso the paradigmatic figure of the survivor,
albeit a privileged one. This privileged status enabled him to continue his work,

and to leave behind the most extensive and exciting body of work done during the Occupation from the point of view of a person at risk.

Picasso had not gone to New York in the prewar period when showings of his works had taken place, and in the summer of 1940 he had not responded to the bid from Alfred Barr and the Emergency Rescue Committee formed in New York by Frank Kingdom to extricate from Europe those believed to be in greatest danger. Although a "foreigner," he had been spared the fate of Spanish and German refugees whom the French government interned during the Phony War. Neither did he accept the invitation of his Mexican friends in 1941.[2] The works shipped to New York for his 1939 New York retrospective (including *Guernica*) were intentionally left there by the artist after the show closed.[3]

A number of works from the Royan stay, dated 11 June 1940 to 7 July 1940, expressively record Picasso's forebodings. As he later told Kahnweiler, "When the Germans arrived in France I was in Royan, and one day I did a portrait of a woman—it was Dora Maar—and when the Germans arrived a few days later (the armistice took effect on 25 June 1940), I saw that the head resembled a German helmet."[4]

What Picasso does not say is that in this group of works, including the *Head of a Woman*, dated 26 June 1940 and singled out by Leo Steinberg for analysis, the head can also be read as a skull.[5] A triangular set of references associating the German occupation, Jews, and death may well be implied in the portrait of Dora Maar.

Fearful as he was, Picasso had made up his mind by August 1940 to leave Royan for Paris, possibly, says his Royan landlady, Andrée Rolland, because "the situation of foreigners was becoming untenable there. They were the victims of the Germans' distrust and of the xenophobia of some Frenchmen; the very ones, by the way, who were then making their accommodations with the [German] occupiers, and among them were the powerful of the day. Picasso from the start could not understand this opportunism."[6] According to Sabartès, "On 23 August, Picasso left Royan for good with his chauffeur, Kazbeck (the dog), and all his baggage."[7]

What prompted Picasso's decision to remain in France and live in occupied Paris can only be surmised. He had already experienced one world war as an outsider in France, with effects on his art and his behavior.[8] Now he may have calculated that world opinion would protect him.[9] The decision by Kahnweiler—who regularly sold his works—to stay in France may also have influenced him.

To Françoise Gilot, who met Picasso in the spring of 1943 and had asked him

why he had run the risk of staying, the artist replied that he simply had no desire to leave:

> Oh, I'm not looking for risks to take, but in a sort of passive way I don't care to yield to either force or terror. I want to stay here because I'm here. The only kind of force that could make me leave would be the desire to leave. Staying on isn't really a manifestation of courage; it's just a form of inertia. I suppose it's simply that I prefer to be here. So I'll stay, whatever the cost.[10]

Did he receive guarantees of safety as long as he did not exhibit his work? According to Christian Zervos, "at the express request of Franco's ambassador to France, the Germans had let Picasso know that they could not authorize him to exhibit."[11] The Franco regime was here punishing not only the creator of *Guernica*, a work with anti-Franco sentiments, but an ex-director of the Prado Museum under the Loyalist government and a benefactor of Spanish refugees.

Did the French police shield Picasso from Gestapo agents who, according to Françoise Gilot, were often nosing about his studio, hoping to discover papers incriminating enough to arrest him?[12] André-Louis Dubois, who had worked at the Paris prefecture and had supplied exit visas to a number of persons in danger at that time, was a frequent visitor to the artist's studio. In his memoirs, Dubois confirms his role of protector: "For five years I had a fixed appointment, almost daily, around 11:00 in the morning. It was rue des Grands Augustins."[13]

On at least one occasion, he may have had a role in saving the artist from arrest:

One day, the phone rings:

"It's Dora. They are at Picasso's."

"I'm coming."

I hurry. I get there. I meet two men in green raincoats in the courtyard. They were leaving alone. Everything was all right. They stop me and ask where I'm headed. I answer "to see Picasso" (he was the only tenant).

"Are you French?"

"Yes."

"Your papers."

They examine them, return them to me, then leave. I arrive at Picasso's. A

mess. Some canvases are slashed. Picasso is smoking. He has an impassive mask.

Picasso says, "They insulted me, called me a degenerate, a communist, a Jew. They kicked the canvases. They told me, 'We'll be back.' That's all. . . ."

They did not come back.[14]

Dubois, by the way, also tells of protecting Soutine.[15]

Whatever motives Picasso may have had for staying and whatever guarantees he may have received, his remaining in France when he had opportunities to leave gave him immense prestige in the eyes of artists and their sympathizers who could not leave, yet were determined to see France liberated. There is a well-known exchange on this subject between the poet Jacques Prévert and the photographer Brassaï:

BRASSAÏ: He stayed. His presence among us is a comfort and a stimulant not only for us his friends, but even for those who do not know him.

PRÉVERT: I completely agree. We must be thankful. It was an act of courage. This man is no hero. He is afraid like all those who have something to defend. . . . He took the risk. He came back to occupied Paris. He is with us. Picasso is a good guy.[16]

Some forty years later, Noèl Arnaud, a young Surrealist poet at that time, queried by the author on the subject of Picasso's wartime record, which in recent years has come under close scrutiny, wrote back: "The presence of Picasso in Paris (especially after the attempt against Hitler had eliminated from the high army command all officers who were against or tepid to the regime) became an uncontestable act of courage and of hope."[17]

So Picasso reappeared in occupied Paris after his sojourn in Royan. What he did between 15 August 1940 and 25 January 1941 cannot be documented by the dating of his paintings, for a gap appears in the Zervos catalogue between these two dates.[18] According to Werner Spies, his sculpture production also shows a gap.[19] *Desire Caught by the Tail*, a play begun by Picasso on 14 January 1941 and said to have been written in three days, reveals what little we are allowed to know about Picasso's early reactions to occupied Paris. In a disguised, indirect, and somewhat Surrealist way, the play manages to convey how the artist exorcised his physical and emotional misery during these first months of readaptation in a changed Paris. Through the voice of Silence, a minor character buried discreetly in the play, Picasso bids his adieux to the hardships that had kept him

silent—lack of milk and difficult milkmaids—and reiterates his belief that HE is the winner. "Silence: '1800! Farewell misery, milk, eggs and milkmaid! I am master of the jackpot!'"[20]

"Most certainly, it is not a time for the creative man to fail, to shrink, or to stop working,"[21] Picasso told an interviewer who had noted the accumulation of works in Picasso's studio when he visited him shortly after the liberation of Paris in August 1944.

To solve the material problems involved in the resumption of his work, Picasso availed himself of the ruses used by those with his means and needs. Fearing a shortage of bare canvas, Picasso, according to Brassaï, had alerted antique dealers to let him know whenever an old painted canvas came into their possession so that he could buy it and build up a stock of them on which to paint.[22] Brassai also tells of having witnessed one day at Picasso's studio the unloading of dozens of bare canvases and, on another occasion, Picasso showing someone a group of drawings made on fine Japan paper and saying, "I paid through the nose."[23]

Asked by Brassaï how he was able to turn so many plaster casts into bronze when bronze was at a premium and public statuary was being melted down, he explained: "It's a long story. . . . A few devoted friends transported the plaster casts at night in lorries to the foundries. . . . And it was even more dangerous to bring them back in bronze under the noses of the German patrols . . . the 'merchandise' had to be camouflaged."[24] One should note that Picasso's sculpture at that time abounds in assemblages of found materials, that many of the bronzes are small and many of the sculptured works are made from the most ephemeral of materials—corrugated cardboard, cigarette boxes, matchboxes, a piece of bread.

As for how Picasso was going to fulfill his determination neither to "fail" nor to "shrink" now that he had broken with Silence, a drawing coincidentally found underneath the words "Act I, Scene I" of the written scenario for the play *Desire*
Fig. 61   *Caught by the Tail*, his first creative project after his return to occupied Paris, gives a hint on that subject.[25] The curtain is open on a kitchen interior and platters of food, glasses, and bottles scattered on a plain table suggest a banquet of sorts at which men and women have been gathered, as evinced by the presence under the table of the diners' legs and feet. (Some people are going to gorge on the new situation, the artist seems to be saying to himself.)

The hand that has drawn this peculiar image is stiff, nervous, but makes no concession to fashionable idealized classicizing; Picasso is not going to revert to the Ingresque mode that he turned to during World War I, a mode that might

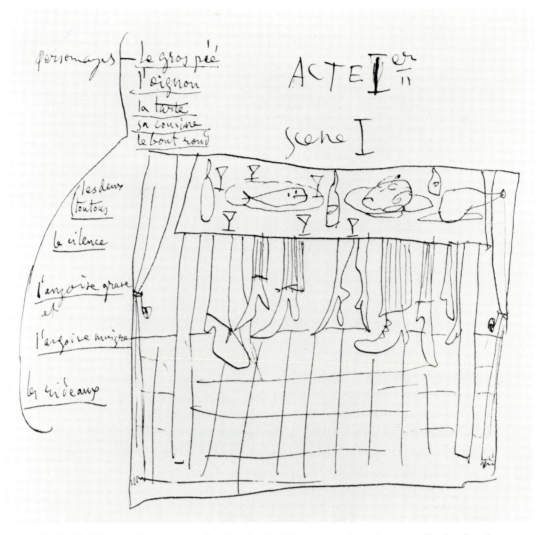

61. Pablo Picasso. Frontispiece for the play *Le Désir attrapé par la queue* (Desire Caught by the Tail), by Pablo Picasso, 1941.

have kept him from being labeled "degenerate." The thinking at work is at the same time detached commentary and macabre imagination. On closer examination, the diners' legs seem to be suspended rather than touching the tile floor, their dangling above the ground reminiscent of the abandoned pose of hanging victims. Furthermore, a human head, possibly Picasso's, is readable as the double of the chicken on the middle platter. One false move on my part, the artist seems to be thinking, and the feasting turns into capital punishment. A banal tabletop—which reappears in the *Charnel House* of 1945—occupies center stage, separating the realm of feasting and of death simultaneously depicted here. "Lying low" is indeed the best posture for surviving treacherous times.

Unlike the work exhibited by French painters at that time, which safely stayed away from loaded subject matter, the fears and traumas of the underdogs, the rejoicing of the winners are readable in the drawing underneath "Act I Scene I." What I propose is that, whatever apologies need to be made for Picasso's "Resistance" record, Picasso's sympathies were unquestionably on the side of freedom, and the artist did not indulge in the kind of escapist art visible in the galleries of occupied Paris at that time.

THE WAR IN PICASSO'S ART

The poet Jacques Prévert would say of Picasso during those years, "More than any other painter labeled 'a painter of reality,' Picasso reacts to what is around him. Each of his works is a response to something he has seen [or] . . . felt that surprised and moved him."[26]

Since Picasso reputedly refused the heating fuel being offered to him by the Germans with the words "a Spaniard is never cold,"[27] he, like all Parisians, had to find other ways of staying warm in the damp Paris winters. In a photograph taken by Brassaï, Picasso is seen seated next to a gigantic pot-bellied stove that he had apparently bought from a collector. (It did not work.) Brassaï recalls that a large bathroom became the artist's sculpture studio because it was the warmest place in the house, heated by a powerful electric radiator. Picasso would commemorate the lack of central heating in *Interior View of the Atelier rue des Grands Augustins* (1943).

Fig. 62

Superficially, Picasso's motif fell in line with the "still life before a window" theme found in many paintings by Estève, Bazaine, Pignon, and other tricolor painters at that time. But when Picasso approached it, it was not in a cheerful or prayful mood. In *Interior View of the Atelier rue des Grands Augustins*, the shapes of roofs outside the window are like blocks of ice, and the zigzagging

62. Pablo Picasso. *Interior View of the Atelier rue des Grands Augustins*, 1943.

lines defining the radiator top simulate shivers. As Prévert remarks, "Any other painter would have suppressed the radiator, judging it ugly, vulgar, unesthetic, . . . whereas it is precisely the radiator that dominates this work."[28]

Food, which some could obtain at black-market prices while others nearly starved, also makes an appearance in Picasso's art. Food receives homage in a series of paintings entitled *Le Buffet du Catalan*, the sideboard at the black market restaurant Au Catalan where Picasso met his friends. It invades not only the conventional still-life motif, but mischievously appears as an adornment on a

woman's hat. (In a time of clothing coupons, fashionable women took to wearing extravagant hats.) Food is also evoked in a small, ephemeral sculpture made from bread.

An obsession with death is a constant in the Spaniard's oeuvre. It became an obsession in the lives of many individuals then. While it is true that the artist's personal life was affected by the death of his friend the sculptor Julio Gonzales, Fig. 63   on 27 March 1942 (the series of *Still Lifes with the Skull of a Bull* is frequently mentioned as Picasso's response to this event), and that Picasso was afraid that his own life was about to end—apparently Max Jacob had predicted that that would occur in the 1940s—the abundance of skull images in his wartime production cannot help connote a more generalized atmosphere of death. (Surprisingly few images of skulls were seen in the galleries of occupied Paris.) The theme of the bull skull has also been read as "the loss or subjugation of the freedom to create"[29] by Mary Margaret Goggin, who has studied in great detail possible ties between Picasso's iconography and specific historic events during the period Fig. 64   1940–44. Picasso's first three-dimensional *Head of a Bull* (1942), also a skull form from that time, made from a bicycle saddle and handlebars, has a humorous though timely reference, as bicycles became part of the street landscape of the French capital.

The composite views of Paris parks in the 1943 *Vert galant* series may have been Picasso's way of commemorating the ritual walks with his dog between his apartment on the Right Bank and his studio on the Left Bank and the visits to Marie Thérèse on boulevard Henri IV. (He abandoned his Right Bank apartment in 1942 and lived thereafter in his working studio on rue des Grands Augustins.) One reason Picasso gave André Malraux as to why he painted landscapes during the war was that since he could no longer travel, he walked along the Seine with his dog. "One day all these things registered in me, unbeknownst to me, began to come out."[30] But a pedestrian's view of Paris was the common lot of Parisians from all walks of life who, lacking other means of transportation, took to covering great distances on foot.

The abundance of female images—no longer women in tears but often women with impenetrable, sometimes accusing glances, or, in *Woman with Artichoke*, the stance of someone ready to kill her attacker—undoubtedly had a personal meaning for Picasso at that time. In *Desire Caught by the Tail*, there are allusions to his annoyance over the jealousy between his two mistresses, Dora Maar and Marie Thérèse; the artist's lust is also amply documented. But one cannot dismiss the lopsided ratio of women to men visible in France because so many men were in German prison camps, nor forget the bravery of women in the French

63. Pablo Picasso. *Head of a Bull on a Table*, 5 April 1942.

64. Pablo Picasso. *Head of a Bull*, 1942.

Resistance movement. In short, the average French person's hardships and obsessions with cold, with food, with the absence of means of transportation; the shortage of men; the courage of women; and even the ambiance of terror that accompanied the daily life of resisters, Jews, and other persecuted individuals can all be read between the lines.

With the exception of those who were benefiting from the Vichy regime and the German occupation, few people living in France during those exceptional times could fail to be aware of a sense of imprisonment and anxious waiting for the war to end. To his friend Lee Miller, who went to see Picasso right after the liberation of Paris, Picasso said, "There was nothing to do but work and struggle for food, see one's friends quietly, and look forward to the day of freedom."[31] Although this accurately describes the situation of refugee artists in the free zone of France, their art rarely contends in visual terms with the tension of waiting and with signs of confinement. Picasso often engages the subject, albeit in forms perhaps only obvious to those who endured these years in particularly intense expectation.

As a semiotics of gesture suggests, the clasped hands resting on the lap in Picasso's sitting figures convey waiting, as does the seat itself when put in the context of a remark Picasso made to André Malraux in 1945. "When I paint a woman in an armchair, the armchair is old age and death, no?"[32] The armchair is thus associated with waiting for death. In *Seated Woman with Hat* (1941–42) Fig. 65 from the Kunstmuseum in Basel, probably a portrait of Dora Maar, the setting resembles a prison cell. There are parallel bars behind and above the seated figure. The woman turns her back on the window as if to dispel the impossible dream of escape. The hands are clasped and their wringing in despair would seem to have been displaced to the woman's "twisted" or tortured head— two simultaneous aspects of the same face turned along a single axis. The Fig. 66 *Woman with Fish Hat* (1942), in the Stedelijk Museum, also evokes waiting and death. The seated woman's extravagant hat, which is readable as a dead fish on a dinner plate, combines the idea of frivolity and finitude, as in the traditional "Vanitas."

It is also tempting to hypothesize that his rocking-chair image alludes to idle waiting, particularly when one notes that one arm of the rocking chair is in the form of a spiral, the symbol of unfolding time. But even *L'Aubade* (4 May 1942), Fig. 67 when returned to its historic context, yields signs of waiting and of confinement while waiting. Picasso told Seckler after the war: "It is simply a nude and a musician. I painted it for myself. When you look at a nude made by someone else, he uses the traditional manner to express the form, and for the people, that repre-

65. Pablo Picasso. *Seated Woman with Hat*, 1941.

66. Pablo Picasso. *Woman with Fish Hat*, 19 April 1942.

sents a nude. But for me, I use a revolutionary expression. In this painting there is no abstract significance. It's simply a nude and a musician."[33]

What concerns us here is not so much the ambiguous way in which Picasso uses the word "revolutionary," since indeed his nude "revolves" around an axis to reveal several simultaneous aspects, but his simplification of the image as just "a nude and a musician." The nude on the striped mattress is, in one of her poses, lying on her back with arms folded behind her head, seemingly "staring" at the ceiling. The seated musician is not playing but watching and "waiting," one hand holding onto the instrument while the other rests quietly on her lap. As in the Basel portrait, the atmosphere is lugubrious and cell-like. Both paintings belong to a particularly somber epoch in the Occupation period, when the Germans appeared to have the upper hand everywhere on the military front.

It seems to me that the signs of waiting change but do not disappear when hope for liberation intensifies after the landing of the Allies in North Africa in November 1942. I propose that the theme of burning candles (April 1943 onward), and even more poignantly the theme of tomatoes ripening on increasingly brittle and dry stems, a theme that preoccupies the artist during the very days when the Allies were approaching the French capital, allude to the fact that by then the end of the wait was in sight. The candle would soon be consumed; the Fig. 68 tomato would drop from its stem.

Conscious of the danger posed by the Germans watching over his work, Picasso seems to have held back his partisanship intensely. In fact, he depicts in the same style Martin Fabiani, a dealer known for his contacts with Germans at that time, and Nush Eluard, a Resistance activist; *Man with the Sheep*, heavy with symbolism, and the animal illustrations for Buffon's *Histoire naturelle*.

But a social or even a political subtext can often be detected. In *Head of a Bull on a Table* (5 April 1942) (see fig. 63), "the bull's head, a skull upon a table, is like a death mask set upon the shoulders of one whose cape cloaks his wooden anatomy and whose elbow akimbo suggests a victorious toreador."[34] If the elbow akimbo image truly connotes the toreador's victory, it appears elsewhere in disguise. The same symbolism can be read in the elbowlike handles of anthropomorphized coffeepots, the subject of paintings from 24 March 1943 on.[35] In the still life signed 6 April 1944, the coffeepot is actually "dancing"!

What emerges here is that while the images themselves were cautiously thought out, and in all likelihood had to do with personal experiences, including the sexual conquest of Françoise Gilot, viewers favorably predisposed toward Picasso since the *Guernica* episode were able to imbue specific images with pro-Resistance messages. For example, Emile Szittya, writing his "notes on Picasso"

67. Pablo Picasso. *L'Aubade*, 4 May 1942.

68. Pablo Picasso. *Tomato Plant*, August 1944.

in the *Courrier des arts et des lettres* in 1947, would say: "The works of Picasso, particularly those that he created during the Occupation, all demonstrate a barely concealed action against fascism. The strange forms, the dirty grey colors . . . the heads with two or three noses, the broken line, remind us that during these years we were living not with human beings but with monsters."[36]

To a visitor who saw him shortly after the liberation of Paris, Picasso said: "I have not painted the war . . . because I am not the kind of painter who goes out like a photographer for something to depict. But I have no doubt that the war is in these paintings I have done. Later on perhaps the historians will find them and show that my style has changed under the war's influence. Myself, I don't know."[37]

The first critic to notice something new in Picasso's style was Picasso's dealer Kahnweiler. Writing from his refuge near the village of St.-Léonard-de-Noblat to Gertrude Stein, who had found her haven in the unoccupied zone near the Swiss border, he asked her on 19 December 1941: "I don't know if you have seen photos from Pablo's new works . . . several views of the same head, each rather realistic, together on the canvas, the total result being of course far from realism."[38] Although several views of the same thing were nothing new in Picasso's art, Kahnweiler sensed—though he did not formulate it—that this was no Cubist reprise.

Several observers have suggested that the emblem of Picasso's wartime "style" had to do with these "monstrous" distortions. Roland Penrose has observed: "As early as the autumn of 1939 we find a 'portrait' of Dora Maar in which distortion is carried so far that it might be expected that all resemblance to the human head has been forfeited."[39] One reads in the Janises' 1946 book on Picasso: "The distortions and displacements of human features are disquieting. It is obvious that the extent and special quality of horror in this new phase were at least heightened and their advent quickened by war."[40] For Leo Steinberg, "the extremes that are being conflated are lady and animal; the front of a bovine snout ingrown as a single visage with the lost profile of a beautiful woman; and sometimes a feminine head shared with a bare skull."[41]

Steinberg is not content with observing the "conflation of extremes" in Picasso's rendering of the human figure. He observes how in *L'Aubade*, but also in the still-life motif, pairs of oblique lines suggesting contrary perspectival views frequently originate at various points at or near the edge of the canvas. Rather than faceting the objects on which they alight, their disparate origins reveal, according to Steinberg, Picasso's multiple facets, his own "natura duplex." Such an expression also qualified the Paris milieu frequented by Picasso, which

Fig. 69

69. Pablo Picasso. *Flower Vase on a Table*, 1942.

his friend Georges Hugnet later described as "dubious," "unhealthy," full of "anxiety and thirst for life . . . cautiousness and incautiousness, calculation and disinterestedness."[42]

NAVIGATING THROUGH TROUBLED WATERS

To the American journalists who came in droves to visit Picasso right after the liberation of Paris, Picasso repeatedly said that he had continued to work all through the war, but for himself. To one he explained, "I have worked on. They would not let me exhibit but I worked and all my work is here."[43] To another he said that he was forbidden to show and sell his work. " 'Decadence, eh?' Picasso said softly. 'Do you know Hitler himself did me the honor of naming me in one of his speeches as a wicked corrupter of youth? So for four years, I have been personally forbidden to show or sell my works.' "[44] We know now the circumstances that made it impossible for Picasso to be exhibited in Paris during the war. It was Spain's Franco that exerted pressure to that effect.

No Picasso exhibition was held during the occupation of Paris. In fact, from an interview with the then director for publications of the Galerie Charpentier, the Marquis de Masclari, it is clear that whenever a painting by Picasso was seen hanging up front in a gallery, the work was immediately removed by order of the censors, who checked on all exhibitions prior to their opening. In the Charpentier incident, the work ordered removed (which did not come from Picasso's studio but belonged to a collector) stayed on view in the private office of the director of the gallery, as my witness told me with a proud smile.[45] Symbolic gestures of disobedience were common in occupied France.

In order, however, to counteract the banning of exhibitions of his work, Picasso continued to allow a stream of visitors into his studio on the rue des Grands Augustins. "There were always quite a few people waiting to see him: some in the long corridor on the lower floor, where Sabartès held forth; others in the large painting atelier on the floor above," Françoise Gilot, who herself became a regular visitor, recalls in her memoirs.[46] Sometimes the mob of visitors was overwhelming. Brassaï: "Monday 29 November 1943. Today such a mob invades Picasso that in a state of exasperation he seeks refuge in the atelier where I am photographing the latest of his large sculptures."[47]

From this eyewitness of some credibility, since he went to Picasso's studio regularly on a professional basis, an aperçu of those who went to the studio emerges. They seem to fall into three main, though overlapping, categories. Those who were trying to sell or interest him in something formed one group. There was old Baron Molet, who had found a chest for Picasso "for close to nothing." A Madame M. M. wanted to sell Picasso an El Greco. Picasso's paint dealer had a house he wanted to trade with Picasso for a still life he particularly admired. A second group comprised friends and acquaintances interested in seeing his work. The third group of visitors mentioned by Brassaï was made up of professional art dealers and art publishers.

Contrary to what Picasso told American journalists, activity around his work continued right through the war. The poets Paul Eluard and Georges Hugnet, both of them active in the Resistance and close friends of Picasso's during the war, bought quite a few works. *Cahiers d'art, 1940–1944* (1944) reproduces a number of Picassos from the war, with Georges Hugnet listed as owner. In a book on Picasso published in 1946, we read that Paul Eluard "owned numerous portraits of Nush and of the war."[48]

"He [Picasso] did sell paintings to my sister-in-law, of course,"[49] Kahnweiler volunteered in the Crémieux interview. Louise Leiris, Kahnweiler's sister-in-law (married to Michel Leiris, who belonged to the Musée de l'Homme Résistance

group), was then the official owner of Kahnweiler's gallery. Anyone interested in seeing Picassos could always ask Mme Leiris if they could visit the back room of her gallery where the Picassos were hung.

If the Leirises had connections with the Resistance, the other dealer who makes an appearance in Brassaï's memoirs had connections on the other side. Martin Fabiani had taken over Ambroise Vollard's gallery after the latter's death in a car accident in July 1939, and he fell heir to the projects Vollard had started with Picasso. Fabiani thus saw to the publication of Buffon's *Histoire naturelle*, which Vollard had commissioned Picasso to illustrate, and which Picasso finished during the war. The book came out in May 1942 in an edition of 226 copies. Gilot says that Fabiani apparently acquired a number of works by Picasso during the war by means of exchanges.

According to Gilot, a painting by the Douanier Rousseau, traded between Picasso and Fabiani, turned out to have come from a Jewish collection that the Nazis had seized, and Picasso dutifully returned it to its proper owner when, back from exile in the United States, she came to claim it after the war.[50] Fabiani was among the dealers called to testify by the Liberation tribunals for having helped the Germans dispose of art seized from Jewish art dealers and art collectors. The Paris dealer Louis Carré also purchased Picassos at that time, some of which he exhibited at his New York gallery after the war, in 1952.

Among the art-book publishers mentioned by Brassaï is Christian Zervos, who stopped publishing *Cahiers d'art* in 1940 and went into seclusion in Vezelay, but who went to Paris in 1943 and proposed an album of Picasso drawings.[51] He also continued to work on the catalogue raisonné of Picasso's oeuvre, but published nothing on Picasso during that period. Also mentioned is Editions du Chêne, owned by Maurice Girodias,[52] for whom Brassaï was photographing Picasso's sculpture production, and who put out an illustrated book on Picasso's most recent paintings, with a text by Robert Desnos, another of Picasso's friends active in a Resistance network.[53]

Even a German publisher apparently approached Picasso, according to Brassaï, who quotes Picasso as follows: "Publishers are funny people. This morning in the mail, a German publisher proposes to do an album of my paintings. Toward the end of his letter—mind you—he has the nerve to write: 'I hope, Mr. Picasso, that thanks to my book, you sell many pictures!' I think that it is he rather who will sell many of his books thanks to my work."[54]

Brassaï's memoirs deflate the notion spread by Picasso himself that he had worked for himself in isolation during the war. Some activity, it turns out, con-

tinued around him during that time. And Brassaï's testimony discreetly points out the eclecticism of his business connections.

But Brassaï's recollections are also notable for their silence on Picasso's German visitors. Possibly Brassaï was unaware of such visits. From two of the three Germans who have left written testimonies of their encounters with Picasso, one gets the sense that Picasso may have been alone to greet them. Visitor number 1 (Ernst Jünger): "On a piece of paper, the little word 'ici' written on it in blue pencil was taped to the narrow door. I rang and a short man in a simple smock opened the door for me, Picasso himself."[55] Visitor number 2 (Gerhardt Heller): "We [Jean Paulhan and he] ring, Picasso himself comes to open the door."[56]

Ironically, the reports on Picasso that came out in the American press right after the Liberation showed him unforgiving toward the French intellectuals and artists who he said had collaborated: "Picasso noted with pleasure yesterday's suspension from the French Académie of the writers Abel Bonnard and Abel Hermant. He was bitter about Albert [sic] Vlaminck, another distinguished painter and once a friend, who after the fall of Paris suddenly appeared with an article denouncing Picasso as a Jewish degenerate. . . . [57] Of Derain, a more conventional and less gifted artist, there are similar questions."[58]

In the *Art Digest*, John Groth reported that Picasso had told him that "he hoped Derain would be shot."[59] To a *Newsweek* reporter he repeated his denunciations of Vlaminck.[60] In conversations with the author, Françoise Gilot confirmed that Picasso urged his friends *never* to initiate contact with the Germans.[61] Curiously, Picasso readily admitted that Germans had come to see him: "Simple soldiers used to visit me," he told a *Time* magazine reporter.[62] "Yes, occasionally there were Germans who came with the pretext of admiring my paintings," he told the reporter from *Lettres françaises*. "I used to distribute reproductions of my *Guernica* and say to them 'take it, souvenir, souvenir,'"[63] he said to S. Tery, so as to put to rest the apocryphal anecdote that when Ambassador Abetz had asked Picasso if "he had done that [*Guernica*] too," Picasso had answered, "No, you did it."

At least one soldier who came to see Picasso went away with more than a reproduction of *Guernica*. On the occasion of a recent Picasso exhibition at the Stuttgart Staatsgalerie, the soldier, who was also a collector, told his interviewer: "I would have liked to acquire a painting, but I was too shy to ask Picasso. Probably I wouldn't have been able to pay the price. Around six o'clock I took my leave. When I visited Mme Bucher [who had arranged the visit] again three days later, Picasso had sent her a drawing for me, for a very small price."[64]

Not surprisingly, many of the memoirs by Germans on their contacts with the French intelligentsia during World War II contain insinuations (usually unverifiable) that co-opt those they met into the collaborationist camp, while making the authors appear to have been anti-Nazis. The novelist Ernst Jünger, a German officer stationed in Paris and a writer who, according to Lottman, "carefully concealing his misgivings about Hitlerism, became a welcome guest at the house of the most prominent literary and artistic personalities of occupied Paris,"[65] was one of them. To him Picasso allegedly said, "The two of us, sitting here together, could work out a peace treaty this very afternoon. By nightfall all men could turn on their lights."[66] (Europe was then under night curfew.)

Another visitor, Gerhardt Heller, the officer in charge of the censorship of literature in occupied Paris, apparently was told by Picasso he could come back another time. "In front of the *Still Life with the Skull of a Bull* he told us: 'I painted that at night because, these days, I prefer night light to natural light. . . . You ought to come back at night to see it.'"[67] According to Lottman, Heller was "the Germans' self-appointed troubleshooter."[68] Not, however, when it came to saving the life of Max Jacob, the French poet who had been arrested as a Jew in his retreat at St.-Benoit, and whose friends were desperately trying to free him. When Youki, the wife of Robert Desnos, sought to intercede with Heller on Jacob's behalf, Heller reportedly replied to her: "Max Jacob is a Jew, Madame, those people, they are like vermin."[69]

In *La Littérature de la défaite et de la collaboration*, Gérard Loiseaux calls untrustworthy the published testimonies by German intellectuals who present themselves as having been protectors and friends of the Parisian intelligentsia. Speaking of Heller's *Un Allemand à Paris*, he goes so far as to say, "It would take a special study to catch all the counter-truths, silences, and impostures that can be found in this book."[70]

To Picasso's credit, it must be said that in their memoirs of their encounters with Picasso, Heller and Jünger concur that Picasso made them extremely uneasy. They were terrified by him and felt mysterious forces that needed to be "domesticated" in his paintings.[71] Jünger: "I had the impression that I was meeting a sorcerer, an impression that on the first occasion had been heightened by his wearing a little pointed green hat."[72] Heller: "One time at the performance of the *Jeanne au Bûcher* by Claudel and Honegger at the Opéra, I felt myself pierced as by electric waves that I could not attribute to the music alone. Looking around I saw, three boxes away, Picasso, who was staring at me with his large, burning eyes."[73]

Even so, visits by German soldiers and officers, discussions on peace with German intellectuals, and exchanges with a dealer who was trading in art sequestered from Jews are difficult to reconcile with the existential hero who, in October 1944, was honored as a symbol of the Resistance at the first Salon d'Automne after the liberation of Paris.[74]

PICASSO AND THE RESISTANCE

In January 1945,[75] the *Museum of Modern Art Bulletin* (New York) published a glowing description of Picasso as a Resistance hero, based on recent newspaper accounts. Peeved by a letter from Christian Zervos that contained mostly negative comments,[76] the author of the article, MOMA's chief curator Alfred Barr, undertook his own research. As he was in the process of updating the catalogue *Picasso: Forty Years of His Art* (it would become *Picasso: Fifty Years of His Art*), Barr decided to make up a set of questions on the artist's entire career and send the questionnaire to Picasso. Concerning the World War II years, Barr zeroed in on the very points he hoped would substantiate a flattering view of Picasso's wartime behavior.

For example, Barr wanted to know whether Derain or Vlaminck had really denounced him, and where he could find evidence of these denunciations. Picasso eventually obliged and, through his secretary, provided Barr with a short list of articles and books in which Picasso had been maligned during the war.[77]

Barr also questioned Picasso on whether Picasso's studio had been a rallying point for the FFI. Question 33A: "Did the FFI (Forces Françaises de l'Interieur) meet in his atelier during the Occupation?" Picasso's answer to question 33A: "No."[78]

As Barr was to discover, while no armed fighters working on the Allies' side had gathered at Picasso's studio, he manifested his sympathies for the forces of freedom in other ways. In a letter dated 22 September 1945, Juan Larrea, who had headed the rescue committee for Spanish loyalist refugees in France, replied to Barr's inquiry on Picasso's Resistance activities during the Spanish civil war and the occupation of France as follows:

In regard to the gifts which Picasso made to the Spanish Republic . . . his official contributions, if I remember correctly, were:

1. The proceeds of the sale of the series of etchings titled "Dreams and Lies of Franco."

2. An actual contribution to buy milk for the children of the Spanish Republic, followed by another contribution for the purpose of having places where people could get free meals which began to function in Barcelona and Madrid. The two together amounted to 400,000 francs, if I am not mistaken, and might have been followed by others to keep the free meal places going.
3. When the disaster followed, Picasso made other donations to the committees that helped the exiled intellectuals, committees which began to spring up immediately in Paris.

To the 550,000 francs—the sum to which the above donations must have amounted more or less—one should add the many individual instances of help which Picasso distributed among his friends from the beginning of the war and especially at the end, among acquaintances or simply compatriots who appealed to his generosity.[79]

In a letter to the author, the Surrealist poet Noèl Arnaud, the leading light of La Main à Plume and the publisher of its review, confirmed Picasso's involvement in the Spanish Loyalist cause:

Yes, it is fashionable today to throw malevolent insinuations at the Picasso of the '40s. . . . I can only speak about what I was witness to: Through various avenues, numerous escapees from Spanish Republicans' internment camps were—all precautions having been taken (and I was on occasion the one to organize these precautions)—greeted by Picasso and received from him travelling moneys (sometimes sizable) and addresses of safe refuges. I observe without wishing to reach any conclusion concerning his political preferences that his help went toward former FAI and POUM militants.

But according to Arnaud, Picasso went beyond assisting only his compatriots:

The gifts made by Picasso to *La Main à plume* were spent first to finance the publications and second (and in parallel) to help with the daily survival of the members of the group who entered clandestinity in larger and larger numbers. The gifts of Picasso were either gifts in money or in graphics [one such graphic, dated 21 May 1941, belongs in the same series of reclining female nudes as the German soldier's Picasso drawing. It does not appear in Zervos]; several of them were intended to fatten up the de luxe editions of publications, which then sold well, or, when their format precluded that, were sold separately (after having been reproduced in small size in our pub-

lications). We never sold directly these de luxe copies of *La Main à plume*: Georges Hugnet was, for three years, our regular buyer and hence the seller. Then, the last year, a few art galleries, Augustinci particularly.[80]

Keenly aware of his public image, Picasso had lied to the American press about his behavior when he said that he had not been allowed to sell his work. Something of Picasso's double nature undoubtedly thrived in the climate of ambiguity favored by the presence of Germans in an uneasy armistice with the French. Overall, Picasso's war was incommensurably softer than that of artist refugees in the free zone.

There are plenty of grounds for finding Picasso guilty by association, if only because of his friendly conversations with German intellectuals, the sale of a drawing to a German collector, and the bizarre phrase he said to Ernst Jünger: "the two of us sitting here together could work out a peace treaty this very afternoon." It seems as if Picasso had his own line of conduct—as if he had deconstructed the idea of resistance and of collaboration, and had acted on the basis of his personal morality and judgment. On the other hand, in spite of his dubious connections, there is abundant evidence that he had given generously to the cause of freedom through his art and through his wealth, as Alfred Barr's research and the testimony of Noèl Arnaud reveal.[81] If Picasso "simply kept his dignity"—the expression used by Christian Zervos[82]—it is more than can be said of those who accepted commissions from the Third Reich, and complied with German requests and invitations.

EPILOGUE

Collaboration, Resistance, Art,
and Artists

> The more prestigious the reputation of an artist, the more important is his engagement, whatever his writings might be.

> At the time, I believed that poetry was situated above or outside of contingencies, or—even better—that its revolutionary force acted by itself wherever the text appeared.
>
> *Emile Guillevic*

A COSTLY "FREE" TRIP

As French territory was liberated thanks to the progress of Allied troops, "purge" committees went into action in the affected areas. In Paris—liberated in late August 1944—the painter André Fougeron, a Communist and a leading figure in the Resistance network of artists, ran such a committee. It was made up of artists and presided over by Picasso (who had just joined the Communist party). Its role was to convoke and hear artists accused of having "favored the enemy's endeavors, hindered the war effort, or impeded the resistance of the French,"[1] listen to witnesses, and impose sanctions. Over the next months and years the *Journal officiel* would periodically announce the sanctions that had been imposed on collaborators in various domains. A decision published in the *Journal officiel* on 26 June 1946 described the punishment for artists.

Despiau and Bouchard were forbidden to exhibit and to sell for two years beginning 1 September 1944; Jean Janin, Derain, Vlaminck, van Dongen, Friesz, Oudot, Legueult, Lejeune, and Belmondo were forbidden to exhibit and to sell for one year beginning 1 September 1944; Dunoyer de Segonzac was forbidden to exhibit and sell for three months starting 1 September 1944.[2] An earlier decree, dated 27 June 1944,[3] had announced the disciplinary sanctions against public servants. As a result, Bouchard lost his post of professor at the Ecole des

Beaux Arts, as did four other professors there. Legueult and Oudot were dismissed from their posts at the Ecole des Arts Décoratifs. (All were eventually reinstated.) The Société du Salon d'Automne administered its own punishment. Maillol and Despiau were not allowed to participate in the Salon d'Automne of 1944. There were exclusions at the other salons, too.

Naturally, artists accused of collaboration were disqualifed from applying for government-sponsored commissions in honor of the Resistance.[4] Such was the case with Albert Bouquillon, the Prix de Rome winner for sculpture in 1934 who had allowed his larger-than-life statue in bronze of a male nude entitled *The Perfect Athlete* to be exhibited in the show Le Juif et la France. The premise of this sociological exhibition, held at the Palais Berlitz in Paris in the fall of 1941, was the physical and moral inferiority of Jews in comparison with Aryans and their nefarious influence on French society.[5]

Fig. 70

Asked by the author in 1984 what criterion had been used to determine who should be punished, Fougeron answered "Le voyage."[6] He was alluding to the trip to Germany offered to French artists by the German Ministry of Propaganda in October and November 1941. Although over half of France was then suffering under the German boot, the invitation was accepted by thirteen French artists, including several major figures of the prewar avant-garde, plus a journalist and an interpreter.

Fig. 71

Those who went on the trip were three Salon artists: Bouchard, president of the Salon; Landowski, head of the Ecole Nationale des Beaux Arts until his replacement by Tournon; and Lejeune, also a member of the Académie des Beaux Arts; the figurative sculptors Despiau and Belmondo; five painters once associated with the Fauve movement, Vlaminck, Derain, van Dongen, Friesz and Segonzac; the painters of poetic reality Oudot and Legueult, who were then teachers at the Ecole des Arts Décoratifs; and a painter and set designer originally from Switzerland, Jean Janin (or Jannin). Maillol had been excused because of his age, and Maurice Denis was among those who found an excuse not to go. Bernard Poissonnier was the accompanying journalist, and Adrion, an Alsatian painter, the interpreter. Their guides were two German officers, Oberleutnant Lucht, who headed the "Kultur" section of the Propaganda-Abteilung in Paris, and Officer Ehmsen, from the art censorship office there.

Over a period of about two weeks, the artists visited the major cities of Germany: Berlin, Munich, Nuremberg, Dresden, Potsdam, Dusseldorf, and Vienna (then part of the Third Reich). At the Munich Kunsthaus, they were shown works by Thorak, Breker, and their painter counterparts. Segonzac found Gulbranson to be a marvelous draftsman.[7] In Berlin, they visited Hitler's new Chancellery; in

70. Le Juif et la France at Palais Berlitz, 1941.

71. French artists and their German guides at Gare de l'Est, October, 1941. From left to right, Charles Despiau (polka-dot bow tie), Othon Friesz (light-color overcoat), André Dunoyer de Segonzac (mustache), Maurice de Vlaminck (black overcoat), Kies van Dongen (white beard), André Derain (behind and to the right of van Dongen).

Nuremberg, the new stadium and other "prodigious constructions." They saw gargantuan bronze horses being readied for the top of an arch leading to the entrance of the Berlin autobahn. The scale of the statuary dwarfed and bewildered them. They also made a stop at Sans Souci, Frederick the Great's hideaway, and they saw the farm near Vienna where Beethoven is reputed to have composed his *Pastorale*. In Dresden and in Dusseldorf, they visited artists' ateliers. They were entertained by Professor Ziegler, the head of the German Chamber of Culture, by local heads of artists' chambers, and by the sculptor Breker, whose unbelievably large workshops near Berlin they were shown.[8]

Back in Paris, most of the artists refrained from talking to the press. Three, however, did not. In addition to the report of Bernard Poissonnier,[9] *Comoedia* published the enthusiastic remarks by the sculptor Despiau and the painter Dunoyer de Segonzac. Despiau, for one, marveled that German artists could now produce, "safe from all material worries."[10] Segonzac acknowledged that, in Germany, "the state is passionately interested in art."[11] As for Bouchard, he wrote in *L'Illustration* that in Nazi Germany artists led a fairy-tale life: "They are the cherished children of the nation," he said.[12]

One of the leitmotifs of the reports was the organizational talent of their German peers and the pleasant management of their trip. Segonzac, for one, wondered how the French would handle a reciprocal gesture.[13] Within a year, the opportunity arose. The very same group that had gone on the German trip was put on the honorary committee that sponsored the mammoth retrospective of Hitler's favorite sculptor, Arno Breker, at the Orangerie in Paris in May–July 1942. Maillol was also on the committee.[14]

The true motive of the trip may never be known. It seems that it was organized as a diplomatic gesture of goodwill between Vichy France and the occupying authorities, and that the artists were promised that their visit would result in the liberation of artist comrades who were war prisoners. The selection of the artists asked to go on the trip remains mysterious as well, except that there was an aura of reconciliation involved at all levels: Germany and France, Salon and non-Salon figurative artists, Derain and Vlaminck.[15]

At the time, the trip and the retrospective of Arno Breker sculpture in a Paris museum that followed a few months later were considered evil enough to stir anti-German artists to meet and organize Le Front National des Arts, a Resistance group that after the Liberation, instigated purges in the artists' milieu. Since then, revisionist attitudes have tended to minimize the responsibility of those who participated in this famous trip—they were promised the liberation of fellow artists from German prison camps, they were coerced, they were naive.

Taking these excuses into account, I hope to demonstrate in this epilogue that collaborationist behavior was predictable due to prewar circumstances, but that that does not mitigate the responsibility of those who engaged in it. My presupposition here is that whatever the pressures placed on them, they, as individuals, grappled with choices. At some point what Sartre—quoting Auguste Comte—calls "the *passage* into subjectivity"[16] could and did assert itself.

Two avenues of research into the source of pro-German sentiments have proved fertile. One lead is the Arno Breker connection. The other is an exhibition of French art by living artists, organized by a branch of the French Ministry of Foreign Affairs (Association Française d'Action Artistique) in 1937 in Berlin, under the patronage of Hermann Goering and of the French ambassador to the Third Reich. In the first case the fact that Breker, once a Parisian expatriate sculptor, had become the official sculptor of the Third Reich and Hitler's confidant, did not deter certain artists he had known in the 1930s from seeing him.

What the 1937 Berlin exhibition suggests is that there were plenty of French artists willing to exhibit in a country where countless Jewish artists and others tagged as Judeo-Marxist-decadent could not show. This revealed to the Germans a lack of solidarity that they were to exploit when the ban against Jewish artists was extended to France. Before the Germans had defeated the French army and "collaboration" with the Nazi regime had become official Vichy policy, a number of French artists, either on account of an earlier tie to Arno Breker, or on the basis of their participation in the Berlin show, or on both counts, were budding "collaborationists."

Pro-German Sentiment in Artists' Ranks

Shortly after the liberation of his area, Maillol was summoned by a purge committee to justify his behavior during the Occupation years. He sent his son to appear in his stead. The son—who had joined the French *milice* (an adjunct to the Gestapo used to combat the Resistance and arrest Jews)—was thrown in jail in Perpignan.[17] In late September 1944, Maillol died, a few days after the car in which he was a passenger had skidded into a tree. He had come to Perpignan to intercede with the authorities on his son's behalf and was found, depressed and at loose ends, by his friend Dr. Nicolau, after an unsuccessful meeting with justice officials. Maillol was on his way to rejoin Dufy in the doctor's company when the accident happened.

Despiau was also among those called by a purge committee. Harassed by anonymous letters and phone calls concerning his pro-German behavior during the Occupation, Despiau, depressed and ill, died in 1946. According to Lucien

Rebatet, "both Maillol and Despiau leaned toward us or, in the words of Brasillach, they did not push us away."[18] Both artists had been "friends" of Arno Breker.

Breker (1900–91) was not unknown to a certain Paris artistic milieu when he appeared there after the June 1940 armistice. The middle-of-the-road figurative sculptor Yencesse, whom I interviewed in 1984, remembered clearly the first time he had seen Breker's clay figurines "with a Rodinesque allure to them" in the window of a Paris gallery; it must have been around 1929. Yencesse went in to inquire who had made them and was told that they were by a young German artist named Breker who lived in Paris; Yencesse met him shortly thereafter.[19]

In his memoirs, *Hitler, Paris, et moi,* and in an interview with the author, Breker evoked his life in Paris in the late 1920s in glowing terms. Among the art world personalities who, he says, befriended him were the art dealer Jeanne Castel and the poet Jean Cocteau. He was also part of the entourage of Flechtheim, the German dealer for Derain and Vlaminck.[20] Breker claims to have passed through Bourdelle's atelier, but his visit to Maillol in his Banyuls retreat at the Spanish border during his first summer in France made the greatest impression on him. Like Maillol and Despiau, whose esthetics (middle-of-the-road and figurative) coincided with his own, Breker was not a product of academic indoctrination. "He only wished for art what others wanted in politics, and at the same time," wrote Paul Morand in *La Voix Française* (12 June 1942).[21]

Breker was apparently not alone in thinking that there was something especially attractive to a German mind about Maillol. The former director of the German Institute in Paris during the Occupation years, Karl Epting, writing his diary in jail in 1945, went so far as to call Maillol more German than French. "I try to describe to myself a few of Maillol's statues; the temperament of Maillol is not

Fig. 72 French. Although southern, Provençal, and pagan, it could be German."[22]

The transformation of Arno Breker from Parisian-German bohemian into Hitler's official sculptor shows the odd turn events can take. According to Breker, in 1929, he began negotiations with a dealer he met in Paris. (Could it have been Flechtheim, who put him in a show titled De Carpeaux à Breker in 1930?) After a year in Fascist Rome, in 1933, at Villa Massimo, Breker returned to Germany. A convert to "street art,"[23] he changed style—his surfaces became

Fig. 73 smooth and shiny, he oversimplified as he monumentalized scale—and started competing for state commissions. In 1936, he won a silver medal for an *Athlete* and a *Victory* in the Olympic games competition.

In 1938, he earned the attention of "le chef," as he called the Chancellor of the Third Reich when he spoke to me in French, with a proposal for a fountain. "When Hitler saw my project for the fountain, he immediately declared: 'From

72. Aristide Maillol, *Ile de France*, 1925.

73. Arno Breker. *Berufung* (The Active Man).

now on Breker must work for no one else, he must only work for Berlin.' "[24] And indeed, Breker received huge commissions from Hitler and his architect Speer.

During World War II, over one hundred people worked for him at his studio near Berlin (Jackelsbrüch), including French war prisoners who happened to be specialists in foundry work, as well as two young French male secretaries, one the son of the publisher Flammarion, the other the son of the prefect of Paris,[25] both of them in the age group Germany was recruiting for forced labor in German factories.

He also became a close confidant of Hitler, and his emissary among French artists during the Occupation period. Small wonder that when, in 1941, Yencesse, walking home, saw a German car that turned out to be Breker's parked in front of his building—it was Breker, come to pressure him to go to Germany on a cultural mission with other French painters and sculptors—he greeted him with something less than the joy one feels at seeing an old friend. The talented German sculptor who used to mingle with Montparnasse bohemians now held the Parisian milieu that had befriended him at his mercy. Yencesse disuaded Breker from taking him on the propaganda trip by telling him he was afraid of being held hostage for his brother, who had escaped from a German prison camp.[26] But, as noted earlier, a number of prestigious French artists did go.

Though remembered as utterly charming and without pretense by those who knew him both before and during the war, Breker was perfectly cast in the ambiguous and sometimes sinister role of Hitler's cultural envoy. In his eagerness to maintain a Paris address, he asked Ambassador Abetz to "Aryanize" for his benefit Helena Rubinstein's apartment on the Ile St.-Louis.[27] He was, however, in a position to arrange for individuals held in prison camps, work camps, and concentration camps to be allowed to work in his mammoth workshop, and he could obtain the release of persons threatened with deportation. He succeeded in preventing the deportation to Auschwitz of Maillol's young Jewish model, Dina Vierny.

Vierny was apparently arrested as part of a Resistance group that helped foreign refugees across the border to Spain. The Maillol atelier, a few kilometers from Banyuls, was situated along a brook that could be followed upstream toward the Spanish border. Breker explained to me in our interview how old Mme Maillol had begged him not to interfere on Dina's behalf, claiming that she and her husband were the happiest they had been together for years, but that he did not listen to her because he knew that Maillol could not work without his model in front of him.[28] He also says he intervened on Picasso's behalf when the artist was threatened with arrest for sending money to Spanish Loyalist refugees in Soviet Russia through Sweden.[29]

Gestures of sympathy toward the culture of the new German state in general (the trip was supposed to accomplish that goal), and toward Breker's sculpture in particular, were expected in return. No less than the Orangerie museum in Paris, which had recently held a Rodin retrospective, now scheduled one of Breker's work from 15 May to 31 July 1942.

It was Benoist Méchin, minister for French prisoners, who, according to Breker, initiated the idea of a museum show in Paris for him. Breker says that at

first he had "qualms about going through with it and then changed his mind after a year."[30] Rudier, the French founder, was liberated from Fresnes, a military prison, so as to be able to cast the works intended for the exhibition. It required thirty tons of bronze, the source of which, the art historian Yvon Bizardel intimates,[31] came from melted-down French bronze statues. Indeed, a first sculpture purge affecting French monuments in bronze was signed into law under pressure from the occupying forces on 11 October 1941, and quantities of statues subsequently disappeared from their pedestals; some were hidden from the Germans' grasp for the duration of the Occupation,[32] but many more have never been recovered and are assumed to have been destroyed.[33]

Arno Breker's prewar friend Despiau signed a monograph on Breker's sculpture. Another of Breker's prewar acquaintances, Maillol, was fetched from his Banyuls retreat in the Pyrénées Orientales so he could attend the opening, although, as he told a friend, Breker's grandiloquent works did not appeal to him: "Breker works too big these days. He showed me a relief he's making of Apollo pursuing Daphne. It should be this small, in order to stay graceful. He is going to make something immense. Figures three meters high with big legs like that. What will it mean? Nothing at all anymore."[34]

The statuary of the German sculptor, so overbearing in scale, so solemn looking and exaggeratedly theatrical, made even the most ardent French supporters of collaboration uneasy,[35] but on that occasion, the German censor imposed on the French press the same rules it did on its own. "No value judgment is ever adequate for looking at Breker's work," the regulation said.[36]

Breker, confusing beauty in art and in nature, appropriated the physique of the most beautiful contemporary male models he knew (and some females too). Besides magnifying human scale far beyond the normal, he made visible each set of muscles—in maximal tension. In order to obtain a highly reflective, smooth surface, he developed a moulage technique (for which he claimed antique Greek statuary as his precedent) that enabled him to work from the negative, smoothing out all the imperfections with special tools before casting the work in bronze.[37]

With much fanfare, the show opened on 15 May 1942. Speeches were delivered by French officials—Laval, Bonnard, and Méchin—at the opening, and the newspaper *La Gerbe* reprinted them on its front page.[38] There were several receptions beginning in April, with one for the press held at the Press Club du Lido (recorded in *Les Nouveaux Temps*, 4 April 1942). Then, at the time of the opening, Laval gave a luncheon (reported in *Le Petit Gatinais*, 25 May 1942); Méchin held a reception (reported in *Aujourd'hui*, 16 May 1942), as did the director of the *Petit Parisien* (reported in *Aujourd'hui*, 18 May 1942). The Grandes

Conférences de Paris organized a demonstration in his honor at the Théâtre Hébertot (see *Aujourd'hui*, 18 May 1942). A reception was also held at the Musée Rodin by its curator, Georges Grappe, head of the Section des Arts Plastiques du Groupe Collaboration (as reported in *Les Nouvelles* [Versailles], 28 May 1942). Even Derain offered champagne at Fauchon, according to Jean Galtier Boissière.[39]

Otto Abetz of the German Embassy and Karl Epting of the German Institute gave parties in the sculptor's honor. There was also a reception at the Ritz given by Arno Breker for his many friends. The German Institute in Paris dispatched a Dr. Bolongaro-Crevenna on a lecture tour to promote Breker. According to *La Petite Gironde*, Georges Grappe went to Bordeaux and gave a talk entitled "From Auguste Rodin to Arno Breker."[40]

The exhibition received wide coverage in the French press. There were reviews by Diehl in *Aujourd'hui*,[41] by d'Espezel in *Je suis partout*,[42] by Paul Morand in *La Voix française*,[43] by Campagne in *Les Nouveaux Temps*.[44] *Comoedia* not only reprinted an excerpt of the Despiau text (16 May 1942)[45] and had its regular critic review the show (23 May 1942), but it published Cocteau's "Salute to Breker," more of an ode to the male bodies celebrated in Breker's sculpture than to the art of the German sculptor.[46]

The most insidious article was by Vlaminck, also in *Comoedia*, because, although Vlaminck's piece did not directly speak in praise of Breker's statuary, the timing of his severe indictment of Picasso's art, coinciding with the opening of Breker's exhibition, was designed to help the cause of Breker against not only Picasso but all those who claimed Picasso among their forebears.[47]

To look at the compromising photographs of French artists and officials seen in his company in 1942, it would hardly seem that France and Germany were at war (notwithstanding the fragile armistice signed in June 1940). In an uncropped photograph, Louis Hautecoeur, making collaboration in the visual arts official, is

Fig. 74   seen posing with Breker, Maillol, and Despiau. In another one taken during the official speeches, Cocteau is visible behind Breker, a few feet away from sinister SS officers (members of Hitler's elite corps) seated in the front row. In the Breker album published by Jacques Damase in 1981,[48] one photograph shows a somewhat despondent Vlaminck posing for Breker in the process of making his bust. (Breker completed a bust of Maillol in 1943. He also did one of Derain and one of Segonzac, both of which have disappeared,[49] and he made busts of Cocteau and Jean Marais in the 1960s.)

One might well ask oneself if all the hoopla surrounding the Breker show was not a diversionary tactic. While the French press preoccupied itself with Breker's

74. The sculptors Arno Breker, Charles Despiau, and Aristide Maillol with France's
head of the fine arts department in the Ministry of Education and Youth,
Louis Hautecoeur, at the Breker exhibition in Paris, May 1942.

art, news of human interest—such as the Vel d'Hiv Stadium roundup by the Gestapo on 16 and 17 July 1942 of twenty-thousand Parisian Jews, who became the first contingent to perish in the gas chambers of Auschwitz—was nowhere to be found.

The devotion shown toward Breker by French personalities from Cocteau to Maillol remains mystifying, even after my own visit with Hitler's official sculptor in 1984. Considering his life-style and his elegant house, surrounded by immaculately kept gardens dotted with replicas of his statues, he appeared to me excessively bitter. In one breath, he maintained that art, including his own, had nothing to do with politics, and that he had always been free to sculpt as he pleased. The next moment, he would exonerate himself of the taint of Nazism by referring to the many people he had saved during the war. He said: "The CIA knew of my work during the war and vouched for me after the war." His ignorance of the artistic accomplishments of his countrymen in recent years was shocking. The name of the contemporary German painter Anselm Kiefer meant

nothing to him. Mention of Maillol, whom he claims was "murdered," and of his sculpture triggered, however, unmitigated praise.[50]

Maillol, like Despiau, shared with other turn-of-the-century avant-gardists of their generation—including the Fauves—a never-assuaged bitterness because critical attention, after having been focused on them briefly, had shifted to art they neither understood nor sympathized with. Not until they became old men did they feel honored in their own country. Only in 1937 did Maillol and Despiau gain their due at the survey of independent art that the city of Paris organized in the context of the Paris World's Fair.[51] Maillol expressed this bitterness in comments like "I hate them [most people], they are wretched beings. I prefer my cat or a frog,"[52] and "The French? They don't give a damn about art."[53]

Germany, by contrast, had been very good to Maillol, starting with Count Kessler in the early years of the century. In an essay by Hans Albert Peters, the extent of the German involvement with Maillol's art since 1905 has been amply documented.[54] Several articles were published in the German press, and collectors and museums bought his works. It also appears that, thanks to a committee composed of Breker, Count Kessler, Kolbe, and Kogan (the latter moved to Paris after Hitler came to power and died a victim of Hitler's gas ovens in 1943), Maillol had a major showing of sculpture at the Flechtheim Gallery in Berlin in 1928. Some eleven years later, during the Nazi regime, in May 1939, Breker included Maillol in a group show of sculptors ranging from Rodin to himself, at the Alex Vomel gallery in Düsseldorf.

Not only was Maillol not considered degenerate, but his work was praised as exemplary in an article in the official German Art magazine *Die Kunst* in 1937. Hans Eckstein wrote: "He [Maillol] showed the way to a new European monumental art. The genuine Greekness of this art is the basis for the fact that it breaks through the boundaries of nineteenth-century bourgeois art and demands by its very nature a wider sphere, a place under the open sky connected to nature, to architecture, to the world and the folk." The article went on to praise Maillol's appeal to the "folk" in the following words: "Maillol's sculpture . . . can be called popular art [*Volkskunst*], meaning that it is not art that makes concessions to the miseducated taste of the time. It is art for the people as Greek art was: naive, blunt, healthy, unromantic, true to nature (not naturalistic). All Classicist art appears thin-blooded in comparison to Maillol."[55]

In return, Maillol admired Germany.[56] He once confided to a friend who was asking him about his German visitors: "You understand, I am so famous in Germany. Much more so than in France. So all those who know that I am here, those who love art, they want to come. They are poets, musicians, you see." (Here,

Maillol omits the visit of the sculptor Arno Breker, who came to finish his bust in 1943.) "I cannot refuse to receive them. Imagine me throwing out an artist? I would not be an artist anymore." And the friend also heard, "[In Germany,] there is a love of art that does not exist here."[57] After a visit to Paris during the Occupation years when he attended a concert of Wilhelm Kempf, he told this same friend: "We became good friends. What can I tell you, I like these people a lot. They have such honesty, an enthusiasm."[58] The idea that artists live by a politics different from that of anyone else was certainly not Maillol's alone. We have encountered it in Matisse and even in Picasso. But Maillol's continued relations with Arno Breker, his admiration for Germany, and his son's involvement in the despicable *milice* are too consistent to be merely coincidental.

The German response to the show of French art held in Berlin in 1937[59] is the other lead I wish to explore for an explanation of pro-German feelings among certain French artists, the Fauves in particular. It should be noted here that Great Britain was also given the opportunity to show British artists in Nazi Germany then, and said no.

The Association Française d'Action Artistique (a branch of the French Ministry for Foreign Affairs at Quai d'Orsay), which sponsored the show of French art by living artists at the Berlin Art Academy in 1937, had a clear goal: to export French know-how in the visual arts. In the catalogue, the artists were presented in light of their participation in the decoration of buildings then going up in Paris: Bonnard, Boussingault, Brianchon, Céria, Dufresne, Oudot, Planson, Roussel, Souverbie, Belmondo, Costa, Niclausse, Pommier, Wlerick, and Yencesse were named in conjunction with their work at the new Palais du Trocadéro (Palais de Chaillot); Courmes and Gromaire were associated with murals at the Pavillon des Manufactures de Sèvres; Aujame, d'Espagnat, Lhote, and Poncelet were connected with murals at the Palais de la Découverte.

Experience in tapestry cartoons was attached to the names of Rouault and Braque; experience in stage design for the Paris Opéra was mentioned with regard to Brianchon and Legueult. Since Germany under Hitler had undertaken an unprecedented public building and arts program and 2 percent of all costs were to be spent on art, the angle of presentation of French art made sense. French artists might be offered commissions by the new German state.

The presence in the exhibition of members of the Académie des Beaux Arts (Bouchard, Baschet, J. E. Blanche, Maurice Denis, Desvallières, Devambez, Sabatté, Boucher, and Landowski), and of artists identified as winners of the Prix de Rome (Yves Brayer, Dupas, and Lejeune), gave the show an aura of safety

and tradition. However, the name of Maillol was accompanied by the comment "one of the two most influential sculptors today." The other was Despiau. "Student of Despiau" (Auricoste, Belmondo) or "student of Maillol" (Costa and Gimond) also appeared as prestigious labels. Matisse, Derain, Camoin, Marquet, and Vlaminck were mentioned with the "Fauve" tag, Vlaminck becoming the "leader" of the Fauve movement.

The show, although held under French auspices, had respected the Nazi ban against Jews. And there were only French artists in the show (no recently naturalized French citizens). The only Cubists were Léger, Lhote, Gromaire, and Braque. No Surrealist works or abstract artworks of any sort were present. It must be noted that Pignon, Bazaine, Desnoyer, Estève, and other future tricolor painters who, in 1937, were also working on the decoration of Popular Front constructions had not been included (or had declined to participate) in this exhibition.

The French curator of the exhibition had been Robert Rey (described as Inspecteur Général des Beaux Arts and Professor at the Ecole du Louvre), who was going to publish, in 1942, a text on modern art that Rebatet called "a Fascist treatise": "If I were not afraid . . . of stirring up trouble for this French *fonctionnaire*—whose political views I do not know—I would say that he has written a sort of Fascist treatise on the condition of the fine arts. Hence the sympathetic way in which I read it," Rebatet said of Robert Rey's *La Peinture moderne*.[60]

The show was reviewed in *Die Kunst* by Fritz Hellwag,[61] who illustrated his comments with *Huts* by Vlaminck, among other works. The reader was directed to Derain, "whose marvelously balanced, wooded landscape exudes a great sense of peace." Vlaminck also received enthusiastic notice. Speaking of *Huts*, the reviewer said: "It shows a sparkling red and yellow field under a billowing blue sky, which unfortunately cannot be adequately reproduced in black and white."

Landscapists in general were applauded. Utrillo was admired for his "usual intensive use of space," but also noted was "a small river landscape steeped in moody mists" by Marquet, a small painting of a pond laid out in very simplified forms by Robert Lotiron, and a delicately sketched marine landscape by Paul Gernez, among many landscape artists included in this exhibition. Rebatet's adoption of landscape painting may well have been inspired by this text.

The review continued with remarks on figure paintings and portraits by Laurencin, Brianchon, and Friesz, and mentioned "a very self-contained portrait of a girl in flat, wide, yellow and pale green brushstrokes by Matisse." As far as genre painting was concerned, the reviewer noted that it was better represented by older painters than by the young ones, and named Lucien Simon's lively *Fair*

(illustrated in the article), Dufy's *View of a Lighted Stage Seen beyond the Orchestra in a Pit*, and Brayer's *The Dinner at the Embassy*. The German ended his remarks with compliments to the following artists: "The master of the still life is still Georges Braque with the handsome harmony of his famous brown-blue hues. Dunoyer de Segonzac is represented by an incandescent symphony in red, and another young painter, Marguerite Louppe, has created a marvelous sense of space in the juxtaposition of *The Two Armchairs*."[62]

Not only does the selection of art for this exhibition prefigure the exclusion of "foreigners" and the triumph of "non-Jewish" French art that characterized the Vichy epoch, it also corrected certain misapprehensions. In particular, the old Fauves who had reason to believe that they appeared on Hitler's list of "degenerate art" must have been pleasantly surprised by the warm reception of their paintings.

One factor that remains unknown is how many of the artists either befriended by Arno Breker or participants in the Berlin exhibition eventually received offers of work from the Nazi state. In a letter to the author, Breker mentioned that Derain and Maillol received sizable commissions.[63] Yencesse, in an interview with the author, spoke of "irresistible financial offers made by officials of the Third Reich."[64] He was vague as to when these commissions were proposed.

The French government's idea of exporting French art irrespective of the politics of the host country was bound to boomerang. Bureaucratic neutrality in 1937 tended to produce pro-German behavior in the period 1940–44. Soon after the June 1940 armistice, Vlaminck could be seen walking arm in arm with a couple of Germans in officers' uniforms;[65] he was going to corral Derain into taking the German trip by forcing a reconciliation between them. As noted earlier, at the time of the Breker retrospective at the Orangerie, Vlaminck published in *Comoedia* a diatribe against Picasso in which Picasso was held responsible for decadence in the visual arts,[66] and Derain offered champagne in honor of the German sculptor.

A pro-German attitude would be noted in Friesz and Despiau, who were in charge of the hanging of work at the Salon des Tuileries and who excluded any artist the Germans did not want exhibited there.[67] Despiau and Segonzac's interviews in *Comoedia* after the trip indicated their high regard for the German way of running culture, as did Bouchard's report in *L'Illustration*.

Bouchard's pro-German sentiments went so far as to echo German wishes on the desirability of a chamber of artists in France that would function on the German model, as a means of control and of exclusion. "Would it not be efficient,"

Bouchard asked in his 1941 speech, "if, on the model of a great neighboring nation, an organization were to be founded at home that would protect artists, establish their social organization, justly regiment their relationship to the state, the city of Paris and the private galleries, distribute paint tubes and other things through which the materials necessary to the execution of artworks would be controlled?"[68] Finally, all thirteen artists who went on the trip in November 1941 had been part of the 1937 Berlin exhibition of French art.

Not all the prestigious painters who had participated in the Berlin show became collaborators, of course. The old Fauve Marquet, for one, remained away from Paris after the armistice and lived in seclusion in Algeria, refusing to exhibit in Paris "as long as that city was under the Nazi boot."[69] Fernand Léger left for the United States; Gromaire joined a Resistance network; many artists simply did not have the occasion to show their feelings one way or the other.

MANIFESTATIONS OF ANTI-GERMAN FEELING AMONG ARTISTS

Nothing is harder to evaluate than the efficacy of the Resistance movement, particularly among artists. According to Christian Zervos, "there were heroes in France but they either paid for it with their lives, or ask that there be silence on their actions. As for painters who retired to the countryside, they are precisely those who did the best work. Unfortunately, their heroism was much greater than the quality of their oeuvre."[70]

According to Edouard Pignon, the Resistance movement among artists was organized in Paris in response to the propaganda trip taken by their peers. "After the trip of the painters to Germany, we protested. Liaisons (meaning contact with someone already part of a network) were very slow, but memberships came in, so as to protest against it."[71] This network, known as the Front National des Arts, began modestly with five painters. Fougeron and Pignon were prewar Communists, though not card-carrying members. André Marchand and Francis Gruber, 1930s French Expressionists in the miserabilist tradition, had been close to Giacometti and Antonin Artaud before the war. The fifth one was Goerg,[72] at whose studio they first met and who, like all four others, had participated in the activities of the Association des Peintres et Sculpteurs de la Maison de la Culture in the 1930s.[73] Later on, two printmakers, Amblard and Aujame, plus the old Cubist Lhote; Montagnac, vice president of the 1943 Salon d'Automne; and the old academician Maurice Denis joined the leadership in Paris.

– 169 –

Its major initiative, and what brought the five painters together in the first place, was the planning of a newsletter. *L'Art français*, composed and printed   Fig. 75 under the supervision of Fougeron, who had turned his atelier into a clandestine printing plant, came out five times between 1942 and the Liberation (fifteen hundred to two thousand copies per issue). The first issue, which has disappeared, contained the shared outrage of the five about the propaganda trip.[74]

In an exhortative style, the newsletter attempted to rally friendly persons to action by reporting information totally missing from the official press. In issue 2, dated October 1942, one reads: "They are killing children. The *boches* are surpassing themselves in their crimes. Thousands of Jewish children, most of them born in France, have been deported to Germany in cattle cars, separated from their mothers."—a counterargument to the cliché that no one knew until the camps were discovered in 1945 that death lay at the end of the train ride. In issue 3, dated November 1942, one finds: "The French artistic patrimony is in danger. Hence, it is necessary that in all museums, patriot functionaries form a committee of the Front National and alert the local patriots of the town whenever a threat arises." (The Germans were claiming to be the rightful owners of certain artworks found in French museums.) In issue 4, dated November 1943: "Artists, like other French people, must fight against deportations by helping young workers obtain papers and shelter, food tickets, money, and a little work that will direct them toward the *maquis*." (The Germans were short-handed and were coercing young Frenchmen to go to work in German factories.)

In its March 1944 issue, the newsletter also announced the esthetics of the Front National des Arts. Considering the influence of Communist artists like Fougeron and Pignon in the artists' Resistance network, the tone of this pamphlet—*Tribune libre*—was unusually conciliatory. As a gesture toward social usefulness, multiples—engravings and lithographs—were said to be better suited to the cause of freedom than painting, "so long as there is no confusion between the painter who sublimates and the polemicist who serves." The *Tribune libre* concluded that whatever the mode chosen, the supreme vocation of art—to question the greatest problems: love, hunger, liberty, death—must never be forgotten. (Behind such generalities lay the potential for divisiveness, as social relevance, problems of hunger, and liberty were placed on par with eternal themes such as love and death. A split between Abstractionists and realist painters was also latent.)

Besides the newsletter, the Front National des Arts planned a tribute to Honoré Daumier, which did not materialize, and it organized a celebration of the centennial of the Douanier Rousseau, which took place in December 1944, after the

PAR PHOTO-LITHO

L'ART FRANÇAIS

numero : 4   novembre 1943

A propos du Salon

Lorsque le Nationalsocialisme était au faîte de sa puissance, il pourchassait avec une haine feroce toute production artistique imbue d'un esprit de rénovation. Les peintres appartenant aux écoles de l'Expressionnisme ou du Cubisme furent traités de dégénérés. Leurs tableaux furent rassemblés dans des "expositions d'horreur". Des brutes nazies futurs incendiaires des musees de Kiev et de Kharkov et des philistins pédants munis du diplôme de "Kunstkritiker" fustigeaient avec suffisance l'art "abâtardi par les juifs" et exaltaient la beauté et l'essence raciale, germanique, du pompiérisme le plus ossifié.

Aujourd'hui, le Dokter Goebbels est trop occupé à verser du courage dans le coeur de ses concitoyens pour avoir le temps de commander leurs goûts artistiques. Après les victoires de l'Armée Rouge, qui en douze mois ont conduit la Wehrmacht de Grodny et de Stalingrad à 100 km au delà de Kiev, il lui faut chaque jour inventer de nouvelles explications "strategiques" pour faire tenir ses hommes un nouveau quart d'heure de plus. Des "positions herissons" il a fallu en venir à la "défense élastique". Celle-ci s'avérant dépourvue de toute élasticité, il fallut passer au "décrochage" et au "colmatage des brèches". Et dans les pays occupés, il y a bien trop à faire en vue de discrediter les réfractaires et les Francs-Tireurs, en vue de conjurer le danger qu'ils representent dans le dos d'une Allemagne exsangue et découragée pour qu'il soit possible d'y appliquer la

politique "culturelle" nazie esquissée du temps de l'exposition Breker et des voyages artistiques en Allemagne, qui avait pour but de domestiquer l'art français.

Ainsi, les combats de nos alliés, ainsi l'heroisme des soldats français sans uniforme, la resistance de tout notre peuple à la déportation, permettent à la France d'avoir encore un Salon d'Automne comme celui de 1943, d'avoir encore un art national, d'avoir encore la possibilité

(suite p.2 .....)

Les artistes et le devoir de l'heure

La proportion des réfractaires à la déportation a été de 100 % parmi les élèves de l'Ecole des Beaux-Arts Sans risquer de se tromper, on peut dire que c'est là un indice du patriotisme qui existe dans tous les milieux d'artistes. Aussi un Comité de Resistance adhérent au Front National s'est-il formé, il y a deja près de deux ans, parmi les peintres et sculpteurs. Ce journal modeste en a été le moyen d'expression. Ce Comité s'est élargi aujourd'hui aux meilleurs noms de toutes tendances et écoles de l'Art français. Mais aujourd'hui, nous ne pouvons plus nous contenter d'un seul Comite, aussi representatif puisse-t-il être de nos professions. Il faut que chaque peintre, chaque sculpteur puisse dire après la libération : j'ai participé au combat.

Le combat cela ne consiste pas seulement en une participation

75. Front page, *L'Art français*, November 1943.

liberation of Paris. It also published, in early 1944, an album sold for the benefit of the Resistance. When this collaborative album of lithographs called *Vaincre* was published, it hardly included the best-known artists living in France at that time, especially when compared with the list of those who had gone on the propaganda trip to Germany in November 1941. They were Aujame, Bartholomé St.-André, Fougeron, Goerg, Ladureau, Montagnac, Pignon, and Taslitzky. Allegedly, difficulties of communication prevented Desnoyer, living in Montauban, Gromaire in Aubusson, Lurçat in St.-Céré, and Marquet in Algiers from handing in their contributions; Denis had died unexpectedly. As for the absence of the preface promised by Paul Eluard, according to Fougeron, the liaison person, Annie Hervé, arrested on the way to delivering the manuscript, had had to swallow it.[75]

Not one of the black-and-white prints included in the album was done in a formally advanced style. All of them had a readily identifiable subject. Several depicted Nazi atrocities expressionistically. Two caricatured Vichy prime minister Pierre Laval. The most biting image in the album was a portrait of Pétain entitled *Judas*. Drawn in a rigorous Classical style, Pétain was shown staring   Fig. 76 frontally at the viewer from within an enlarged postage stamp adorned with the Nazi swastika and the marshal's emblem (the *francisque*). On his head was not the French kepi but the hat of a German SS officer; on his collar, both the Nazi and the Vichy emblems appeared. The value of the stamp, "30 deniers," was a reference to the Roman coins Judas accepted in return for betraying Jesus. The title of the drawing, the notation on the stamp, the dress of the subject, the use of both Nazi and Vichy emblems, and the appropriation of the Classical style typical of National Socialist taste—all these elements converged toward the message that Pétain had betrayed France and was playing according to the German game plan.

"Purely plastic resistance was difficult to organize because it was difficult to publish one's works with one's own style. One had to use camouflage in order not to be caught, and it is difficult to camouflage one's style," Pignon told Debu-Bridel.[76] Besides the *Vaincre* album of 1944, not much remains of these clandestine publications, usually found in small brochures along with poems with Resistance themes. In *Poésie 41* (October–November 1941), there appeared an etching by Gromaire next to a poem by Aragon ("La Liberté au cachot," signed Blaise d'Ambérieux, a pseudonym). A collaboration between Eluard and the painter Jean Hugo produced a small brochure, *En Avril 44, Paris respire encore*; in "Digne de vivre," Fautrier also collaborated with Eluard. "Prière pour les déshérités," a poem by Martial d'Auvergne, was illustrated by Fougeron;

76. Pierre Ladureau. *Judas*, 1944.

"Blason," a poem by Maurice Scève, by Pignon. Picasso illustrated poems by Hugnet, Eluard, and Desnos, and by the young poets of *La Main à plume*, the clandestine review. Among the tapestries produced by Jean Lurçat during the Occupation years was one woven clandestinely at Aubusson by Goubely in 1943 in which lines from Eluard's poem "Liberté" appeared.

Curiously, the most obvious way of helping the Resistance cause—donating the proceeds of the sale of artworks to a Resistance fund—does not seem to have been a common practice. Mention is made in *L'Art français* of a donation by Marquet, then living in North Africa, to the Gaullist cause.[77] Picasso's gift of two original artworks to *La Main à plume* seems exceptional. Picasso's generosity extended to signing works made by an artist who needed to survive in total clandestinity as his own.[78]

This being said, offers of shelter to a person in danger were probably the most useful and earliest demonstrations of pro-Resistance feeling among artists. Since until the June 1941 attack by Hitler on Soviet Russia, Germany and the USSR were bound by a nonaggression pact, French Communists trying to reorganize subversive activities were hounded not by the Germans but by Vichy. Also hounded by the French police and by the Gestapo right after the armistice were foreign political refugees without papers. When Germany attacked the USSR, Russian nationals (including Russian Jews) also became political enemies who had to lead clandestine lives. Later in the war, English and American pilots downed in France, members of a Resistance network under surveillance, young people who refused forced labor in Germany, and Jews threatened with deportation were also at risk of arrest and death.

To artists in need of shelter, the more fortunate ones offered the use of their work studios. Pignon, who took over Lipchitz's house in Paris after the sculptor had emigrated to the United States in order to save it from "Aryanization" (illegal seizure), apparently offered the ground floor to the Musée de l'Homme Resistance network.[79] Also during those early days of the Pétain regime, the tapestry-maker Lurçat provided work and shelter to the Communist painter Taslitzky at Aubusson, until the French police began asking questions about this "assistant," who then fled to the Lot in the free zone of France.[80] The sculptor Laurens sheltered the Spaniard Lobo, who had fought on the Loyalist side of the Spanish civil war, in his Paris home throughout the war years.[81]

In Paris, Tita, a young Surrealist painter (and a Jew) hid Manuel Viola, until her arrest in the first roundup of June 1942. She was going to die at Auschwitz.[82] Viola, who used the name J. V. Manuel, was a painter, poet, and protégé of Picasso. He had fought in the Spanish civil war and, at the tender age of eighteen,

had become a Commissaire of the POUM (Partido Obrero de Unificación Marxista, a Trotskyite organization). He had joined the Foreign Legion to avoid being interned in a French concentration camp. A deserter, he had no valid identity papers. These are a few examples that have come to my attention, not a comprehensive survey.

Other subversive activities included the manufacture of tracts and of fake identity cards. Using a crude printing press, the artists would have the subversive messages printed on various pieces of paper, the back of post-office *mandats*, toilet paper, or ordinary paper, according to the Surrealist painter Henri Goetz, who with his wife Christine Boumeester was one of the creators of such messages. "We distributed the *mandats* in their usual box at the post office, and in the pages of telephone books. We placed the toilet paper in the rest rooms of cafés, and the ordinary sheets, we left on church benches." As for fake identity cards, "things were well organized. Weekly, I handed over a batch of my work to M. François, whose real name I did not know, at the same time as he would ask me for a light in a little park near the Denfert Rochereau Métro station. He'd also hand me a new batch with instructions," Goetz recalled. Goetz apparently learned to make fake identity cards from the Surrealist painter Dominguez.[83] Jacques Hérold, another Surrealist living in France during the Occupation years, also participated in this activity.

As far as being helpful to the Resistance cause was concerned, a few art dealers played a key role. The prewar dealer René Gimpel (a Jew) joined a Resistance network, was caught, was deported, and died in 1945. Jean Séligman (also a Jew) was killed as a hostage in 1941. The gallery bookstore owned and run by the prewar Surrealist poet Georges Hugnet was the main distribution center for clandestine publications in Paris. In his memoirs, Hugnet, speaking of the changes that the end of the Occupation years brought to his life, said: "These days . . . mean that I will not have to fear the visits of the Gestapo, that they will no longer show up, and leaning their elbows on a pile of clandestine publications, ask me questions on my activities and those of my friends, and that a tapestry rolled up in the bathroom will no longer be used to conceal dozens of false identity cards."[84]

A look at the guest books of art galleries, however, reveals that there were non-Gestapo Germans, such as art reviewers from the *Pariser Zeitung*, attending openings. Among Germans who bought art during the Occupation years were Dr. Werner Rusche from Cologne, Dr. Bernhard Sprenger from Hannover, and even Baron Von Hirsch (an ennobled Jew then living in Switzerland). The unavoidable commingling at art openings had its advantages for French resisters. Accord-

ing to Fougeron,[85] the meeting between himself and Maurice Denis, at which Denis agreed to become the honorary chairman of the Front National des Arts, took place at an art opening. The presence of Germans at art openings made galleries particularly unsafe places for such discussions, but they were a political no-man's-land where all sorts of business (including asking for the liberation of a friend) could be conducted in relative anonymity.

When Jean Moulin, de Gaulle's delegate to the internal Resistance, needed a professional cover, he decided to open a gallery in Nice, which he called Galerie Romanin, from his nom de plume in the 1930s. In the memoirs of Paul Pétridès, one reads that Moulin quickly learned the métier of dealer from Pétridès, and that Pétridès consigned a number of artworks to him.[86] Moulin was himself a collector. He was also a cartoonist[87] and an etcher. (His prewar illustrations for Tristan Corbière's epic poem "Armor" were frighteningly prescient.)[88]   Fig. 77

Another gallery, L'Esquisse, Quai des Orfèvres, in Paris, which on 7 April 1944 held a private showing of works by Kandinsky, Domela, Alberto Magnelli, and the young de Stael, was also a front for Resistance activities.[89] At the Drouin gallery, Gildo Caputo, who became director in 1943 after the dismissal of Georges Maratier (whose dealings with the Germans had become an embarrassment), used his role as a talent scout to leave Paris on secret missions for the Resistance.[90]

Pierre Villon was an architect, a Jew, and a key figure in the Front National, the Resistance network of Communist artists and intellectuals. (He took over after Politzer, who early on had organized the Musée de l'Homme network of intellectuals, was caught and killed with four others, and the women participants were shipped to concentration camps.)[91] Villon observed in a postwar interview how "among painters, outside of purely political action against the Occupiers and their allies, it was difficult to find something for artists to do in their domain."[92]

Since at that time both de Gaulle and Pétain claimed to be the representatives of the French tricolor flag, the tricolor paintings done by Pignon and others remain ambiguous at best. If artists were to show their Resistance via politically correct art, their images needed to be unambiguously pro-de Gaulle. One such image has come to my attention. Entitled *Hommage à Jacques Callot*, it was painted by Francis Gruber, a member of the Resistance front of artists (who himself was not a Jew but was married to the daughter of the Jewish playwright Henry Bernstein). *Hommage à Jacques Callot* (1942) showed a young woman   Fig. 78 lying nude in a landscape of desolation and devastation, a tricolor bouquet in her right hand (France after the Armistice?). On a broken chair was a copy of the *Beggar with the Wooden Leg*, a drawing by Jacques Callot, a seventeenth-cen-

77. Jean Moulin. *La Fosse de conlie*, 1932.

tury etcher known for his series *Les Malheurs et les Misères de la Guerre* and also for a visual commemoration of the siege of La Rochelle, won by Louis XIII. In order fully to appreciate its subversive subtext, it is necessary to know that Callot, born in Lorraine, was said to have declined the king's commission to commemorate the siege of Nancy, the capital of Lorraine—as he had done for La Rochelle, telling the king that his allegiance was to his native province, and to Charles, prince of Lorraine. The hidden reference to another Charles from Lorraine, General de Gaulle, could hardly have been accidental.[93]

78. Francis Gruber. *Hommage à Jacques Callot*, ca. 1942.
(Color Plate 5)

Even the German censor who went to inspect the work prior to its exhibition at Galerie Friedland in the context of a show entitled "Homage to Our Ancestors" was unable to eliminate its Resistance message. Discerning a political statement in the presence of a tricolor bouquet in the hands of the defeated figure lying on the ground, he apparently ordered the artist to paint over the bouquet.[94] The pentimento memory of the bouquet is visible as tiny droplets of red, white, and blue in the area where the bouquet used to be. But what the censor overlooked was the identity of the artist to whom homage was paid, and what he reputedly had done when confronted with the demands of a powerful monarch of his own time.

In defending the politically correct poetry of the Resistance, Tristan Tzara expressed ideas that were fulfilled in the painting described above: It "does not need to express a reality. It is itself reality. But in order to be valid, it must be included in a larger reality, that of the world of the living." Tzara also asked questions that were pertinent to politically correct art then (and might be worth thinking about today): "Could we think one way and write another? Could we separate our being into two parts, thinking and acting for the liberation of the country on the one hand, thinking and writing according to a disembodied abso-

lute on the other hand? Did all of our poetry not have at the base of its nourishment the concrete life of *seen images* . . . ?"[95]

If the purpose of a clandestine network of artists was to disseminate news that was otherwise unavailable, the Front National des Arts proved a success. That its chief artistic endeavor, an album of lithographs, did not rally more famous names is a sign of the political indifference of many French artists. If the goal of artistic resistance was to offer art "made in France" to the public in order to keep German National Socialist productions from infiltrating the Paris art scene, this goal was also reached. If one could not work for a Resistance network, sheltering Jews and active Resisters was without doubt a useful initiative. However, many collaborators later used this argument to show that they had been double agents and to seek clemency for acts of collaboration.

That instances of unambiguous pictorial resistance were so rare reveals the mistaken belief, all too common at that time, that Formalist avant-gardism alone could express political opposition: "Deep down, there was resistance each time a painting that the Germans declared to be Judeo-Marxist-decadent stood up to official art," Pignon told an interviewer after the war. "In a way, avant-garde painting was like a Resistance voice."[96] Fortunately, not all anti-German artists were taken in by this point of view. When a leaflet circulated among artists telling them that they were not expected to serve like ordinary citizens but must cultivate what was most precious within them, namely their art, it prompted the sarcastic comment in *Les Lettres françaises*: "Decidedly, France is a very civilized country!"[97]

CONCLUSION: ART, PREJUDICE, AND PERSECUTION IN FRANCE, 1940–44

France, recently humiliated on the battlefield, allegedly because of a lack of national fervor among governments and leaders, was supposed to be rejuvenated through the rediscovery of purely French values and French traditions. To rediscover a common identity and a shared culture was the sine qua non of moral rebirth. In the fields of painting and sculpture, this policy expressed itself through the official promotion of exhibitions of purely French talent both in France and abroad (in Switzerland and Spain). Controversial international modernists and Jewish artists disappeared underground, and a unique experiment unfolded: the nurturing of purely French art and the transformation of prewar French underdogs of the Paris art world into the standard-bearers of the new culture.

Ironically, some of the very artists who praised national values and traditions in art invoked internationalism as the law of artists in order to explain their above-politics attitude during the Occupation years or their continued friendship with Arno Breker. In fact, the state sponsorship of art allegedly practiced in Nazi Germany greatly appealed to artists intent on bureaucratic careers.

By encouraging his last visitors freely to trample over his paintings—and by trampling them himself—Robert Delaunay expressed pessimism about the future of formally advanced art that seemed attuned to the aftermath of the debacle and of Hitler's successes. What could be the function of such art at a time, 1940–44, when all energies ought to be directed toward liberating France from Nazism? In the context of such a gesture, the move toward a new abstraction with spiritual connotations carried out by Bazaine, Estève, and other tricolor painters reveals a reverence for art that comes out of another consciousness, the attitude toward art for which Matisse was the model.

Ignorance, the argument invoked to this day for justifying life as usual under the German boot, finds its visual counterpart in the escapist tendencies of the art that passed censorship, whether among the Romantic realists, the tricolor paint-ers, or the Salon network. From a psychological perspective, escapism records the stance of a social group that repressed what it did not want to know. Depic-tions of dramas taking place daily in Vichy France are as absent from the art as they are from the authorized press. Censorship and self-censorship collaborated. Since in the early 1940s escapism was fashionable, art opposing escapism—not formal inventiveness—would have been better suited to aid the Resistance cause. *Hommage à Jacques Callot*, by Francis Gruber, and many of Picasso's wartime images showed the way.

Instead, a number of French artists saw themselves as "resisters" because they resisted the style of Social Realist painting and sculpture. The presence of their work in official contexts, and the positive commentary they received in a German publication, dampens those claims. Distributed by clandestine means, the album called *Vaincre* (1944), with its devastating representations of Vichy leaders and Nazi practices, was more to the point—although a bit tardy.

The study of artistic networks from the June 1940 armistice to the Liberation is not without surprises. Paradoxically, those whom the Pétain regime called "foreigners" and who found themselves excluded from the life of the arts in France did not generally follow the example of Robert Delaunay. It was they who unwittingly "returned to the soil" in a literal fashion, and managed to make art out of the materials at hand—even as internees in French concentration camps.

Of the models proposed as expressive possibilities for intellectual resistance, the first one, "speaking between the lines," might be said to apply to much of Picasso's production during that time, and to Gruber's *Hommage*. The second model, that of Ketman, with its garbled message, might have something remotely to do with the incommunicability and esotericism of the Surrealists' production at that time, particularly that of Victor Brauner. As for the Derridaen model of a "double edge," it might be said to apply to tricolor painting, and to Picabia's appropriation of Nazi photographic pseudo-realism.

Considering Hitler's witch-hunt against degenerate art in his own country, his tolerance of "decadent" art made by Aryan French artists is another paradox. Yet the selection of modern French art sent to Berlin by the French Ministry of Foreign Affairs in 1937 foretold the favored treatment of certain Modernist French artists, including the Fauves, during the Occupation. It also prefigured collaboration in that the selections were already subjected to the racist exclusions practiced in the Third Reich.

Lucien Rebatet's abhorrence of academic Salon art is another surprising finding in light of the pro-German and Pétainist outlook of key academicians. The fragmentation of points of view among avengers of decadence is evident here. The art that Rebatet praised, although it included sculpture by such senior figures as Maillol and Despiau, embodied the values of a new right wing, whereas Salon art was representative of the old Maurrassian traditionalism.

Depending on the arbiter, the inclusions and exclusions of "decadent" art varied. Naturally, on the false assumption that "foreign" artists practiced an art that was alien to French sensibilities, they were excluded. But no one except the most conservative members of the Académie des Beaux Arts rejected Impressionism, including the *Intimisme* of Bonnard, in painting. Only the most rabid supporters of the Académie and the more timid middle-of-the-road artists were ready to sacrifice Fauvism in the name of decadence. There were even partisans of Cubism, particularly if it was French and Catholic in lineage, among the rhetoricians of decadence. Rather than a consensus about form, there seems to have been agreement that from now on French art would be "judenrein," harmonious, decorative, joyful, and uplifting, and that art probing the seedy sides of life and of the psyche should remain out of sight. Women artists appear to have remained very much in the background in this antidecadence rampage.

Michèle C. Cone
January 1991

APPENDIXES

APPENDIX 1: REPORT OF THE PROPAGANDA-ABTEILUNG ON THE VISUAL ARTS, JANUARY 1944

Propaganda-Abteilung Frankreich   Paris, den 31.Januar 1944

Gruppe Kultur

B e r i c h t

über den Monat Januar 1944

Bildende Kunst:

Die Zensurtätigkeit des Referates erfasste alle im Laufe der Berichtszeit eröffneten Kunstausstellungen privater und offizieller Art. Auf Grund der bestehenden Anmeldepflicht werden die Ausstellungsvorhaben vor der Eröffnung gesichtet, um dann später an Ort und Stelle im Rahmen der Kontrollbesuche der Galerien nochmals überprüft zu werden. Die grossen offiziellen Veranstaltungen erfordern die Anwesenheit des Referenten bei den in engem Rahmen stattfindenden Eröffnungsfeierlichkeiten, den sogenannten Inaugurationen. Sind auch diese Eröffnungen, deren 2 bis 3 je Woche stattfinden, sehr zeitraubend, so muss jedoch darauf Wert gelegt werden, dass der Militärbefehlshaber im Kreise der eröffnenden Minister und führenden Persönlichkeiten auf dem Gebiete der Kunst durch die zuständigen Sachbearbeiter vertreten ist und derartige Reunions jederzeit kontrolliert werden.

Dem Kolonialgedanken und der Sehnsucht nach den verlorengegangenen Kolonien ist die Ausstellung "L'Influence Coloniale sur le décor de la vie française" gewidmet. - Die letzten Schöpfungen auf dem Gebiete der Bildteppiche sind in der Orangerie "Cartons et Tapisseries modernes des Manufactures nationales" zu sehen. Viele Tapisserien verdienen dabei keineswegs als Bildteppiche angesprochen zu werden, sondern bleiben gewebte Gemälde. Wo bleibt da die Tradition; gerade Frankreich hat in dieser Kunstgattung ja Vorbildliches geleistet. - In der Zeit

APPENDIXES

zwischen dem Wintersalon und dem Salon der Unabhängigen wurde
im Palais de Tokio der "Salon des Femmes peintres et sculp-
teums" eröffnet. Unter den Frauen gibt es bekanntlich einige
grosse Künstlerinnen wie die Morisot, Valadon, Cassat, die
hier auch in einer Gedächtnisschau zu sehen sind, aber der
grösste Teil der Frauen lernte als Pensionstochter u.a. auch
etwas malen. Die Ergebnisse derartiger Versuche sind nun zum
60. Male als schleierumwobene Porträts oder "zartduftende"
Blumenarrangements zu bewundern. Das Mannweib fehlt aber auch
nicht und stellt mit viel Kraft und Farbenmut herunterge-
strichene Leinwände aus. - Die im Verlaufe des Jahres in der
Provinz stattgefundenen Ausstellungen wie "Salon de Guyenne"
in Bordeaux, Salon de Rouen, Caen, Orléans etc. werden im Musée Galliera in einer zusammenfassenden Schau als "Salon des
Provinces" ausgestellt.

Viel beobachtet wird auch die von der Stadt Paris veran-
staltete Ausstellung von architektonischen Entwürfen zur Umgestaltung von wichtigen Plätzen der französischen Hauptstadt,
die auf Grund eines Wettbewerbes für kriegsgefangene Architek-
ten entstanden. Neben der Umgestaltung des Place Clichy und
des Val de Grâce verdienen die Entwurfe für die Porte Sainte Denis und die Porte St.Martin besonderer Beachtung. Die Ausstellung,
an der 448 Kriegsgefangene beteiligt sind, zeigt erneut die
freizügige Behandlung in den deutschen Lagern.

Von den Privatausstellungen verdienen die neusten Maillol-
zeichnungen bei Carré erwähnt zu werden. diese wunderbaren
Zeichnungen des menschlichen Körpers legen erneut die klassi-
sche Grösse des jetzt 82-jährigen Bildhauers dar.- Mit wieviel
Sorgfalt der Plakatmaler Jules Chéret seine Affichen entwarf,
zeigen die Studienblätter, die die Galerie Ruaz ausstellt. Ne-

APPENDIXES

- 3 -

ben den Entwürfen sind die wenige1 geschaffenen Bilder zu sehen, die durch den Charm ihrer figürlichen Darstellung ent-
zücken. -

Mit den Kunstreferenten der verschiedenen Dienststellen,
wie den Herrn Konsul Wuester (Deutsche Botschaft), Dr.Lohse
(Einsatzstab Rosenberg) und Professor Möbius (Kunstschutz) ,
fanden verschiedene Besprechungen statt, in denen Fragen des
öffentlichen Kunstlebens geklärt und die Stellungnahme gegen-
über den französischen Behörden eindeutig festgelegt wurden.
Es wurde beschlossen, alle in Zukunft auftretenden Fragen ge-
meinsam zu erörtern und auf eine eindeutige Haltung abzustimmen.

Die von der General-Bau-Inspektion der Reichshauptstadt
in Auftrag gegebenen Pantographen sind fertiggestellt. Vor dem
Versand nach Deutschland wurden sie montiert und werden augen-
blicklich vom Referat mit Hilfe der nötigen Fachkräfte nach
ihrer Brauchbarkeit überprüft, damit eventuell sich ergebende
Mängel vor dem Abtransport noch behoben werden können. Die Far-
benlieferungen für die Reichskammer der Bildenen Künste gingen
laufend nach Deutschland, sowie Gips, Werk u.a. Rohstoffe für
die General-Bau-Inspaektion.

Einige Bildhauer wurden an die reichseigenen.Breker-Werk-
stätten nach Wriezen/Oder verpflichtet. Im Rahmen der Dienst-
verpflichtung wurde gleichfalls in die Breker-Werkstätten der
Sohn des bekannten Verlegers Flammarion als Bibliothekar verpflichtet, wo der Sohn des Pariser Polizeipräfekten Bussière
schon seit einem halben Jahr als Sekr tär tätig ist

Zur Aufrechterhaltung der guten Beziehungen fanden sei-
tens des Referates zum Jahreswechel verschiedentlich Besuche

APPENDIXES

in den Ateliers bekannter Künstler statt. - Auf Grund einer
Rücksprache mit dem Hafenkommandanten in Port Vendre kann
der Bildhauer Meillol trotz der Evakuierungsmassnahmen in
Banyuls-sur-mer verbleiben, um seine angefangenen Arbeiten
zu beenden.

Propaganda Division, France   Paris, 31 January 1944
Cultural Affairs Group

REPORT ON THE MONTH OF JANUARY 1944

The censorship activities of the Department comprised all exhibitions of a public or private nature opened during the reporting period. As a result of the ongoing duty to give advance notice, all projected exhibitions are viewed prior to opening, and later they are once more inspected at the exhibition site within the framework of supervisory visits to the galleries. Important official functions require the presence of the Department Head at opening ceremonies held within a more intimate framework, the so-called inaugurations. Even if the attendance at these ceremonies is very time consuming, since there are two or three of them in any given week, it is important that the Military Commander be represented by an authorized agent within the circle of ministers and leading art-world personalities present at each opening, and that such gatherings be monitored at all times.

An exhibition dedicated to the idea of colonialism and nostalgia for the lost colonies is entitled "L'Influence Coloniale sur le décor de la vie française." The latest creations in the field of tapestry can be viewed at the Orangerie's "Cartons et Tapisseries modernes des Manufactures nationales." Many of these tapestries in no way deserve to be called Bildteppiche [tapestries—literally, "picture-carpets"], since they remain mere woven paintings. What has this tradition been reduced to? It was in this genre that France had formerly produced exemplary work. In the interim period between the Winter Salon and the Salon des Independants an exhibition entitled "Salon des Femmes peintres et sculpteurs" opened at the Palais de Tokyo. Among the women there are a few well-known artists such as Morisot, Valadon, and Cassat, who can also be viewed here in a commemorative show, but the majority of the women seem to be pensioners' daughters who have taken a few painting lessons. The result of this sort of effort can be admired here for sixty-odd times in mist-veiled portraits and "daintily-scented" flower arrange-

ments. The masculine woman is not absent either, but is represented here with canvases daubed in bold strokes and daring colors. Exhibitions that had taken place in the provinces in the course of the year, such as the "Salon de Guyenne" in Bordeaux, and the Salons of Rouen, Caen, Orleans, etc., are currently shown at the Musée Galliera in a comprehensive show entitled "Salon des Provinces."

Another well-attended exhibition is the one organized by the city of Paris showing architectural design sketches for the alteration of important sites in the French capital, which originated as a result of a competition among prisoner-of-war architects. In addition to new designs for the Place Clichy and Val de Grace, the sketches for the Porte St.-Denis and the Porte St.-Martin deserve special notice. This exhibition, in which 448 prisoners of war have taken part, is a renewed proof of generous treatment in the German camps.

Among the private exhibitions, the recent show of Maillol drawings at the Carré deserves mention. These marvelous drawings of the human body once more prove the classical greatness of this now eighty-two-year-old sculptor. How much care the poster artist Jules Cheret invests in his designs can be seen in the preliminary sketches exhibited at the Galerie Ruaz. In addition to these sketches, one can see the less finished paintings, whose charming figurative subjects provide sheer delight.

Various talks were held by the art specialists at the various administrative departments, among them Consul Wuester (German Legation), Dr. Lohse (Rosenberg's operational task force), and Professor Moebius (Art Protection), in which questions regarding public art activities were discussed, and an unambiguous position with regard to the French authorities was established. It was decided that any future questions would be discussed jointly and that a clear and unanimous position would then be decided by a vote.

The pantographs ordered by the General Buildings Inspection Department of the German Capital have been completed. They have been mounted and are now being inspected by the Department with the help of needed specialists, so that any flaws that might surface can be remedied now, before they are shipped to Germany. The shipments of paints for the Reichskammer for the Arts are continually being made to Germany, along with plaster and other raw materials required by the general building inspection department.

Several sculptors were engaged ["verpflichten," implying obligation or force] for the Reich-owned Breker workshops at Wriezen-Oder. Within the framework of such a service engagement, the son of the well-known publisher Flammarion was also assigned to the Breker workshops as a librarian. The son of the Paris prefect of police has already been on duty there as a secretary for the last six months.

In order to maintain good relations, the Department made several visits to the studios of well-known artists at year's end. Based on a request from the port commander at Port Vendre, permission has been granted to the sculptor Maillol to remain in Banyuls sur Mer in spite of evacuation procedures, so that he might complete work already in progress.

(Translated by Juliana Biro.)

LA SEMAINE ARTISTIQUE

Programmes et calendriers du 16 au 22 Mai 1941

Les Musées ouverts au public :

CARNAVALET, 24, rue de Sévigné : Tous les jours, sauf le lundi, de 10 à 12 heures et de 14 à 18 heures. Entrée : 3 francs. Entrée gratuite pour les militaires en uniforme.

CERNUSCHI, 7, avenue Vélasquez : Ouvert tous les jours, sauf le lundi.

MUSÉE DE L'ARMÉE, tous les jours, Hôtel des Invalides, sauf lundi de 10 h. à 5 h.

MUSÉE DES ARTS DÉCORATIFS, Pavillon de Marsan, 107, rue de Rivoli.

MUSÉE DES ARTS MODERNES, quai de Tokio. Jusqu'au 31 mai : *Le Salon*.

MUSÉE COGNACQ-JAY, 25, boul. des Capucines. Exposition organisée par l'Entraide des Artistes « Paris vu par les Peintres ». (Entrée libre).

MUSÉE DE L'HOMME, Palais de Chaillot, aile Passy : De 10 à 16 heures, sauf le lundi.

MUSÉE DE LA FRANCE D'OUTRE-MER, 293, avenue Daumesnil : Tous les jours, sauf le lundi, de 13 h. 30 à 16 h. 30.

MUSÉE GALLIERA, av. Pierre 1er de Serbie : Salon de l'Imagerie Française.

MUSÉE DU LOUVRE, quai du Louvre : Les salles des Antiques sont ouvertes les mardi, jeudi, samedi et dimanche, de 11 à 16 heures. Entrée : 1 franc, gratuite le dimanche.

MUSÉE DES MONUMENTS FRANÇAIS, Palais de Chaillot, aile Paris : De 10 à 16 heures, sauf le lundi.

MUSÉE DE L'ORANGERIE. A partir du vendredi 4 avril, Peintures de la Donation P. Jamot.

MUSÉE RODIN, 77, rue de Varennes : De 13 à 17 heures, sauf le lundi.

Le Calendrier des Galeries :

GALERIE L'ARCHIPEL, 10, r. J.-du-Bellay, 2 au 9 mai : Bériole, Charlemagne, Chopard, Delatousche, Koepil, Feuillatte, J. Moreau, Parlurier.

GALERIE BERRI-RASPAIL, 99, bd Raspail : du 17 mai au 14 juin : Exposition rétrospective de Mar. Luce.

GALERIE BRAUN : 18, rue Louis-le-Grand : Jeunes Peintres de la Tradition Française.

GALERIE ARMAND DROUANT, 35, rue de Seine : Exposition *Le Tournier*.

GALERIE CLAUSEN, 14, r. des Beaux-Arts : R. Besse, M. Maillet, H. Le Pesqueur, Pierrepont.

GALERIE D'ART CONTEMPORAIN, 40, r. Bonaparte : Tableaux modernes.

AU BON GOUT DE L'ART ANCIEN, 53, rue Vivienne : Expos. perm. et sculp. de P. de Léonardi.

BARTEIRO, 30, rue de Seine : *Tableaux modernes*. Renoir, Courbet, Derain, Vuillard, etc. J.-M. BERNARD, 8, r. Jacques-Callot : Expos. Mad. Luka, du 19 mai au 9 juin.

BERNIER, 10, rue Jacques-Callot : *Tableaux et sculptures modernes*, 35, rue de Berri. *GALERIE DE BERRI*, 12, rue de Berri. Paysages par F. Salbat, du 10 au 23 mai.

Jacques BLOT, 29, rue La Boëtie (Anj. 38-63) : *Tableaux des XIXe et XXe siècles*.

GALERIE BORGHÈSE, 35, Champs-Elysées, (Elys. 11-97) : *Tableaux anciens et modernes*.

J. BUCHER, 9 ter, boul. du Montparnasse : Exp. A. Bauchand, jusqu'au 30 mai. *GALERIE Mme BENEZIT*, 23, bd Haussmann, Pastels, Aquarelles de Degas, Renoir, Pissaro.

GALERIE BRETEAU, 70, rue Bonaparte, 14 à 19 h, Peint. de M. de Béchillon.

GALERIE CARMINE, 51, r. de Seine, Derain, Dufy, Guillaumin, Luce, Marquet, Renoir, etc.

GALERIE Louis CAIRÉ, 10, av. de Messine : Exposit. de dessins de Jean Cocteau.

GALERIE CARREFOUR, 141, boul. Raspail Imagerie pop. anc. Objets anc. Océanie.

Jeanne CASTEL, 32, av. Matignon : *Peintures*.

CASTELUCHO, 125 bd du Montparnasse (Métro Vavin) : *Peintures modernes*.

GALERIE DES CHAMPS-ÉLYSÉES, 79, Champs-Elysées : *Maîtres contemporains*.

GALERIE F. CLAIR, Grand-Hôtel, 12, boul. des Capucines : *Tableaux modernes*.

GALERIE J. DESSEINTENNE, 10, aven. du Parc-Montsouris : Expos. de Félix Labbé.

GALERIE DE L'ÉLYSÉE, 69, faub. Saint-Honoré : Peintures d'Henzé du 7 au 21 mai.

GALERIE L'ESPLANADE, 90, rue de Rennes, (Lit. 73-44) : *Tableaux anciens et sculptures du moyen âge, qu'au XVIIIe siècle*.

GALERIE DES QUATRE-CHEMINS, Éditart, 19, rue de Marignan (Bal. 39-16) : *Tableaux modernes, livres d'art*, de 14 h. à heures.

GALERIE RENOU ET COLLE, 164, Fbg St-Honoré : Georges d'Espagnat.

GALERIE RIVE GAUCHE, 44, r. de Fleurus (Lit. 04-91) : *Tableaux de Lebourg, Utrillo, Marie Laurencin, Foujita, Bauchant et Oudot*.

GALERIE DU TROIS, 3, rue Jacques-Callot : *Tableaux modernes*.

RAPHAËL GÉRARD, 4, avenue de Messine : *Tableaux modernes*, de 9 à 12 heures

Marcel GUIOT, 4, rue Volney: *Gravures et Dessins anciens et modernes*.

LUCY KROGH, place Saint-Augustin : Peintures et Emaux de Jean Serrière, du 16 au 30 mai.

R. LEJEUNE, 12, r. Jacques-Callot : *Tableaux anciens*, de 10 à 12 heures et de 14 à 19 h. 30.

MAISON DE LA GRAVURE, Gravures, cartes et dessins anciens. 52, faub. St-Honoré.

ALICE MANTEAU, 14, rue de l'Abbaye : *Tableaux anciens et sculptures*

LE NOUVEL ESSOR, (G. Jacquart), 40, r. des Sts-Pères : Despiau, Segonzac, Boussingault.

LA PEAU DE CHAGRIN, 2, rue des Beaux-Arts : Aquar. et décors de J.-A. Bonnaud.

PÉTRIDES, 6, av. Delcassé : *Tableaux modernes*. Renoir, Pissaro, Bonnard, Wlaminck, etc.

GALERIE PITTORESQUE, 133, bd Raspail : *Peintures contemp. et objets 1830 à 1900*.

Paul PROUTÉ, 74 rue de Seine : E. Blérg.

ROTGÉ, 140, faub. Saint-Honoré : 3, des Annonciades : Charigny, M. Doiton-Toulouse et R. Fernier, du 16 mai au 1er juin.

APPENDIX 3: GALLERY GUIDE, PARIS, NOVEMBER 1943

LES BEAUX-ARTS
Le Journal des Arts
139, Faub. Saint-Honoré, Paris-8ᵉ
BALzac 35-15 et la suite

ABONNEMENTS :
Un an, **160 fr.** — Six mo's, **80 fr.**
Trois mois, **45 fr.**
ÉTRANGER : Un an, **340 fr.**

Editions ART ET TECHNIQUE
Compte Chèques Postaux Paris 3076-17
R. C. Seine 283-108 B
POUR LA ZONE NON OCCUPÉE
les abonnements doivent être adressés aux
Messageries Hachette, Service Beaux-Arts
12, rue Bellecordière, Lyon.
Compte Chèques Postaux, Lyon 218.

Comité de Publication :
MM. **Jean Babelon**, conservateur du Cabinet des Médailles de France ; **Pierre du Colombier** ; **Pierre d'Espezel** ; **Bernard Faÿ**, administrateur général de la Bibliothèque Nationale ; **Philippe Gangnat** ; **Georges Grappe**, conservateur du Musée Rodin ; **Louis Hautecœur**, secrétaire général des Beaux-Arts ; **Charles Picard**, membre de l'Institut ; **Louis Réau**, professeur à la Sorbonne ; **Jean-Louis Vaudoyer**, administrateur de la Comédie-Française.

Rédaction : Rédacteur en chef : Pierre d'Espezel ; Secrétaire général : Pierre Imbourg.

Les Musées

AERO-CLUB DE FRANCE, salle des fêtes, 6, rue Galilée : **Peintres et Sculpteurs de l'Aviation 1943.**
CARNAVALET, 24, rue de Sévigné. Tous les jours, de 10 h. à 12 h. et de 14 h. à 17 h. 30. (Fermé le lundi.)
CERNUSCHI, 7, av. Vélasquez. Ouvert tous les jours, sauf lundi : **Art d'Extrême-Orient.**
PAVILLON DE MARSAN, 107, rue de Rivoli : **Société des Décorateurs français.**
MUSÉE GALLIERA, av. Pierre-Iᵉʳ-de-Serbie : Exposition du Timbre.
MUSÉE COGNACQ-JAY, 25, boul. des Capucines : Exposition « La Samothrace », jusqu'au 21 novembre.
MUSÉE DE L'HOMME (Trocadéro) : Exposition des Pionniers et Explorateurs de notre Empire colonial.
MUSÉE DU LOUVRE. Tous les jours, de 10 à 17 h., sauf lundi. Entrée : 1 franc, gratuit le dimanche.
MUSÉE DE LA MARINE (Palais de Chaillot) : tous les jeudis, vendredis, samedis et dimanches, de 10 à 18 h.
MUSÉE DES MONUMENTS FRANÇAIS. Palais de Chaillot, aile Paris. De 10 à 17 heures, sauf lundi.
MUSÉE DE L'OPÉRA. Théâtre de l'Opéra. Tous les jours, sauf dimanches et fêtes, de 13 h. à 17 h. 30.
MUSÉE RODIN, 77, rue de Varennes. De 13 à 18 heures, sauf le lundi.

Salon des Provinces Françaises

GASCOGNE-LANGUEDOC, Toulouse, Musée des Augustins, jusqu'au 28 novembre.
LIMOUSIN-MARCHE, Limoges, salle des fêtes de la mairie. Vernissage le 20 novembre. Jusqu'au 5 décembre.

ACADÉMIE MONTMORENCY
49, Av. des Sycomores - PARIS-XVIᵉ
"Villa Montmorency"   JASmin 93-00
PEINTURE   DESSIN
MODÈLES VIVANTS

Les Galeries

1ᵉʳ Arrᵗ   RIVE DROITE

René DROUIN, 17, pl. Vendôme (Opé. 94-00) : Fautrier, vernissage le 18 novembre.
P. HENAUT, 3, place des Pyramides : A. Calbet, A. Béronneau, K. Terlow.
ROUX, 13, av. de l'Opéra (Opé. 34-79) : Brun-Buisson, du 12 au 22 novembre.
SILEX, 12, rue des Pyramides : Tableaux modernes.
TROIS QUARTIERS, bd de la Madeleine : « Intimité », œuvres de contemporains.

2ᵉ Arrᵗ

ALLARD-MALESHERBES, 20, rue des Capucines : Nicolas Eekman, aquarelles et dessins. Vernissage le 12 novembre.
LA CIMAISE, 15, bd Poissonnière (Gut. 80-20) : Tabl. anciens et mod.

8ᵉ Arrᵗ

GALERIE D'ANJOU, 9, bd Malesherbes (Anj. 62-41) : P. Jouffroy, jusqu'au 21 novembre.
Cie des ARTS FRANÇAIS, 116, fg St-Honoré (Ely. 78-53) : Tapisseries, jusqu'au 20 novembre.
GALERIE DE L'ART MODERNE, 56, rue La Boétie (Ely. 78-53) : Tableaux de Maîtres modernes.
GALERIE DE BERRI, 12, rue de Berri (Ely. 14-56) : Nicolas Eekman, jusqu'au 18 novembre.
Jacques BLOT, 29, rue La Boétie (Anj. 38-63) : Laprade. Vern. le 19 nov.
LA BOÉTIE, 83, rue La Boétie : Romana-Nemours, jusqu'au 30 nov.
BORGHÈSE, 35, Champs-Elysées (Ely. 11-97) : Peintures modernes.
F.-E. BUFFA, 36, rue de Miromesnil (Anj. 35-26) : Tableaux contemporains.
Laurence CAJET, 6, av. Percier (Bal. 04-19) : Tableaux modernes.
Louis CARRE, 10, av. de Messine : Exposition Ch. Camoin.
CHAMPS-ELYSÉES, 79, Ch.-Elysées : Maîtres contemporains.
GALERIE CHARPENTIER, 76, fg Saint-Honoré : Rétrospective Emile Bernard ; La jeune Sculpture française. Tous les jours, sauf lundis.
GALERIE DE L'ORFÈVRERIE CHRISTOFLE, 12, rue Royale (Opé. 70-43) : « Gravures Orfèvrerie » : Daragnès, Dignimont, Galanis, M. Laurencin, Touchagues, de Waroquier.
GALERIE G. DENIS, 33, rue de Miromesnil : Tableaux modernes.
DROUANT-DAVID, 52, fg St-Honoré (Anj. 79-45) : Arthur Greuell.
ELYSÉE, 69, fg St-Honoré (Bal. 27-87) : Œuvres récentes de Heuzé, jusqu'au 23 novembre.
M. FABIANI, 26, avenue Matignon : Tableaux modernes.
GABRIELLE FRANC, 35, av. Friedland (Ely. 15-77) : Tableaux anciens et modernes.
GALERIE DE FRANCE, 3, fg Saint-Honoré (Anj. 69-37) : Loutreuil (1885-1925), peintures.
FROISSARD, 12, rue La Boétie (Anj. 93-65) : De Lapeyrière et C. Oliveda. A partir du 18 : Deparis.
GALERIE JOS HESSEL (H. Joly, Succ'), 26, r. La Boétie (Ely. 19-58) : Tableaux modernes.
André HURTREZ, 252, fg Saint-Honoré (Car. 38-68) : Antiquités. Tableaux anciens et modernes.
Lucy KROHG, 10 bis, pl. St-Augustin (Lab. 69-78) : Marie Pigelet.
MAISON DE LA GRAVURE, 52, fg Saint-Honoré : Gravures, dessins anciens du XVIIIᵉ.
GALERIE PARVILLEE, 104, boulevard Haussmann (Eur. 35-07) : Œuvres de maîtres contemporains.
PETRIDES, 6, avenue Delcassé (Bal. 47-43) : Peintures modernes.
RAPHAEL GERARD, 4, avenue de Messine : Tableaux modernes.
RENEVEY PIERRE, 174, faubg Saint-Honoré : Tableaux de maîtres.

RENOU ET COLLE, 164, fg Saint-Honoré (Ely. 35-95) : Tableaux modernes.
GALERIE ROYALE, 11, rue Royale, IIIᵉ Salon des moins de trente ans, jusqu'au 27 novembre.
CH. VANDAMME, 70, Champs-Elysées (Ely. 46-20) : Maîtres contemporains.

9ᵉ Arrᵗ

ART PLACE PIGALLE, 13, boulev. de Clichy (Tru. 88-30) : Peintures modernes, meubles. Ouv. le dimanche.
GALERIE D'ART DU PRINTEMPS, 64, bd Haussmann : « Moissons et Vendanges », vues par les peintres contemporains. Jusqu'au 13 nov.
LE GARREC et CORDIER, 8, rue de la Victoire : Adolphe Hervier (1821-1879), jusqu'au 20 nov.

16ᵉ Arrᵗ

MARCEAU, 55, avenue Marceau (Klé. 56-78) : Société d'artistes.

17ᵉ Arrᵗ

O.-C. CLAUDET, 6, bd de Courcelles (Car. 90-68) : Peintures de pêche.
ART DE L'ETOILE, 30, avenue des Ternes : Groupe contemporain.
GALERIE VILLIERS, 10, avenue de Villiers : Les peintres qui plaisent.

18ᵉ Arrᵗ

AU VIEUX MONTMARTRE, 91, rue Lepic (Mon. 31-28) : Jeunes peintres d'aujourd'hui.
GALERIE 102, 102, rue Lepic (Métro : Lamarck) : J. d'Esparbès, Creixams, Leprin.
GALERIE D'ORSEL, 46, rue d'Orsel (Pro. 30-45) : Corbellini, Dot Lewis, P.-V. Baullieu, H. Verbrugghe.

6ᵉ Arrᵗ   RIVE GAUCHE

Galerie ANDRE, 3, r. des Saints-Pères (Lit. 61-44) : Jean Dufy, gouaches.
L'ARC-EN-CIEL, 17, rue de Sèvres (Lit. 17-29) : Nelly Huchet, du 12 au 26 novembre.
BARREIRO, 30, rue de Seine (Dan. 46-70) : Tableaux modernes.
BERNIER, 10, rue Jacques-Callot : Exposition Limouse, du 12 novembre au 2 décembre.
BERRI-RASPAIL, 99, boul. Raspail (Lit. 48-86) : Tableaux de Maîtres et de Jeunes.
BOURDEIX, 62, rue Bonaparte (Odé. 02-05) : André Favory et Pompon.
BRETEAU, 70, rue Bonaparte (Dan. 40-96) : Bertholle, du 12 au 27 novembre.
Jeanne BUCHER, 9 ter, bd du Montparnasse (Ség. 64-32) : Louis Marcoussis, vernissage le 18 novembre.
GALERIE CARMINE, 51, rue de Seine (Dan. 91-10) : Tableaux de maîtres.
GALERIE CHARDIN, 5, rue de Seine (Dan. 99-38) : Vingt peintres du Salon d'Automne.
LE CHEVAL BLEU, 1, r. Guénégaud : Tableaux anc. et mod. Antiquités. Décoration (Séverin Mars et Fils).
Else CLAUSEN, 14, rue des Beaux-Arts (Dan. 74-33) : Peintures naïves.
LE DRAGON, 26, rue du Dragon : S. de Calà, peintures.
LA GENTILHOMMIÈRE, 67, bd Raspail (Lit. 35-14) : Exposition de groupe.
GALERIE GUENEGAUD, 35, rue Guénégaud (Odé. 22-40) : Tableaux anciens et modernes.
LEFRANC et ENGRAND, 13, rue de l'Abbaye (Odé. 23-21) : J. Le Tournier, aquarelles.
LE GARREC, 24, rue du Four (Dan. 43-48) : Jeune gravure contemporaine.
LEJEUNE, 12, r. Jacques-Callot (Dan. 99-73) : Tableaux anciens.
N.-D.-DES-CHAMPS, 116, bd Raspail (Lit. 24-74) : Leprin, Maufra, Céria.
PELLETAN-HELLEU, 125, bd Saint-Germain : Les Peintres de la Galerie.
PROUTE Paul, 74, rue de Seine : « Le Monde à Table », gravures du XVIᵉ au XIXᵉ siècle.

APPENDIXES

Appendix 4: Artists in the Inaugural Exhibition of the Musée National d'Art Moderne, Paris, August 1942

Liste alphabétique des Artistes
dont les œuvres sont exposées

I. - PEINTURES, DESSINS, AQUARELLES et GRAVURES

(Les numéros qui suivent les noms des artistes sont ceux des Salles.)

ALIX. 213, 228.
AMAN-JEAN. 206.
ANDRÉ (ALBERT). 207.
ANTRAL. 224.
ASSELIN. 217.
AUJAME. 230.
BAIGNÈRES. 206.
BALANDE. 206.
BASCHET. 206.
BEAUFRÈRE. 228.
BELTRAND. 228.
BÉRARD. 230.
BÉRAUD. 206.
BERNARD (ÉMILE). 208.
BERSIER. 224, 228.
BERTRAM. 224.
BESNARD. 206.
BEURDELEY. 228.
BEZOMBES. 230.
BILLOTEY. 216.
BILOUL. 206.
BISSIÈRE. 213.
BLANCHE. 206.
BOMPARD (MAURICE). 206.
BONNARD. 209, 210.
BOUCHAUD (JEAN). 224.
BOUCHE. 217.
BOUNEAU. 230.
BOUSSINGAULT. 216, 217, 228
BRAQUE. 213.
BRAYER. 224.
BRIANCHON. 230.
CAILLARD. 230.

CAMOIN. 210.
CAPON. 224.
CAVAILLÈS. 230.
CÉRIA. 217.
CHABAS. 206.
CHABAUD. 224.
CHAMAILLARD. 207.
CHAPELAIN-MIDY. 230.
CHARLEMAGNE. 217.
CHARLOT. 206.
CHASTEL. 230.
CHÉRIANE. 224.
COCHET. 217, 228.
CORNEAU. 224, 228.
COTTET. 206.
COURNAULT. 228.
COUTAUD. 214.
CROSS. 207.
DARAGNÈS. 224.
DAUCHEZ. 206.
DAVID (HERMINE). 217, 228.
DELAUNAY. 213.
DENIER. 224.
DENIS (MAURICE). 208, 209, 218.
DERAIN. 210.
DÉSIRÉ-LUCAS. 206.
DESNOYER. 214, 230.
DESPIERRE. 230, 216.
DESPUJOLS. 206.
DESVALLIÈRES. 210.
DEVAMBEZ. 206.
DÉZIRÉ. 206.

25

26

APPENDIXES

II. - SCULPTURES, DESSINS de Sculpteurs, MÉDAILLES

27

MEUBLES et LAQUES

28

APPENDIX 5: STATE ACQUISITIONS OF MODERN ART
BETWEEN 1941 AND 1947

Artist	Title	Year Bought
Oudot	*Cérès*, 1941	1941
Brianchon	*Le mur gris*, 1941	1941
	Le Bois de Boulogne, 1943	1943
Legueult	*Figure à la rose*, 1939–41	1941
Humblot	*La Sardinière*	1942
	Port de Villefranche	1943
	Nature morte à la lampe	1943
Rohner	*Nature morte au crâne*	1942
	Sommeil	1946
Pignon	*Nature morte*	1942
	Catalane, 1946	1947
Gischia	*Les brioches*	1942
	Les toiles, 1944	1945
Le Moal	*Le Port*	1944
Manessier	*Combat de coqs*, 1944	1944
Singier	*Nu à la plante ornementale*	1945

Source: Musée National d'Art Moderne, *Catalogue Guide*, Paris, 1947.

APPENDIX 6: DISTRIBUTION OF SCULPTURE COMMISSIONS BETWEEN SALON EXHIBITORS (S) AND OTHERS IN 1941

	Artist	Commission (in francs)
Conservatoire de Musique	Bouquillon (S)	35,000
Collège de France	Chauvel	35,000
	Geminiani	40,000
	Jegou	40,000
Faculté de Pharmacie	Niclausse (S)	62,000
	Crouzat (S)	52,000
	Lacroix	52,000
	Deschamps (S)	52,000
Eglise St.-Esprit	Bazin	36,000
	Dufresne	36,000
	Fenaux (S)	36,000
	Fenerstein	45,000
	Gibert (S)	45,000
	Homs	36,000
	Leleu	36,000
	Martel, Jean	36,000
	Martel, Joel	36,000
	Mocquot (S)	40,000
	Morlaix (S)	36,000
	Munziger (S)	45,000
	Prat (S)	54,000
	Serraz	36,000
Orangerie Meudon	Auricoste	50,000
	Cornet	50,000
	de Jaeger	40,000
	Duparcq (S)	40,000
	Muller (S)	7,000
Pont Autoroute étoile de Maintenon	Belmondo	60,000
	Le Bourgeois	80,000

	Artist	Commission (in francs)
Entrée tunnel, Autoroute de St.-Cloud	Biaggi (S)	12,000
	Brule	8,000
	Cadenat	20,000
	Debarre	20,000
	Dumont (S)	30,000
	Grattesat (S)	20,000
	Halbout (S)	20,000
	Joffre (S)	60,000
Autoroute de St.-Cloud	Lagriffoul (S)	20,000
	Ottany (S)	35,000
	Petit (S)	20,000
	Ridet	8,000

Source: French National Archives (F21 4760 6).

NOTES

PREFACE

1. Bertrand Dorléac, *Histoire de l'art*.

2. I thank M. Cézard, now retired from the French National Archives in Paris, for pointing me toward A J 40 1001.

3. On the cinema under Vichy, see Ehrlich, *Cinema of Paradox*, which contains a bibliography of French authors on the subject.

4. On literature, the most interesting source is Loiseaux, *Littérature de la défaite*.

5. This is the view espoused by Moulin in *French Art Market*, pp. 20–21.

6. Lehmann-Haupt, *Art under a Dictatorship*, p. 72.

7. Haraszti, *Velvet Prison*, p. 14.

8. Ibid.

9. I am indebted to Prof. Gerald L. Bruns of the University of Notre Dame, whose paper on Beckett and the Resistance delivered at the 1990 Iowa Conference in French Studies inspired these thoughts. I thank Professor Bruns for making his paper, "Persecution and the Art of Writing," available to me.

10. See Strauss, *Persecution*, chap. 2.

11. Quoted by Bruns (see n. 9 above) in "Persecution and the Art of Writing," p. 5.

12. See Derrida, "Like the Sound of the Sea."

13. Paxton, *Vichy France*, p. 249.

14. Céline, *L'Ecole des cadavres*, pp. 138–39. "A qui je vous demande un petit peu a profité le Front Populaire? Aux Juifs strictement et aux maçons (Juifs synthétiques). Les Aryens ont tout paumé. Bourgeois, ouvriers, paysans, petits commerçants, artistes, petits fonctionnaires: repassés. . . . Mais enfin, ça va se terminer. Ça peut pas durer toujours, les sursis."

15. Winock, *Edouard Drumont et Cie*, p. 40.

16. Ibid., pp. 40–48.

17. Sartre, *Situations II*, p. 28. In this passage, Sartre is talking about the worker, not the artist.

18. Alloway, *Network*, pp. 4–5.

19. Becker, *Art Worlds*, pp. 24–25.

20. Jauss, *Pour une esthétique de la réception*, p. 85.

CHAPTER 1

1. Hélion, *They Shall Not Have Me*, pp. 44–46. Hélion later escaped from a German work camp and made his way back to the United States.

2. Kahnweiler, *My Galleries and Painters*, p. 111.

3. Soutine's collector during that last period was Madeleine Castaing, who was also his neighbor.

4. Max Ernst has given a vivid account of the experience in *Ecritures*, p. 62.

5. Buffet-Picabia, *Aires abstraites*, p. 123. She was Francis Picabia's first wife.

6. Information on the whereabouts of artists whose residence changed several times during these weeks is not always certain.

7. See Centre de la Vieille Charité, *Planète affolée*, p. 56. Joe Bousquet (1897–1950) came to the financial rescue of Max Ernst when the artist was a stateless person, and he also helped Bellmer. During the war, he sheltered fugitives and protected resisters although he was confined to his bed. He became president of a purge tribunal in his area after the Liberation.

8. Goldfarb-Marquis, *Marcel Duchamp*, p. 262. Beckett was also in Arcachon at the time.

9. Ibid. Among those who had left France either during or shortly before the Phony War began—that is, during the period between the September 1939 declaration of war with Germany and the German attack of May 1940—were Mondrian, Tanguy, Onslow Ford, Matta, Kay Sage, Dali, Pahlen, Man Ray, Kurt Seligman, Hayter, and Ozenfant (Centre d'Art et de Culture Georges Pompidou, *Paris-Paris*, p. 86).

10. Sabartès, *Picasso: An Intimate Portrait*, p. 219.

11. Grosshans, *Hitler and the Artists*, p. 88.

12. A bonfire was set in the courtyard of the Berlin Central Fire Department on 20 March 1939, and an untold number of "decadent" artworks were engulfed in flames.

13. This exception has gone unnoticed because of other indications of Hitler's intentions, namely the removal of artworks, including Fauve paintings, from German museums between 1933 and 1939, and the auction of art from German museums held in Lucerne, Switzerland, in 1939, which included Fauve paintings. From the detailed lists of artworks removed from German museums between 1933 and 1939 found in Rave, *Kunstdiktatur im Dritten Reich*, it is possible to arrive at the following numbers of Fauve works: thirteen Matisses, eight Vlamincks, and nine Derains, a rather modest number compared to the fifty-nine Chagalls, thirty-five Kogans, fifty-seven Kandinskys, nineteen Picassos, and fourteen Freundlichs. According to the catalogue of the Lucerne auction, the following works by artists then living in France were included among the 125 put on the block: *Odalisque, Three Women*, a still life, and a landscape by Matisse; *The Soler Family, Two Harlequins, The Absinthe Drinker*, and *Head of a Woman* by Picasso; a still life by Braque; *Blue House, Winter*, and *The Rabbi* by Chagall; *View out of the Window* and *The Pond* by Derain, and *Path in the Wood* and a landscape by Vlaminck. The titles are not always correct, and the dates do not appear in the catalogue. What the Lucerne auction suggests is that, in German art politics, certain artworks that did not fit National Socialist criteria might well continue to be tolerated for trade on the world art market as a means of raising cash.

14. See Brenner, *Politique artistique du national-socialisme*, chaps. 1 and 2.

15. *Hitler's Table Talk*, p. 489.

16. Brenner, *Politique artistique du national-socialisme*, p. 166.

17. Institut Goethe, *Munich 1937*, 15 March–17 May 1987. The catalogue includes the list of names in the Entartete Kunst exhibition, the speech given by Ziegler for its inauguration, and long excerpts from Hitler's speech on the occasion of the opening of the Great Exhibition of German Art, 18 July 1937, in Munich. Picasso's name also appears in the list compiled by Rave in *Kunst diktatur im Dritten Reich*. However, in the catalogue of the Degenerate Art exhibition at the 1991 Los Angeles County Museum, no mention is made of Picasso.

18. Wilson, "Collaboration in the Fine Arts, 1940–1944," p. 104.

19. *Cahier d'art* (1936): 212.

20. Akademie der Kunste, *Ausstellung Franzosischer Kunst der Gegenwart*, Berlin 1937, sponsored by L'Association Française d'Action Artistique. Neither Picasso nor any of the Surrealists participated.

21. "Une Exposition d'Art Français à Berlin," *Cahiers d'art* (1937): 62.

22. Stein, *Wars I Have Seen*, p. 87.

23. Quoted in Loiseaux, *Littérature de la défaite*, p. 354.

24. Rémond, *Right Wing in France*, p. 310.

25. Ibid., p. 311.

26. Ibid., p. 313.

27. Ibid., p. 314.

28. See Valéry, "autre digression" in "Pièces sur l'art," pp. 1205–6. "L'invention a disparu. La composition s'est réduite à l'arrangement. . . . Comment en est-on arrivé à ce point de relâchement?"

29. In *Histoire de l'art*, p. 109, Bertrand Dorléac discusses the views of the architectural and art historian Louis Hautecoeur, the very person Pétain would place at the head of the Department of Fine Arts at the Ministry of Education and Youth. His *Considérations sur l'art d'aujourd'hui* (1929) (together with Robert Rey's 1941 *Peinture moderne*) "reveal once again the assimilation that was to take place between artistic decadence and foreign influences on French art." In a text of which Bertrand Dorléac was probably unaware, Hautecoeur collapses the meaning of foreigner with that of *israélite* (Jew). See Chapter 4, pp. 81, 82.

30. Golan, "*Ecole Française* vs. the *Ecole de Paris*," p. 86.

CHAPTER 2

1. At the Musée des Arts Décoratifs in 1941, exhibitions entitled Les Arts Décoratifs Contemporains, Poupées d'Autrefois, La Seine à Paris, and a bicycle retrospective were organized. At the Musée de l'Orangerie in 1940, the Monet-Rodin centenary was celebrated; in 1941, the Paul Jamot donation was exhibited, and a show of Berthe Morisot

took place. At the Musée Galliéra, shows on the theme of sports and art (Le Sport dans l'Art), on the theater, (Le Théatre à Paris), art by French war prisoners (Le Salon du Prisonnier), French popular imagery, (L'Imagerie Française), and children's art done in homage to the marshal all took place in 1941 and early 1942.

2. Pierre du Colombier, "La Vie artistique en 1941," *Les Beaux Arts: Journal des arts* (6 February 1942): 5.

3. Letter from Le Conseiller d'Etat, Secrétaire Général des Beaux Arts, to Monsieur le Commissaire Général aux Questions Juives, dated 1 May 1942 (CDJC, document xxi-6): "Comme suite à votre lettre no. 13–19215 en date du 7 avril courant par laquelle vous avez exprimé le désir que les locaux des Administrations publiques ne soient mises à la disposition des organisateurs d'expositions d'oeuvres d'art que dans la mesure où les associations s'engageraient à ne présenter aucune oeuvre juive, j'ai l'honneur de vous faire connaitre que j'ai avisé de cette mesure M. le Préfet de la Seine et les organismes intéressés." This letter was merely a reminder, since the exclusion of Jews from exhibitions had begun in the autumn of 1940. Persons then living in the occupied zone who could not prove that they had two non-Jewish grandparents were kept from entering public places, theaters, and department stores and, as of 7 June 1942, made to wear the yellow star. Starting in June 1942, they were subject to roundups and deportation.

4. Jeanne Bucher, originally from Switzerland, went to Paris after World War I and opened a bookstore-gallery on the rue du Cherche Midi. She became a friend of the tapestry maker Lurçat and showed his work, as well as that of Arp, Lipchitz, Pascin, Marcoussis, and Gromaire. Her neighbor during World War II was Georges Hugnet, who also ran a bookstore-gallery.

5. Beauvoir, *Force de l'age*, p. 478.

6. This weekly, edited by Delange and appearing officially in occupied Paris, is typical of the ambiguities of the times. During the Occupation years, it was not seen as pro-German, but according to Pascal Ory, among others, its status was highly equivocal. See Ory, *Collaborateurs* p. 205. A rare interview with Cézanne's son, "Cézanne vu par son fils," appeared in *Comoedia* (15 May 1943).

7. René Drouin, an interior architect, had opened a gallery with Leo Castelli on Place Vendome in 1939. Drouin kept it going during the Occupation years, first with Georges Maratié as director, then with Gildo Caputo. It was Caputo's idea to show Fautrier in 1943.

8. *Le Rouge et le bleu*, edited by a former minister in the Blum cabinet, Spinasse, adopted pro-Vichy positions and advocated collaboration in its first editorial. It disappeared in August 1942. See Ory, *Collaborateurs*, p. 137.

9. Lesbats became known as Franck Elgar in the postwar years.

10. See Bellanger et al., *Histoire générale*, pp. 16–18. "Rien n'échappait au zèle des censeurs allemands." A Dr. Hibbelen insinuated himself into publishing houses and in the press, whose majority ownership he gained. Toward the end of the Occupation he

controlled 45 to 50 percent of the Parisian press. Ambassador Abetz had private funds of one billion francs at his disposal.

11. *Le Journal officiel* (18 October 1940). *"Statut des Juifs*: . . . Article 5: Les Juifs ne pourront, sans condition ni réserve, exercer l'une quelconque des professions suivantes: Directeurs, gérants, rédacteurs de journaux, revues, agences ou périodiques, à l'exception de publications de caractère strictement scientifique." Louis Vauxcelles changed his name to Thérèse Vallier. Nothing of Waldemar George or Florent Fels was seen in print. André Salmon (who may not have been Jewish) succeeded in publishing under his own name in *Comoedia* a review of a show in homage to the poet Guillaume Apollinaire.

12. Some see the beginning of Modernism as coinciding with the French Revolution; Romanticism is often named as its first intellectual manifestation; and the painters Courbet and Manet are frequently given as its starting point for art.

13. Boime, in *Academy and French Painting*, p. 10, has pointed out the role that a style of art situated between extremes had played for the regime of Louis Philippe: "This epithet [*juste milieu*] was used during the time of Louis Philippe and demonstrates how conscious was the desire to create a middle-of-the-road style, to find a compromise that would reconcile the antagonistic trends of the period—a characteristic of the political and cultural outlook of Louis Philippe himself."

14. Silver, "Esprit de Corps," p. 51.

15. Golan, "Moral Landscapes," chap. 1.

16. In *"Ecole Française* vs. The *Ecole de Paris*," p. 84, Romy Golan suggests that the Ecole Française (as distinguished from the Ecole de Paris) was a hotbed of middle-of-the-roadism and that a number of Ecole de Paris Jewish artists conformed to its values.

17. See Université de St.-Etienne, *Retour à l'ordre*; Centre d'Art et de Culture Georges Pompidou, *Réalismes*; Dérouet, "Beaux Arts"; and Ceysson, *Rappel à l'ordre*.

18. Ceysson, *Rappel à l'ordre*, p. 22.

19. Ibid., p. 37.

20. Ibid.

21. Nochlin, "Return to Order," p. 77. Forces Nouvelles was the French counterpart in the 1930s of the Italian Novecento and the German Neue Sachlichkeit.

22. See Ceysson, *Rappel à l'ordre*, p. 23. The debates were first published in 1936 and have recently been reissued under the same title (Paris: Cercle d'art, 1987).

23. Ceysson, *Rappel à l'ordre*, p. 22.

24. Founded in 1932, it was suspended in May 1940 for its attacks against the government of Paul Reynaud and for its demoralizing antiwar campaign. Two of its staff members, Lesca and Laubreaux, were briefly interned by order of Georges Mandel, minister of the interior during the Phony War. See Bellanger et al., *Histoire générale*, p. 57. In a letter from the Commissariat aux Questions Juives to Achenbach, an official at the German Embassy, Rebatet's name appears among those considered to head the arts section of the Institut des Questions Juives. CDJC, documents CXIII and XXII–13.

25. This view ignores the particularly distasteful personality to whom this talent belonged.

26. It started in February 1941 at 125,000 and doubled during its first year, according to Ory, *Collaborateurs*, p. 117.

27. Rebatet, "Entre le Juif et le pompier," *Je suis partout* (14 February 1941).

28. Rebatet, *Décombres*, p. 20.

29. Brasillach, *Notre avant guerre*, p. 186.

30. Rebatet, *Décombres*, p. 28.

31. Ibid.

32. Pryce-Jones, *Paris in the Third Reich*, p. 262.

33. Lucien Rebatet, "Chas Laborde et Utrillo," *Je suis partout* (2 May 1942).

34. Rebatet, *Décombres*, chaps. 25 and 26, offers unusual insight into the early days of the government in Vichy, confirming the view that Vichy was fragmented, but that extremists like Rebatet were not welcomed by Pétain.

35. Rousso, "Collaborer," p. 57.

36. Lucien Rebatet, "Le Salon des artistes français," *Je suis partout* (9 May 1942).

37. Ibid.

38. Lucien Rebatet, "Obscène Bourgoisie," *Je suis partout* (21 May 1943).

39. Lucien Rebatet, "Entre le Juif et le pompier," *Je suis partout* (14 February 1941).

40. Lucien Rebatet, "L'Offensive des pompiers," *Je suis partout* (12 March 1941).

41. Lucien Rebatet, "De Giotto au Sieur Poughéon," *Je suis partout* (5 May 1944).

42. Ralph Soupault, "Un Scandale permanent, l'offensive de la peinture juive," *Je suis partout* (7 February 1942). Rebatet was not beyond naming in his columns the hiding (or meeting) places of political refugees and Jews. The Café Cintra in Marseille, where, among others, Breton and his Surrealist friends had often met in the winter of 1940–41, was a case in point. In "Marseille la juive," *Je suis partout* (30 August 1941), Rebatet denounced the Café Cintra as a place where Jews met, and called it an active center of Gaullist agitation. According to Lottman, a witness at the trial of Rebatet testified in 1945 that shortly after the publication of the article "the witness was indeed arrested with forty-three other persons, some of whom were deported by the Germans and never heard from again" (Lottman, *Purge*, p. 141).

43. Lucien Rebatet, "Les Indépendants," *Je suis partout* (21 March 1941): 7. "On peut reconnaître que *Le Baptème* de l'Espagnol Creixames est d'un peintre dont la couleur violacée se souvient beaucoup trop encore de la pourriture Juive."

44. Lucien Rebatet, "Les Arts et les lettres," *Je suis partout* (25 November 1943): 4.

45. Rebatet, *Décombres*, p. 568. The postwar edition of the memoirs was renamed *Les Mémoires d'un fasciste*. See introduction by J. J. Pauvert, p. v.

46. Kogan had emigrated from Germany because of Hitler, and had become a regular exhibitor in French salons. In *Je suis partout* (12 May 1941), Rebatet, learning that in Toulouse "along with painters from Normandy, Berry, and Provence, [Chagall] the

imagist of the Russian ghetto was exhibiting," complained that nothing had been done to "dejudaize French art" in the free zone.

47. Palmier, *Expressionisme comme révolte*, p. 119.

48. Foucault, *Birth of the Clinic*, p. 158. Foucault calls attention to the word "degeneration" as indicative of a change in the scientific language on morbidity that occurred in the nineteenth century.

49. Rebatet, "La Femme dans l'art contemporain," *Je suis partout* (17 January 1942).

50. Dérouet, "Beaux Arts," p. 397.

51. Lucien Rebatet, "Des plus grands peintres aux autres," *Je suis partout* (25 February 1944).

52. Lucien Rebatet, "Le Salon des Tuileries," *Je suis partout* (23 June 1944).

53. See Dorival, *Etapes de la peinture française contemporaine*, pp. 256–64. In *Les Maitres de demain*, a collection headed by Francis Carco, monographs on Roland Oudot (text by Pierre Gueguen), Kostia Terechkovitch (text by Louis Cheronnet), Raymond Legueult (text by René Jean), André Planson (text by Jacques de la Prade), and Maurice Brianchon (text by Robert Rey) came out during the Occupation.

54. Lucien Rebatet, "Le Salon des Tuileries," *Je suis partout* (23 June 1941). "On s'aperçoit que presque tous les Français même les moins habiles sont d'instinct des harmonistes." Rebatet's admiration for the Salon des Tuileries did not extend to the other salons. The Salon des Indépendants, where the least academic artists, including foreigners, had shown in the 1930s, Rebatet found too egalitarian, and he objected that ersatz Jewish art done by non-Jewish artists was shown there. "The liquidation of the Indépendants must be inscribed into the cleansing program of France," he wrote (21 March 1941). As for the Salon d'Automne, he found the presentation of art there far too confusing. "It resembles a department store, a Uniprix where the buyers have mixed up, for mere fun, all of the articles" (11 October 1941). It is undeniable from looking at the lists of exhibitors that the Salon des Tuileries, where on and off between 1941 and 1944 so many major French artists "showed their cards" (Rebatet's expression about three who in 1943 stopped showing their cards, namely Derain, Matisse, and Dufy), was an important institution and that, in spite of obvious absences and omissions, it managed to sustain a certain level of liveliness. Even Fautrier and the non-French Magritte showed there one year during the Occupation.

55. Ibid.

56. Lucien Rebatet, "A travers les galeries," *Je suis partout* (5 March 1943).

57. Lucien Rebatet, "Chas Laborde et Utrillo," *Je suis partout* (2 May 1942).

58. Kléophas Bogailei (a pseudonym) was an artist from central Europe who may have given to the Gestapo the names of Jewish colleagues during the Occupation years. He was executed shortly after the Liberation. Interview with Jacques Bazaine.

59. Lucien Rebatet, "Le Salon des Tuileries," *Je suis partout* (23 June 1941).

60. Vlaminck, *Portraits avant décès*, p. 179.

61. Lucien Rebatet, "Les Paysagistes de Corot à nos jours," *Je suis partout* (3 July 1942).

62. Lucien Rebatet, "Des plus grands peintres aux autres," *Je suis partout*, (25 February 1944).

63. French National Archives, F 12 9631.

64. Lucien Rebatet, "A travers les galeries," *Je suis partout* (5 March 1943).

65. Galerie Charpentier, *Un Siècle d'aquarelle*.

66. Lucien Rebatet, "Les Paysagistes de Corot à nos jours," *Je suis partout* (3 July 1942).

67. Galerie Charpentier, *Fleurs et les fruits*.

68. Lucien Rebatet, "Les Paysagistes de Corot à nos jours."

69. Lucien Rebatet, "Fleurs et fruits depuis le romantisme," *Je suis partout* (8 January 1943).

70. Roger Lannes, "Air de Paris," *Fontaine* (October 1942): 467.

71. It became known as the Prix de !a Fondation Américaine.

72. Oudot, Legueult, and Brianchon had done sets and costumes for *Griselidis* in 1922, for *La Naissance de la lyre*, and for *Valses nobles et sentimentales* in 1938 at the Paris Opéra.

73. *Répertoire des ballets de l'Opéra de Paris*, Bibliothèque et Musée de l'Opéra, Paris.

74. André Derain, interviewed by Pierre Lagarde, *Comoedia* (21 June 1941).

75. *Hitler's Table Talk*, pp. 439–40. The failure of the reform of art schools and curriculums in Nazi Germany and the failure of the show of new German art in Munich are being investigated by Karl Otto Werckmeister of Northwestern University.

76. Debu-Bridel, *Résistance intellectuelle*, p. 63.

CHAPTER 3

1. Before World War II, there had been two museums for modern art, one devoted to French art in the Palais du Luxembourg, and the other to foreign schools at the Musée du Jeu de Paume. During the 1930s, two structures for art were commissioned by the French government along the Quai de Tokyo. One wing was going to be a national museum of modern art, the other the city of Paris's own museum of modern art. Although a retrospective of French art had been held there during the Paris World's Fair in 1937, no art had yet been installed permanently, as the imminence of war had sent the art patrimony into hiding in the French provinces.

2. These matters are amply documented in Cassou, *Pillage*, and in Valland, *Front de l'art*. See below, chap. 4, note 46.

3. See Hautecoeur, *Beaux Arts en France*, p. 200; Hautecoeur, "Evacuation," p. 3; Valland, *Front de l'art*, pp. 5, 17; also see Cassou, *Vie pour la liberté*, p. 131. Fearing Nazi incursions into the French art patrimony, French officials, starting in the summer of

1938, had made plans for the evacuation of art, archives, and libraries from Paris. As the chateaux in which much of the art had been hidden wound up in the occupied zone, a second hasty departure took place to regions left in the free zone of France, such as the Dordogne. The chateau de Montal belonging to Robert de Billy became "a bastion for the defense of artworks."

4. L'Action Artistique à l'Etranger was (and still is) an arm of the French Ministry of Foreign Affairs for the dissemination of French culture abroad. During World War II its director was Michel Florisone. For more details see Bertrand Dorléac, *Histoire de l'art*, pp. 282–85.

5. Huyghe, *Contemporains*, p. 108. Dorival wrote in *Etapes de la peinture française contemporaine*, p. 296: "Après l'armistice de 40, un seul parti restait aux Français, semble-il: ressaisir toutes leurs forces pour aller de l'avant. Tenir n'eut pas suffi; pour ne pas disparaitre il fallait agir, foncer devant soi, non seulement pour se reconquérir, mais aller plus loin que soi même. Et c'est ce qu'ils firent, dès 1940." Christian Zervos wrote in *Cahiers d'art* (1944): 7: "Ça a été pour eux une cause d'étendre encore leur vue et leur experience . . . d'atteindre à une plus grande force." Francastel, in *Nouveau Dessin, nouvelle peinture*, p. 14, writes: "En ce moment même en pleine catastrophe, une évolution importante de la peinture [se prépare]."

6. Although Bazaine names twenty-one names, the show is associated with twenty artists. Pignon says that twenty artists were contacted and only twelve responded. See Debu-Bridel, *Résistance intellectuelle*, p. 224.

7. Wilson, "Les Jeunes Peintres de tradition française," in Centre de l'Art et de Culture Georges Pompidou, *Paris-Paris*, p. 106.

8. Ibid.

9. In Gaston Diehl's manuscript, "Le Nouvel art contemporain, 1925–1944," the group Témoignage is said to have included Bertholle and Le Moal at the 1937 Salon d'Automne of Lyon; Bertholle, Le Moal, and Manessier at the group show of 1938 at Galerie Matière in Paris; and Bertholle and Le Moal in 1939 at Galerie Matières et Formes. Témoignage apparently published a review titled *Le Poids du monde*.

10. Severini, *Témoignages*, p. 144. The discussions on art took place in 1932, leading to a manifesto drafted by Pierre Courthion on which the entire group could never agree. At the outset, the group included Chagall, Beaudin, Gilles de la Tourette, Gino Severini, Edmond Humeau, Ivan Denis, Pablo Gargallo, Suzanne Roger, and Pierre Courthion.

11. Ibid., p. 244. *Union sacrée*, or "sacred union," designates the type of government to which France resorted during World War I in order to mobilize all existing political forces toward victory over Germany. Pétain-style *union sacrée* was short on anti-German feelings but did attempt a corporatist union of conflicting economic interests so as to avoid class warfare.

12. Diehl, "Nouvel art contemporain." From the Témoignage manifesto: "Héritiers surchargés, nous ne pouvions que donner des Témoignages de ferveur, de reconnaissance, de foi, d'où le titre de ce groupement spontané. . . . Nous croyons pouvoir écrire

que le groupe Témoignage est la première manifestation collective qui, en parfaite con-
naissance de cause des mouvements cubistes et surréalistes (l'influence de ces deux mouvements est sensible chez chacun de nous) soit sortie du feu brillant mais désespéré de
l'art contemporain pour mordre à l'espoir des réalités essentielles."

13. Bertrand Dorléac, *Histoire de l'art*, pp. 176–79. Jean Bazaine, in an interview
with the author, 5 May 1984, said that the name chosen for the exhibition at Galerie
Braun, Peintres de Tradition Française, had been Bazaine's idea, an idea that "was to
lend itself to many confusing interpretations" but which "had had no other purpose than
to mislead the German authorities so as to allow us to realize our project." By this, Bazaine meant that with the word "tradition," which smacked of Pompierism, the show
connoted safe art rather than the daring art he believed his show represented. Bazaine
also said that the Galerie Braun had been selected because "it was the only one willing
to take a chance. The others were scared." Braun was an art-publishing house that belonged to Alsatian Jews and hence was in all likelihood closed or "Aryanized."

14. Winock, *Histoire politique de la revue Esprit*, p. 222.

15. Loubet del Bayle, *Non-Conformistes*, p. 411.

16. Sénarclens, *Mouvement Esprit*, p. 287.

17. Sternhell, *Ni droite ni gauche*, p. 299.

18. Sénarclens, *Mouvement Esprit*, p. 114.

19. Namer, "Politique artistique," p. 270.

20. Clark, "Jackson Pollock's Abstraction," p. 176.

21. Jean Bazaine, "La Peinture bleu-blanc-rouge," *Comoedia* (11 January 1943). For
a short bibliography on the semiotics of the colors of national flags, see Gage, "Color in
Western Art," p. 519 n. 8.

22. Bosson, *Jean Bazaine*, p. 42.

23. Debu-Bridel, *Résistance intellectuelle*, p. 229.

24. Diehl had been a journalist at the Popular Front weekly *Marianne* in the 1930s and
became the art critic at *Aujourd'hui* during the Occupation years. He was extremely active during that time, writing numerous catalogue essays, organizing exhibitions, and
writing books on modern art. He contributed to the revival of Fauvism, writing on the
Fauves and interviewing them (including Matisse). His anthology of texts on art,
Problèmes de la peinture, was published by *Confluences* in 1945. His history of modern
art, "Le Nouvel Art contemporain, 1925–1944," exists only in galleys, which the author
kindly let me read.

25. Galerie de France, *Douze Peintres d'aujourd'hui*.

26. Galerie Berri Raspail, *Etapes du nouvel art contemporain* 7, p. 1.

27. Jean Marc Campagne, "Esprit, es-tu là?" *Les Nouveaux Temps* (19 February
1942). Campagne, an astute critic, no doubt ruined his career by associating his name
with the catalogue essay that accompanied the show of Hitler's favorite sculptor, Arno
Breker, held in Paris in 1942. Alfred Courmes is an interesting artist whose use of popular culture imagery anticipates Pop. Ino, Marembert, and Janin formed the group Gravi-

tations, whose manifesto of Transhylism expressed "a desire to remain in touch with the earth, with life, while producing an art of magic."

28. Jacques Bazaine, interview with the author, 19 June 1984.

29. Francis Gruber died in December 1948. He was considered by his peers the most promising painter of his generation. A retrospective of his work was held at the Bern Kunsthalle in 1976.

30. A Communist, Magritte must have decided that the context was wrong. The photographic Surrealism of Magritte (like that of Pierre Roy) was acceptable in the collaborationist circle of Jean Marc Campagne.

31. The "anciens" paid homage to were the Le Nain brothers, Poussin, Delacroix, Daumier, Cranach, Carpaccio, Chardin, Bosschaert, the masters of the Ecole de Fontainebleau, Breughel, Seurat, and Cézanne. (Galerie Friedland exhibition catalogue.)

32. De Gaulle's and Churchill's memoirs are classic sources. In addition to *Vichy France* by Paxton, whose focus is on one country, Gilbert, *Second World War*, contains the most up-to-date bibliography on the subject. See also the controversial *Wartime* by Paul Fussell.

33. Paxton, *Vichy France*, p. 292.

34. Ibid., p. 280.

35. Jean Marc Campagne, "Le Salon d'Automne," *Les Nouveaux Temps* (10 October 1943). "Là, cette année se pressent les champions de la couleur pure, du cubisme sans cesse renaissant, de l'imagerie décorative, tant et si bien que le public est fondé à croire que les seules tendances vivantes de la jeune peinture se résolvent en des essais décoratifs où la plupart du temps la notion de l'humain est étrangement absente."

36. Lucien Rebatet, "Révolutionnaires d'arrière garde," *Je suis partout* (29 October 1943).

37. Paxton, *Vichy France*, p. 281.

38. Ibid., p. 282.

39. The idea that abstract-art-as-the-expression-of-freedom is an ideological construct has been examined by Serge Guilbaut in *How New York Stole the Idea of Modern Art*.

40. See Musée National d'Art Moderne, *Exposition inaugurale* (Paris, 1942), exhibition catalogue in appendix 4.

41. Galerie de France, *Fauves*, essay by Gaston Diehl.

42. Diehl, *Fauves*, p. 3.

43. Two radio interviews are partially transcribed in Barr, *Matisse*, appendix i, p. 562. "Si vous êtes libre Dimanche 27 Juin a 14 heures 30, prenez la TSF, à Radio diffusion nationale, Nice. Vous entendrez un reportage sur Nice dans lequel je parle et mes oiseaux chantent," Matisse wrote Bonnard. See Clair, "Correspondance Matisse-Bonnard," p. 98; N. G. Vedrès, "Chez Matisse, parmi ses toiles et ses Oiseaux," *Le Rouge et le bleu* (6 June 1942); and Vedrès, "Matisse réclame la disparition du concours de Rome," *Le Rouge et le bleu* (11 July 1942). An interview with Francis Carco and a conversation with Aragon have been transcribed in Flam, *Matisse on Art*. Also see Gaston Diehl, "Henri

Matisse, le Méditerraneen nous dit," *Comoedia* (7 February 1942); and Diehl, "Avec Matisse le classique," *Comoedia* (12 June 1943).

44. The dealers Fabiani, Pétrides, and Maeght, the French collectors Henri Joly and René Herscher, and the German collector Von Hirsch are named as owners of paintings reproduced in *Matisse: Seize peintures* of 1943. One of the reproduced works, *La Conversation*, was apparently sold to Georges Renand. It came up at the Drouot auction of the Georges Renand collection, 20 November 1987.

45. Diehl, "Henri Matisse, le Méditerranéen nous dit," *Comoedia* (7 February 1942).

46. Ibid. Pierre Levy, a collector who visited Matisse in Nice, also speaks of exotic birds, flowers, and tropical plants in *Artistes et un collectionneur*, p. 94.

47. Diehl, *Peintres d'aujourd'hui*, p. 26.

48. Clair, "Correspondance Matisse-Bonnard," p. 95. "Heureusement, l'armistice est arrivé," Bonnard exclaimed in his letter.

49. Ibid. The armistice had caught him at Ciboure near St.-Jean-de-Luz. He made his way to Nice during the summer of 1940, going to St.-Gaudens (for three weeks), then Carcassonne, then Marseilles, before reaching his destination (Fourcade, *Henri Matisse*, p. 277).

50. Ibid., p. 99.

51. Ibid., p. 54.

52. Besides the *Thêmes et variations* book and the *Pasiphaé* illustrations, mention is made of illustrations for a book of Ronsard poems (*Florilèges des amours de Ronsard*, 1948) and for poems by Charles d'Orleans (*Les Poèmes de Charles d'Orleans*, 1950). Other collaborative works and other projects underway during the war were *Le Signe de vie*, by Tristan Tzara; *Visages*, by Pierre Reverdy; *Lettres Portugaises de Marianne d'Alcaforado*, which came out in 1946; *Jazz* and *Repli*, which came out in 1947.

53. Gaston Diehl, "Henri Matisse, le Méditerraneen nous dit," *Comoedia* (7 February 1942).

54. Gaston Diehl, "Avec Matisse le classique," *Comoedia* (12 June 1943).

55. See *Le Rouge et le bleu* (11 July 1942). See also a letter from Matisse to Bonnard (undated): "La date du 8 Novembre 1941 marquera dans les annales intellectuelles et artistiques de la France: c'est celle du rassemblement sur son propre sol de cette élite que constituent les prix de Rome, dit *l'Eclaireur de Nice* de ce jour. . . . Mais, mon cher Bonnard, parlons sérieusement" (Clair, "Correspondance Matisse-Bonnard," p. 63).

56. One hypothesis for this omission is the fact that jazz music was considered decadent and was forbidden during the Occupation years. However, if the title *Jazz* did not come to Matisse until the spring of 1944, as proposed by Isabelle Monod-Fontaine in Centre National d'Art et de Culture Georges Pompidou, *Oeuvres d'Henri Matisse*, this hypothesis does not stand up.

57. See Matisse, "Lettre à Pierre Matisse," 1 September 1940, in Fourcade, *Henri Matisse*, p. 278.

58. Quoted in Université de St.-Etienne, *Art face à la crise*, p. 389n. See also Kenneth Silver, "Matisse's Retour à l'Ordre," *Art in America* (June 1987).

59. Jünger, *Second Journal parisien*, p. 173.

60. Heller, *Allemand à Paris*, p. 120.

61. Paul Strecker, "Visage Français: Considérations sur le Salon d'Automne," *Pariser Zeitung* (24 October 1943, weekly edition).

62. Speer, *Inside the Third Reich*, p. 184.

63. So much for the contention that the French art scenes were being protected by independent-minded German intellectuals.

64. Michel Tapié, in *Art autre*, brought together an international roster of its practitioners—among them Fautrier, Dubuffet, and Jackson Pollock.

65.
> Ta voix chante les longs passages
> de nos frères multipliés
> aux horizons, et leurs messages
> noués au tronc des peupliers;
> les noirs charniers des jours torrides,
> les faims, les soifs insatiables
> et le rire égrèné des sables
> déchirant des poitrines vides;
> Les griffes, l'emprunte des dents
> les flammes vacillantes dans
> la nuit des plaines infinies
> la sèche attente des momies
> le dur et blanc dédain des os
> l'ordre frappe sur la peau morte
> roulant aux ailes des échos,
> et tout ce que la terre porte.

66. See Lesbats, *Cinq Peintres d'aujourdhui*; Bertrand Dorléac, *Histoire de l'art*, pp. 182–84.

67. Charbonnier, *Monologue du peintre*, p. 83.

68. Jean Bazaine, "La Jeune Peinture," *Nouvelle Revue française* (June 1942).

69. Bazaine, *Notes sur la peinture d'aujourd'hui*, p. 51.

70. Ibid., p. 49.

71. Jean Bazaine, "La Jeune Peinture," *Nouvelle Revue française* (June 1942).

72. *New York Times*, art page (13 June 1943).

73. Ibid.

74. Speaking of the funeral, Valéry told his and Bergson's peers at the Académie Française: "It was necessarily a summary affair. No procession, no words. Only a silent homage on the part of some thirty persons" (*Institut, Séances Publiques*, Discours 1941). Bergson was a Jew who, although he had converted to Catholicism, had declared his Jewishness at the Paris préfecture.

75. Bazaine, *Notes sur la peinture d'aujourd'hui*, p.73. When I interviewed Bazaine in 1984, he told me of having met his American peers at the Carnegie International after the war. Whereas he felt a strong affinity with Baziotes, the chaos of Pollock's art had no impact on him whatsoever. "Expressionism and Surrealism are an abomination," he told me, "and further they are totally alien to the French sensibility." Bazaine's *Notes* are a denigration of Surrealism in its visual manifestations. In particular, Bazaine makes the point that "between conscious and unconscious states there is no sufficiently powerful barrier to prevent an exchange between the two" (p. 25). What Bazaine's esthetics suggest is that the barrage against Surrealism noted by Guilbaut in his *How New York Stole the Idea of Modern Art* (à propos of Motherwell and Clement Greenberg in New York around 1943–44) was not unique and existed as a strong force in French art as well.

76. Salon des Jeunes Indépendants, Club des Architectes de l'Exposition de '37, sponsored by the Société des Amateurs d'Art et Collectionneurs. Diehl, "Nouvel Art contemporain."

77. Jean Bazaine, "Chronique de la peinture," *Nouvelle Revue française* (August 1941): 225.

78. Oskar Schlemmer, "Letter of Protest to Minister Goebbels," 25 April 1933, in *Letters and Diaries*, p. 310.

79. See illustrations of pencil sketches in Baltimore Museum of Art, *Oskar Schlemmer*, p. 33.

CHAPTER 4

1. "L'Art au service de la Révolution Nationale" (unsigned editorial), *Atalante* 1 (1941): 6.

2. The Salon de la Société des Artistes Français was the oldest of the salons, and the most conservative. In 1939 there were 1,600 painters and 272 sculptors. During the Occupation years, the numbers never exceeded 700 painters and 134 sculptors (Salon catalogues, 1939 to 1944). The withdrawal was probably an expression of distaste for the direction taken by the Société after the armistice.

3. "Le Point de vue d'*Atalante*" (unsigned proclamation), *Atalante* 1 (1941): 7.

4. Henri Bouchard, "Le Passé de nos salons" (unpublished speech, date uncertain [March 1941?]), Musée Atelier Bouchard Archives, p. 12. Bouchard succeeded Albert Tournaire, who resigned under pressure from the occupying forces.

5. Ibid.

6. Hinz, *Art in the Third Reich*, p. 10.

7. "L'Art au service de la Révolution Nationale," *Atalante* 1 (1941): 6.

8. The Prix de Rome was awarded for painting, sculpture, or architecture yearly to students being graduated from the Ecole des Beaux Arts. A two-tiered competition, it was so competitive and prestigious that students tried for it as many as five times. The immediate reward was a sojourn of several years at the Villa Médicis in Rome.

9. The Académie des Beaux Arts has a long history, dating from the seventeenth century, when it was called Académie Royale de Peinture et Sculpture. It was abolished during the French Revolution and replaced by the Institut, founded in 1795, which combined intellectuals and artists. During the Napoleonic era, the Académie des Beaux Arts reappeared as one of five sections that made up the Institut. In 1942, Maurice Denis was president of the Académie des Beaux Arts, Henri Le Riché was vice president, and Adolphe Boschot was *secrétaire perpétuel*. There were thirteen painters, eight sculptors, six architects, three etchers, six composers, nine *académiciens libres*, and seven foreign associate members listed for that year.

10. It is worth noting that when Claude Roger Marx spoke of the possibility of even more progressive artists joining the Académie, the names he thought of were Bonnard, Despiau, Maillol, and Segonzac (*La Renaissance* [March 1938]: 68). None of the Roger Marx candidates was voted in during the Occupation years, even though nine new members, Lejeune, Dupas, Montézin, Biloul, Tournon, Pougheon, A. Perret, Désiré Lucas, and Niclausse, became academicians during that time.

11. Vallier, *Henri Bouchard*. Vauxcelles, a Jew, was forced to use this pseudonym to be able to publish.

12. Marie Bouchard, interview with the author, 12 May 1984.

13. Moulin, *Marché de la peinture*, p. 267.

14. The Delaunays, Fernand Léger, Henri Laurens, and Jacques Lipchitz were among the recipients. See Musée d'Art Moderne de la Ville de Paris, *Paris 1937: Cinquantenaire*.

15. Mady Menier, "A propos de la sculpture dans la section Française de l'expo de 1937," in Université de St.-Etienne, *Art face à la crise*, p. 101.

16. See Bernadette Contensu, in Musée d'Art Moderne de la Ville de Paris, *Paris 1937: L'Art indépendant*, p. 16.

17. Laurent, *Arts et pouvoirs*, p. 140.

18. Bouchard, "Apollon," p. 11. Compare this sum with the thirty-eight thousand francs paid to Laurens for his sculpture (Mady Menier, in Université de St.-Etienne, *Art face à la crise*, p. 101).

19. Bouchard, "Apollon," p. 10.

20. Boime, *Academy and French Painting*, p. 15.

21. Hinz, *Art in the Third Reich*, p. 16.

22. Lehmann-Haupt, *Art under a Dictatorship*, p. 98.

23. Brenner, *Politique artistique*, p. 179.

24. Cointet-Labrousse, *Vichy et le fascisme*, pp. 75–77. Paul Marion is described by the author as "a bona fide Fascist who was to place at the service of his latest convictions the talent he had acquired within the Communist party where he had held important responsibilities in the agitation and propaganda section."

25. Bertrand Dorléac, *Histoire de l'art*, p. 42.

26. An inventory of these cult objects appears in Museé d'Histoire Contemporaine, *Propagande sous Vichy*, pp. 272–79.

27. Fauré, *Projet culturel de Vichy*, p. 159.

28. Not much is known about this "Parc de la Petite France," to be called Parc Philippe Pétain, which was supposed to be inaugurated in 1947 between Le Bourget and St.-Denis, north of Paris, on the site of a slum. Le Corbusier was apparently approached about creating a "green city" at the edge of this park. According to an undated press report, it was to have a model farm and three artificial lakes connected to a river to be used by water sports buffs. The park would have included several sports facilities at the periphery and gardens with walking paths as in the Bois de Boulogne.

29. Guyot and Restellini, *Art Nazi*, p. 176.

30. Maxime Real del Sarte won the Grand Prix National in 1921.

31. Mme Chapaux-Letulle had been a student of Landowski and Mengue.

32. Pierre Traverse and Robert Busnel had been students of Injalbert. François Cogné had studied with Barrias.

33. Jacques Baschet, "Le Salon," *L'Illustration* (16 May 1942).

34. Catalogue and album of the Salon de la Société des Artistes Français, 1942. Montézin died in 1946. One such harvest scene brought 40,100 francs at auction on 8 May 1942 (Bénézit).

35. Louis Hourticq, "Art Français et Europe Nouvelle," *L'Illustration* (18 July 1942).

36. Jacques Baschet, "Le Salon," *L'Illustration* (16 May 1942).

37. Bouquillon, born in Douai in 1908, was a student of Injalbert and Bouchard. A "Sociétaire des artistes français," he received a silver medal in 1933 and the Prix de Rome in 1934.

38. Hautecoeur, *Considérations sur l'art d'aujourd'hui*, p. 85.

39. CDJC, document XCVI–80. One Vichy delegate substituted for de Brinon, the French ambassador to the German Occupation authorities in the occupied zone, the other for Vallat, Commissaire Général aux Questions Juives. There was also a delegate of the prefect of police. Jacques Lesdain, from *L'Illustration*, and Buscher, the representative of the German ambassador, Otto Abetz, were also at the opening.

40. See French National Archives, Paris, 68 A J 312. See also Bizardel, "Statues parisiennes."

41. See "Adolf Hitler, Speech Inaugurating the 'Great Exhibition of German Art 1937,' Munich," reprinted in part in Chipp, *Theories of Modern Art*, pp. 474–82.

42. Lottman, *Pétain*, p. 236.

43. Arno Breker, interview with the author, 25 July 1984.

44. Aside from Hitler's, Goering's, and other German leaders' personal interest in artworks, particularly those belonging to Jews, the redressing of alleged wrongs committed by the French against the German art patrimony since the sixteenth century turned out to be at the root of these maneuvers. For details, see the Kummel report that contains the list of artworks from foreign museums that the Third Reich intended to repatriate to Germany.

45. In light of article 56 of the Hague treaty on the protection of national art treasures in times of war, the French governments in office in 1938 and 1939 might well have chosen to let artworks belonging to the French state stay in place, or follow the advice of Louis Hautecoeur to have them stored in local underground quarries (the Val de Grace and the Observatoire in particular) to protect them against bombings. Instead, comprehensive plans for the eventual removal of art from locations deemed dangerous for their security were made by the fine arts administration under Georges Huisman, the director since 1934 (Huisman had replaced Emile Bollaert), as if there were good reasons to suspect that, in the event of a German invasion, the Nazis might not honor the Hague treaty. Hautecoeur's solution was based on the commonly held view that the main threat to the art patrimony was an air war against civilian targets (see Paret, *Makers of Modern Strategy*, p. 630). The Huisman solution responded to fear of an air war and to the possibility of looting and—in the case of modern art deemed degenerate in Hitler's Germany—destruction. (The unusually large participation of French museums in the 1939 New York World's Fair was also intended to shelter art in case of war, as was Picasso's New York retrospective in 1939.) Beginning in the summer of 1938, according to a note dated 22 July 1938 (French National Archives, F 21 4904 3j) from the Ministry of Education and Youth to Georges Huisman, the sum of ten million francs was allocated for measures of protection. Evacuation plans for art, archives, and libraries were made. Curators and specialists in historic monuments scouted the countryside in search of suitable chateaux that could eventually shelter not only national art treasures but the personnel responsible for their maintenance. Chateaux on the Loire river were taken over. The Chateau de Chambord, a state-owned property, became a central depot, and the ultimate destination of art collections was to be determined from there. Lists were made, choices of art proposed, discussions held, crates readied, artworks numbered. "For modern artworks, those by dead artists whose talent is recognized, and those by living artists marking a date in their career were selected," said Louis Hautecoeur in a radio speech on the evacuation of French artworks ("Evacuation," p. 3). Two days before the Munich conference, the first convoys of trucks had left the Louvre headed for Chambord. After the Munich lull, the evacuation process resumed and, from 27 August to 28 December 1939, some thirty-seven convoys transported masterpieces of painting and sculpture from the Louvre first to Chambord and then to some fifteen other locations. "Convoy no. 29," says Rose Valland, a Louvre curator, in her memoirs, "contained the Venus de Milo" (*Front de l'art*, p. 5). Prefiguring, though in a far more orderly fashion, the slow, relentless flight that would take place on those same roads in June 1940, convoys of trucks escorted by museum personnel in private automobiles headed south. Included in the move were a number of noted private art collections of old masterpieces and of modern art, those of eminent Jews and of others with contacts in the art bureaucracy, who suspected that they might have to flee Paris in a hurry. According to Jean Cassou, briefly a curator for modern art under Pétain, the painter Fernand Léger, at the suggestion of Huisman, had also placed a group of his paintings in the trust of national museums (Cassou, *Vie pour la*

liberté, p. 131). Peggy Guggenheim's holdings were, however, rejected as too recent and controversial. Still, it was the first time in French history that a protective policy for works of art and documents had been articulated in terms of actual geographic movement on such a massive scale.

46. Almost instantly, however, a group of trucks accompanied by male and female curators and guards moved southward again. Chaperoned by René Huyghe, head of the paintings department at the Louvre, the convoy reached the southern town of Montal, where a chateau belonging to Robert de Billy had been readied for the precious cargo. In the words of Rose Valland, whose actions against German incursions also saved important works of the French art patrimony, "Until the end of the war, this center of protection offered itself as a bastion for the defense of art works" (Valland, *Front de l'art*, p. 17). Such a bastion proved necessary, for no sooner had the armistice been signed than ordinances concerning the French art patrimony were promulgated in Berlin. By the ordinance of 30 June 1940, the Führer declared that all artworks, those belonging to the French state and those belonging to private individuals, especially to Jews, were to be "put under the protection" of the German military as a pledge for peace negotiations: "The Führer . . . has given the order to place in safekeeping—besides art objects belonging to the French state—art objects and historic documents belonging to individuals, notably Jews. This measure is not an expropriation but a transfer under our protection which will serve as a pledge for peace negotiations." See Cassou, *Pillage*, document 1, p. 77. By ordinance of 15 July 1940, all art objects worth over one hundred thousand francs were to be declared by their owners. No art was to be moved except with the authorization of the German military (document 4, pp. 80–81). Teams of German officials showed up at the depots in occupied France and made inventories of the works still there. In Paris, too, inspections accompanied by inventories went on. Jean Cassou reports on the strange sight of Picasso in his bank vault in Paris, witnessing the examination by a German officer of old Picassos and of works from his personal art collection (Cassou, *Vie pour la liberté*, p. 162). Meanwhile, German military guards were posted at each of the remaining depots in occupied France and, on 31 August 1940, Ambassador Otto Abetz was ready to send to Berlin complete documentation on all the paintings found in the occupied zone (Valland, *Front de l'art*, p. 32).

47. For a description of the role of the Einsatzstab-Reichsleiter Rosenberg (EER) and its infamous leader, Alfred Rosenberg, in the looting of art collections belonging to Jews throughout Europe, see "A Legacy of Shame: Nazi Art Loot in Austria," *Art News* (December 1984), pp. 54ff. See also Rorimer and Rabin, *Survival*, and Howe, *Salt Mines and Castles*.

48. These matters have been amply documented in Jean Cassou, *Pillage*, and in Valland, *Front de l'art*.

49. For Pétain's initial measure concerning the property of those who left France, see "Loi du 23 Juillet 1940 relative à la déchéance de la nationalité à l'égard des Français qui ont quitté la France," *Le Journal officiel* (24 July 1940), article 2. For the use of this law

by French officials to prevent Jewish property from leaving France, see document 40 in Cassou, *Pillage*, dated Paris, 28 February 1941. See also id., document 46.

50. Georges Preuilly, "Les Echanges artistiques franco-espagnols," *Comoedia* (2 August 1941).

51. For the *Diane au Bain* request and several others successfully or unsuccessfully fended off by M. Hautecoeur's fine arts department, see Hautecoeur, *Beaux Arts en France,* p. 206.

52. See Bertrand Dorléac, *Histoire de l'art*, chap. 2.

53. Pierre du Colombier, "Un Statut des musées de France," *Comoedia* (13 December 1941).

54. Hautecoeur, *Beaux Arts en France*, p. 154. The clause dealing with the percentage on art was done away with; a "commission d'achats et de commandes" was put in charge of all purchases and commissioning of all art except that falling under the label of charitable "secours." L'Entr'aide aux Artistes was solely responsible for aid to needy artists. It also distributed canvas, colors, and oils.

55. See "Lois et Décrets—Journal Officiel 1 July 1940 to 31 December 1942," *Revue des beaux arts de France* (August–September 1943). This publication was the official periodical of the fine arts department of the Ministry of Education and Youth.

56. Bertrand Dorléac, *Histoire de l'art*, p. 50.

57. Ordinarily, a new French government inherits from its predecessors an administrative corps that has served successive governments irrespective of political changes. In the case of the Vichy administration, this situation did not hold, at least with regard to bureaucrats who were affected by the decree of 17 July 1940, which "permitted the state to remove any civil servant without formality during the next three months, if he seemed likely to be an 'element of disorder, an inveterate politician, or incapable.'" Paxton, in *Vichy France* (p. 156), says that this initial measure was directed against political opponents. On 3 October, the first measures against Jews in public service would be promulgated by Vichy. The Pétain government chose not only new ministers but also administrators to replace those affected by the July decree. Georges Huisman, head of the fine arts administration, was one of them. Hautecoeur and Huisman had often been at loggerheads during the Popular Front era and the preparation for the orderly exodus of French artworks. During the exodus, Huisman had gone first to Chaumont; then he had rejoined the French government officials and parliamentarians who embarked on the ship *Massilia*, headed for North Africa, a decision that in the eyes of Pétain and his supporters was tantamount to desertion. Meanwhile, Hautecoeur had escorted a convoy of artworks to the Abbaye du Loc Dieu in the Aveyron and there received a phone call from Mireaux, former editor in chief at *Le Temps*, briefly the minister of education under Pétain. Thus he went to Vichy and was hired. During the four years of the Vichy regime, Hautecoeur would find Pétain on his side whenever conflicts arose with Pétain's ministers, and with Laval in particular. Finally, in March 1944, a Laval protégé was appointed in his place. Hautecoeur was a graduate of the Ecole

Normale and an amateur painter, and in 1940 had already published *Considérations sur l'art d'aujourd'hui* (1929), *L'Architecture française au XIXème siècle* (1925–26), *L'Architecture en Bourgogne* (1929), *De l'architecture* (1938), and *L'Architecture française de la Renaissance à nos jours* (1940). *Littérature et peinture en France du XVIIème au XXème siècle* and *Histoire de l'architecture classique en France, 1495–1900*, volume 1, would come out in 1942. Working under him were Jacques Jaujard, Director of French national museums and of the Ecole du Louvre, Pierre Ladoué, head curator of the Department of Modern Art, and Bernard Dorival, who became curator at the Musée National d'Art Moderne (Jean Cassou, hired by Hautecoeur for that post, was immediately fired for his Communist affiliations). These names appear on the masthead of *La Revue des beaux arts de France*. For more details, see Bertrand Dorléac, *Histoire de l'art*, pp. 282–85.

58. Hautecoeur, *Beaux Arts en France*, p. 149. This text is a memoir and an attempt to justify the author's role as head of the Department of Fine Arts under Vichy.

59. See Musées Nationaux, *Louvre*. Vuillard died on 21 June 1940 at the house of his friend Hassel, according to Hautecoeur, *Beaux Arts en France*, p. 211.

60. Other acquisitions mentioned in Bertrand Dorléac, *Histoire de l'art*, p. 56, include stained glass by Rouault and *Mother and Children* by Bonnard. She also mentions the important donation of Paul Jamot in 1939.

61. See *Pierre Ladoué, "Les Achats et les commandes de l'état aux artistes en 1941," La Revue des beaux arts de France* (October–November 1942): 23–30, and Ladoué, "Les Achats et les commandes de l'état aux artistes en 1942," *La Revue des beaux arts de France* (April–May 1943): 213–22. See also Stéphane Galanon, "L'Autoroute de l'Ouest," *Les Beaux Arts: Journal des arts* (10 April 1942).

62. French National Archives, F 21 4760, box 6.

63. Pierre Imbourg, "Pour Une politique des beaux arts: Une importante interview de Georges Hilaire, secrétaire général des beaux arts," *Comoedia* (4 August 1944).

64. French National Archives, F 21 4759, box 5.

65. "Le Discours du Maréchal à Commentry," *Le Nouvelliste* (2 May 1941).

66. "Le Voyage du Maréchal Pétain dans le Limousin," *Le Figaro* (17 June 1941).

67. "Le Premier Mai, à Thiers, le Maréchal Pétain s'est adressé aux artisans de France," *Métiers de France* (May 1942).

68. Ibid.

69. Mayet, "L'Artisanat, l'art, et le gout," *Métiers de France* (May 1943).

70. Ibid.

71. Hautecoeur, *Considérations sur l'art d'aujourd'hui*, p. 57.

72. The inventor of the emblem was a jeweller named Capt. Rober Ehret, who was recommended to Dr. Ménétrel by an officer in Pétain's entourage named Bonhomme. The insignium distributed to those deemed worthy of the Order of the Francisque was a brass pin enamelled in blue, white, and red and adorned with ten gold stars.

73. See *La Revue des beaux arts de France* (December 1942–January 1943): 120.

74. Fauré, *Projet Culturel de Vichy*, p. 158.

75. Silverman, *Art Nouveau in Fin de Siècle France*, p. 278.

76. See Abetz, *Pétain et les Allemands*, p. 19.

77. See Veillon, *Mode sous l'Occupation*.

78. Mainardi, *Art and Politics*, p. 20.

79. Such a view coincided with the corporatism of Gustave Thibon and René Gillouin whereby "artificial class groupings that emphasized conflicting interests ... would be replaced by 'natural' economic units whose members all shared a common interest in the success of their products." See Paxton, *Vichy France*, p. 211.

80. Léger, "The Machine Aesthetic—The Manufactured Object—The Artisan and the Artist," reprinted in Tate Gallery, *Léger and Purist Paris*, pp. 88–89.

81. Hautecoeur, *Beaux Arts en France*, p. 159.

82. Silverman, *Art Nouveau in Fin de Siècle France*, p. 132.

83. Ibid., p. 278.

84. Hautecoeur, *Considérations sur l'art d'aujourd'hui*, p. 72.

85. Museo Nacional de Arte Moderno, Exposicion de artistas franceses contemporaneos, n.p.

CHAPTER 5

1. Lincoln Kirstein, "Letter from France," *Magazine of Art* (January 1945): 3–6.

2. Sartre, "Paris sous l'Occupation," in *Situations III*, p. 37, reprinted from *La France libre* (London, 1944). "Le mal était partout tout choix était mauvais et pourtant il fallait choisir et nous étions responsables."

3. John Pudney, "A Glimpse in Sunlight," *The New Statesman and Nation* (16 September 1944), Barr Archives, Picasso IX.A.3.

4. G. H. Archambault, "Picasso, the Painter Who Defied the Germans, Finds Himself the Hero of a Revolutionary Mood," *New York Times* (29 October 1944), Barr Archives, Picasso IX.A.3.

5. John Groth, "Letter from Paris," *Art Digest* (1 December 1944), Barr Archives, Picasso IX.A.3. The article identifies John Groth as follows: "John Groth, while covering the European Theatre of Operations as a war correspondent for the Marshall Field Publications (*The Chicago Sun, Parade*) was the first American artist to enter Paris with the armies on Liberation Day. He returned to Montmartre and Montparnasse, visited the galleries and art shops, met the artists, and interviewed Picasso."

6. Gladys Delmas was secretary to the United States commission for the Paris International World's Fair in 1937 and worked for the Museum of Modern Art in Paris and New York. She was married to a Parisian publisher, according to the biographical note that accompanied her article.

7. Gladys Delmas, "A New Group of French Painters," *Magazine of Art* (November 1945): 268–71.

8. René Huyghe, "Letter from Paris: Conflicting Tendencies," *Magazine of Art* (November 1945): 272–73.

9. All sorts of rumors had circulated concerning Picasso since the time of the Phony War: he had been interned, fled to Mexico incognito, and so forth.

10. Alfred Barr, Jr., "Picasso 1940–1944: A Digest with Notes," *Museum of Modern Art Bulletin* 12, no. 3 (January 1945).

11. Emlen Etting, "First Report from Paris," *Art News* (1 November 1944), Barr Archives, Picasso IX.A.3. Emlen Etting was the correspondent for *Art News*, whose editor described him thus: "Eyewitness to the first fabulous week of Paris' liberation, versatile Emlen Etting spoke with artists, young and old, saw their work, investigated what was happening to theatre, movies, photography and brings his first-hand report exclusively to *Art News*."

12. Rousso, *Syndrome de Vichy*, p. 319.

13. Ibid., p. 21.

14. René Huyghe, "Letter from Paris: Conflicting Tendencies," *Magazine of Art* (November 1945): 273.

15. Huyghe, *Contemporains*, p. 108.

16. Hautecoeur, *Littérature et peinture*, p. 306.

CHAPTER 6

1. Stein Archives, Yale University, 76.

2. Stein, *Wars I Have Seen*.

3. Stein Archives, Yale University, 78.

4. Ibid., 81.

5. Arp, *Jours effeuillés* (author's translation). Sophie entered a Resistance network that sent Jewish children to Switzerland by clandestine means.

6. Meyer, *Marc Chagall*, p. 431.

7. The American Rescue Committee, presided over by Frank Kingdom in New York, was under the patronage of Eleanor Roosevelt. Varian Fry had been a journalist prior to his assignment in Marseilles as the American representative there of the committee. In *Surrender on Demand*, he explains how he had been chosen to go to France during his summer vacation to rescue a small number of intellectuals and artists recommended to him by various refugees already living in New York, and also by Alfred Barr from the Museum of Modern Art. Discovering the magnitude of his task, he decided that he must stay. He stayed thirteen months (and would have stayed even longer, had he not been expelled by the Vichy government), organized an office in Marseilles, and hired interviewers to screen the cases of desperate and not-so-desperate individuals who came knocking at the office's doors. He found illegal means for those he felt were most exposed to get out through secret passes over the Pyrenees; the name of Fry's book, *Surrender on Demand*, is based on a line from article 19 of the Armistice Commission, which

stipulated that any person wanted by the Germans was to be "surrendered on demand" by the Pétain government. An homage to Varian Fry will inaugurate the Holocaust Memorial Museum in Washington, D.C., in 1993.

8. Ibid., p. 432. In an unpublished manuscript, Varian Fry, describing the behavior of refugees, says that "if some of the refugees in France were overanxious, others were not anxious enough," and that Lipchitz and Chagall had to be prodded to leave (Fry Archives, Columbia University).

9. Wols, born Wolfgang Schulze in 1913 in Dresden, went to Paris in 1933. A photographer in the 1930s, he began to draw and to paint at that time, but it was as an internee in a French camp that he discovered himself as an artist. A leading figure of postwar art ("Tachism"), he died of alcoholism in 1951.

10. Galerie Michel Couturier, *Wols, Cités et navires*.

11. Fry, *Surrender on Demand*, p. 113. The house, some kind of Provençal *mas*, three stories high, has since disappeared. The rent was paid by Mary Jayne Gold, the "angel" of the Emergency Rescue committee. Gold, described by Daniel Bénédite as tall, attractive, blond, intelligent, and rich, was an expatriate from the American Midwest (Bénédite, *Filière marseillaise*). Gold explains in her memoirs, *Crossroads, Marseilles*, how, stranded in Marseilles, she became involved with the Rescue Committee practically from the start of its Marseilles operations, not only for the high motive of saving intellectuals and artists but because she was having an affair with a local thug. There were eight bedrooms. Though their population changed over the months, the initial occupants were Varian Fry, Daniel Bénédite and his wife, Theo, Jean Ghemaling, Mary Jayne Gold, and Miriam Davenport, all of whom worked for the Emergency Rescue Committee, plus the Victor Serge and Breton families. Max Ernst, Victor Brauner, Peggy Guggenheim, and Consuelo de Saint-Exupery stayed there on occasion. Davenport screened the artists. Fry's right-hand man, Daniel Bénédite, a former employee at the prefecture in charge of *permis de sejour* (identity cards for refugees), was recommended to Fry by Gold (who had been a guest at Bénédite's mother's Paris pension) and went to work for the committee starting about 20 October 1940 (*Filière marseillaise*). Jean Ghemaling, unbeknownst to the others, was in a Resistance network. He was imprisoned, liberated, and survived the war. At the Emergency Rescue Committee headquarters, this team was assisted by several German refugees to whom Daniel Bénédite rightly pays homage in his book.

12. Lambert, "Jeu de Marseille," p. 66. Hérold went to France from Romania in 1933 and was befriended by Breton. The Galerie Henriette had given him a show before the war. He died in 1986.

13. Consuelo de Saint-Exupéry, *Oppède*, pp. 34–36. She was the wife of the pilot-novelist Antoine de Saint-Exupéry, who preceded her to New York. Described by Bénédite as vivacious, cheerful, energetic, and "chirping" like a bird from the islands (*Filière marseillaise*, p. 212), she was alleged to be the niece of the then-president of San Salvador. Her memoirs, written after her arrival in New York in 1942, are not the easiest

of sources, for she has changed the names of the protagonists. She apparently left Air Bel after three weeks and eventually rejoined her husband in New York.

14. Breton, "Le Jeu de Marseille," in *Clé des champs*, p. 66. Breton's presence in Marseilles after a stint in the army attracted other Surrealists, and his residency at Air Bel, the home of the Emergency Rescue Committee hierarchy, gave him a renewed aura among old friends, including some—like Max Ernst—with whom he had broken off relations.

15. The first to mention this project is Mellow in *Charmed Circle*, p. 445. In her monograph *Picabia*, p. 419, Borras writes: "Gertrude Stein too (Picabia was the other) seemed to agree with the stand taken by the Marshal. . . . A few months later she was to begin the English translation of Pétain's *Paroles aux français: Messages et écrits, 1934–1941*, which was never published." The manuscripts are at Yale.

16. How, from the number of refugee intellectuals in the Marseilles area, Breton and Victor Serge with their respective families were chosen to live in the company of the Committee hierarchy is explained by Daniel Bénédite in *Filière marseillaise*. Bénédite had first befriended Victor Serge when the latter had needed a new *permis de séjour*, and Bénédite, then an official at the Paris prefecture, had succeeded in getting him one. He had taken a great liking to the man and would say of Victor Serge that "he personifies a humanist Socialism, deeply opposed to that which Stalinism perverted and betrayed." The two men met again in Marseilles, where, after numerous misadventures, both had landed, "Serge terribly down, at the end of his rope, feeling like an outcast in this reactionary country." Bénédite then invited him to live at Air Bel. According to Bénédite, no sooner had Serge heard of his good fortune than he brought to Bénédite's attention the case of André Breton, who was also in need of living quarters for himself and his family. After some hesitation, Bénédite agreed to speak to "the others"; "his euphoria [at having found a place to live] made him convincing and André Breton was unanimously accepted." Breton and Serge knew the intellectual milieu of refugees well, unlike Fry and the other Americans in Marseilles, and hence became useful advisers.

17. Serge, *Mémoires d'un révolutionnaire*, p. 385.

18. Saint-Exupéry, *Oppède*, p. 40.

19. Arp Archives, Meudon. The Arps let slip two opportunities to leave, one by the *Nyassa* and the other by the *Serpa Pinto*. See letters to the Arps in the Arp Archives from (a) the American Consulate, signed L. Bradford, dated 5 May 1942, (b) the Centre Américain de Secours, June 1942, and (c) the Union des Sociétés Israelites de Toulouse, 11 August 1942. The last communication has led to the conclusion that Taeuber-Arp was a Jew. Rather, there were several groups active in aiding people emigrate that functioned interdenominationally, according to a source at the Fondation Arp.

20. Clébert, *Mythologie d'André Masson*, p. 64.

21. Ballard, "Passage à Marseille d'André Breton, 1929–39," in Musée Cantini, *André Masson*.

22. *Cahiers du sud* was a prewar intellectual periodical from Marseilles, sympathetic to the literary aspects of Surrealism. In the 1930s, it had published some of the writings of German refugees, including Walter Benjamin. During the war, it continued publication, harboring spiritualist tendencies close to those at *Esprit*. It was also a book-publishing venture. Jean Ballard, born in 1893, edited the review through the Occupation years and until his death in 1973.

23. This double portrait is a mine of intuitions and interpretations. See, for example, Lanchner, "André Masson: Origins and Development," in Museum of Modern Art, *André Masson*, p. 158.

24. Letter from Otto Freundlich to Kosnick Kloss dated 22 August 1940, Freundlich Archives, Pontoise. Freundlich had lived in France permanently since 1924. His first sojourn dated from 1909–14, when he was a neighbor of Picasso and Max Jacob at the Bateau Lavoir. He was not a French citizen. Kosnick Kloss was an artist in her own right, and not a Jew.

25. Young-Bruehl, *Hannah Arendt*, p. 159. In *Surrender on Demand* (p. 16), Fry confirms how "you would get them prepared with their passports and their visas in order and a month later they would still be sitting in a Marseilles café waiting for the police to come and get them."

26. Among the architects were Georges Brodovitch, whose brother had in fact discovered the site, Jean Auproux, Albert Conil, Paul Herbé, and Jean Le Couleur. (Letter from Auproux to the author dated 14 April 1987.) The painter Zelman died of tuberculosis in 1942 (ibid.).

27. Saint-Exupéry, *Oppède*, p. 73.

28. The painting, which Hérold thought had disappeared, has been found. It was among the works assembled for the exhibit *"La beauté convulsive": Exposition André Breton* at the Pompidou Center in Paris (25 April–26 August 1991).

29. Bernard Zehrfuss, "Oppède essai de renaissance," *Cahiers du sud* (February 1941): 68.

30. Ibid., p. 69.

31. Ibid.

32. The area from Cassis to Sanary on the Mediterranean coast had become a home for German refugees long before the war. Meier Graefe and Walter Bondy were the catalysts. See Guindon, "Sanary sur mer: Capitale Mondiale de la Littérature Allemande," in *Camps en Provence*.

33. Silver, "Jewish Artists in Paris, 1905–1945," in *Circle of Montparnasse*, p. 53.

34. Musée Regional d'Art et d'Histoire, *Six Artistes de Grasse*. Stahly was in danger because, although a German-Italian by birth, he had fought in the French army and was "wanted" by both the German and Italian police. Susi Magnelli, interview with the author, 24 May 1984.

35. Susi Magnelli, interview with the author, 24 May 1984.

36. Musée Regional d'Art et d'Histoire, *Six Artistes de Grasse*, Magnelli text.

37. Susi Magnelli, interview with the author, 24 May 1984.

38. Blatter and Milton, *Art of the Holocaust*, p. 124.

39. In Centre d'Art et de Culture Georges Pompidou, *Arp*, Christian Dérouet explains that the technique of *papiers froissés* involved complicating the relatively simple cuisine of collage by "nourishing them with gouache and India ink which thicken, butter and sugarcoat the paper sheets," a language which he finds befitting the time of shortages when they were done (p. 40).

40. Jean, *History of Surrealism*, p. 333.

41. Musée Regional d'Art et d'Histoire, *Six Artistes de Grasse,* Magnelli text.

42. Haftmann, *Marc Chagall*, pp. 89–90.

43. In Clébert, *Mythologie d'André Masson*, p. 62. Masson explains: "Le paysage était marécageux (il y avait des marais autour de l'endroit que j'habitais) et dans ce paysage s'érige, avec une solidité flagrante, une sorte de tour en forme de femme."

44. Webb, *Hans Bellmer*, p. 129.

45. Meyer, *Marc Chagall*, p. 433.

46. Lafranchis, *Louis Marcoussis*, p. 183. "A few of these drawings and gouaches are humble observations of nature. Others disguise under an outwardly innocent realism a strange force that rejoins the Surrealism of his Brittany landscapes. Some landscapes also are among those drawings from 1940–1941."

47. Tanning, *Birthday*, p. 53: "It was dark in the brick oven. Drawing was harder than digging, but then, you see, you were *required* to draw. They wanted their portraits, the vain posturing officers of Les Milles." Who could have guessed that the portrait genre, which, according to Kenneth Silver (*Circle of Montparnasse*, pp. 42–44) flourished among the Montparnasse artists in the 1920s, would be put to such a use during World War II?

48. Max Jacob, a Jew converted to Catholicism, lived in a convent at St.-Benoit near Orleans in the occupied zone of France. He was arrested as a Jew and died at the camp of Drancy outside Paris in early 1944, just as his friends had finally obtained his release.

49. Musée d'Art Moderne de la Ville de Paris, *200 Dessins d'André Masson*.

50. O'Connor, "Psychodynamics," 171.

51. Ibid., p. 179.

52. Ibid., p. 185.

53. Ibid., p. 201.

54. Quoted by Carolyn Lanchner in Museum of Modern Art, *André Masson*, p. 157.

55. Ibid., p. 155.

56. Bozo, *Victor Brauner*.

57. Alexandrian, *Victor Brauner*, p. 40.

58. Arp, *Jours effeuillés*.

59. Reported in McCabe, *Artistic Collaborations in the Twentieth Century*, pp. 37–38.

60. André Gide lived in Cabris near Grasse before moving to Algeria in 1942.

61. Bénédite, *Filière marseillaise*, p. 125. Bénédite mentions among the visitors Dominguez, Hérold, Brauner, Lam, Max Ernst, the writers Pierre Hébrart and Jean Malaquais, and the actor Sylvain Itkine.

62. Breton, "Le Jeu de Marseille," in *Clé des champs*, p. 66.

63. Photos taken at Marseilles show that indeed almost every Surrealist male was accompanied by a female companion.

64. Lambert, "Jeu de Marseille," p. 65.

65. Gold, in *Crossroads, Marseilles*, p. 252, recalls how one evening Dominguez, whose turn preceded hers, stealthily pulled pubic hair from his crotch and used that in lieu of drawing for that night's game of Exquisite Corpse.

66. Lambert, "Jeu de Marseille," p. 65.

67. Bénédite, *Filière marseillaise*, p. 144.

68. Mabille, "Jeu de cartes surrealistes."

69. In Breton, *Clé des champs*. Breton, who apparently studied the history of playing cards at the library in Marseilles, noted: "Les historiographes de la carte a jouer tombent d'accord pour noter que les modifications qu'elle a subies au cours des siècles ont toujours été liées à de grands revers militaires" (p. 67). And he added "Ce qui ici est récusé par nous de l'ancien jeu de carte, c'est d'une manière générale tout ce qui indique en lui la survivance du signe à la chose signifiée."

70. Of the sixteen new cards, the design for Hegel and Helen Smith (a twentieth-century seer) fell to Brauner; Breton was responsible for Paracelsus; Max Ernst drew Pancho Villa; Hérold did Sade and Lamiel (a female character from an unfinished novel by Stendhal), Masson did Novalis and the Portuguese nun, Dominguez did Freud and Lautréamont, and Lam did Baudelaire and Alice. Of the four aces, Breton did the keyhole of Knowledge, Max Ernst drew the ace of Love, Jacqueline Lamba the wheel of Revolution, Lam and Dominguez the ace of Dream. The joker was Ubu. Lambert, "Jeu de Marseille," pp. 65–66. See Mabille, "Jeu de cartes surrealists."

71. Breton, *Clé des champs*. In his letter of condolences to Breton's widow dated 9 October 1966 (Fry Archives, box 12) Varian Fry recalled with admiration the "gentle-manly behavior" of Breton even in the most "distressing circumstances" and his sense of humor: "Finalement il y avait son inépuisable et son inoubliable sens de l'humour, un sens de l'humour qui n'était jamais noir, mais au contraire toujours prèt à remonter le moral de n'importe qui, même dans les circonstances les plus désespèrées telles que l'étaient les circonstances dans lesquelles nous ètions tous."

72. Another project involving Zelman and Zehrfuss was the redecoration of a villa at Bonnieux with frescoes by Zelman (letter to the author from Zehrfuss, 1 February 1985).

73. Ibid.

74. Jacques Hérold, interview with the author, 17 July 1985.

75. Mentioned in Lanchner's chronology in Museum of Modern Art, *André Masson*, p. 216.

76. Jacques Hérold, interview with the author, 17 July 1985.

77. Guiraud, "Vie culturelle," p. 82.

78. Ibid.

79. Ibid., p. 85.

80. Boris Taslitzky, interview with the author, 20 July 1984.

81. Darmon, *Camp des Milles* p. 27. See also Fontaine, *Camp de concentration.*

82. Webb, *Hans Bellmer*, p. 118. Osmosis of pictorial ideas was common at that time. The idea of symbolic portraits was probably introduced by Masson; the hieratic pose of face cards affected the manner of Brauner who may also have borrowed from Bellmer's dolls for a series of drawings involving strangely limbed figures, the *Palladiste* of 1943 and the sculpture *Nombre*, also of 1943.

83. Musée Regional d'Art et d'Histoire, *Six Artistes de Grasse*, Springer text.

84. Ibid., Stahly text.

85. Lambert, "Jeu de Marseille," p. 66. Wifredo Lam had arrived in Paris from Spain in 1937. Admired by Picasso, he had had a show at the Galerie Pierre, June–July 1939.

86. Musée Regional d'Art et d'Histoire, *Six Artistes de Grasse*, Magnelli text.

87. Letter from Sophie Taeuber-Arp to unknown correspondent dated 17 April, Fondation Arp, Meudon.

88. Arp, *Jours effeuillés.*

89. Delaunay, *Nous irons jusqu'au soleil*, p. 130.

90. Hautecoeur, *Beaux Arts en France*, pp. 88–89.

91. Ibid., p. 149. "Je pus obtenir des Finances de substantielles augmentations de crédit et disposer en 1942 et 1943 d'une dizaine de millions chaque année pour les achats et les commandes. Certes toutes les oeuvres acquises ne furent pas des chef d'oeuvre, en de telles circonstances la philantropie dut parfois primer sur le mécènat."

92. Ibid, p. 21.

93. Guggenheim, *Confessions of an Art Addict*, pp. 77–78. For more information on André Farcy, see Gaudibert, "André Farcy."

94. See Centre d'Art et de Culture Georges Pompidou, *Paris-Paris*, on the Lipchitz controversy, which ended in the removal of the *Prometheus* under pressure of the Paris Conseil Municipal after the closing of the Paris World's Fair of 1937 (p. 58).

95. Solomon Guggenheim, whose New York adviser was Hilla Rebay, also had a Paris contact.

96. Laure de Buzon-Vallet, "Le groupe Témoignage," in Centre d'Art et de Culture Georges Pompidou, *Paris-Paris*, p. 90. The names associated with the Lyons group include Marcel Michaud, the originator of the group Témoignage, André Warnod, a reporter for *Le Figaro*, and Raymond Cogniat, a critic on the acquisitions committee of the fine arts department of the Ministry of Education.

97. Georges Raillard, "Marseille, passage du surréalisme," in Centre de la Vieille Charité, *La Planète affolée*, p. 51.

98. See Fauré, *Histoire du surréalisme sous l'Occupation.*

99. The editor of *Confluences* was Bernard Tavernier, that of *Cahiers du sud*, Jean Ballard. Noèl Arnaud edited *La Main à plume* and refused to abide by censorship procedures; hence the clandestine nature of the little magazine, and the Resistance involvement of most of its participants.

100. "Peindre est une gageure" was reprinted in the British journal *Horizon* in 1943 under the title "Painting Is a Wager." The article, which Masson had discussed in some

detail with his dealer Kahnweiler (see "Correspondence Masson-Kahnweiler: Extraits" in Will-Levaillant, *André Masson*) was also given as an address in amended form at the Baltimore Museum shortly after the artist's arrival in America in conjunction with a show of his work (31 October–22 November 1941). An important piece of writing, it would probably have left a trail of controversy had artistic issues been on people's minds in France at that particular time and had the publication reached a larger public. For one thing, it continued to condemn on various grounds the achievements and beliefs of abstract artists, accusing abstract (geometric) art of "representing unconscious escapism in the face of the contradictions offered by our torn-asunder epoch," and of "resolving these contradictions through the absurd, proclaiming the coming about of pure representation, the abandon of any emotional content, of allusions to reality." Masson accused the practitioners of abstraction of isolating themselves in the "arid realm where indifference reigns." Curiously, in the American lecture, this passage does not appear. As far as the Surrealists' own lack of concern for external reality was concerned, Masson made several points that showed a significant divergence from earlier Surrealist thinking. Now, Masson suggested, neither pure automatism nor the photographic rendering of dreams represented true Surrealist creation. It was all right for an artist to open his or her eyes on to the external world (sometimes) so long as he or she did not see things "in their learned generality but in their revealed individuality." "Est-ce a dire qu'il faudra donner le pas à la réflexion sur l'instinct ou à l'intelligence sur ce qu'il est convenu d'appeler l'inspiration. Nullement: la fusion des éléments hétérogènes mise en jeu par le peintre-poête s'accomplira avec la rapidité fulgurante de la lumière. L'inconscient et le conscient, l'intuition et l'entendement devront opérer leur transmutation dans la surconscience, dans la rayonnante unité." Will-Levaillant, *André Masson*, p. 18.

101. Bénédite, *Filière marseillaise*, and Guggenheim, *Confessions of an Art Addict* It was on one of these visits that the affair between Peggy Guggenheim and Max Ernst began.

102. Susi Magnelli, interview with the author, 24 May 1984. M. Carré bought paintings from Matisse, which explains Carré's visits to the Côte d'Azur.

103. Interview with Michel Hertz, who had been Brauner's assistant, 2 December 1986.

104. Tape of conversation between Eda Maillet and Mrs. Rudolph Gutman, Freundlich Foundation Archives, Pontoise.

105. Letter dated 5 November 1941, Fondation Arp, Meudon.

106. Letter found on a small piece of paper dated 1941, Freundlich Archives, Pontoise.

107. Bénédite, *Filière marseillaise*, p. 219.

108. Guiraud, *Vie intellectuelle*, p. 71.

109. Corti, *Souvenirs désordonnés*, pp. 224–26. In their memoirs, Edwige Feuillère, Dr. Ferdière, and André Roussin also pay homage to the talent and generosity of Sylvain Itkine.

110. Ibid.

111. Guiraud, *Vie intellectuelle*, p. 71. A slogan attributed to André Breton went as follows: Je pense, donc je suis (Descartes)—Je mange, donc je croque fruit (sans carte).

112. Fauré, *Histoire du surréalisme sous l'Occupation*, pp. 166–67.

113. Musée Regional d'Art et d'Histoire, *Six Artistes de Grasse*.

114. Guiraud, *Vie intellectuelle*, p. 72.

115. See Golan, "Moral Landscapes."

CHAPTER 7

1. Hinz, *Art in the Third Reich*, p. 24.

2. Marrus and Paxton, *Vichy France and the Jews*, pp. 54–58. In May 1938, decrees were signed facilitating the expulsion of refugees; in November 1938 a new decree made it possible to strip new French citizens of their citizenship if they were judged unworthy.

3. Ibid., p. 57.

4. Blatter and Milton, *Art of the Holocaust*, p. 256.

5. As harsh as conditions in these camps may sound, they were the least oppressive. "Repressive" camps—Roland Garros, La Petite Roquette prison in Paris, Le Vernet and Rieucros in the provinces—and "semi-repressive" camps such as Gurs were far worse.

6. Lingerat and Narbutt, "Allemagne et les Allemands," p. 60 n. 36.

7. Miscellaneous correspondence, Freundlich Archives, Pontoise.

8. Max Ernst's letter of thanks to Paul Eluard is cited in Centre de la Vieille Charité, *Planète affolée*, p. 73.

9. Otto Freundlich's correspondence with Gacon and the president of the Société du Salon des Indépendants is found at the Freundlich Archives, as is the official notification of his liberation.

10. *Camps en Provence*, p. 54. The following is an excerpt of the letter from Walter Benjamin to Jean Ballard written while he was interned in Nevers, dated 23 October 1939:

Cher Monsieur Ballard,

Je suis certain que vous savez . . . que les réfugiés provenant d'Allemagne se trouvent actuellement dans des camps de rassemblement. C'est mon cas également . . . Paul Valéry et Jules Romains m'ont bien voulu donné leur appui. . . . Adrienne Monnier m'a donné maintes signes d'une amitié indéfectible. Hier encore j'ai reçu la lettre touchante entre tous que Paul Desjardins m'a écrit d'une main, hélas, défaillante. Je serais très heureux de joindre un môt de vous à ces documents précieux.

Walter Benjamin.

On 30 October, Ballard wrote the letter Benjamin asked him for, and around 20 November 1939, the critic was liberated, according to his letter to Jean Ballard dated 20 November 1939 (*Camps en Provence*, p. 56).

11. Barbara Vormeier, "La Situation des réfugies en Provenance d'Allemagne," in *Camps en Provence*, pp. 90–91.

12. André Fontaine, "L'Internement au camp des Milles et dans ses annexes," in *Camps en Provence*, p. 122.

13. Ernst, *Ecritures*, p. 62.

14. Susi Magnelli, interview with the author, 12 April 1984.

15. Carrington's sudden departure after selling the house at St.-Martin-des-Ardèches to an innkeeper with whom she had accumulated drinking debts, Max Ernst's return to the house occupied by a gang of toughs, his arrest once more by the gendarmes, and his flight ("See him running across the hills, hiding in barns, avoiding the roads, the towns. Bridges are the worst. A bridge is guarded at both ends. The sleepy peasant lets him hold the reins, the sleepy horse pulls him across") are narrated in Tanning, *Birthday*, pp. 51–53. In Ernst, *Ecritures*, p. 63, the alleged sale of the country house by Carrington is not mentioned. Ernst says he reoccupied his house, and that he started a second version of *Europe after the Rain* at that time.

16. Miscellaneous correspondence, Freundlich Archives.

17. *Camps en Provence* contains a letter from Walter Benjamin written from Lourdes to Jean Ballard, dated 16 August 1940 (p. 57). In this letter, Benjamin tells Ballard that he is about to go to Marseilles and then to embark for America. Benjamin owed his American visa to the intervention of Max Horkheimer. The possibility of leaving by ship did not materialize, as we know, probably because Benjamin did not have the proper exit visa.

18. Ibid., p. 93.

19. Ibid.

20. Ernst, *Ecritures*, p. 64. "The day before his departure from St.-Martin-des-Ardèches, the mailman would show up with his end-of-the-year calendars."

21. *Camps en Provence*, p. 93.

22. Ibid., pp. 91–93.

23. Ibid., pp. 94–95.

24. Ibid., p. 94.

25. Ibid.

26. Varian Fry, "Operation Emergency Rescue," manuscript, Fry Archives, Columbia University. "But for a while all requests for exit visas had to be referred to Vichy, which was said to refer them to the German authorities" (p. 17).

27. Bénédite, *Filière marseillaise*, pp. 133–34.

28. For Benjamin's suicide, see Grunfeld, *Prophets without Honour*, pp. 248–49; for the death of Carl Einstein, p. 250. The woman who led Walter Benjamin to the Spanish border on foot, Lisa Fittko, published a memoir, which has been translated from German into French under the title *Le Chemin des Pyrénées—Souvenirs, 1940–1941*.

29. Ernst, *Ecritures*, p. 62. Ernst relates how arriving at the border town of Campfranc, he was told by the *chef de gare* that his papers were not in order and were out of

date. In the customs room where he went anyway, he unpacked his belongings, including paintings, which he spread out.

"Bonito! Bonito! Les douaniers sont émerveillés. Les treize voyageurs du train aussi. Reste le chef de gare (français). Il demande à Max de sortir avec lui pour entrer dans son bureau. Là, il lui déclare: 'Monsieur, j'adore le talent. Monsieur, vous avez beaucoup de talent. Je l'admire.' Il lui rend son passeport et l'emmène jusqu'au quai ou se trouvaient deux trains. 'Le premier, explique-t-il est celui qui va vers l'Espagne; l'autre, celui qui rentre à Pau, la préfecture la plus proche.' Et il ajoute: 'Faites bien attention de ne pas vous tromper de train.' Après quoi, il rentre gentiment dans son bureau de contrôle des passeports sans plus se préoccuper du voyageur. Max Ernst a suivi le conseil que le chef de gare n'avait pas ôsé lui donner explicitement: il s'est trompé de train et, dix minutes plus tard, se trouvait en Espagne, à destination de Madrid et de Lisbonne.

30. Marrus and Paxton, *Vichy France and the Jews*, p. 69.

31. Ibid., p. 14.

32. Fry, *Surrender on Demand*, p. 206.

33. See André Fontaine, Jacques Grandjonc, and Barbara Vormeier, "Les Déportations a partir des Milles, Aout–Septembre 1942," in *Camps en Provence*, p. 199.

34. Ibid.

35. Blatter and Milton, *Art of the Holocaust*, p. 260.

36. The visit of Pétain to Marseilles is vividly evoked in at least three memoirs: Fry, "The Marshal Comes to Town," in *Surrender on Demand*; Gold, chap. 20, *Crossroads, Marseilles*; and Bénédite, "La Visite du Maréchal," in *Filière marseillaise*. It is also evoked in Breton, *Entretiens avec André Parinaud*.

37. *Le Figaro* was published out of Lyons in the free zone of France. It is hard to detect at this date the presence of sarcasm in this headline.

38. See Breton, *Entretiens avec André Parinaud*, p. 196. *L'Anthologie de l'humour noir*, ready at the printer, was not allowed to come out. An interview Breton gave to *Le Figaro* was censored and Breton's letters to the newspaper remained unanswered. His poem *Fata Morgana* was also denied publication.

39. Fry Archives, Columbia University, box 8.

40. See "American Seized by French Police," *New York Times* (1 September 1941). The departure of Fry did not put an end to the activities of the committee. Lipchitz, Mane Katz, Zadkine, and Moise Kisling managed to get out, as did Marcel Duchamp, the last client of the Committee. Duchamp sailed out of Marseilles for Casablanca in May 1942, made his way to Lisbon, and took another ship from there to New York.

41. Fry Archives, Columbia University, box 4.

42. Ibid., box 3, letter from Théo Bénédite to Fry, dated 12 March 1942.

43. Ibid., Bénédite report to the Committee, dated 2 September 1941, p. 13.

44. Corti, *Souvenirs désordonnés*, p. 226.

45. Jacques Hérold, interview with the author, 17 July 1985.

46. See Fauré, *Histoire du surrealisme sous l'Occupation*, p. 330.

47. Susi Magnelli, interview with the author, 12 April 1984.

48. Silver, "Jewish Artists in Paris, 1905–1945," in *Circle of Montparnasse*, p. 53.

49. Stein, *Wars I Have Seen*, p. 50.

50. Borras, *Picabia*, p. 423.

51. [Picabia] Mohler, *Für Francis Picabia*, p. 121.

52. Ibid., p. 125.

53. Freundlich Archives.

54. Ibid.

55. Ibid.

56. Ibid.

57. Ibid.

58. Ibid.

59. Ibid.

60. Ibid. In a postwar letter, a Red Cross worker who had met Freundlich after his arrest wrote to Freundlich's common-law wife, Kosnick Kloss, portraying Freundlich with great compassion.

61. Freundlich, "Idées et intuitions d'un artiste," 1942, reprinted in *Deux Sculptures monumentales*. A longer extract follows:

> Cette force d'une ambiance vitale sur-individuelle, que nous sommes partis chercher dans notre jeunesse, s'était dévoilée pour les peintres et sculpteurs, simultanément, dans les deux moyens d'expression. N'oublions pas que nous ne partions ni de la chose, ni de l'objet, ni de l'individu, mais du signe comme symbole de cette ambiance vitale. L'artiste crée à partir de son émotivité humaine et de son activité humaine, qui sont liées dans sa morale de responsabilité vis-à-vis du monde des apparences, exprimée par les moyens de l'art. Les exigences qui se sont presentées à lui l'obligeaient à examiner les moyens conventionnels d'expressions artistiques. . . .
>
> Notre tâche nous imposait de nous défaire du monde des objets, sachant qu'il réapparaitrait quand le grand ordre de l'être' l'entourerait."
>
> Otto Freundlich, St.-Paul-de-Fenouillet (P.O.), 1942.

62. "Eighty Jewish artists from Montparnasse died in the Holocaust," writes Silver in "Jewish artists in Paris, 1905–1945," in *Circle of Montparnasse*, p. 53. A symposium held at Goethe House, April–June 1988, on the German Resistance movement, 1933–1945, revealed the name of yet another German refugee artist victim of the Holocaust, Charlotte Salomon. *Take Good Care of It—It's My Whole Life: Charlotte Salomon 1940–1942* (1986), a film by Hannelore Schafer, features the artist, a German refugee in France, who died at Auschwitz in 1943.

63. Tzara, *Les Ecluses de la Poésie*, in *Oeuvres complètes*, p. 649 n. 38.

CHAPTER 8

1. The Zervos catalogue lists 1,473 paintings and drawings in the period between September 1939 and August 1944. In *Picasso*, Sidney and Harriet Janis propose "3 to 400 as the number of oils on canvas, five times that many sketches and drawings in ink, pencil, oil on paper" (p. 5).

2. "Calling Picasso," *Art Digest* (15 May 1941): 12, shows how poor communications with the Continent were: "Germany having swept into France caught up with the noted Spaniard and for his patriotic activites tossed him, according to reliable reports, into a concentration camp. Since then, a group of Mexican artists and writers, including Rivera and Orozco, have obtained an entry permit to Mexico for Picasso." Barr Archives, Picasso IX.A.3.

3. Françoise Gilot, interview with the author, 15 March 1985.

4. Kahnweiler, *My Galleries and Painters*, p. 118.

5. Steinberg, "The Skulls of Picasso," in *Other Criteria*, p. 205.

6. Rolland, *Picasso et Royan*, p. 33.

7. Sabartès, *Picasso: An Intimate Portrait*, p. 220.

8. See Silver, *Esprit de Corps*, for a thorough analysis of these effects. Silver describes the changes that took place in Picasso's art during World War I, and also tells of the artist's unpopularity for not being in the military.

9. This was Alfred Barr's supposition. In *Picasso*, p. 226, Barr writes: "His stature and worldwide fame as an artist gave him a certain immunity in the eyes of Nazi officials."

10. Gilot and Lake, *Life with Picasso*, p. 38.

11. Barr Archives, Picasso VIII.B.3, letter from Christian Zervos to Alfred Barr, dated 28 March 1945, quoted in full in note 76.

12. Françoise Gilot, interview with the author, 15 March 1985.

13. Dubois, *A travers trois républiques*, p. 132.

14. Ibid., p. 145. Arno Breker was alerted and says that he intervened on Picasso's behalf. As far as Picasso's alleged Jewish ancestry goes, I refer the reader to Picasso's birth certificate in Sabartès, *Picasso: Documents iconographiques*, p. 302.

15. Ibid, p. 151. An alcoholic, Soutine suffered from ulcers and was too weak for the long automobile trip to Paris when he fell ill in his refuge. He died on the operating table at the Paris clinic to which he had been transported.

16. Brassaï, *Conversations avec Picasso*, p. 82.

17. Noèl Arnaud, letter to the author, 16 April 1984.

18. Zervos, *Pablo Picasso*, vol. 11, no. 90 (15 August 1940); no. 91 (1941).

19. Spies, *Sculptures de Picasso*, p. 144.

20. First English translation of Picasso, *Desire Caught by the Tail*, p. 38.

21. John Pudney, "Picasso: A Glimpse in Sunlight," *The New Statesman and Nation* (16 September 1944), Barr Archives, Picasso IX.A.3.

22. Brassaï, *Conversations avec Picasso*, p. 149.

23. Ibid., p. 84. "Ça m'a couté les yeux de la tête."

24. Ibid., p. 65.

25. The play was performed for the first time in January 1944 at the home of Louise and Michel Leiris, with Michel Leiris, Dora Maar, Georges Hugnet, Simone de Beauvoir, and Jean-Paul Sartre in leading roles and Albert Camus as director. See Beauvoir, *Force de l'age*, p. 583. According to Beauvoir, the roles were attributed as follows: Leiris, Gros Pied; Sartre, Bout Rond; Dora Maar, L'Angoisse grasse; Hugnet's wife, L'Angoisse maigre; Zanie Campan, La Tarte; Beauvoir, La cousine. André-Louis Dubois, in *A travers trois republiques*, who attended the performance, has made a slightly different description: "La Tarte—Zanie Aubier, La cuisine [sic]—Beauvoir, ... l'Oignon—Raymond Queneau, Le silence—Jacques Bost, Les rideaux—Jean Aubier, l'accompagnement musical—G. Hugnet" (p. 136). Dubois's list is interesting in emphasizing the culinary aspects of the play. "La cuisine" instead of "la cousine" is a curious slip in light of Picasso's accent.

26. Brassaï, *Conversations avec Picasso*, p. 77.

27. Penrose, *Picasso*, p. 333.

28. Brassaï, *Conversations avec Picasso*, p. 76.

29. Goggin, "Picasso and His Art," p. 166.

30. Malraux, *Corde et les souris*, p. 428.

31. In *Vogue* (15 October 1944), Lee Miller's visit is recorded with photographs and her notes on Picasso: "He said that painting in wartime required [an equal amount of] ingenuity, that it was easier to work seriously and devotedly in wartime isolation than before." Barr Archives, Picasso IX.A.3.

32. Malraux, *Corde et les souris*, p. 428.

33. Quoted in Goggin, "Picasso and His Art," p. 175.

34. Janis and Janis, *Picasso*; see text adjacent to pl. 101.

35. Zervos, *Pablo Picasso*, vol. 12, nos. 290, 317; vol. 13, nos. 22, 169, 247–56, 264–65.

36. Emile Szittya, "Notes sur Picasso," *Courrier des arts et des lettres* (1947): 24.

37. Peter D. Whitney, "Picasso Is Safe," *San Francisco Chronicle* (3 September 1944), Barr Archives, Picasso IX.A.3.

38. Stein-Kahnweiler correspondence, Stein Archives, Yale University, 81.

39. Penrose, *Picasso*, p. 339. It has been said that Maar's half-Jewish origins (her full name was Markovitch) led Picasso to suggest her anxiety through these distortions. His particular fascination with deconstructing her nose may also be imputed to her vaguely Semitic features.

40. Janis and Janis, *Picasso*, p. 28.

41. Steinberg, *Other Criteria*, p. 205.

42. Hugnet, *Pleins et déliés*, p. 28.

43. John Pudney, "Picasso: A Glimpse in Sunlight," *The New Statesman and Nation* (16 September 1944), Barr Archives, Picasso IX.A.3.

44. Peter D. Whitney, "Picasso Is Safe," *San Francisco Chronicle* (3 September 1944), Barr Archives, Picasso IX.A.3.

45. Marquis and Marquise de Masclari, interview with the author, 20 May 1984.

46. Gilot and Lake, *Life with Picasso*, p. 21.

47. Brassaï, *Conversations avec Picasso*, p. 113.

48. Eluard, *Picasso. Tête de l'homme barbu* (1941), *Tête de femme* (1943), *Tête, le baiser, 30 Decembre 1943* (Stedelijkmuseum), and *Nature morte, 23 Juillet 1944* (Musée de St.-Etienne) are mentioned. Paul Eluard was the "turntable" of the Comité National des Ecrivains in the occupied half of France, and adviser to Jean Bruller of Les Editions de Minuit publishing house. Eluard spent many hours writing at Picasso's studio. According to Françoise Gilot, Picasso made financial contributions to Les Editions de Minuit. Georges Hugnet, who ran a gallery bookstore specializing in rare Surrealist materials, entered a Resistance network as soon as he was let out of the army. He and Picasso saw each other at the Flore café and dined regularly together at the Catalan restaurant.

49. Kahnweiler, *My Galleries and Painters*, p. 116.

50. Françoise Gilot, interview with the author, 15 March 1985.

51. This must be the book of Royan drawings that came out in 1947 (*Carnet de Royan, 1940*).

52. See Michèle Cone, "Desnos, Picasso, Girodias, trois comparse de fortune," *L'Herne* (1987): 205–11. Maurice Girodias was the son of the publisher of Obelisk Press, the first publisher of Henry Miller, Lawrence Durrell, Anaïs Nin, and others. At the onset of war, after the death of his father, he took his mother's name (his father's name was Kahane) and founded, at age twenty-one, a new publishing house, Editions du Chêne.

53. The Picasso book was one in a series that included Matisse, Bonnard, and "Cinq Peintres d'Aujourdhui." Robert Desnos, the Surrealist poet, worked at the newspaper *Aujourd'hui* while also belonging to a Resistance network called Agir. He was another Catalan restaurant regular. Desnos was arrested when a young boy carrying tracts was stopped and searched by the Nazis, and revealed, among other names, that of Desnos and his address. He died of typhus at the camp of Teresin moments after the camp had been liberated. Aside from the text in the Picasso book, Desnos also wrote on Picasso for *Confluences*, a publication in the free zone ("Le Buffet du Catalan" [1945]).

54. Brassaï, *Conversations avec Picasso*, pp. 143–44.

55. Jünger, *Premier Journal parisien*, p. 158.

56. Heller, *Allemand à Paris*, p. 118.

57. Both Derain and Vlaminck were among the artists who participated in the trip to Germany organized by the Propaganda Staffel. Vlaminck wrote a virulent article against Picasso in the weekly *Comoedia*. See Epilogue.

58. Peter D. Whitney, "Picasso Is Safe," *San Francisco Chronicle* (3 September 1944), Barr Archives, Picasso IX.A.3. Picasso even insinuated that Georges Braque had "lent himself to Nazi propaganda by giving a show in Munich shortly after the debacle."

59. John Groth, "Letter from Paris," *Art Digest* (1 December 1944).

60. *Newsweek* (24 September 1944), Barr Archives, Picasso IX.A.3.

61. Gilot quotes Picasso as saying, "Il ne faut surtout pas le chercher [contact with Germans]." Interview with the author, 15 March 1985.

62. *Time* (25 September 1944), Barr Archives, Picasso IX.A.3.

63. Quoted in Ashton, *Picasso on Art*, p. 149.

64. "Ein Stuttgarter Samler als Soldat bei Picasso in Paris," in Stuttgart Staatsgalerie, *Picasso*, p. 36. For a full translation of the text, see Cone, "Art and Politics in France," pp. 263–65. The drawing, dated 21 May 1941, does not appear in Zervos.

65. Lottman, *Left Bank*, p. 200.

66. Jünger, *Premier Journal parisien*, p. 159.

67. Heller, *Allemand à Paris*, p. 118.

68. Lottman, *Left Bank*, p. 175.

69. Desnos, *Confidences de Youki*, p. 218.

70. Loiseaux, *Littérature de la défaite*, p. 474. Corroborating Loiseaux's view is an example of Heller's unattributed quote on the subject of Picasso. Heller: "He was then selecting his subjects from ordinary daily life: the roofs from his windows, a chair from his atelier, the Parisian landscapes which the impossibility of traveling forced him to look at with keen attention. Pont Neuf, Pont St.-Michel, the trees, and the quays." It is a longer version of Leymarie, *Picasso* (p. 256): "Sometimes his subjects are the commonplace things of daily life: the view from his window, a chair in his studio, etc."

71. Heller, *Allemand à Paris*, p. 119.

72. Jünger, *Premier Journal parisien*, pp. 158–59.

73. Heller, *Allemand à Paris*, p. 127.

74. In an interview with the author, 28 July 1984, the Communist painter André Fougeron, who was named head of the Purge Tribunal for artists at the time of the liberation of Paris, took full responsibility for engineering the Picasso homage by interceding in turn with Montagnac, president of the Salon d'Automne, with Joseph Billiet, the head of Instruction Publique in the Liberation government, and with Picasso himself.

75. Alfred H. Barr, Jr., "Picasso 1940–1944; A Digest with Notes," *Museum of Modern Art Bulletin* 12, no. 3 (January 1945).

76. Barr Archives, Picasso VIII.B.3 (original letter in French).

28 March 1945

Dear Mr. Barr,

I have just read the notes you have published on Picasso-as-Resistance worker in the Bulletin of the Museum. For the love of Picasso, do not include these notes in a book on this artist. Everything that has been recounted is bad journalism and most

of the time false. The anecdotes are false, the participation of Picasso in the Resistance is false. Picasso simply kept his dignity during the Occupation the way millions of people did here. But he never got involved in the Resistance. Realize that his work itself IS the greatest form of resistance, not only against an enemy but against millions of pretentious imbeciles. The only truth is that at the express request of the ambassador of Franco in France, the Germans let him know that they could not authorize him to exhibit. . . . [He goes on to deny that the young men Picasso drew in August 1944 were resisters.]

Do not let yourself be influenced by nonexisting heroisms. There were heroes in France, but they either paid for it with their lives, or ask that there be silence on their actions. As for painters who retired to the country, they are precisely those who did the best work. Unfortunately, their heroism was much greater than the quality of their oeuvre. In any case, the countryside was primarily the place where many sublime actions took place. I lived in the country, in the forests, among marvelous men whom I will never forget, men of unimaginable generosity who knew how to remain humble, contrary to men of letters and journalists.

77. Barr Archives, Picasso VIII.B.2.

78. Barr Archives, Picasso VIII.B.2. To question 35, "Est-ce que Picasso a fourni des fonds à la République Espagnole pour des avions ou des tanks? Pour des ambulances, pour la nourriture, ou pour quels autres fins?" Sabartès answered, "A ce sujet Picasso répond que c'est son affaire à lui."

79. Barr Archives, Picasso VIII.B.3.

80. Letter from Noèl Arnaud to the author, 16 April 1984.

81. Much has been made of Picasso's alleged indifference to the plight of Max Jacob. Max Jacob's arrest, his friends' efforts to get him out of the French concentration camp of Drancy, and his sudden death, are evoked in Cocteau, *Journal*, pp. 481–82, 484, 486–87. "Max Jacob est mort. C'est effroyable. Hier soir à dix heures Prades me téléphone que sa libération est signée. Ce matin la nouvelle de sa mort nous arrive par le maire de Saint-Benoit." In note 3 Cocteau mentions the "Spanish side and its efforts." (Was Picasso involved?: "Mème conscience d'un inutile succès du coté esgagnol, selon Misia: 'L'ordre de libération que Sert finit par obtenir arriva trop tard' (A. Gold et R. Fizdale, *Misia*, p. 342)." For a fair judgment on this matter, see Richardson, "Interview Barbara Rose," p. 73. See also the exchange between the author and Arianna Stæ opoulos Huffington in the *Atlantic Monthly* (September 1988): 6.

82. Barr Archives, Picasso VIII.B.3.

EPILOGUE

1. *Le Journal officiel*, 31 May 1945.
2. *Le Journal officiel*, 26 June 1946.
3. *Le Journal officiel*, 6 July 1944.

4. Albert Bouquillon, interview with the author, 18 June 1984.

5. The show opened on 5 September 1941 at the Palais Berlitz, a former movie house near the Opéra. Organized by the Institut d'Etudes des Questions Juives, a "Nazi-sponsored propaganda outlet," staffed by French individuals "but with an ample budget from the Germans" and under tight Gestapo control (Marrus and Paxton, *Vichy France and the Jews*, p. 211), the exhibition informed the French public about why Jews could never be French, or for that matter nationals of any country. Differences between the Jewish mentality and physique and their Aryan counterparts were intended to corroborate this view. The show used images as well as texts and graphs to make its points. The walls of one room were hung with panels reproducing in large print the official Vichy legislation toward Jews as it appeared in *Le Journal officiel*; the marshal's emblem was seen atop each panel. In another room, statistics indicated the percentages of Jews in professional activites. In the entrance hall, the triumph of the purely Aryan tradition over the Jewish one was symbolized by a giant image in plaster showing a mother holding an infant, her foot down on the despised possessor of the earth, a hook-nosed Jew with a globe in his arms. The author, the sculptor René Perron (Peron?), was also responsible for the caricatures seen throughout the show, for the cover of the catalogue, and for the immense plaster head of a man, seemingly a caricature of the archetypal Jewish physiognomy. According to *L'Illustration* (September 1941), "In order to illustrate this lesson in anthropology, numerous photographs show the most diverse types of Jews. For contrasting effects, Aryan types—among them the most famous French personalities—face them side by side. . . . There are anonymous images representing French peasants from our provinces . . . , and handsome young men with athletic forms, all of them of the purest Aryan blood." Albert Bouquillon (who was located through a French art magazine announcing an exhibition of his sculpture) conceded in an interview with the author, 18 June 1984, that he needed money at that time and had accepted five thousand francs for allowing the statue to appear in the show.

6. André Fougeron, interview with the author, 28 July 1984.

7. Maximilien Gauthier, "Impressions d'Allemagne: Chez Dunoyer de Segonzac," *Comoedia* (29 November 1941).

8. This information has been pieced together from reports of the trip provided by the travelers to the press.

9. Bernard Poissonnier, "Peintres et sculpteurs français en Allemagne," *Comoedia* (22 November 1942).

10. Maximilien Gauthier, "Impressions d'Allemagne: Chez Charles Despiau," *Comoedia* (29 November 1941).

11. Ibid. "La politique n'est pas plus mon rayon que le vôtre. Qu'il me soit cependant permis de dire que là bas l'Etat s'intéresse passionément aux artistes et qu'un intérèt énorme pour les arts a été déterminé dans le public par certains môts d'ordre venus de haut. On a nettement l'impression qu'un souffle puissant, exterieur à eux mêmes, soutient les artistes allemands."

12. Henri Bouchard, "La Vie d'artiste dans l'Allemagne actuelle," *L'Illustration* (7 February 1942): 85–88.

13. Maximilien Gauthier, "Impressions d'Allemagne: Chez Dunoyer de Segonzac," *Comoedia* (29 November 1941).

14. The Arno Breker catalogue shows the following names on the Comité d'Honneur: Président: Abel Bonnard. Membres: Belmondo, Bouchard, Brasillach, J. Chardonne, A. de Chateaubriant, René Delange (editor of *Comoedia*), A. Derain, C. Despiau, J. C. Dondel, van Dongen, Drieu La Rochelle, A. Dunoyer de Segonzac, O. Friesz, H. Greber, L.Hautecoeur, J. Jannin, P. Landowski, R. Legueult, L.Lejeune, A. Maillol, R. Oudot, A. Perret, M. de Vlaminck, and Jean Walter (the architect and second husband of Mme Paul Guillaume).

15. The painter Georges Papazoff claims to have effected the reconciliation shortly before the trip by having the two artists drink champagne at La Coupole so that Derain would have someone to talk to during the trip. See Papazoff, *Derain mon copain*, pp. 69–84.

16. Sartre, *Situations II*, p. 27.

17. Puig, "Vie misèrable et glorieuse," p. 58.

Samedi 16 Septembre 1944, Maillol revenait de la Citadelle [the jail in Perpignan where his son had been incarcerated]. Vers midi, sortant de chez le docteur Bassères, il errait non loin de la Promenade aux alentours de la maison du docteur Nicolau. Celui-ci parti le matin pour Vernet-les-Bains, avait du revenir à la suite d'incidents automobiles. Ce retour inopiné fit qu'il rencontra Maillol errant comme une âme en peine; il lui proposa de venir passer deux jours chez lui à la campagne ou se trouvait déjâ Raoul Dufy. Une solution automobile ayant été trouvée, Maillol, le Dr. Nicolau et son fils ainé partirent pour Vernet-les-Bains.

Il faisait doux et humide. Vers Prades, il pleuvait légèrement. La route était glissante pour les pneus usés de la petite voiture, une Simca 5 de l'époque. Elle fit un tête à queue au tournant en S qui est à deux kilomètres avant Prades et se retrouva en direction de Perpignan, plaquée contre l'un des beaux platanes qui ont été abattus au printemps 1964. A cette époque, sans voiture et sans essence, les automobilistes étaient rares. L'un d'eux enfin recueillit les blessés. Maillol fut déposé à l'hopital de Prades."

According to this witness, an infection of the prostate led to terminal uremia.

18. Rebatet, *Mémoires d'un fasciste*, vol. 2, p. 106.

19. Hubert Yencesse, interview with the author, 17 February 1984.

20. Breker, *Paris, Hitler, et moi*; Breker, interview with the author, 25 July 1984.

21. Paul Morand also explained in *La Voix française* (12 June 1942) that Breker had had difficult beginnings because he had not looked for official support the way academic artists did.

22. Epting, *Réflexions d'un vaincu*, p. 146.

23. Arno Breker, interview with the author, 25 July 1984.

24. Noèl, *Arno Breker et l'art officiel*, p. 7.

25. Breker provided the author with xerox copies of two articles on the idyllic life of the French and Italian prisoners who worked for him, one from *Signal*, the other from *Reflets*.

26. Interview with Hubert Yencesse, 17 February 1984.

27. See letter of 3 June 1942 from Dr. Zeitschel to Rahn on the subject of an apartment for Prof. Arno Breker, CDJC, LXXI–98.

28. Arno Breker, interview with the author, 25 July 1984.

29. Ibid.

30. Ibid.

31. Bizardel, *Sous l'occupation*, p. 107. Some of the bronze was probably used to cast Rodin's *Gates of Hell* for Hitler's projected museum at Linz.

32. French National Archives 68 A J 312, letter dated 14 October 1944, from the Groupement d'Importation et de la Répartition des Métaux to the Commissariat des Métaux Non Ferreux. Bureaucrats at the Ministry for Industrial Production, under whose orders the purge was conducted, had taken measures to have as much of the statuary as was possible hidden in secret emplacements underground. As soon as France was liberated, a list of the hidden works and their location was divulged so that they could be put back in their proper places. Mayors in the local communities where the threatened statues were found also frequently removed them ahead of the vandals and hid them.

33. By the law of 28 October 1943, a second purge was ordered. Louis Hautecoeur, and the sculptor Henri Bouchard seem to have been the main arbiters of this vandalism. Among the victims were *Gambetta* by Aube, *La Porteuse de pain* by Coutan, and *La Faneuse* by A. Boucher, three works cited by Hautecoeur in his *Histoire de l'Art* (1959) as mediocre works. The sculptor Barrias, who had been Bouchard's teacher at the Ecole des Beaux Arts, was one of those most victimized by the vandalism. His *Victor Hugo* on Place Victor Hugo was ordered removed and Bouchard received the commission (one hundred thousand francs) to make a new effigy of the bard in stone. For details on the statues that disappeared, see Bizardel, "Statues parisiennes," pp. 134–48.

34. Frère, *Conversations avec Maillol*, p. 250.

35. In *Comoedia* (23 August 1941), Henri Rabu points out that the revival of sculpture like Breker's coincided with the revival of state-sponsored architecture, an alliance that had been severed in the early 1900s when sculpture became atelier art, and, says the author, "uncertainties in the search for a style had become translated into abstract forms and expressionism."

36. See Brenner, *Politique artistique du national-socialisme*, on the suppression of art criticism in Nazi Germany. On the orders received by the French press on how to review the Breker show, see Magdalena Bushart, "Arno Breker (geb. 1900)—Kunstproduzent im dienst der Macht" in Akademie der Kunste, *Skulptur und Macht*, p. 157.

37. A booklet published by Breker and Marco (Bonn, 1983) contains an aperçu of the technique and of the tools used by Breker for obtaining his shiny smooth surfaces. Gift of Breker to the author.

38. "Le 'Sculpteur' ouvre les perspectives," *La Gerbe* (28 May 1942).

39. Galtier-Boissière, *Mémoires d'un Parisien*, p. 69.

40. Dossier Breker, Musée Rodin, Paris.

41. *Aujourd'hui* (16, 18, and 24 May 1942).

42. Pierre d'Espezel, "Arno Breker ou le triomphe de la jeunesse," *Je suis partout* (23 May 1942).

43. *La Voix française* (12 June 1942).

44. *Les Nouveaux temps*, where Jean Marc Campagne, the author of the catalogue essay on Breker's show, officiated as art critic, published an interview with Breker on 15 May 1942, an article about Breker on 17 May 1942, another one on 21 May 1942, and also reported on the Press Club reception held in April.

45. *Comoedia* (16 and 23 May 1942). From the Despiau text, these words: "Son souci d'artiste arrivé est de faire à Paris l'hommage de sa gloire. Eh bien, je suis fier d'être le premier à saisir cette main d'artiste tendue."

46. Jean Cocteau, "Salut à Breker," *Comoedia* (23 May 1942).

47. Maurice de Vlaminck, "Opinions libres sur la peinture," *Comoedia* (6 June 1942).

48. Probst, *Arno Breker*.

49. Arno Breker, interview with the author, 25 July 1984.

50. Ibid.

51. Maillol had sixty-one works in the exhibition. See Musée d'Art Moderne de la Ville de Paris, *Paris 1937: L'Art independant*.

52. John Rewald, "Maillol Remembered," in Solomon R. Guggenheim Museum, *Aristide Maillol*, p. 15.

53. Frère, *Conversations avec Maillol*, p. 270.

54. Hans Albert Peters, "Maillol in Deutschland—Deutsche und Maillol," Staatliche Kunsthalle, *Maillol*.

55. Hans Eckstein, "Maillol, au seinem 75 Geburstag," *Die Kunst* 75 (January 1937). *Die Kunst* was published in Munich.

56. Although not pro-Nazi, according to his nephew, Maillol was a royalist and had noble blood on his mother's side. Interview with Maillol's nephew, Yvon Berta, 2 December 1985.

57. Frère, *Conversations avec Maillol*, p. 270.

58. Ibid., p. 253.

59. Akademie der Kunste, *Ausstellung Franzosischer Kunst der Gegenwart*.

60. Lucien Rebatet, in *Je suis partout* (14 February 1942): 6.

61. Fritz Hellwag, "Ausstellung Franzosischer Kunst der Gegenwart," *Die Kunst* (August 1937).

62. Ibid.

63. Breker, letter to the author dated 25 June 1984. "Les artistes Français qui ont recu à l'époque une commande passé sont Aristide Maillol et André Derain. Tous les deux avaient une grande comande pour Berlin. Maillol devait faire une fontaine et Derain un fresque monumental mural."

64. Hubert Yencesse, interview with the author, 17 February 1984.

65. Debu-Bridel, "Edouard Pignon raconte la bataille du Front National des Artistes," in *Résistance intellectuelle*, p. 222.

66. Maurice de Vlaminck, "Opinions libres sur la peinture," *Comoedia* (6 June 1942).

67. André Fougeron, interview with the author, 28 July 1984.

68. Henri Bouchard, "Le Passé de nos salons," Atelier Bouchard Archives. Even Hautecoeur, who was put in charge of preparing the French project for organizing artists into a "chamber," found the issue highly charged. He appointed Bouchard and Maurice Denis to work on the final decree but discovered that they held opposite views. An official decree was signed on 7 July, which announced the creation of a Comité d'Organisation des Arts Graphiques et Plastiques. Denis was listed as president, Jean Dupas the delegate of painters, Landowski the delegate of sculptors. All three were academicians, Dupas of recent vintage, as his nomination in the *Journal officiel* was dated 3 July 1941. Denis, however, resigned immediately, saying "I refuse, and I beg you to discharge me. It is an artist hostile to the reform who has been chosen to head it." Denis was well aware of the political underside of this organization, which could be used to filter out undesirables. Another government project on the same issue was revived when Hilaire succeeded Hautecoeur as Secrétaire Général des Beaux Arts in March 1944. This time, the middle-of-the-road group of artists, starting with Maillol, was solicited. The end of the Occupation came too soon for results to emerge.

69. Reported in *L'Art français* (November 1942).

70. Barr Archives, Picasso VIII, box 3.

71. Debu-Bridel, *Résistance intellectuelle*, p. 222.

72. Goerg, born in 1893, had already shown his antifascist sympathies during the Spanish civil war.

73. This association, which regrouped Communist and non-Communist members, organized exhibitions and lectures. For our purposes, it is worth noting that there were no future collaborators in their midst. Among the names kindly supplied by Pascal Ory in a conversation with the author on 29 March 1988 were those of Lurcat, Tazlitsky, Gromaire, Pignon, Fougeron, Goerg, and Gruber. In 1939, they organized a Picasso exhibition.

74. Four numbers can be consulted at the Bibliothèque Nationale Reserve, Res G 1470.

75. André Fougeron, interview with the author, 28 July 1984.

76. Debu-Bridel, *Résistance intellectuelle*, p. 223.

77. *L'Art français* 2 (1 October 1942).

78. Interview with Noèl Arnaud, 18 August 1984.

79. Debu-Bridel, *Résistance intellectuelle*, pp. 222–23.

80. Boris Taslitzky, interview with the author, 20 July 1984.

81. Mady Menier, "Un Sculpteur devant la crítique, Henri Laurens," in Université de St.-Etienne, *Art et idéologies*, p. 197.

82. Fauré, *Histoire du surréalisme*, pp. 48 and 169, for details concerning her arrest.

83. Goetz, "Ma vie, mes amis (Journal)," p. 302.

84. Hugnet, *Pleins et déliés*, p. 233.

85. André Fougeron, interview with the author, 28 July 1984.

86. Pétridès, *Ma chance et ma réussite*, p. 191. On the Pétridès case during the "épuration" period, see French National Archives, F 12 9631.

87. *Le Rire*, *Gringoire*, and *Ric Rac* published his cartoons.

88. For more on Jean Moulin, a visit to the Fondation Jean Moulin in Bordeaux is suggested. The first volume by Jean Moulin's secretary, Cordier, has now been published. A publication of the Ministère de l'Education Nationale, *Jean Moulin (dossier pédagogique)*, reproduces some of his own artworks. A sibylline telegram addressed by Laure Moulin to Colette Jacques, dated 16 July 1943, marked the end of the gallery venture: "Vendez comme convenu" (chancellerie de l'Ordre de la Libération, *Exposition résistance et déportation*).

89. See "Notes et documents sur les dernières années de V. Kandinsky," *Cahiers du Musée national d'art moderne* 9 (1982): 101 n. 3; 99.

90. Gildo Caputo, interview with the author, 2 February 1987.

91. See Michel, *Paris résistant*, p. 59.

92. Debu-Bridel, *Résistance intellectuelle*, p. 222.

93. This anecdote is mentioned in Hadjinicolaou, *Histoire de l'art et lutte des classes*, p. 92. "Callot pria Sa Majesté, avec beaucoup de respect, de vouloir l'en dispenser parce qu'il était Lorrain."

94. Jacques Bazaine, interview with the author, 19 June 1984.

95. Tzara, "Les Ecluses de la poésie," *Oeuvres complètes*, p. 75.

96. Debu-Bridel, *Résistance intellectuelle*, p. 226.

97. *Les Lettres françaises* (April 1944).

BIBLIOGRAPHY

ARCHIVES

Barr, Alfred H., Jr., Museum of Modern Art, New York.

Bazaine, Jacques, Paris.

Bibliothèque de l'Institut, Paris.

Centre de Documentation Juive Contemporaine (CDJC), Paris.

Diehl, Gaston, Paris.

Fondation Arp, Meudon, France.

French National Archives, (Archives Nationales), Paris. (A J 40, F 21, F12, 68 A J 312.)

Freundlich, Otto, Pontoise, France.

Fry, Varian, Columbia University, New York.

Galerie Charpentier, Paris.

Galerie de France, Paris.

Musée Atelier Bouchard

Musée d'Histoire Contemporaine (formerly Musée des Deux Guerres Mondiales), Paris.

Musée du Louvre, Paris

Stein, Gertrude, Yale University, New Haven.

INTERVIEWS

Arnaud, Noèl, poet and editor of *La Main à plume*. 18 August 1984.

Asse, Geneviève, artist and army nurse during World War II. 7 April 1984.

Barr, Mrs. Alfred H., Jr. 5 October 1984.

Bazaine, Jacques, cousin of Jean Bazaine; owner of Galerie Friedland. 19 and 27 June 1984.

Bazaine, Jean, artist and head of the visual arts section of Jeune France. 5 May 1984.

Berta, Yvon, owner of the Maillol vineyard and nephew of the artist. 2 December 1985.

Bouchard, Marie, daughter-in-law of Henri Bouchard. 12 May 1984.

Bouquillon, Albert, academic sculptor and contributor of The *Perfect Athlete* to the show Le Juif et la France. 18 June 1984.

Breker, Arno, Hitler's official sculptor. 25 July 1984.

Brieu, Alain, bookseller, sheltered by the poet Robert Desnos. 2 June and 16 July 1985.

Campagne, Jean Marc, critic at *Les Nouveaux Temps* and author of the essay on Arno Breker in the Orangerie catalogue. 17 June 1984.

Caputo, Gildo, director of Galerie Drouin as of 1943 and contributor to *Tempo*, the Italian-language newspaper in Paris. 2 February 1987.

Castelli, Leo, part-owner of Galerie Drouin. 5 November 1986.

Courmes, Alfred, painter and lecturer for Jeune France. 17 May 1984.

Diehl, Gaston, critic at *Aujourd'hui*. 28 March, 10 May, and 24 July 1984.

Fougeron, André, artist and active member of the Resistance network of artists. 28 July 1984.

Gilot, Françoise, painter in the Picasso entourage. 15 March and 3 June 1985.

BIBLIOGRAPHY

Hérold, Jacques, Surrealist painter. 17 July 1985.

Hugnet, Mme Georges, widow of the Surrealist poet and bookseller. 12 March 1984.

Jaeger, Jean-François, current director of Galerie Jeanne Bucher. 23 May 1984.

Kellerman, Michel, dealer of André Derain. 23 July 1984.

Lévy, Pierre, collector and friend of André Derain. 16 July 1984.

Littman-Wolf, Peter, artist interned with Max Ernst. 3 May 1987.

Louttre [pseud.], painter and son of Roger Bissière, a muralist in the 1930s. 27 May 1984.

Masclari, Marquise de, wife of the head of publishing at Galerie Charpentier. 20 May 1984.

Namuth, Hans, photographer and visitor at Air Bel and at the Pastré estate. 22 August 1985.

Rohner, Georges, Forces Nouvelles painter. 1 March 1984.

Rolando, Mlle, secretary to M. Nasenta at Galerie Charpentier. 10 May 1984.

Taslitzky, Boris, Communist artist in the Resistance deported to Buchenwald; active in the Maison de la Culture in the 1930s. 20 July 1984.

Yencesse, Hubert, middle-of-the-road sculptor and acquaintance of Arno Breker in the 1930s. 17 February 1984.

PUBLISHED CORRESPONDENCE, AUTOBIOGRAPHIES, JOURNALS, AND REPORTS OF CONVERSATIONS

Arp, Hans. *Jours effeuillés*. Paris: Gallimard, 1966.

Barr, Margaret S. "Rescuing Artists in World War II." Statement dated 7 January 1980. Barr Archives, Museum of Modern Art, New York.

Beauvoir, Simone de. *La Force de l'age*. Paris: Gallimard, 1960.

Bénédite, Daniel. *La Filière marseillaise*. Paris: Clancier Guénaud, 1984.

Bizardel, Yvon. *Sous l'occupation: Souvenirs d'un conservateur de musée, 1940–1944*. Paris: Calman-Levy, 1964.

Bousquet, Joe. *Correspondance*. Paris: Gallimard, 1969.

Brasillach, Robert. *Notre avant guerre*. Paris: Plon, 1941.

Brassaï. *Conversations avec Picasso*. Paris: Gallimard, 1964.

Breker, Arno. *Hitler, Paris, et moi*. Paris: Presses de la Cité, 1970.

Breton, André. *La Clé des champs*. Paris: Sagittaire, 1953.

———. *Entretiens avec André Parinaud, 1913–1952*. Paris: Nouvelle Revue française, 1954.

Buffet-Picabia, Gabrielle. *Aires abstraites*. Geneva: Cailler, 1957.

Carcopino, Jérome. *Souvenirs de sept ans*. Paris: Flammarion, 1953.

Cassou, Jean. *Une Vie pour la liberté*. Paris: Laffont, 1981.

Clair, Jean, ed. "Correspondance Bonnard–Matisse." *Nouvelle Revue française* (July, August 1970): 82–100, 54–70.

Cocteau, Jean. *Journal, 1942–1945*. Paris: Gallimard, 1989.

Corti, José. *Souvenirs désordonnés*. Paris: Corti, 1983.

Debu-Bridel, Jacques. *La Résistance intellectuelle: Textes et témoignages*. Paris: Juillard, 1970.

Delaunay, Sonia. *Nous irons jusqu'au soleil*. Paris: Laffont, 1978.

Denis, Maurice. *Journal III: 1921–1943*. Paris: Colombe, 1959.

Dérouet, Christian. "Vassily Kandinsky: Notes et documents sur les dernières années du peintre." *Cahiers du Musée national d'art moderne* 9 (1982): 84–107. Includes letters.

Desnos, Youki. *Les Confidences de Youki.* Paris: Fayard, 1957.

Dubois, André-Louis. *A travers trois républiques: Sous le signe de l'amitié.* Paris: Plon, 1972.

Epting, Karl. *Réflexions d'un vaincu: Au cherche-midi à l'heure française.* Bourg, France: ETL, 1953.

Ernst, Jimmy. *A Not So Still Life.* New York: St. Martin's, 1984.

Ernst, Max. *Ecritures.* Paris: Nouvelle Revue française, 1970.

Ferdière, Gaston. *Les Mauvaises Fréquentations.* Paris: Simoen, 1978.

Fittko, Lisa. *Le Chemin des Pyrénées: Souvenirs, 1940–1941.* Paris: Maren Sell, 1987.

Flam, Jack, ed. *Matisse on Art.* New York and London: Phaidon, 1973.

Fourcade, Dominique, ed. *Henri Matisse: Ecrits et propos sur l'art.* Paris: Hermann, 1972.

Frère, Henri. *Conversations avec Maillol.* Geneva: Cailler, 1946.

Fry, Varian. *Surrender on Demand.* New York: Random House, 1945.

Galtier-Boissière, Jean. *Mémoires d'un Parisien.* Paris: Table Ronde, 1960–63.

———. *Mon journal pendant l'occupation.* Garas: Jeune Parque, 1944.

Gilot, Françoise, and Carlton Lake. *Life with Picasso.* London: Nelson, 1965.

Girodias, Maurice. *The Frog Prince: An Autobiography.* New York: Crown, 1980.

Goetz, Henri. "Ma vie, mes amis (Journal)." *Cahiers du Musée national d'art moderne* 10 (1982): 296–315.

Gold, Mary Jayne. *Crossroads, Marseilles.* New York: Doubleday, 1980.

Guéhenno, Jean. *Journal des années noires.* Paris: Gallimard, 1973.

Guggenheim, Peggy. *Confessions of an Art Addict.* New York: Macmillan, 1960.

Hautecoeur, Louis. *Les Beaux Arts en France, passé et avenir.* Paris: Picard, 1948.

Hélion, Jean. *They Shall Not Have Me.* New York: Dutton, 1943.

Heller, Gerhardt. *Un Allemand à Paris, 1940–1944.* Paris: Seuil, 1981.

Howe, Thomas Carr, Jr. *Salt Mines and Castles.* New York: Bobbs-Merrill, 1946.

Hugnet, Georges. *Pleins et déliés: Témoignages et souvenirs, 1926–1972.* Paris: Authier, 1972.

Jünger, Ernst. *Premier Journal parisien: Journal II, 1941–1943; Second Journal parisien: Journal III, 1943–1945.* Paris, 1980.

Kahnweiler, Daniel-Henry. *My Galleries and Painters.* New York: Viking, 1971.

Lambert, J.-C. "Le Jeu de Marseille: Entretien avec Jacques Herold." *Opus International* 19–20 (October 1970): 65–66.

Lania, Leo [pseud.]. *The Darkest Hour: Adventures and Escapes.* Boston: Putnam, 1941.

Levy, Julien. *Memoir of an Art Gallery.* Boston: Putnam, 1977.

Lévy, Pierre. *Des Artistes et un collectionneur.* Paris: Flammarion, 1976.

Lingerat, Petra, and Sybille Narbutt. "L'Allemagne et les Allemands dans les *Cahiers du sud* de 1933 à 1942." In *Les Camps en Provence: Exil, internement, déportation, 1933–1942.* Preface by Jacques Grandjonc and Benjamin Fondane. Aix-en-Provence: Editions Al-

inea, 1984. With letters from Walter Benjamin.

Loeb, Pierre. *Voyage à travers la peinture.* Paris: Bordas, 1945.

Malraux, André. *La Corde et les souris.* Paris: Gallimard, 1976.

Marevna. *Life with the Painters of La Ruche.* New York: Macmillan, 1972.

Martin du Gard, Maurice. *La Chronique de Vichy, 1940–1944.* Paris: Flammarion, 1975.

Mourlot, Fernand. *Gravés dans ma mémoire.* Paris: Laffont, 1979.

Musée Cantini. *André Masson.* Marseilles: Musée Cantini, 1968.

Musée Régional d'Art et d'Histoire. *Six Artistes de Grasse, 1940–1943.* Grasse: Musée Régional d'Art et d'Histoire, 1967.

Papazoff, Georges. *Derain mon copain.* Paris: Valmont, 1960.

Paulhan, Jean. *Correspondance avec Francis Ponge, 1923–1968.* Paris: Gallimard, 1986.

Pétridès, Paul. *Ma chance et ma réussite.* Paris: Plon, 1978.

(Picabia) Mohler, Olga. *Fur Francis Picabia: Das Album von Olga Picabia-Mohler.* Notes by Maurizio Fagiolo. Berlin: Brinkmann and Bose, 1981.

Pol, Heinz. *Suicide of a Democracy.* New York: Raynal and Hitchcock, 1940.

Rebatet, Lucien. *Les Décombres.* Paris: Denoel, 1942.

———. *Les Mémoires d'un fasciste.* 2 vols. Paris: Pauvert, 1976.

Robbe-Grillet, Alain. *Le Miroir qui revient.* Paris: Minuit, 1984.

Rolland, Andrée. *Picasso et Royan aux jours de la guerre et de l'occupation.* Paris: Imp. Nouvelle, 1967.

Roy, Claude. *Somme toute.* Vol. 1, *Moi je*; vol. 2, *Nous.* Paris: Gallimard, 1969–72.

Sabartès, Jaime. *Picasso: An Intimate Portrait.* New York: Prentice-Hall, 1948.

Saint-Exupéry, Consuelo de. *Oppède.* New York: Brentano, 1945.

Sartre, Jean Paul. *Situations II.* Paris: Gallimard, 1948.

———. *Situations III.* Paris: Gallimard, 1949.

Schlemmer, Oskar. *Letters and Diaries,* edited by Tut Schlemmer, translated by Krishna Winston. Middletown, Conn.: Wesleyan University Press, 1972.

Serge, Victor. *Mémoires d'un révolutionnaire, 1901–1941.* Paris: Seuil, 1951.

Severini, Gino. *Témoignages: Cinquante ans de reflexion.* Rome: Art Moderne, 1963.

Skilton, John D., Jr. *Défense de l'art européen: Souvenirs d'un officier américain "spécialiste des monuments."* Paris: Editions Internationales, 1948.

Sorlier, Charles. *Mémoires d'un homme de couleurs.* Paris: Pré aux clercs, 1985.

Speer, Albert. *Inside the Third Reich.* New York: Collier, 1970.

Sperber, Manes. *Ces temps là.* Vol. 3, *Au delà de l'Oubli.* Paris: Calmann-Levy, 1979.

Stein, Gertrude. *Wars I Have Seen.* New York: Random House, 1945.

Tanning, Dorothy. *Birthday.* San Francisco: Lapis Press, 1986.

Tzara, Tristan. *Oeuvres complètes.* Vol. 5. Paris: Flammarion, 1982.

Valland, Rose. *Le Front de l'art.* Paris: Plon, 1961.

Vlaminck, Maurice de. *Portraits avant décès.* Paris: Flammarion, 1943.

Will-Levaillant, Françoise, ed. *André Masson, le rebelle du surréalisme: Ecrits*: Paris: Hermann, 1976.

———. "André Masson et le temps des *Cahiers du sud.*" *Cahiers du Musée*

national d'art moderne 10 (1982): 213–46. Includes letters.

Zay, Jean. *Souvenirs et solitude.* Paris: Juillard, 1945.

ART ESSAYS; CONTEMPORARY AND
RETROSPECTIVE STUDIES

Akademie der künste. *Skulptur und Macht: Figurative Plastik im Deutschland der 30er und 40er Jahre.* Berlin: Akademie der Künste, 1983.

Alexandrian, Sarane. *Victor Brauner, l'illuminateur.* Paris: Editions Cahiers d'art, 1954.

Alloway, Lawrence. *Network. Art and the Complex Present.* Ann Arbor: UMI Research, 1984.

Ashton, Dore, ed. *Picasso on Art.* New York: Viking, 1972.

Assouline, Pierre. *L'Homme de l'art: D.H. Kahnweiler, 1884–1979.* Paris: Balland, 1988.

Baltimore Museum of Art. *Oskar Schlemmer.* Baltimore: 1986.

Barr Alfred, H., Jr. *Matisse: His Art and His Public.* New York: Museum of Modern Art, 1951.

———. *Picasso: Fifty Years of His Art.* New York: Museum of Modern Art, 1946.

Bazaine, Jean. *Notes sur la peinture d'aujourd' hui.* Paris: Seuil, 1953.

Bertrand Dorléac, Laurence. *Histoire de l'art: Paris 1940–1944: Ordre national, traditions, et modernités.* Paris: Sorbonne, 1986.

Bizardel, Yvon. "Les Statues parisiennes fondues sous l'Occupation (1940–1944)." *Gazette des beaux arts* (March 1974): 134–48.

Blatter, Janet, and Milton, Sybil. *Art of the Holocaust.* New York: Rutledge, 1981.

Boime, Albert. *The Academy and French Painting in the Nineteenth Century.*

Reprint. New Haven: Yale University Press, 1986.

Borras, Maria Lluisa. *Picabia.* New York: Rizzoli, 1985.

Bosson, Viveca. *Jean Bazaine.* Paris: Galerie Maeght, 1975.

Bouchard, Marie. "L'Apollon du Palais de Chaillot." *Bulletin de l'Association des amis d'Henri Bouchard* 33 (November 1983): 3–23.

Bozo, Dominique. *Victor Brauner.* Paris: Musée National d'Art Moderne, 1972.

Cassou, Jean, ed. *Le Pillage par les Allemands des oeuvres d'art et des bibliothèques appartenant à des Juifs en France.* Paris: Centre de Documentation Juive Contemporaine, 1947. Documents.

Centre d'Art et de Culture Georges Pompidou, Musée National d'Art Moderne. *Arp: Le Temps des papiers déchirés.* Text by Christian Dérouet. Paris: Centre d'Art et de Culture Georges Pompidou, 1983.

———. *Oeuvres d'Henri Matisse: 1869–1954.* Text by Isabelle Monod-Fontaine. Paris: Centre d'Art et de Culture Georges Pompidou, 1979.

———. *Paris-Paris 1937–1957: Créations en France.* Paris: Centre d'Art et de Culture Georges Pompidou, 1981.

———. *Paul Eluard et ses amis peintres.* Paris: Centre d'Art et de Culture Georges Pompidou, 1982.

———. *Les Réalismes 1919–1939.* Paris: Centre d'Art et de Culture Georges Pompidou, 1981.

Centre Atlantico de Arte Moderno. *El Surrealismo entre Viejo y Nuevo Mundo.* Las Palmas: Centre Atlantico de Arte Moderno, 1990.

Centre de la Vieille Charité. *La Planète affolée: Surréalisme, dispersion et influence, 1938–1947.* Paris: Flammarion, 1986.

Ceysson, Bernard. *Le Rappel à l'ordre: L'Art en France dans les années trente.* St.-Etienne: Musée d'Art et d'Industrie, 1979.

Chancellerie de l'Ordre de la Libération. *Exposition résistance—déportation: Création dans le bruit des armes.* Paris: Chancellerie de l'Ordre de la Libération, 1980.

Charbonnier, Georges. *Le Monologue du peintre.* Paris: Juillard, 1959.

Chipp, Herschel B., ed. *Theories of Modern Art.* Berkeley and Los Angeles: University of California Press, 1969.

Clark, Timothy. "Jackson Pollock's Abstraction." In *Reconstructing Modernism: Art in New York, Paris, and Montreal, 1945–1964,* edited by Serge Guilbaut. Cambridge, Mass.: MIT Press, 1990.

Clébert, J. P. *Mythologie d'André Masson.* Geneva: Cailler, 1971.

Combes, André, Michel Vanoosthuyse, and Isabelle Vodoz, eds. *Nazisme et anti-Nazisme dans la littérature & l'art Allemands, 1920–1945.* Lille: Presses universitaires de Lille, 1986.

Cone, Michèle. "Art and Politics in France during the German Occupation, 1940–1944." Ph.D. diss., New York University, 1988.

———. "Desnos, Picasso, Girodias, trois comparses de fortune." *L'Herne* (1987): 205–11.

———. *The Roots and Routes of Art in the Twentieth Century.* New York: Horizon, 1975.

Dérouet, Christian. "'Beaux Arts' en travers la peinture." *Cahiers du Musée national d'art moderne* 7–8 (1981): 386–407.

Desnos, Robert. *Picasso.* Paris: Editions du Chêne, 1943.

Diehl, Gaston. *Les Fauves.* Paris: Editions du Chêne, 1943.

———. "Le Nouvel Art contemporain, 1925–1944." Unpublished mss.

———. *Peintres d'aujourd'hui.* Paris: Comoedia Charpentier, 1943.

———, ed. *Problèmes de la peinture.* Paris: Confluences, 1946.

Dorival, Bernard. *Les Etapes de la peinture française contemporaine, 1911–1944.* 6th ed. Paris: Gallimard, 1946.

Eluard, Paul. *Picasso.* Geneva: Trois Collines, 1946.

Fauré, Michel. *Histoire du surréalisme sous l'Occupation.* Paris: La Table Ronde, 1982.

Focillon, Henri. *Art d'occident: Le moyen Age roman et gothique.* Paris: Armand Colin, 1938.

Francastel, Pierre. *Nouveau Dessin, nouvelle peinture.* Paris: Médicis, 1946.

Freundlich, Otto. *Deux Sculptures monumentales d'Otto Freundlich.* Paris: Galerie Claude Bernard, 1962.

Gage, John. "Color in Western Art: An Issue?" *The Art Bulletin* 72, no. 4 (December 1990): 518–41.

Galerie Michel Couturier. *Wols, cités et navires.* Paris: Galerie Michel Couturier, 1964.

Galeries Nationales du Grand Palais. *Bazaine.* Paris: Skira, 1990.

———. *Estève.* Paris: Réunion des musées nationaux, 1987.

Gaudibert, Pierre. "André Farcy et le pre-

mier musée d'art moderne de France à Grenoble." *Cahiers du Musée national d'art moderne* 9 (1982): 128–33.

Gee, Malcolm. *Dealers, Critics, and Collectors of Modern Painting: Aspects of the Parisian Art Market between 1910 and 1930*. New York: Garland, 1981.

Goggin, M. M. Picasso and His Art during the German Occupation, 1940–1944. Ph.D. dissertation. Stanford U., August 1985.

Golan, Romy. "The *Ecole Française* vs. the *Ecole de Paris*." In Kenneth E. Silver and Romy Golan, *The Circle of Montparnasse: Jewish Artists in Paris, 1905–1945*. New York: Universe Books, 1985.

———. "Moral Landscapes: Organic Images of France between the Two World Wars." Ph.D. diss., Courtauld Institute, London, 1989.

Goldfarb-Marquis, Alice. *Marcel Duchamp: Eros, c'est la vie: A Biography*. Troy, N.Y.: Whitston, 1981.

Grosshans, Henry. *Hitler and the Artists*. New York: Holmes & Meier, 1983.

Guilbaut, Serge. *How New York Stole the Idea of Modern Art: Abstract Expressionism, Freedom, and the Cold War*. Chicago: University of Chicago, 1983.

Guiraud, Jean-Michel. "La Vie culturelle à Marseille sous le Maréchal Pétain," *Revue d'histoire de la deuxième guerre mondiale* 113 (January 1979).

———. *La Vie intellectuelle et artistique à Marseille à l'époque de Vichy et sous l'Occupation*. Marseille: Centre Regional de Documentation Pedagogique, 1987.

Guyot, Adeline, and Restellini, Patrick. *L'Art Nazi 1933–1945*. Brussels: Editions Complexe, 1987.

Haftmann, Werner. *Marc Chagall. Gouaches, Drawings, Watercolors*. New York: Abrams, 1984.

———. *Verfemte Kunst. Bildende Kunstler der inneren und ausseren Emigration in der Zeit des Nationalsozialismus*. Cologne: DuMont, 1986.

Haraszti, Miklos. *The Velvet Prison. Artists under State Socialism*. New York: Basic Books, 1987.

Hautecoeur, Louis. *Considérations sur l'art d'aujourd'hui*. Paris: Librairie de France, 1929.

———. "Discours d'ouverture Musée d'art moderne." Manuscript. Paris: Bibliothèque de l'Institut, August 1942.

———. "L'Evacuation des oeuvres d'art françaises." Radio speech. Paris: Bibliothèque de l'Institut, MS 6910, May 1940.

———. *Histoire de l'art*. Paris: Flammarion, 1959.

———. *Littérature et peinture du XVIIème au XXème siecle*. Paris: Armand Colin, 1942.

———. *Sculpture décorative*. Paris: Moreau, 1937.

Hemming Fry, John. *L'Art décadent sous le règne du communisme et de la démocratie*. Paris: Colas, 1942.

Hilaire, Georges. *Derain*. Geneva: Cailler, 1969.

Hinz, Berthold. *Art in the Third Reich*. New York: Pantheon, 1979.

Huyghe, René. *Les Contemporains*. Paris: Pierre Tisné, 1949.

Institut Goethe. *Munich 1937: L'Art acclamé—l'art diffamé*. Paris: Institut Goethe, 1987. Pamphlet with excerpt from Hitler's speech.

Janis, Sidney, and Harriet. *Picasso—The Recent Years, 1939–1946*. Garden City, N.J.: Doubleday, 1946.

Jean, Marcel. *History of Surrealism*. New York: Grove Press, 1960.

Kjellberg, Pierre. *Le Guide des statues de Paris*. Paris: Bibliothèque des Arts, 1973.

Lafranchis, Jean. *Louis Marcoussis*. Paris: Editions du Temps, 1961.

Lesbats, Roger. *Cinq Peintres d'aujourd'hui*. Paris: Editions du Chêne, 1943.

Letourneur, René. *La Sculpture française contemporaine*. Monaco: Documents d'art, 1944.

Leymarie, Jean. *Picasso, The Artist of the Century*. Translated by James Emmons. New York: Viking, 1972.

Los Angeles County Museum. *"Degenerate Art": The Fate of the Avant-Garde in Nazi Germany*. New York: Abrams, 1991.

Lukach, Joan. *In Search of the Spirit in Art*. New York: Braziller, 1983.

Mabille, Pierre. "Le Jeu de cartes surréalistes." *Vrille* (1945).

McCabe, Cynthia. *Artistic Collaborations in the Twentieth Century*. Washington, D.C.: Smithsonian, 1984.

Mainardi, Patricia. *Art and Politics of the Second Empire: The Universal Expositions of 1855 and 1867*. New Haven and London: Yale University Press, 1989.

Mauclair, Camille. *La Crise de l'art moderne*. Paris: CEA, 1944.

———. *La Farce de l'art vivant: Une campagne picturale, 1928–1929*. Paris: Nouvelle Revue critique, 1929.

Meyer, Franz. *Marc Chagall: Life and Works*. New York: Abrams, 1983.

Moulin, Raymonde. *Le Marché de la Peinture en France*. Paris: Minuit, 1967. Translated by Arthur Goldhammer, under the title *The French Art Market: A Sociological View*. New

Brunswick: Rutgers University Press, 1987.

Musée d'Art Moderne de la Ville de Paris. *L'Aventure de Pierre Loeb*. Paris: Musée d'Art Moderne de la Ville de Paris, 1979.

———. *200 Dessins d'André Masson*. Paris: Musée d'Art Moderne de la Ville de Paris, 1976.

———. *Fautrier*. Paris: Musée d'Art Moderne de la Ville de Paris, 1989.

———. *Forces nouvelles, 1935–1939*. Paris: Musée d'Art Moderne de la Ville de Paris, 1980.

———. *Paris 1937: L'Art indépendant*. Paris: Musée d'Art Moderne de la Ville de Paris, 1987.

———. *Paris 1937. Cinquantenaire de l'exposition internationale des arts et des techniques dans la vie moderne*. Paris: Musée d'Art Moderne de la Ville de Paris, 1987.

Musée Cantini. *André Masson*. Marseilles: Musée Cantini, 1968.

Museum of Modern Art. *André Masson*. New York: Museum of Modern Art, 1976.

Nochlin, Linda. "Return to Order." *Art in America* (September 1981): 74–83, 209–11.

Noèl, Bernard. *Arno Breker et l'art officiel*. Paris: Damase, 1981.

O'Connor, Francis. "The Psychodynamics of the Frontal Self-Portrait." *Psychoanalytical Perspectives on Art*, edited by M. M. Guedo, 1:169–221. Hillsdale, N.J.: Analytic Press, 1985.

Orangerie des Tuileries. *Soutine*. Paris: Orangerie des Tuileries, 1973.

Palmier, Jean Michel. *L'Expressionisme comme révolte*. Paris: Payot, 1983.

Penrose, R. *Picasso: His Life and Work*. Berkeley: U. of California Press, 1981.

Picasso, Pablo. *Desire Caught by the Tail.* New York: Philosophical Library, 1948.

Probst, Volker G. *Arno Breker, Soixante ans de sculpture.* Paris: Damase, 1981.

Puig, René. "La Vie misérable et glorieuse d'Aristide Maillol." *Tramontane* 403–4 (1965): 1–59.

Rave, Paul Ortwin. *Kunstdiktatur im Dritten Reich.* Hamburg: Gebr. Mann, 1949.

Rey, Robert. *La Peinture moderne.* Paris: Que Sais-je, 1941.

Richardson, John. "Interview with Barbara Rose." *The Journal of Art* (February 1991).

———. *A Life of Picasso.* Vol. 1, *1881–1906.* With Marilyn McCully. New York: Random House, 1991.

Roche-Pézard, Fanette. "Du Futurisme au Novecento: Un Engagement politique?" *Cahiers du Musée National d'Art Moderne* 7–8, 1981.

Roh, Franz. *Entartete Kunst: Kunstbarberei im Dritten Reich.* Hannover: Fackelträger-Verlag Schmidt-Kustler, 1962.

Rorimer, James, and Gilbert Rabin. *Survival: The Salvage and Protection of Art in War.* New York: Abelard, 1950.

Sabartès, Jaime. *Picasso, Documents iconographiques.* Geneva: Cailler, 1954.

Schapiro, Meyer. *Romanesque Art.* New York: Braziller, 1977.

Silver, Kenneth E. "Esprit de Corps: The Great War and French Art, 1914–1925." PhD. dissertation, Yale University, 1981.

———. *Esprit de Corps: The Art of the Parisian Avant-Garde and the First World War, 1914–1925.* Princeton: Princeton University Press, 1990.

Silver, Kenneth E., and Romy Golan. *The Circle of Montparnasse: Jewish Artists in Paris, 1905–1945.* New York: Universe Books, 1985.

Silverman, Deborah L. *Art Nouveau in Fin de Siècle France: Psychology and Style.* Berkeley and L.A.: University of California Press, 1989.

Solomon R. Guggenheim Museum. *Aristide Maillol, 1861–1944.* New York: Solomon R. Guggenheim Museum, 1975.

Spies, Werner. *Les Sculptures de Picasso.* Lausanne: Clairefontaine, 1971.

Staatliche Kunsthalle. *Maillol.* Baden-Baden: Staatliche Kunsthalle, 1978.

Steinberg, Leo. *Other Criteria.* New York: Oxford University Press, 1972.

Stuttgart Staatsgalerie. *Picasso in der Stuttgart Staatsgalerie.* Text by Gunther Thiem and Karin Maur. Stuttgart: Stuttgart Staatsgalerie, 1981.

Tapié, Michel. *Un Art autre ou il s'agit de nouveaux dévidages du réel.* Paris: Gabriel-Giraud, 1952.

Tate Gallery. *Léger and Purist Paris.* With texts by Fernand Léger, including "The Machine Aesthetic—The Manufactured Object—The Artisan and the Artist." London: Tate Gallery, 1971.

Université de St.-Etienne. *L'Art face à la crise: L'Art en occident, 1929–1939.* Travaux, 26. St.-Etienne: CIEREC, 1980.

———. *Art et ideologies: L'Art en occident, 1945–1949.* Travaux, 20. St.-Etienne: CIEREC, 1976.

———. *Le Retour à l'ordre dans les arts plastiques et l'architecture, 1919–1925.* Travaux, 8. St.-Etienne: CIEREC, 1986.

Valéry, Paul. "Pièces sur l'art." In *Oeuvres complètes.* vol. 2. Paris: Pleiade, 1960.

Vallier, Thérèse. *Henri Bouchard.* Paris: Horizon de France, 1943.

Vanderpyl. *L'Art sans patrie—Un Mensonge: Le Pinceau d'Israel.* Paris, 1942.

Webb, Peter. *Hans Bellmer.* New York and London: Quartet Books, 1985.

Willett, John. *Art and Politics in the Weimar Period: The New Sobriety.* New York: Pantheon, 1978.

Widerstand statt Anpassung: Deutsche Kunst im Widerstand gegen den Faschismus 1933–1945. Berlin: Elefanten Press Verlag, 1980.

Zervos, Christian. *Pablo Picasso.* 33 vols. Catalogue raisonné. Volumes 10–14. Paris: Editions Cahiers d'Art, 1932–.

ART EXHIBITION CATALOGUES, 1937–1947

Note: Because of the unusual circumstances of the German Occupation, exhibition catalogues have frequently disappeared. This list is based on the resources of libraries and of private archives that were opened to the author.

Museum Catalogues

Akademie der Kunste. *Ausstellung Franzosischer Kunst der Gegenwart.* Sponsored by L'Association Française d'Action Artistique. Berlin, 1937.

Athénée de Genève. *Jeune Peintres français et leurs maitres.* Sponsored by L'Association Française d'Action Artistique. Text by Jacques Guenne. Exhibition traveled to Zurich, Bern, Lucerne, Basel, September 1942-March 1943. Geneva, 1942.

Baltimore Museum of Art. *An Exhibition of Paintings and Drawings by André Masson.* Baltimore, 1941.

Kaiser, Fritz. *Austellungsfuhrer Entartete "Kunst."* Brochure in lieu of catalogue for the show of degenerate art held in Munich in 1937. Berlin: Verlag für Kultur und Wirtschaftswerbung, 1937.

Musée National d'Art Moderne. *Catalogue Guide.* Text by Jean Cassou. Paris, 1947.

———. *Exposition inaugurale, Palais de Tokyo.* Paris, 1942.

Musées Nationaux. *Louvre, nouvelles acquisitions, septembre 1939–septembre 1945.* Text by Georges Salles. Paris, 1945.

Museo Nacional de Arte Moderno. *Exposicion de artistas franceses contemporaneos.* Sponsored by L'Association Française d'Action Artistique. Text by Louis Hautecoeur. Madrid, 1943.

L'Orangerie. *Arno Breker.* Text by Jean Marc Campagne. Paris, 1942.

Art Gallery Exhibition Catalogues

Galerie Berri Raspail. *Les Etapes du nouvel art contemporain 1–7.* Text by Gaston Diehl. Paris, 1941–42.

Galerie Charpentier. *L'Automne.* Text by Germaine Beaumont. Paris, 1944.

———. *Chas Laborde.* Text by André Salmon. Paris, 1942.

———. *La Femme et les peintres et sculpteurs contemporains.* Paris, 1942.

———. *Les Fleurs et les Fruits depuis le romantisme.* Text by Colette. Paris, 1942.

———. *Jardins de France.* Text by Louise de Vilmorin. Paris, 1943.

———. *La Jeune Sculpture française.* Text by Pierre du Colombier. Paris, 1943.

————. *Le Paysage français de Corot à nos jours*. Text by Jean Marc Campagne. Paris, 1942.

————. *La Quinzaine d'art espagnol*. Paris, 1942.

————. *Scenes et figures parisiennes*. Text by Jean Cocteau. Paris, 1943.

————. *Un Siecle d'aquarelle*. Text by Louis Réau. Paris, 1942.

————. *Treize Peintres; sculpteurs contemporains*. Text by Jean Marc Campagne. Paris, 1943.

————. *La Vie familiale*. Paris, 1944.

Galerie Drouin. *Dubuffet*. Text by Jean Paulhan. Paris, 1944.

————. *Fautrier*. Text by Jean Paulhan. Paris, 1943.

————. *Le Portrait français*. Text by Louis Hourticq. Paris, 1943.

Galerie de France. *Dix Peintres subjectifs*. Text by Bernard Dorival. Paris, 1944.

————. *Douze Peintres d'aujourd'hui; sculptures de Chauvin*. Text by Gaston Diehl. Paris, 1943.

————. *Les Fauves, 1903–1908*. Text by Gaston Diehl. Paris, 1942.

————. *Jacques Villon peintures, 1909–1941; Duchamp Villon sculpture*. Text by René Jean. Paris, 1942.

————. *Les Néo-Impressionistes*. Text by Paul Signac. Paris, 1942–43.

Galerie Friedland. *Exposition d'inauguration*. Alix, Brianchon, Coutaud, Despierre, Esteve, Goerg, Gruber, Jannot, Legueult, Marchand, Oudot, Pignon, Planson, Tal Coat, Walch. Paris, 1942.

————. *Hommage aux anciens*. Text by Bernard Champigneulle. Paris, 1942.

————. *Peints par eux-mêmes: Auto-portraits*. Text by Bernard Champigneulle. Paris 1943.

Galerie Louis Carré. *Dessins d'Henri Matisse*. Text by Henri Matisse. Paris, 1941.

————. *Dessins de Maillol*. Paris, 1942.

————. *Dominguez*. Text by Paul Eluard. Paris, 1943.

————. *Rouault*. Text by Bernard Dorival. Paris, 1942.

Salon Catalogues and Albums

Le Salon d'Automne, 1940–44.

Le Salon des Tuileries, 1941–45.

Le Salon de la Société des Artistes Français et de la Nationale 1941–45.

Auction Catalogues

Galeries Fischer, Grand Hôtel National. *Tableaux et sculptures des maitres modernes provenant des musées d'Allemagne*. Auction sale at Lucerne, Friday, 30 June 1939.

IDEOLOGY, SOCIAL LIFE, AND POLITICS; COMPARATIVE CULTURE STUDIES

Abetz, Otto. *Pétain et les Allemands: Memorandum d'Abetz sur les rapports Franco-Allemands*. Paris: Gaucher, 1948.

Amouroux, Henri. *La Vie des français sous l'occupation*. Paris: Fayard, 1961.

Becker, Howard S. *Art Worlds*. Berkeley: University of California Press, 1982.

Bellanger, Claude, et al. *Histoire générale de la presse française*. Vol. 4, *1940–1958*. Paris: Presses universitaires de France, 1975.

Brenner, Hildegard. *La Politique artistique du national-socialisme*. Translated from

the German by Lucien Steinberg. Paris: Maspéro, 1980.

Les Camps en Provence: Exil, internement, deportation, 1933–1944. Preface by Jacques Grandjonc and Benjamin Fondane. Aix-en-Provence: Alinea, 1984.

Céline, Louis-Ferdinand. *L'Ecole des cadavres.* Paris: Dénoèl, 1938.

Cointet-Labrousse, Michèle. *Vichy et le fascisme.* Brussels: Editions Complexe, 1987.

Derrida, Jacques. "Like the Sound of the Sea Deep within a Shell: Paul de Man's War." *Critical Inquiry* 14, no. 3 (Spring 1988): 590–652. See subsequent issues for discussion.

Dunan, Elizabeth. "La Propaganda Abteilung de France: Tache et organisation." *Revue d'histoire de la deuxième guerre mondiale,* no. 4 (1951).

Ehrlich, Evelyn. *Cinema of Paradox: French Filmmaking under the German Occupation.* New York: Columbia University Press, 1985.

Fauré, Christian. *Le Projet culturel de Vichy.* Lyons: Editions du Centre National de Recherche Scientifique, 1989.

Fontaine, André. *Un Camp de concentration à Aix-en-Provence: Le Camp d'étrangers des milles, 1939–1943.* Aix-en-Provence: EDISUD, 1989.

Foucault, Michel. *The Birth of the Clinic: An Archeology of Medical Perception.* New York: Vintage, 1973.

Fouché, Pascal. *L'Edition française sous l'occupation, 1940–1944.* 2 vols. Paris: Bibliothèque de Littérature Française Contemporaine de l'Université Paris 7, 1987.

Fussell, Paul. *Wartime: Understanding and Behavior in the Second World War.* New York: Oxford University Press, 1989.

Gilbert, Martin. *The Second World War: A Complete History.* New York: Holt, 1989.

Grunfeld, Frederic V. *Prophets without Honour: A Background to Freud, Kafka, Einstein, and Their World.* New York: Holt, Rinehart, and Winston, 1979.

Hadjinicolaou, Nicos. *Histoire de l'art et lutte des classes.* Paris: Maspero, 1974.

Halimi, André. *Chantons sous l'occupation.* Paris: Olivier Orban, 1976.

Henri-Lévy, Bernard. *L'Idéologie française.* Paris: Grasset, 1981.

Hitler's Table Talk: His Private Conversations, 1941–1944. Translated by Norman Cameron and R. H. Stevens. London: Weidenfeld and Nicolson, 1973.

Hoffmann, Stanley. "Aspects du régime de Vichy." *Revue française de science politique* (January–March 1956).

———. "Collaborationism in Vichy France." *Journal of Modern History* (September 1968).

———. *In Search of France.* Cambridge, Mass.: Harvard University Press, 1963.

Jackman, Jarrell C., and Carla Borden, eds. *The Muses Flee Hitler: Cultural Transfer and Adaptation, 1930–1945.* Washington, D.C.: Smithsonian, 1983.

Jauss, Hans Robert. *Pour une esthétique de la réception.* Paris: Gallimard, 1978.

Jeune France: Principes, directions, esprit. Lyon: Audin, 1941.

Kaplan, Alice Yaeger. *Reproductions of Banality: Fascism, Literature, and French Intellectual Life.* St. Paul: University of Minnesota Press, 1986.

Laurent, Jeanne. *Arts et pouvoirs.* St.-Etienne: CIEREC, 1982.

Lehmann-Haupt, Helmut. *Art under a Dic-*

tatorship. New York: Oxford University Press, 1954.

Lévy, Claude. "L'Organisation de la propagande allemande en France." *Revue d'histoire de la deuxième guerre mondiale* 64 (October 1966).

Loiseaux, Gérard. *La Littérature de la défaite et de la collaboration.* Paris: Sorbonne, 1984.

Loiseaux, Jean Claude. *Les Zazous.* Paris: Sagittaire, 1977.

Lottman, Herbert. *The Left Bank: Writers, Artists, and Politics from the Popular Front to the Cold War.* Boston: Houghton Mifflin, 1982.

————. *Pétain.* Paris: Seuil, 1984.

————. *The Purge.* New York: Morrow, 1986.

Loubet del Bayle, Jean Louis. *Les Non-Conformistes des années trente: Une Tentative de renouvellement de la pensée politique française.* Paris: Seuil, 1969.

Madajczyk, Czeslaw, ed. *Inter Arma non silent Musae: The War and the Culture, 1939–1945.* Warsaw: Institute of History, 1977.

Marchetti, Stéphane. *Images d'une certaine France: Affiches, 1939–1945.* Lausanne: Edita, 1982.

Marrus, Michael, and Robert Paxton. *Vichy France and the Jews.* New York: Basic Books, 1981.

Mellow, James R. *Charmed Circle: Gertrude Stein and Company.* New York: Praeger, 1974.

Michel, Henri. *Paris résistant.* Paris: Albin Michel, 1982.

————. *Pétain, Laval, Darlan: Trois politiques.* Paris: Flammarion, 1972.

Musée d'Histoire Contemporaine and Bibliothèque de Documentation Internationale Contemporaine. *La France et les français de la libération, 1944–1945.* Paris: Bibliothèque de Documentation Internationale Contemporaine, 1984.

————. *La Propagande sous Vichy, 1940–1944.* Paris: Bibliothèque de Documentation Internationale Contemporaine, 1990.

Namer, Luce. "La Politique artistique du gouvernement de Vichy: Hommes et structures." Master's thesis, Fondation Nationale des Sciences Politiques, Paris, 1983.

Noguères, Henri. *Histoire de la résistance en France.* Paris: Laffont, 1967.

Novick, Peter. *The Resistance vs. Vichy: The Purge of Collaborators in Liberated France.* New York: Basic Books, 1968.

Ory, Pascal. *Les Collaborateurs, 1940–1945.* Paris: Seuil, 1976.

Palmier, Jean Michel. *Weimar en exil: Le destin de l'émigration intellectuelle allemande anti-Nazie en Europe et aux Etats-Unis.* 2 vols. Paris: Payot, 1988.

Paret, Peter. *Makers of Modern Stretegy from Machiavelli to the Nuclear Age.* Princeton: Princeton University Press, 1986.

Paxton, Robert O. *Vichy France: Old Guard and New Order, 1940–1944.* New York: Columbia University Press, 1972.

Pryce-Jones, David. *Paris in the Third Reich: A History of the German Occupation, 1940–1944.* London: Collins, 1981.

Ragache, Gilles, and Jean-Robert. *La vie quotidienne des écrivains et des artistes sous l'occupation, 1940–1944.* Paris: Hachette, 1988.

Rémond, René. *The Right Wing in France from 1815 to de Gaulle.* Translated by James M. Laux. Philadelphia: University of Pennsylvania Press, 1966.

Rich, Norman. *Hitler's War Aims: The Establishment of a New Order.* New York: Norton, 1974.

Rioux, Jean-Pierre. "Ambivalences en rouge et bleu: Les pratiques culturelles des Français pendant les années noires." *Cahiers de l'Institut d'histoire du temps présent,* no. 8 (June 1988): 27–38.

———, ed. *Cahiers de l'Institut d'histoire du temps présent,* no. 8 (June 1988).

Rousso, Henry. "Collaborer." *L'Histoire* 80 (1986): 48–61.

———. *Le Syndrome de Vichy.* Paris: Seuil, 1987.

Schorske, Carl E. *Fin de Siècle Vienna.* New York: Knopf, 1961.

Sénarclens, P. de. *Le Mouvement Esprit, 1932–1941: Essai critique.* Lausanne: L'Age d'homme, 1974.

Séghers, Pierre. *La Résistance et ses poêtes.* Vols. 1 and 2. Paris: Marabout, 1978.

Siclier, Jacques. *La France de Pétain et son cinéma.* Paris: Veyrier, 1981.

Steinberg, Lucien. *Les Autorités allemandes en France occupée: Inventaire commenté de la collection des documents conservés au Centre de documentation juive contemporaine.* Paris: Centre de Documentation Juive Contemporaine, 1966.

Sternhell, Zeev. *Ni droite ni gauche: L'Idéologie fasciste en France.* Paris: Seuil, 1983.

Strauss, Leo. *Persecution and the Art of Writing.* New York: Free Press, 1952.

Veillon, Dominique. *La Mode sous l'Occupation.* Paris: Payot, 1990.

Wilson, Sarah. "Collaboration in the Fine Arts." In *Collaboration in France— Politics and Culture during the Nazi Occupation, 1940–1944.* Edited by Gerhard Hirshfield and Patrick S. Marsh, pp. 103–25. London: Berg, 1989.

Winock, Michel. *Edouard Drumont et Cie: Antisémitisme et fascisme en France.* Paris: Seuil, 1983.

———. *Histoire politique de la revue Esprit.* Paris: Seuil, 1975.

Wyman, David. *The Abandonment of the Jews: America and the Holocaust, 1941–1945.* New York: Pantheon, 1984.

———. *Paper Walls: American Policy toward the Emigration of Refugees from Nazism.* Boston: University of of Massachusetts, 1968.

Young-Bruehl, Elizabeth. *Hannah Arendt: For Love of the World.* New Haven: Yale University Press, 1982.

Press: Dailies, Weeklies, and Periodicals, 1937–1947

Art Digest (New York, 1944–45)
L'Art français (Paris, 1942–44)
Art News (New York, 1 November 1944)
Atalante (Paris, 1941–43)
Aujourd'hui (Paris, 1941–44)
Au Pilori (Paris, 1941–44)
Les Beaux Arts: Journal des arts (Paris, 1940–44)
Cahiers d'art (Paris, 1937, 1944)

Cahiers du sud (Marseilles, 1940–42)
Comoedia (Paris, 1941–44)
Confluences (Lyons, 1943–44)
Courrier des arts et des lettres (Paris, 1947)
Le Figaro (Lyons, 1941)
Fontaine (Algiers, 1942–44)
La Gerbe (Paris, 1941–44)
L'Illustration (Paris, 1941–43)
Je suis partout (Paris, 1941–44)

BIBLIOGRAPHY

Le Journal officiel (Paris, 1941–46)

Die Kunst (Munich, January and August 1937)

Magazine of Art (New York, January and November 1945)

La Main à plume, with a different title each issue: *Transfusion du verbe, La Conquète du monde par l'image, Le Surréalisme encore et toujours*, others (Paris, 1941–44)

Métiers de France (Paris, 1942)

Museum of Modern Art Bulletin (New York, January 1945)

New Statesman and the Nation (New York, 16 September 1944)

New York Times Sunday Magazine (New York, 29 October 1944)

Les Nouveaux Temps (Paris, 1941–44)

La Nouvelle Revue française (Paris, 1940–43)

Pariser Zeitung (Paris, 1942–44)

Revue des beaux arts de France (Paris, 1942–43)

Le Rouge et le bleu (Paris, 1941–42)

San Francisco Chronicle (San Francisco, 3 September 1944)

Signal (Paris, 1941–43)

Le Spectateur des arts (Paris, 1944)

La Voix française (Paris, 1942)

Vrille (mantes, 1945)

INDEX

INDEX